AutoCAD® 2000i Tutorial

Second Level: 3D Modeling

Randy H. Shih
Oregon Institute of Technology

SDC PUBLICATIONS

Mission, Kansas

Schroff Development Corporation
P.O. Box 1334
Mission KS 66222
(913) 262-2664
www.sdcACAD.com

Shih, Randy H.
AutoCAD® 2000i Tutorial / Second Level: 3D Modeling

Randy H. Shih

ISBN 1-58503-061-9

Printed and bound in the United States of America.

Preface

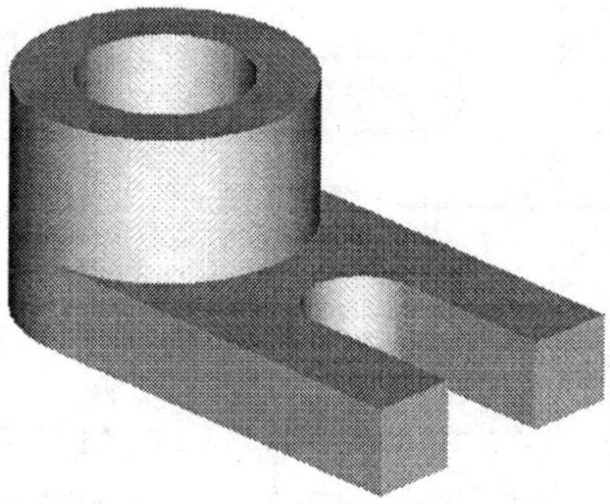

The primary goal of ***AutoCAD® 2000i Tutorial: 3D Modeling*** is to introduce the aspects of **Computer Three Dimensional Modeling**. This text is intended to be used as a training guide for students and professionals. This text covers *AutoCAD® 2000i* and the chapters proceed in a pedagogical fashion to guide you from constructing 3D wireframe models, 3D surface models and 3D solid models to making multiview drawings. This text takes a hands-on, exercise-intensive approach to all the important 3D modeling techniques and concepts. This textbook contains a series of ten tutorial style chapters designed to introduce CAD users to 3D modeling with **AutoCAD® 2000i**. This text is also helpful to AutoCAD users upgrading from a previous release of the software. The new improvements and enhancements of the software are incorporated into the tutorials. The 3D modeling techniques and concepts discussed in this text are also designed to serve as the foundation to the more advanced feature-based CAD/CAE packages such as AutoCAD® Mechanical Desktop, AutoCAD® Architectural Desktop, and Autodesk Inventor. The basic premise of this book is that the more 3D designs you create using AutoCAD® 2000i, the better you learn the software. With this in mind, each tutorial introduces a new set of commands and concepts, building on previous chapters. This book does not attempt to cover all of AutoCAD® 2000i's features, only to provide an introduction to the software. It is intended to help you establish a good basis for exploring and growing in the exciting field of Computer Aided Engineering.

Acknowledgments

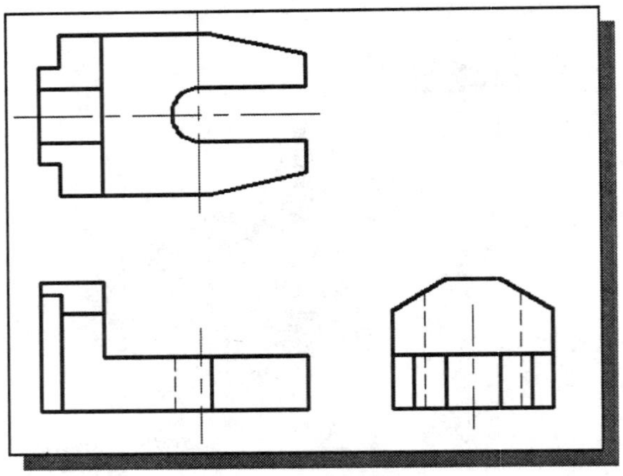

This book would not have been possible without a great deal of support. First, special thanks to two great teachers, Prof. George R. Schade of University of Nebraska-Lincoln and Mr. Denwu Lee, who taught me the fundamentals, the intrigue, and the sheer fun of Computer Aided Engineering.

The effort and support of the editorial and production staff of Schroff Development Corporation is gratefully acknowledged. I would especially like to thank Stephen Schroff and Mary Schmidt for their support and helpful suggestions during this project.

I am grateful that the Mechanical and Manufacturing Engineering Technology Department of Oregon Institute of Technology has provided me with an excellent environment in which to pursue my interests in teaching and research. I would especially like to thank Professor Brian Moravec and Emeritus Professor Charles Hermach for helpful comments and encouragement.

Finally, truly unbounded thanks are due to my wife Hsiu-Ling and my daughter Casandra for their understanding and encouragement throughout this project.

Randy H. Shih
Klamath Falls, Oregon

Table of Contents

Chapter 3
3D Wireframe Modeling

Chapter 4
UCS, Viewports and Wireframe Modeling

Chapter 5
3D Surface Modeling

Chapter 6
Solid Modeling - Constructive Solid Geometry

Chapter 1
Getting Started

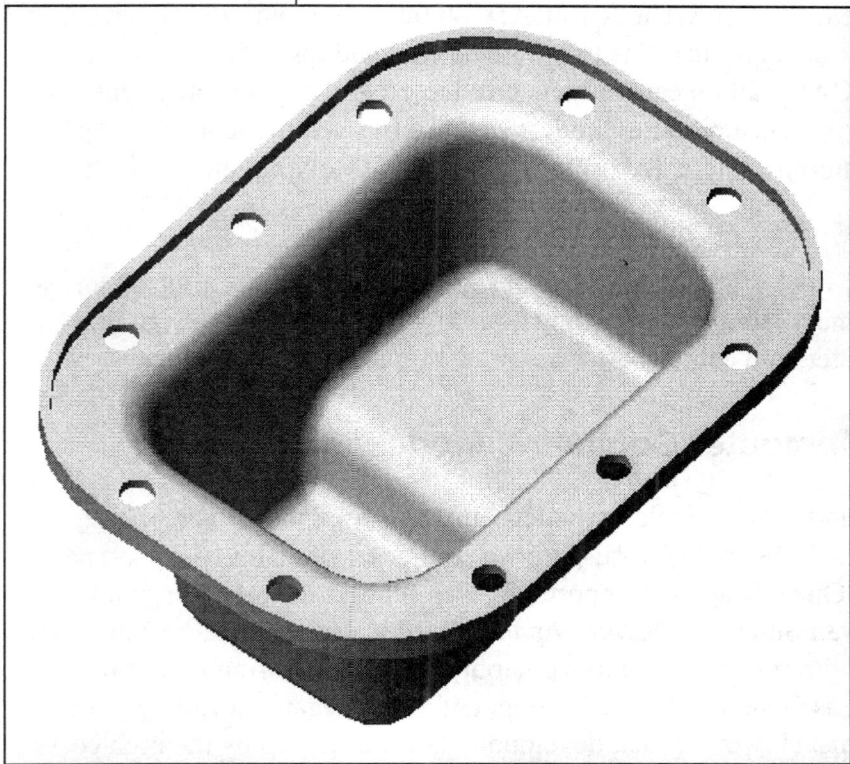

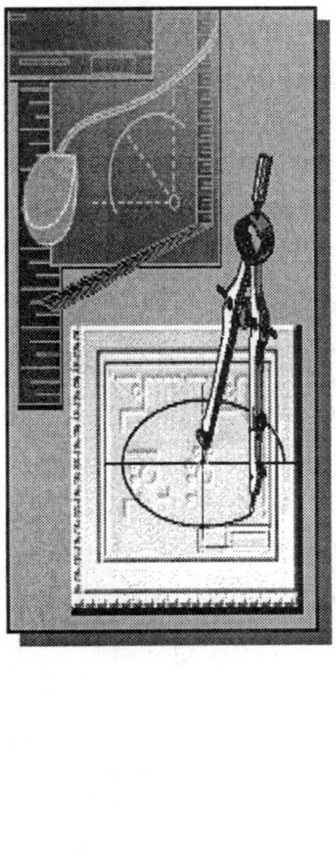

Learning Objectives

- Development of Computer Aided Design
- Why use AutoCAD 2000i?
- Getting Started with AutoCAD 2000i
- The AutoCAD Today dialog box and Units Setup
- AutoCAD 2000i Screen Layout
- Mouse Buttons

Introduction

Computer Aided Design (CAD) is the process of doing designs with the aid of computers. This includes the generation of computer models, analysis of design data, and the creation of the necessary drawings. **AutoCAD® 2000i** is computer aided design software developed by *Autodesk Inc.* The **AutoCAD® 2000i** software is a tool that can be used for design and drafting activities. The two-dimensional and three-dimensional models created in **AutoCAD® 2000i** can be transferred to other computer programs for further analysis and testing. The computer models can also be used in manufacturing equipment such as machining centers, lathes, mills, or rapid prototyping machines to manufacture the product.

The rapid changes in the field of computer aided design have brought exciting advances in industry. Recent advances have made the long-sought goal of reducing design time, producing prototypes faster, and achieving higher product quality closer to a reality.

Development of Computer Geometric Modeling

Computer geometric modeling is a relatively new and rapidly expanding area. The transistor was invented in 1948, and general-purpose computers were invented soon after, in the 1950s and 1960s. One of the most important developments in computer graphics was the publication of Ivan Sutherland's ***Sketchpad*** (MIT doctoral dissertation) in 1963. This is considered the beginning of interactive computer graphics. During that time, several companies, such as General Motors, Boeing, and IBM, began development of interactive CAD programs. However, such developments were slowed by the high cost of computer hardware, the high programming cost, and the non-portability of software.

The 1970s were marked by significant progress in the development of microprocessors. It was in 1971 that Ted Hoff developed the first microprocessor. The era of the personal computer (PC) had begun through the development of large-scale integrated circuits (LSIC) in which all circuitry of the central processing unit (CPU) is on one chip. In the 1980s, improvements in computer hardware brought the power of mainframes to the desktop.

Computer modeling technology advanced along with computer hardware. CAD programs evolved into design tools rather than just drafting tools. During these years of development, modeling schemes progressed from two-dimensional (2D) wireframe to three-dimensional (3D) wireframe, to surface modeling and, finally, to solid modeling.

The development of three-dimensional modeling schemes started with three-dimensional (3D) wireframes. Wireframe models are models consisting of locations of points and lines between appropriate pairs of points. The lines are used to represent transitions, such as from surface to surface. Lines are also a very economical way of representing geometry.

The first generation CAD packages were 2D wireframe **Computer Aided Drafting** programs, basically the electronic equivalents of the drafting board. For typical models, this required that several to many views of the object be created individually as they would be on the drafting board. The 3D model remained in the designer's mind, not in the computer database. Although such systems have some advantages over manual drafting, they are still tedious and labor intensive.

The development of the 3D wireframe modeler was a major leap in the area of computer modeling. The computer database in the 3D wireframe modeler contains the locations of all the points in space coordinates and it is sufficient to create just one model rather than multiple models. This single 3D model can then be viewed from any direction as needed. The 3D wireframe modelers require the least computer power and achieve reasonably good representations of 3D models. However, because surface definition is not part of a wireframe model, all wireframe images have the inherent problem of ambiguity.

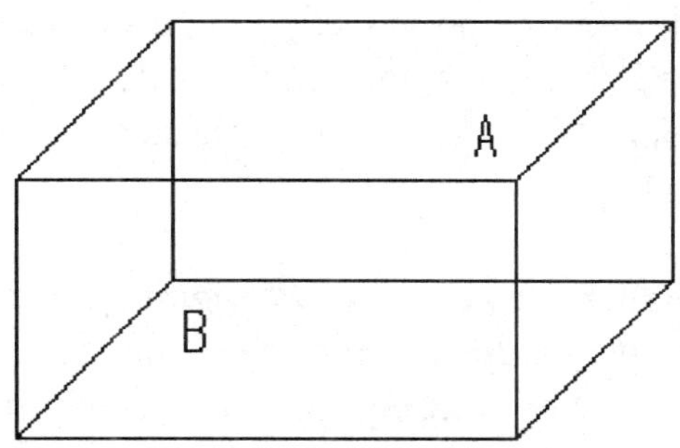

Wireframe Ambiguity: Which corner is in front, A or B?

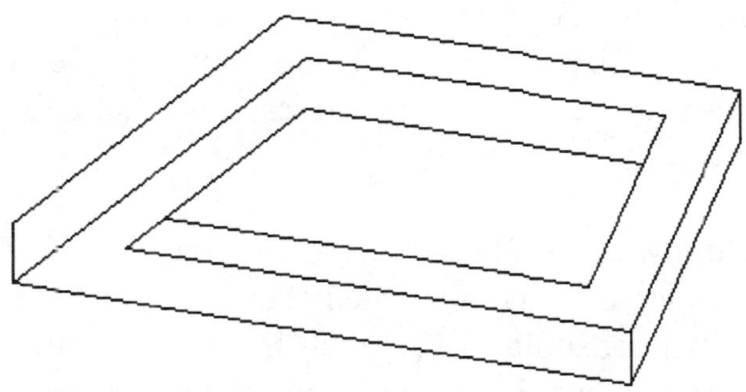

A non-realizable object: Wireframe models contain no surface definitions.

Surface modeling is the logical development in computer geometry modeling to follow the 3D wireframe modeling scheme by organizing and grouping edges that define polygonal surfaces. Surface modeling describes the part's surfaces but not its interiors. Designers are still required to interactively examine surface models to insure that the various surfaces on a model are contiguous throughout. Many of the concepts used in 3D wireframe and surface modelers are incorporated in the solid modeling scheme, but it is solid modeling that offers the most advantages as a design tool.

In the solid modeling presentation scheme, the solid definitions include nodes, edges, and surfaces, and it is a complete and unambiguous mathematical representation of a precisely enclosed and filled volume. Unlike the surface modeling method, solid modelers start with a solid or use topology rules to guarantee that all of the surfaces are stitched together properly. Two predominant methods for representing solid models are **constructive solid geometry** (CSG) representation and **boundary representation** (B-rep).

The CSG representation method can be defined as the combination of 3D solid primitives. What constitutes a "primitive" varies somewhat with the software but typically includes a rectangular prism, a cylinder, a cone, a wedge, and a sphere. Most solid modelers allow the user to define additional primitives, which can be very complex.

In the B-rep representation method, objects are represented in terms of their spatial boundaries. This method defines the points, edges, and surfaces of a volume, and/or issues commands that sweep or rotate a defined face into a third dimension to form a solid. The object is then made up of the unions of these surfaces that completely and precisely enclose a volume.

By the 1980s, a new paradigm called *concurrent engineering* had emerged. With concurrent engineering, designers, design engineers, analysts, manufacturing engineers, and management engineers all work closely right from the initial stages of the design. In this way, all aspects of the design can be evaluated and any potential problems can be identified right from the start and throughout the design process. Using the principles of concurrent engineering, a new type of computer modeling technique appeared. The technique is known as the *feature-based parametric modeling technique*. The key advantage of the *feature-based parametric modeling technique* is its capability to produce very flexible designs. Changes can be made easily and design alternatives can be evaluated with minimum effort. Various software packages offer different approaches to feature-based parametric modeling, yet the end result is a flexible design defined by its design variables and parametric features.

In this text, we will follow a logical order, parallel to the development of computer geometric modeling, in learning the fundamental concepts and commands of **AutoCAD® 2000i.** We will begin with creating 2½D models by modifying the entities properties of 2D designs and then move toward creating 3D wireframe and surface models. We will also discuss and demonstrate several procedures for creating three-dimensional solid models. The techniques presented in this text will also serve as the foundation for entering the world of advanced three-dimensional solid modeling using packages such as **AutoCAD Mechanical Desktop, AutoCAD Architectural Desktop** and **Autodesk Inventor**.

Why use AutoCAD® 2000i?

AutoCAD® was first introduced to the public in late 1982, and was one of the first CAD software products that were available for personal computers. Since 1984, **AutoCAD®** has established a reputation for being the most widely used PC-based CAD software around the world. By 2000, it is estimated that there are over 3.5 million **AutoCAD®** users in more than 150 countries worldwide. **AutoCAD® 2000i** is the sixteenth release, with many added features and enhancements, of the original **AutoCAD®** software produced by *Autodesk Inc.*

CAD provides us with a wide range of benefits; in most cases, the result of using CAD is increased accuracy and productivity. First of all, the computer offers much higher accuracy than the traditional methods of drafting and design. Traditionally, drafting and detailing are the most expensive cost element in a project and the biggest bottleneck. With CAD systems, such as **AutoCAD® 2000i,** the tedious drafting and detailing tasks are simplified through the use of many of the CAD geometric construction tools, such as *grids*, *snap*, *trim,* and *auto-dimensioning*. Dimensions and notes are always legible in CAD drawings and, in most cases, CAD systems can produce higher quality prints compared to traditional hand drawings.

CAD also offers much-needed flexibility in design and drafting. A CAD model generated on a computer consists of numeric data that describe the geometry of the object. This allows the designers and clients to see something tangible and to interpret the ramifications of the design. In many cases, it is also possible to simulate the operating conditions on the computer and observe the results. Any kind of geometric shape stored in the database can be easily duplicated. For large and complex designs and drawings, particularly those involving similar shapes and repetitive operations, CAD approaches are very efficient and effective. Because computer designs and models can be altered easily, a multitude of design options can be examined and presented to a client before any construction or manufacturing actually takes place. Making changes to a CAD database is generally much faster than making changes to a traditional hand drawing. Only the affected components of the design need to be modified and the drawings can be plotted again. In addition, the greatest benefit is that, once the CAD model is created, it can be used over and over again. The CAD models can also be transferred into manufacturing equipment such as machining centers, lathes, mills, or rapid prototyping machines to manufacture the product directly.

CAD, however, does not replace every design activity. CAD may help, but it does not replace the designer's experience with geometry and graphical conventions and standards for the specific field. CAD is a powerful tool, but the use of this tool does not guarantee correct results; the designer is still responsible for using good design practice and applying good judgment. CAD will supplement these skills to ensure that the best design is obtained.

CAD designs and drawings are stored in binary form, usually as CAD files, to magnetic devices such as diskettes and hard disks. The information stored in CAD files usually requires much less physical space in comparison to traditional hand drawings. However, the information stored inside the computer is not indestructible. On the contrary, the electronic format of information is very fragile and sensitive to the environment. Heat or cold can damage the information stored on magnetic storage devices. A power failure while you are creating a design could wipe out the many hours you spent working in front of your computer monitor. It is a good habit to save your work periodically, just in case something might go wrong while you are working on your design. In general, one should save one's work onto the disk at an interval of every 15 to 20 minutes. You should also save your work before you make any major modifications to the design. It is also a good habit to periodically make backup copies of your work and put them in a safe place.

Getting started with AutoCAD® 2000i

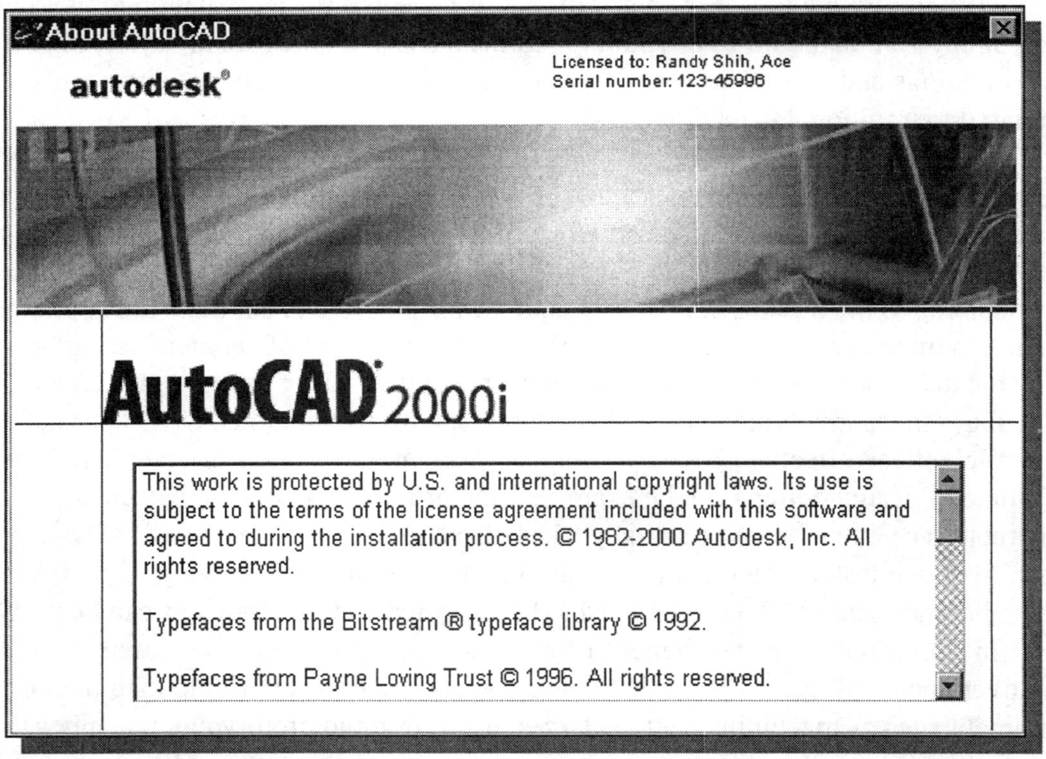

How to start **AutoCAD® 2000i** depends on the type of workstation and the particular software configuration you are using. With most *Windows* systems, you may select the **AutoCAD® 2000i** option on the *Start* menu or select the **AutoCAD® 2000i** icon on the *Desktop*. Consult with your instructor or the technical support personnel if you have difficulty starting the software.

The program takes a while to load, so be patient. Eventually the AutoCAD® 2000i *drawing screen* and the *AutoCAD Today startup dialog box* will appear on the screen.

The tutorials in this text are based on the assumption that you are using AutoCAD® 2000i's default settings. If your system has been customized for other uses, some of the settings may not work with the step-by-step instructions in the tutorials. Contact your instructor and/or the technical support personnel to restore the default software configuration.

The AutoCAD Today dialog box and Units Setup

Once the program is loaded into the memory, the AutoCAD® 2000i startup dialog box, ***AutoCAD Today***, appears at the center of the screen.

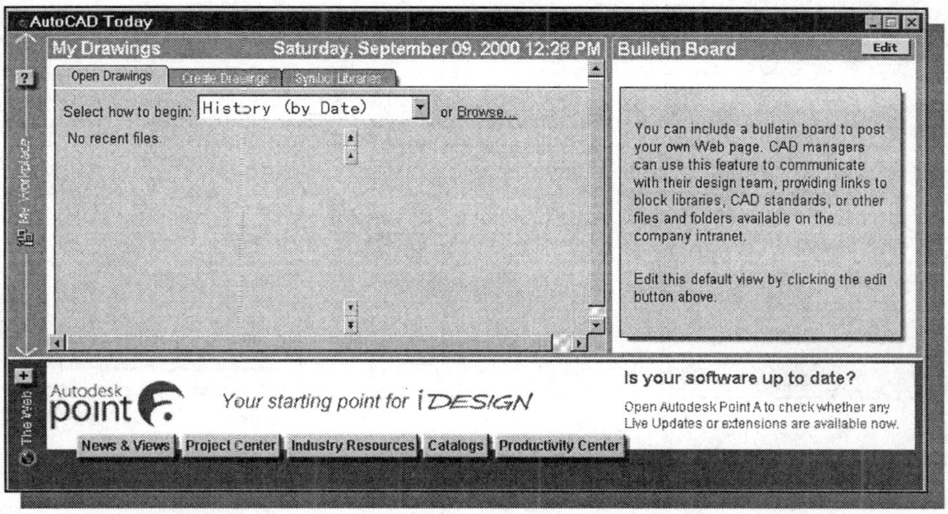

- The *AutoCAD Today* startup dialog box is divided into two sections: ***My Workplace*** and ***The Web***. Using these options, we can communicate our designs to other members of the design team and/or customers around the world.

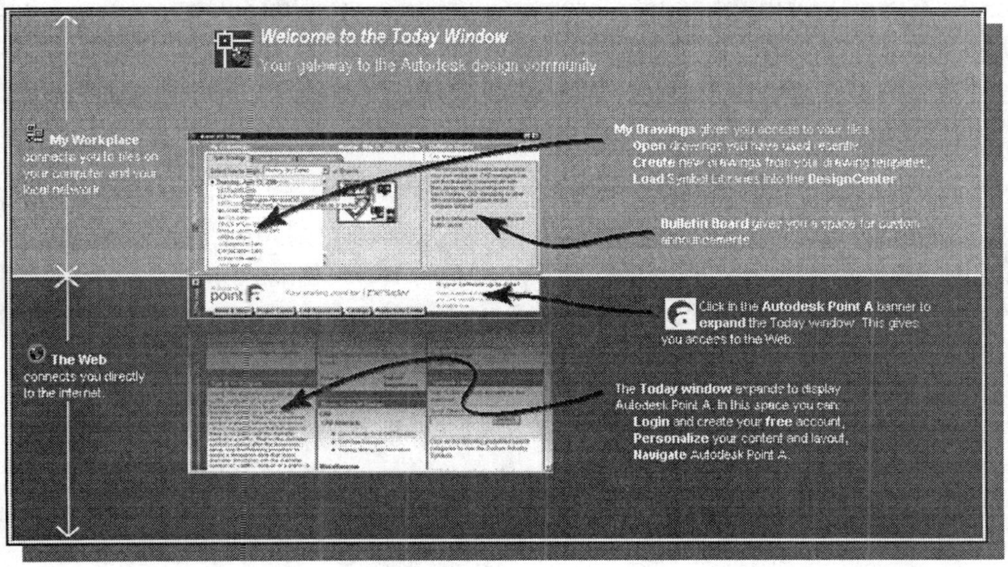

In the *My Drawings* section of the *AutoCAD Today* dialogue box, the following three startup options are available: *Open Drawings*, *Create Drawings*, and *Symbol Libraries*. We can *open existing files*, *create new drawings* or access the AutoCAD *symbol libraries* options.

- Select the **Create Drawings** tab with a single click of the left-mouse-button in the *My Workplace* section of the *AutoCAD Today* dialogue box.

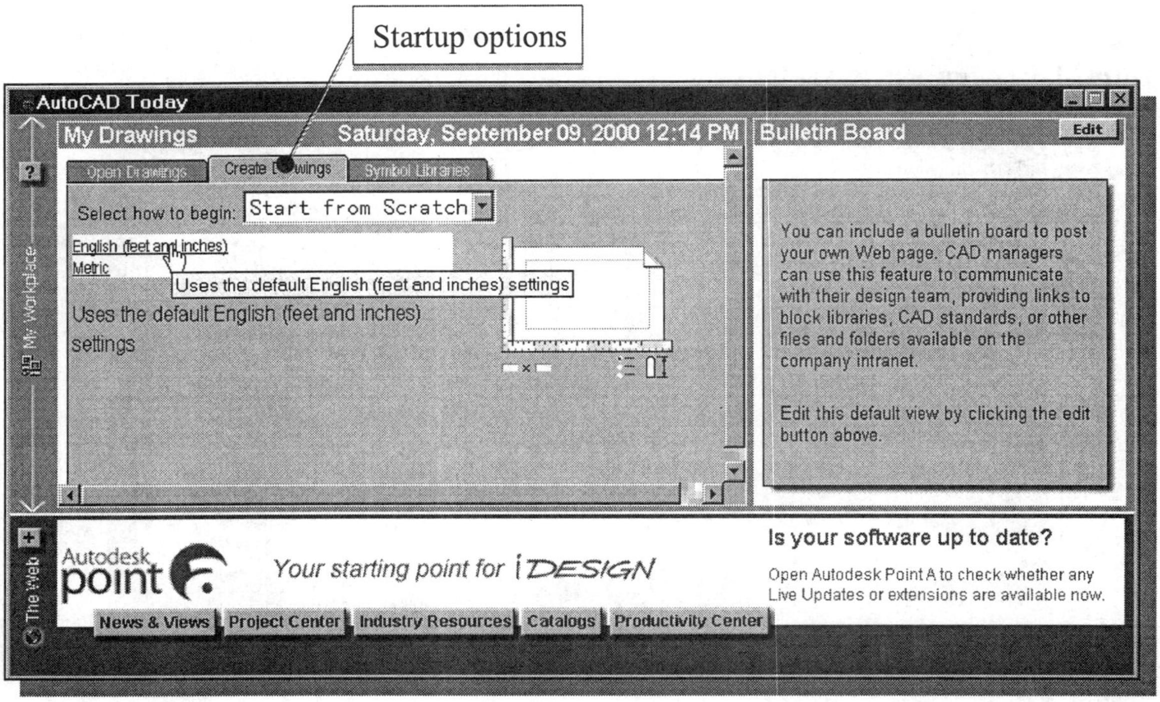

Under the **Create Drawings** tab, three options are available: *Start from Scratch*, *Use a Template*, and *Use a Wizard*. The default *Start from Scratch* option allows us to start a new CAD file without setting any preferences. We will explain and demonstrate the use of the other options in the following chapters.

Below the *Startup* option icons is the *Default Settings* section, which lets us specify the units to be used with the CAD file. When starting a new CAD file, the first thing we should do is choose the units we would like to use. We will use the default **English (feet and Inches)** setting for this example.

- Move the cursor on top of the **English (feet and inches)** option and notice a brief explanation of the option is displayed as shown in the above figure.

- Use the left-mouse-button to select the **English (feet and Inches)** units as the units to be used for the design.

AutoCAD® 2000i Screen Layout

The default AutoCAD® 2000i drawing screen contains the *pull-down* menus, the *Standard* toolbar, the *Object Properties* toolbar, the *Draw* toolbar, the *Modify* toolbar, the *command prompt area*, the *Status Bar* and the *AutoCAD Active Assistance*. A line of quick help text appears at the bottom of the window as you move the *mouse cursor* over different icons. You may resize the AutoCAD® 2000i drawing window by click and drag at the edges of the window, or relocate the window by click and drag at the window title area.

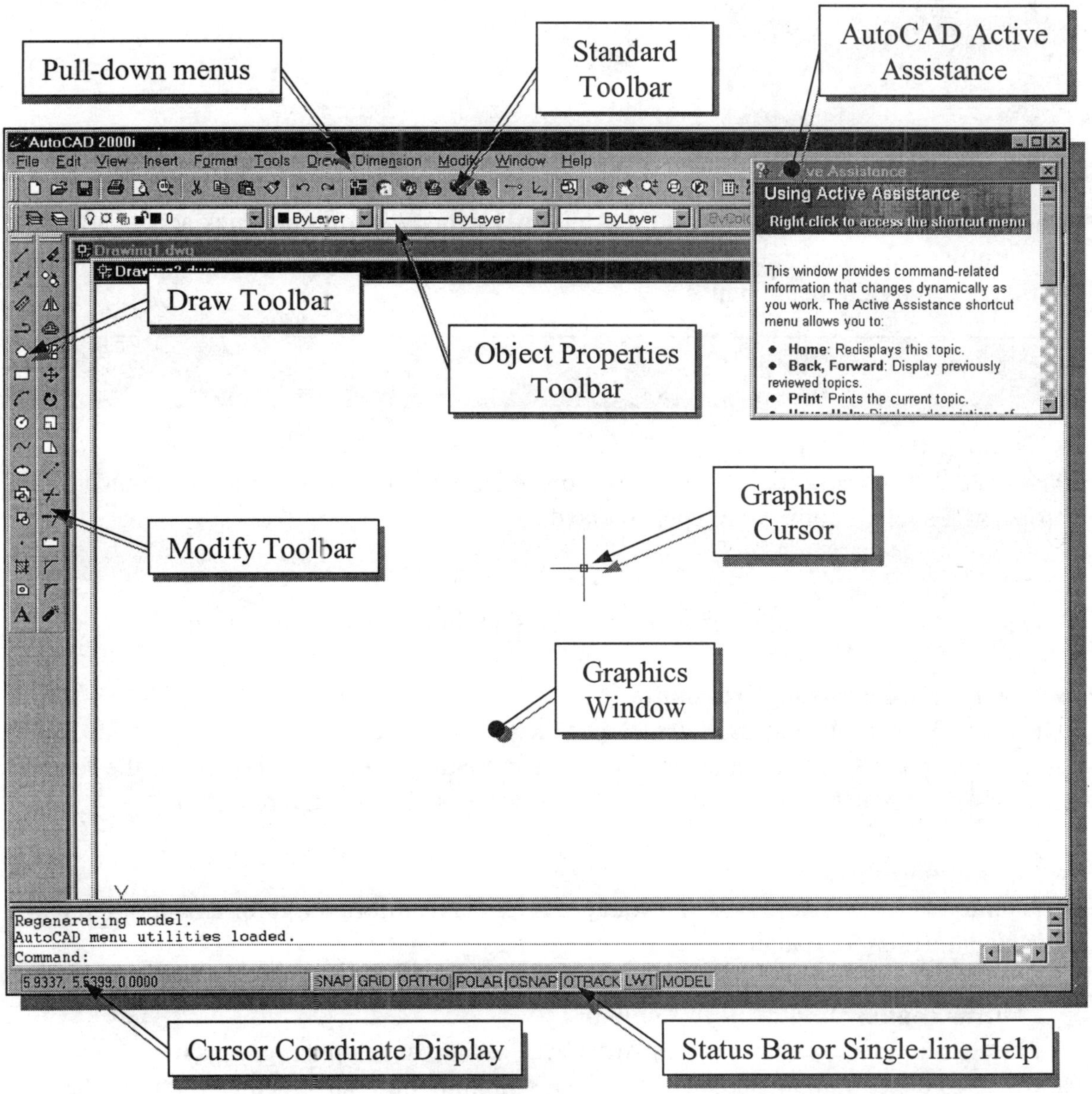

- **Pull-down Menus**

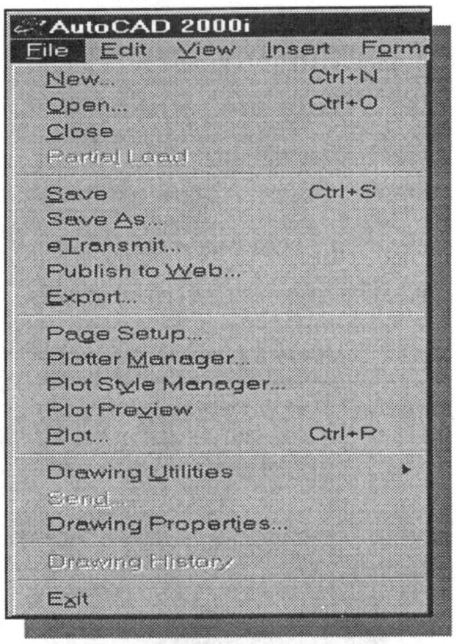

The *pull-down* menus at the top of the main window contain operations that you can use for all modes of the system.

- **Standard Toolbar**

The *Standard* toolbar at the top of the AutoCAD window allows us quick access to frequently used commands. We can customize the toolbar by adding and removing sets of options or individual commands.

- **Object Properties Toolbar**

The *Object Properties* toolbar contains tools to help manipulate the graphical object properties, such as color, line type, and layer.

- **Graphics Window**

The *graphics window* is the area where models and drawings are displayed.

- **Graphics Cursor or Crosshairs**

The *graphics cursor*, or *crosshairs*, shows the location of the pointing device in the graphics window. The coordinates of the cursor are displayed at the bottom of the screen layout. The cursor's appearance depends on the selected command or option.

- **Command Prompt Area**

The bottom section of the screen layout provides status information for an operation and it is also the area for data input.

- **Draw Toolbar and Modify Toolbar**

Additional toolbars are available in AutoCAD® 2000i, and contain groups of buttons that allow us to pick commands quickly, without searching through a menu structure. The *Draw* toolbar and *Modify* toolbar contain icons for basic draw and modify commands.

Mouse Buttons

AutoCAD® 2000i utilizes the mouse buttons extensively. In learning AutoCAD® 2000i's interactive environment, it is important to understand the basic functions of the mouse buttons. It is highly recommended that you use a mouse or a tablet with AutoCAD® 2000i since the package uses the buttons for various functions.

- **Left mouse button**

The **left-mouse-button** is used for most operations, such as selecting menus and icons, or picking graphic entities. One click of the button is used to select icons, menus and form entries, and to pick graphic items.

- **Right mouse button**

The **right-mouse-button** is used to bring up additional available options. The software also utilizes the **right-mouse-button** as the same as the **ENTER** key, and is often used to accept the default setting to a prompt or to end a process.

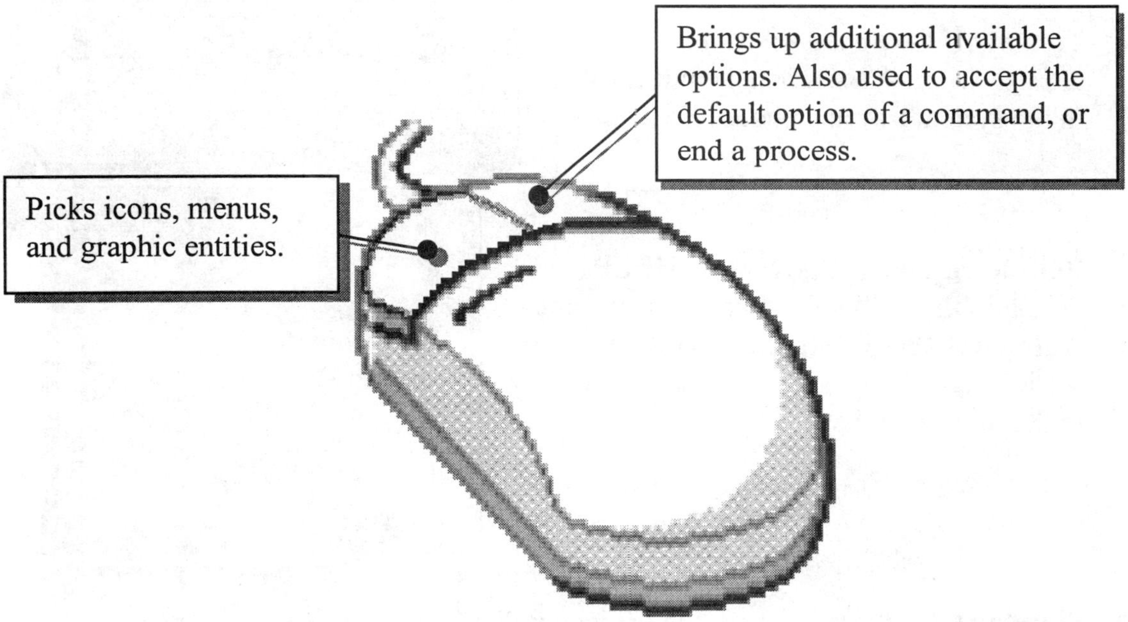

[Esc] - Canceling commands

The [Esc] key is used to cancel a command in AutoCAD® 2000i. The [Esc] key is located near the top-left corner of the keyboard. Sometimes, it may be necessary to press the [Esc] key twice to cancel a command; it depends upon where we are in the command sequence. For some commands, the [Esc] key is used to exit the command.

On-Line Help

❖ Several types of on-line help are available at any time during an AutoCAD 2000i session. The AutoCAD 2000i software provides many on-line help options:

- **Active Assistance**: The *Active Assistance* window provides an instant help that dynamically displays information on the activated command. The guidance from the *Active Assistance* system enables users to quickly get started on performing desired tasks. In the *Active Assistance* window, links to additional information are also available. Clicking a blue-text-link expands the current *Active Assistance* topic.

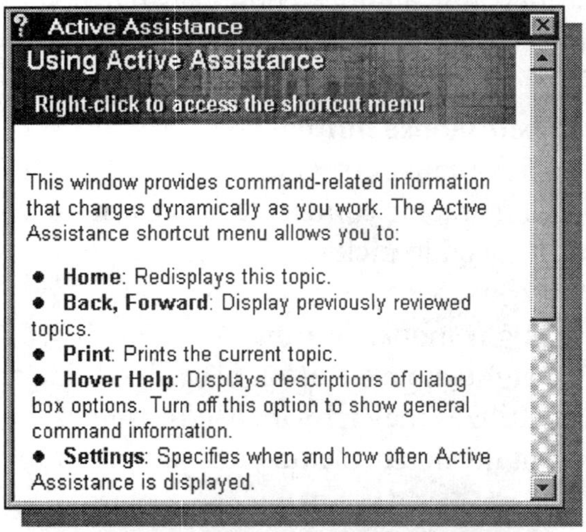

- To turn off the *Active Assistance*, right-click the *Active Assistance* icon located in the system tray and choose **Exit**.

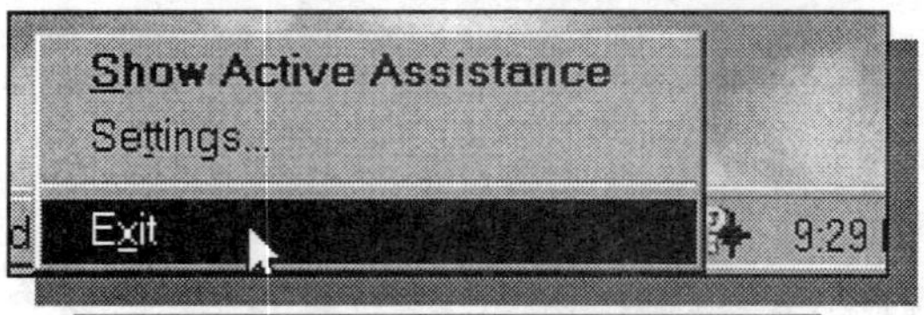

- **Pull-down menu**: Click on the **HELP** option in the pull-down menu to access the **AutoCAD 2000i Help menu system.** Notice the different help options available in the pull-down list.

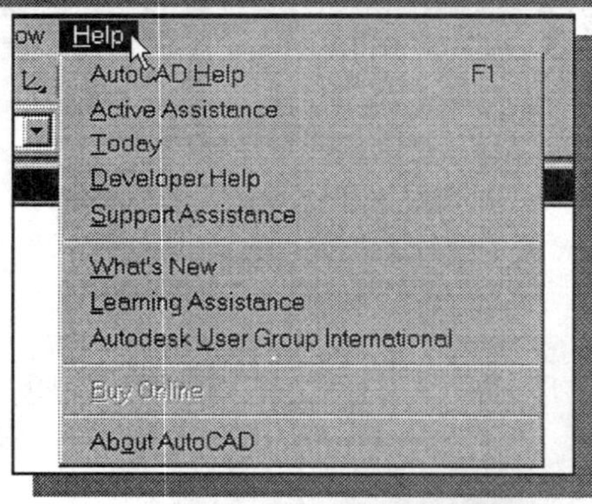

- **Standard Toolbar**: Click on the [?] icon in the *Standard* toolbar to access Autodesk On-line Help: User Documentation. Note the *Active Assistance* icon is located right next to the *Help* icon.

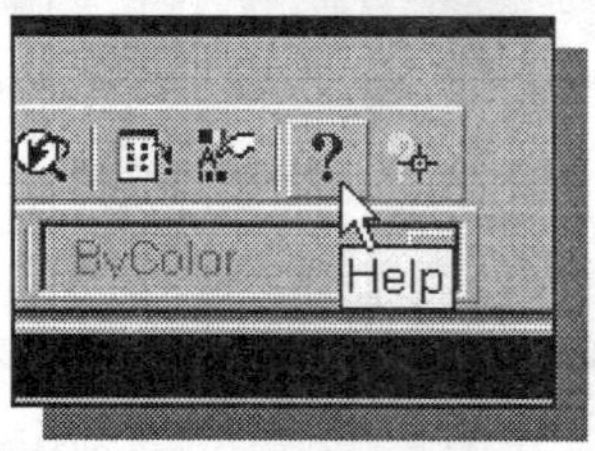

- **Command line and function key [F1]**: Press the [F1] key or enter a question mark [?] at the command prompt to access the **AutoCAD On-line Help** system.

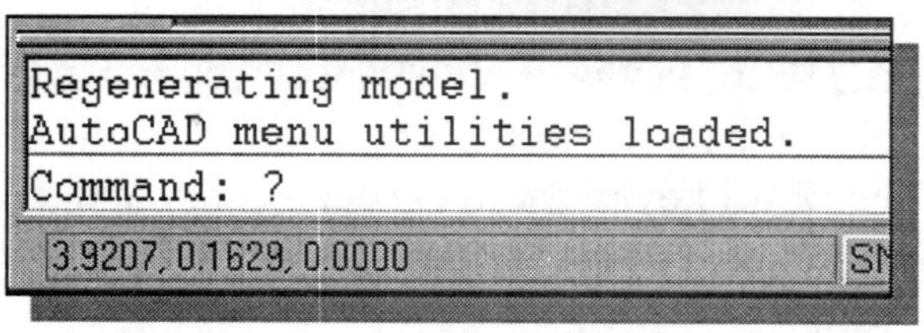

Leaving AutoCAD® 2000i

To leave AutoCAD® 2000i, use the left-mouse-button and click on **File** at the top of the AutoCAD® 2000i window, then choose **Exit** from the pull-down menu or type ***QUIT*** in the command prompt area.

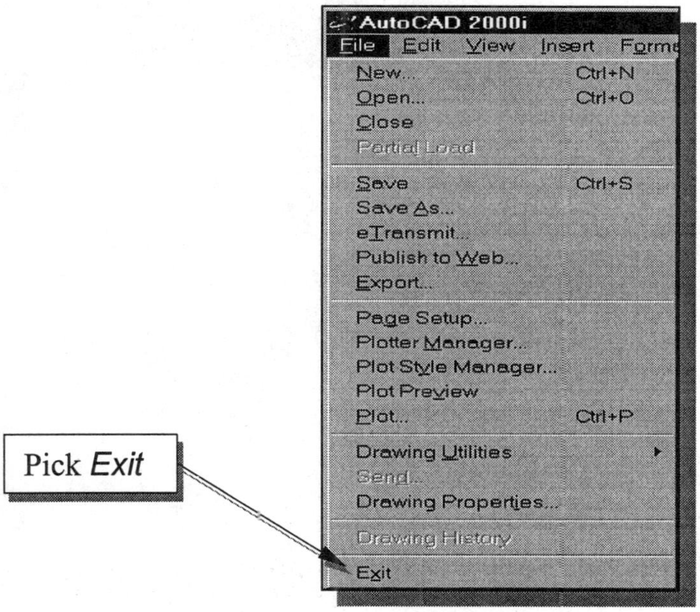

Creating a CAD file folder

It is a good practice to create a separate folder to store your CAD files. You should not save your CAD files in the same folder where the AutoCAD® 2000i application is located. It is much easier to organize and back up your project files if they are in a separate folder. Making folders within this folder for different types of projects will help you organize your CAD files even further. When creating CAD files in AutoCAD® 2000i, it is strongly recommended that you *save* your CAD files on the hard drive. However, if you do want to save your files on a floppy drive, be sure to exit the AutoCAD® 2000i program before removing the diskette from the drive. The better alternative is to save the files on the hard drive and then copy the files onto a floppy diskette under the operating system.

To create a new folder:

1. In *My Computer*, or start the **Windows Explorer** under the *Start* menu, open the folder in which you want to create a new folder.

2. On the **File** menu, point to **New**, and then click **Folder**. The new folder appears with a temporary name.

3. Type a name for the new folder, and then press **ENTER**.

Notes:

Chapter 2
User Coordinate System and the Z-Axis

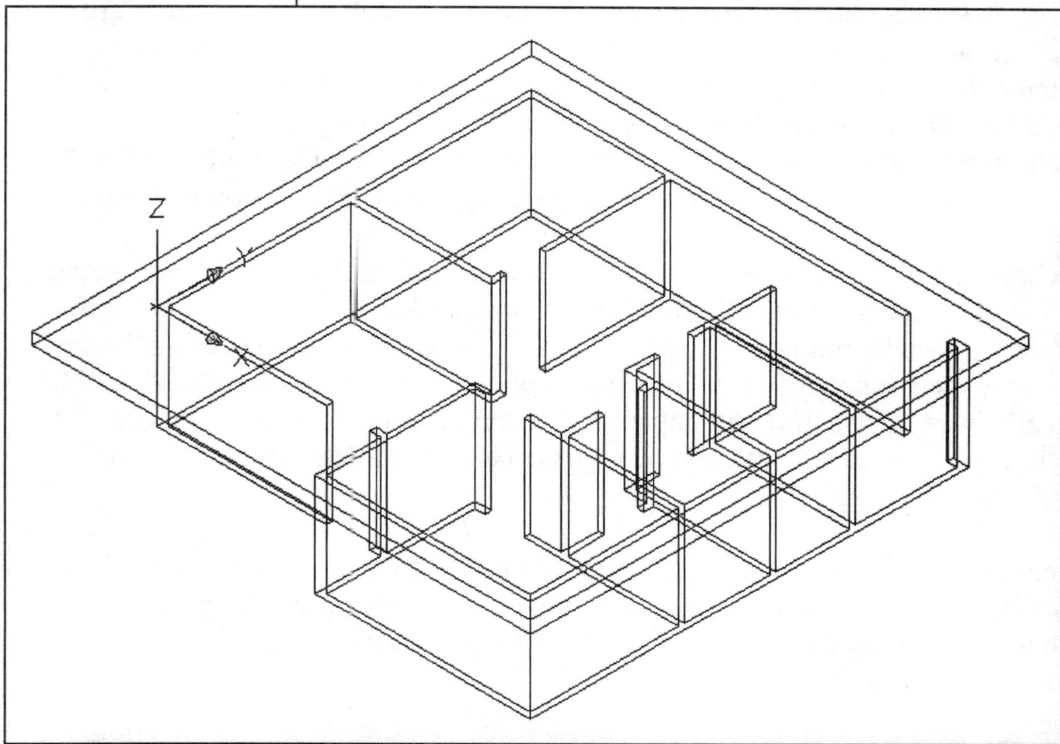

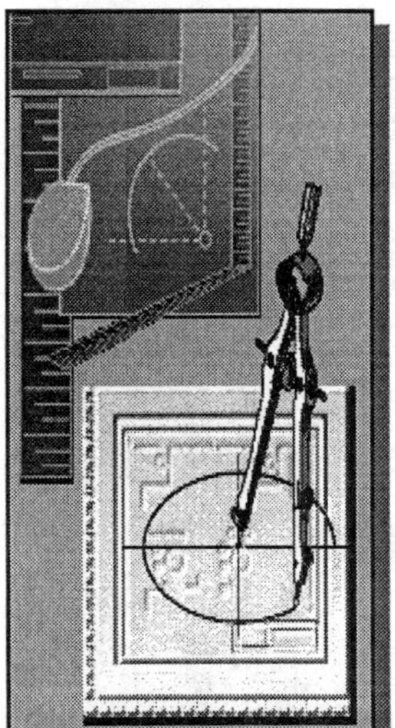

Learning Objectives

- Using the AutoCAD Quick Setup wizard.
- Understand and use the THICKNESS option.
- Understand the AutoCAD UCS.
- Be able to switch to predefined views.
- Pre-selection of objects.
- Controlling Object Properties
- Viewing with the Hidden option.

Introduction

Creating three-dimensional models on a CAD system provides us a means to check the integrity of a design. Creating realistic three-dimensional models helps us visualize our final design much more clearly than we can with 2D representations of the design. Several different approaches are available in AutoCAD that allow us to quickly create 3D models. The simplest approach is to use the THICKNESS variable to perform an extrusion in the third dimension of 2D geometries. In AutoCAD, the Thickness variable can make certain 2D objects look like 3D objects. It is important to realize that this approach is somewhat limited and that the objects created are not true solids. This approach allows us to start considering the complexity involved in creating 3D models.

In this chapter, we will explore the virtual 3D environment in AutoCAD. Understanding how to maneuver in the virtual 3D environment and the use of a *User Coordinate System* (UCS) are the foundations and perhaps the most difficult part of 3D modeling. We will also examine the basic viewing and rendering options that are available in AutoCAD. Specifically, we will use the Hide options to create hidden-line-removed images. The hidden-line-removed image makes it easier to visualize the model because the back faces are not displayed.

In this chapter, we will begin with the construction of a 2D floor plan design. This tutorial will also serve as a review of some of the 2D CAD construction techniques. The main goal of this chapter is to provide you with a basic understanding of the 3D environment of AutoCAD.

The Floor Plan Design

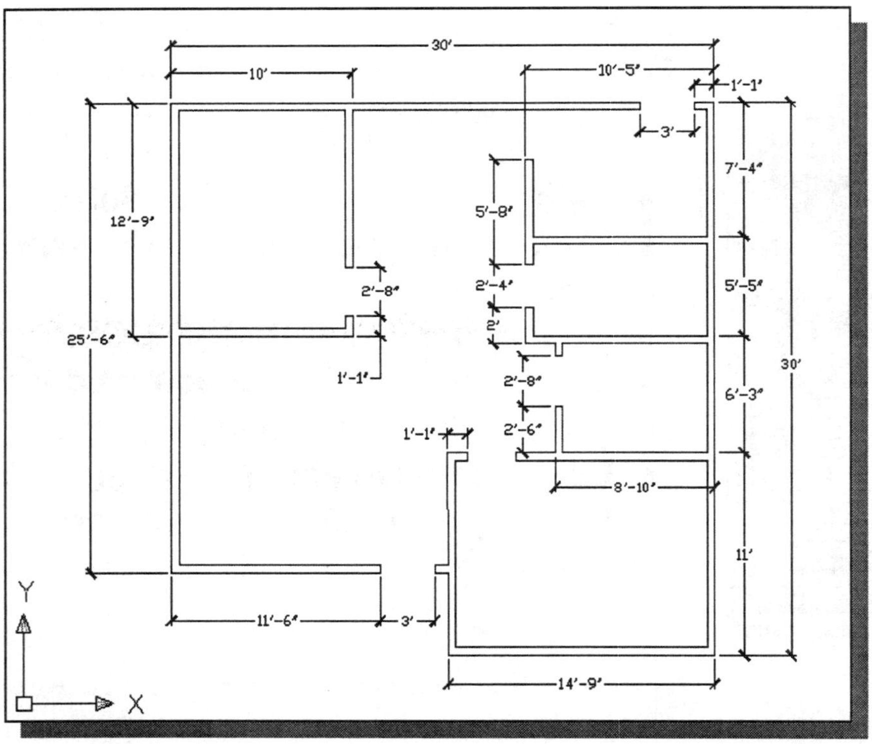

Starting Up AutoCAD® 2000i

1. Select the AutoCAD® 2000i option on the *Program* menu or select the AutoCAD® 2000i icon on the *Desktop*. Once the program is loaded into memory, the AutoCAD® 2000i drawing screen and the *AutoCAD Today* startup dialog box will appear on the screen.

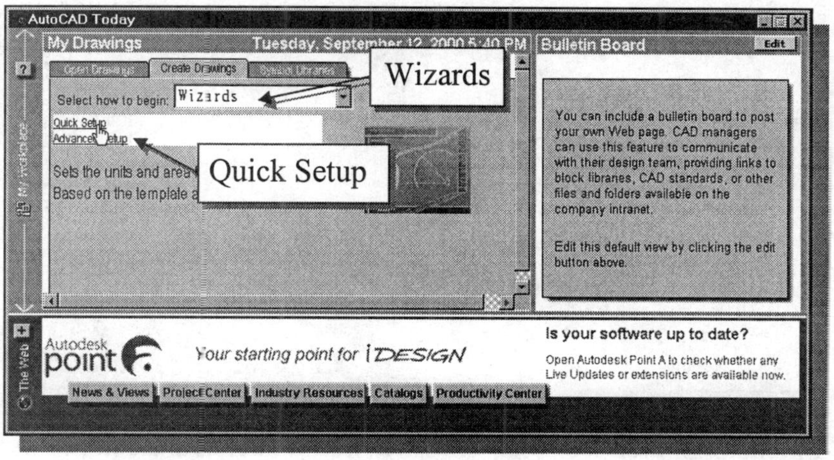

2. In the *AutoCAD Today* startup dialog box, select the **Create Drawings** tab with a single click of the left-mouse-button.

3. In the startup dialog box, select the ***Wizards*** option as shown in the above figure.

4. In the *Wizards* section, pick ***Quick Setup***.

- AutoCAD setup wizards allow us to customize several of the AutoCAD settings depending upon the wizard we choose. The *Quick Setup* wizard sets the units and grid display area. Choices for units include *Decimal, Engineering, Architectural, Fractional,* and *Scientific*. We can also specify the width and length of a two-dimensional area to establish the extents of the *grid* displayed, also known as the *limits* of the working area.

Drawing Units Setup

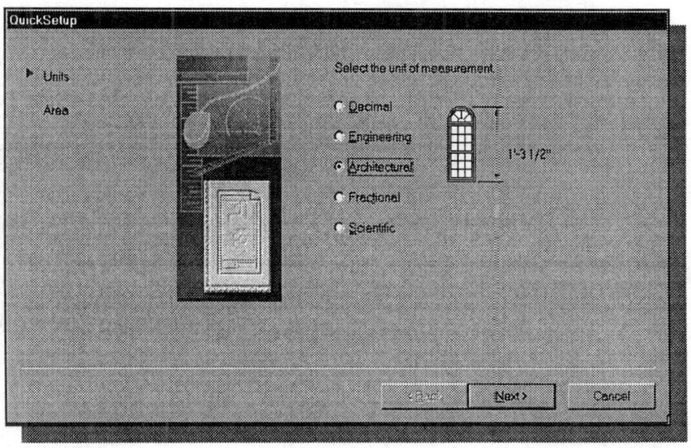

1. In the *Quick Setup - Units* option, select ***Architectural***.

2. Click **Next** to continue with the *Quick Setup* settings.

Reference Area Setup

1. In the *Quick Setup - Area* option, enter ***60'*** and ***40'*** for the width and length.

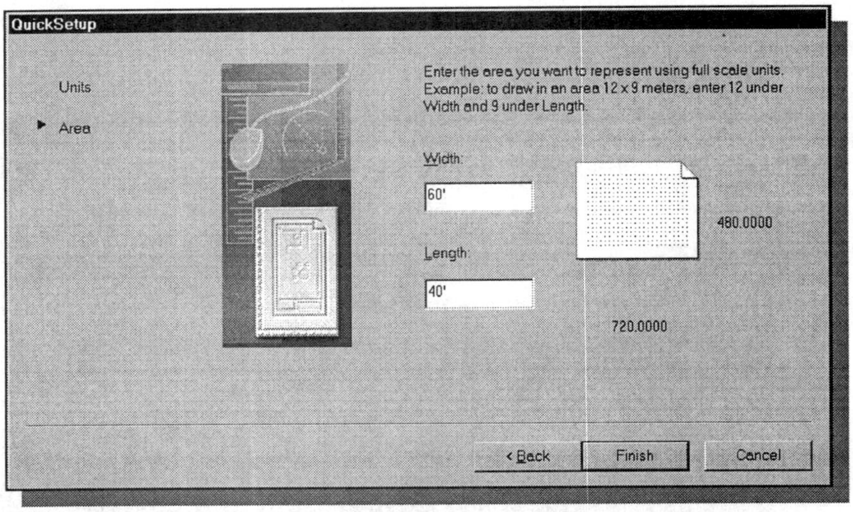

- The two-dimensional area we set up in *Quick Setup* is called the *limits* in AutoCAD. Setting the *limits* controls the extents of the display of the *grid*, and also provides the following functionality:
  - Serves as a visual reference that marks the working area.
  - Serves as a tool that can be used to prevent construction outside the grid limits.
  - Serves as a plot option that defines an area to be plotted/printed.

2. Pick **Finish** to accept the settings and end the *Quick Setup* wizard.

- We have two drawing windows opened in the AutoCAD window. Note that the units setting of *Drawing1* is set to the default system units. The *Drawing2* window is set up through the AutoCAD *Quick Setup* wizard, which set the units to the architectural style. To avoid any confusion in following through the tutorial, let's close the *Drawing1* window.

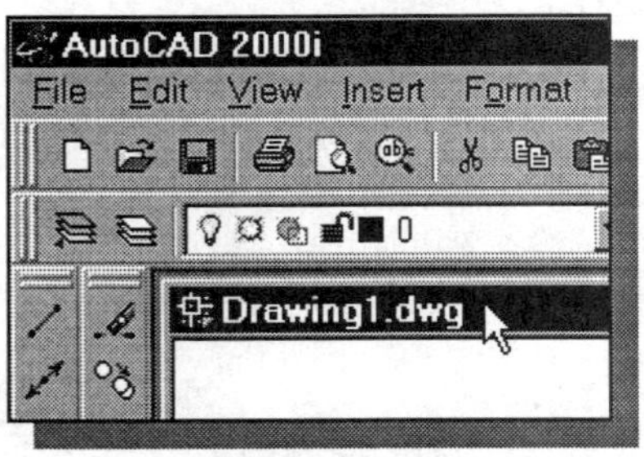

3. Switch to the *Drawing1* window by left-clicking once in the title area of the window.

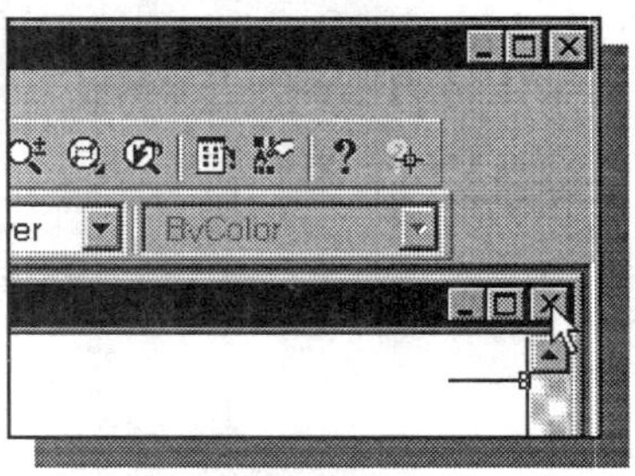

4. Close the window by clicking the ***Close*** icon located at the upper-right-corner of the *Drawing1* window.

GRID and *SNAP* intervals Setup

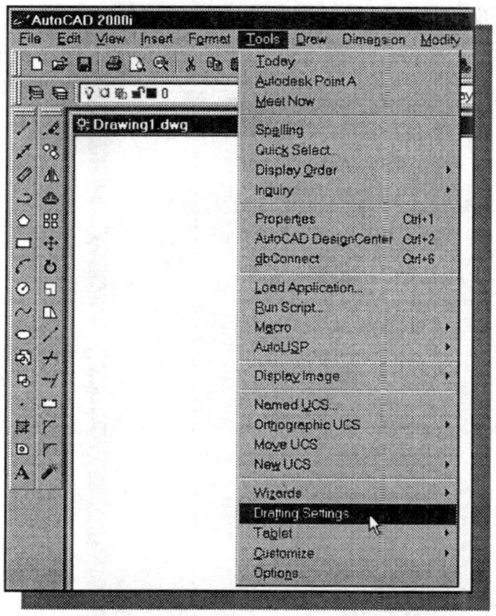

1. In the pull-down menus, select:
   [Tools] => [Drafting Settings]

2. In the *Drafting Settings* dialog box, select the **SNAP and GRID** tab if it is not the page on top.

3. Change *Grid Spacing* to ***6"*** for both X and Y directions.

4. Also adjust the *Snap Spacing* to ***6"*** for both X and Y directions.

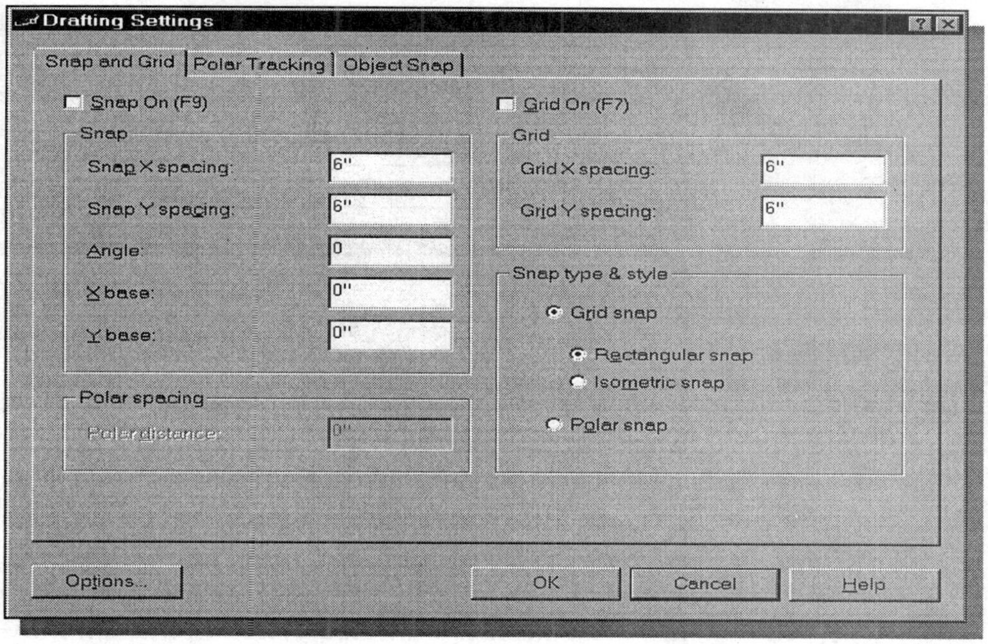

5. Pick **OK** to exit the *Drafting Settings* dialog box.

6. In the *Status Bar* area, reset the option buttons so that only *SNAP, GRID*, and *MODEL* are switched ***ON***.

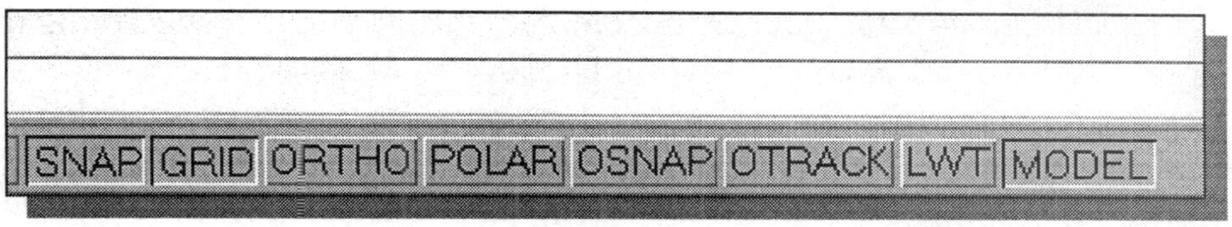

Drawing Polylines

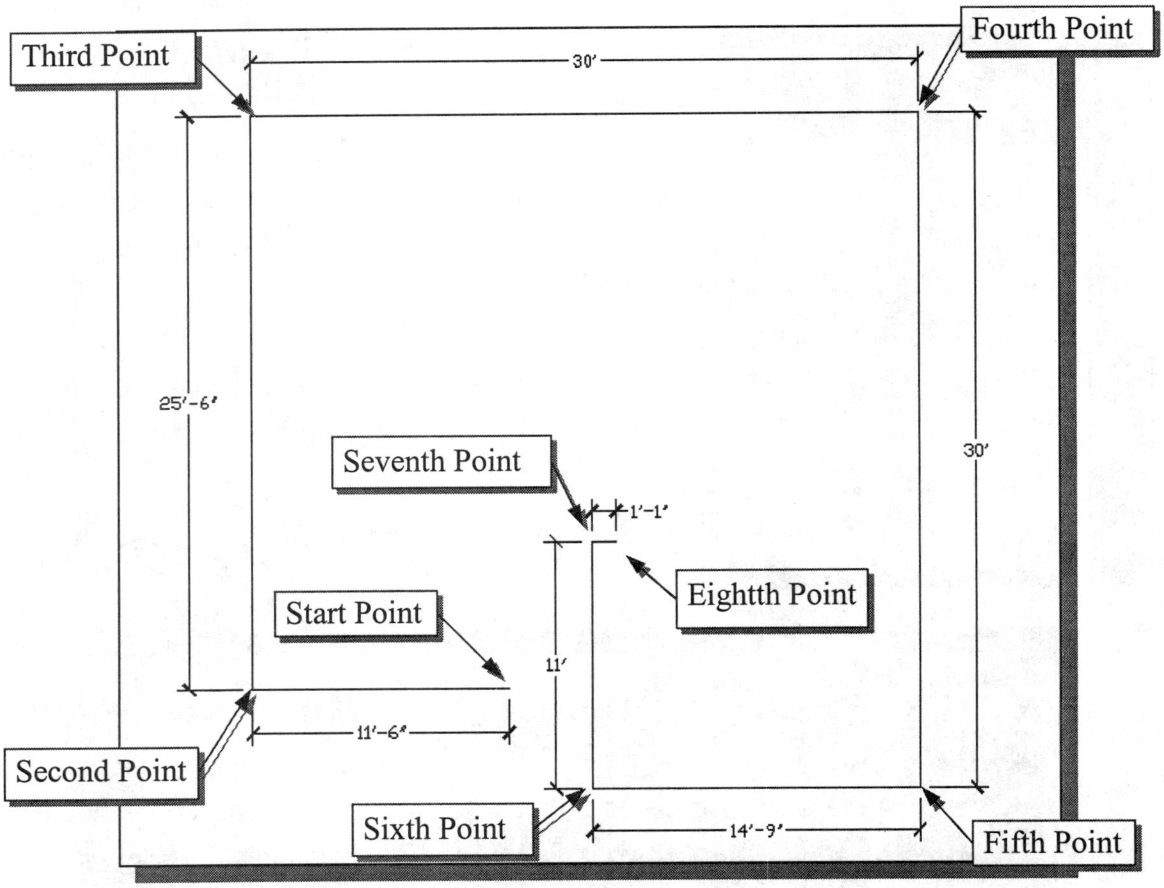

1. Select the ***Polyline*** command icon in the *Draw* toolbar.

2. In the command prompt area, the message *"Specify start point:"* is displayed. AutoCAD expects us to identify the starting location. Select a location near the bottom of the graphics window as the **starting point** of the polyline by left-clicking the mouse.

3. In the command prompt area, create a vertical line by using the *relative rectangular coordinates entry method*, relative to the last point we specified

   Specify next point: **@-11'6" [ENTER]**

4. On your own, complete the polyline by specifying the points, *point three* through *point eight*, as shown.

5. Inside the graphics window, right-mouse-click and select **Enter** to end the *POLYLINE* command.

Creating an offset polyline

- The *OFFSET* command creates a new object at a specified distance from an existing object or through a specified point.

1. Select the ***Offset*** command icon in the *Modify* toolbar. In the command prompt area, the message *"Specify offset distance or [Through]:"* is displayed.

   Specify offset distance or [Through]: **6" [ENTER]**

2. In the command prompt area, the message *"Select object to offset or <exit>:"* is displayed. Pick any line segment on the screen. (Note that all line segments of the polyline are automatically selected.)

3. AutoCAD next asks us to identify the direction of the offset. Pick a location that is *inside* the polyline.

4. Inside the graphics window, **right-mouse-click** to end the *OFFSET* command.

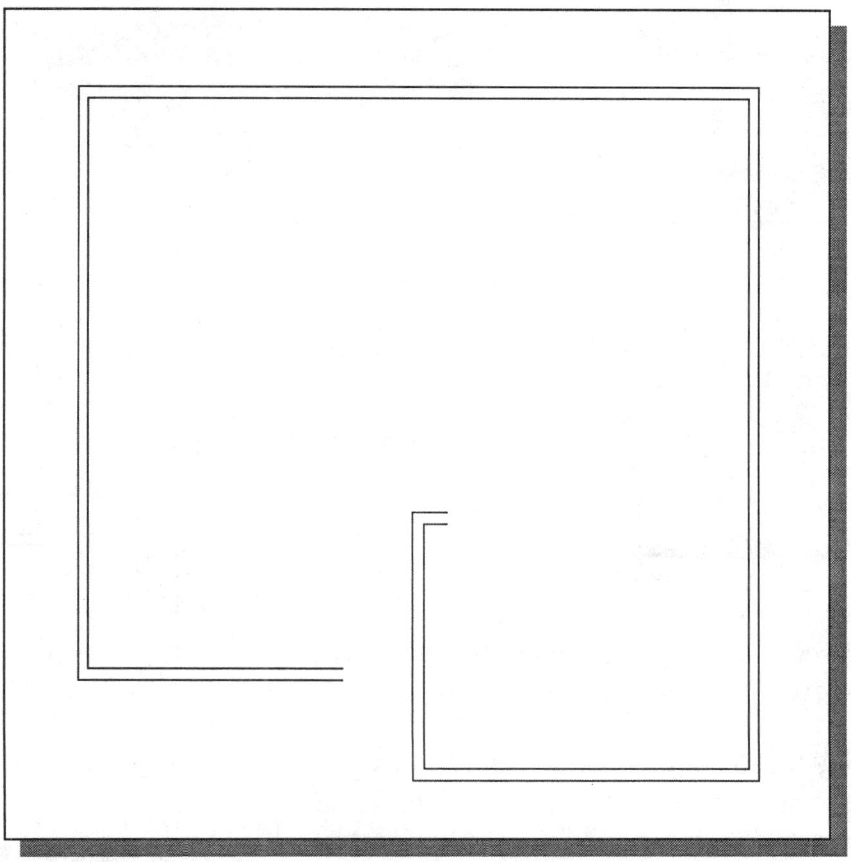

Creating interior walls

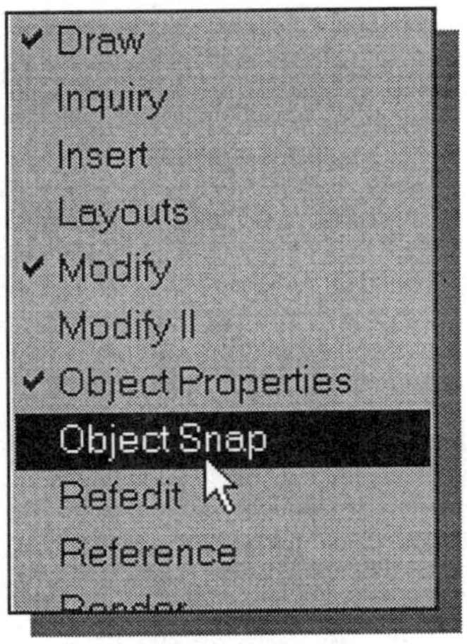

1. Move the cursor on any icon in the *Standard* toolbar area and **right-mouse-click** once to display a list of toolbar menu groups.

2. Select ***Object Snap***, with the left-mouse-button, to display the *Object Snap* toolbar on the screen to assist the construction of the floor plan.

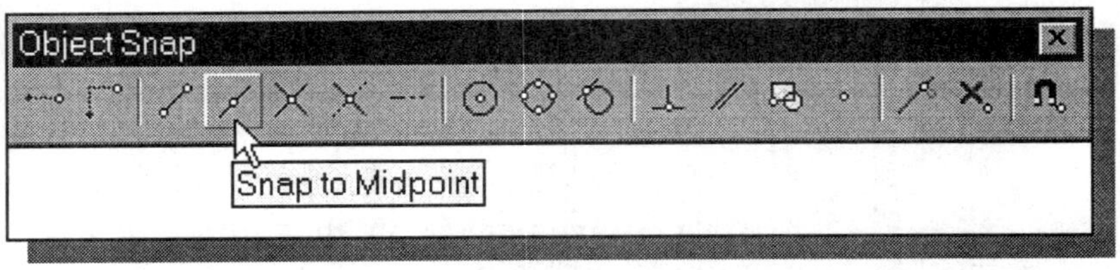

3. Select the ***Polyline*** command icon in the *Draw* toolbar. In the command prompt area, the message *"Specify start point or [Justification/Scale/Style]:"* is displayed.

4. In the *Object Snap* toolbar, pick ***Snap to Midpoint***. In the command prompt area, the message *"_mid of"* is displayed. AutoCAD now expects us to select a geometric entity on the screen.

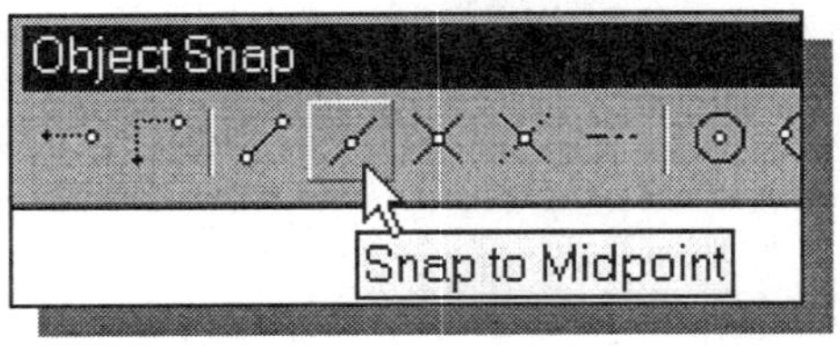

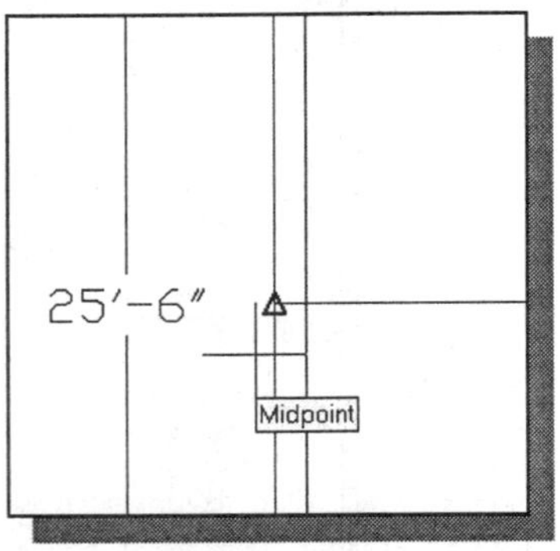

5. Select the vertical line on the left as shown.

6. At the command prompt, enter **@10',0 [ENTER]**.

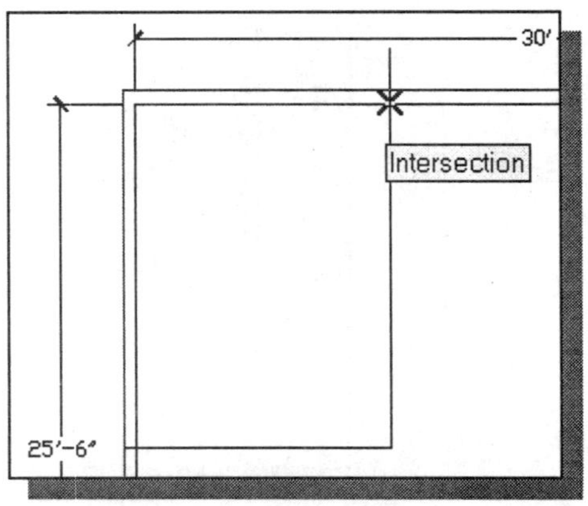

7. Next define a vertical wall by using the intersection option and create a vertical line as shown.

8. Inside the graphics window, **right-mouse-click** and select **Enter** to end the *POLYLINE* command.

9. Select the ***Offset*** command icon in the *Modify* toolbar. In the command prompt area, the message *"Specify offset distance or [Through]:"* is displayed.

   Specify offset distance or [Through]: **6" [ENTER]**

10. In the command prompt area, the message *"Select object to offset or <exit>:"* is displayed. Pick the polyline we just created.

11. AutoCAD next asks us to identify the direction of the offset. Pick a location that is toward the upper-left corner of the design.

12. Inside the graphics window, **right-mouse-click** to end the *OFFSET* command.

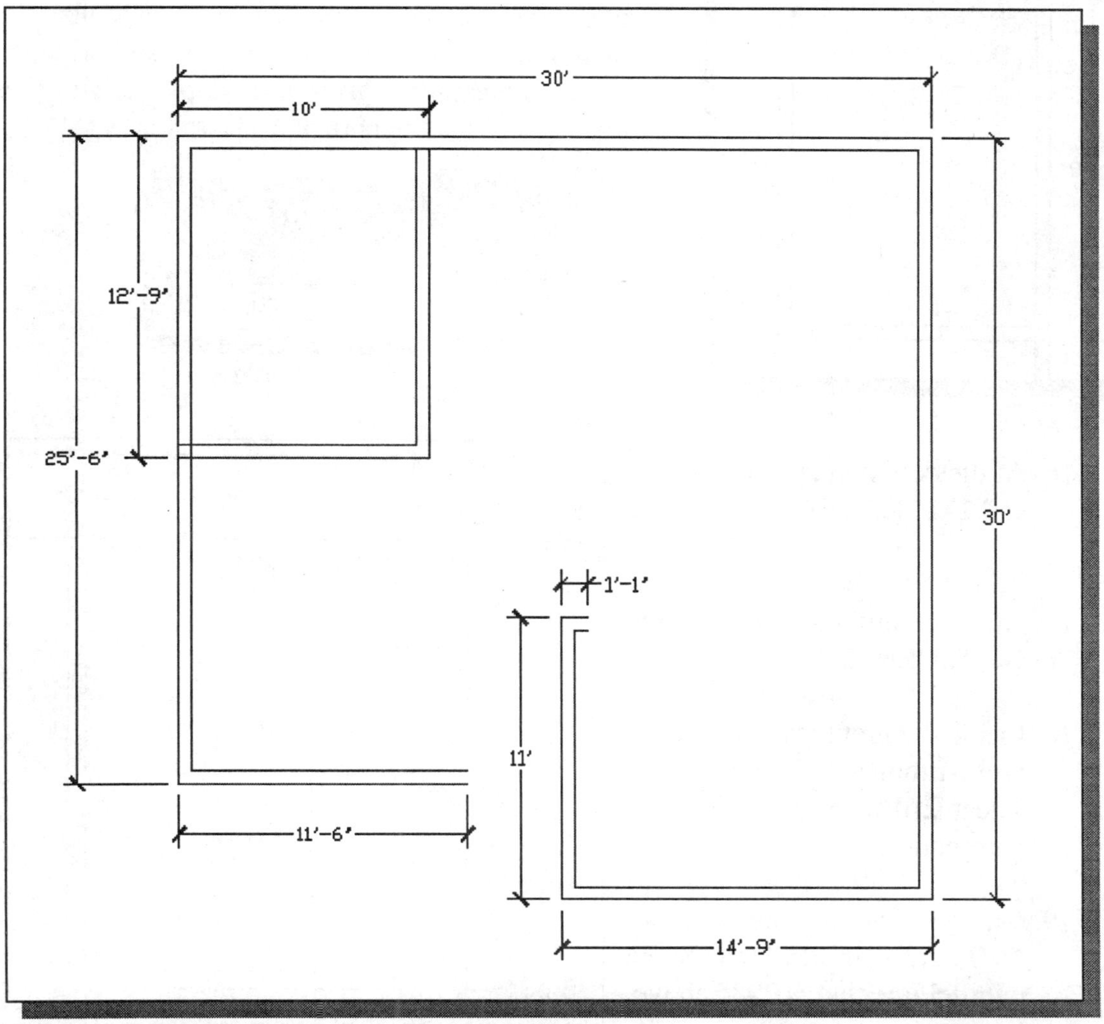

- Next, we will create a 2'-8" doorway.

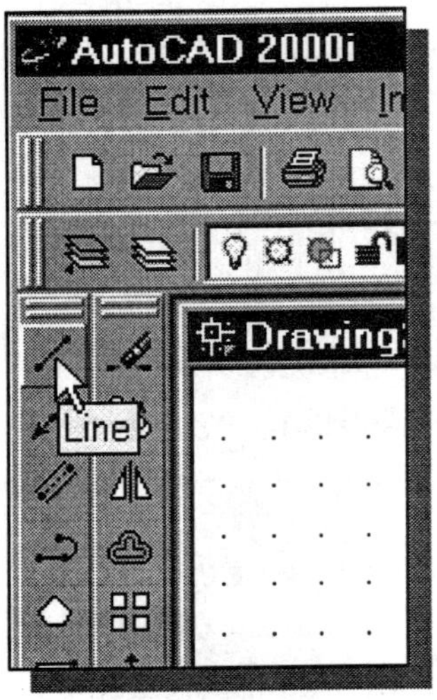

13. Select the ***Line*** command icon in the *Draw* toolbar. In the command prompt area, the message *"_line Specify first point:"* is displayed.

14. In the *Object Snap* toolbar, pick ***Snap From***. In the command prompt area, the message *"_from Base point"* is displayed. AutoCAD now expects us to select a geometric entity on the screen.

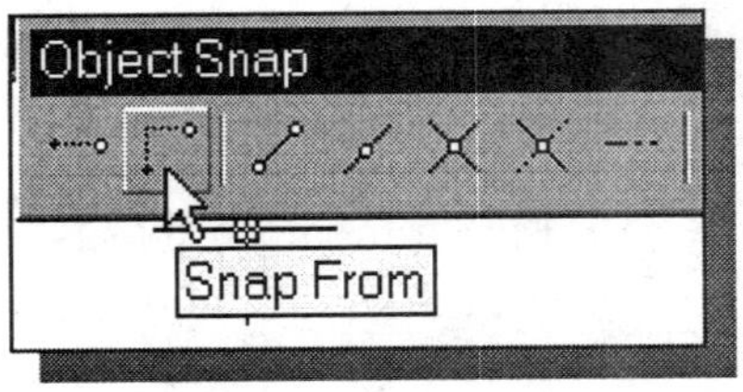

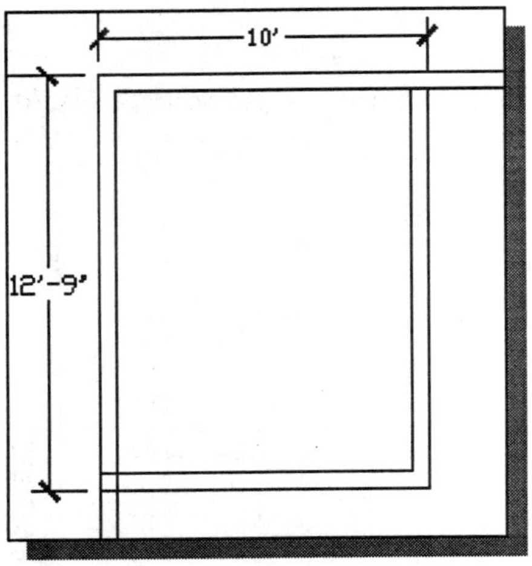

15. We will measure relative to the lower-left corner of the interior wall. In the *Object Snap* toolbar, pick ***Snap to Endpoint***. In the command prompt area, the message *"_from Base point:_endp of"* is displayed. Pick the corner as shown.

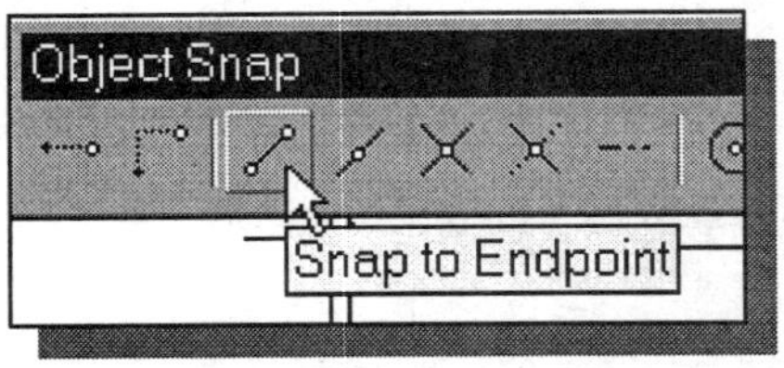

16. At the command prompt, enter **@0,1'-1" [ENTER]**.

17. At the command prompt, enter **@-6",0 [ENTER]**.

18. Inside the graphics window, **right-mouse-click** once and select **Enter** to end the *LINE* command.

19. On your own, use the ***OFFSET*** command to create a parallel line that is 2'-8" above the line we just created.

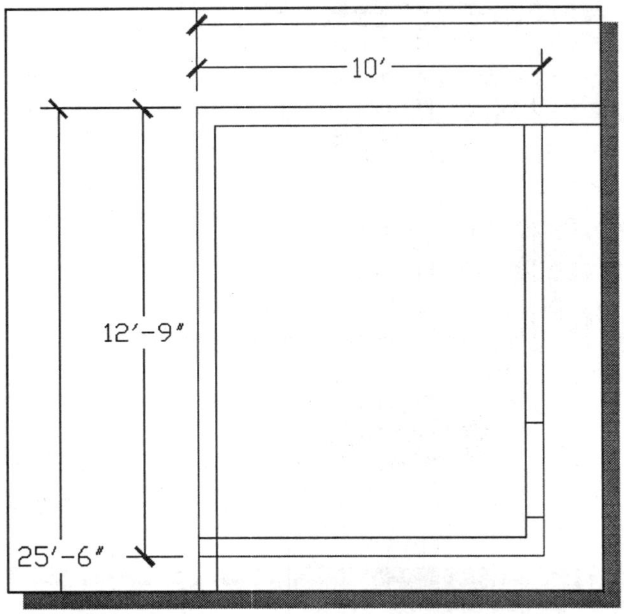

Completing the doorway using *TRIM* command

- The *TRIM* command shortens an object so that it ends precisely at a selected boundary.

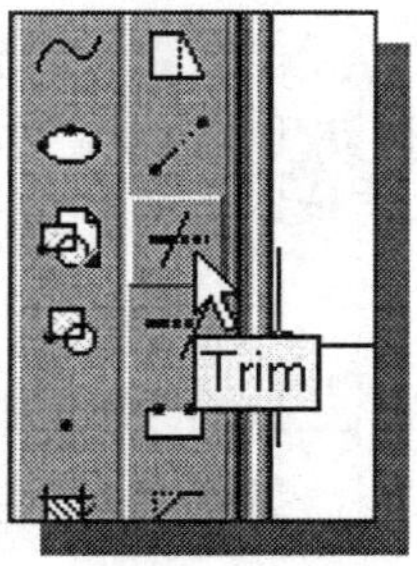

1. Select the ***Trim*** command icon in the *Modify* toolbar. In the command prompt area, the message *"Select boundary edges... Select objects:"* is displayed.

- First we will select the objects that define the boundary edges to which we want to trim the object.

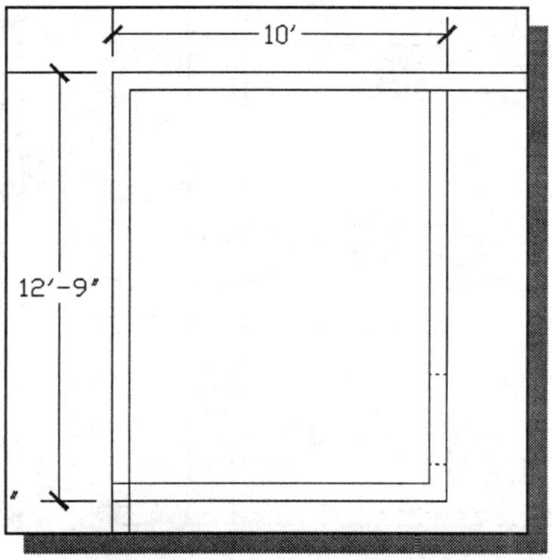

2. Pick the two horizontal lines we just created as the *boundary edges*.

3. Inside the graphics window, **right-mouse-click** to proceed with the *TRIM* command.

4. The message *"Select object to trim or shift-select object to extend or [Project/ Edge/ Undo]:"* is displayed in the command prompt area. Pick the vertical sections bound by the two selected horizontal lines.

5. Inside the graphics window, **right-mouse-click** to activate the option menu and select **Enter** with the left-mouse-button to end the *TRIM* command.

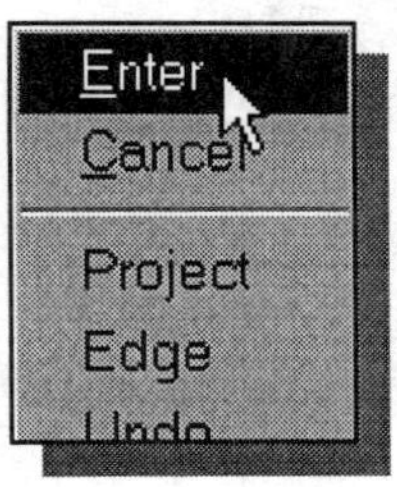

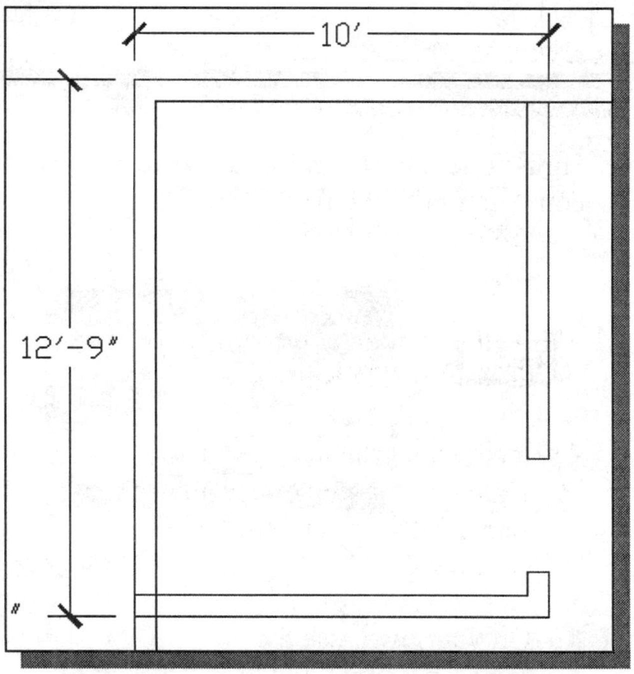

- Using the *POLYLINE* and *LINE* commands, create the additional walls and doorways as shown.

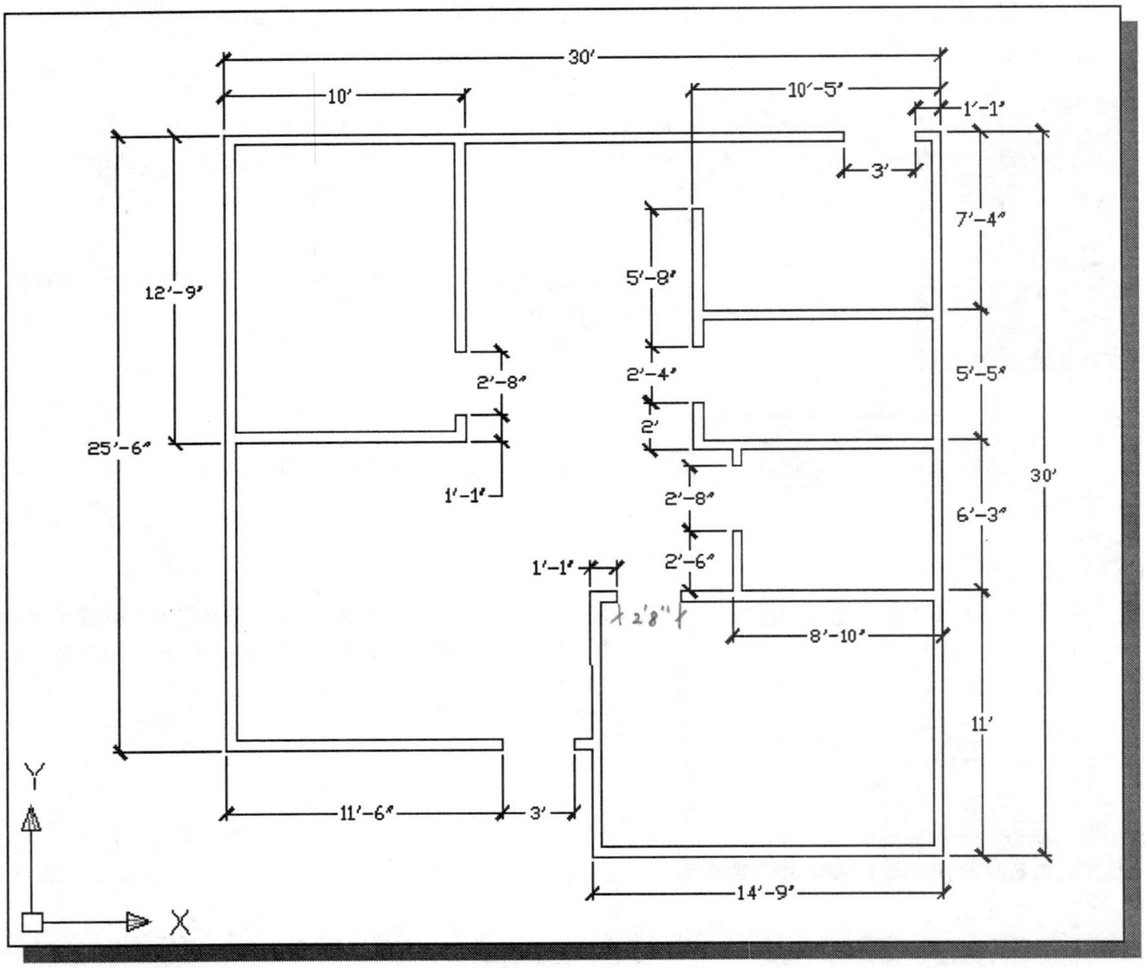

❖ Hints: Use the ***TRIM/EXTEND***, ***UNDO***, and ***ERASE*** commands to assist the construction of the floor plan.

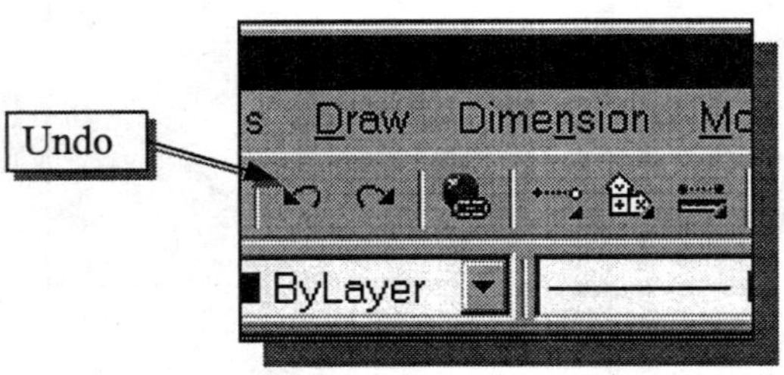

- Now is a good time to save the design. Select **[File] => [Save As]** in the pull-down menu and use ***FloorPlan*** as the *File name.*

User Coordinate System – It is an XY CRT, but an XYZ World

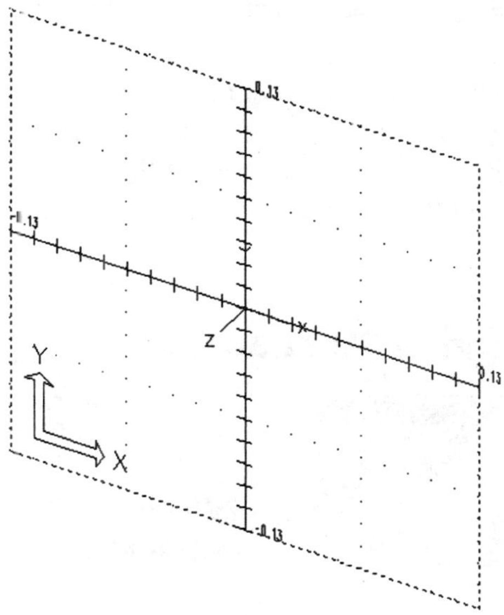

Design modeling software is becoming more powerful and user friendly, yet the system still does only what the user tells it to do. When using a geometric modeler, we therefore need to have a good understanding of what the inherent limitations are. We should also have a good understanding of what we want to do and what to expect, as the results are based on what is available.

In most 3D geometric modelers, 3D objects are located and defined in what is usually called **world space** or **global space**. Although a number of different coordinate systems can be used to create and manipulate objects in a 3D modeling system, the objects are typically defined and stored using the world space. The world space is usually a **3D Cartesian coordinate system** that the user cannot change or manipulate.

In most engineering designs, models can be very complex, and it would be tedious and confusing if only the world coordinate system were available. Practical 3D modeling systems allow the user to define **Local Coordinate Systems (LCS)** or **User Coordinate Systems (UCS)** relative to the world coordinate system. Once a local coordinate system is defined, we can then create geometry in terms of this more convenient system.

Although objects are created and stored in 3D space coordinates, most of the geometry entities can be referenced using 2D Cartesian coordinate systems. Typical input devices such as a mouse or digitizers are two-dimensional by nature; the movement of the input device is interpreted by the system in a planar sense. The same limitation is true of common output devices, such as CRT displays and plotters. The modeling software performs a series of three-dimensional to two-dimensional transformations to correctly project 3D objects onto a 2D picture plane.

The AutoCAD's **User Coordinate System (UCS)** is a special construction tool that enables the planar nature of the 2D input devices to be directly mapped into the 3D coordinate system. The ***UCS*** is a local coordinate system that can be aligned to the world coordinate system, an existing face of a part, or a pre-defined plane. By default, the UCS is aligned to the XY plane of the world coordinate system.

Think of the UCS as the surface on which we can sketch the 2D profiles of designs. It is similar to a piece of paper, a white board, or a chalkboard that can be attached to any planar surface. In the previous sections, we created the 2D design of a floor plan using the default settings where the UCS is aligned to the XY plane of the world coordinate system.

Viewing the 2D Design in 3D space

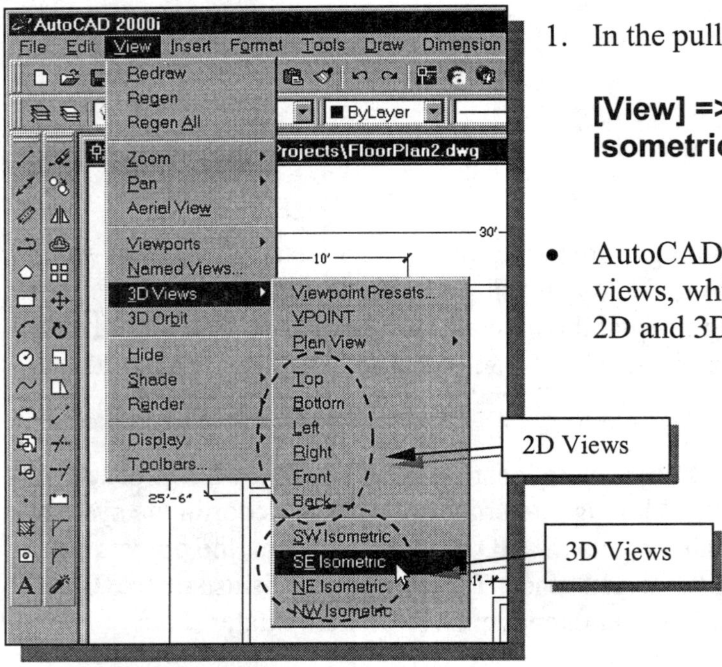

1. In the pull-down menus, select:

   [View] => [3D Views] => [SE Isometric]

- AutoCAD provides a set of pre-defined views, which contains most of the standard 2D and 3D views as shown in the figure.

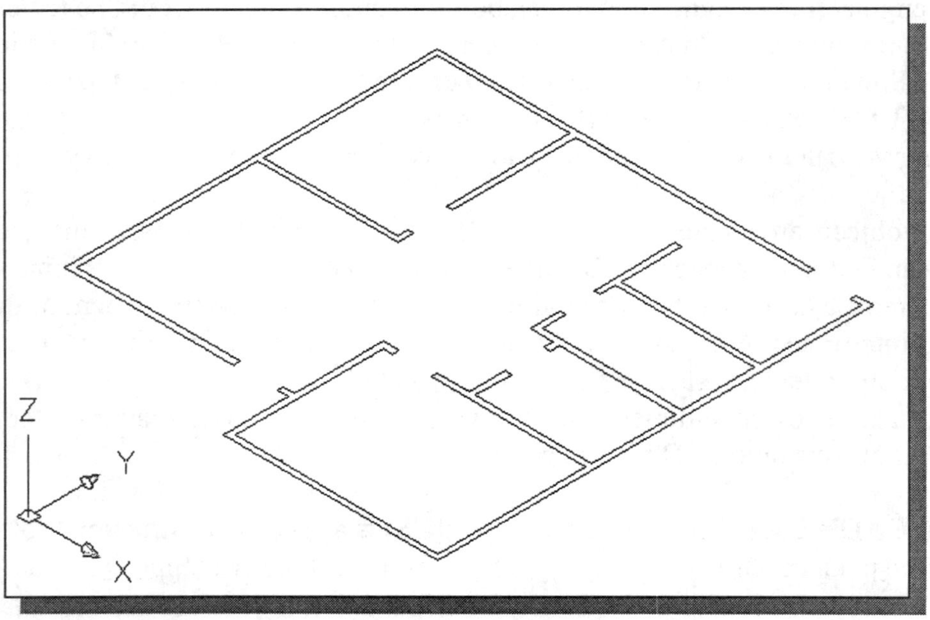

- The orientations of the preset 2D and 3D views are based on the world coordinate system as shown below. Note that the positive Y-axis direction is also identified as pointing toward **North** and the preset 3D views are oriented using the **North**, **East**, **South** and **West** directions.

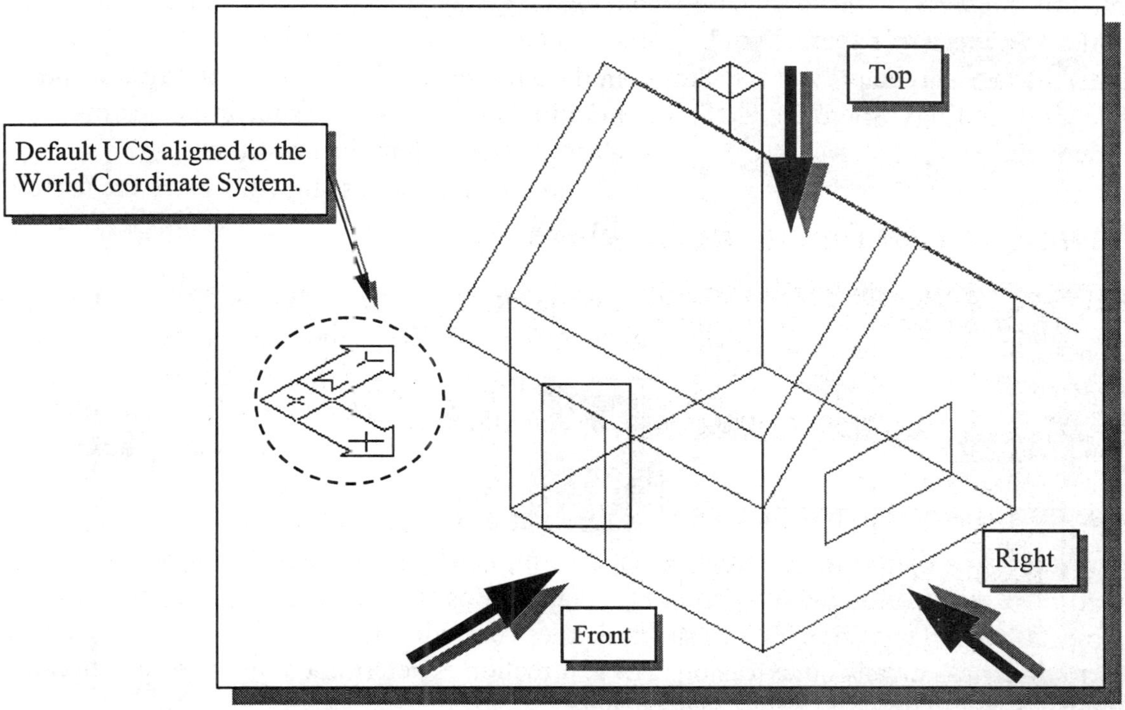

Adding the 3rd dimension to the Floor Plan Design

❖ AutoCAD 2000i provides a flexible graphical user interface that allows users to select graphical entities BEFORE the command is selected (*Pre-selection*), or AFTER the command is selected (*Post-selection*). We can pre-select one or more objects by clicking on the objects at the command prompt (**Command:**). To deselect the selected items, press the **[Esc]** key twice.

1. Inside the graphics window, pre-select all objects by enclosing all objects inside a **selection window** as shown.

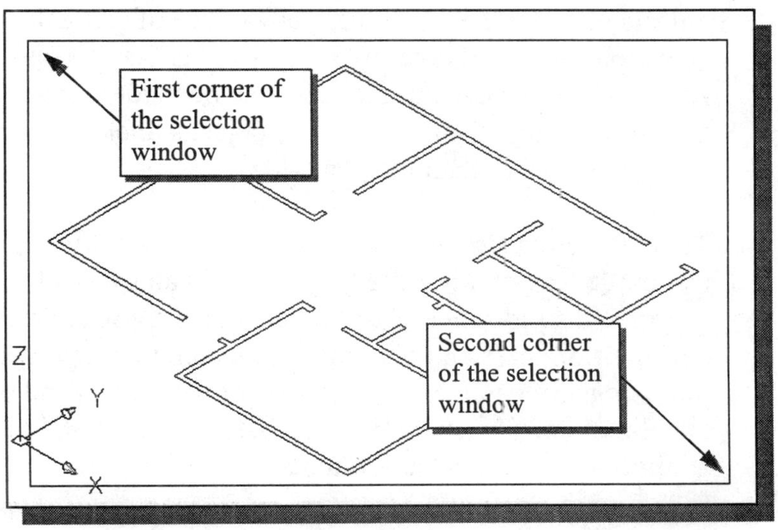

2. In the *Standard* toolbar, click on the ***PROPERTIES*** icon.

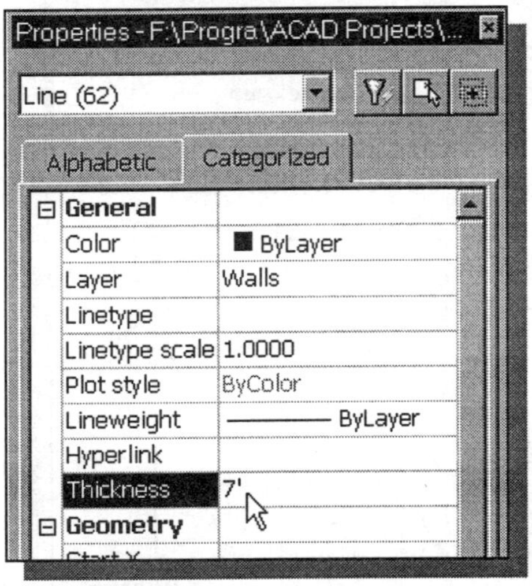

3. In the *Properties* dialog box, properties of the highlighted entities are displayed. Click the **Categorized** tab to display the listing in a categorized manner as shown. Notice the current Thickness is set to 0".

4. **Left-click** the *Thickness* box and enter a new value: **7' [ENTER]** as the new thickness value.

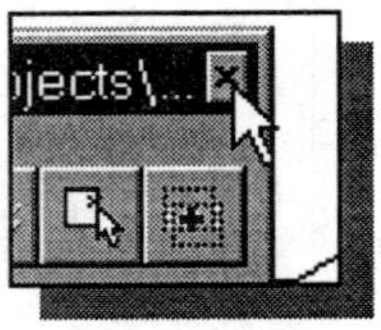

5. Click on the [**X**] button to exit the *Properties* dialog box.

In AutoCAD, the *thickness* of an object determines the distance that the object is extruded above or below its current Z-elevation. Positive thickness will extrude the objects upward (positive Z), negative thickness extrudes downward (negative Z), and zero thickness means no extrusion. The Z direction is determined by the orientation of the UCS at the time the object was created.

Changing the *thickness* of objects changes the appearance of certain geometric objects, such as circles, lines, polylines, arcs, 2D solids, and points. Note that the *Thickness* property is not available on certain geometric objects, such as *Splines* and *Multilines*. We can set the *thickness* of an object with the **Thickness** variable. AutoCAD applies the extrusion uniformly to an object. A single object cannot have different thicknesses for its various points.

Changing the thickness of objects simulates a simple Z-extrusion of creating solid objects in AutoCAD. The main advantage of using the object thickness to create the Z-elevation instead of creating a true solid is that the operation is quick and easy. In AutoCAD, objects with thickness can be hidden, shaded, and rendered as if they are three-dimensional solids. Once an object's thickness is set, we can visualize the results in any view other than the plan view.

This method is also known as the **2½D solid modeling approach**. This modeling technique was first invented in the 1970s and was adopted by several of the first-generation solid-modeling packages. This approach requires no additional 3D construction tools and only minimum computing power is needed. Note that this modeling approach does not create true 3D solids and objects can only be extruded in one direction. This modeling approach is considered to be less flexible and its application is somewhat limited.

Viewing the design using the Hide option

- By default, AutoCAD produces a wireframe image of the constructed 2D/3D design on the screen. All geometric entities are present, including those that should be hidden by other objects. Several options are available in AutoCAD to create more realistic images of 3D designs. In this section, we will introduce the Hide option, which can be used to adjust the display of the design; the Hide option eliminates the hidden lines on the screen.

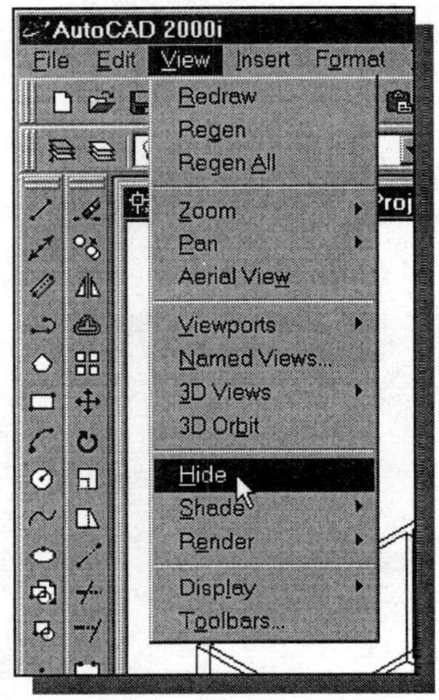

1. In the pull-down menus, select:

   [View] => [Hide]

2. To display the wireframe image, select:

   [View] => [Regen]

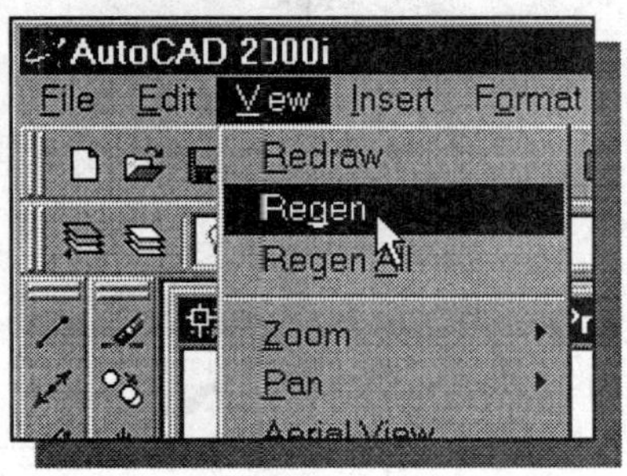

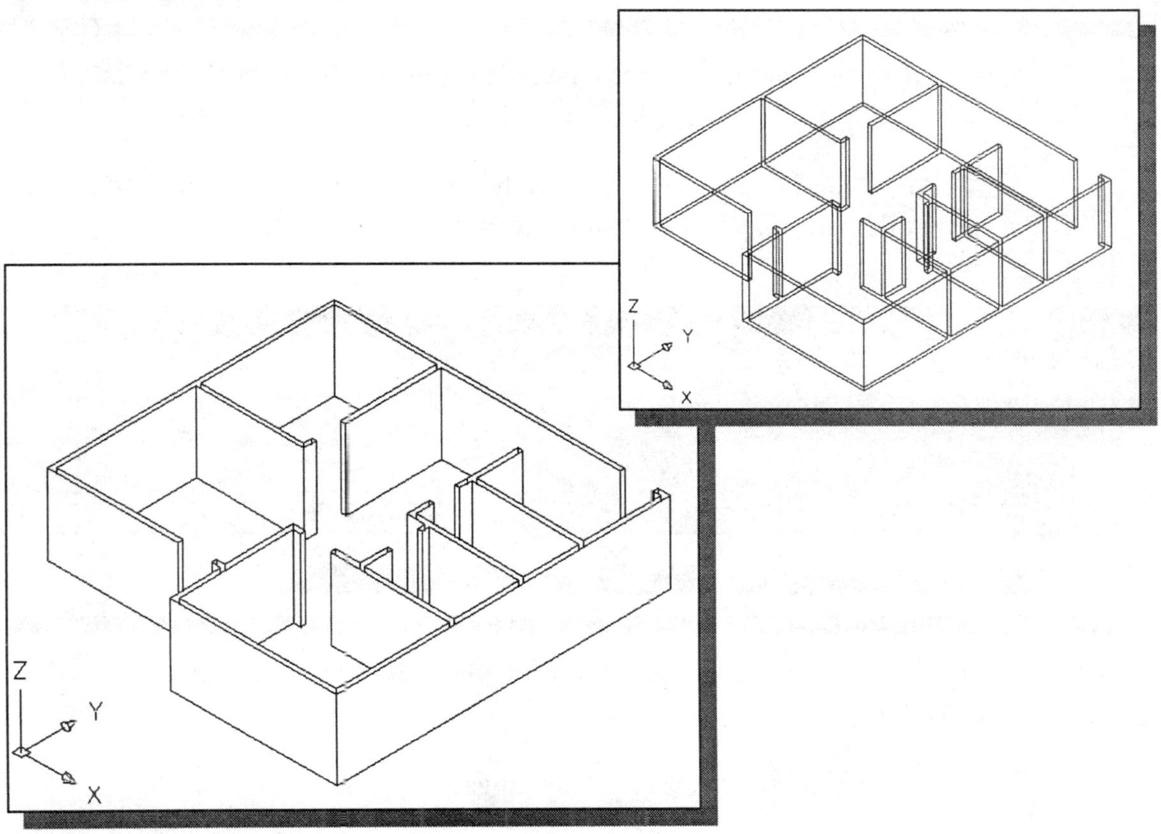

Adding New Layers

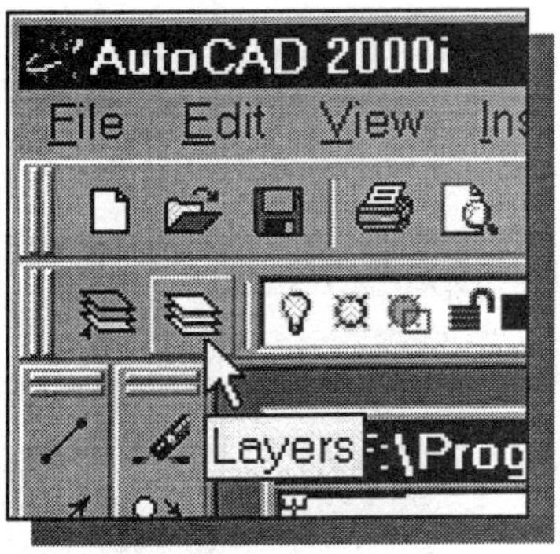

1. Pick ***Layers*** in the *Object Properties* toolbar. The *Layer Properties Manager* dialog box appears. AutoCAD creates a default layer, *layer 0*, which we cannot rename or delete. *Layer 0* has special properties used by the system.

In AutoCAD, we always construct entities on a layer. It may be the default layer or a layer that we create. Each layer has associated properties such as the visibility setting, color, linetype, lineweight, and plot style.

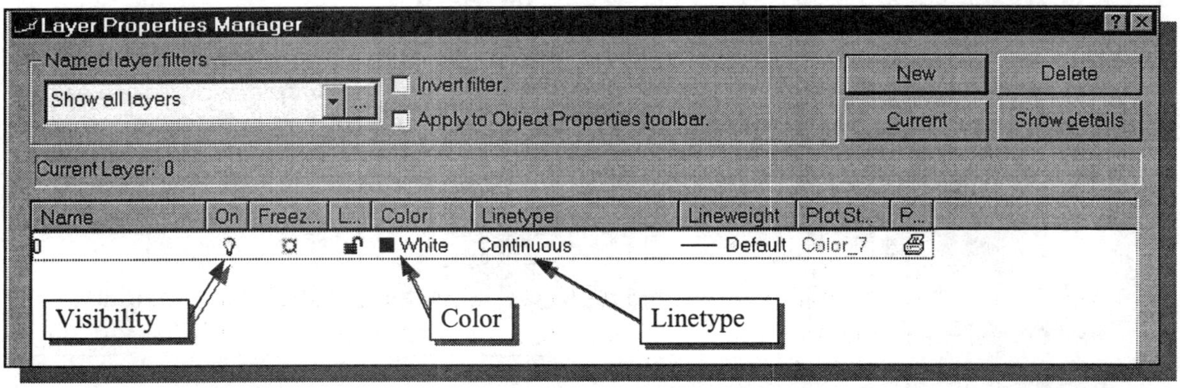

2. Click on the **NEW** button. Notice a layer is automatically added to the list of layers.

3. AutoCAD will assign a generic name to the new layer (*Layer1*). Enter ***Walls*** as the name of the new layer and change the layer color to ***Green***.

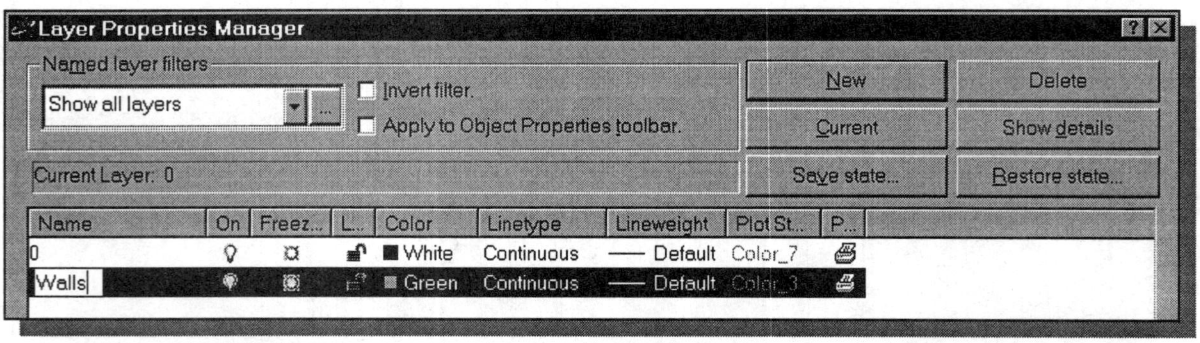

4. On your own, create another layer (layer name: ***Roof***) and change the layer color to ***Blue***.

5. Click on the **OK** button to accept the settings.

Moving entities to a different layer

1. Inside the graphics window, pre-select all objects by enclosing all objects inside a **selection window** as shown.

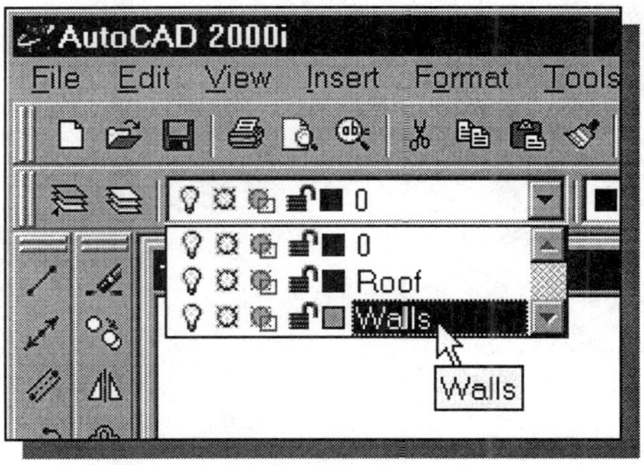

2. On the *Object Properties* toolbar, choose the ***Layer Control*** box with the left-mouse-button.

   Notice the layer name displayed in the *Layer Control* box is the selected object's assigned layer and layer properties.

3. In the *Layer Control* box, click on the *Walls* layer name. The selected objects are now moved to the *Walls* layer.

4. Left-click once the *Roof* layer name to set it as the **Current layer**.

The Move UCS command

- AutoCAD's **User Coordinate System (UCS)** is a special construction tool that enables the planar nature of the 2D input devices to be directly mapped into the 3D coordinate system. The **UCS** is a local coordinate system that can be repositioned and/or reoriented to an existing face of a part, or a pre-defined plane. By default, the UCS is aligned to the XY plane of the world coordinate system. Several options are available to reposition and reorient the UCS in 3D space.

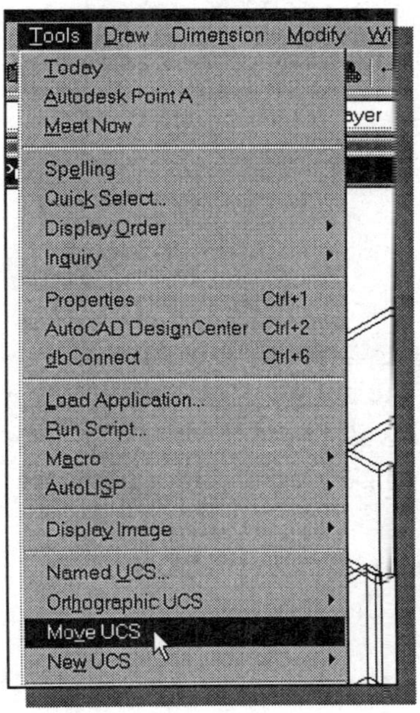

1. In the pull-down menus, select:

   [Tools] => [Move UCS]

2. We will use the *Object Snap* and *Object Tracking* options to aid the repositioning of the UCS. In the *Status Bar* area, reset the option buttons so that the *POLAR, OSNAP, OTRACK* and *MODEL* options are switched ***ON***.

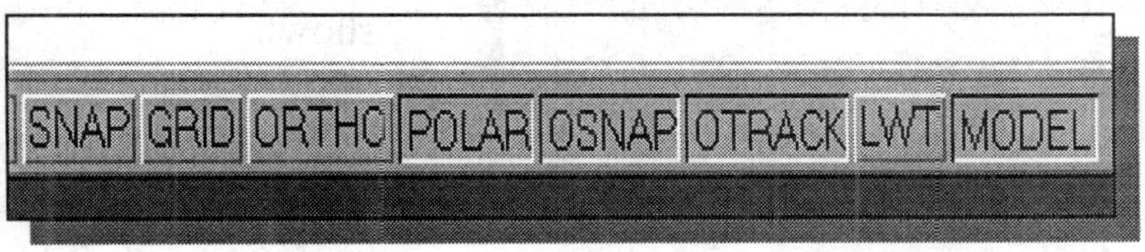

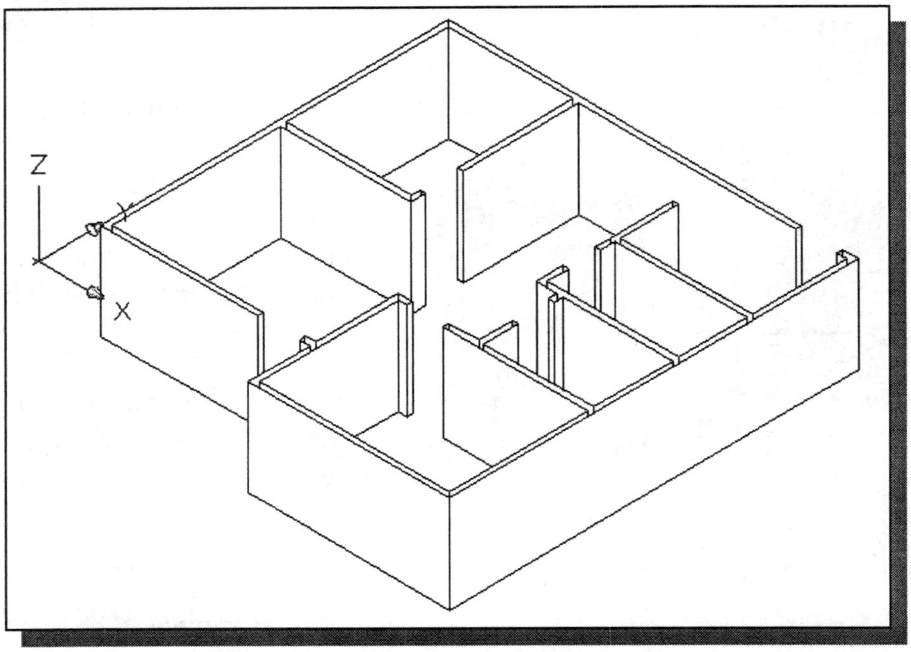

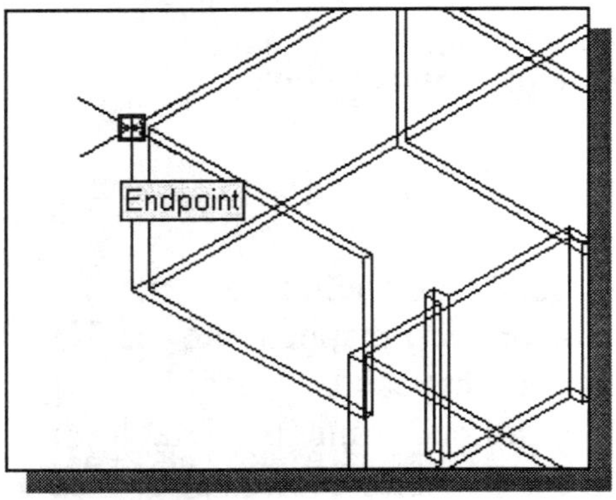

- We will reposition the UCS to the intersection of the left wall and the front wall; the intersection can be found by using the AutoCAD object tracking options.

3. Move the cursor on the top-left corner of the external wall as shown; pause for a few seconds to activate the *OTRACK* option.

4. Move the cursor on the top-front corner of the external wall as shown; pause for a few seconds to activate the *OTRACK* option.

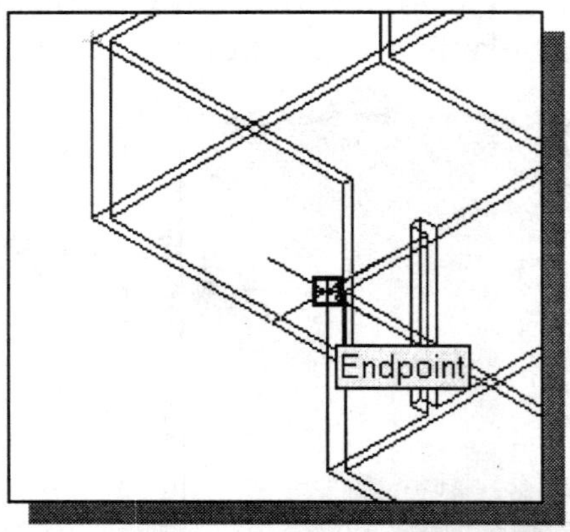

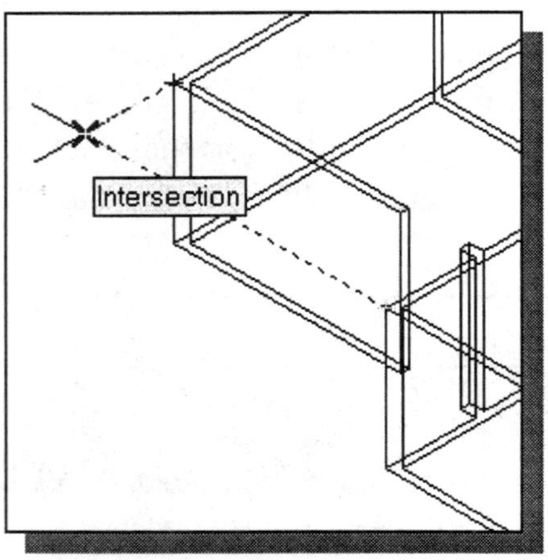

5. Left-click once when the cursor is aligned to the intersection of the left wall and the front wall as shown.

- The UCS is repositioned to the new location as shown. This location is the new origin for any geometric constructions.

Creating the roof

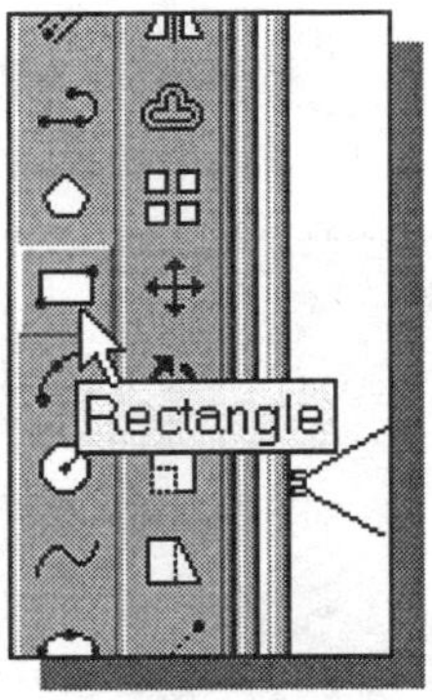

1. Select the ***Rectangle*** command icon in the *Draw* toolbar as shown.

2. In the command prompt area, the message *"Specify first corner point or [Chamfer/Elevation/Fillet/Thickness/Width]:"* is displayed. Move the cursor inside the graphics window and right-mouse-click to display the option menu.

- The thickness of certain geometry entities can be set as they are being created.

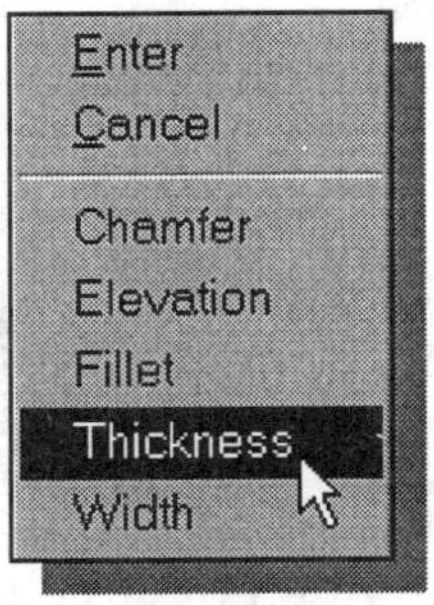

3. In the option menu, select **Thickness** by clicking once with the left-mouse-button.

4. In the command prompt area, the message *"Specify thickness for rectangles <0'-0">:"* is displayed. Enter **10" [ENTER]**.

5. At the command prompt, enter **-2',-2' [ENTER]**.

6. In the command prompt area, the message *"Specify other corner point or [Dimensions]:"* is displayed. Enter **@34',34' [ENTER]**.

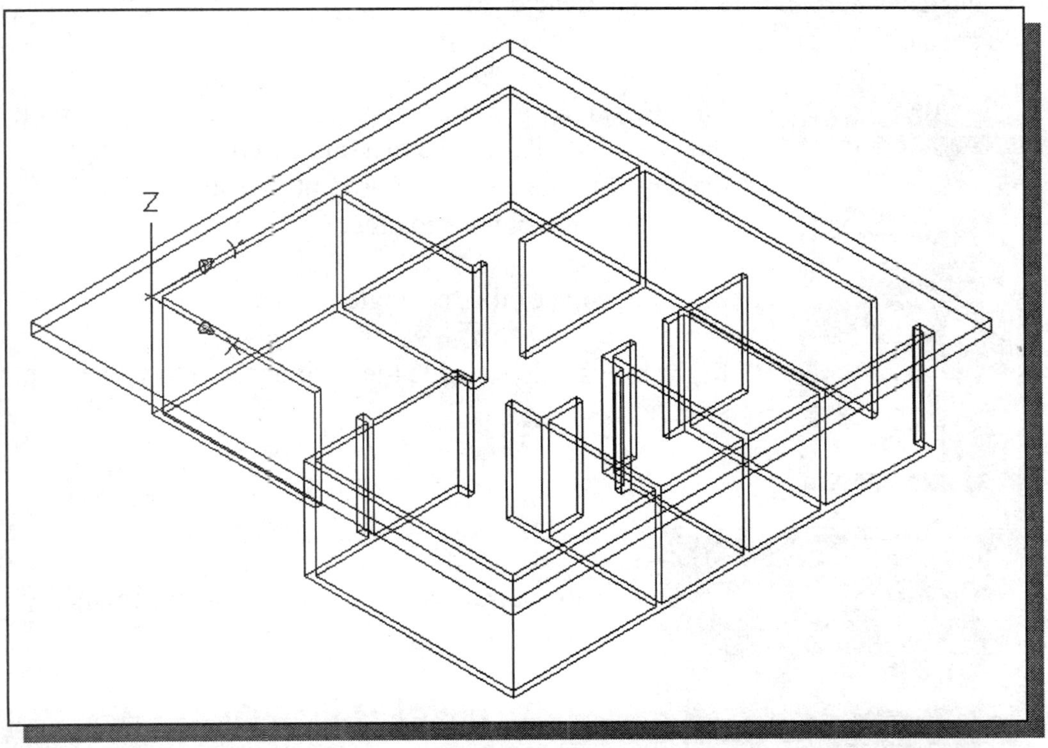

- Note that the coordinates entered are measured relative to the new UCS origin.

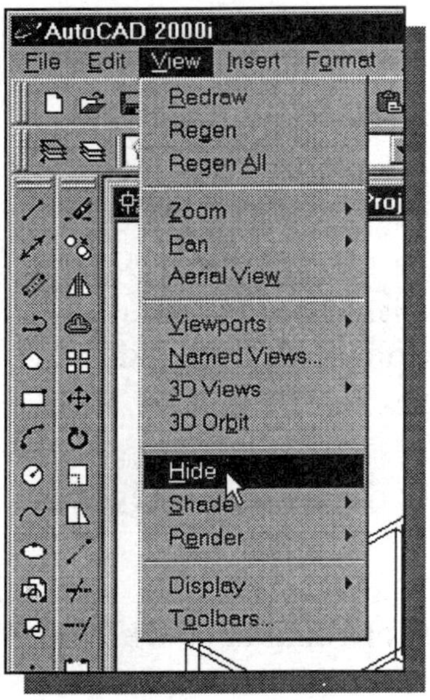

7. In the pull-down menus, select:

[View] => [Hide]

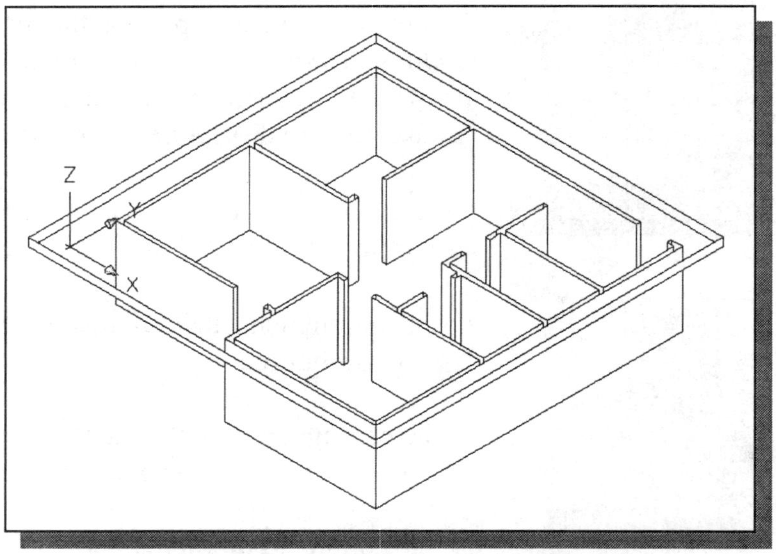

- The *Thickness* option extrudes the 2D design in the positive Z-direction relative to the current UCS, which is at the same Z-elevation of the plane of the 2D design. Note that the *Thickness* option only makes 2D objects look like 3D solids; only surfaces perpendicular to the plane of the 2D design are created. No top or bottom surfaces are created with the *Thickness* option.

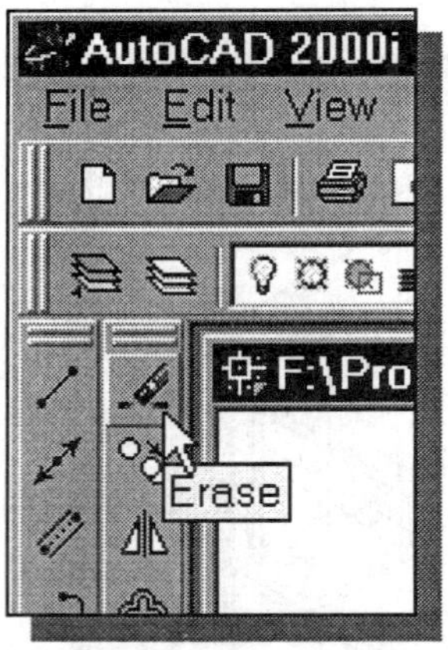

8. Pick ***Erase*** in the *Modify* toolbar. (The icon is the first icon in the *Modify* toolbar.) The message *"Select objects"* is displayed in the command prompt area and AutoCAD awaits us to select the objects to erase.

9. Pick any edge of the rectangle we just created.

10. Right-mouse-click inside the graphics window to accept the selection.

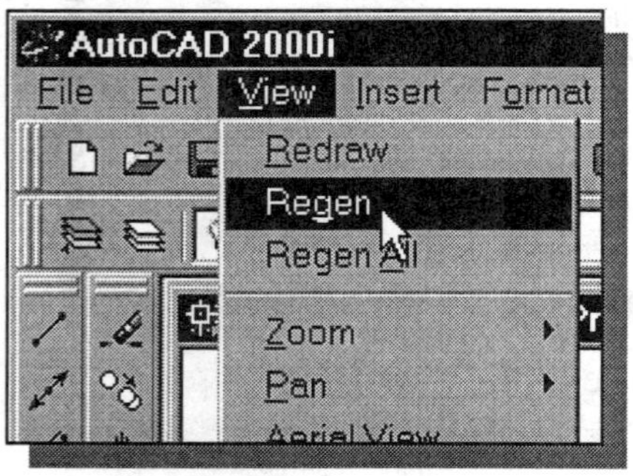

11. Reset the display to the wireframe image by selecting:

[View] => [Regen]

Rotating the UCS

- AutoCAD's **User Coordinate System (UCS)** can be repositioned and reoriented in 3D space. All of the UCS options are organized and can be found in the *Standard* toolbar.

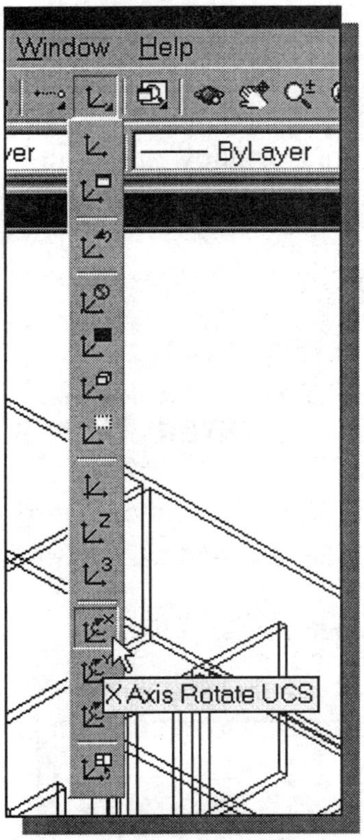

1. In the *Standard* toolbar, press and hold the left-mouse-button on the UCS icon to display the icon stack. Select the ***X Axis Rotate UCS*** option by releasing the left-mouse-button on the icon.

   [UCS] => [X Axis Rotate UCS]

- Notice the other UCS command icons available in the stack.

2. In the command prompt area, the message *"Specify rotation angle aboutX axis<90>:"* is displayed.

   Enter: **90 [ENTER]**.

- The UCS rotation is done using the standard engineering convention, where positive values are treated as rotating counter-clockwise. Also note that the *SNAP*, *GRID*, and *ORTHO* options all rotate in line with the UCS.

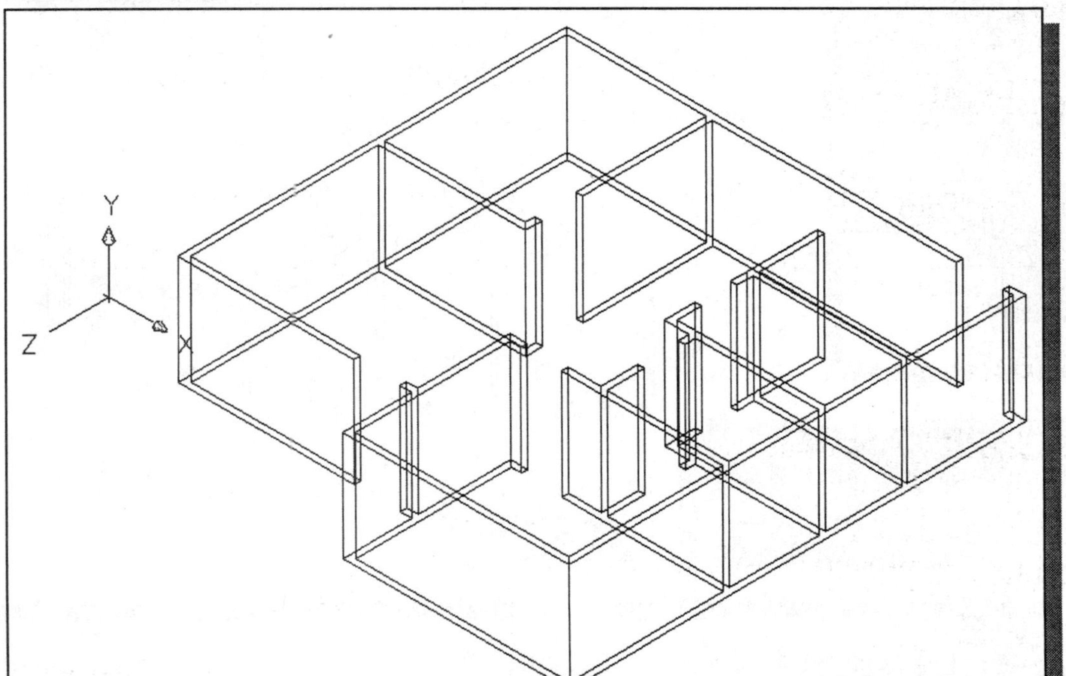

Sketching on the Rotated UCS

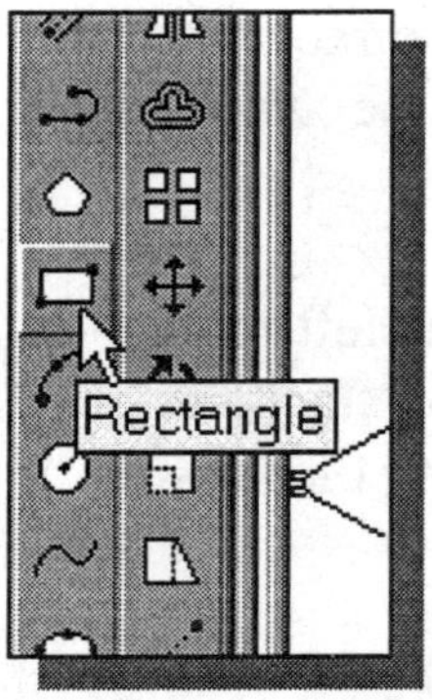

1. Select the ***Rectangle*** command icon in the *Draw* toolbar as shown.

2. In the command prompt area, the message *"Specify first corner point or [Chamfer/Elevation/Fillet/Thickness/Width]:"* is displayed. Move the cursor inside the graphics window and right-mouse-click to display the option menu.

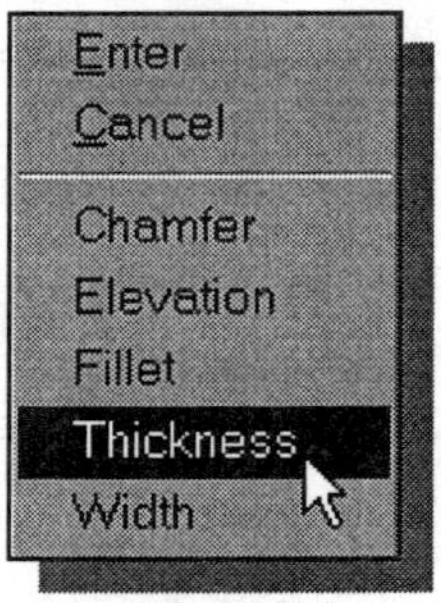

3. In the option menu, select **Thickness** by clicking once with the left-mouse-button.

4. In the command prompt area, the message *"Specify thickness for rectangles <0'-10">:"* is displayed. Enter **–30" [ENTER]**.

5. At the command prompt, enter **-2',0' [ENTER]** as the first corner of the rectangle.

6. In the command prompt area, the message *"Specify other corner point or [Dimensions]:"* is displayed. Enter **@34',10" [ENTER]**.

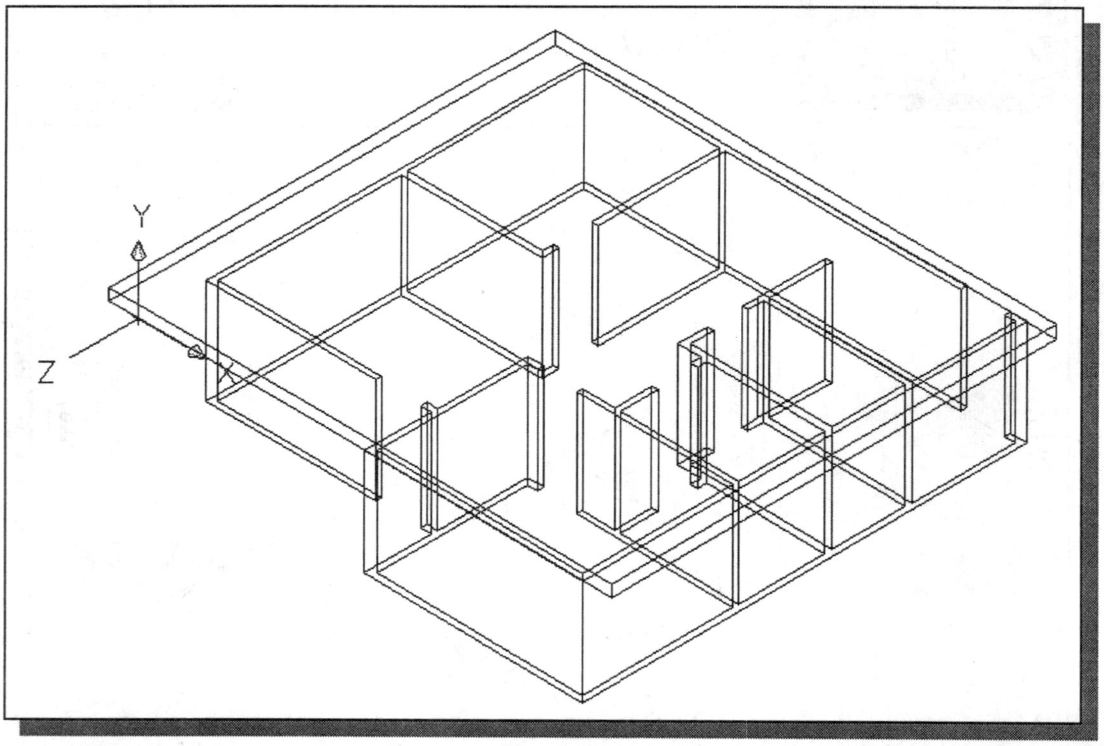

- The negative thickness extrudes the rectangle in the negative Z-direction of the current UCS.

Viewing the design using the Hidden option

- Several options are available in AutoCAD to create more realistic images of 3D designs. The **Shade - Hidden** option can also be used to eliminate the hidden lines on the screen. The **Shade - Hidden** option performs a more complicated calculation of the display and usually produces a better image than the **Hide** option.

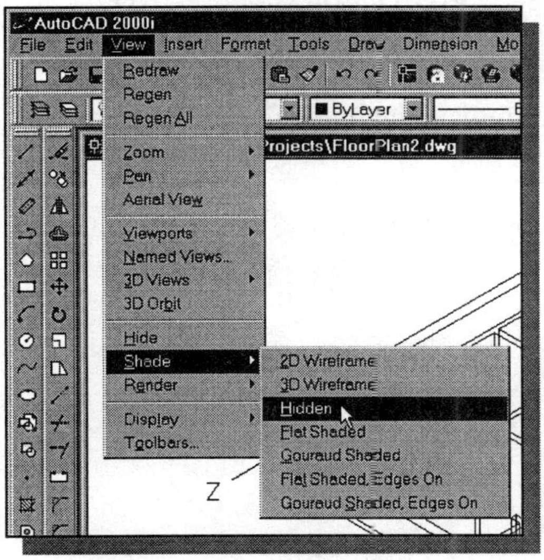

1. In the pull-down menus, select:

   [View] => [Shade] => [Hidden]

2. To display the wireframe image, select:

   [View] => [Shade] => [3D Wireframe]

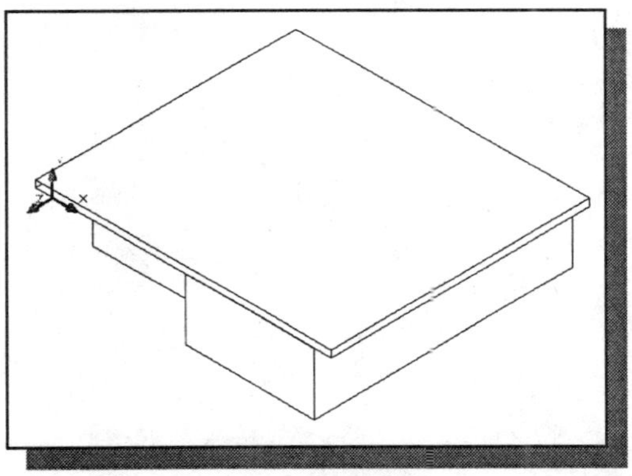

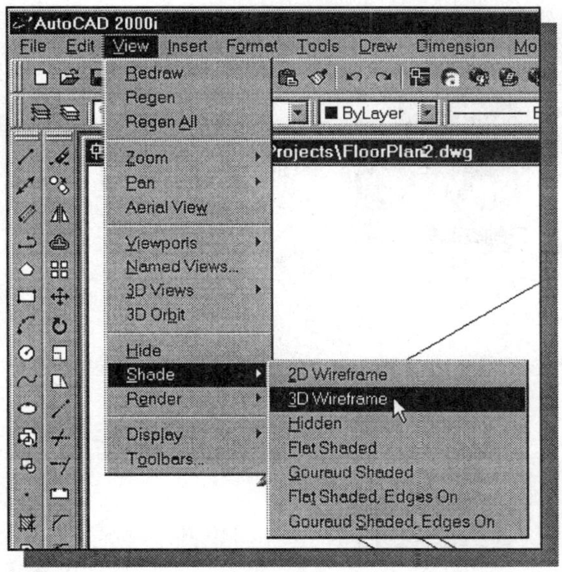

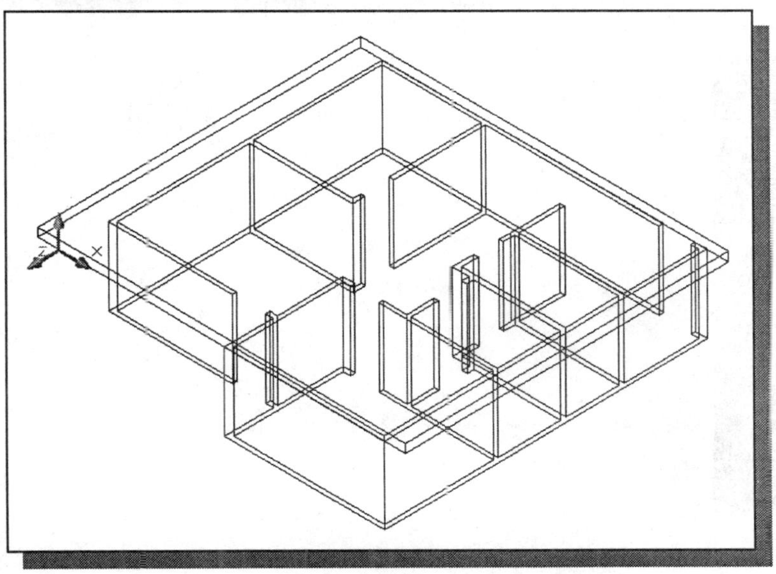

Questions:

1. What is the difference between *WCS* and *UCS*?

2. List and describe two available options to manipulate the UCS.

3. Describe some of the advantages of using the AutoCAD *Thickness* option over creating 2D or 3D models.

4. In the tutorial, which commands were used to eliminate the hidden lines on the screen?

5. What is the difference between a *POLYLINE* and a *LINE*?

6. Identify the following commands:

(a)

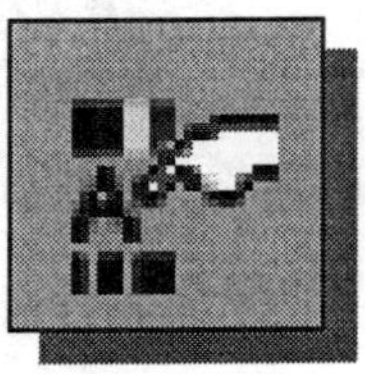

properties

(b)

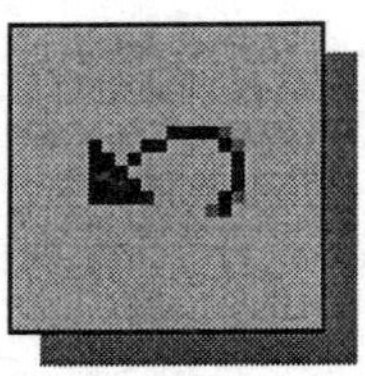

undo

(c)

Polyline

(d)

layers

Exercises:

1. Dimensions are in inches. Thickness : 0.5

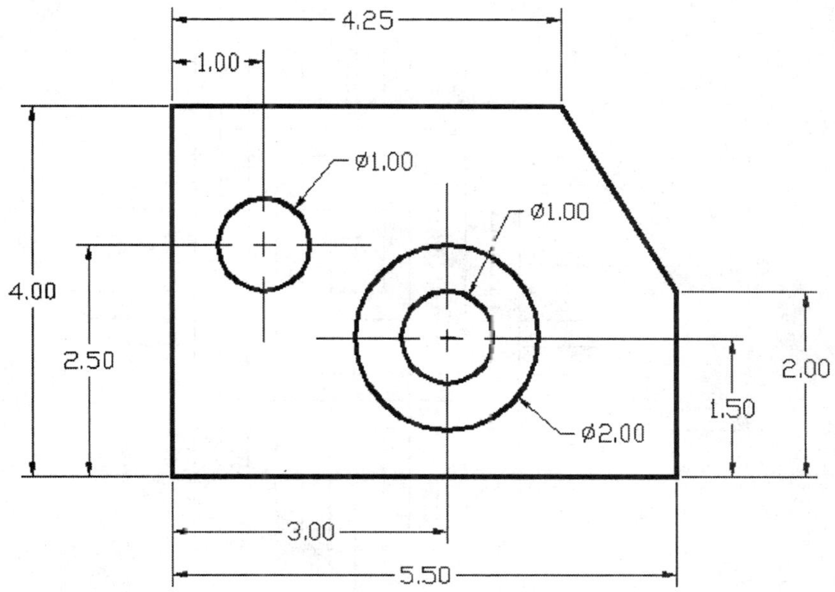

2. Wall thickness: 5 inch, height: 7 feet

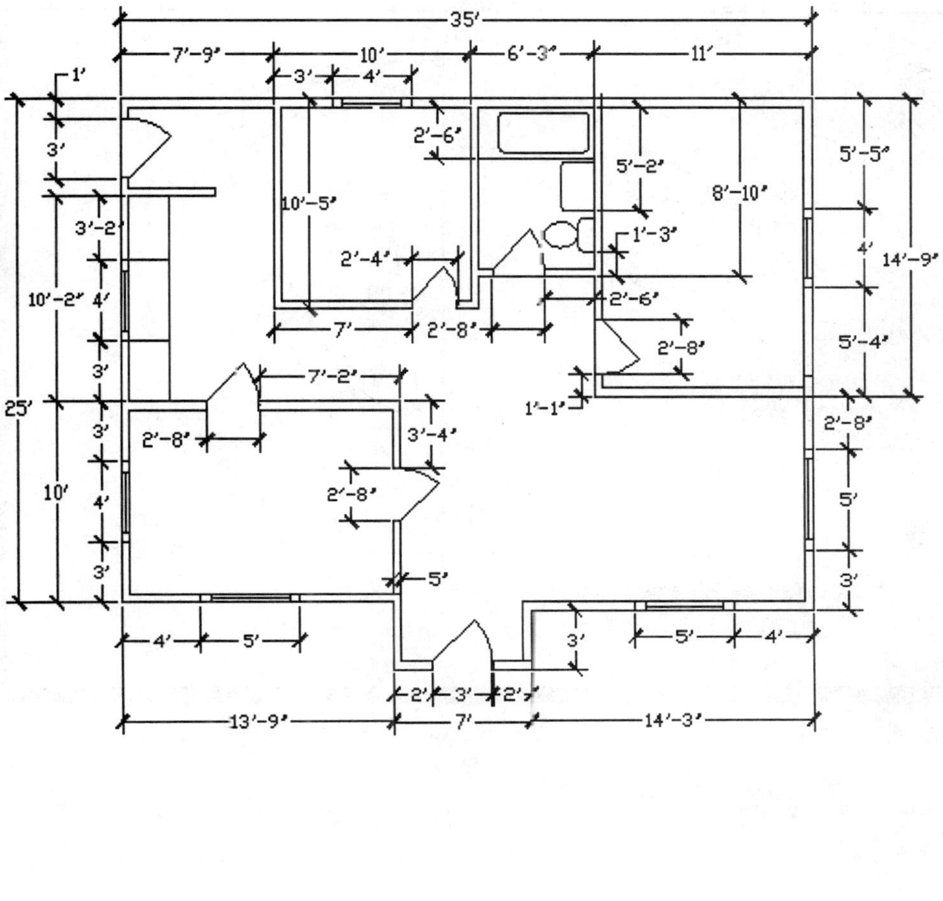

3. **D**imensions are in inches**. Thickness: 0.5**

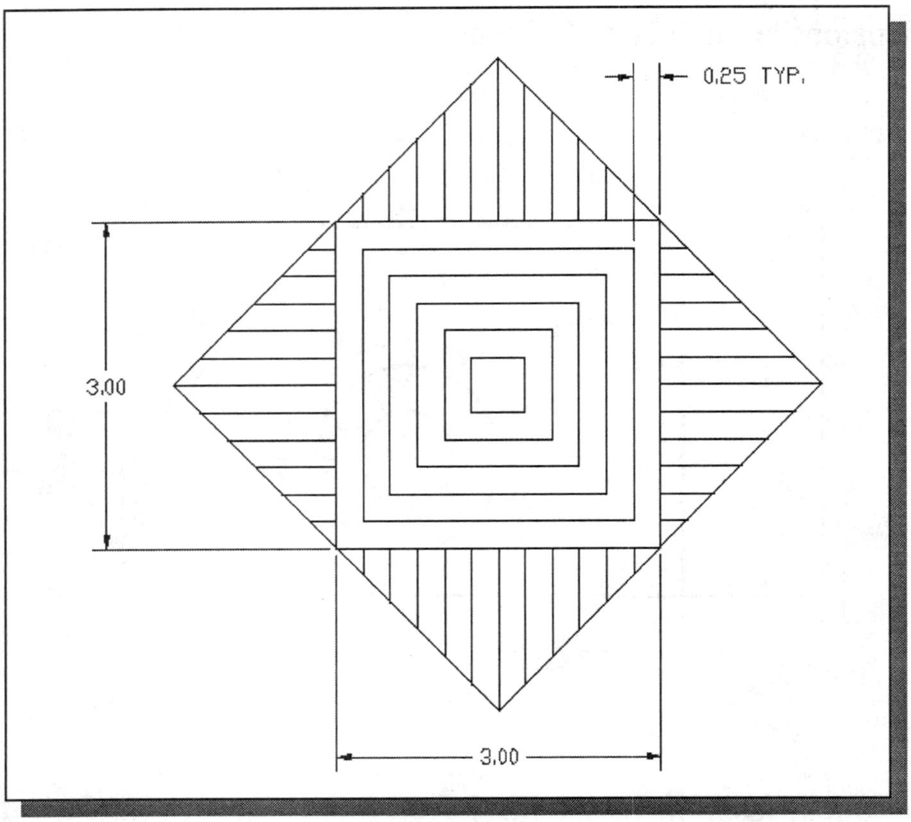

4. **D**imensions are in inches. **Thickness: 0.25**

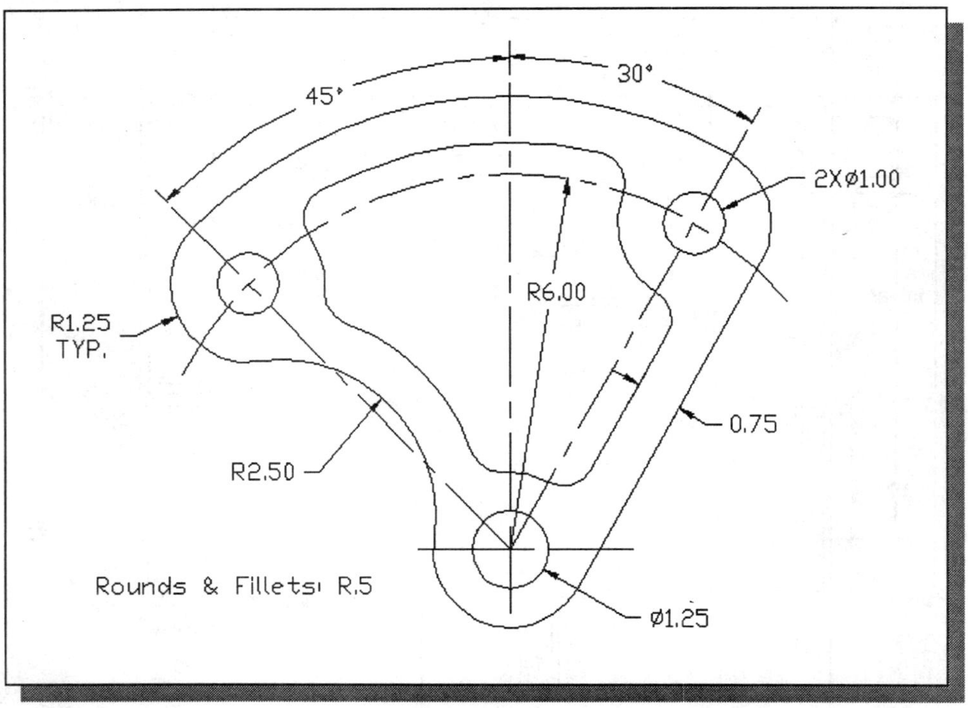

Chapter 3
3D Wireframe Modeling

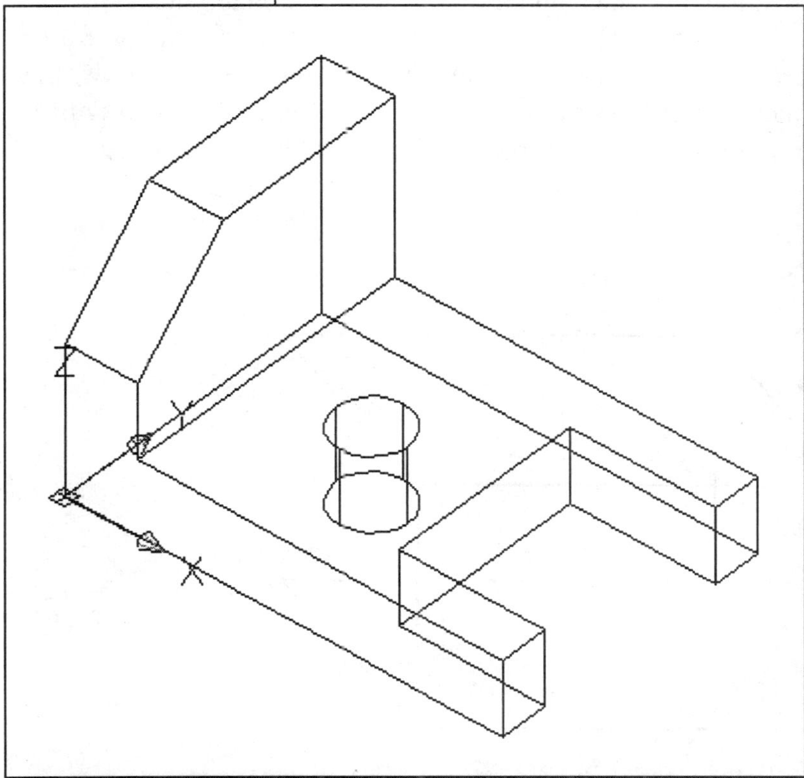

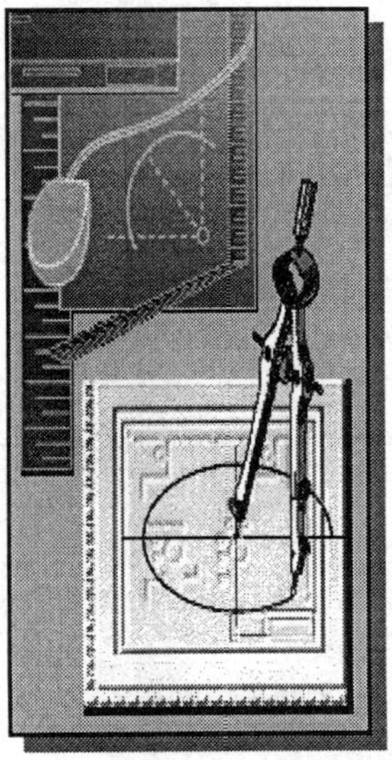

Learning Objectives

- ♦ Create Wireframe Models.
- ♦ Apply the Box method.
- ♦ Construct with the Copy command.
- ♦ Understand and use the available 3D Coordinates input options.
- ♦ Using the View Toolbar.
- ♦ Setup and use the TRIM options.
- ♦ Use the 3D Orbit command.

Introduction

The first true 3D computer model created on CAD systems in the late 1970s was the 3D wireframe model. Computer generated 3D wireframe models contain information about the locations of all the corners and edges in space coordinates. The 3D wireframe models can be viewed from any direction as needed and are in general reasonably good representations of 3D designs. But because surface definition is not part of a wireframe model, all wireframe images have the inherent problem of ambiguity. For example, in the figure displayed below, which corner is in front, corner A or corner B? The ambiguity problem becomes much more serious with complex designs that have many edges and corners.

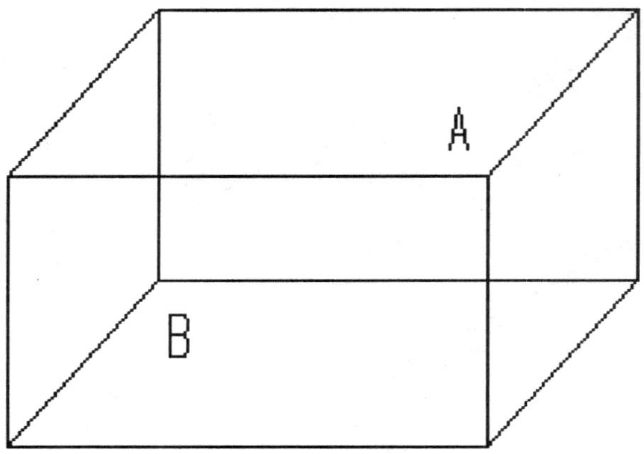

Wireframe Ambiguity: Which corner is in front, A or B?

The main advantage of using a 3D wireframe modeler to create 3D models is its simplicity. The computer hardware requirements for wireframe modelers are typically much lower than that of the requirements for surface and solid modelers. A 3D wireframe model, also know as a stick-figure model or a skeleton model, contains only information about the locations of all the corners and edges of the design in space coordinates. You should also realize that, in some cases, it could be quite difficult to locate some of the corner locations while creating a 3D wireframe model. Note that 3D wireframe modelers are usually used in conjunction with surfacing modelers, which we will discuss in the later chapters of this text, to eliminate the problem of ambiguity.

With most CAD systems, creating 3D wireframe models usually starts with constructing 2D entities in 3D space. Two of the most commonly used methods for creating 3D wireframe models are the **Box method** and the **2D Extrusion method**. As the name implies, the *Box method* involves the creation of a 3D box with the edges constructed from the height, width and depth dimensions of the design. The 3D wireframe model is typically completed by locating and connecting corners within the box.

The *2D Extrusion method* involves making copies of 2D geometries in specific directions. This method is similar to the 2½D extrusion approach illustrated in the previous chapter (Chapter 2) with several differences. First of all, we do not really extrude the wireframe entities; instead we simply make copies of wireframe entities in the desired directions. Secondly, constructed wireframe entities have true 3D space coordinates, while the *thickness* approach creates entities with no true 3D coordinates. And lastly, no surfaces are created in the 3D wireframe models.

In this chapter, we will illustrate the general procedure to construct a 3D wireframe model using both the box method and the 2D extrusion method. To illustrate the AutoCAD 3D construction environment, we will create the wireframe model using only the default UCS system, which is aligned to the world coordinate system. Repositioning and/or reorienting the User Coordinate System can be useful in creating 3D models. But it is also feasible to create 3D models referencing only a single coordinate system. One important note about creating wireframe models is that the construction techniques mostly concentrate on locating the space coordinates of the individual corners of the design. The ability to visualize designs in the form of 3D wireframe models is extremely helpful to designers and CAD operators. It is hoped that the experience of thinking and working on 3D wireframe models, as outlined in this chapter, will enhance one's 3D visualization ability.

The Locator Design

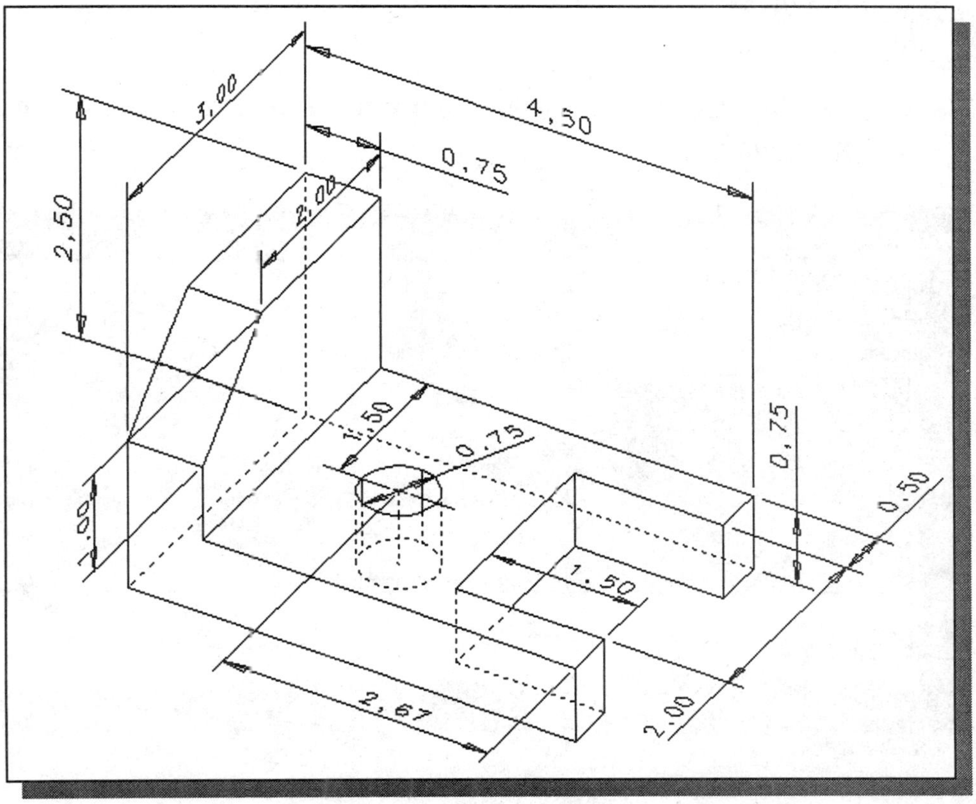

Starting Up AutoCAD® 2000i

1. Select the AutoCAD® 2000i option on the *Program* menu or select the AutoCAD® 2000i icon on the *Desktop*. Once the program is loaded into the memory, the AutoCAD® 2000i drawing screen and the *AutoCAD Today* startup dialog box will appear on the screen.

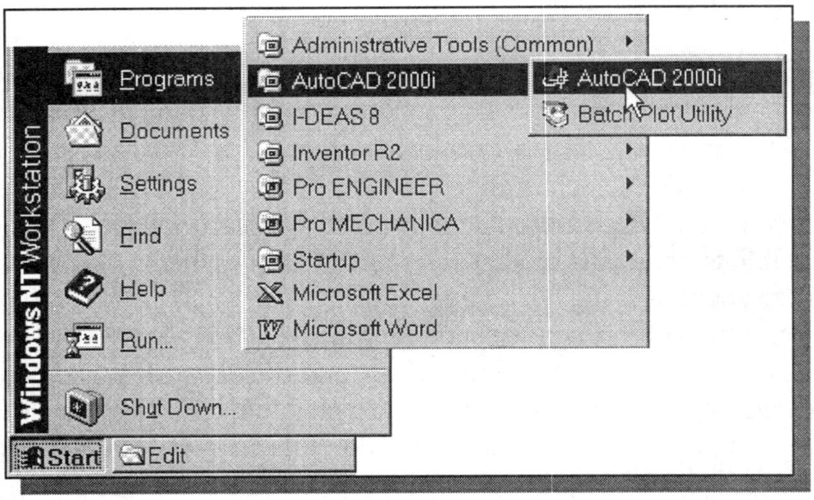

2. In the *AutoCAD Today* startup dialog box, select the **Create Drawings** tab with a single click of the left-mouse-button.

3. Confirm the startup option is set to ***Start from Scratch***, as shown in the figure below.

4. In the *Default Settings* section, pick **English (feet and Inches)** as the drawing units.

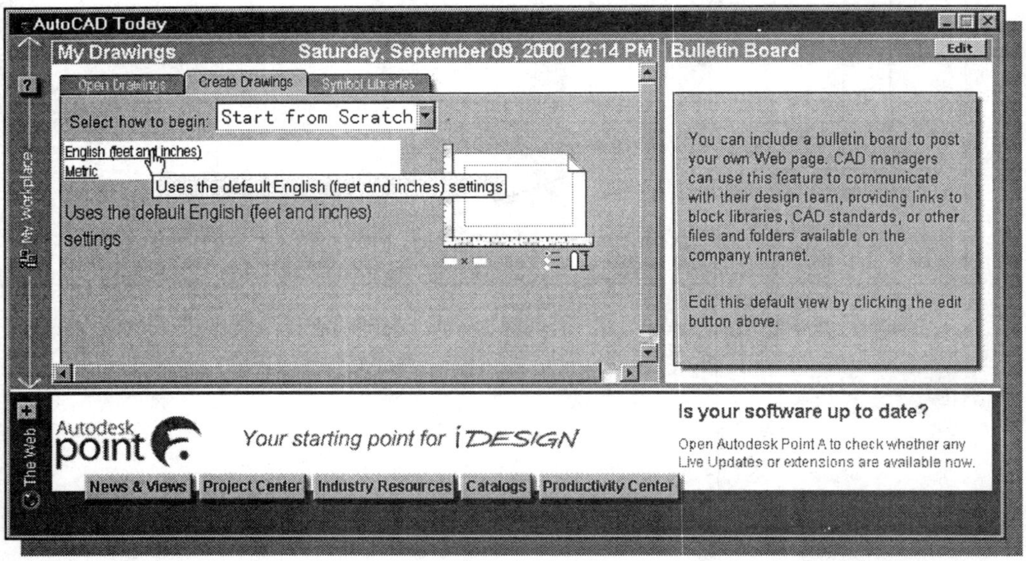

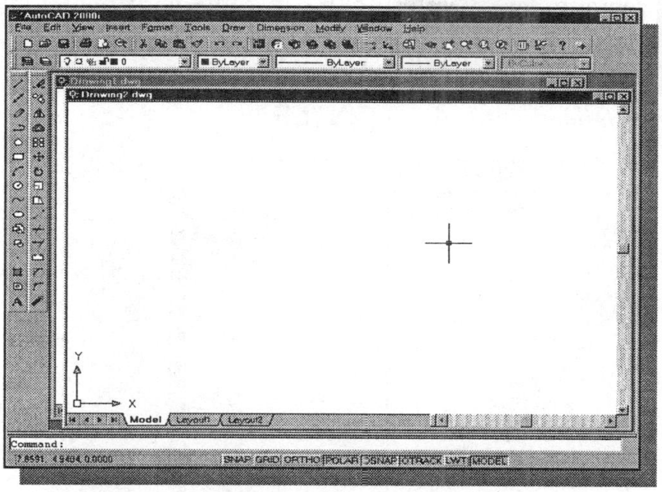

❖ Note that two graphics window are available. The *Drawing1.dwg* uses the default units set during the installation of AutoCAD 2000i. The units used in the second graphics window, the *Drawing2.dwg* window, are set to the English units, inches and feet.

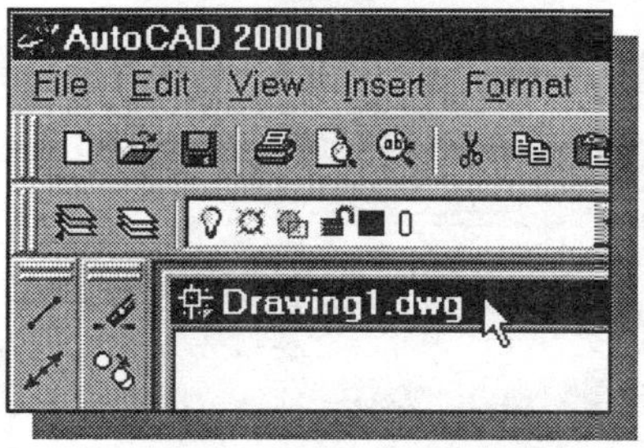

5. Switch to the *Drawing1* window by left-clicking once in the title area of the window.

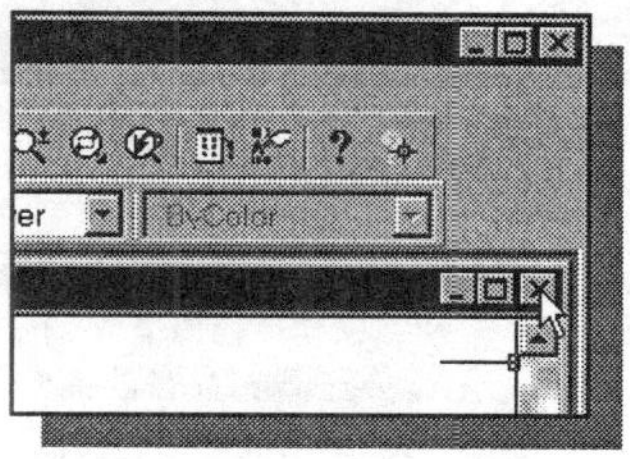

6. Close the window by clicking the ***Close*** icon located at the upper-right-corner of the *Drawing1* window.

Creating the rectangular base of the design

➢ We will first construct the wireframe geometry defining the rectangular base of the design.

1. In the *Status Bar* area, reset the options and turn ***ON*** the *GRID*, *POLAR*, *OSNAP*, *LWT* and *MODEL* options.

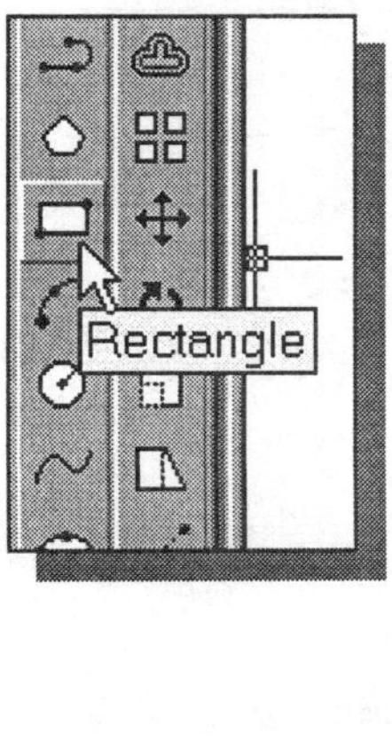

2. Select the ***Rectangle*** icon in the *Draw* toolbar. In the command prompt area, the message *"Specify first corner point or [Chamfer/Elevation/Fillet/Thickness/Width]:"* is displayed.

3. Place the first corner-point of the rectangle at the origin of the world coordinate system.

   Command: _line Specify first point: **0,0 [ENTER]**
   (Type **0,0** in the command prompt area and press the **[ENTER]** key once.)

4. We will create a 4.5"X3.0" rectangular by entering the absolute coordinates of the second corner.

   Specify other corner point or [Dimension]: **4.5,3 [ENTER]**

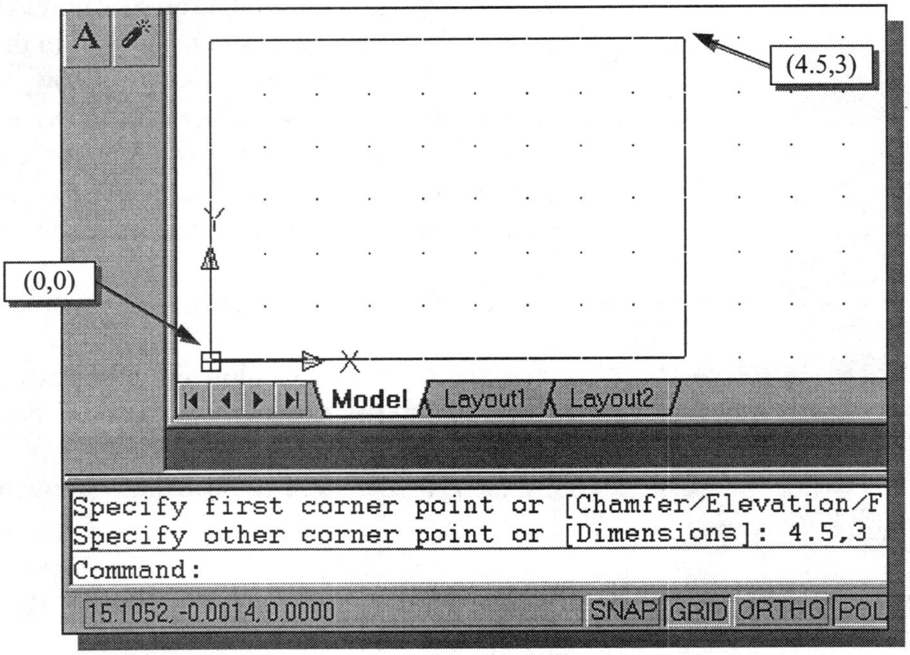

- The *RECTANGLE* command creates rectangles as *polyline* features, which means the four segments of a rectangle are created as a single object. In AutoCAD, rectangles are wireframe entities.

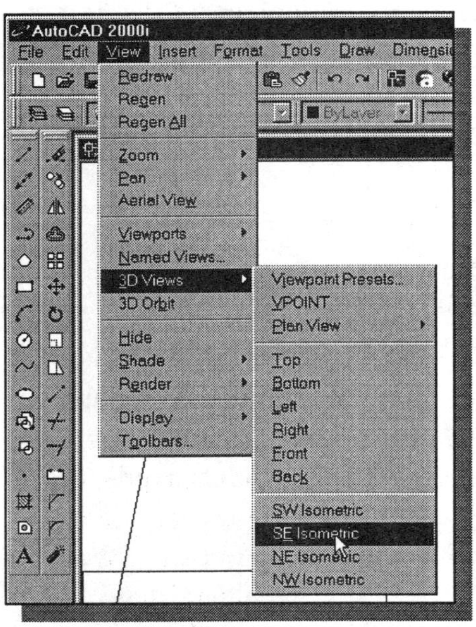

5. In the pull-down menus, select:

   [View] => [3D Views] => [SE Isometric]

- Notice the orientation of the sketched 2D rectangle in relation to the displayed AutoCAD user coordinate system. By default, the 2D sketch-plane is aligned to the XY plane of the world coordinate system.

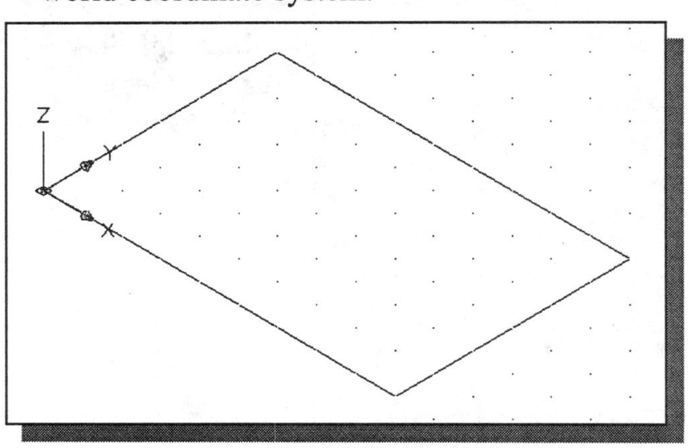

Create a 3D box

- We will create a 3D box to define the 3D boundary of the design. We will do so by placing a copy of the base rectangle at the corresponding height elevation of the design. The dimensions of the 3D box are therefore based on the height, width and depth dimensions of the design.

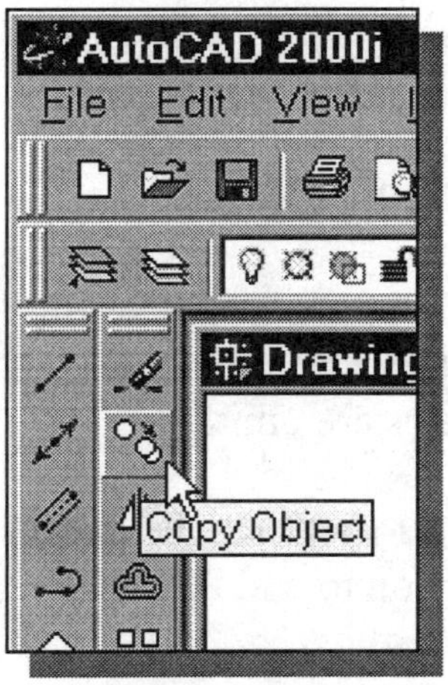

1. Click on the ***Copy Object*** icon in the *Modify* toolbar.
2. In the command prompt area, the message *"Select objects:"* is displayed. Pick any edge of the sketched rectangle.
3. Inside the graphics window, right-mouse-click once to accept the selection.
4. In the command prompt area, the message *"Specify base point or displacement, or [Multiple]:"* is displayed. Pick any corner of the sketched rectangle as a base point to create the copy.
5. In the command prompt area, the message *"Specify second point of displacement or <use first point as displacement>:"* is displayed.

   Enter: **@0,0,2.5 [ENTER]**

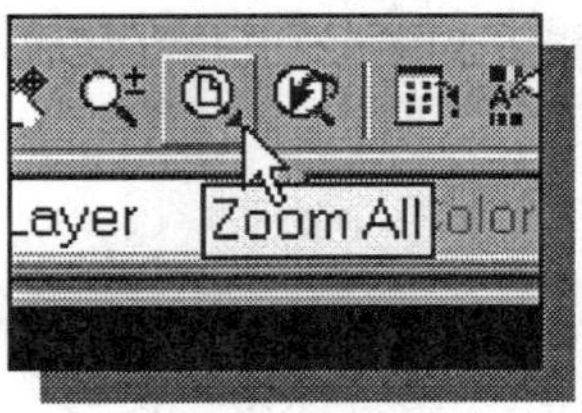

6. Select the ***Zoom All*** icon in the *Standard* toolbar to view the constructed geometry. If the ***Zoom All*** icon is not displayed, choose the icon by pressing down the left-mouse-button on the displayed icon to display the option list.

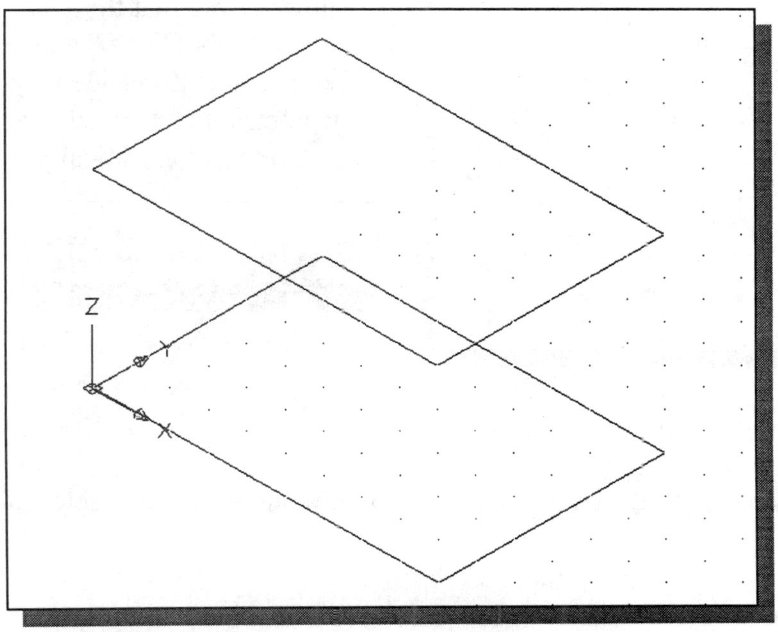

❖ The two rectangles represent the top and bottom of a 3D box defining the 3D boundary of the design. Note that the construction of the second rectangle was independent of the UCS, User Coordinate System; the UCS is still aligned to the world coordinate system.

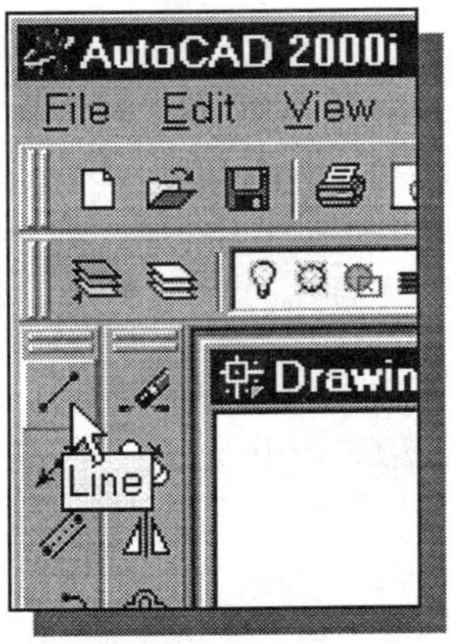

7. Select the ***Line*** icon in the *Draw* toolbar.

8. In the command prompt area, the message *"_line Specify first point:"* is displayed.

   Command: _line Specify first point: **0,0 [ENTER]**

9. In the command prompt area, the message *" Specify next point or [Undo]:"* is displayed.

Command: _line Specify first point: **0,0,2.5 [ENTER]**

❖ Notice the *LINE* command correctly identified the entered 3D coordinates of the second point. The default Z-coordinate, which is set by the AutoCAD UCS, is applied automatically whenever the Z-ccordinates are omitted.

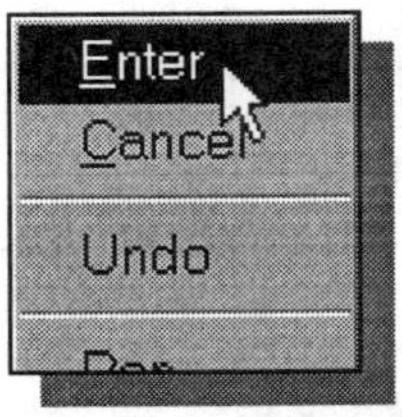

10. Inside the graphics window, **right-mouse-click** to activate the option menu and select **Enter** with the left-mouse-button to end the *LINE* command.

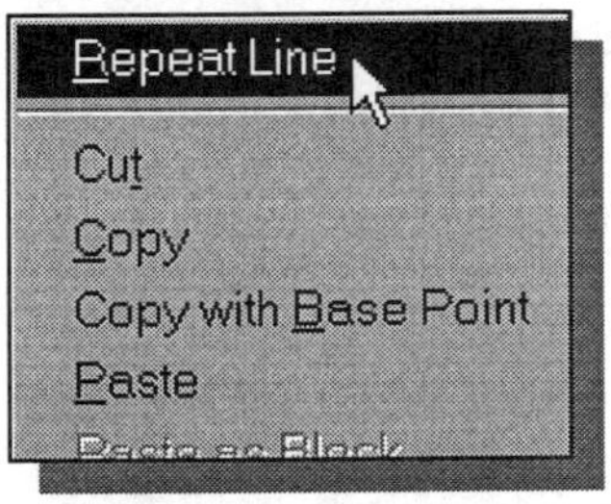

11. Inside the graphics window, **right-mouse-click** to bring up the popup option menu.

12. Pick **Repeat Line** with the left-mouse-button in the popup menu to repeat the last command.

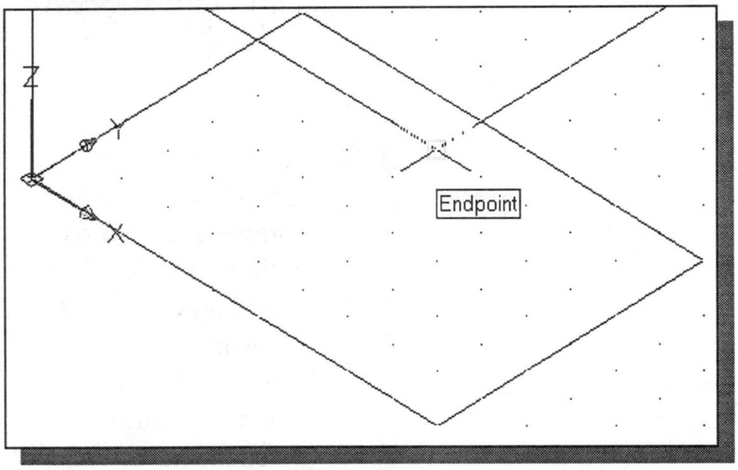

13. Move the cursor on top of the top-front-corner as shown. Note that the AutoCAD's *OSNAP* and *OTRACK* features identify geometric features, such as endpoints, automatically.

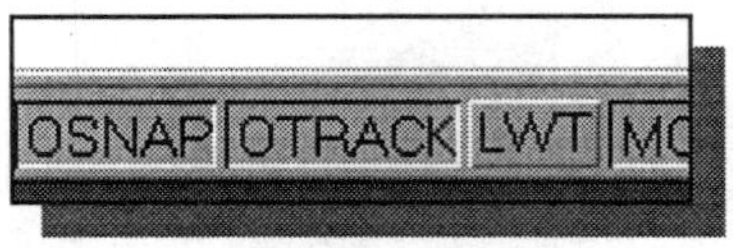

14. Left-click once to select the endpoint as shown.

15. Create a line connecting to the endpoint directly below the previously selected point.

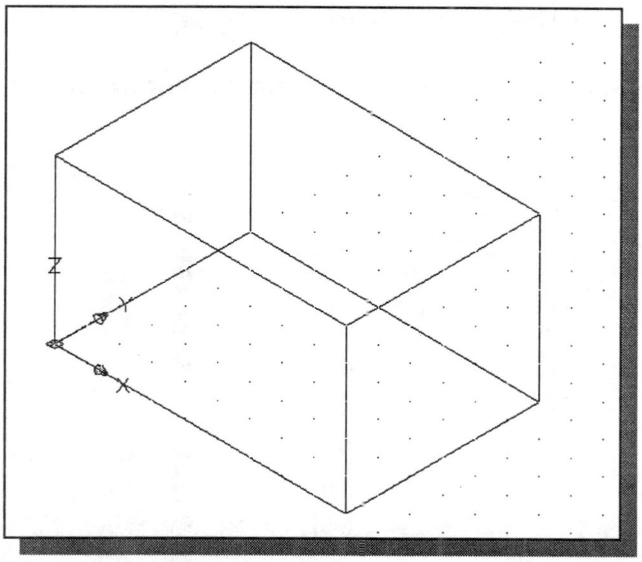

16. On your own, complete the 3D box by creating the two lines connecting the back corners of the 3D box as shown.

Object Snap Toolbar

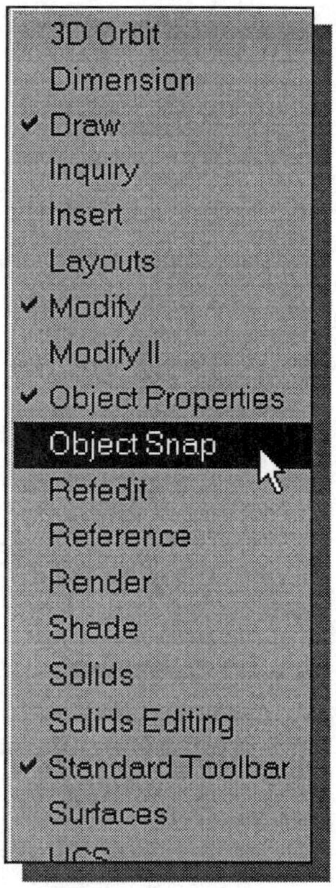

1. Move the cursor to the *Standard* toolbar area and **right-mouse-click** once on any icon in the toolbar area to display a list of toolbar menu groups.

   ❖ AutoCAD provides 24 toolbars for access to frequently used commands, settings, and modes. The *Standard, Object Properties*, *Draw*, and *Modify* toolbars are displayed by default. The *check marks* in the list identify the toolbars that are currently displayed on the screen.

2. Select **Object Snap**, with the left-mouse-button, to display the *Object Snap* toolbar on the screen.

   ❖ ***Object Snap*** is an extremely powerful construction tool available on most CAD systems. During an entity's creation operations, we can snap the cursor to points on objects such as endpoints, midpoints, centers, and intersections. For example, we can turn on ***Object Snap*** and quickly draw a line to the center of a circle, the midpoint of a line segment, or the intersection of two lines.

3. On your own, move the cursor over the icons in the *Object Snap* toolbar and read the description of each icon in the *Status Bar* area.

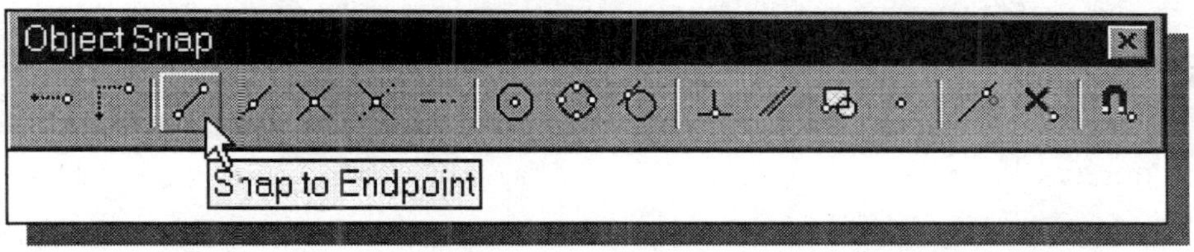

Using the Snap options to locate the top corners

❖ We will use the *Object Snap* options to identify the locations of the top corners of the model.

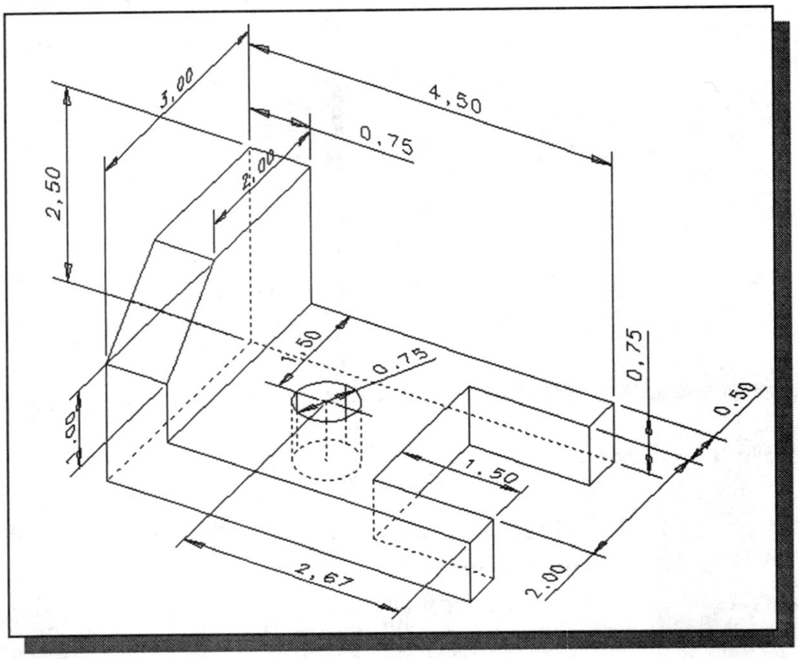

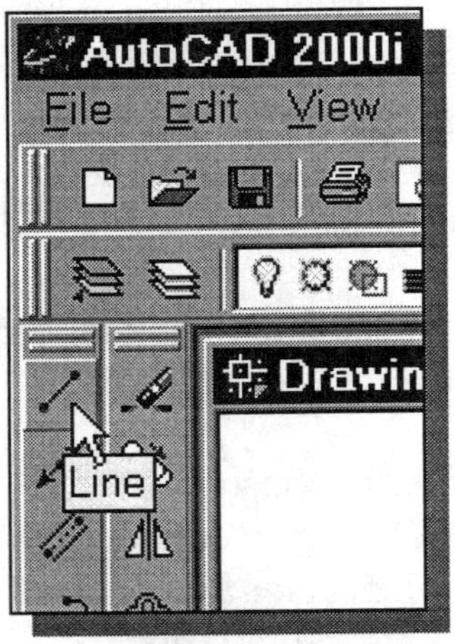

1. Select the ***Line*** icon in the *Draw* toolbar.

2. In the command prompt area, the message *"_line Specify first point:"* is displayed. Select ***Snap From*** in the *Object Snap* toolbar.

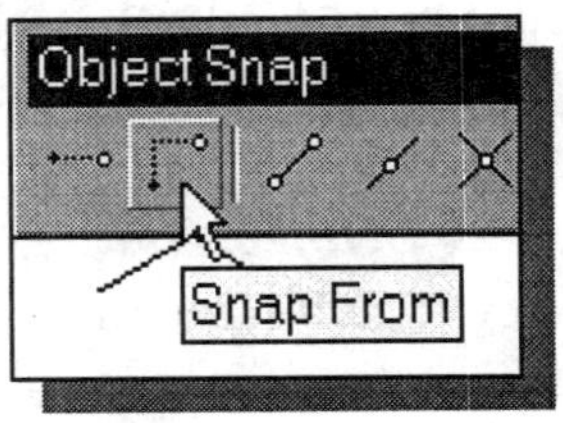

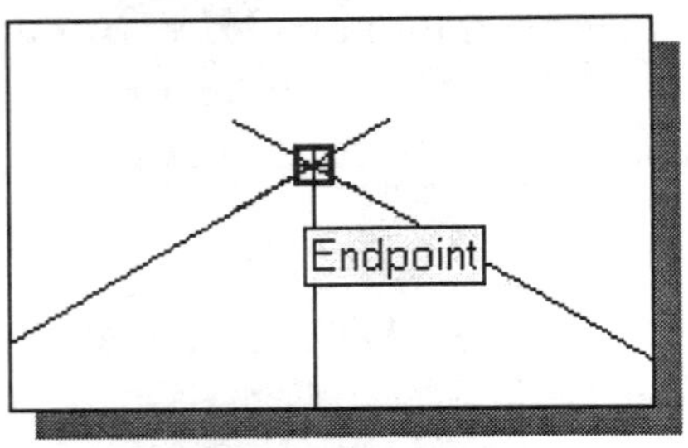

3. Select the **top-back corner** as the reference point as shown.

4. In the command prompt area, the message *"_line Specify first point:_from Base point:<Offset>:"* is displayed.
   Command: **@0.75,0,0 [ENTER]**

❖ By using the relative coordinate input method, we can locate the position of any point in 3D space. Note that the entered coordinates are measured relative to the current UCS.

5. In the command prompt area, the message *" Specify next point or [Undo]: "* is displayed.

   Command: Specify next point or [Undo]: **@0,-2,0 [ENTER]**

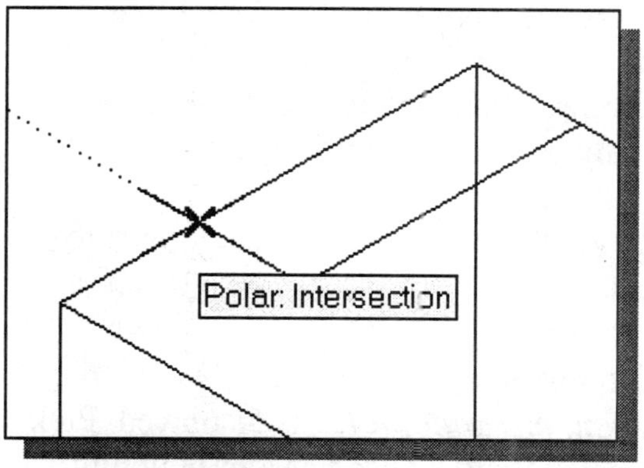

6. Move the cursor toward the left to create a perpendicular line. Select a location that is on the back-line as shown, notice the displayed *Object Snap/Tracking* tips: *Polar Intersection.*

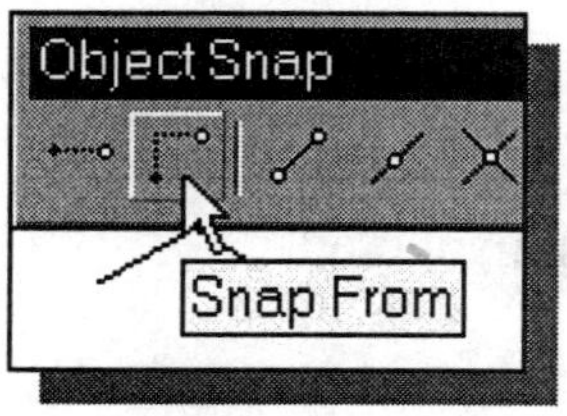

7. In the command prompt area, the message *"Specify next point or [Undo]:"* is displayed. Select ***Snap From*** in the *Object Snap* toolbar.

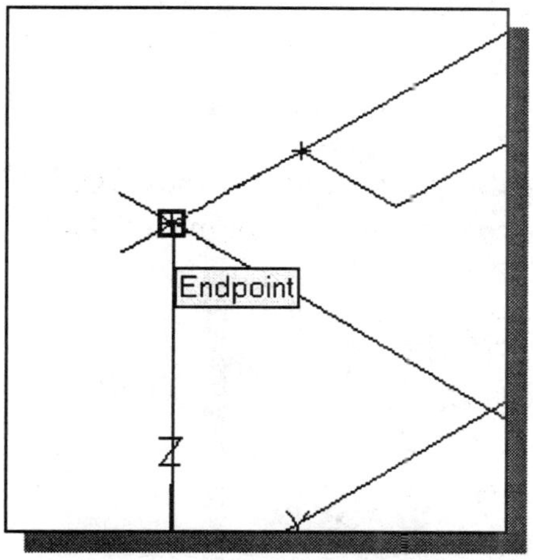

8. Select the **top-front corner** as the reference point as shown.

9. In the command prompt area, the message *"Specify next point or [Close/Undo]:_from Base point <Offset>:"* is displayed.

   Command: **@0,0,-1 [ENTER]**

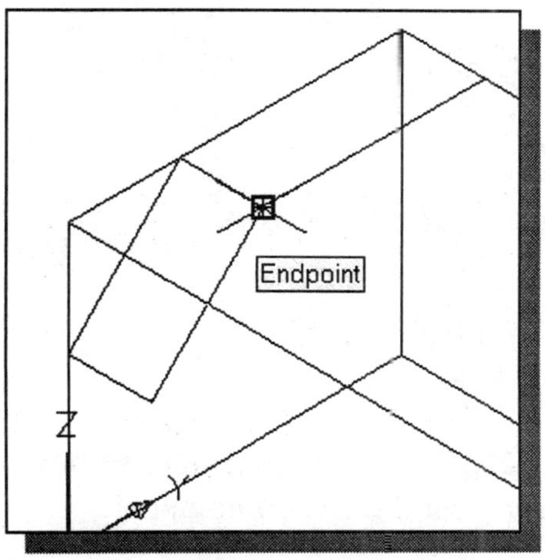

10. In the command prompt area, the message *"Specify next point or [Undo]:"* is displayed.

    Command: **@0.75,0,0 [ENTER]**

11. Move the cursor to the top corner as shown in the figure.

❖ Using the *Object Snap* options and the *relative coordinate input method* allow us to quickly locate points in 3D space.

Using the Copy option to create additional edges

❖ The *Copy* option can also be used to create additional edges of the wireframe model.

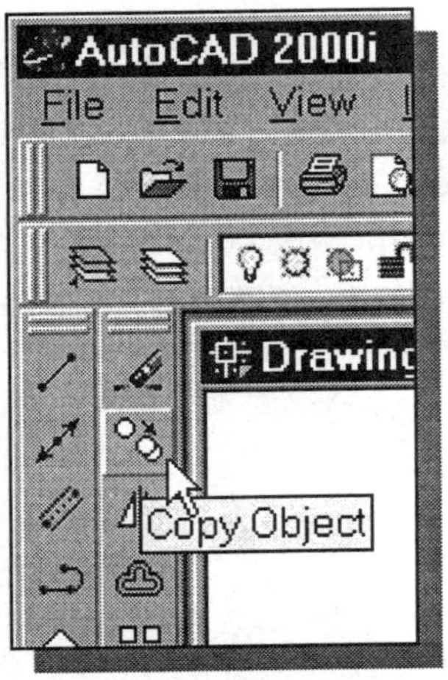

1. Click on the ***Copy Object*** icon in the *Modify* toolbar.

2. In the command prompt area, the message *"Select objects:"* is displayed. Pick any edge of the bottom rectangle.

3. Inside the graphics window, right-mouse-click once to accept the selection.

4. In the command prompt area, the message *"Specify base point or displacement, or [Multiple]:"* is displayed. Pick any corner of the rectangle to be used as a base point to create the copy.

5. In the command prompt area, the message *"Specify second point of displacement or <use first point as displacement>:"* is displayed.

   Enter: **@0,0,0.75 [ENTER]**

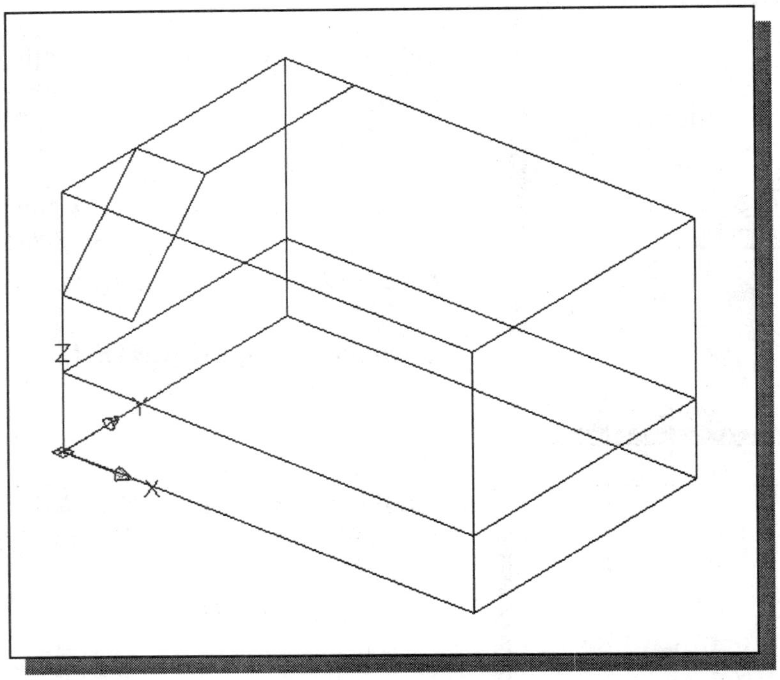

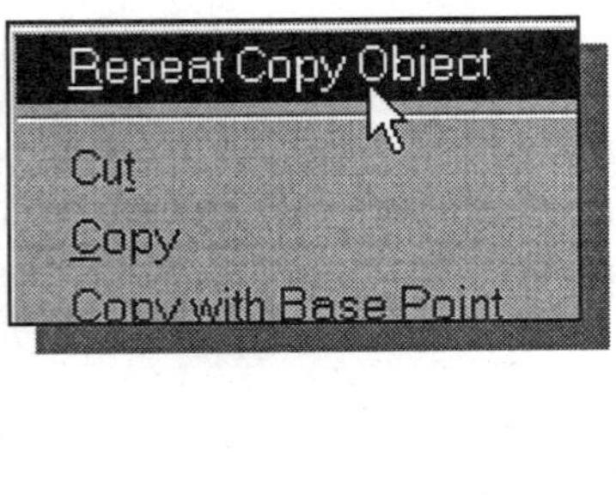

6. Inside the graphics window, **right-mouse-click** to bring up the popup option menu.

7. Pick **Repeat Copy Object** with the left-mouse-button in the popup menu to repeat the last command.

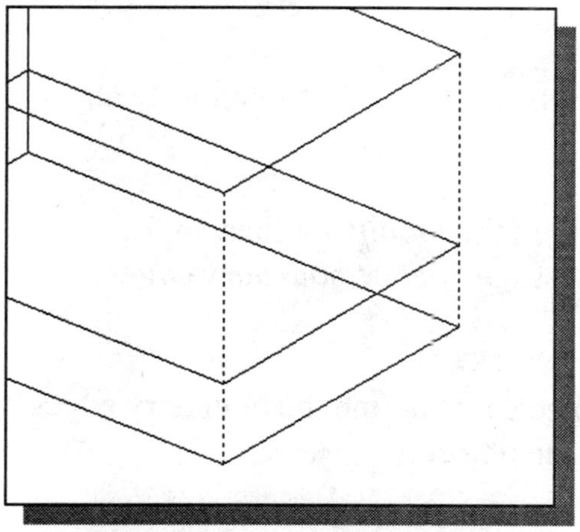

8. Pick the two **vertical lines** on the right side of the 3D box as shown.

9. Inside the graphics window, right-mouse-click once to accept the selection.

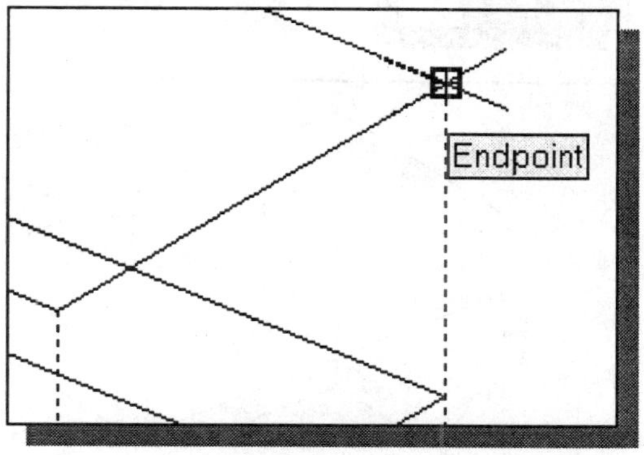

10. In the command prompt area, the message *"Specify base point or displacement, or [Multiple]:"* is displayed. Pick the top-back corner of the wireframe as a base point to create the copy.

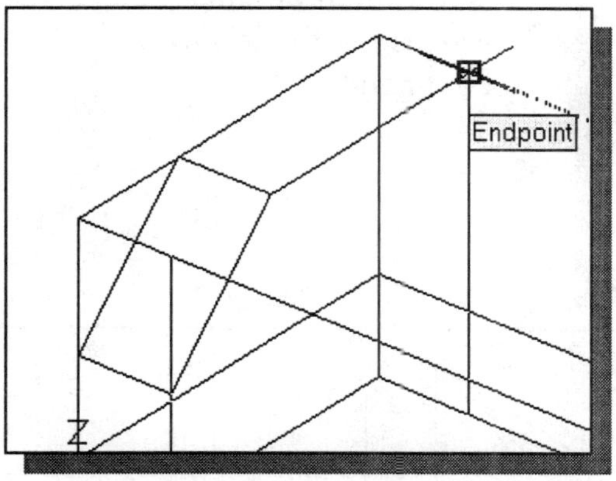

11. In the command prompt area, the message *"Specify second point of displacement or <use first point as displacement>:"* is displayed. Pick the top-back corner of the wireframe model as shown.

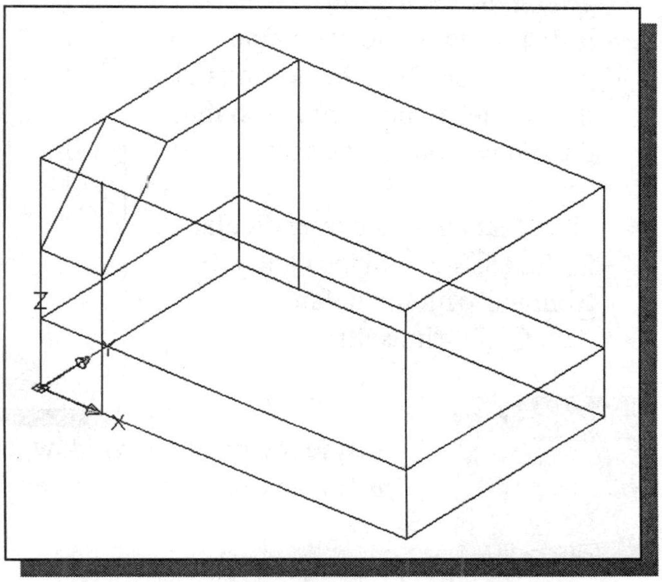

❖ The copy option is an effective way to create additional edges of wireframe models, especially when multiple objects are involved. With wireframe models, the emphasis is placed on the corners and edges of the model.

Using the *TRIM* Command

❖ The *TRIM* command can be used to shorten objects so that they end precisely at selected boundaries.

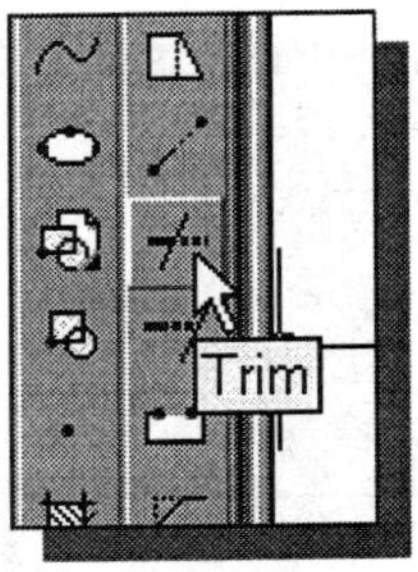

1. Select the ***Trim*** command icon in the *Modify* toolbar. In the command prompt area, the message *"Select boundary edges... Select objects:"* is displayed.

❖ First we will select the objects that define the boundary edges to which we want to trim the object.

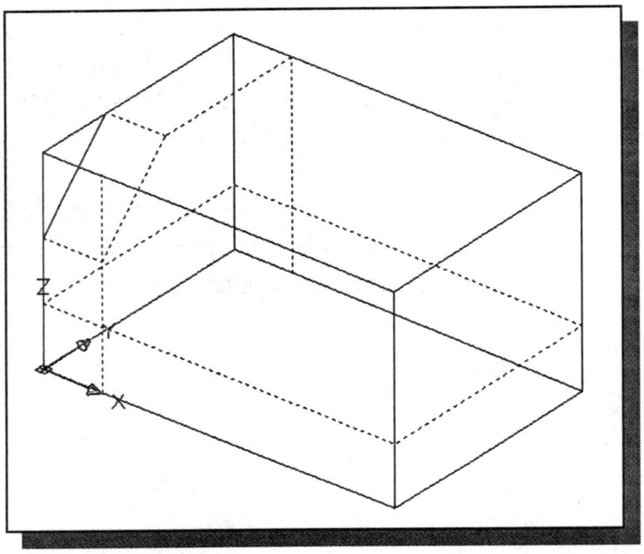

2. Pick the highlighted edges as shown in the figure; these edges are the *boundary edges*.

3. Inside the graphics window, **right-mouse-click** to accept the selection of boundary edges and proceed with the *TRIM* command.

4. The message *"Select object to trim or shift-select object to extend or [Project/Edge/Undo]:"* is displayed in the command prompt area. Pick the portions of the entities to be trimmed so that the model appears as shown.

❖ Note that entities perpendicular to the UCS XY plane cannot be trimmed with the default AutoCAD trim settings.

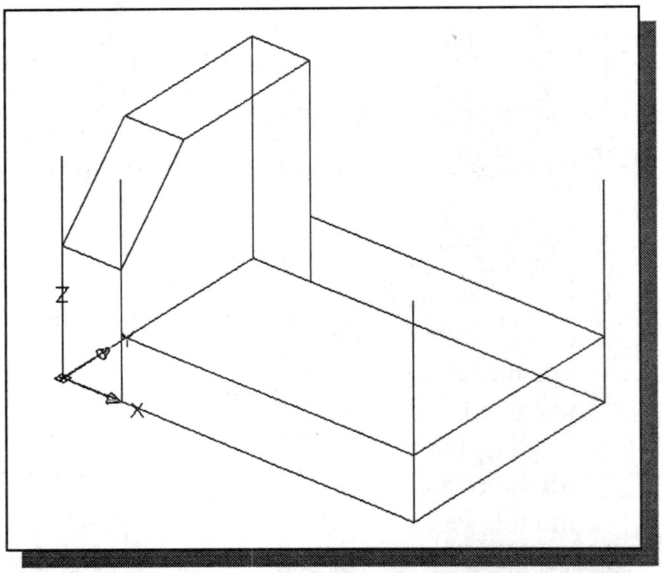

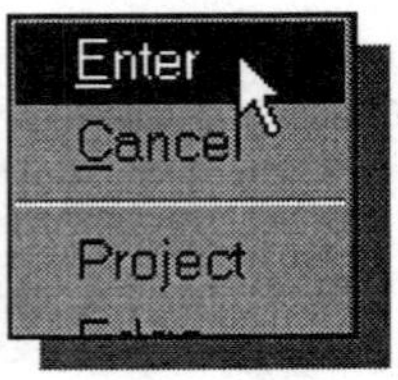

5. Inside the graphics window, **right-mouse-click** to bring up the option menu and select **Enter** to end the *TRIM* command.

Using the Trim-Project-View option

❖ The *Trim-Project-View* option allows us to trim entities that are perpendicular to the UCS XY plane.

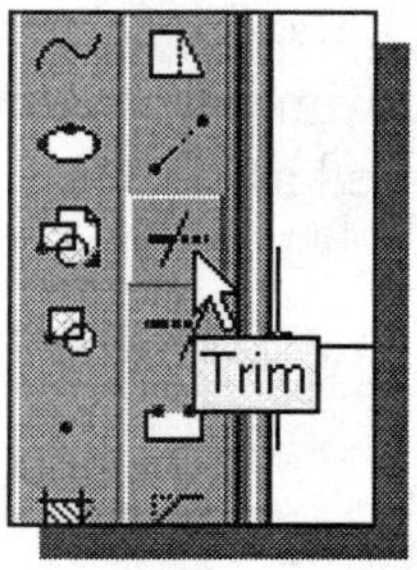

1. Select the ***Trim*** command icon in the *Modify* toolbar. In the command prompt area, the message *"Select boundary edges... Select objects:"* is displayed.

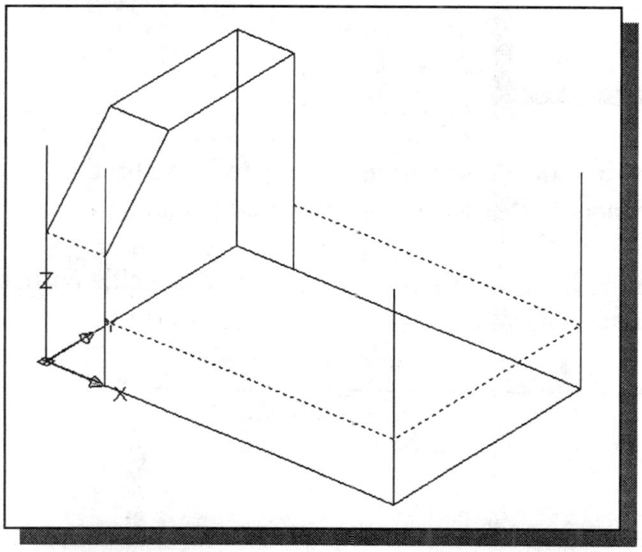

2. Pick the highlighted edges as shown in the figure; these edges are the *boundary edges*.

3. Inside the graphics window, **right-mouse-click** to accept the selected boundary edges.

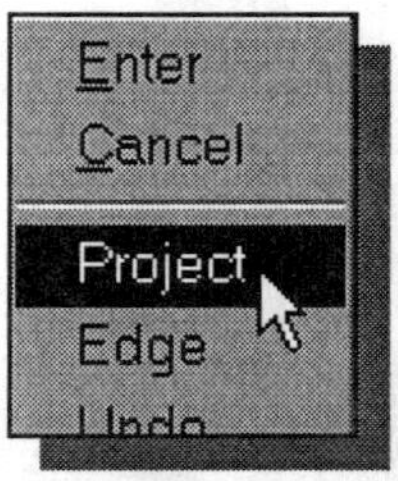

4. The message *"Select object to trim or shift-select object to extend or [Project/Edge/Undo]:"* is displayed in the command prompt area. Inside the graphics window, right-mouse-click to bring up the option menu and select **Project** as shown.

❖ Note that the default *Trim-Projection* is set to the *UCS XY* plane. Any entities that are perpendicular to the projection plane cannot be trimmed.

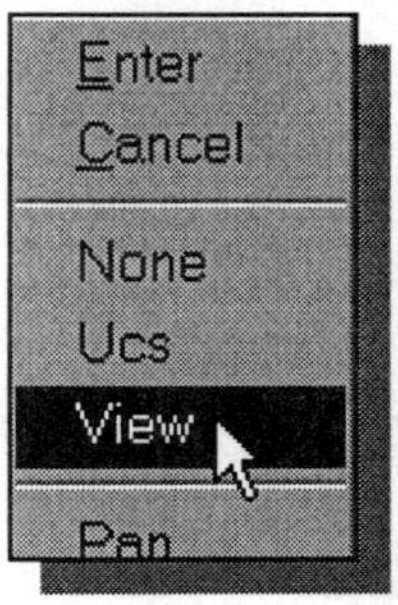

5. The message *"Enter a projection option [None/Ucs/View] <UCS>:"* is displayed in the command prompt area. Inside the graphics window, right-mouse-click to bring up the option menu and select **View** as shown.

❖ Changing the projection setting to *View* allows us to modify basically any viewable entities.

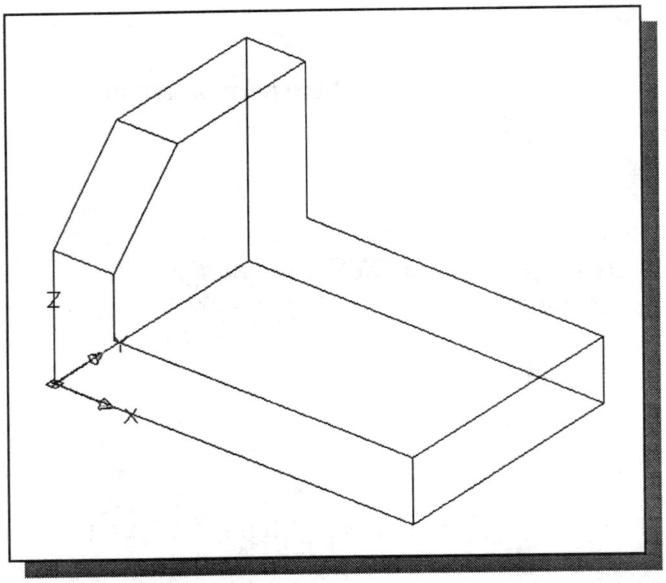

6. The message *"Select object to trim or shift-select object to extend or [Project/Edge/Undo]:"* is displayed in the command prompt area. Pick the portions of the entities to be trimmed so that the model appeared as shown.

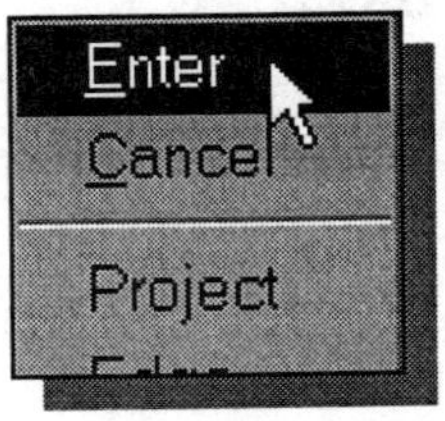

7. Inside the graphics window, **right-mouse-click** to bring up the option menu and select **Enter** to end the *TRIM* command.

8. On your own, use the *LINE* command to complete the inside corner of the wireframe model as shown.

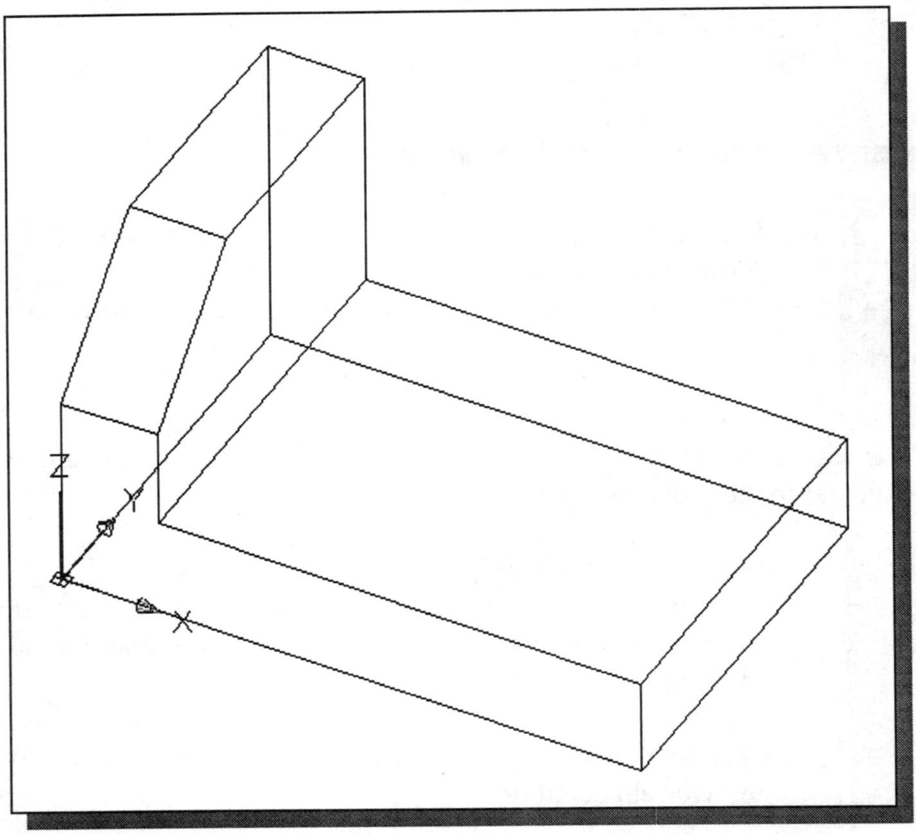

Using the View Toolbar

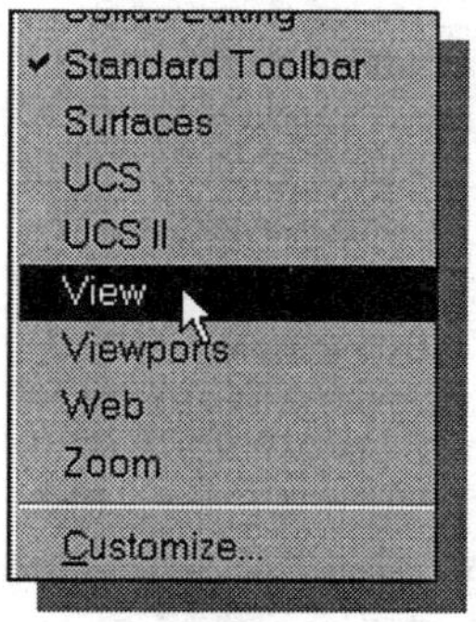

1. Move the cursor on top of any icon and **right-click** on any icon of the *Standard* toolbar to display a list of toolbar menu groups.

2. Select **View**, with the left-mouse-button, to display the *View* toolbar on the screen.

➢ The *View* toolbar contains two sections of icons that allow us to quickly switch to standard 2D and 3D views.

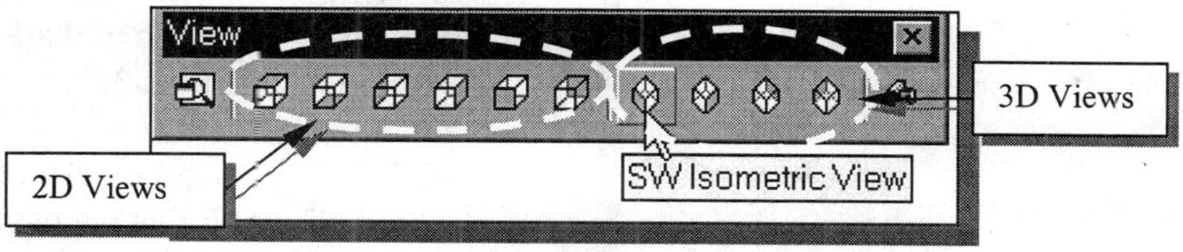

3. On your own, examine the wireframe model by using the different icons in the *View* toolbar.

Dynamic Rotation – 3D orbit

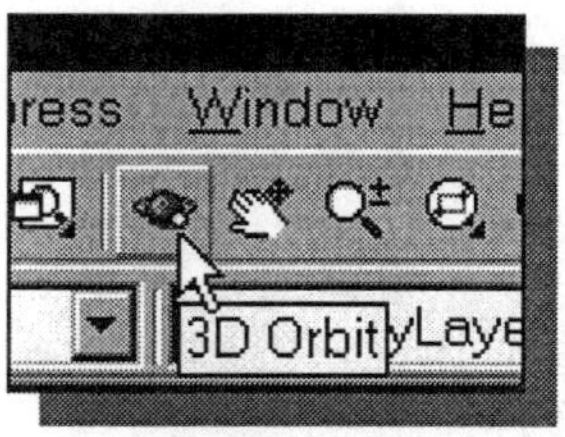

1. Click on the ***3D Orbit*** icon in the *Standard* toolbar.

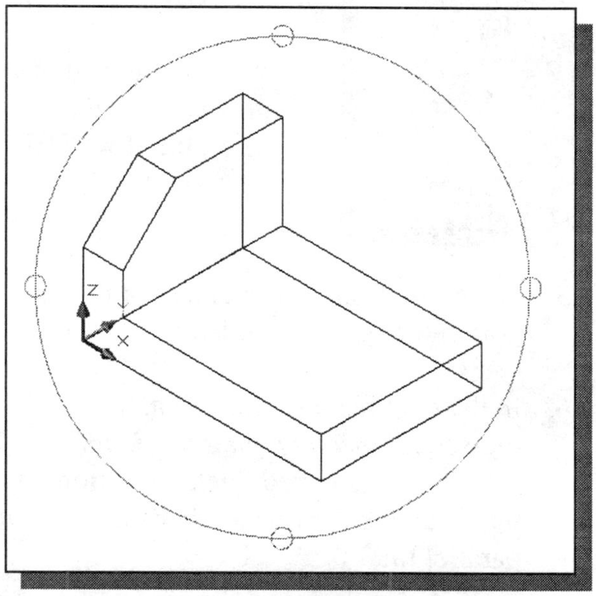

❖ The *3D-Orbit* view displays an ***arcball***, which is a circle, divided into four quadrants by smaller circles. *3D-Orbit* enables us to manipulate the view of 3D objects by clicking and dragging with the left-mouse-button.

2. Inside the *arcball*, press down the left-mouse-button and drag it up and down to rotate about the screen X-axis. Dragging the mouse left and right will rotate about the screen Y-axis.

3. Move the cursor to different locations on the screen, outside the *arcball* or on one of the four small circles, and experiment with the real-time dynamic rotation feature of the *3D-ORBIT* command.

Using the *OFFSET* command to create parallel edges

❖ The AutoCAD *Offset* option can also be used to create edges that are at specific distances to existing 3D wireframe edges. Prior to creating the parallel edges, we will first convert one of the polylines to individual line segments.

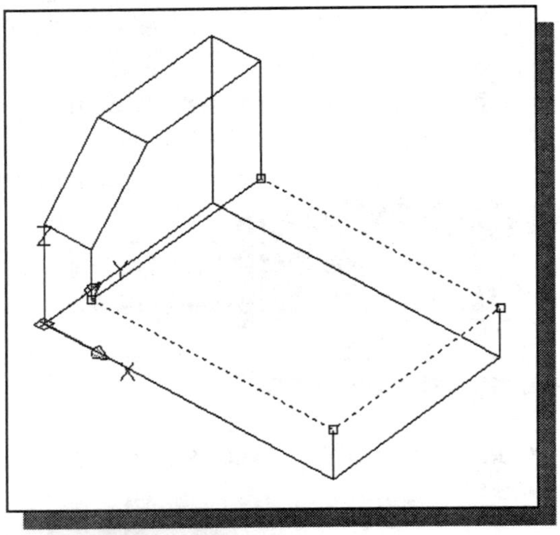

1. Pick the top-right edge of the wireframe model.

- AutoCAD 2000i provides a flexible graphical user interface that allows users to select graphical entities BEFORE the command is selected (*Pre-selection*), or AFTER the command is selected (*Post-selection*). The polyline we have pre-selected consists of three line-segments.

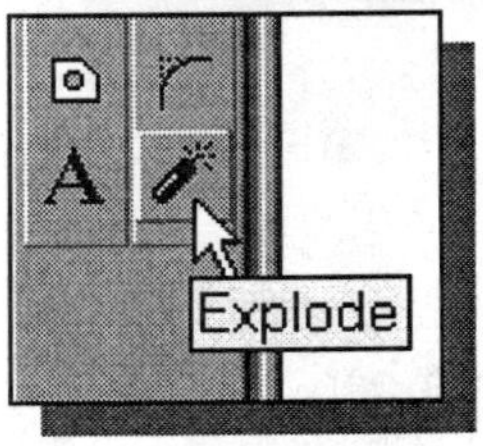

2. Select the ***Explode*** command icon in the *Modify* toolbar as shown.

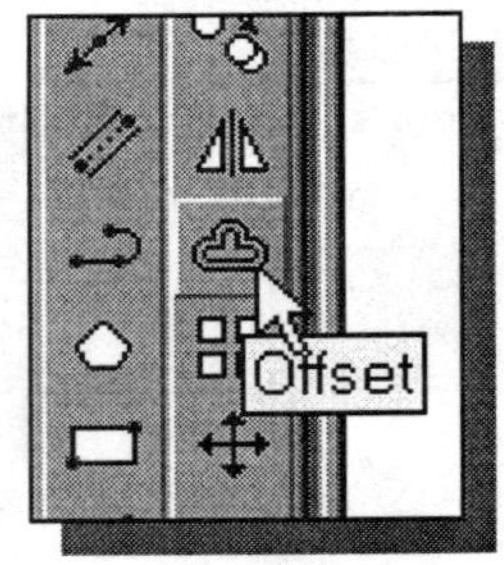

3. Pick ***Offset*** in the *Modify* toolbar as shown.

4. In the command prompt area, the message *"Specify offset distance or [Through] <Through>:"* is displayed.
   Enter: **0.5** **[ENTER]**

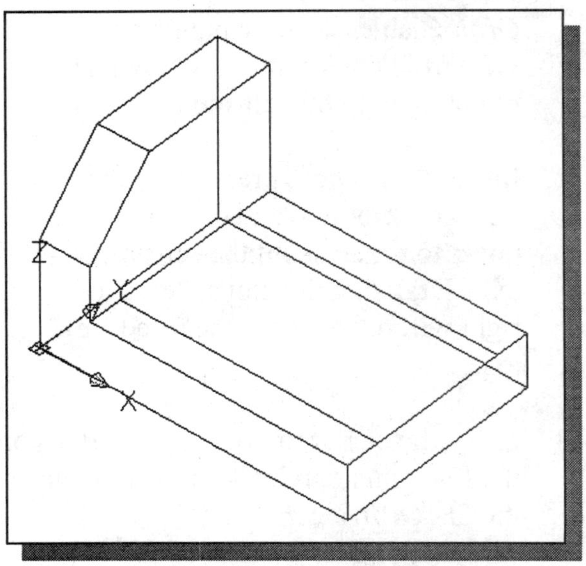

5. Select the front line segment of the polyline we just exploded.

6. In the command prompt area, the message *"Specify point on side to offset:"* is displayed. Pick a location that is above the line to create the first parallel line.

7. Select the back line segment of the polyline we exploded and create another parallel line as shown.

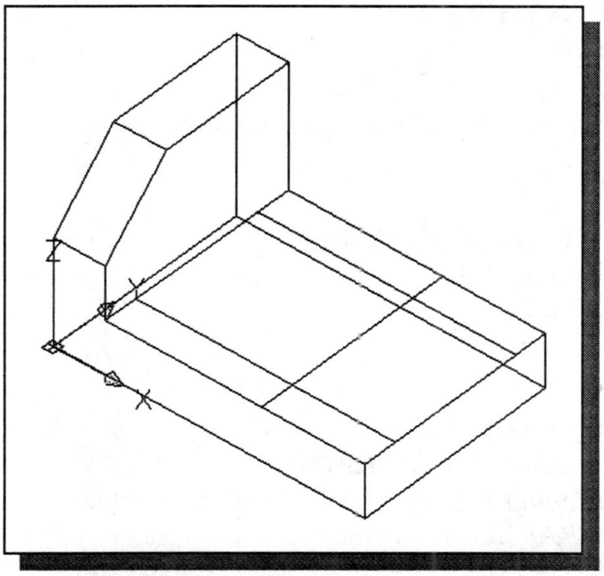

8. On your own, repeat the above steps and create another parallel line (distance: **1.5**) as shown.

   - In creating parallel edges, the *OFFSET* command can be viewed as an alternative to the *COPY* command. In 3D wireframe modeling, the focus is on identifying the edges and corners of the model. Most of the 2D construction tools are also applicable in 3D environment.

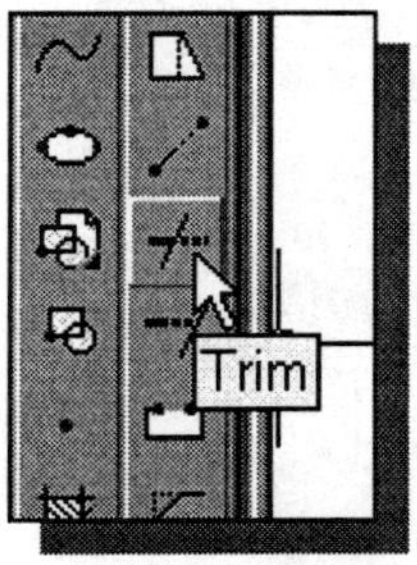

9. Select the ***Trim*** command icon in the *Modify* toolbar.

10. In the command prompt area, the message *"Select boundary edges... Select objects:"* is displayed. Pick the highlighted edges as shown in the figure; these edges are the *boundary edges*.

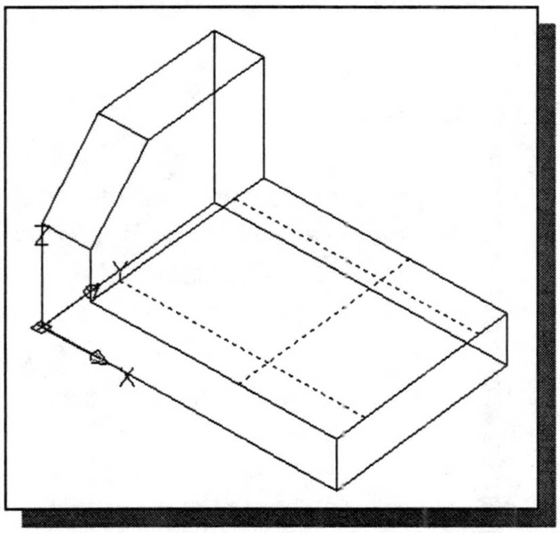

11. Inside the graphics window, **right-mouse-click** to accept the selection of boundary edges and proceed with the *TRIM* command.

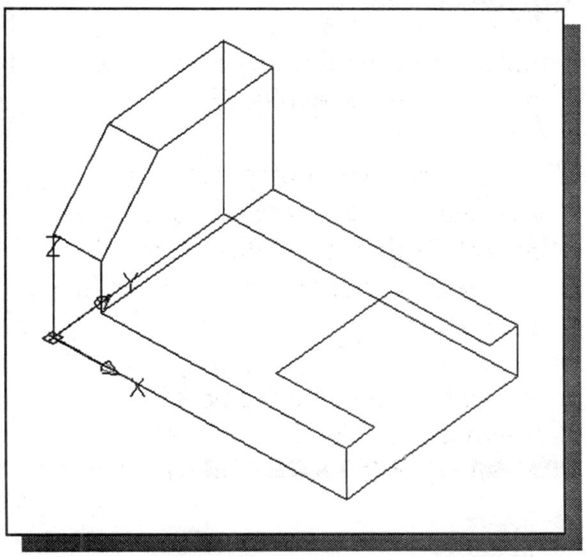

12. On your own, click on the line segments to trim so that the wireframe model appears as shown.

Creating a circle above the UCS XY plane

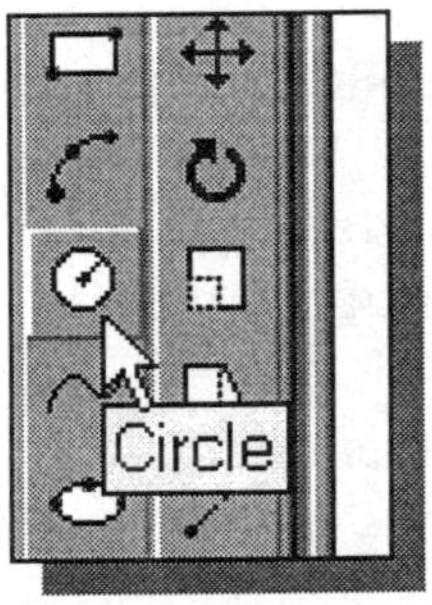

1. Select the ***Circle*** command icon in the *Draw* toolbar.

- By default, the XY plane of the UCS defines the sketching plane for constructing 2D geometric entities.

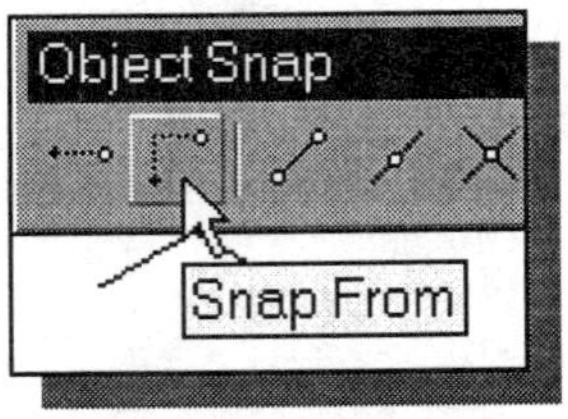

2. In the command prompt area, the message *"_circle Specify center point for circle or[3P/2P/Ttr (tan tan radius)]:"* is displayed. Select ***Snap From*** in the *Object Snap* toolbar.

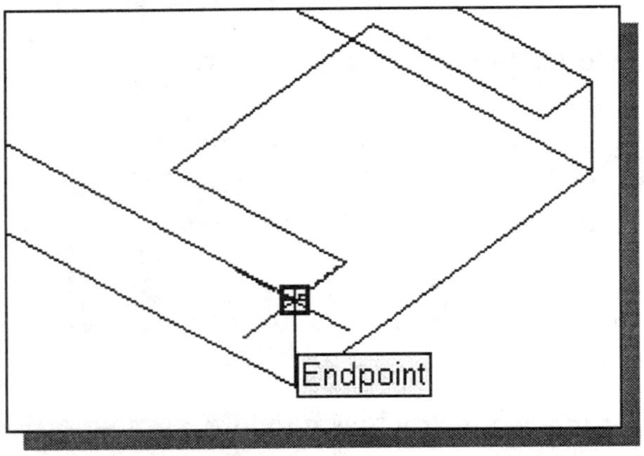

3. Select the **top-right corner** as the reference point as shown.

4. In the command prompt area, the message *"Specify next point or [Close/Undo]:_from Base point <Offset>:"* is displayed.

   Command: **@-2.67,1.5,0 [ENTER]**

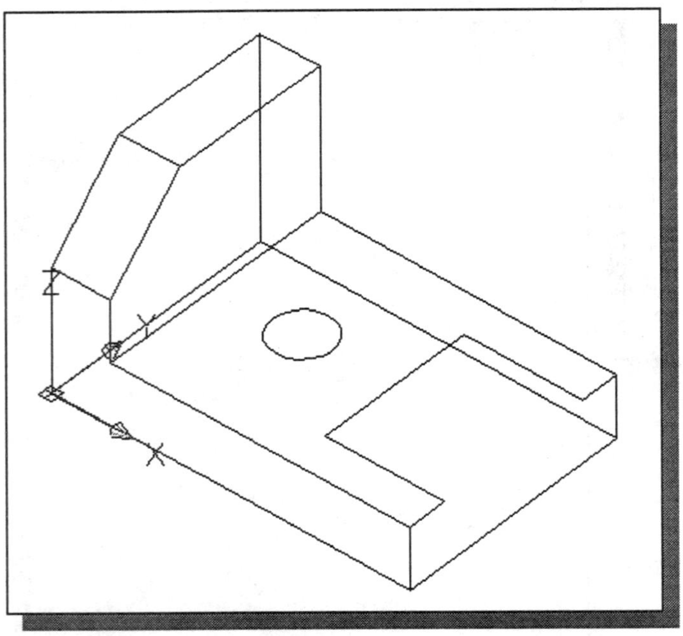

5. In the command prompt area, the message *" Specify radius of circle or [Diameter]:"* is displayed.

   Command: **0.375 [ENTER]**

- The circle is created above the sketching plane by using the ***Snap From*** option.

Completing the wireframe model

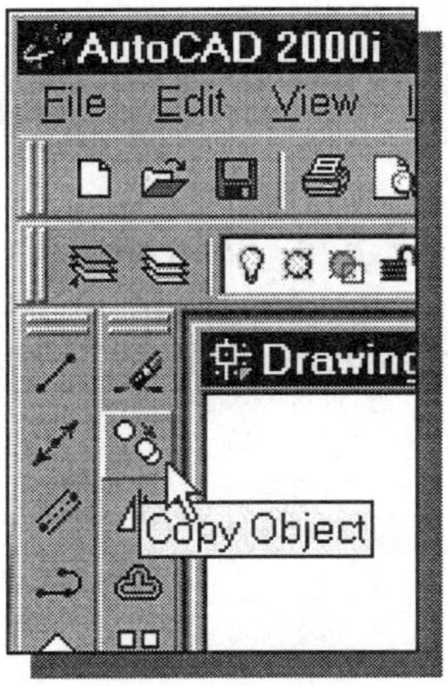

1. Click on the ***Copy Object*** icon in the *Modify* toolbar.

2. In the command prompt area, the message *"Select objects:"* is displayed. Pick the edges and the circle as shown in the figure.

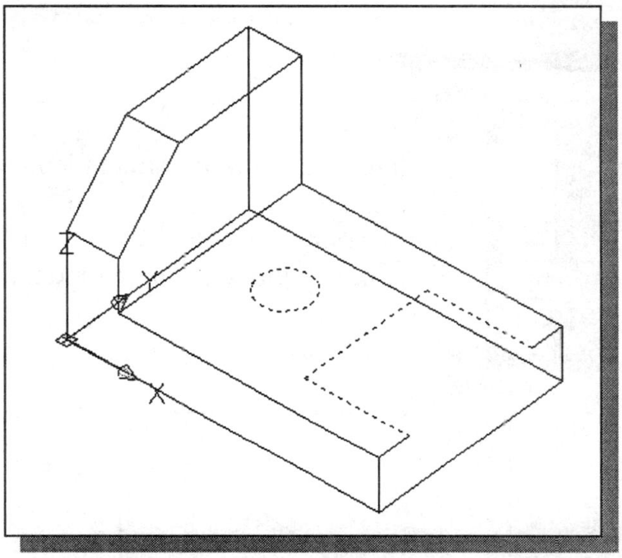

3. Inside the graphics window, right-mouse-click once to accept the selection.

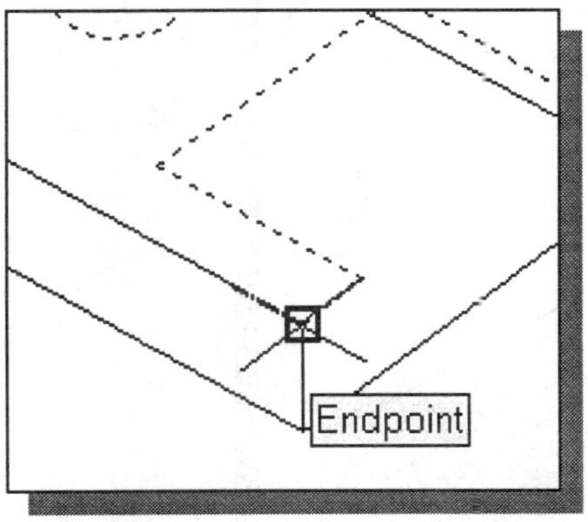

4. In the command prompt area, the message *"Specify base point or displacement, or [Multiple]:"* is displayed. Pick the front-right corner as shown.

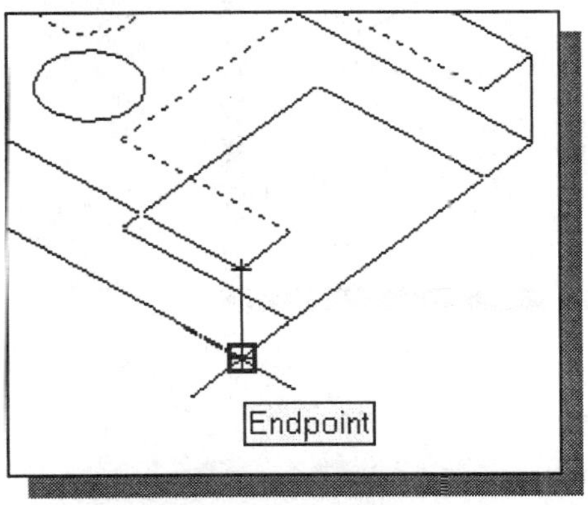

5. In the command prompt area, the message *"Specify second point of displacement or <use first point as displacement>:"* is displayed. Pick the bottom-right corner as shown.

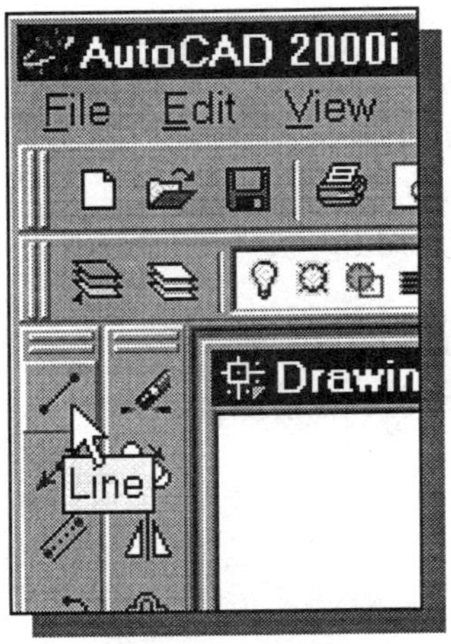

6. Select the ***Line*** icon in the *Draw* toolbar.

7. On your own, create the lines connecting the corners of the created edges as shown.

8. Use the *Snap to Quadrant* option to create edges in between the two circles.

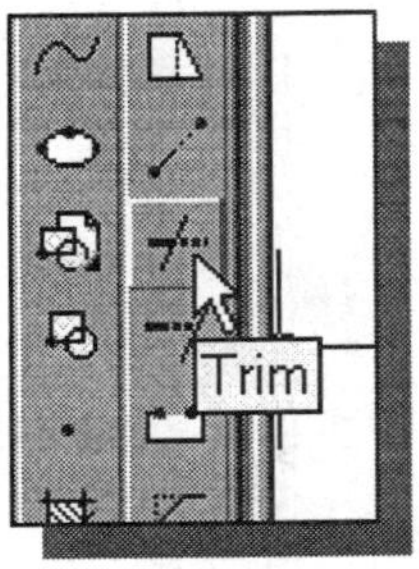

9. Select the ***Trim*** command icon in the *Modify* toolbar.

10. On your own, trim the center portion of the bottom-right and complete the wireframe model as shown.

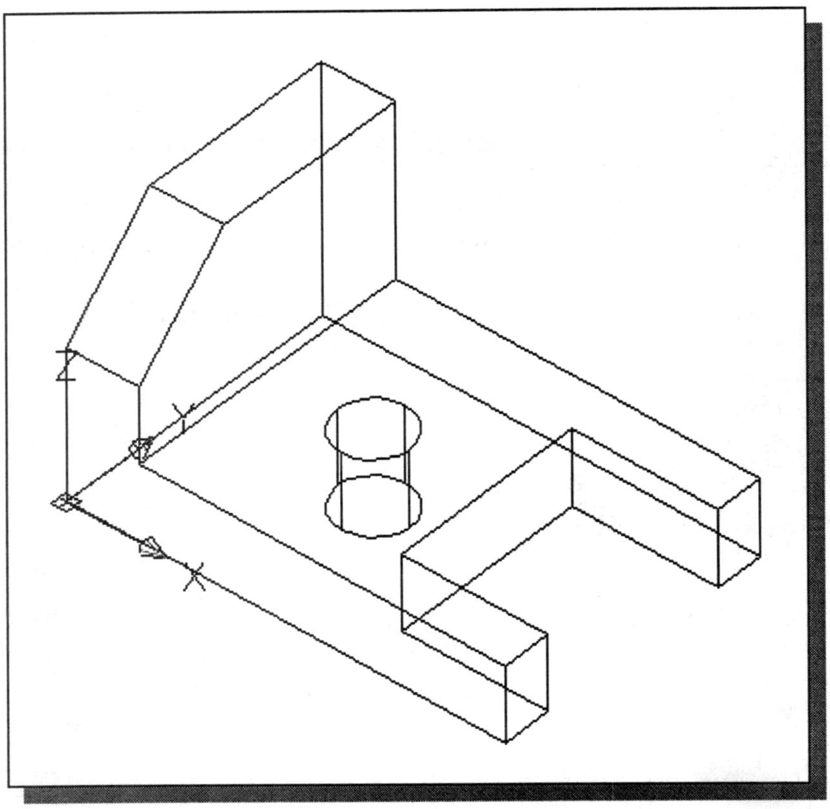

Questions:

1. Describe some of the control option available with the *3D Orbit* command.

2. List two different methods to create 3D edges from existing 3D edges in AutoCAD 2000i.

3. In the chapter tutorial, how many of the UCS options were used to create the wireframe model?

4. When and why would you use the *Trim-Project-View* option?

5. Identify the following commands:

(a)

(b)

(c)

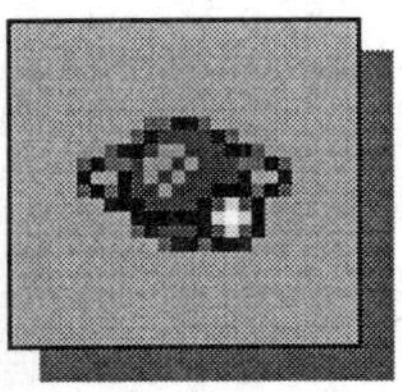

(d)

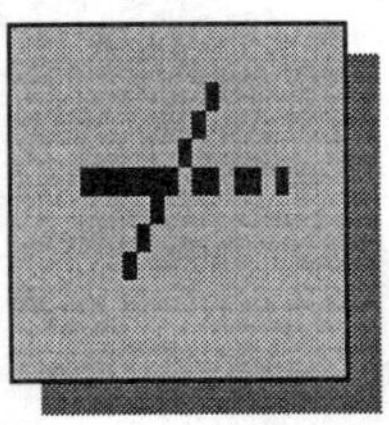

Exercises: All dimensions are in inches.

1.

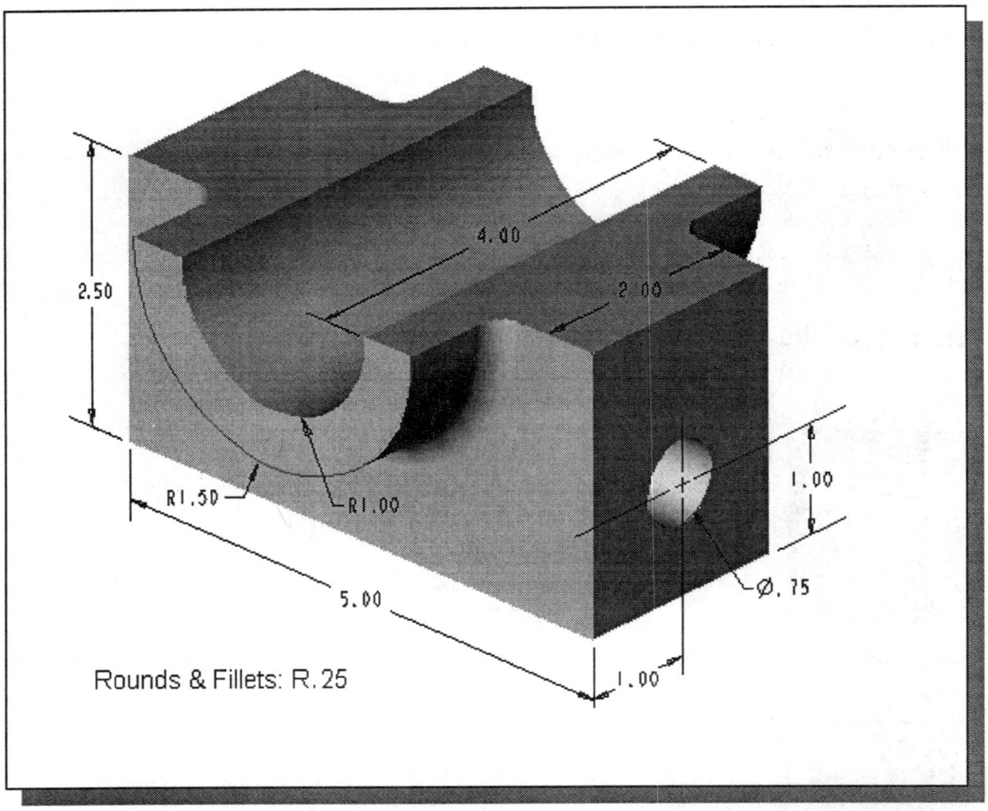

2.

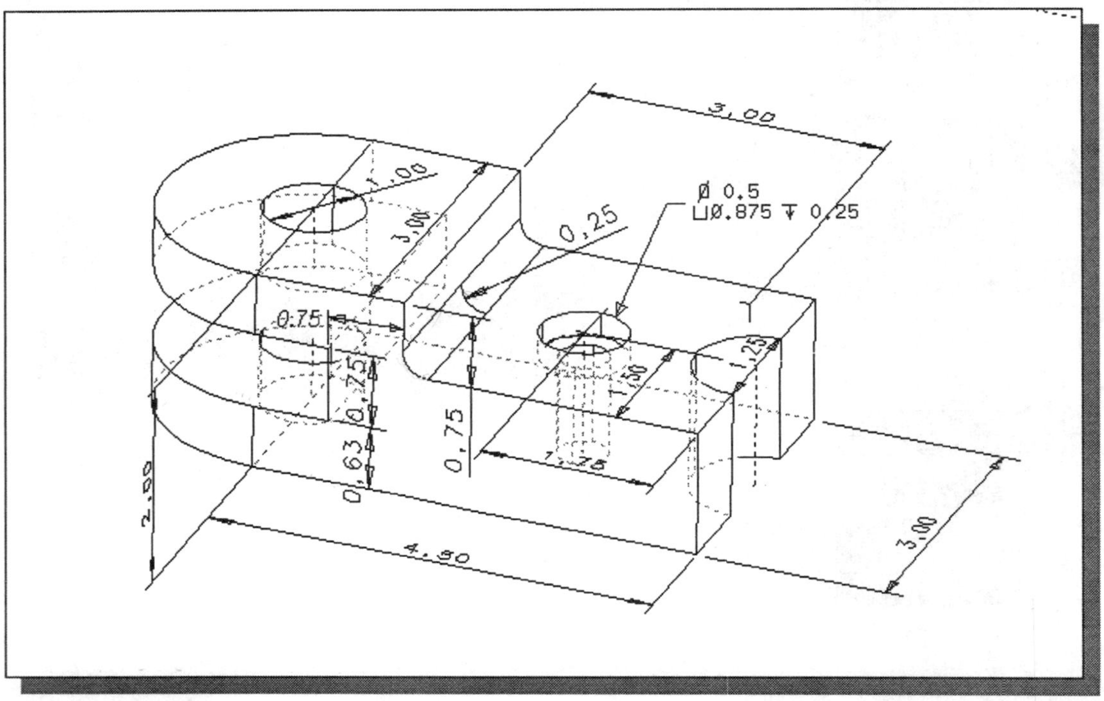

3.

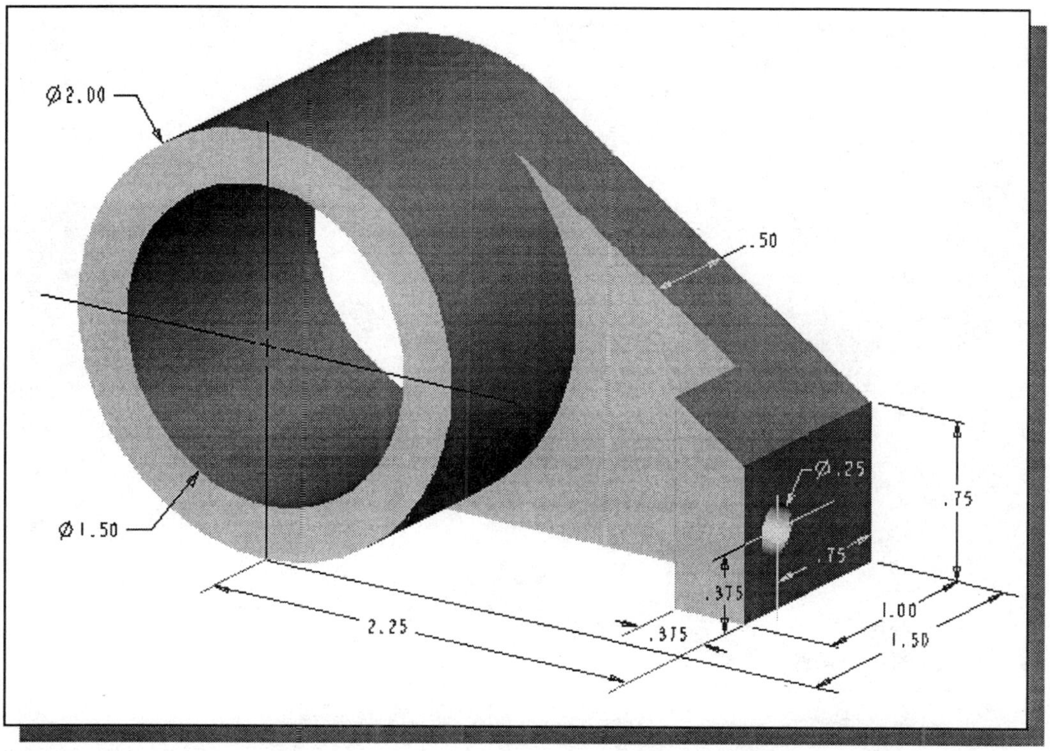
Ø2.00
.50
Ø.25
.75
Ø1.50
.75
.375
2.25
.375
1.00
1.50

4.

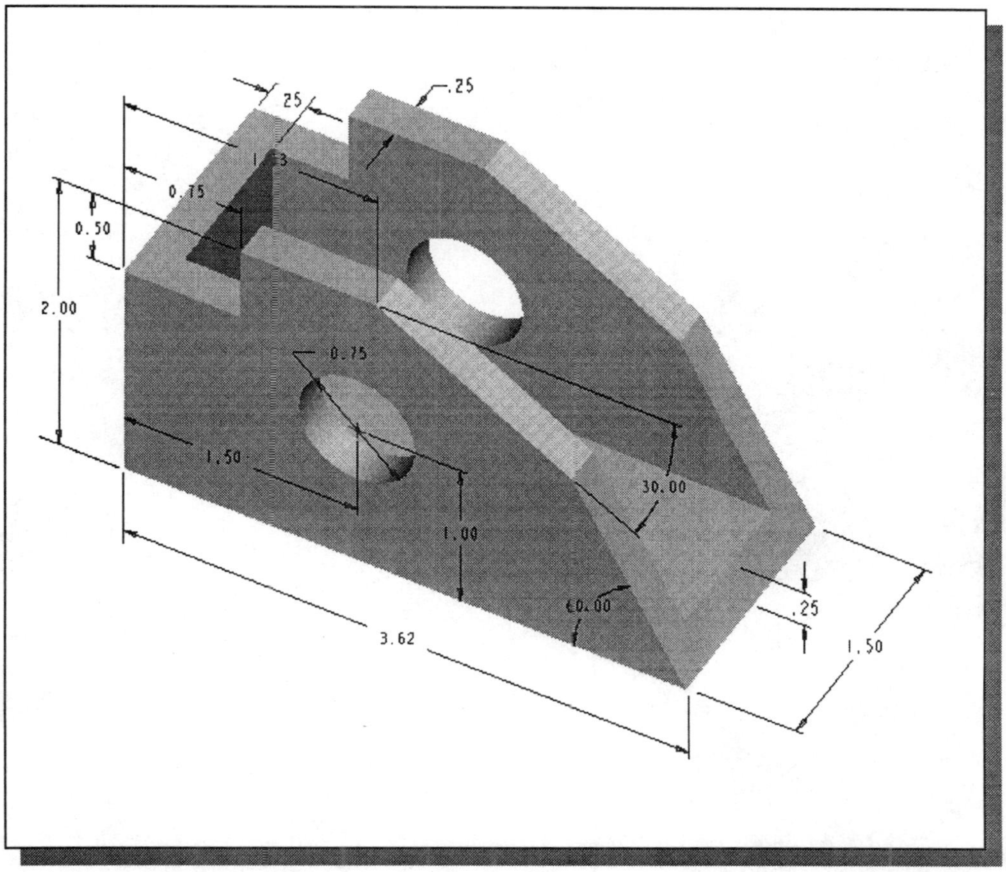
.25
.25
0.75
0.50
2.00
0.75
1.50
30.00
1.00
60.00
.25
3.62
1.50

NOTES:

Chapter 4
UCS, Viewports and Wireframe Modeling

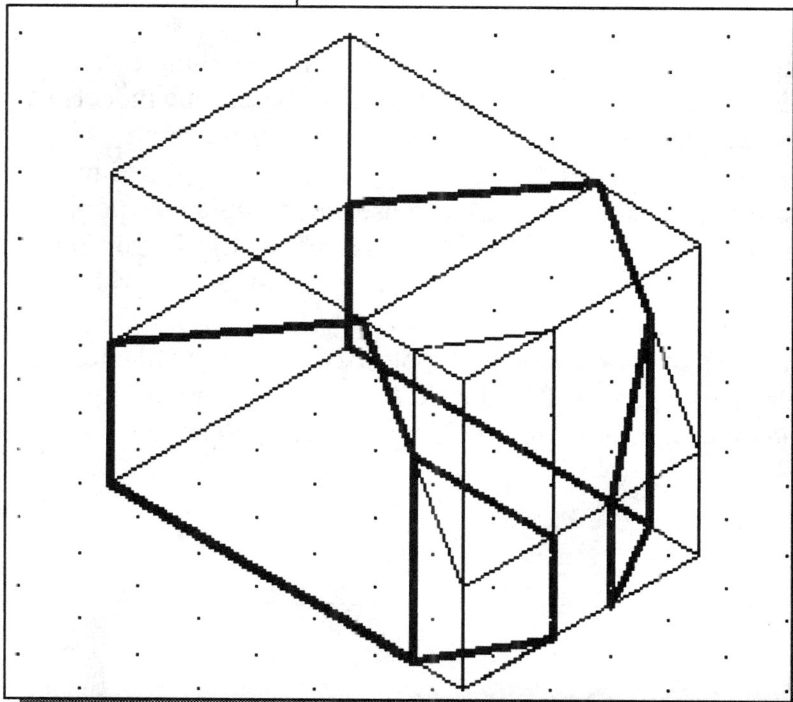

Learning Objectives

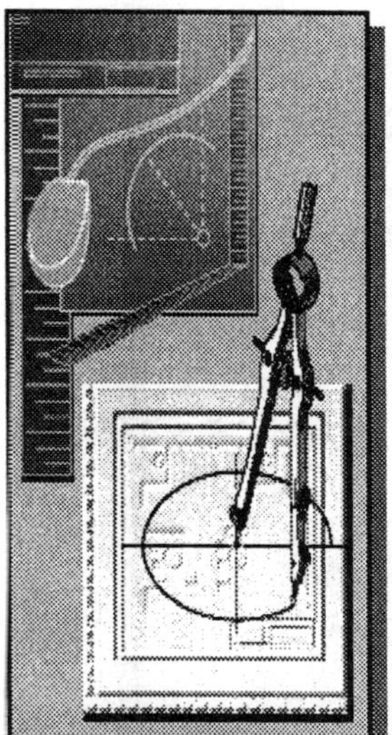

- Understand the use of UCS.
- Display and Orient 3D Views.
- Understand and apply the basic wireframe construction techniques.
- Create 3D Wireframe Models.
- Use the Named Views option.

Introduction

In the previous chapter, we examined some of the basic techniques to create 3D wireframe models. Again, a wireframe model is a skeletal description of a 3D object. There are no surfaces in a wireframe model; it consists only of points, lines, and curves that describe the edges of the object.

In this chapter, we will further discuss the techniques and wireframe modeling tools available in AutoCAD. Instead of creating the corners and edges of wireframe models by entering the precise 3D coordinates, the use of construction lines and referencing techniques are illustrated. The construction of edges in 3D space can be simplified by using the AutoCAD User Coordinate System. We will also use the multiple viewports option, which is available in most CAD systems, to aid the construction of 3D wireframe models.

It is important to point out that most of the construction tools used in creating 2D designs, such as *Object Snap* and *Polar Tracking*, as well as the *COPY*, *MIRROR*, and *ARRAY* commands, are also applicable to the constructions of 3D wireframe models.

The V-Block Design

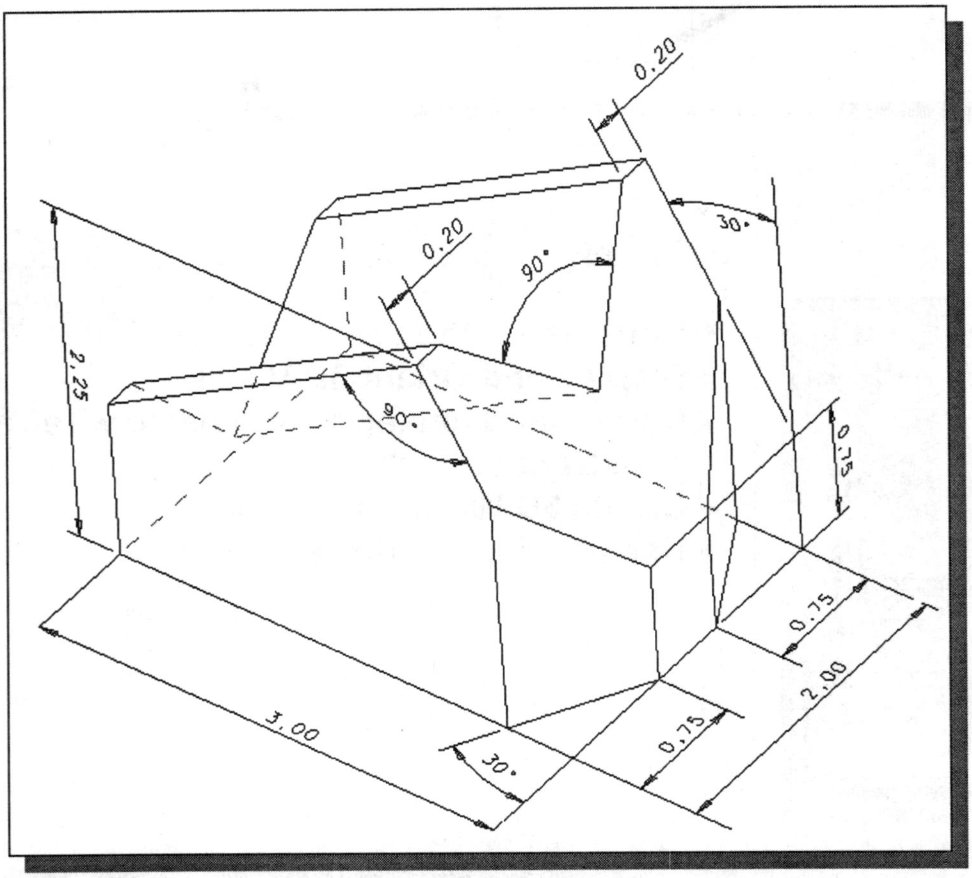

Starting Up AutoCAD® 2000i

1. Select the AutoCAD® 2000i option on the *Program* menu or select the AutoCAD® 2000i icon on the *Desktop*. Once the program is loaded into the memory, the AutoCAD® 2000i drawing screen and the *AutoCAD Today* startup dialog box will appear on the screen.

2. In the *AutoCAD Today* startup dialog box, select the **Create Drawings** tab with a single click of the left-mouse-button.

3. Confirm the startup option is set to ***Start from Scratch***, as shown in the figure below.

4. In the *Default Settings* section, pick **English (feet and Inches)** as the drawing units.

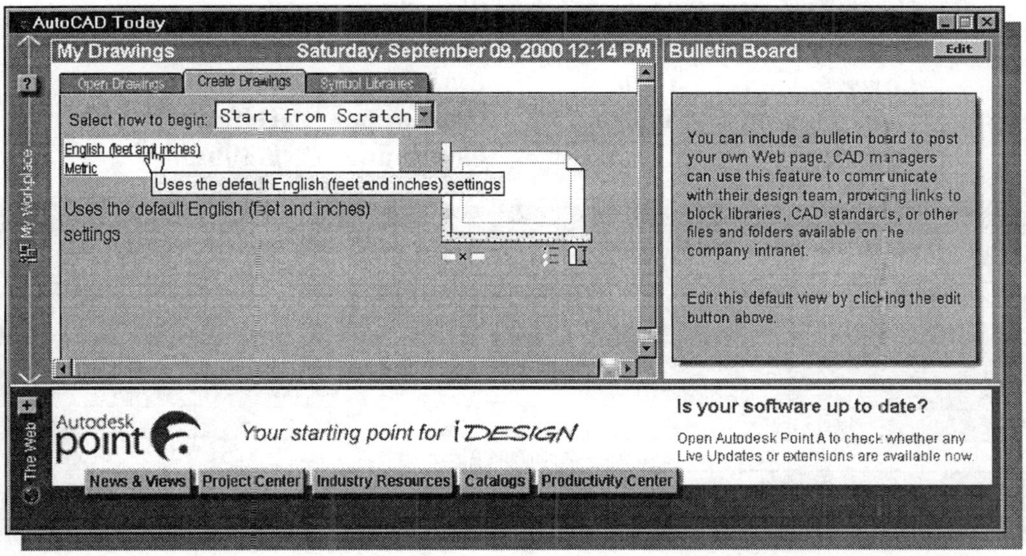

❖ Note that two graphics window are available. The *Drawing1.dwg* uses the default units set during the installation of AutoCAD 2000i. The units used in the second graphics window, the *Drawing2.dwg* window, are set to the English units, inches and feet.

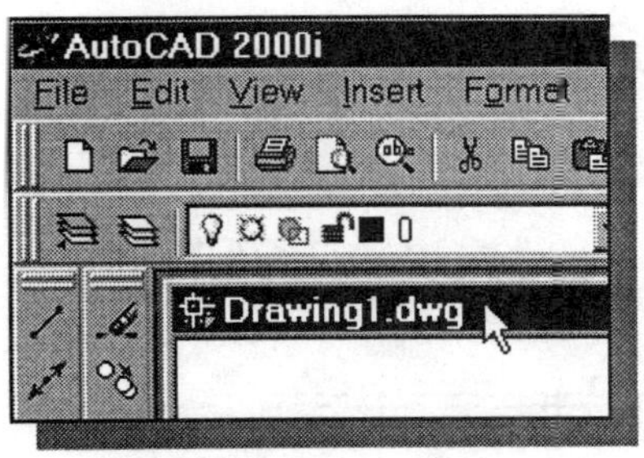

5. Switch to the *Drawing1* window by left-clicking once in the title area of the window.

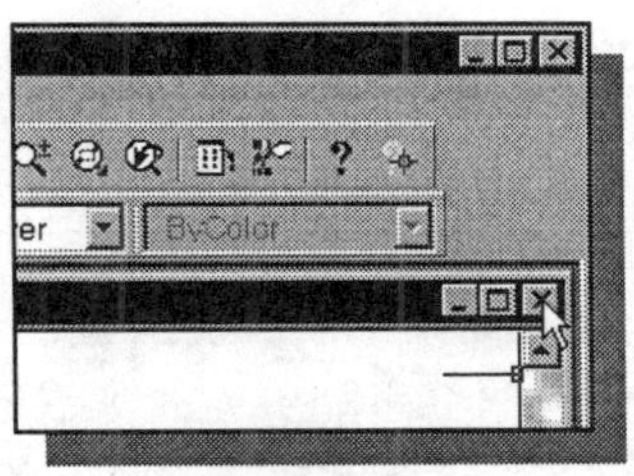

6. Close the window by clicking the ***Close*** icon located at the upper-right-corner of the *Drawing1* window.

Layers setup

1. Pick ***Layers*** in the *Object Properties* toolbar.

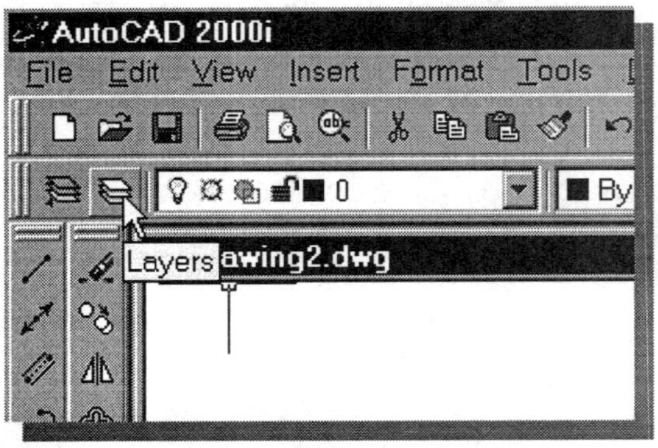

2. Click on the ***New*** icon to create new layers.

3. Create **two new layers** with the following settings:

Layer	***Color***	***LineType***	***LineWeight***
Construction	**White**	**Continuous**	**Default**
Object	**Cyan**	**Continuous**	**0.30mm**

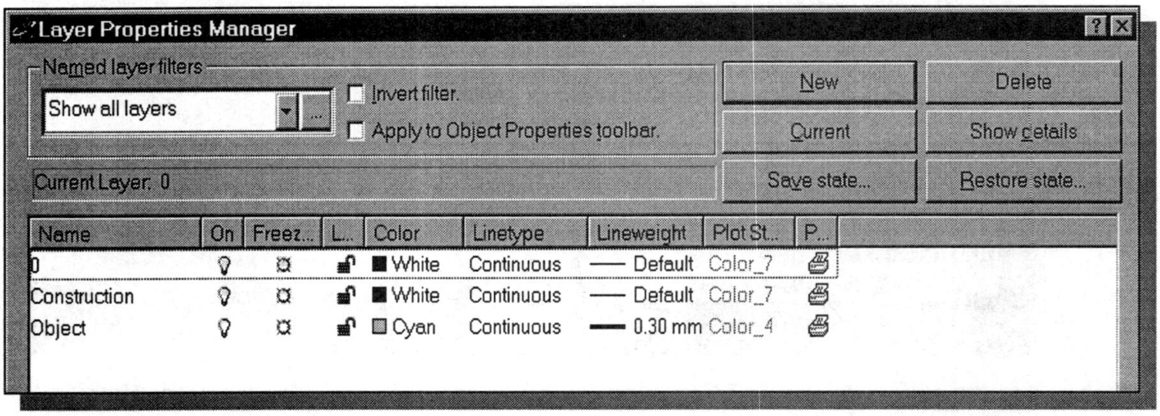

4. Highlight the layer ***Construction*** in the list of layers.

5. Click on the ***Current*** icon to set layer ***Construction*** as the *Current layer*.

6. Click on the **OK** button to accept the settings and exit the *Layer Properties Manager* dialog box.

7. In the *Status Bar* area, reset the options and turn ***ON*** the *GRID, POLAR, OSNAP, LWT* and *MODEL* options.

Creating the rectangular base of the design

➤ We will first use construction geometry to define the outer edges of the design.

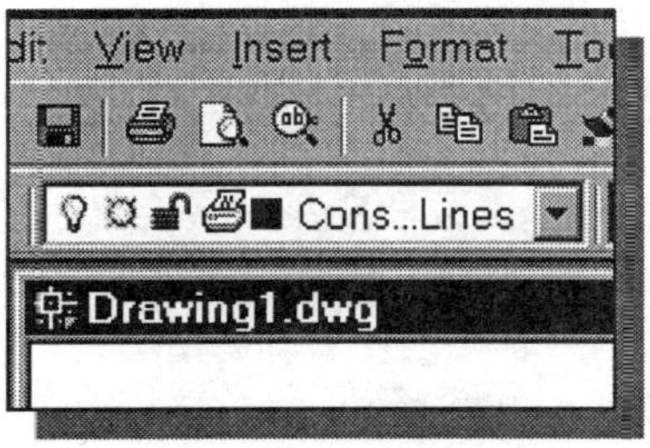

1. In the *Layer Control* box, confirm that layer *Construction_Lines* is set as the *Current layer*.

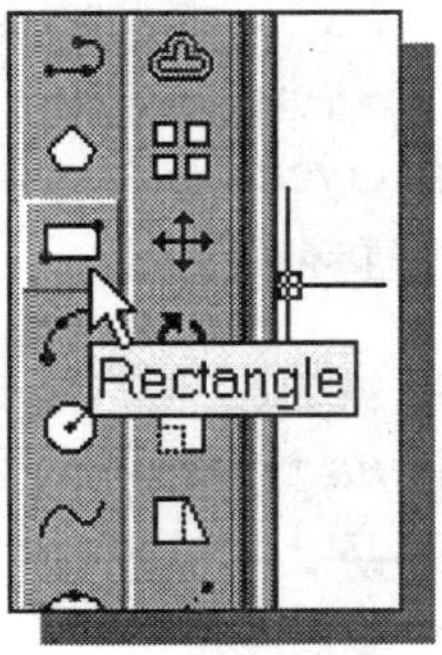

2. Select the ***Rectangle*** icon in the *Draw* toolbar. In the command prompt area, the message *"Specify first corner point or [Chamfer/Elevation/Fillet/Thickness/Width]:"* is displayed.

3. Place the first corner-point of the rectangle near the lower left corner of the screen. Do not be overly concerned about the actual coordinates of the location; the drawing space is as big as you can imagine.

4. We will create a 3" X 2" rectangle by entering the coordinates of the second corner using the relative coordinates input method.

Specify other corner point or [Dimension]: **@3,2 [ENTER]**

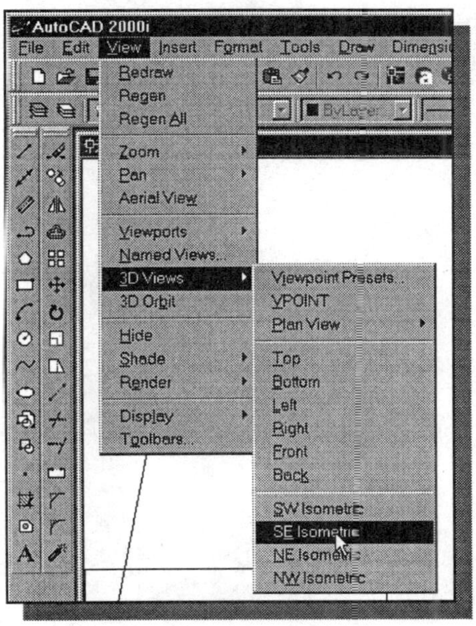

5. In the pull-down menus, select:

   [View] => [3D Views] => [SE Isometric]

- Notice the orientation of the sketched 2D rectangle in relation to the displayed AutoCAD user coordinate system. By default, the 2D sketch-plane is aligned to the XY plane of the world coordinate system.

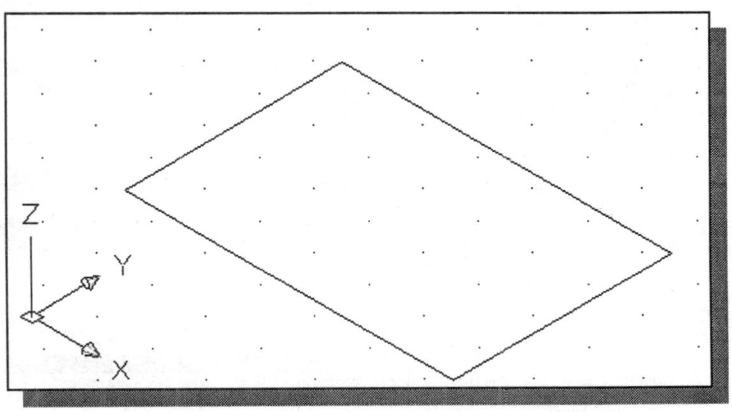

Creating a wireframe Box

- Next, we will use the *COPY* command to define the 3D boundary of the design.

1. Click on the ***Copy Object*** icon in the *Modify* toolbar.
2. In the command prompt area, the message *"Select objects:"* is displayed. Pick any edge of the sketched rectangle.
3. Inside the graphics window, right-mouse-click once to accept the selection.
4. In the command prompt area, the message *"Specify base point or displacement, or [Multiple]:"* is displayed. Pick any corner of the sketched rectangle as a base point to create the copy.
5. In the command prompt area, the message *"Specify second point of displacement or <use first point as displacement>:"* is displayed. Enter: **@0,0,2.25 [ENTER]**

➤ Note that the three values represent the distance measured in the X, Y and Z directions relative to the current UCS.

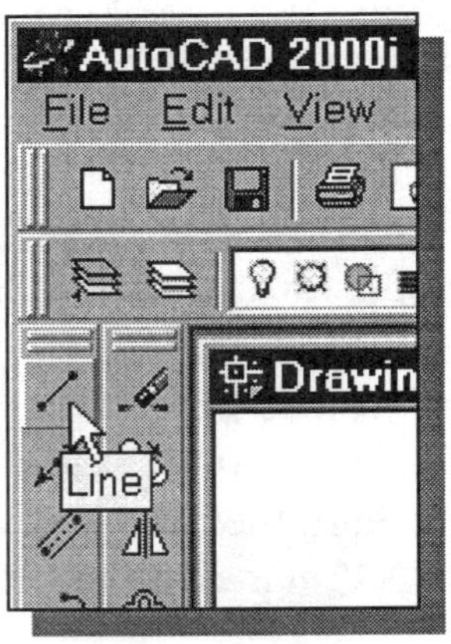

6. Select the ***Line*** icon in the *Draw* toolbar.
7. On your own, create four lines connecting the four-corners of the two rectangles as shown below.

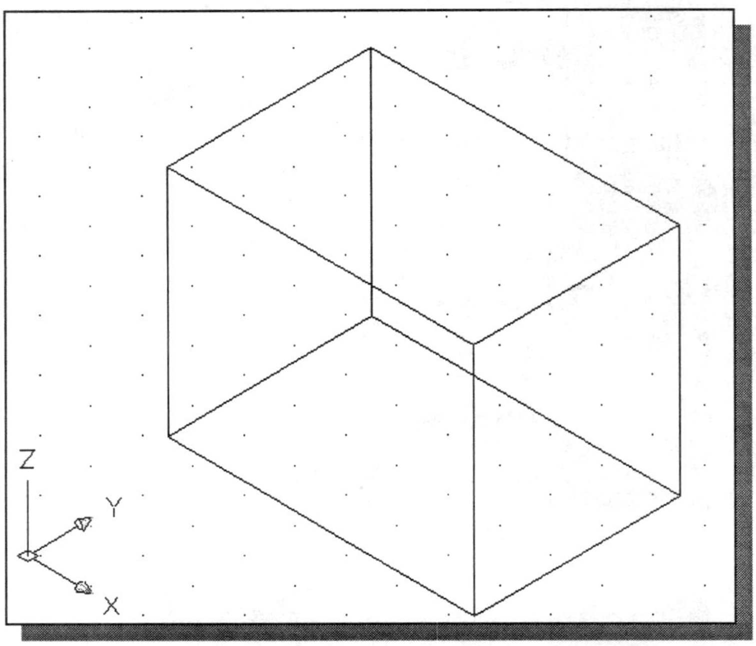

Using the View and the UCS Toolbars

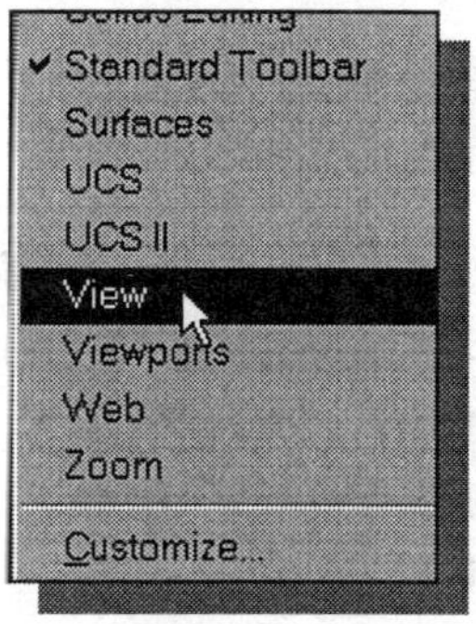

1. Move the cursor on top of any icon and **right-click** on any icon of the *Standard* toolbar to display a list of toolbar menu groups.

2. Select ***View***, with the left-mouse-button, to display the *View* toolbar on the screen.

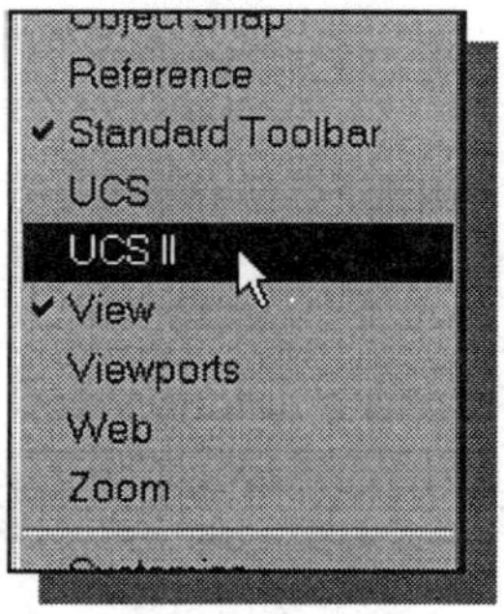

3. Move the cursor to the *Standard* toolbar area and **right-click** on any icon of the *Standard* toolbar to display a list of toolbar menu groups.

4. Select ***UCS II***, with the left-mouse-button, to display the *UCSII* toolbar on the screen.

➢ The options available in UCS II toolbar allow us quickly align the UCS to the preset standard 2D views.

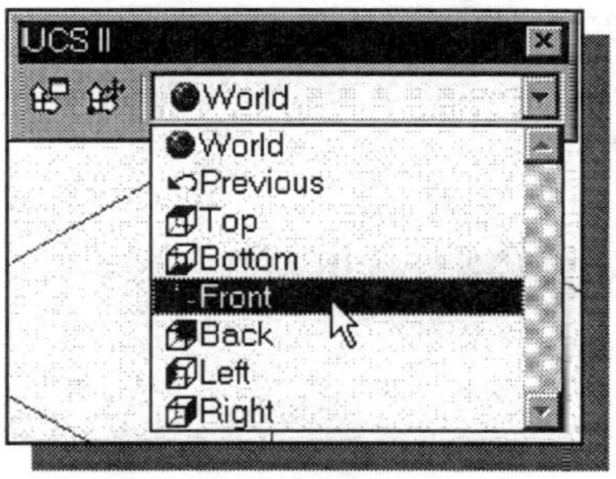

5. Note that the current *UCS* is aligned to the *World Coordinate System*. Select ***Front*** in the *UCS II* toolbar as shown.

➢ Note that the UCS is rotated and it is now aligned parallel to the front view of the wireframe box as shown in the figure.

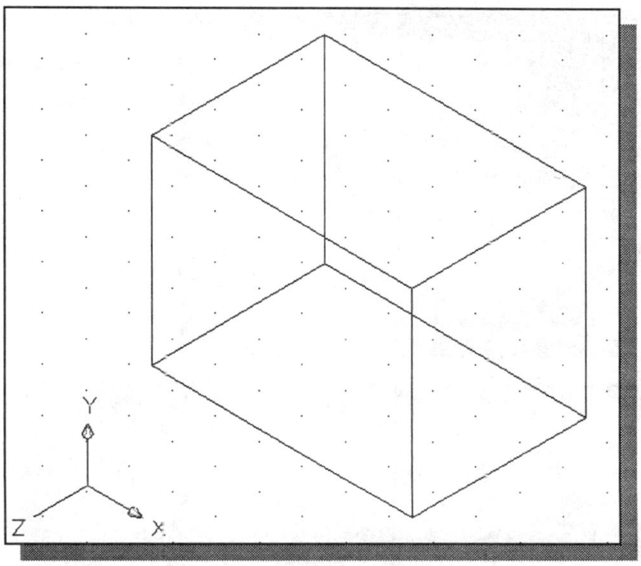

Creating construction lines in the front view

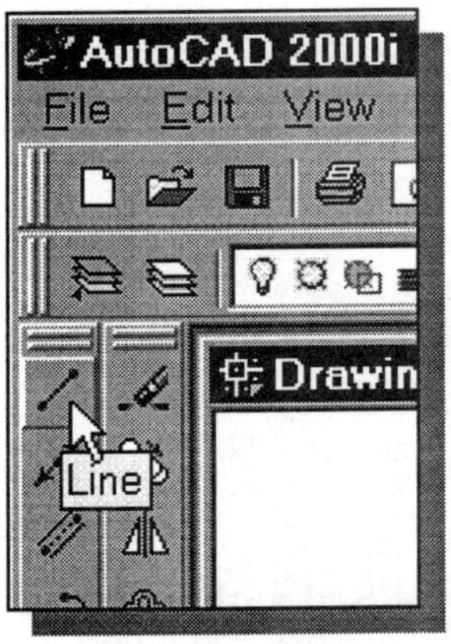

1. Select the ***Line*** command icon in the *Draw* toolbar. In the command prompt area, the message *"_line Specify first point:"* is displayed.

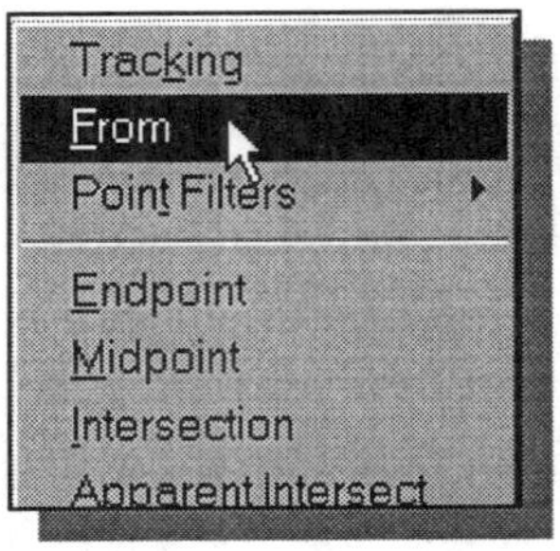

2. Inside the graphics window, hold down the **[SHIFT]** key and **right-mouse-click** once to bring up the *Object Snap* shortcut menu.

3. Select the **From** option in popup window.

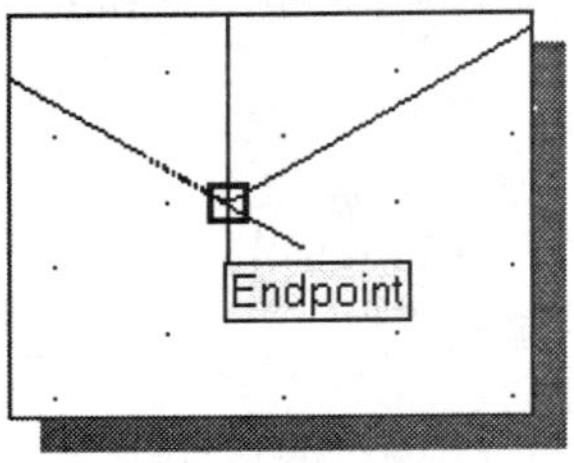

4. Pick the lower-right corner of the bottom horizontal line in the front-view as the base point.

5. In the command prompt area, the message *" Specify next point or [Undo]:"* is displayed. Enter: **@0,0.75 [ENTER]**

6. We will setup the *POLAR* tracking option to assist the creation of the next corner. Right-mouse-click once on the *POLAR* option located at the bottom of the graphics window.

7. In the option menu, select **Settings** by clicking once with the left-mouse-button.

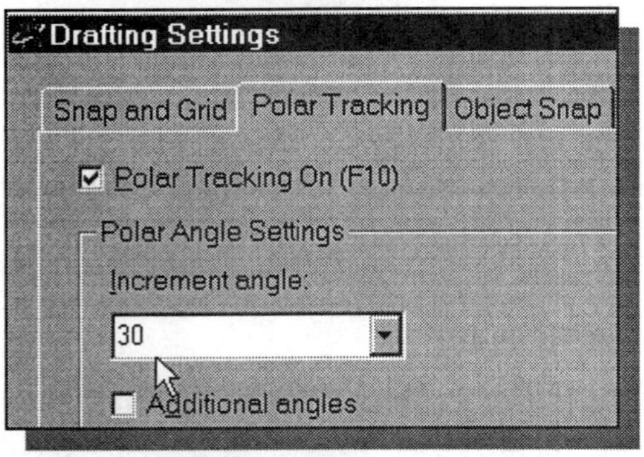

8. In the *Drafting Settings* dialogue box, set the *Polar Increment Angle* setting to 30 degrees.

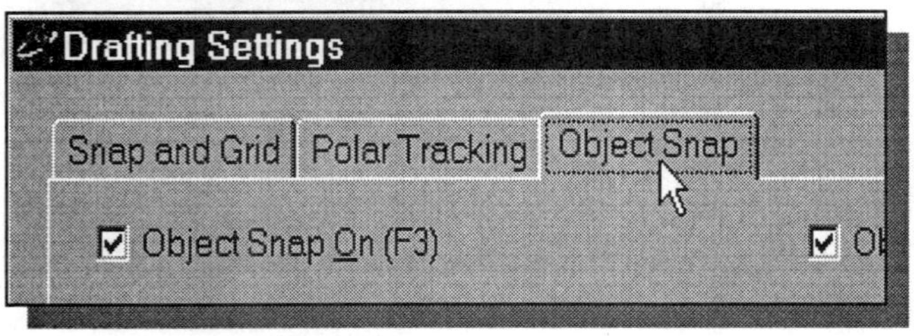

9. Click on the **Object Snap** tab to switch to the *Object Snap* option settings.

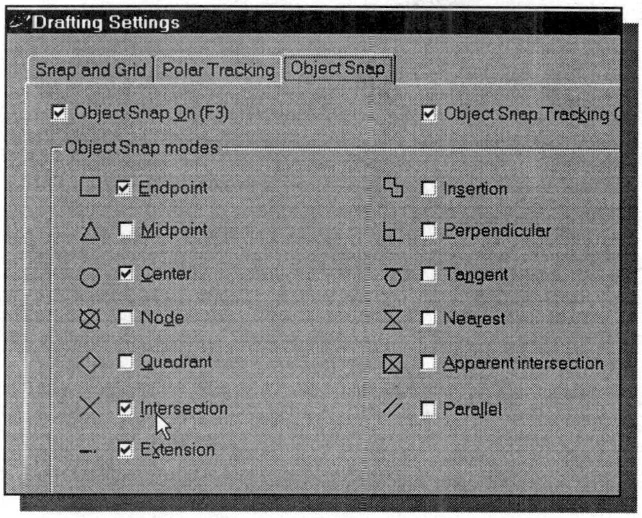

10. Confirm that the *Intersection* and *Extension* options are switched *ON* as shown.

11. Click on the **OK** button to accept the settings.

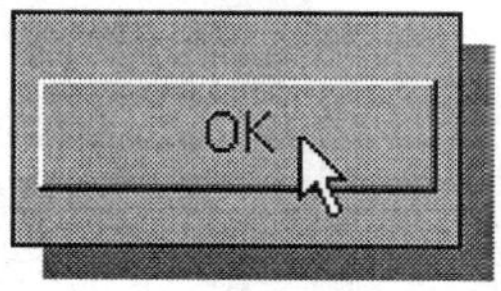

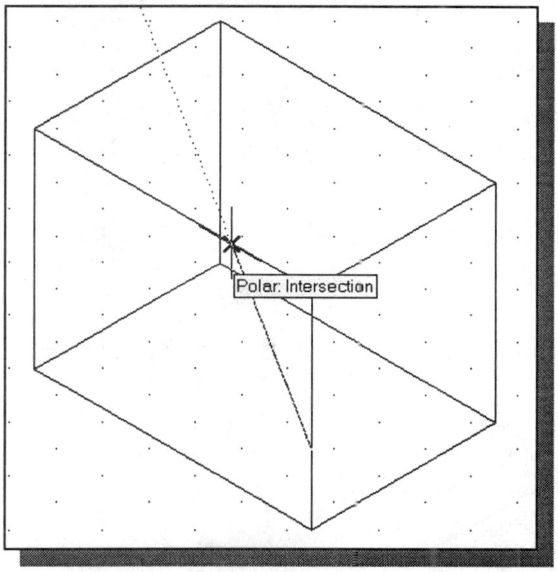

12. In the command prompt area, the message *" Specify next point or [Undo]: "* is displayed. Using the *Polar Tracking* option (30 degrees increment), create a line as shown in the figure.

13. Move the cursor near the left-vertical edge of the front-view and create the second line perpendicular to the last line we created.

14. Inside the graphics window, **right-mouse-click** to activate the option menu and select **Enter** with the left-mouse-button to end the *LINE* command.

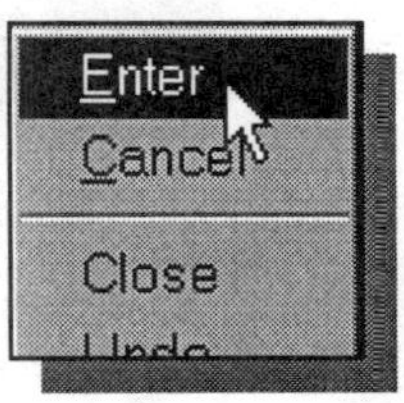

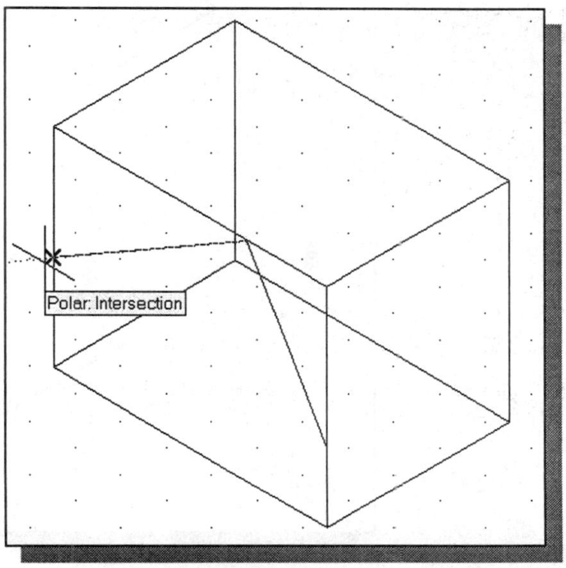

Copying in the negative Z direction

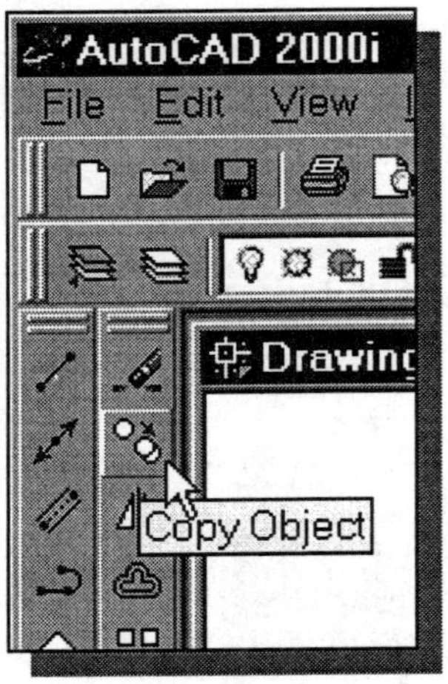

1. Click on the ***Copy Object*** icon in the *Modify* toolbar.

2. In the command prompt area, the message *"Select objects:"* is displayed. Pick the two edges we just created.

3. Inside the graphics window, right-mouse-click once to accept the selection.

4. In the command prompt area, the message *"Specify base point or displacement, or [Multiple]:"* is displayed. Pick any corner of the wireframe mode to use as a base point to create the copy.

5. In the command prompt area, the message *"Specify second point of displacement or <use first point as displacement>:"* is displayed.

   Enter: **@0,0,-2.0 [ENTER]**

➢ Note that the negative value represents the distance measured in the negative Z direction relative to the current UCS.

6. On your own, create three lines to connect the corners of the two sets of lines we just created, as shown below.

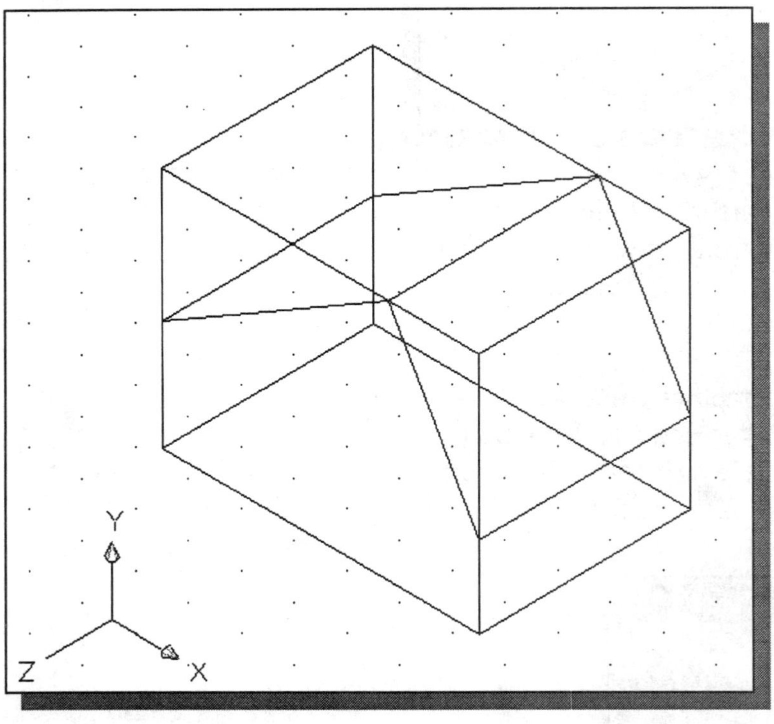

Creating an Inclined Line at the Base of the Model

1. Select ***Top*** in the *UCS II* toolbar as shown.

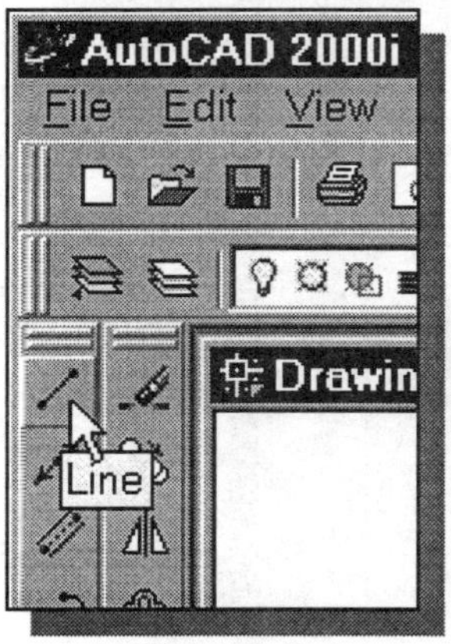

2. Select the ***Line*** command icon in the *Draw* toolbar. In the command prompt area, the message *" _line Specify first point: "* is displayed.

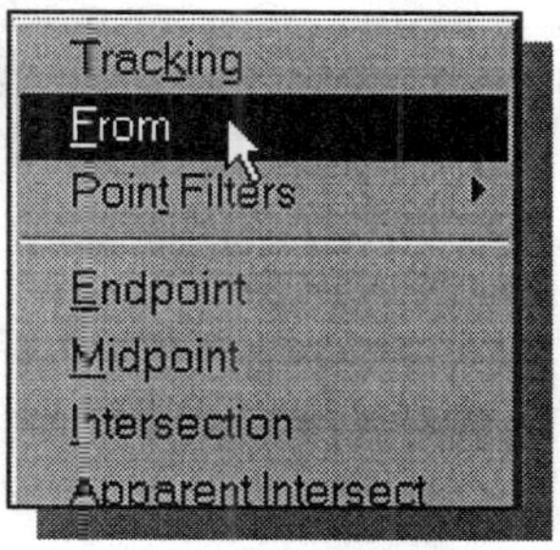

3. Inside the graphics window, hold down the **[SHIFT]** key and **right-mouse-click** once to bring up the *Object Snap* shortcut menu.

4. Select the **From** option in popup window.

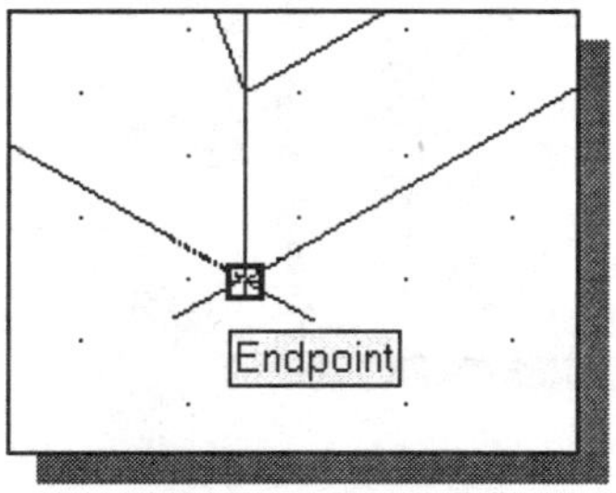

5. Pick the lower-right corner of the bottom horizontal line as the base point as shown in the figure.

6. We will place the first point above the selected corner. Enter: **@0,0.75 [ENTER]**

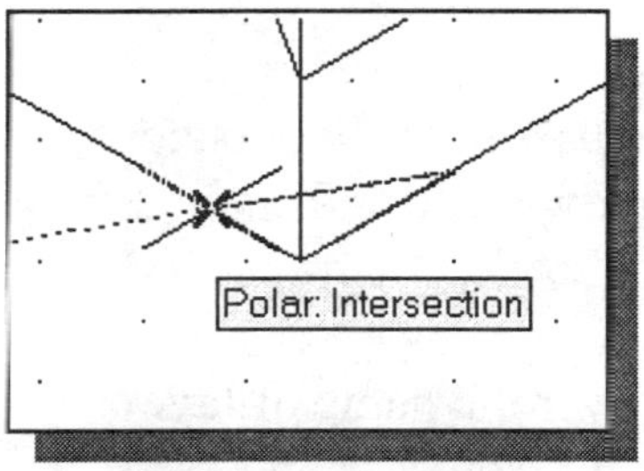

7. In the command prompt area, the message *" Specify next point or [Undo]: "* is displayed. Using the *Polar Tracking* option (30 degrees increment), create a line as shown in the figure.

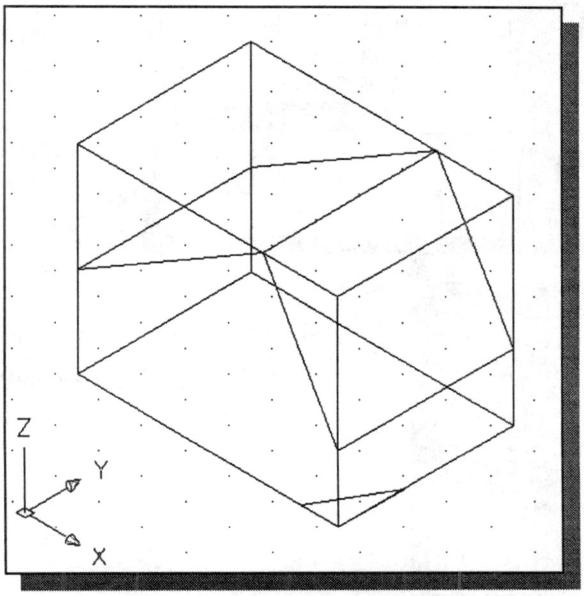

8. Inside the graphics window, **right-mouse-click** to activate the option menu and select **Enter** with the left-mouse-button to end the *LINE* command.

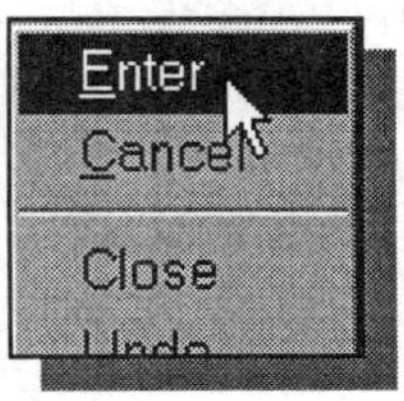

➢ On your own, use the *COPY* and *LINE* commands to create additional edges so that the wireframe model appeared as shown below.

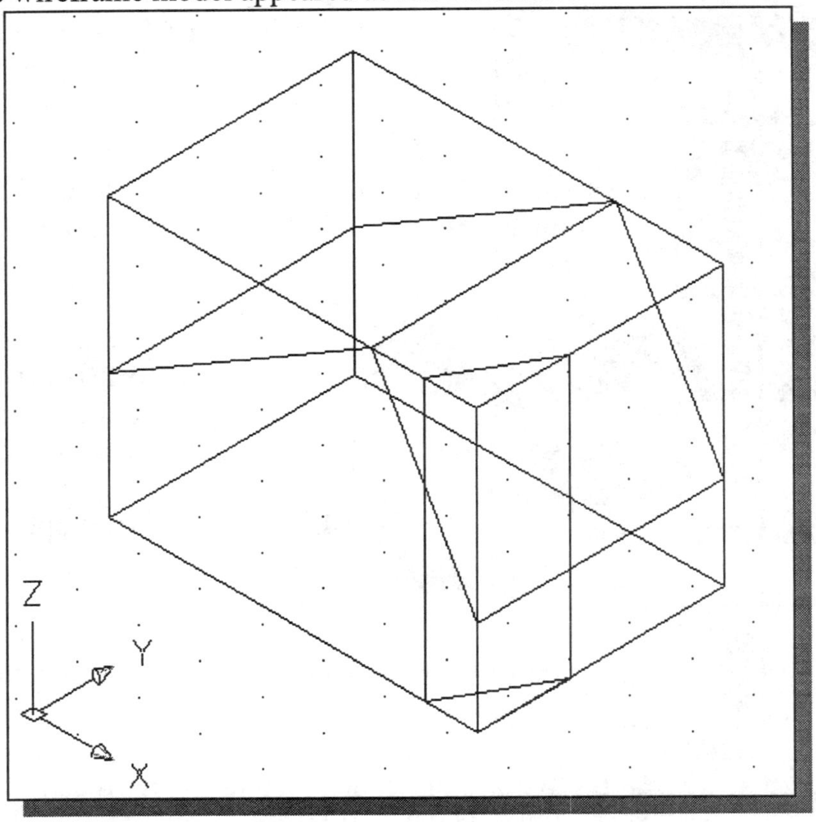

Creating object lines

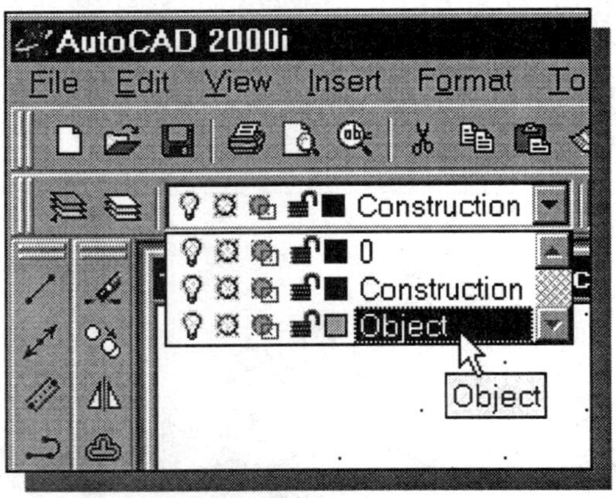

1. On the *Object Properties* toolbar, choose the ***Layer Control*** box with the left-mouse-button.

2. Move the cursor over the name of **layer *Object***; the tool tip *"Object"* appears.

3. **Left-mouse-click once** on the layer name and now layer *Object* is set as the *Current layer*.

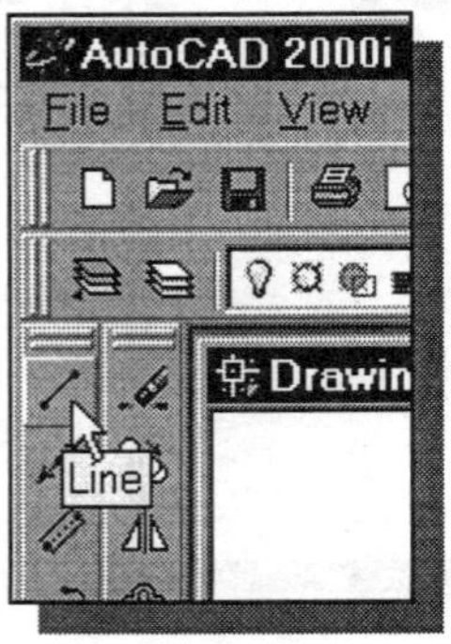

4. Select the ***Line*** command icon in the *Draw* toolbar. In the command prompt area, the message *"_line Specify first point:"* is displayed.

5. Pick the lower-left corner of the bottom of the wireframe model as the starting point and create the four line segments as shown.

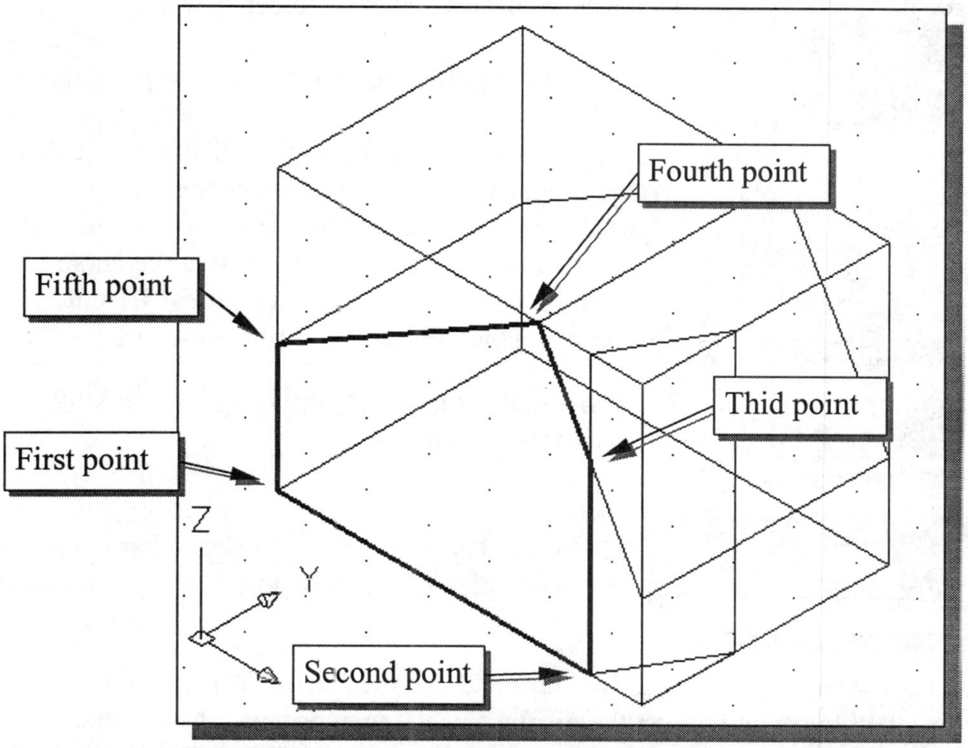

- Note that even though the UCS is aligned to the base plane of the model, the *OSNAP* option enables us to select points on the front plane of the model.

➢ On you own, create three additional lines representing the edges of the inclined face of the design as shown.

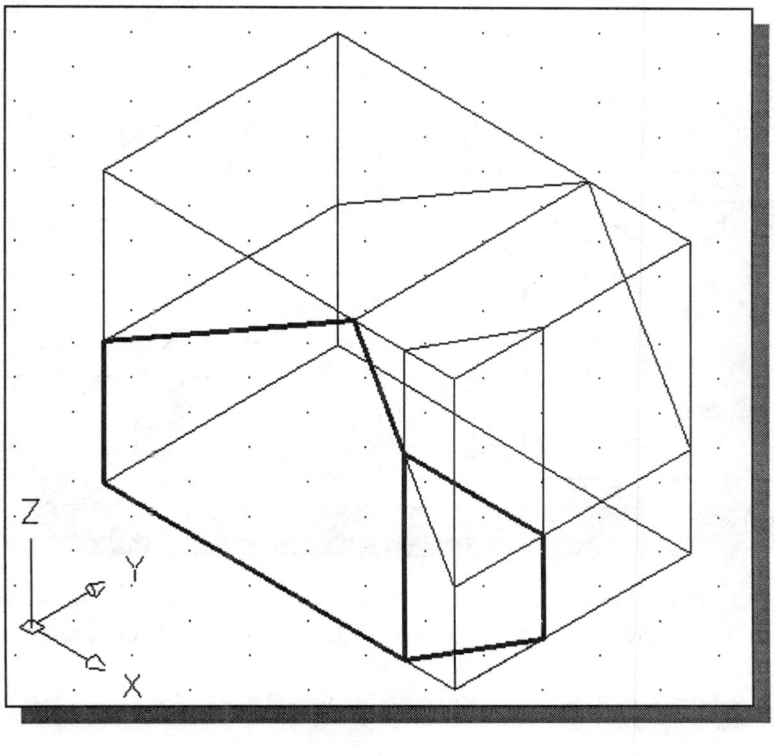

Multiple Viewports

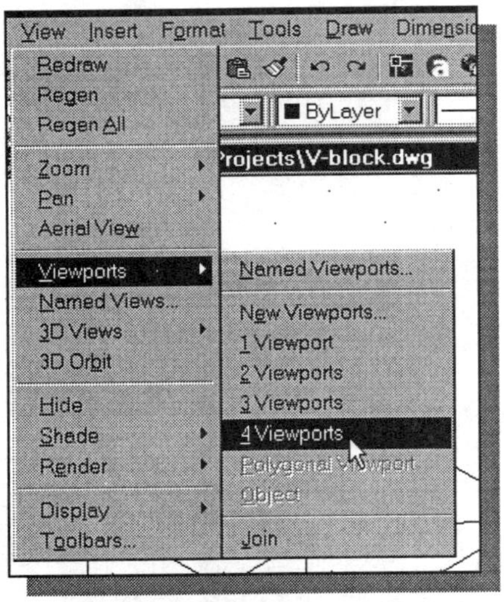

1. In the pull-down menus, select:

   [View] => [Viewports] => [4 viewports]

➢ AutoCAD allows us to display different VIEWS of the model simultaneously. Only one viewport is activated at one time. The viewport with the darker border is the active viewport. Move the cursor inside each viewport and notice the different cursor-display inside the active viewport.

2. Activate the top-left viewport by left-clicking once inside the viewport.

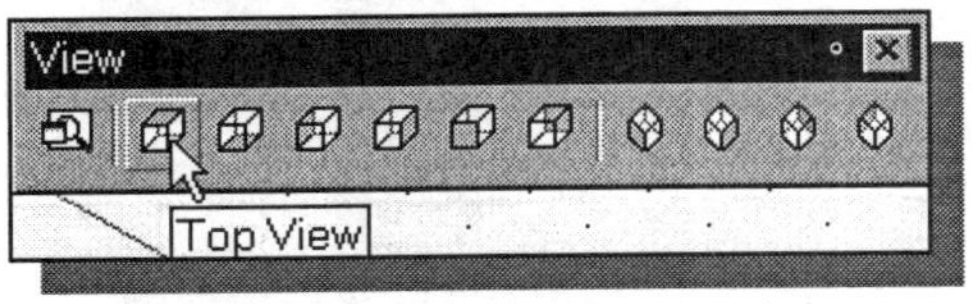

3. Select ***Top View*** in the *View* toolbar to change the display of the viewport.

4. On your own, repeat the above steps and use the *REALTIME ZOOM* command to set and adjust the displays of the viewports as shown below.

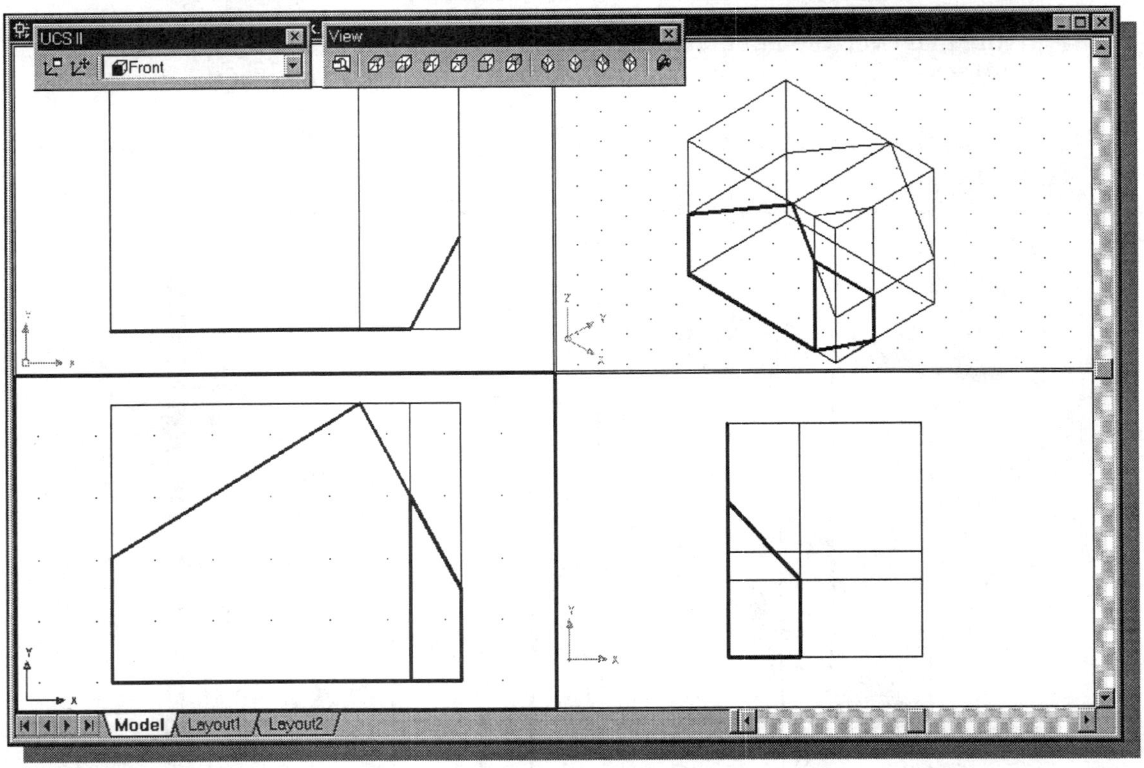

➢ Note that the displayed UCS icons at the lower left corner of each viewport corresponds to the orientation of the wireframe model in each viewport.

Using the *MIRROR* command

1. Activate the top-left viewport by left-clicking once inside the viewport.

2. ***Pre-select*** all the objects in the active viewport by using a selection window.

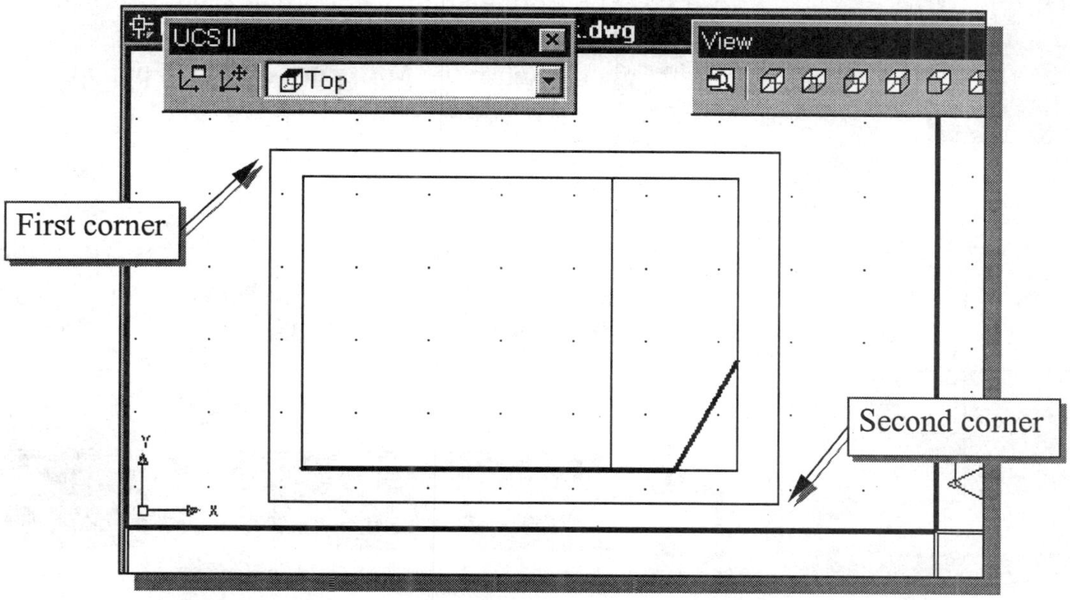

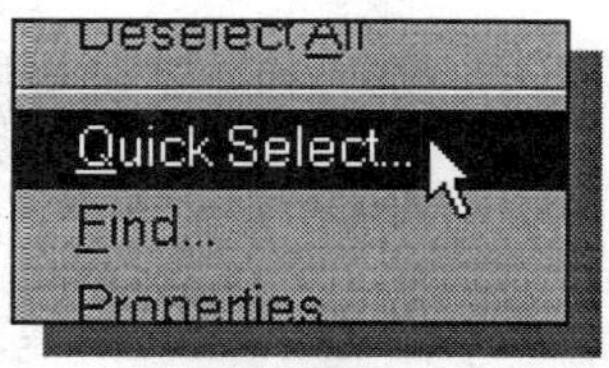

3. Inside the *active viewport*, **right-mouse-click** to bring up the popup option menu and select the **Quick Select** option.

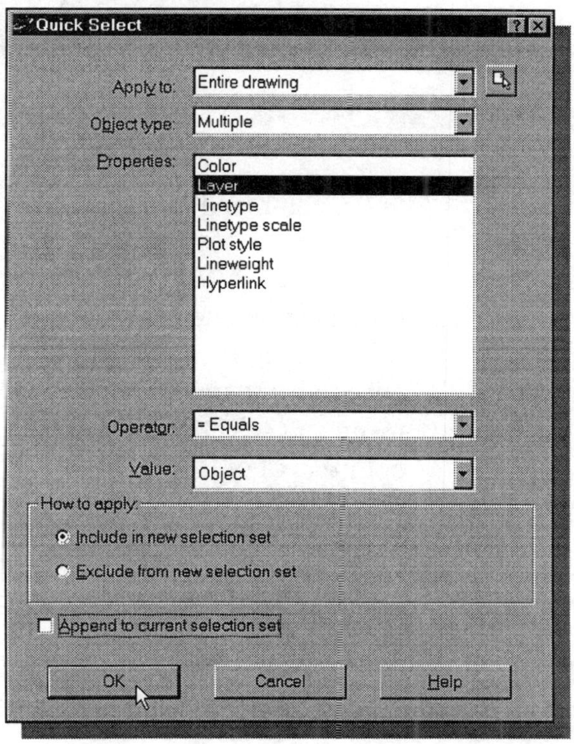

4. In the *Quick Select* dialog box, select ***Layer*** from the *Properties* list.

5. Set the ***Value*** box to *Object_Lines.*

6. In the *How to apply* section, confirm the ***Include in new selection set*** option is selected.

7. Switch *OFF* the *Append to current selection set.*

8. Click on the **OK** button to accept the settings.

- AutoCAD will now **filter out** objects that are not on layer *Object*.

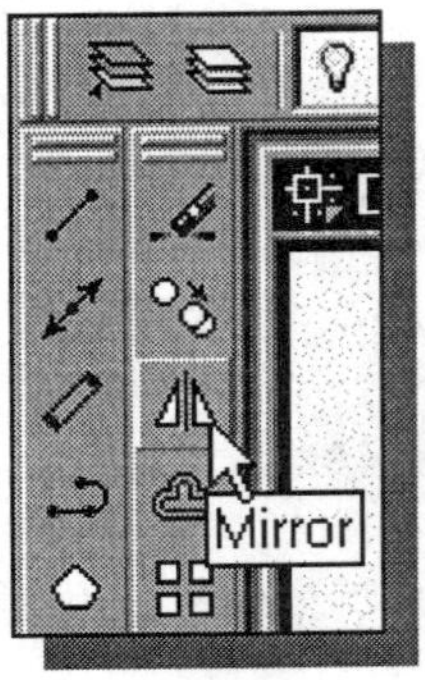

9. Click on the ***Mirror*** icon in the *Modify* toolbar.

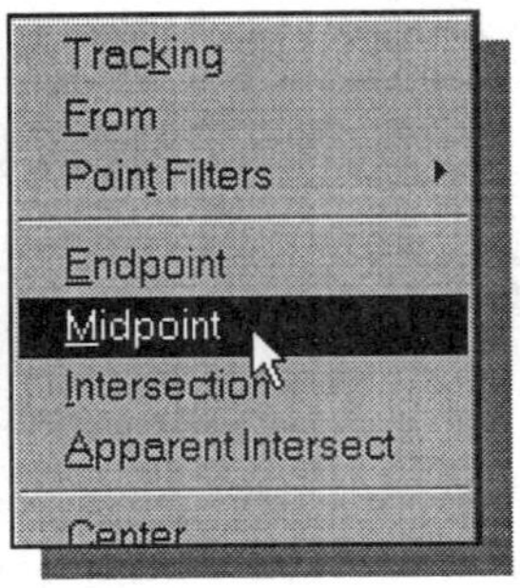

10. Inside the graphics window, hold down the **[SHIFT]** key and **right-mouse-click** once to bring up the *Object Snap* shortcut menu.

11. Select the **Midpoint** option in popup window.

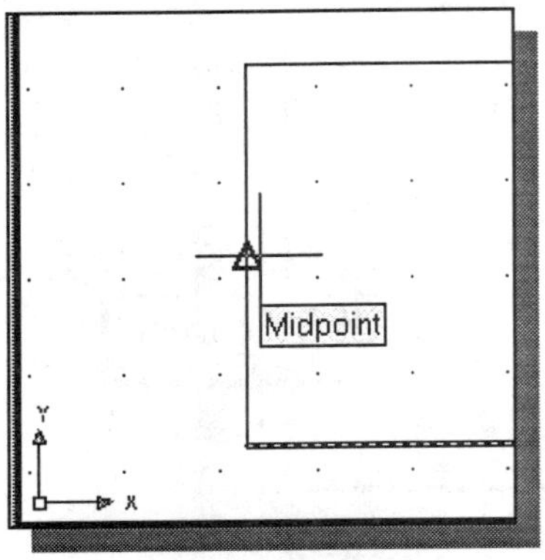

12. Inside the active viewport, click on the left-vertical line of the wireframe model. With the *Midpoint* snap option, the midpoint of the line is selected

13. Move the cursor toward the right-vertical line in the active viewport, left-click once when the ***Polar:Intersection*** tooltip is displayed as shown.

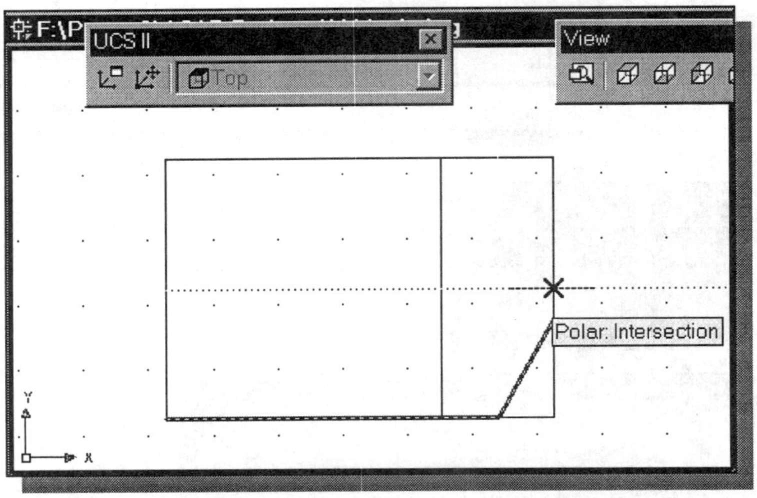

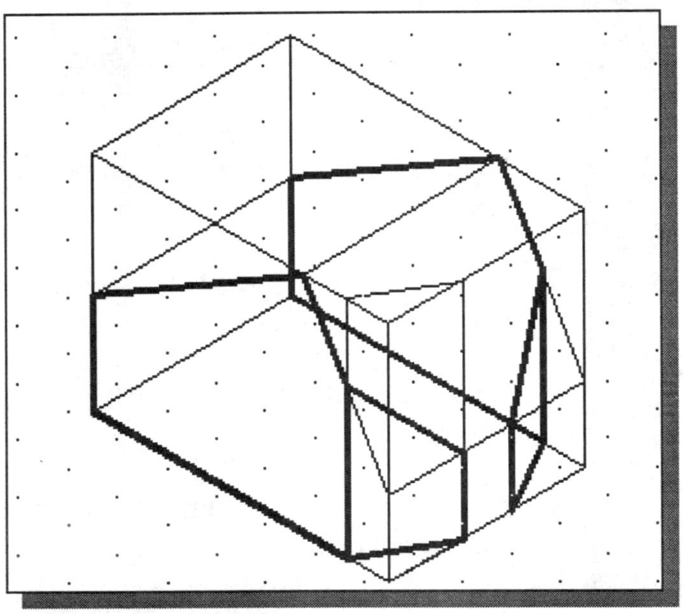

14. In the command prompt area, the message *"Delete Source Objects? [Yes/No] <N>:"* is displayed. Inside the graphics window, **right-mouse-click** once to bring up the option menu and select **No** to keep both sets of objects.

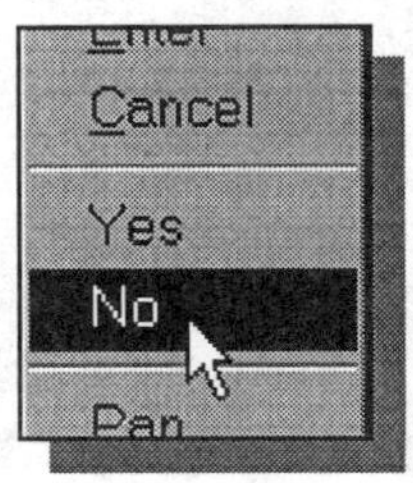

Turn *OFF* the Construction Lines

1. On the *Object Properties* toolbar, choose the ***Layer Control*** box with the left-mouse-button.

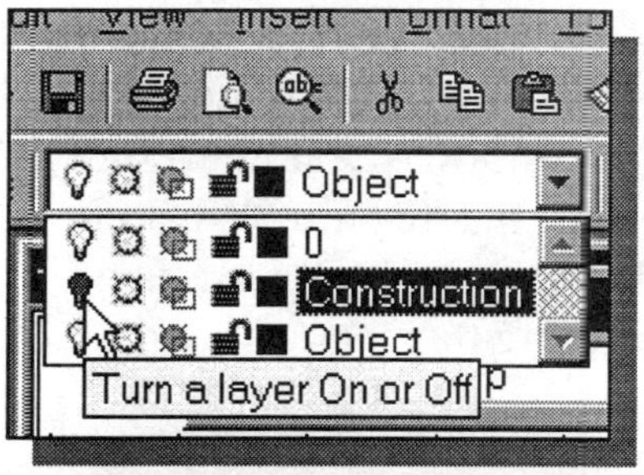

2. Move the cursor over the light-bulb icon for layer *Construction*, **left-mouse-click once**, and notice the icon color is changed to a gray tone color, representing the layer (layer *Construction*) is *turned OFF*.

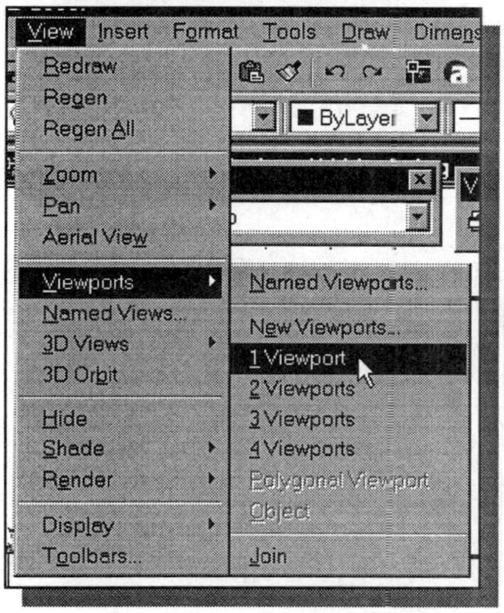

3. In the pull-down menus, select:

   [View] => [Viewports] => [1 viewport]

- Viewports can also be used as a way of checking the integrity of the constructed 3D models. Feel free to switch to multiple viewports in the following sections of this tutorial.

4. On your own, create the additional object lines connecting the two sets of objects as shown below.

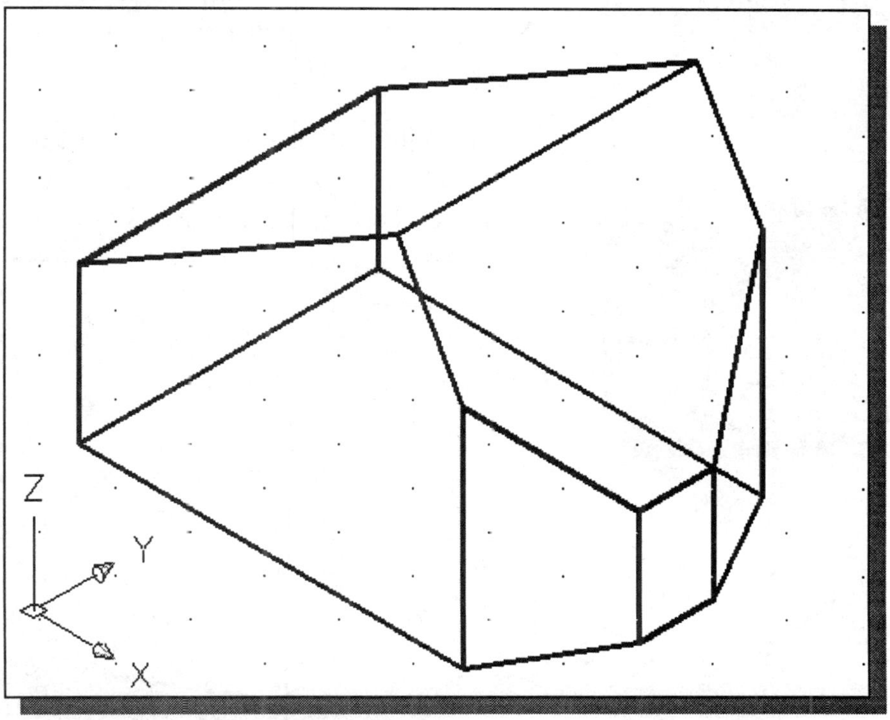

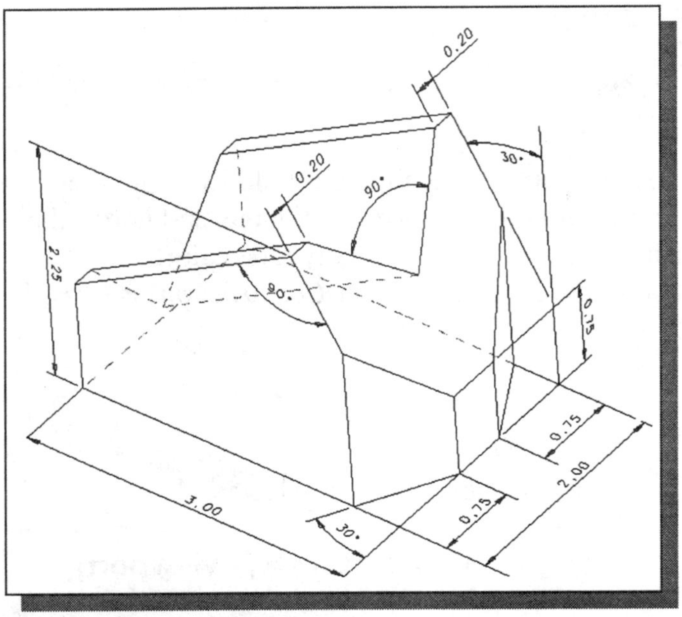

➢ The v-cut feature of the design is the last feature, and perhaps the most difficult one, to create in the CAD system. Based on your knowledge of modeling with AutoCAD, how would you create this feature? What are the more difficult aspects of creating this feature?

Creating a NEW UCS

➢ Besides using the preset UCS planes, AutoCAD also allows us to change our viewpoint and create new UCS planes. We will create an UCS plane aligning to the inclined plane of the design.

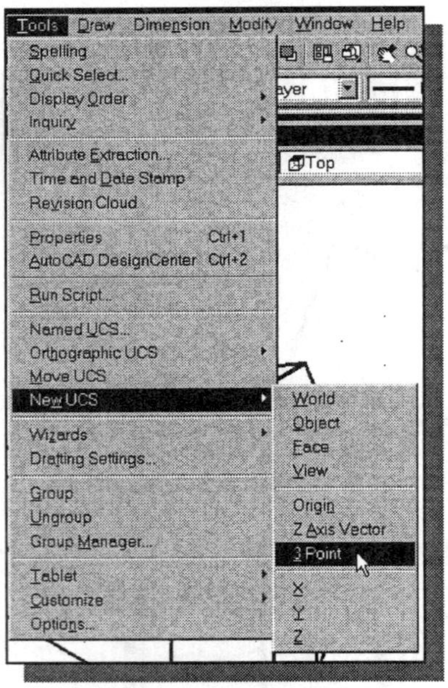

1. In the pull-down menus, select:

   [Tools] => [New UCS] => [3 points]

- Note that other options are also available to aid the creation of new UCS planes.

2. In the command prompt area, the message *"Specify New Origin point <0,0,0>:"* is displayed. Pick the lower-left corner of the inclined plane as shown.

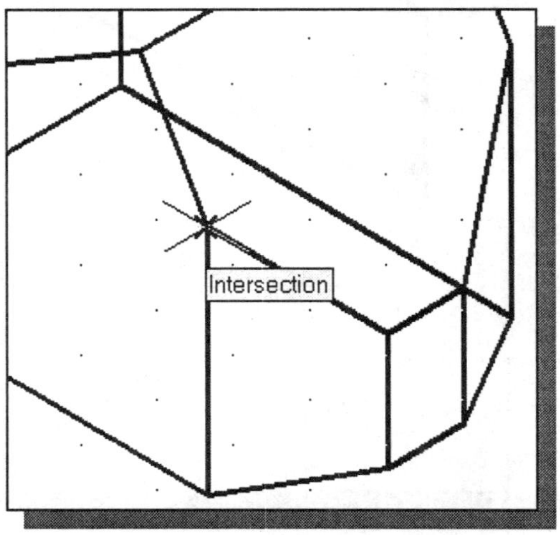

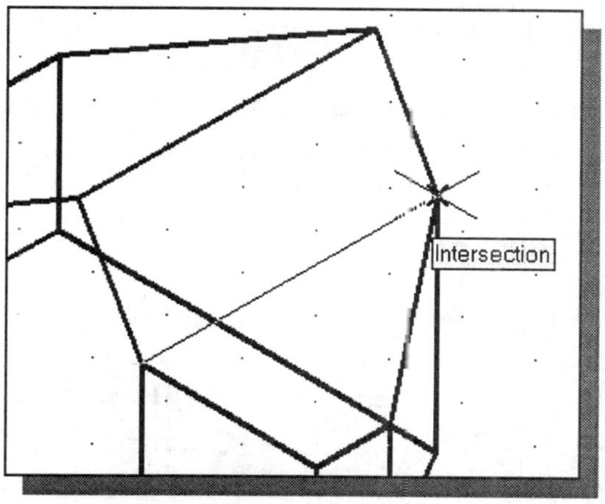

3. In the command prompt area, the message *"Specify point on positive portion of X-axis:"* is displayed. Pick the lower-right corner of the inclined plane as shown.

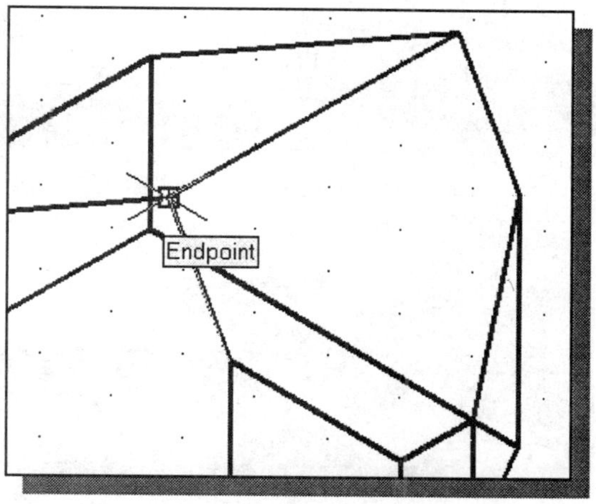

4. In the command prompt area, the message *"Specify point on positive portion of X-axis:"* is displayed. Pick the top-left corner of the inclined plane as shown.

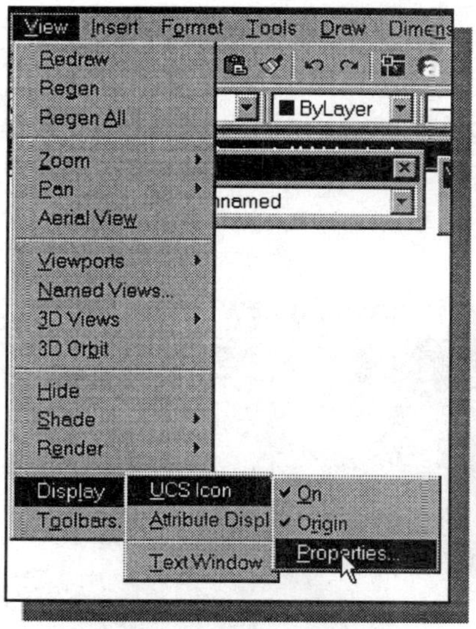

5. In the pull-down menus, select

[View] => [Display] => [UCS Icon] => [Properties]

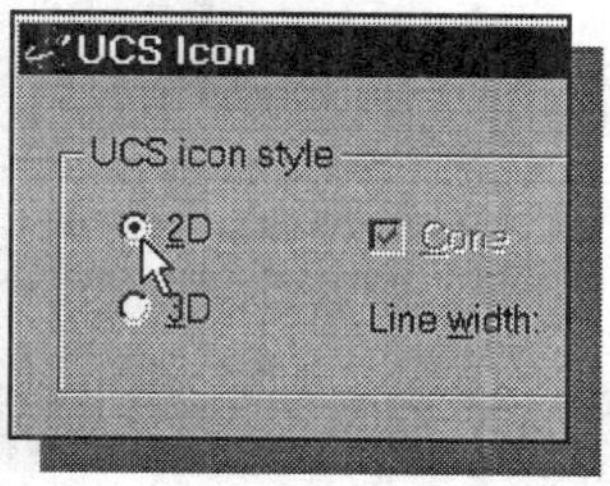

6. In the *UCS Icon* window, switch the *UCS icon style* to ***2D*** as shown.

7. Click on the **OK** button to accept the settings.

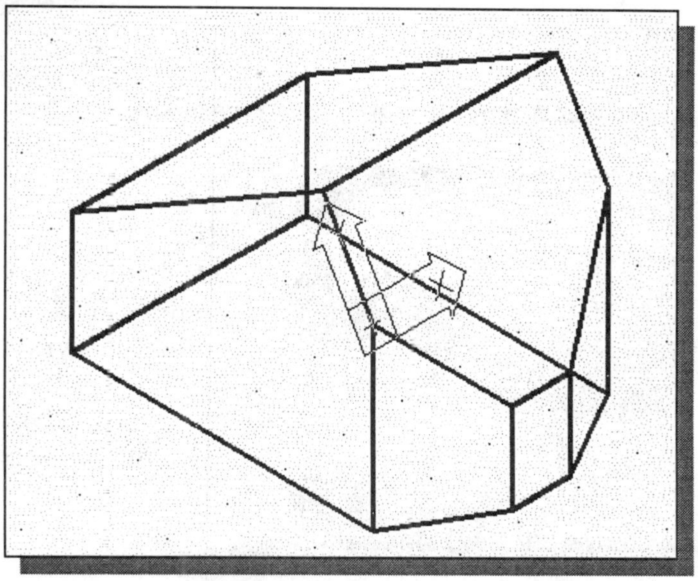

Creating a New Named View

- Besides using the preset views, AutoCAD also allows us to change our viewpoint and create new views, which can be saved and restored by name for convenient access. We will create a new view aligned to the new UCS plane we just created.

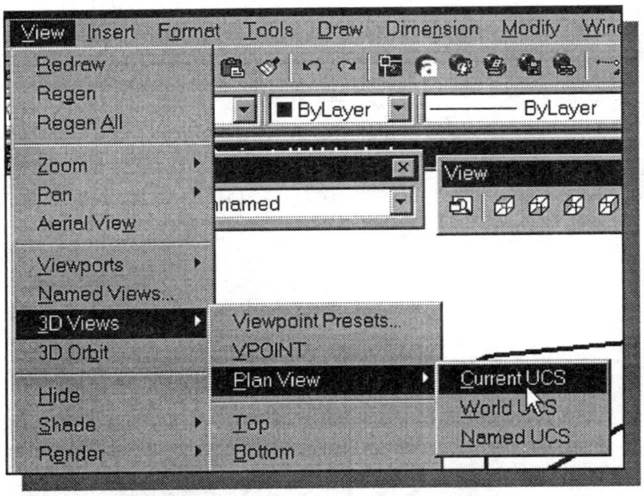

1. In the pull-down menus, select

   [View] => [3D Views] => [Plan View] => [Current UCS]

- The graphics window is now adjusted to display the current UCS plane.

2. Click on the ***Named Views*** icon in the *View* toolbar.

3. In the *View* dialog box, click on the **NEW** button to create a new named view.

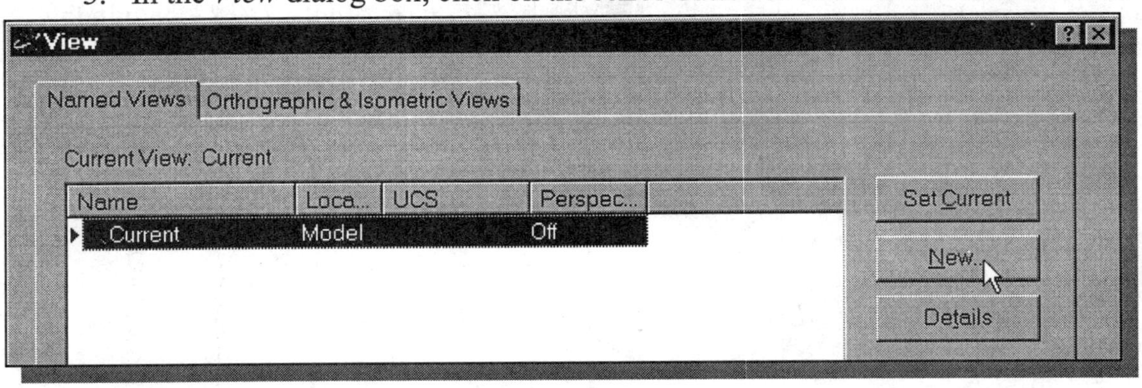

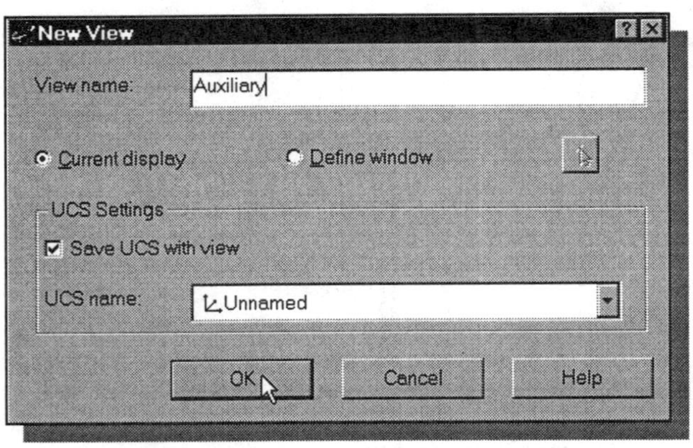

4. In the *New View* dialog box, enter ***Auxiliary*** as the new *View Name* and confirm the ***Current display*** option and the ***Save UCS with view*** option are switched ***ON*** as shown.

5. Click on the **OK** button to accept the settings and create the named view.

6. In the *View* dialog box, the new named view (*Auxiliary*) is added to the *Named Views* list. We can also switch to this view by using the **Set Current** option.

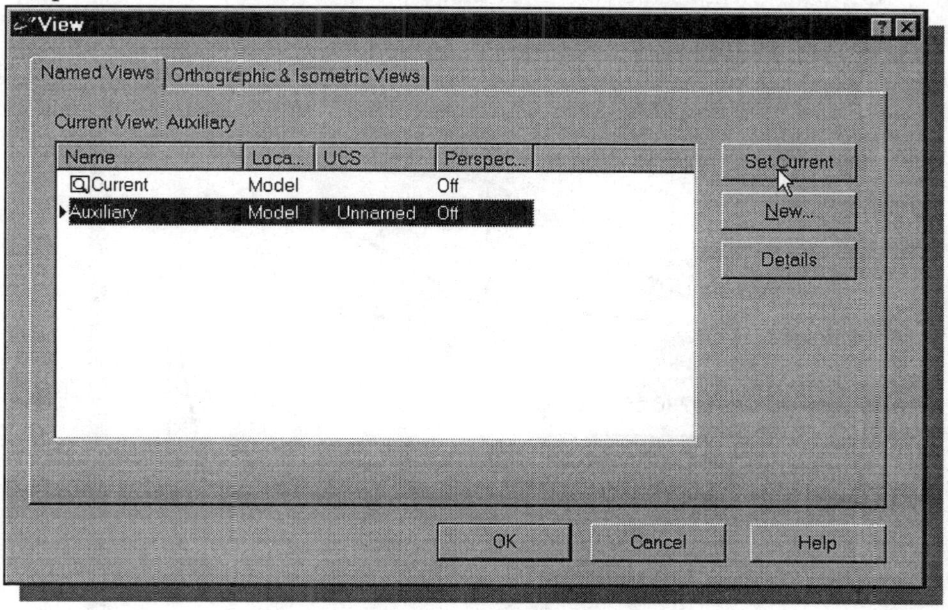

7. Click on the **OK** button to accept the settings.

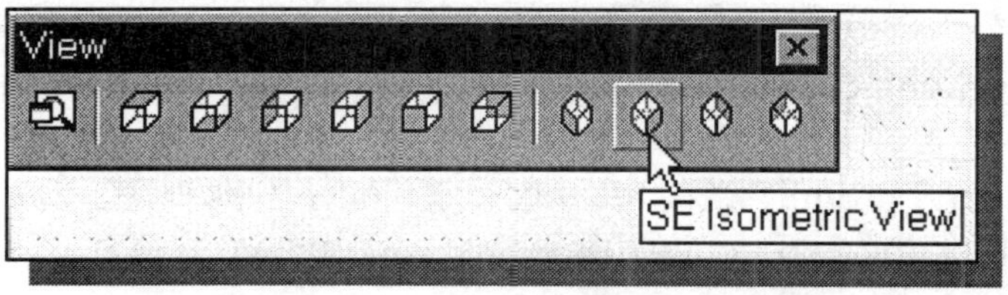

8. In the *View* toolbar, select *SE Isometric View.*

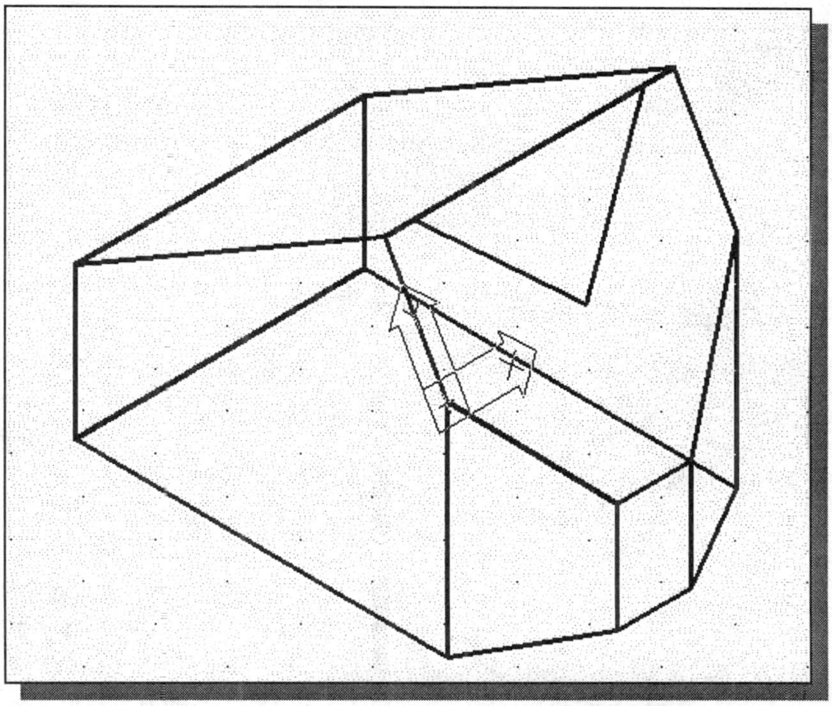

Creating the V-Cut feature on the inclined plane

1. On your own, create two lines that are **0.2"** away from the top corners of the model, which are also rotated **45 degrees** relative to the top-edge of the model.

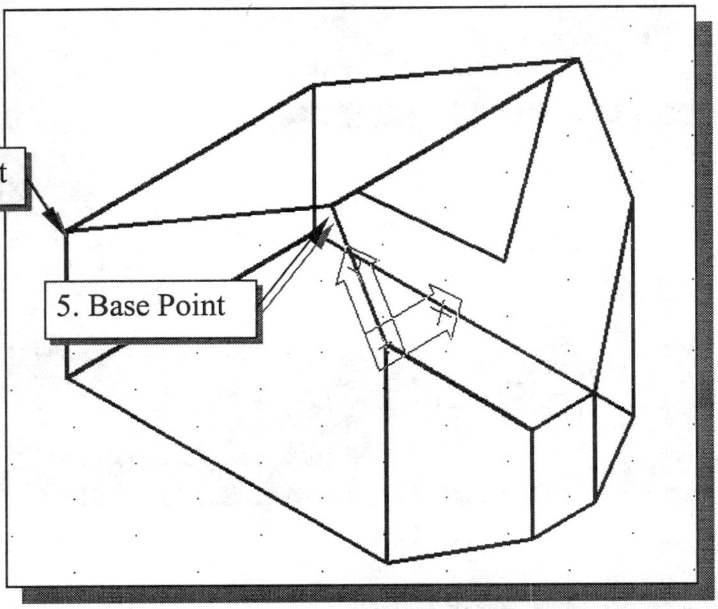

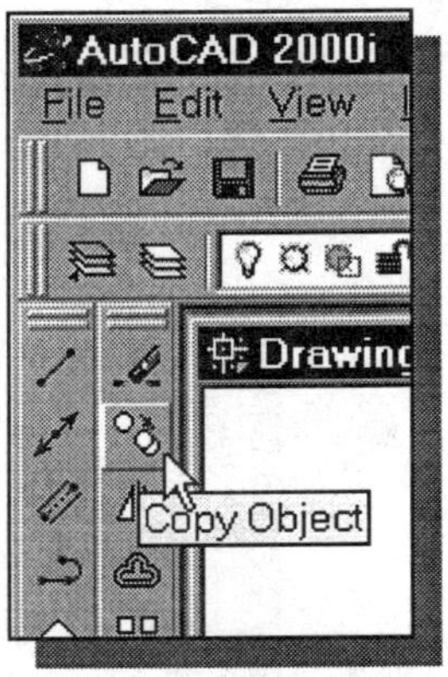

2. Click on the ***Copy Object*** icon in the *Modify* toolbar.

3. In the command prompt area, the message *"Select objects:"* is displayed. Pick the two inclined lines we just created.

4. Inside the graphics window, **right-mouse-click** once to accept the selections.

5. In the command prompt area, the message *"Specify base point or displacement, or [Multiple]:"* is displayed. Pick the top-left corner as the base point to create the copy.

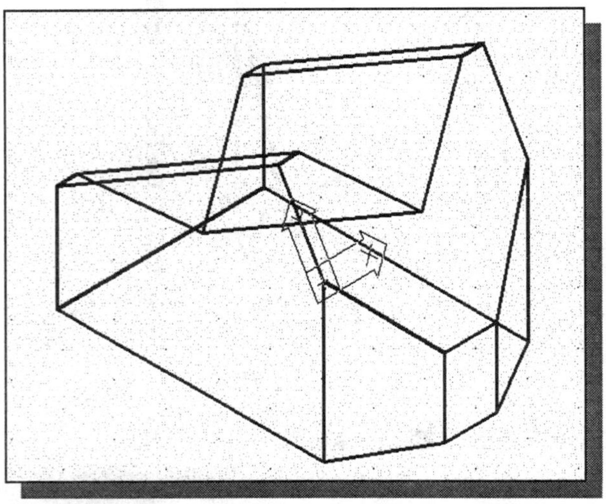

6. In the command prompt area, the message *"Specify second point of displacement or <use first point as displacement>:"* is displayed. Pick the corresponding corner on the backside of the model as shown in the above figure.

7. On your own, create addition lines to define the edges of the V-cut and use the ***TRIM*** command to complete the model as shown below.

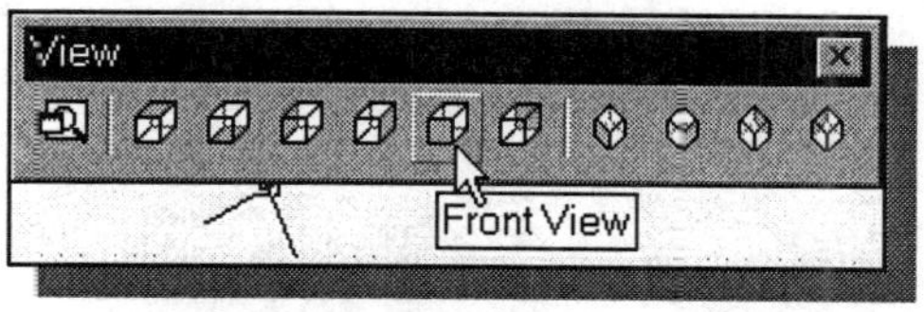

8. Click on the ***Front View*** icon in the *View* toolbar.

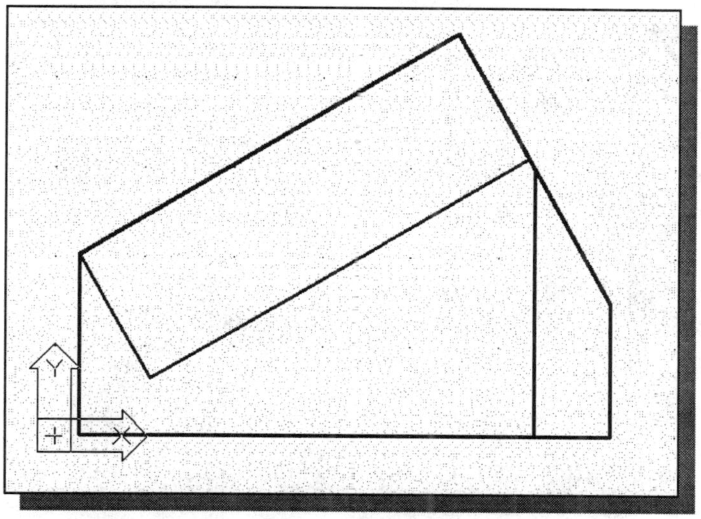

➢ Note that the V-Cut we created, using the copy command, does not represent a cut that passes through the entire block.

Extend the Cut and GRIP Editing

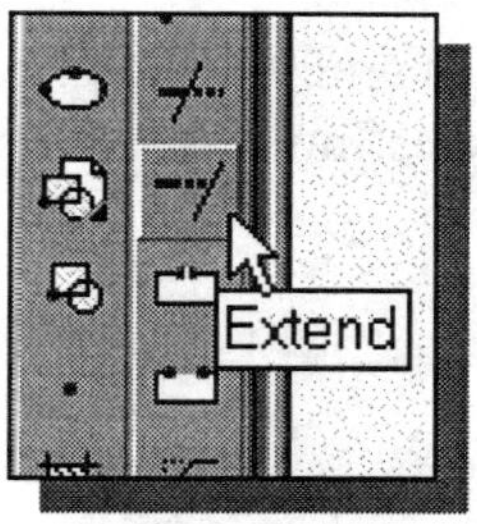

1. Select the ***Extend*** command icon in the *Modify* toolbar.

2. In the command prompt area, the message *"Select boundary edges... Select objects:"* is displayed. Pick the left-vertical line as the *boundary edge.*

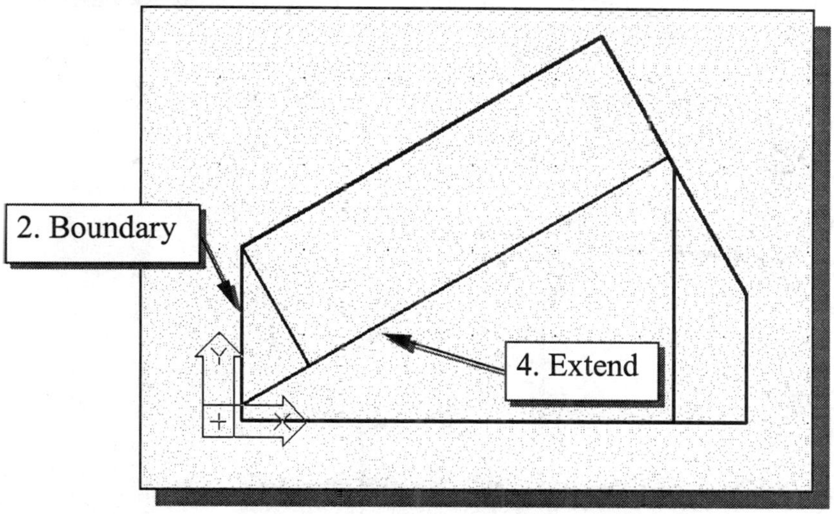

3. Inside the graphics window, **right-mouse-click** to accept the selection.

4. The message *"Select object to Extend or [Project/Edge/Undo]:"* is displayed in the command prompt area. Pick the bottom edge of the V-cut to extend.

5. Inside the graphics window, **right-mouse-click** to activate the option menu and select **Enter** with the left-mouse-button to end the *EXTEND* command.

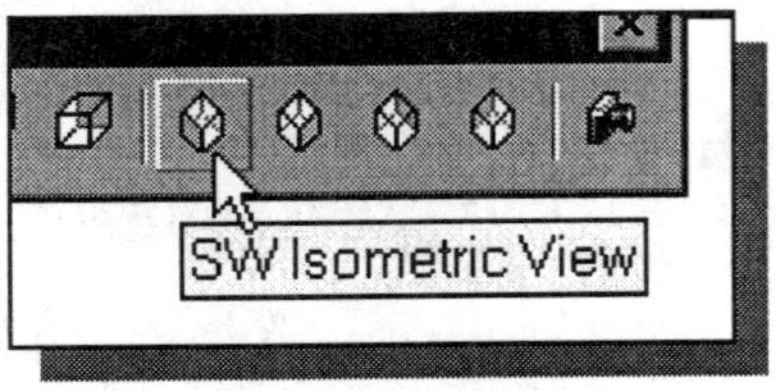

6. Click on the ***SW Isometric View*** icon to reset the display to the preset isometric view.

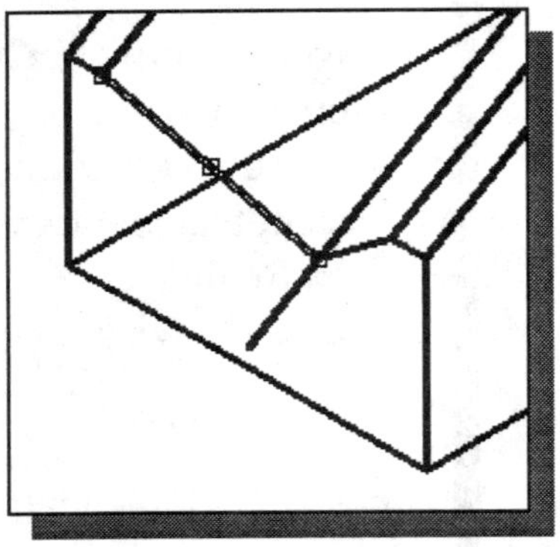

7. ***Pre-select*** the top edge of the V-block as shown.

8. Left-click once on the lower-right-grip-point on the selected line.

- Selecting the grip points located at the end of the line or arc allows us to STRETCH the selected line.

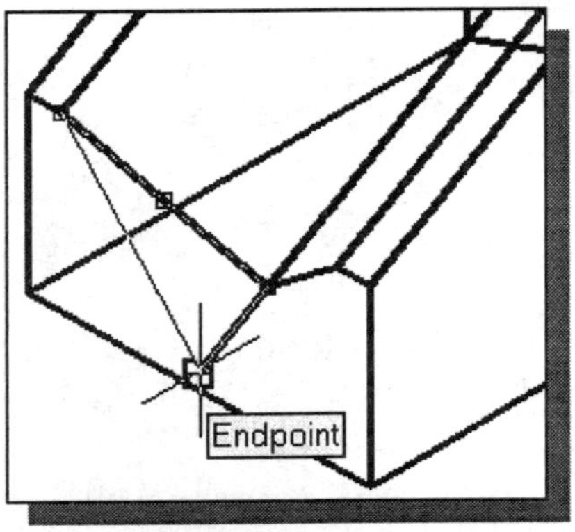

9. Move the cursor toward and select the lower corner of the v-cut as shown.

➢ On your own, repeat the above steps and use the grip editing options and complete the wireframe model as shown below.

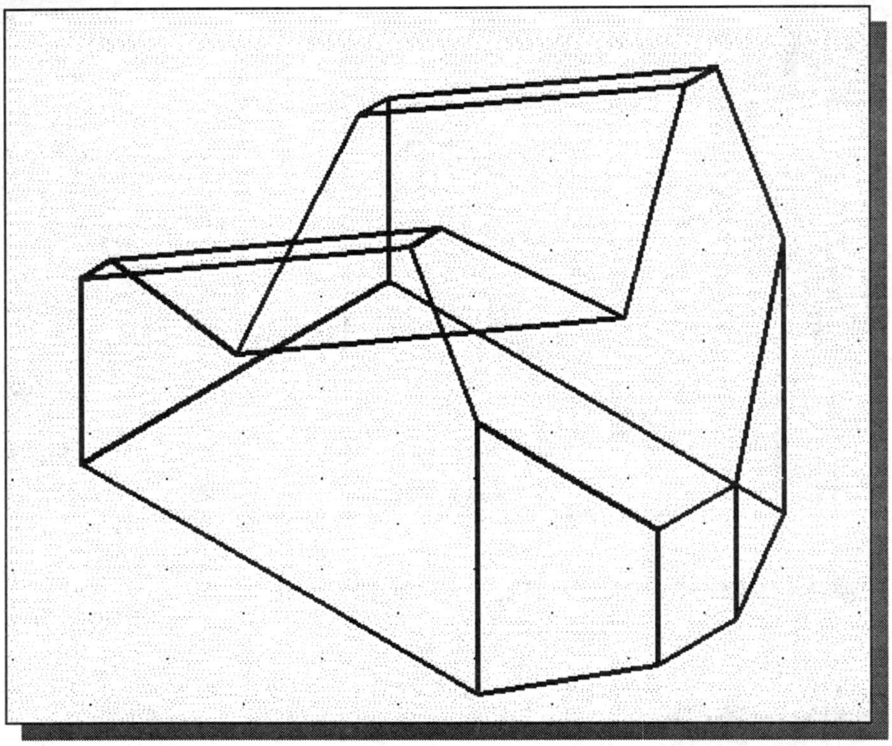

Questions:

1. List and describe three different types of 3D computer geometric modeling software available today?

2. What is a *NAMED VIEW*?

3. What is the difference between *Stretch* and *Extend*?

4. List and describe the methods available in AutoCAD to create a new UCS plane.

5. What is the difference between *COPY* and *MIRROR* in AutoCAD?

6. Identify and describe the following commands:

a)

front view

b)

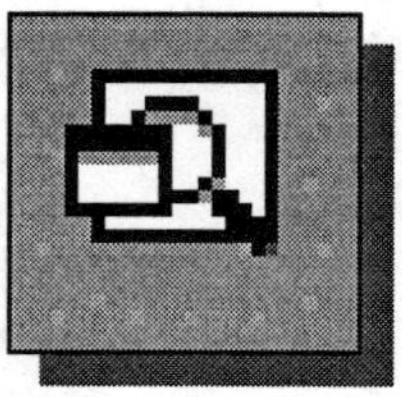

Named Views

c)

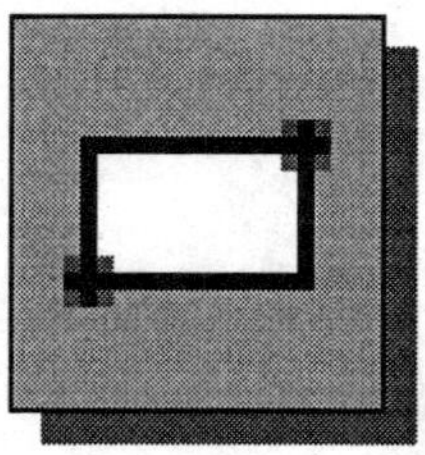

rectangle

d)

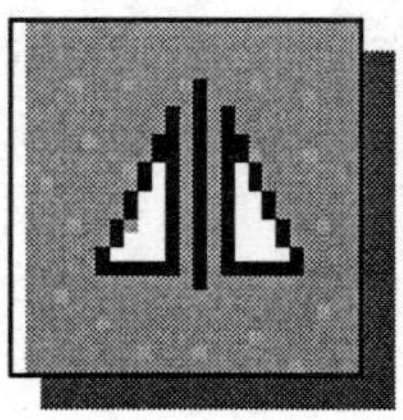

mirror

Exercises:

1.

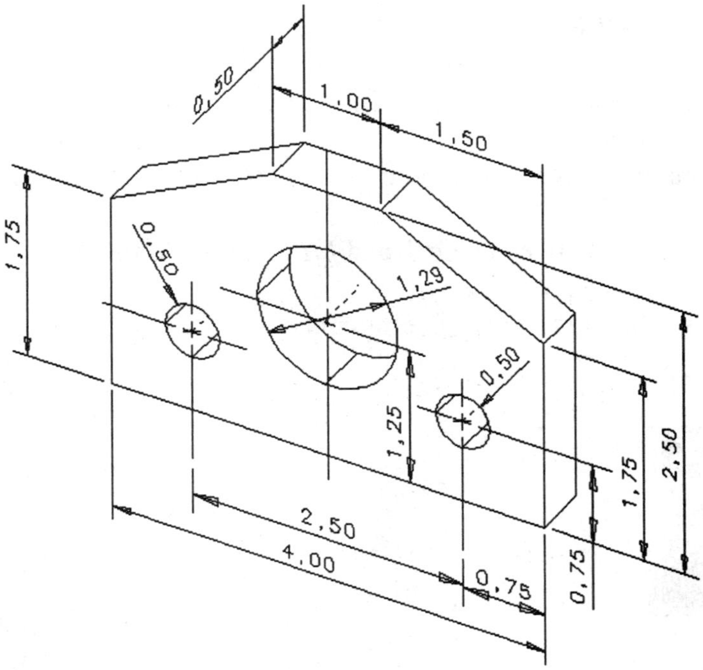

2.

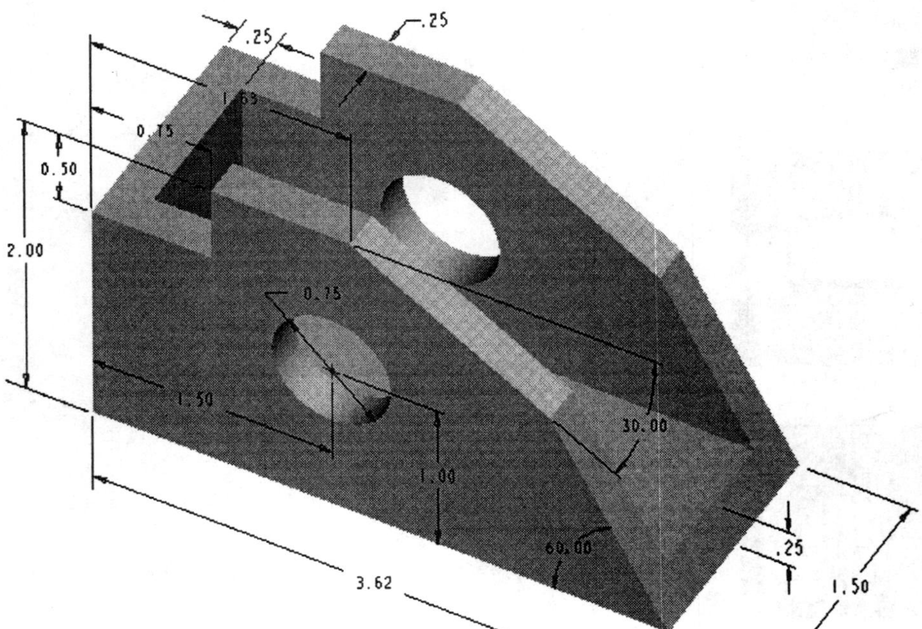

3.

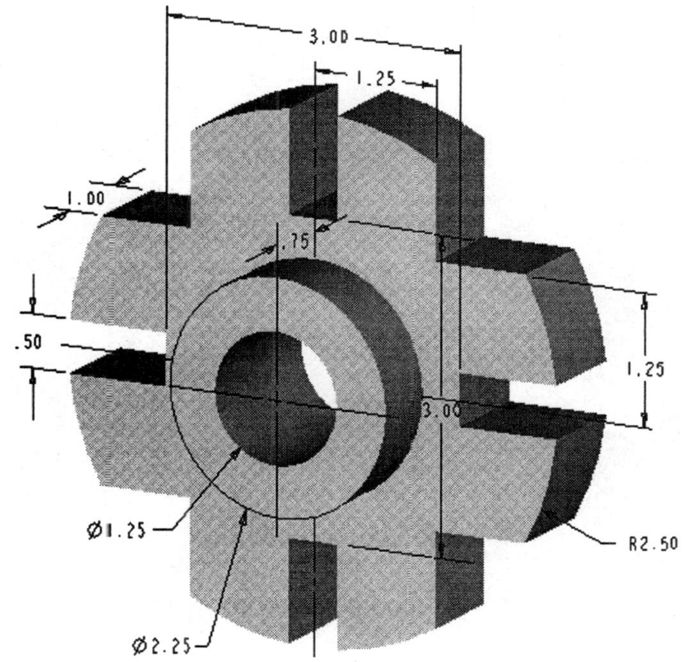
3.00
1.25
1.00
.75
.50
1.25
3.00
Ø1.25
R2.50
Ø2.25

4.

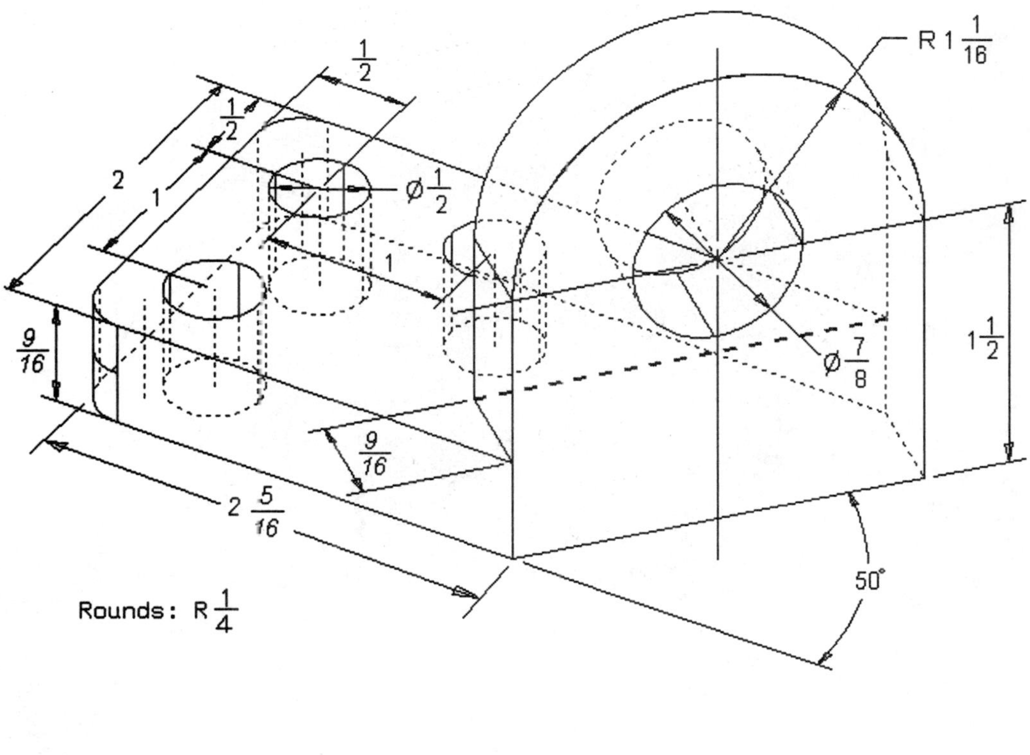
R 1 1/16
1/2
1/2
2
1
Ø 1/2
1
9/16
1 1/2
Ø 7/8
9/16
2 5/16
50°
Rounds: R 1/4

NOTES:

Chapter 5
3D Surface Modeling

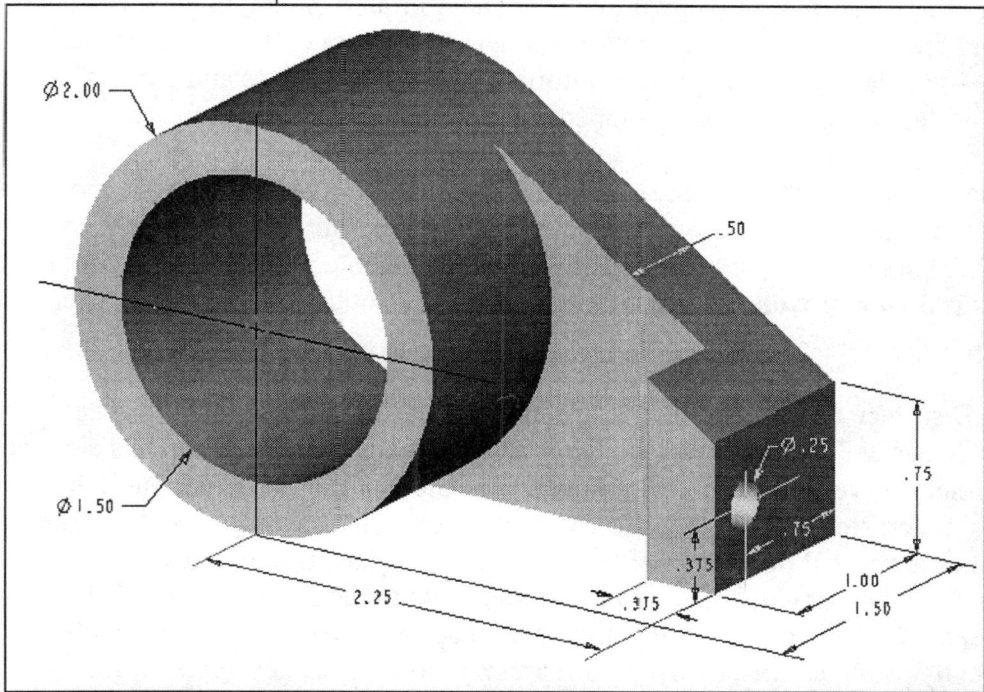

Learning Objectives

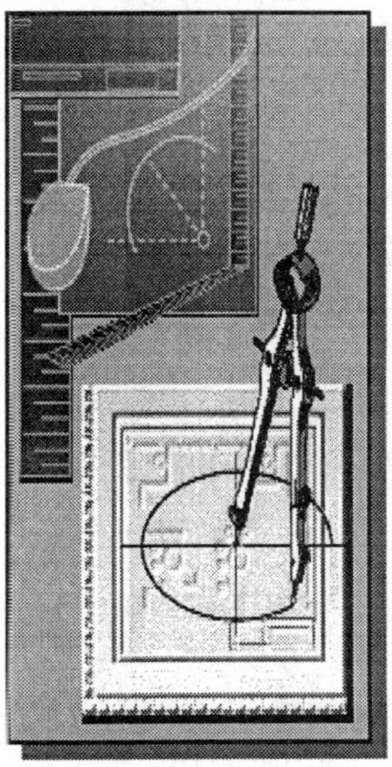

- ♦ Create 3D Surface Models.
- ♦ Apply the available surface modeling techniques.
- ♦ Understand the use of 2D solid command.
- ♦ Using the predefined surface models.
- ♦ Understand the use of 3D Face command.
- ♦ Use the Hidden Edge option.

Introduction

As illustrated in the previous chapters, there are no surfaces in a wireframe model; it consists only of points, lines, and curves that describe the edges of the object. Surface modeling is developed to provide the surface information that is missing in wireframe modeling. Essentially, defining the skin of a design creates a surface model. Although it is possible to create a surface model without using a wireframe model, in most cases it is much easier to create a surface model on top of a wireframe model. In surface modeling, a wireframe model can be used to provide information about the edges and corners so that the desired faces can be easily positioned and placed.

Surface modeling is more sophisticated than wireframe modeling in that surface modelers define not only the edges of 3D objects, but also the surfaces. Surface modeling provides hiding, shading, and rendering capabilities that are not available in wireframe modeling. Surface models do not provide the physical properties that solid models provide, such as mass, weight, center of gravity, and so on.

The AutoCAD surface modeler defines faceted surfaces using a filled polygon. The created faces of surface models are only planar, which means the surface models can only have approximate curved surfaces. It is important to note that the AutoCAD surface modeler does not create true curved surfaces. To differentiate these two types of surfaces, faceted surfaces are called **meshes** in AutoCAD. Because of the use of faceted approximation on true curved surfaces, the computer requirements of most faceted surface modelers are typically much less than that of solid modelers. Faceted surface modeling usually provides reasonably good representations of 3D designs with fast rendering and shading capabilities. Faceted surface models are also useful for creating geometry with unusual surface patterns, such as a 3D topographical model of mountainous terrain.

AutoCAD 2000i provides three basic methods for creating surfaces – the ***2D Solid***, ***3D FACE*** and ***REGION*** commands. The three commands were developed parallel to the historical development of the different types of computer modelers.

- ***2D SOLID***: The first generation surface command available in AutoCAD. Used mostly to fill an area in the sketch plane of the current UCS. This type of surface is not a true 3D surface.

- ***3D FACE***: Creates a true 3D planar surface (allowing X, Y and Z coordinates) of three-sided or four-sided shape. This is the type of surface developed primarily for creating faceted surface models.

- ***REGION***: Creates a 2D surface of arbitrary shape from existing 2D entities. This command creates the most flexible and the most complicated type of surface available in AutoCAD. This command was developed to allow manipulation of 2D surfaces using one of the solid modeling construction techniques, namely, the Constructive Solid Geometry method.

Although all three commands can be used to create planar surfaces, the resulting surfaces are not equal. In fact, the three commands are developed for specific tasks in mind. The ***2D SOLID*** command is mostly used in 2D drawings to create 2D filled area and the ***REGION*** command is designed so that general 2D shapes can be easily transformed into solid models. The ***3D FACE*** command is the only one that is designed specifically for surface modeling and therefore it is the most suitable for such tasks. The use of the ***2D SOLID*** and ***REGION*** commands in 3D surface modeling can be somewhat awkward and at times very difficult. Note that the use of the ***REGION*** command will be focused on in the solid modeling chapters of this text.

As one can imagine, sketching each surface manually can be very time consuming and tedious. AutoCAD also provides additional tools for surface modeling, such as **Predefined surfaces, Tabulated surfaces, Ruled surfaces** and **Revolved surfaces.** These tools are basically automated procedures, which can be used to define and create multiple copies of planar surfaces in specific directions. The principles and concepts used by these tools are also used in creating solid models, which are covered in chapter six through chapter eight of this text. You are encouraged to re-examine these commands after you have finished the solid modeling chapters.

In this chapter, the general procedures to create surface models are illustrated. The use of the ***2D SOLID*** and ***3D FACE*** commands are illustrated and differences discussed. We will also demonstrate the use of the more advanced surface modeling tools. Two wireframe models, which were created in the previous chapters, will be converted into surface models.

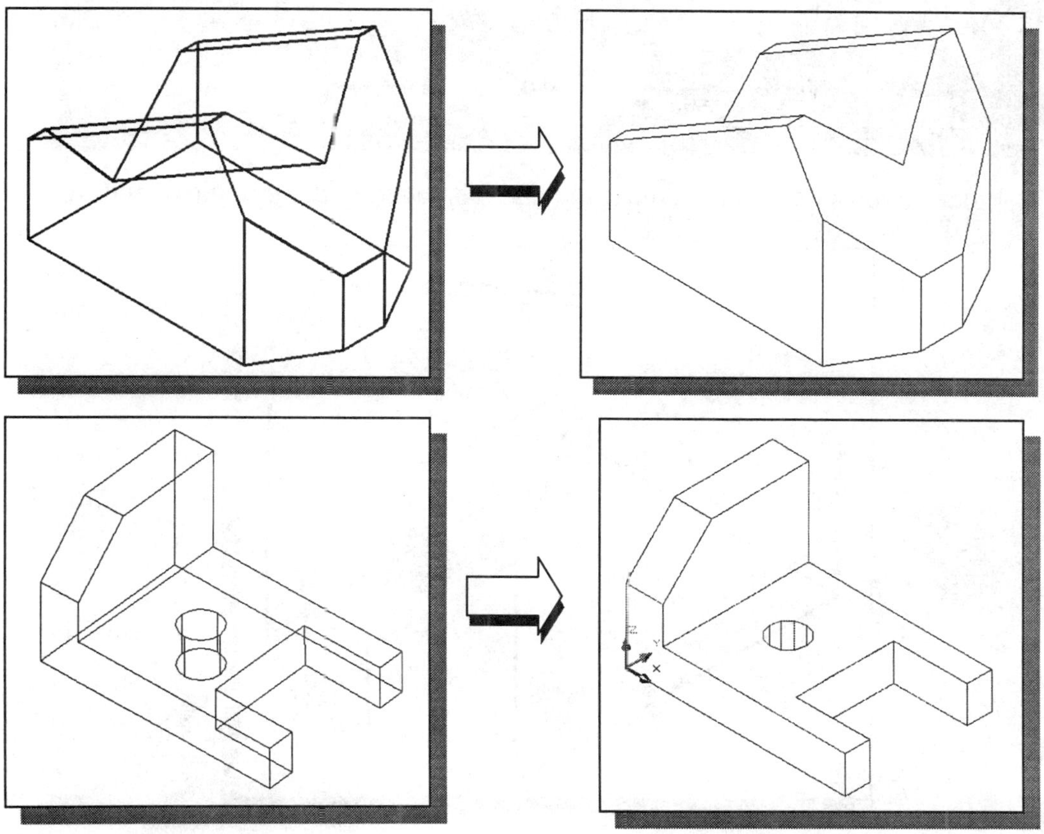

Starting Up AutoCAD® 2000i

1. Select the AutoCAD® 2000i option on the *Program* menu or select the AutoCAD® 2000i icon on the *Desktop*. Once the program is loaded into the memory, the AutoCAD® 2000i drawing screen and the *AutoCAD Today* startup dialog box will appear on the screen.

2. In the *AutoCAD Today* startup dialog box, select the **Open Drawings** tab with a single click of the left-mouse-button.

3. Click on the ***V-block.dwg*** filename to open the *V-block* wireframe model created in the previous chapter. (Use the Browse option to locate the file if it is not displayed.)

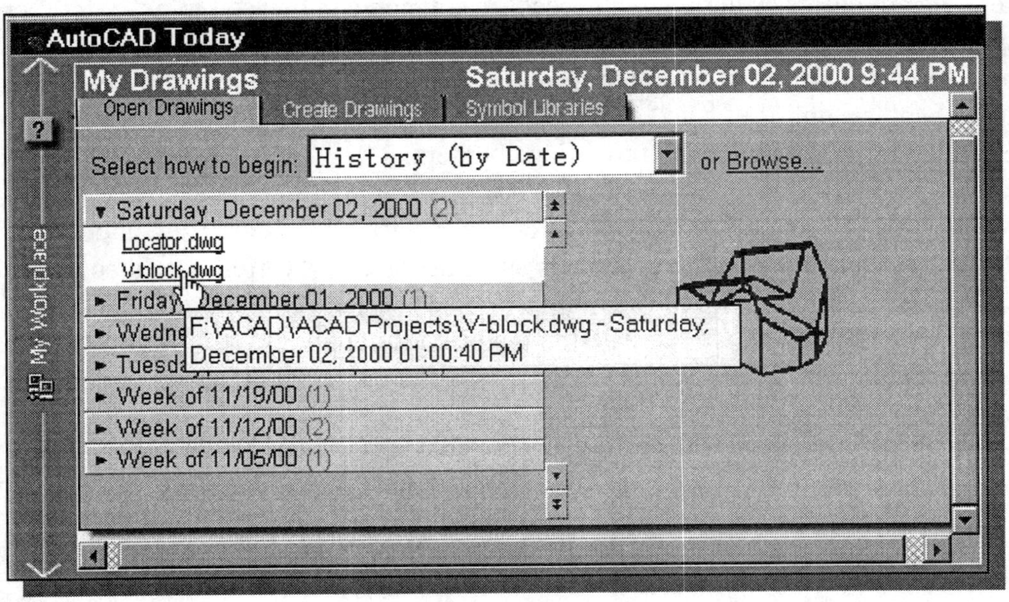

- The V-block wireframe model is retrieved and displayed in the graphics window.

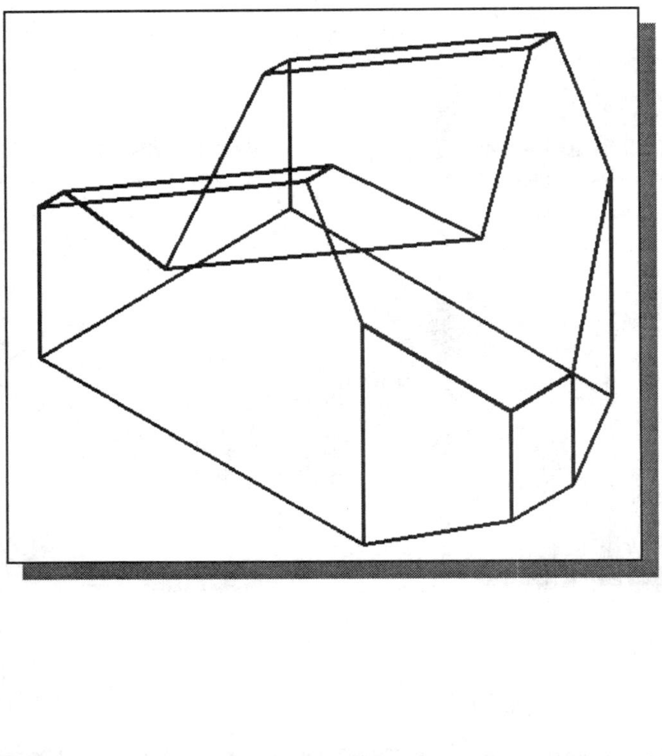

Using the UCS and Surfaces Toolbars

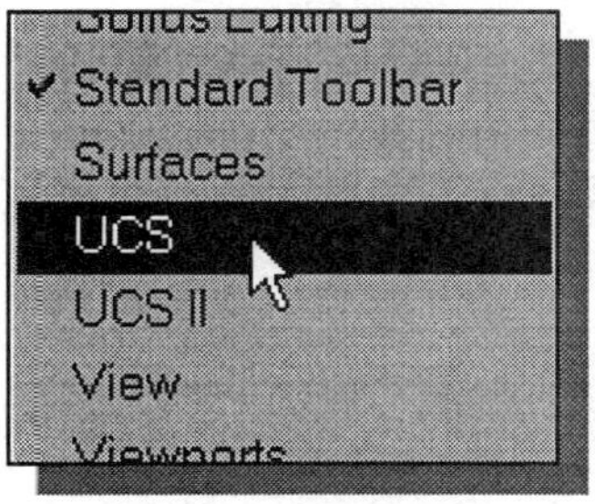

1. Move the cursor to the *Standard* toolbar area and **right-click** on any icon of the *Standard* toolbar to display a list of toolbar menu groups.

2. Select **UCS**, with the left-mouse-button, to display the *UCS* toolbar on the screen.

➢ The options available in the *UCS* toolbar allow us to quickly orient and align the UCS.

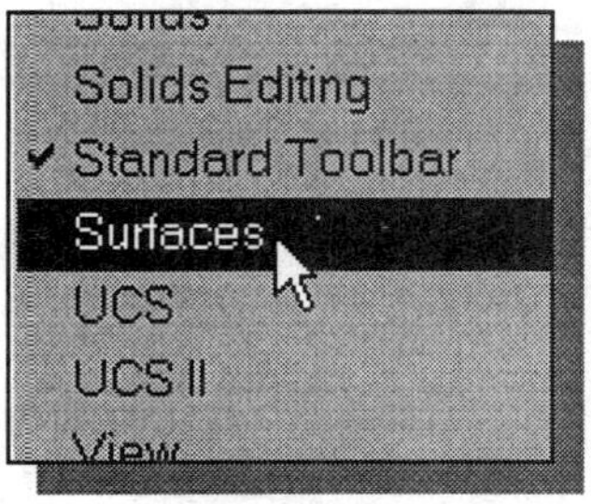

3. Move the cursor to the *Standard* toolbar area and **right-click** on any icon of the *Standard* toolbar to display a list of toolbar menu groups.

4. Select **Surfaces**, with the left-mouse-button, to display the *Surfaces* toolbar on the screen.

- Four groups of options are available in the *Surfaces* toolbar, which allow us to access the surface modeling commands quickly. On your own, move the cursor on top of the different icons and read the brief description of the individual commands in the help-line area.

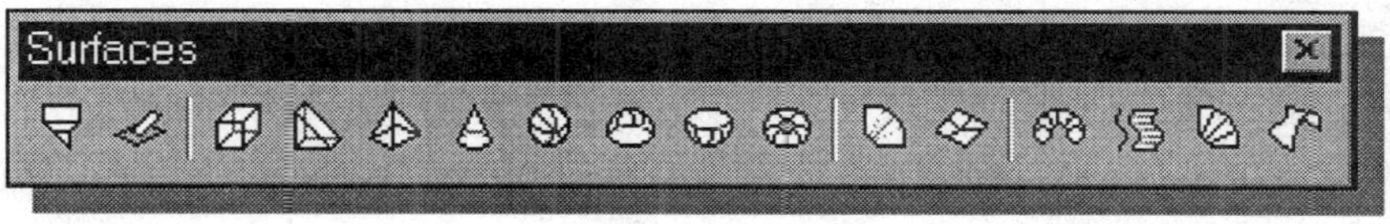

Creating a surface using the *2D SOLID* command

➢ The first generation surface available in AutoCAD is used to fill an area in the sketch plane of the current UCS. It is therefore necessary to properly orient the UCS prior to using the *2D SOLID* command.

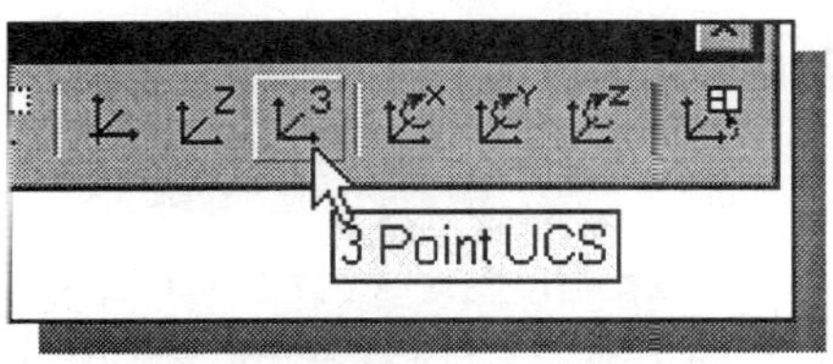

1. Select the ***3 Point UCS*** in the *UCS* toolbar.

- The ***3 point UCS*** option allows us to specify the new X-axis and Y-axis directions to align the UCS.

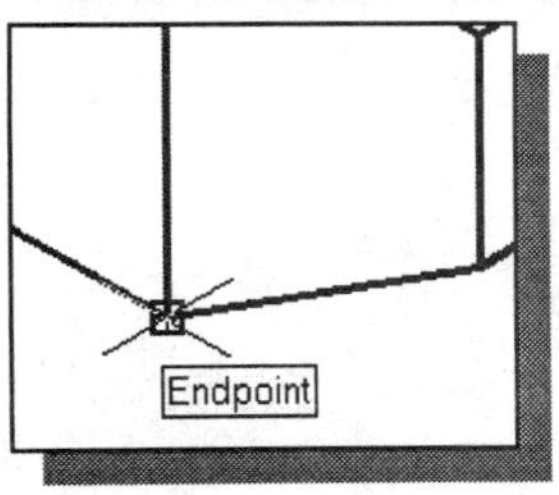

2. In the command prompt area, the message *"Specify new origin point<0,0,0>:"* is displayed. Pick the lower-right corner of the front face of the wireframe model as shown.

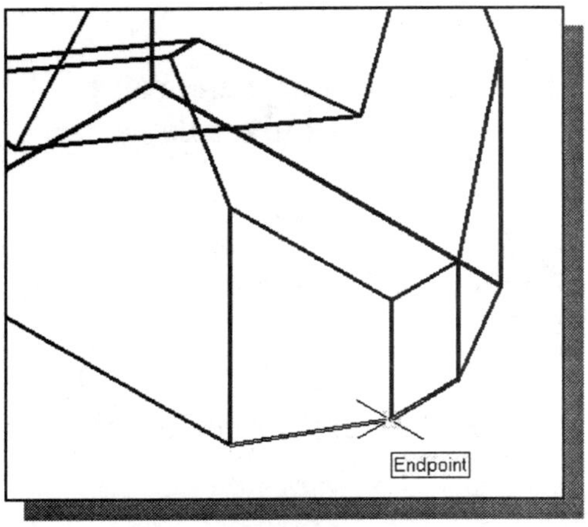

3. In the command prompt area, the message *"Specify point on positive portion of X-axis:"* is displayed. Pick the adjacent corner toward the right side of the model as shown.

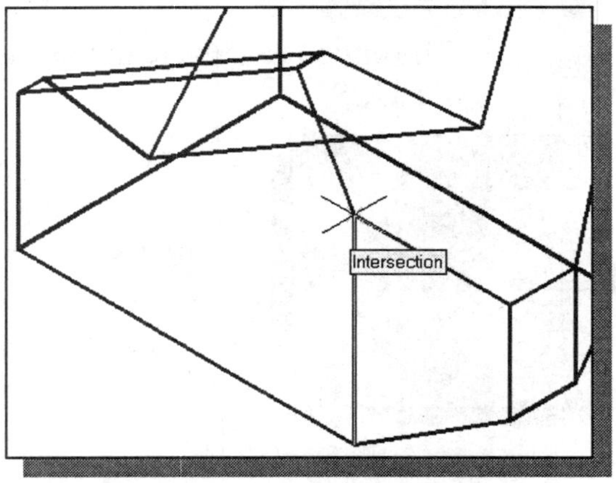

4. In the command prompt area, the message *"Specify point on positive portion of X-axis:"* is displayed. Pick the right corner of the inclined plane as shown.

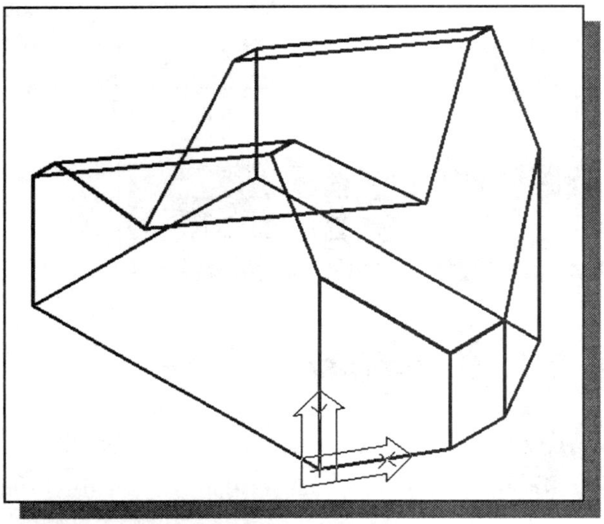

- The new UCS is aligned to the vertical inclined plane as shown.

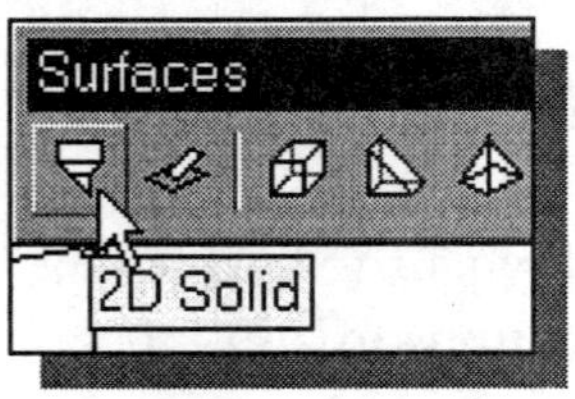

5. Select *2D Solid* in the *Surfaces* toolbar.

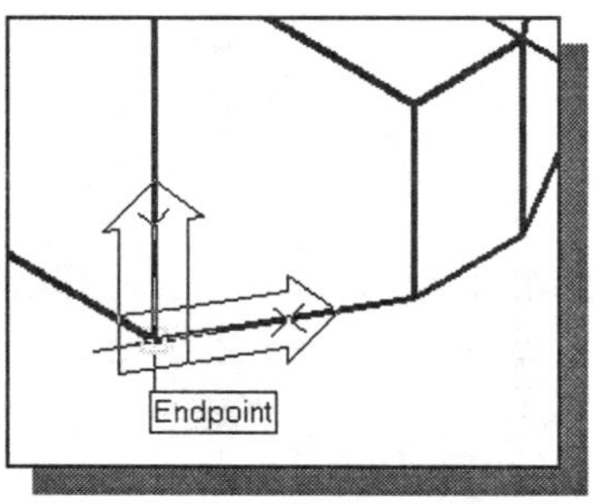

6. Place the first corner-point of the 2D Solid at the origin of the new UCS.

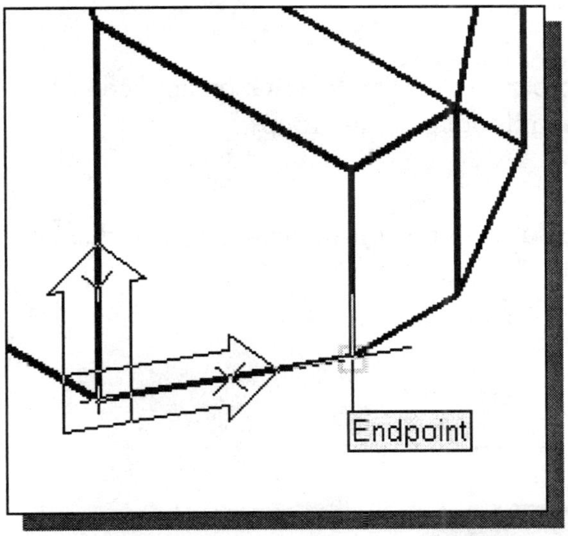

7. In the command prompt area, the message *"Specify second point:"* is displayed. Pick the bottom-right corner of the inclined plane as shown.

8. In the command prompt area, the message *"Specify third point:"* is displayed. Pick the corner directly above the origin of the UCS as shown.

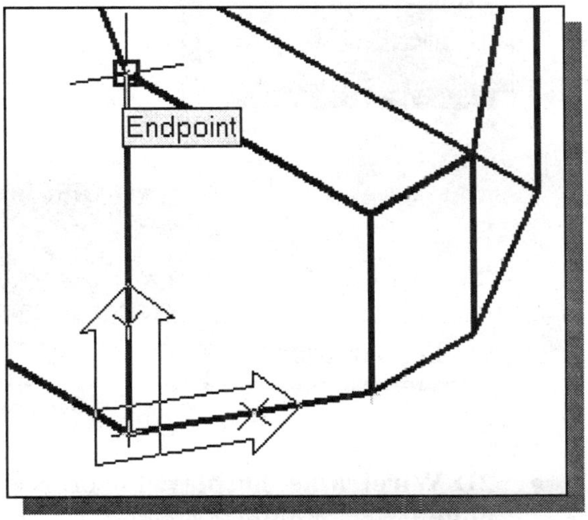

- The *2D SOLID* command requires the third point to be specified diagonally opposite to the second point. This seemly strange way of specifying the third corner was established when the *2D SOLID* command was first introduced back in the mid-1980s. Note that the ***3D FACE*** command, the second-generation surface command in AutoCAD, does not follow this convention.

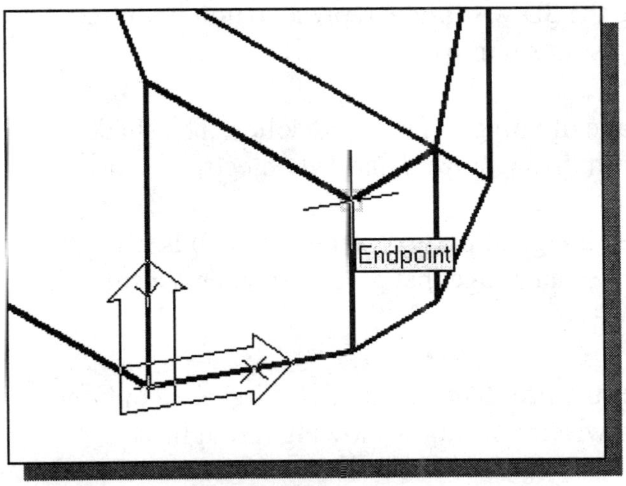

9. In the command prompt area, the message *"Specify fourth point or [Exit]:"* is displayed. Pick the corner directly above the second point we selected as shown in the figure.

10. Inside the graphics window, **right-mouse-click** once to end the *2D SOLID* command.

- The *2D SOLID* command allows the creation of three-sided or four-sided filled polygons, which can be used to represent faces of surface models. Note that in the above steps, we could accept the three-sided polygon after defining the third corner.

Using the Shade Toolbar

1. Move the cursor to the *Standard* toolbar area and **right-click** on any icon of the *Standard* toolbar to display a list of toolbar menu groups.

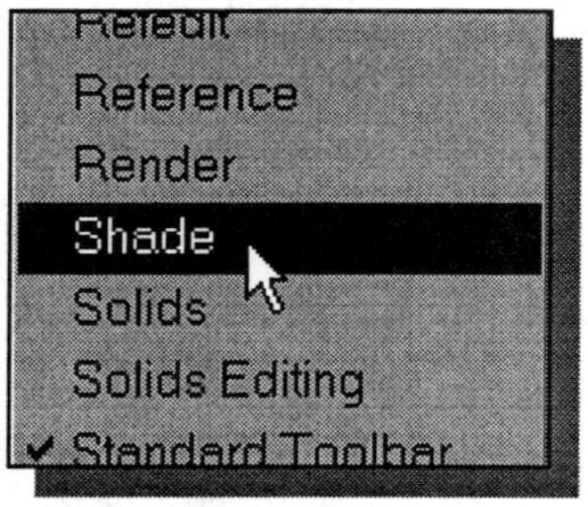

2. Select **Shade**, with the left-mouse-button, to display the *Shade* toolbar on the screen.

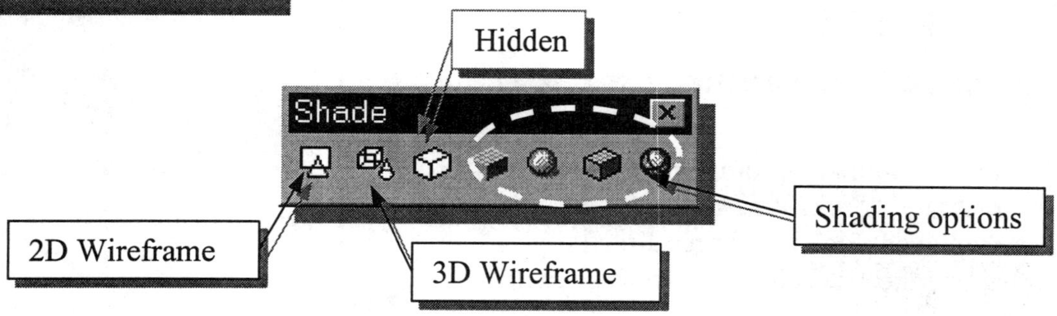

- **2D Wireframe**: Displays the objects using lines and curves to represent the boundaries of objects created. Linetypes and lineweights are visible with this option. Note that this is the default AutoCAD display mode.

- **3D Wireframe**: Displays the objects using lines and curves to represent the boundaries of objects created. Displays a shaded 3D user coordinate system (UCS) icon. Note that linetypes and lineweights are not visible with this option.

- **Hidden**: Displays the objects using the 3D wireframe representation with lines that are located behind surfaces and solids removed.

- **Flat Shaded**: Creates a shaded image of polygon faces and solids. The shaded objects appear flatter and less smooth than *Gouraud Shaded* objects.

- **Gouraud Shaded**: Creates a shaded image of polygon faces and solids using the Gouraud method. This mode generates an image that gives the objects a smooth and realistic appearance.

- **Flat Shaded, Edges On**: Combines the *Flat Shaded* and *3D Wireframe* options. The objects are flat shaded with the wireframe edges showing through.

- **Gouraud Shaded, Edges On**: Combines the *Gouraud Shaded* and *3D Wireframe* options. The objects are Gouraud shaded with the wireframe edges showing through.

3. In the *Shade* toolbar, click on the ***Gouraud Shaded*** icon to display the shaded image of the model. There exist only one surface in our model. The surface was created with the *2D SOLID* command.

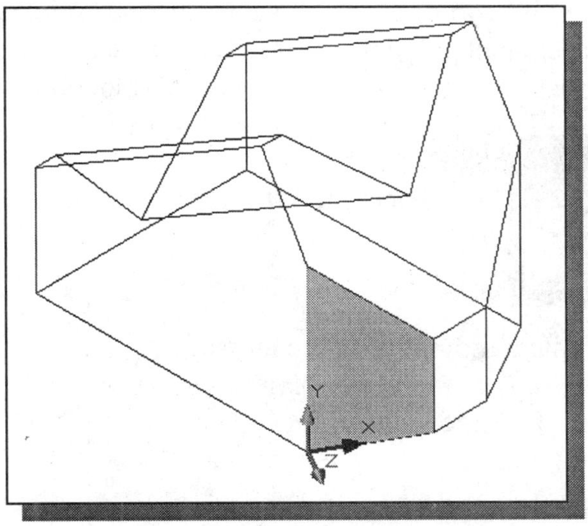

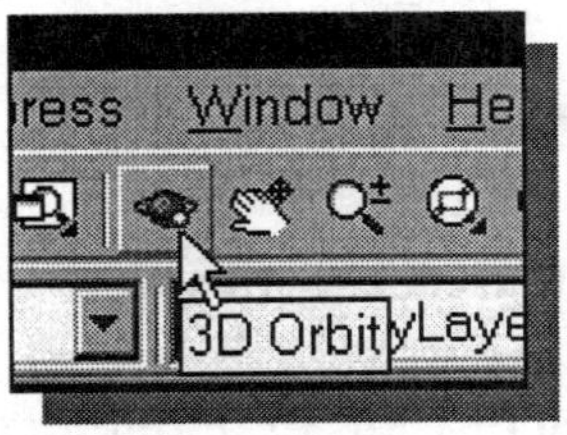

4. Click on the ***3D Orbit*** icon in the *Standard* toolbar.

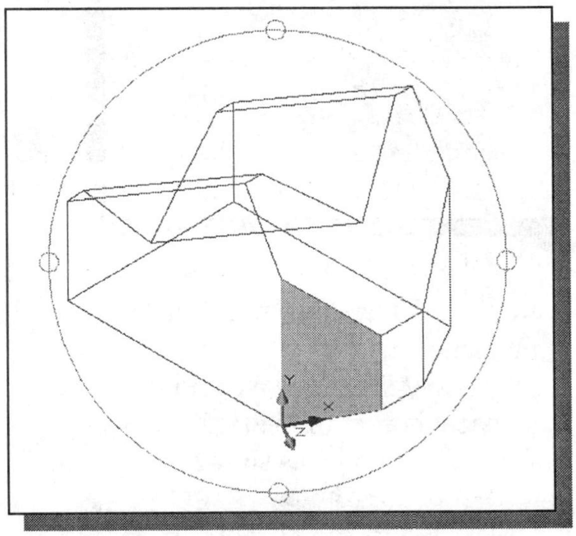

5. Inside the *arcball*, press down the left-mouse-button and drag it to rotate the model freely in 3D space.

- Observe the display of the shaded surface in contrast to the 3D wireframe edges that are located behind it.

6. On your own, reset the display to the SE Isometric view before continuing to the next section.

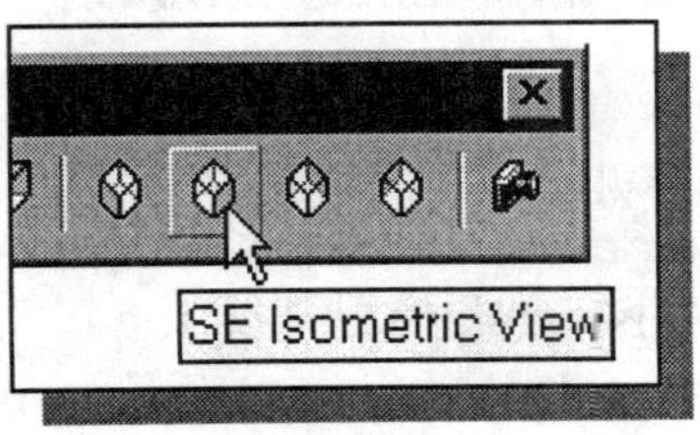

7. In the *UCS* toolbar, select the ***World UCS***. This option reset the UCS to align to the world coordinate system.

Creating a surface using the *3D FACE* command

- The second generation of surface command made available in AutoCAD is the *3D FACE* command. The *3D FACE* command creates a true 3D planar surface allowing the X, Y and Z coordinates of the corners to be selected independently of the current UCS. The created polygon can be a three-sided or four-sided shape. This command is the primary construction tool for surface modeling in AutoCAD.

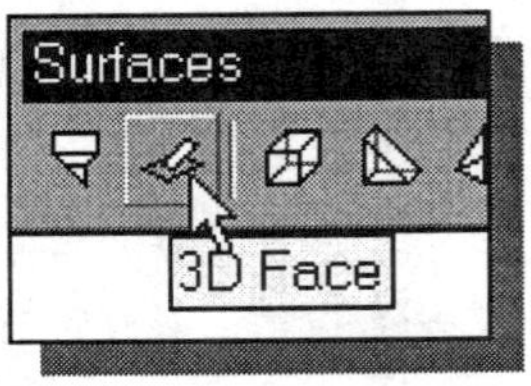

1. Select the ***3D Face*** in the *Surface* toolbar.

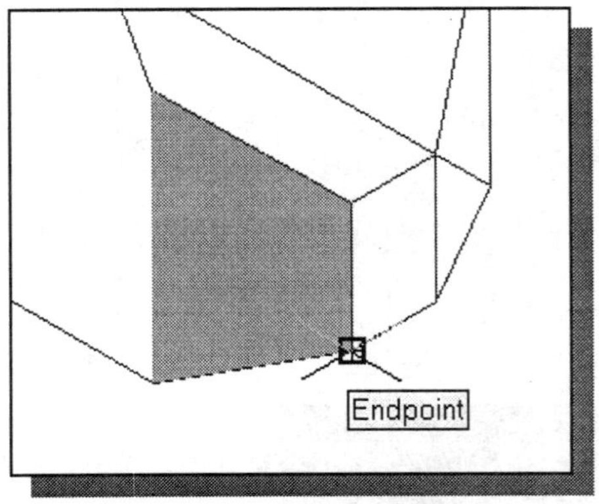

2. In the command prompt area, the message *"_3dface Specify first point or [invisible]:"* is displayed. Pick the lower-right corner of the vertical inclined face of the model as shown.

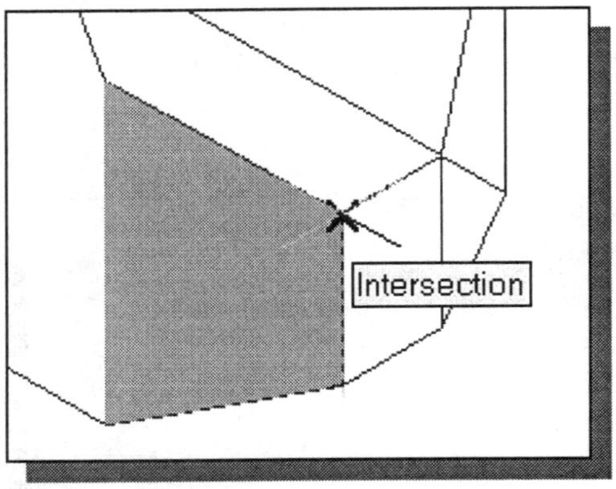

3. In the command prompt area, the message *"Specify second point or [invisible]:"* is displayed. Pick the adjacent corner above the previous selected corner of the vertical inclined face as shown.

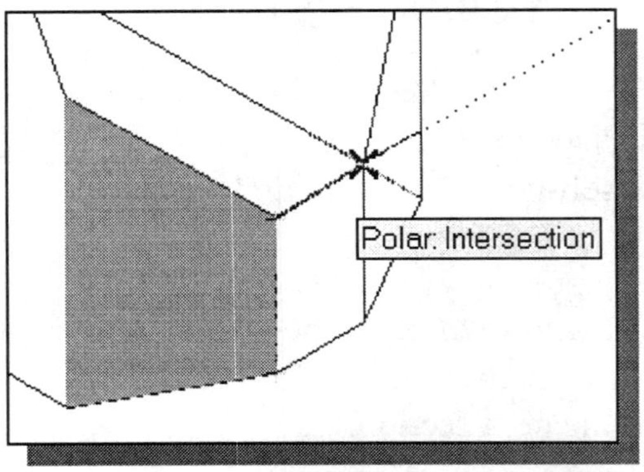

4. In the command prompt area, the message *"Specify third point or [invisible]:"* is displayed. Pick the adjacent corner of the right-vertical face of the model as shown.

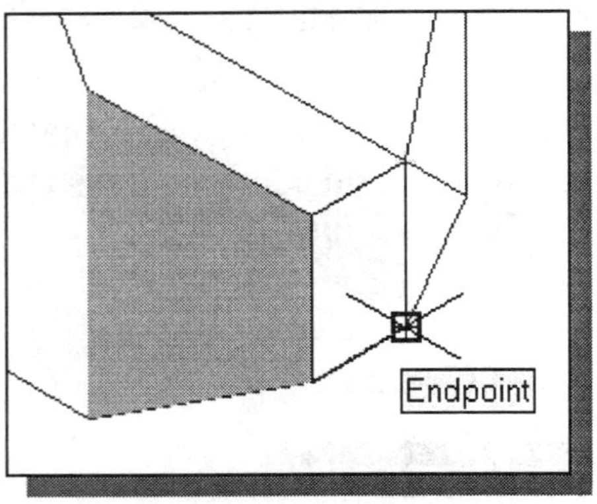

5. In the command prompt area, the message *"Specify fourth point or [invisible] <Create three-sided face>:"* is displayed. Pick the corner below the last selected corner as shown.

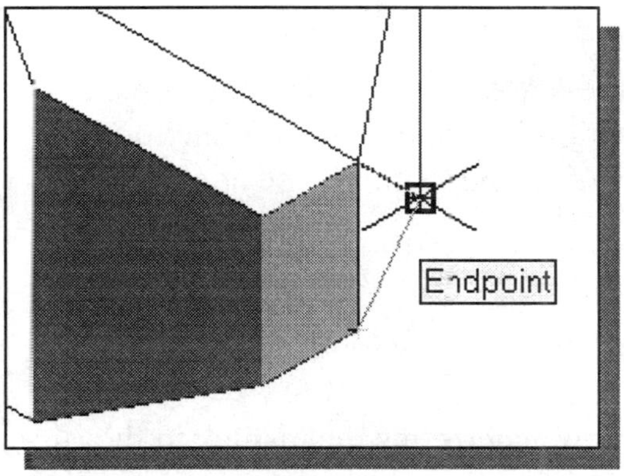

6. In the command prompt area, the message *"Specify third point or [invisible] <exit>:"* is displayed. Pick the back corner of the model as shown.

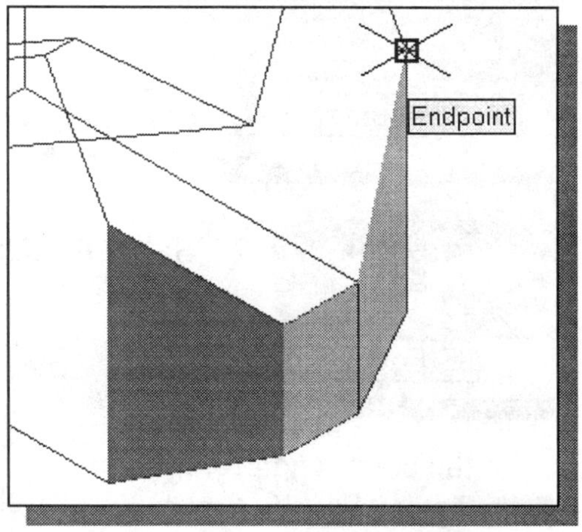

7. In the command prompt area, the message *"Specify fourth point or [invisible] <Create three-sided face>:"* is displayed. Pick the back corner of the model as shown.

- Note that this surface is created independent of the UCS and two corners of the previous face were used to position this face.

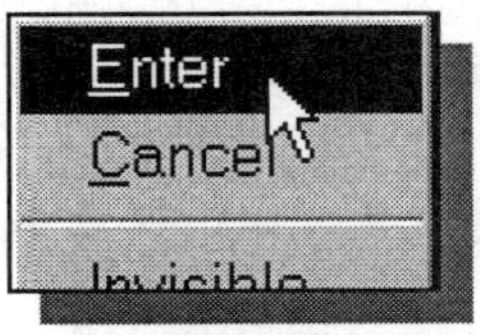

8. Inside the graphics window, **right-mouse-click** to activate the option menu and select **Enter** with the left-mouse-button to end the *3D FACE* command.

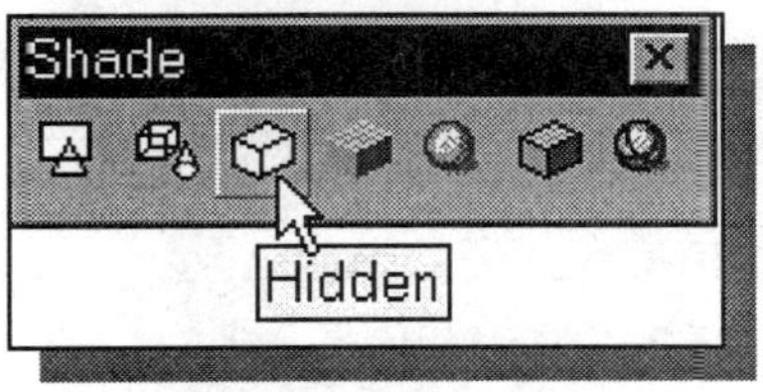

9. In the *Shade* toolbar, click on the ***Hidden*** icon to display the model with hidden lines removed.

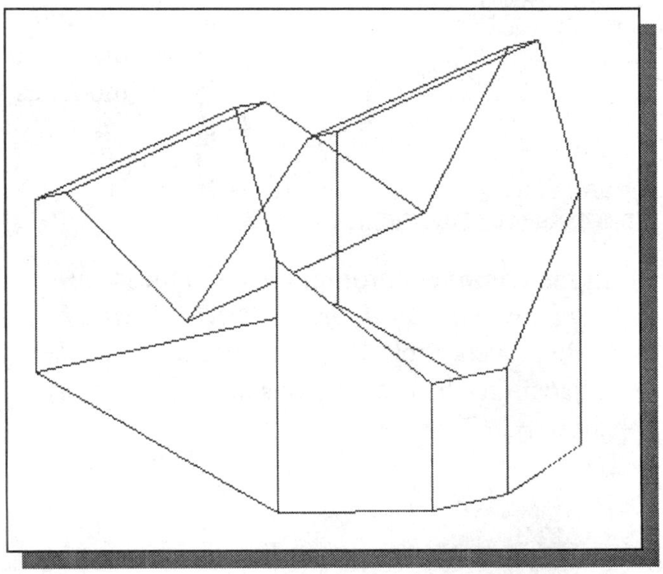

10. Click on the ***3D Orbit*** icon in the *Standard* toolbar.

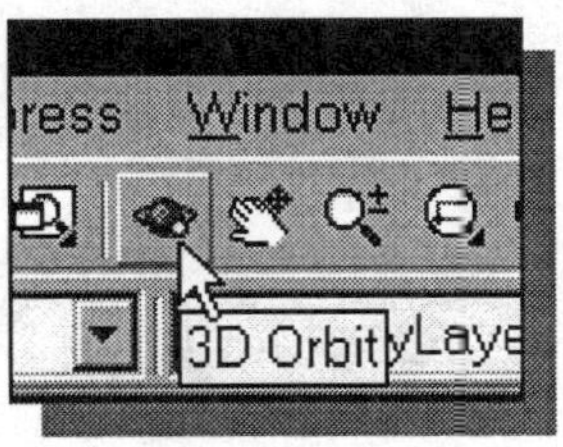

11. Rotate the model in 3D space and examine the constructed surface model.

- Reset the display to SE Isometric view before proceeding to the next section.

Creating a surface of irregular shape

- The ***3D FACE*** command allows us to create three-sided or four-sided polygons. For surfaces of irregular shape, the *Invisible Edge* option is available in conjunction with the *3D FACE* command. Note that the *Invisible Edge* option cannot be applied to polygons created by the *2D SOLID* command.

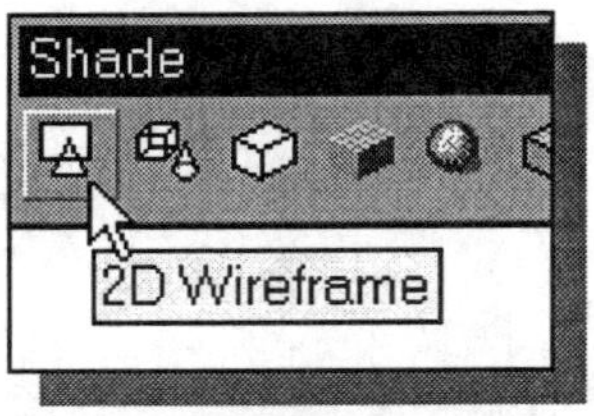

1. Select the ***2D Wireframe*** in the *Shade* toolbar.

- The *2D WIREFRAME* command resets the display to the default AutoCAD display mode

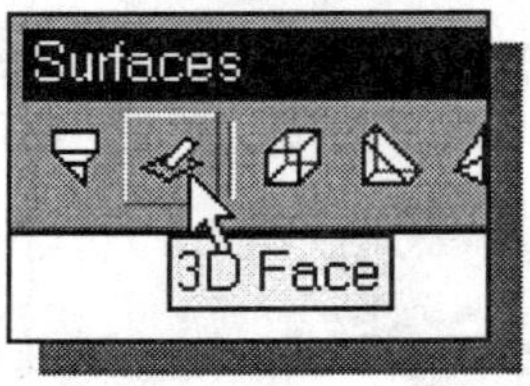

2. Select the ***3D Face*** in the *Surface* toolbar.

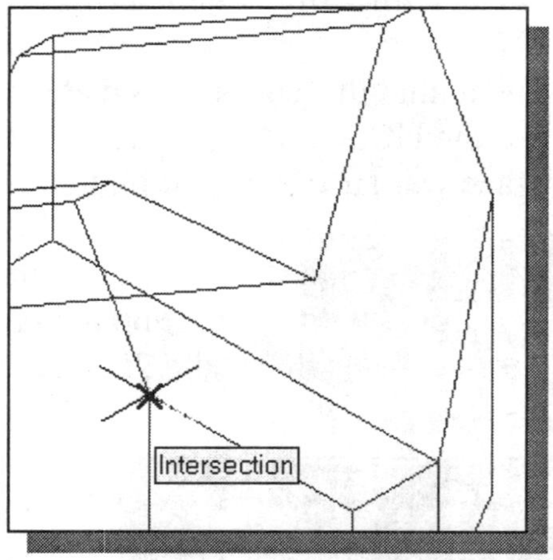

3. In the command prompt area, the message *"_3dface Specify first point or [invisible]:"* is displayed. Pick the top-right corner of the model as shown.

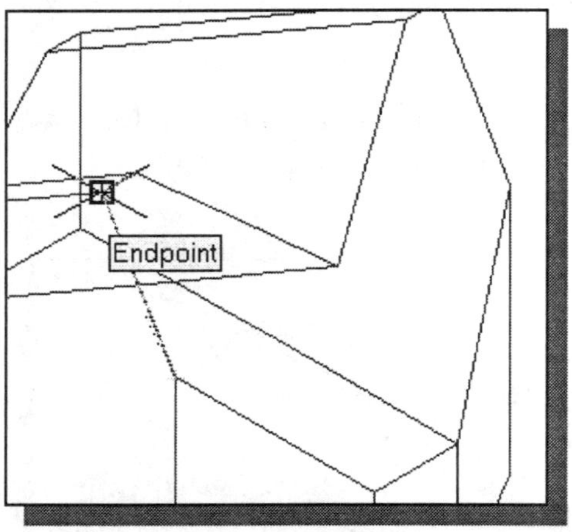

4. In the command prompt area, the message *"Specify second point or [invisible]:"* is displayed. Pick the top-front corner of the model as shown.

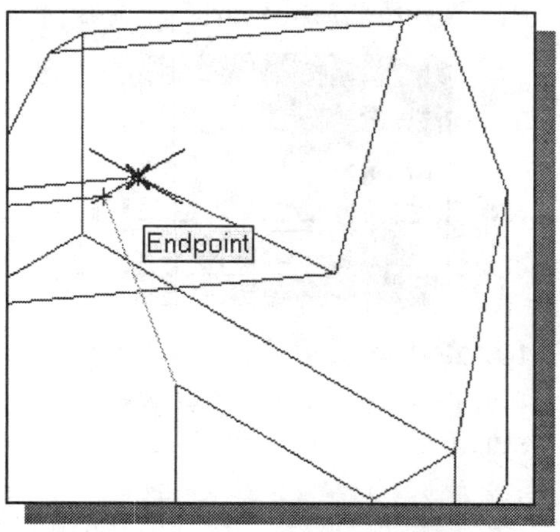

5. In the command prompt area, the message *"Specify third point or [invisible] <exit>:"* is displayed. Pick the top corner of the model adjacent to the previously selected corner as shown.

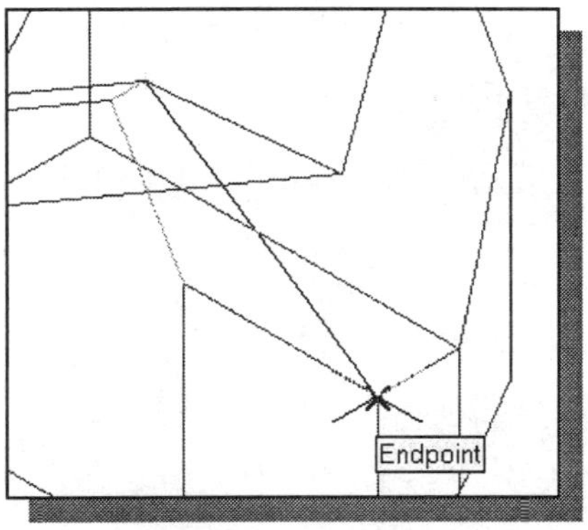

6. In the command prompt area, the message *"Specify fourth point or [invisible] <Create three-sided face>:"* is displayed. Pick the corner below the last selected corner as shown.

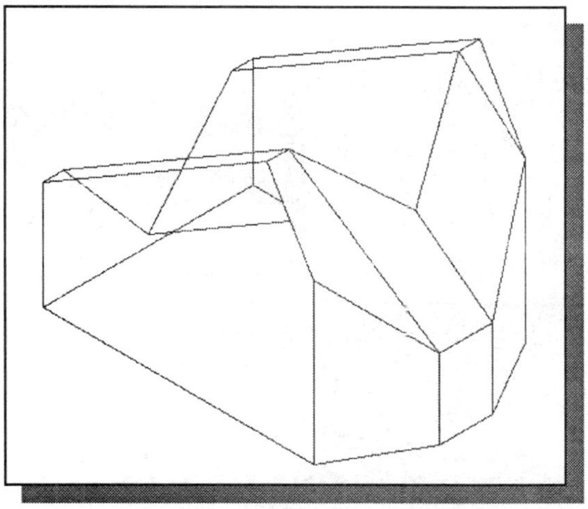

7. On your own, repeat the zigzagging pattern to define polygons until all corners of the inclined surface have been selected and additional polygons are created as shown in the figure. Note that the last polygon we created is a three-sided polygon.

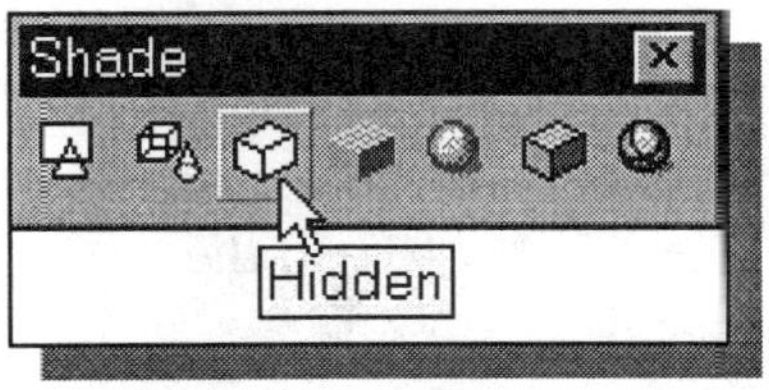

8. In the *Shade* toolbar, click on the ***Hidden*** icon to display the model with hidden lines removed. Note that the edges of the polygons are displayed as shown in the above figure.

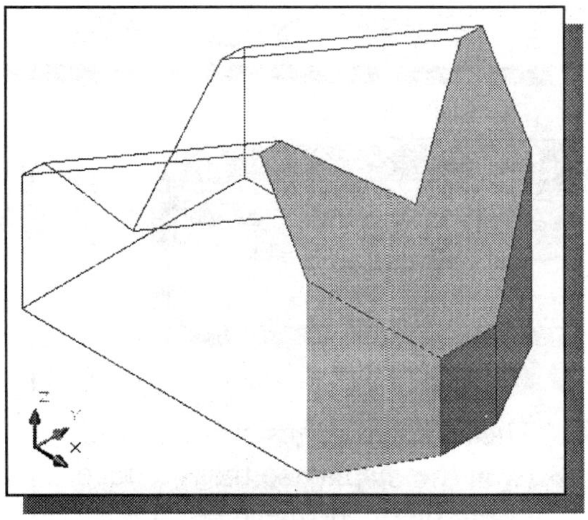

9. In the *Shade* toolbar, click on the ***Gouraud Shaded*** icon to display the shaded image of the model. Note that the edges of the polygons are not visible when a shaded command is performed.

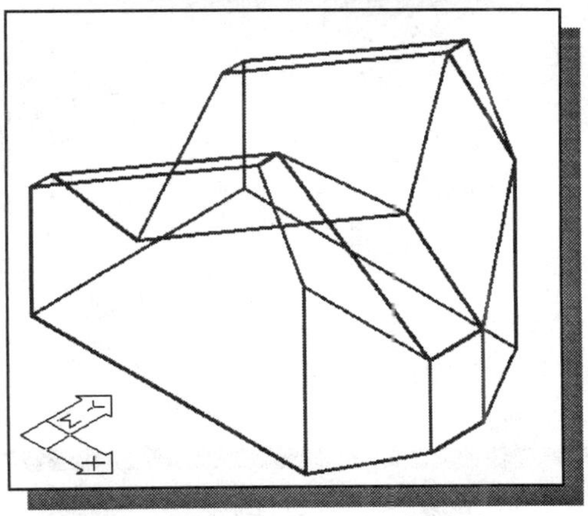

10. Select ***2D Wireframe*** in the *Shade* toolbar to reset the display to the default AutoCAD display mode.

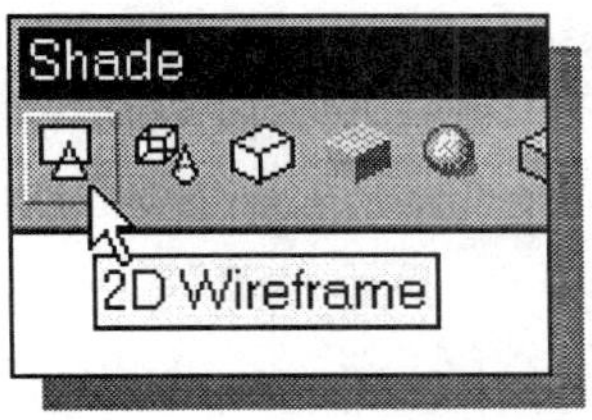

Using the *Invisible Edge* option

- The *Invisible Edge* option is used to turn off the display of selected edges and therefore allow the adjacent polygons, created by the *3D FACE* command, to appear as being joined together.

1. Select ***Edge***, with the left-mouse-button, in the *Surfaces* toolbar.

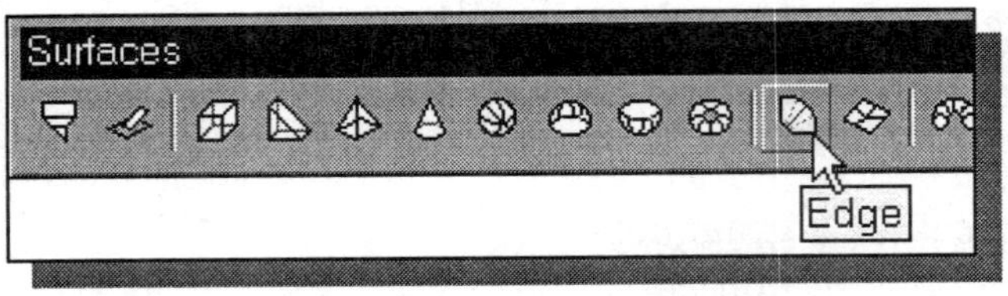

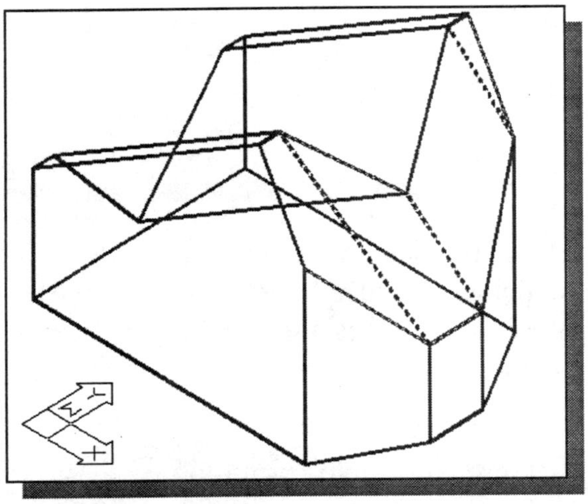

2. In the command prompt area, the message *"Specify edge of 3dface to toggle visibility or [Display]:"* is displayed. Pick the three edges inside the inclined surface as shown.

3. Inside the graphics window, **right-mouse-click** to activate the option menu and select **Enter** to end the *EDGE* command.

4. In the *Shade* toolbar, click on the ***Hidden*** icon to display the model with hidden lines removed.

- The selected edges are removed from the display so that the face of the inclined surface of the model appears to be more realistic.

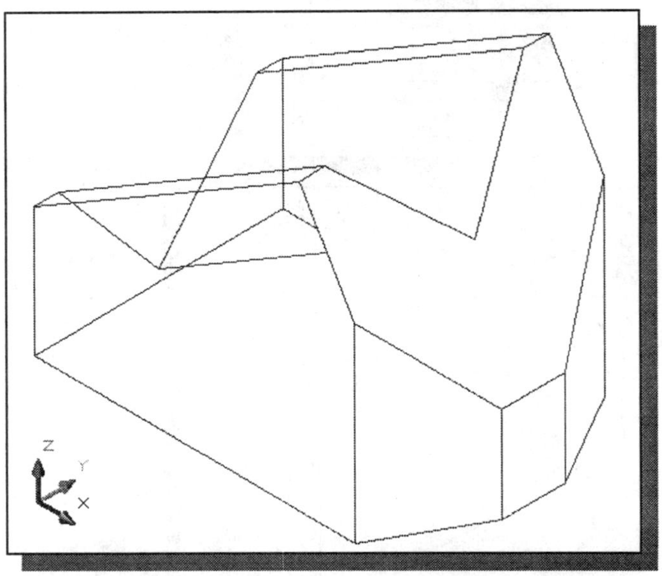

➢ On your own, repeat the above steps and complete the surface model of the design.

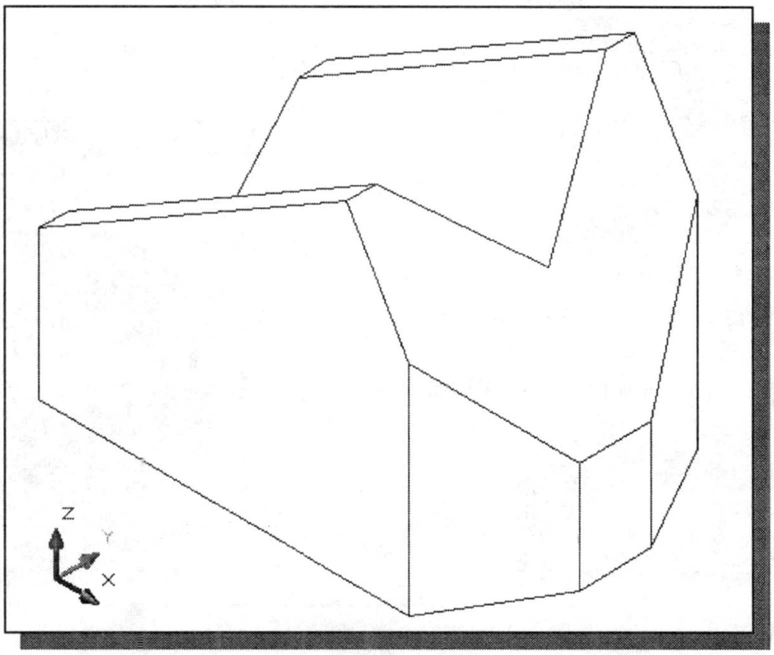

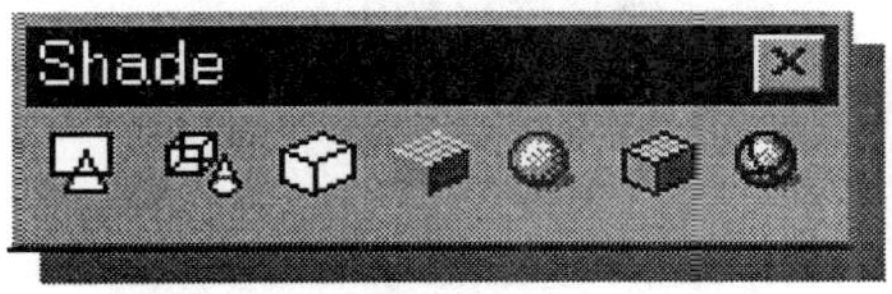

- On your own, examine the completed surface model by using the different shading commands.

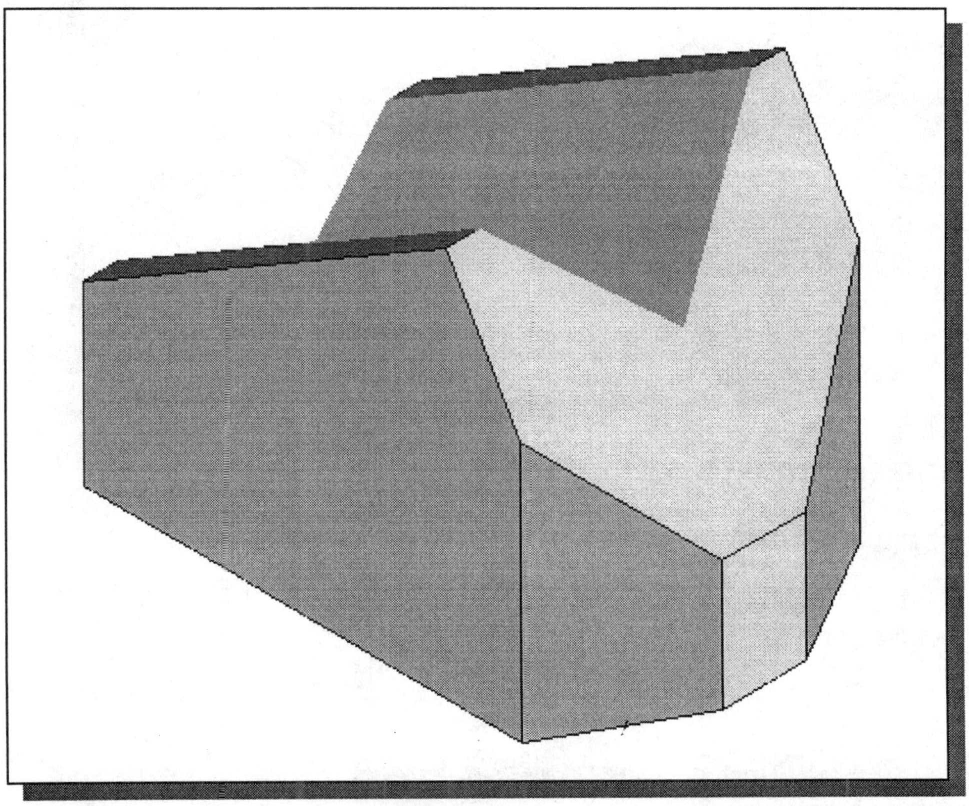

The *Locator* wireframe model

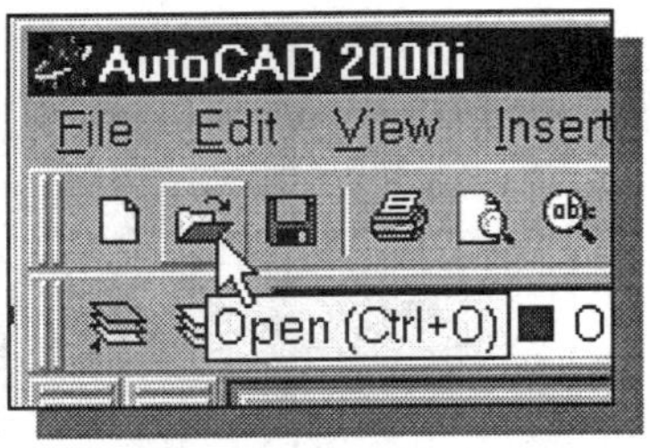

1. Click on the ***Open*** icon in the *Standard* toolbar.

2. In the *Select File* window, pick the ***Locator*** file that was created in chapter three.

3. Click **Open** to open the model file.

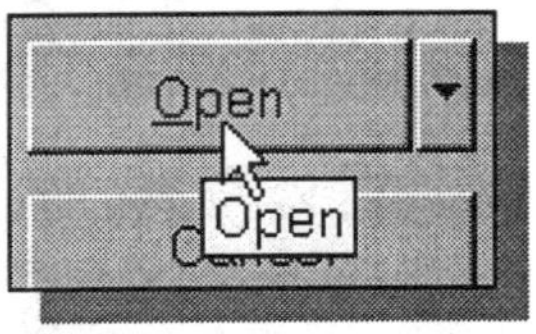

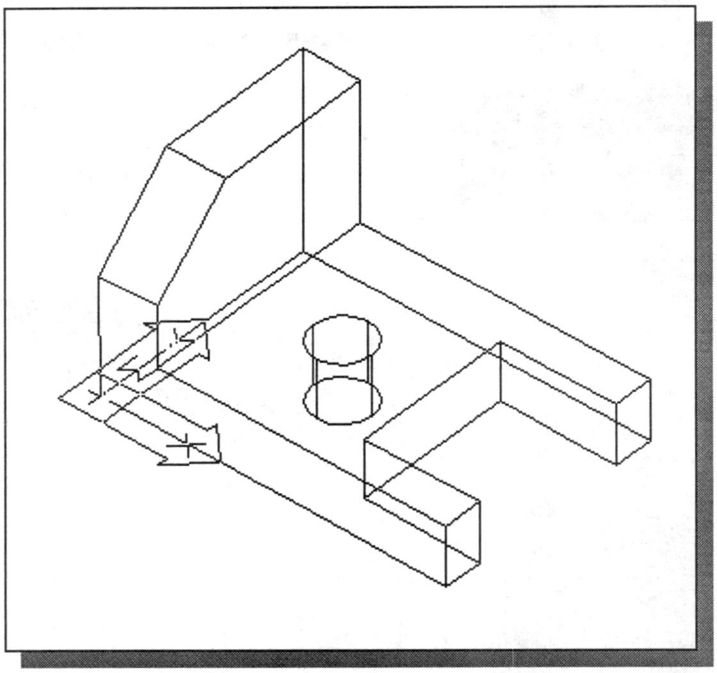

Moving Objects to a different Layer

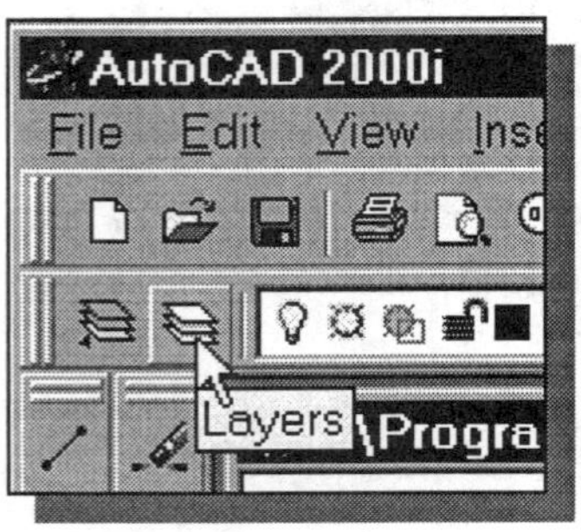

1. Pick ***Layers*** in the *Object Properties* toolbar.

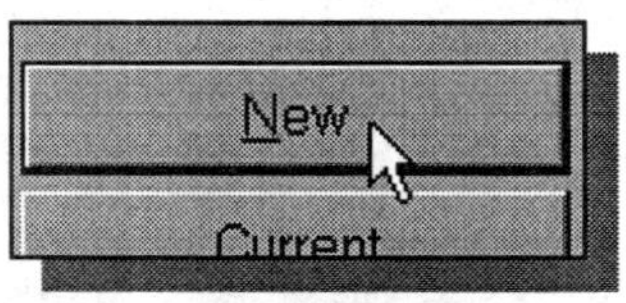

2. Click on the ***New*** icon to create new layers.

3. Create **two new layers** with the following settings:

Layer	*Color*	*LineType*	*LineWeight*
Construction	**White**	**Continuous**	**Default**
Wireframe	**Blue**	**Continuous**	**0.30mm**
Surface	**Cyan**	**Continuous**	**Default**

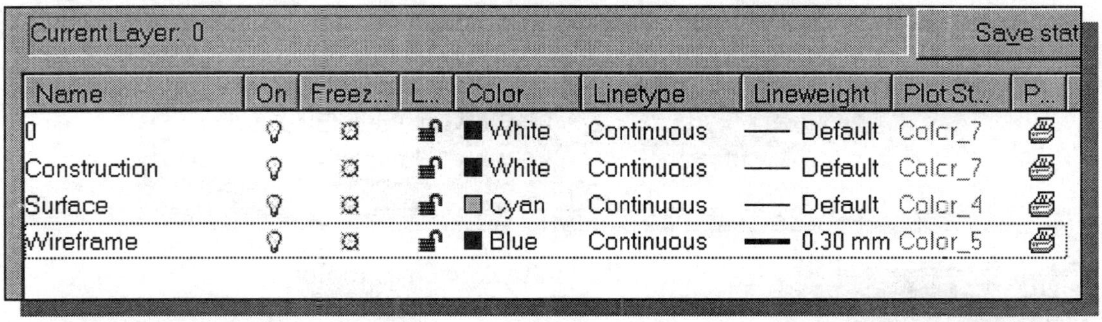

4. Click on the **OK** button to accept the settings and exit the *Layer Properties Manager* dialog box.

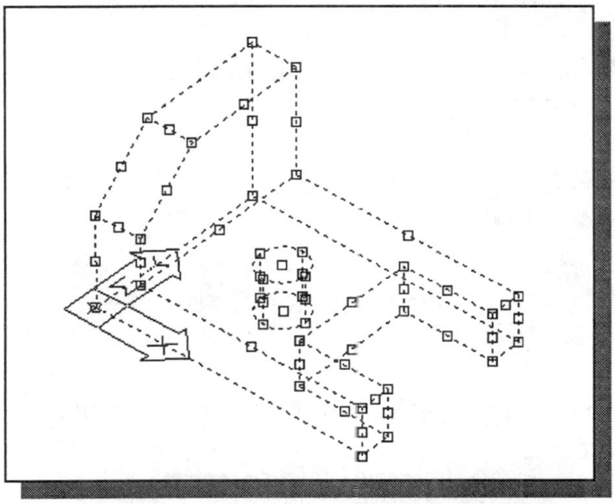

5. Inside the graphics window, pre-select all entities by using the left-mouse-button to create a *selection window* enclosing all entities.

- Note that all selected entities are highlighted.

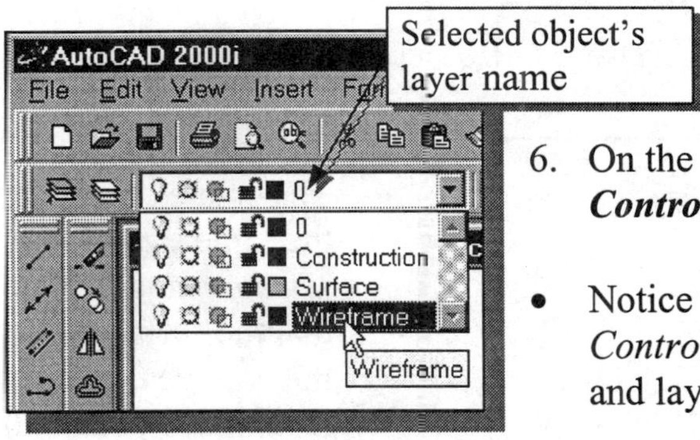

6. On the *Object Properties* toolbar, choose the ***Layer Control*** box with the left-mouse-button.

- Notice the layer name displayed in the *Layer Control* box is the selected object's assigned layer and layer properties.

7. In the *Layer Control* box, click on the ***Wireframe*** layer name as shown.

8. Press the **[ESC]** key twice to deselect all highlighted entities.

- All entities of the *Locator* model are moved to the *Wireframe* layer.

Predefined Surface models

- **Predefined surface models**: AutoCAD provides the following predefined 3D surface models: boxes, cones, dishes, domes, meshes, pyramids, spheres, tori (donuts), and wedges. AutoCAD creates these models by prompting the users to input specific dimensions for the desired models. For example, the length, width and height dimensions are required for the *Box* surface model.

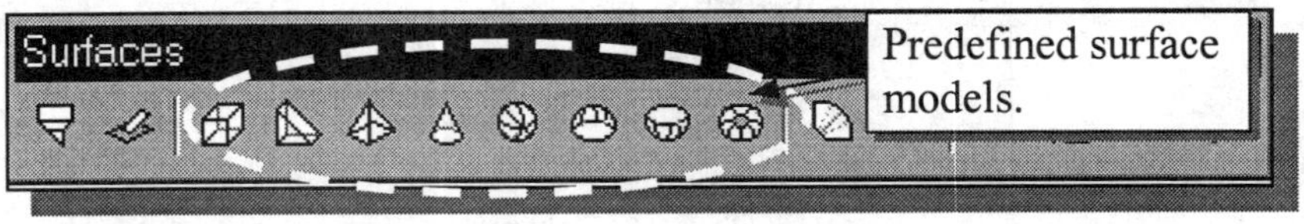

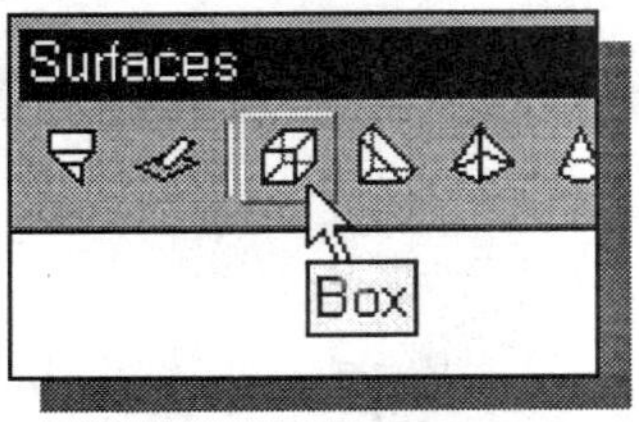

1. Select ***Box*** in the *Surfaces* toolbar.

2. In the command prompt area, the message *"Specify corner point of Box:"* is displayed. Pick a point that is toward the right of the *Locator* model.

3. In the command prompt area, the message *"Specify length of Box:"* is displayed. *Specify length of Box*: **4.5** [**ENTER**]

4. In the command prompt area, the message *"Specify width of Box:"* is displayed. *Specify width of Box*: **3.0** [**ENTER**]

5. In the command prompt area, the message *"Specify height of Box:"* is displayed. *Specify height of Box*: **2.5** [**ENTER**]

6. In the command prompt area, the message *"Specify rotation angle about the Z axis or [Reference]:"* is displayed.
   Specify rotation angle about the Z axis or [Reference]: **0** [**ENTER**]

➢ On your own, use the *HIDDEN*, *SHADED* and *ORBIT* commands to examine the constructed surface model.

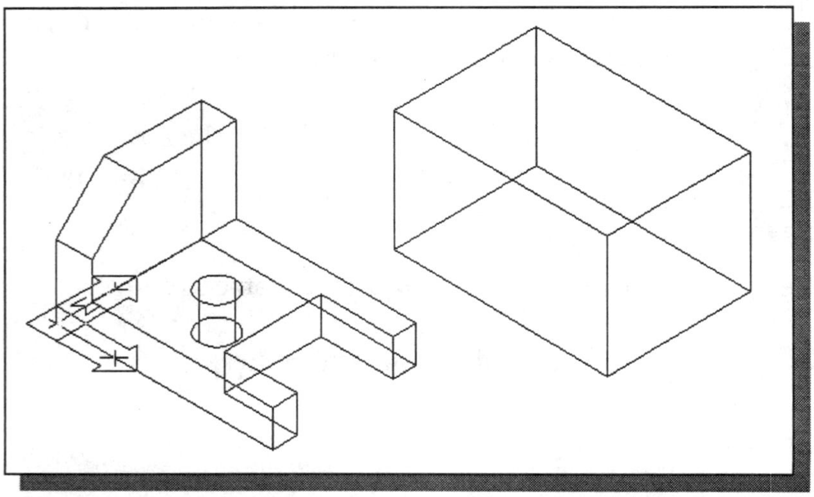

- The created *Box* is of the same size of the *Locator* model. Note that the surfaces of the box are created automatically and all faces of the model are grouped together as a single object.

➤ The predefined surface models can be used as a base for more complex designs. The main difficulty, and disadvantage, of surface modeling is that the constructed surfaces can not be easily modified. In AutoCAD, we can use the grip-editing option to resize the constructed faces.

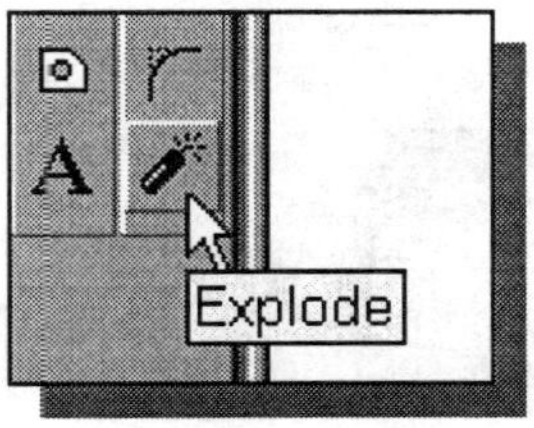

7. Select ***Explode*** in the *Modify* toolbar.

8. In the command prompt area, the message *"Select objects:"* is displayed. Select any edges of the surface model and note that the entire model is selected.

9. Inside the graphics window, right-mouse-click once to accept the selection and the faces are separated into individual objects.

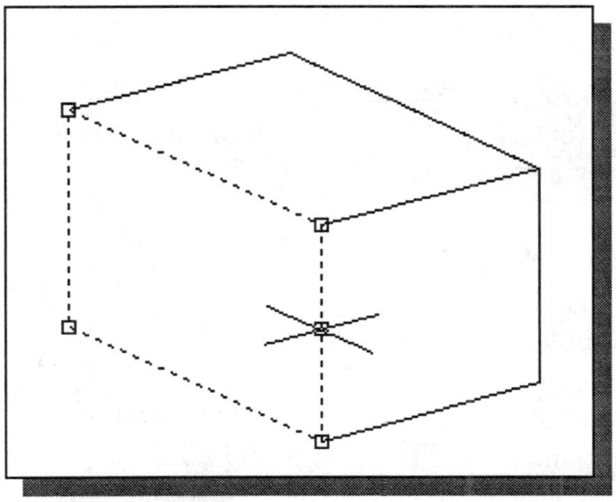

10. Select the front vertical face of the model by clicking on the inside of the front face as shown.

- Four grip points, the small rectangles displayed at the corners of the highlighted polygon, can be used to adjust the size and shape of the highlighted polygon.

11. Select the top-right grip point with the left-mouse-button.

12. Move the cursor to the left, along the top-edge of the model, of its current location as shown. Left-mouse-click once to reposition the grip-point.

13. Press the **[ESC]** key to deselect the highlighted entities.

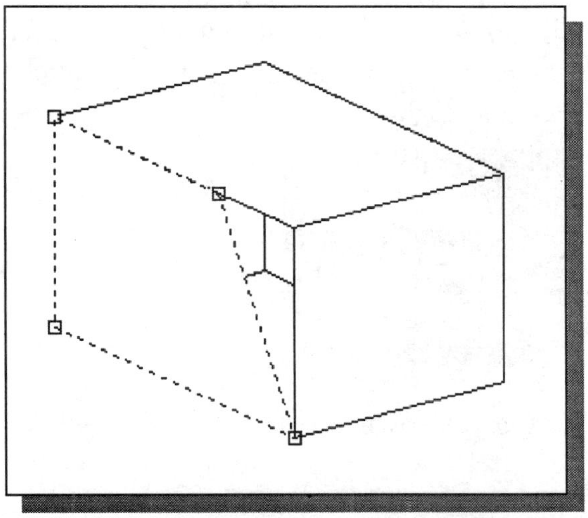

➤ On your own, experiment with creating other predefined surface models that are available in the *Surfaces* toolbar. Delete all surface models before proceeding to the next section.

Advanced Surface Modeling commands

❖ Several of the advanced surface-modeling commands are displayed in the *Surfaces* toolbar. These commands allow us to quickly create and duplicate surfaces in specific manners.

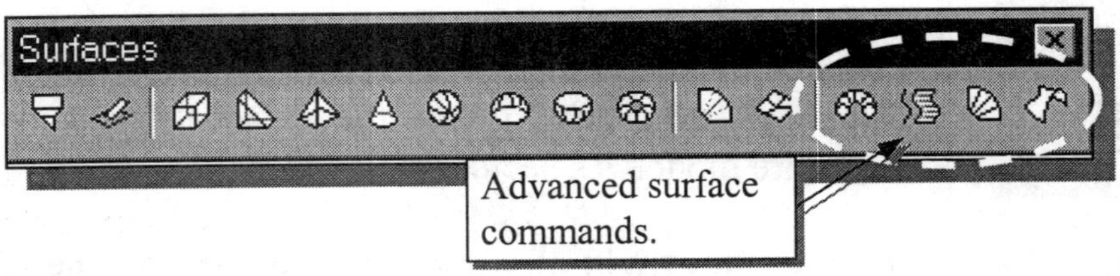

- **Revolved Surface**: Creates a surface mesh by rotating a group of objects about an axis.

- **Tabulated Surface**: Creates a surface mesh representing a general tabulated surface defined by a path curve and a direction vector. The resulting mesh is a series of parallel polygons running along a specified path.

- **Ruled Surface**: Creates a surface mesh between two objects.

- **Edge Surface**: Creates a surface patch mesh from four edges.

Note that there are two AutoCAD system variables used to control the results of the *Ruled Surface* and *Tabulated Surface* commands: **SurfTab1 & SurfTab2.**

SurfTab1 & SurfTab2 system variables: These two variables are used to set the number of increments used by the *Ruled Surface* and *Tabulated Surface* commands. The default values are set to six, which means any curve will be approximated with six straight lines.

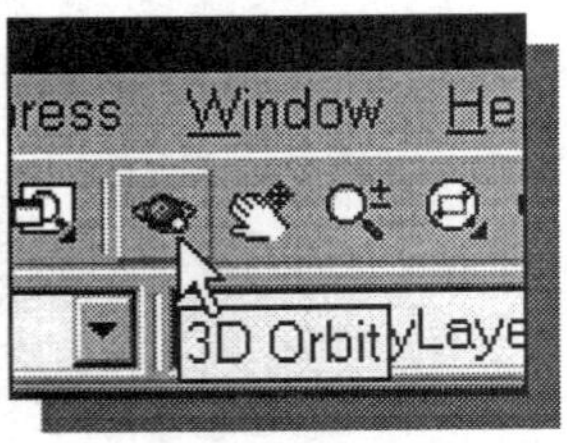

1. Click on the ***3D Orbit*** icon in the *Standard* toolbar.

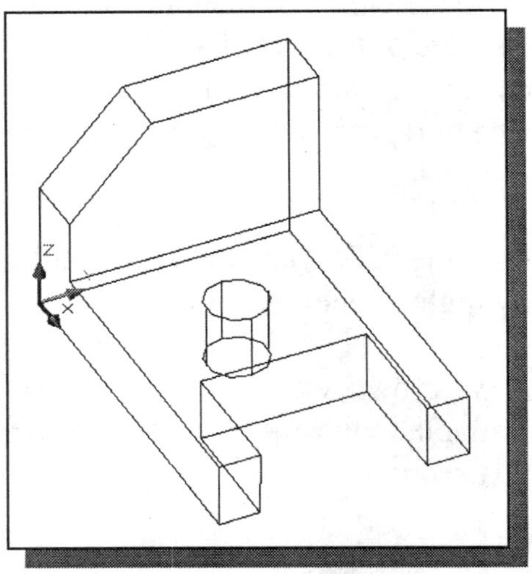

2. On your own, adjust the display of the wireframe model so that the four vertical lines connecting the two circles are visible as shown.

- We will split the top circle into two arcs to illustrate the use of the *Ruled Surface* and *Tabulated Surface* commands.

3. Select ***Break*** in the *Modify* toolbar.

- The *BREAK* command can be used to erase parts of objects or split an object in two. Note that we can only erase parts of a circle. We will therefore erase a portion of the circle and then split the circle into two arcs.

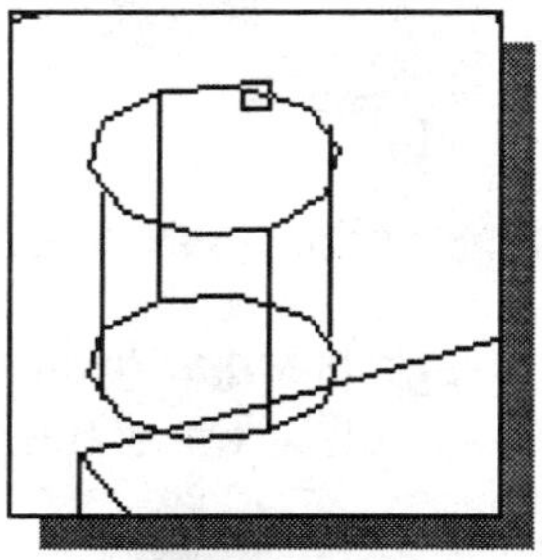

4. Select the top circle as shown. Note that the selected portion will be erased.

- By default, AutoCAD treats the selection point as the first break point. We can override the first point by choosing **First point** in the option menu.

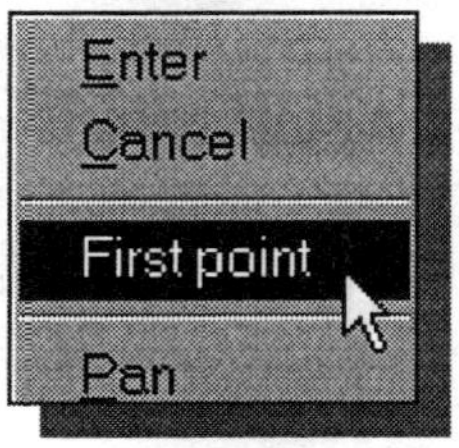

5. In the command prompt area, the message *"Specific second break point or [First point]:"* is displayed. Right-mouse-click once and select **First point** in the option menu.

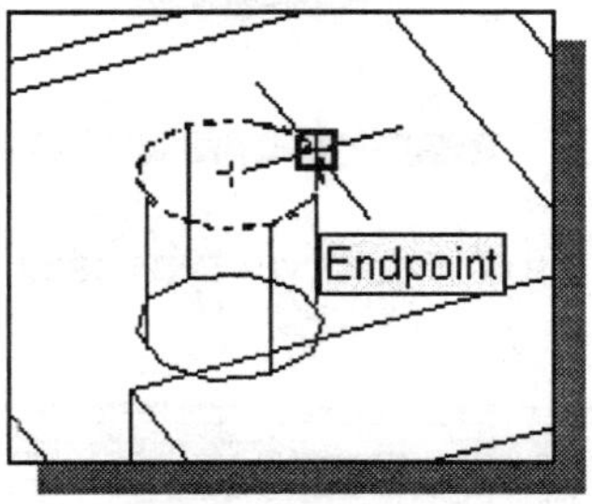

6. In the command prompt area, the message *"Specific first break point:"* is displayed. Choose the top endpoint of the vertical line as shown.

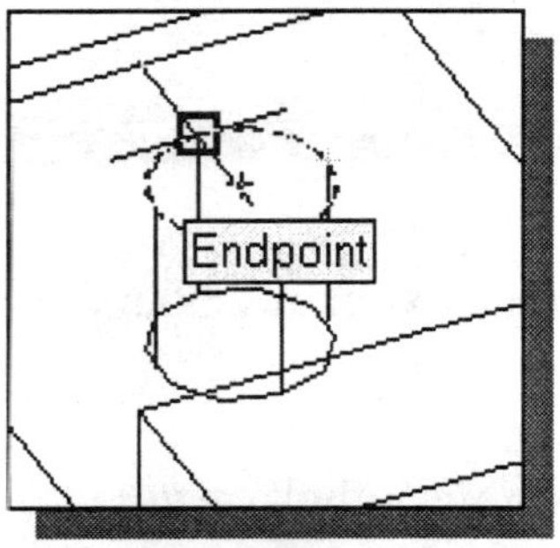

7. In the command prompt area, the message *"Specific second break point:"* is displayed. Choose the top endpoint of the vertical line as shown.

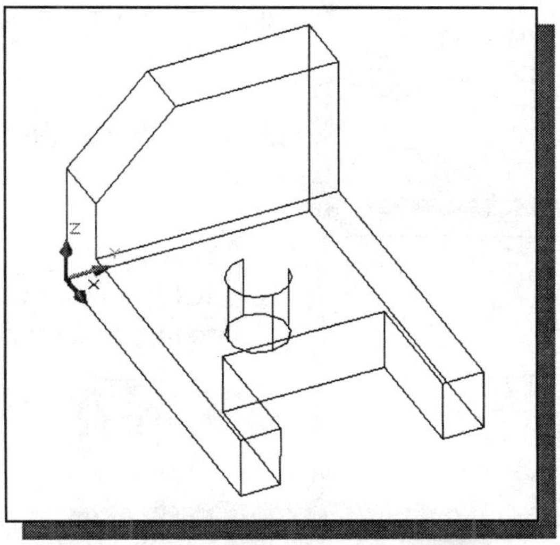

- One quarter of the circle has been erased. We will next split the circle into two arcs using the ***BREAK*** command.

8. Select *Break* in the *Modify* toolbar.

9. Select the top circle as shown. Note that the selected portion will be erased.

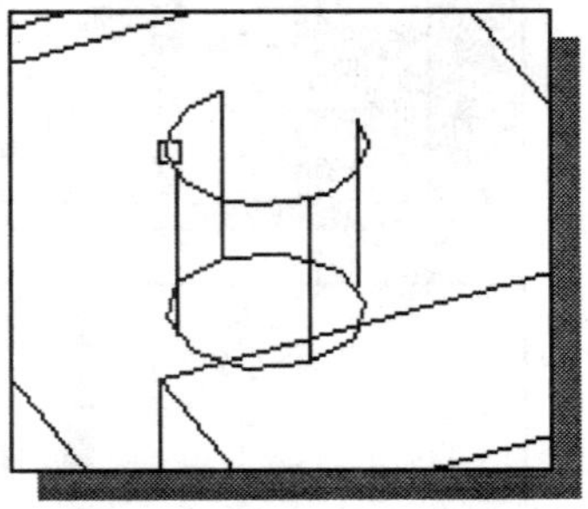

- By default, AutoCAD treats the selection point as the first break point. We can override the first point by choosing **First point** in the option menu.

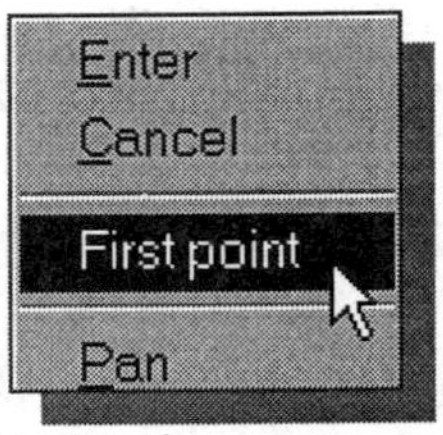

10. In the command prompt area, the message *"Specific second break point or [First point]:"* is displayed. Right-mouse-click once and select **First point** in the option menu.

11. In the command prompt area, the message *"Specific first break point:"* is displayed. Choose the top endpoint of the vertical line as shown.

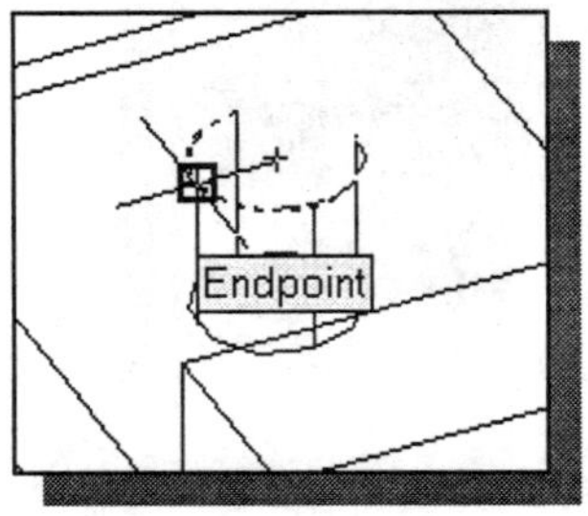

12. In the command prompt area, the message *"Specific second break point:"* is displayed. To split an object, choose the same endpoint that was chosen as the first endpoint.

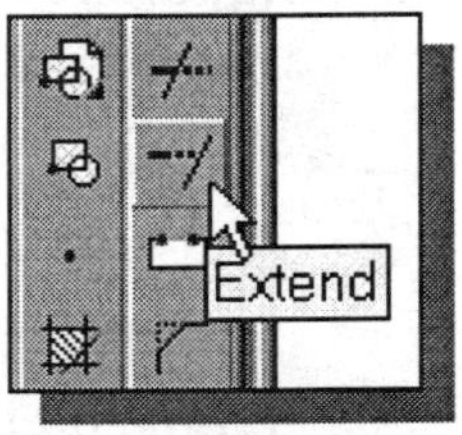

13. Select ***Extend*** in the *Modify* toolbar. Note the *Projection* type is set to *View*, as shown in the prompt window.

```
Current settings: Projection=View, Edge=None
Select boundary edges ...
Select objects:
```

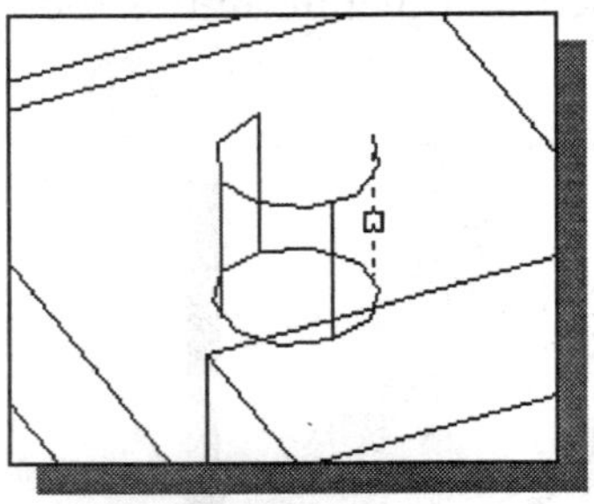

14. Select the right vertical edge to be the extending boundary as shown.

15. Inside the graphics window, right-mouse-click once to accept the selection.

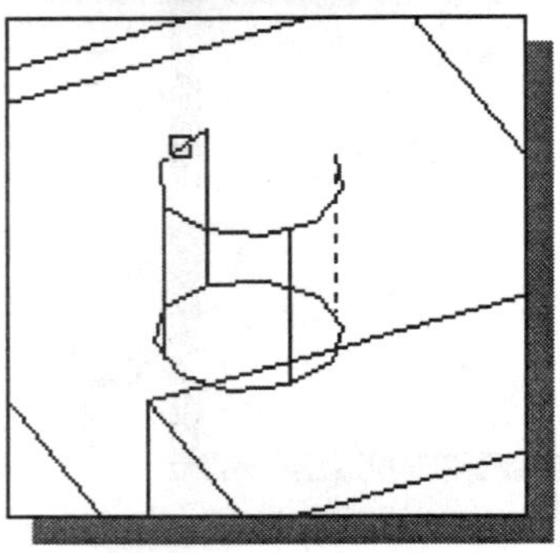

16. Pick the shorter arc near the right endpoint to extend the arc in that direction.

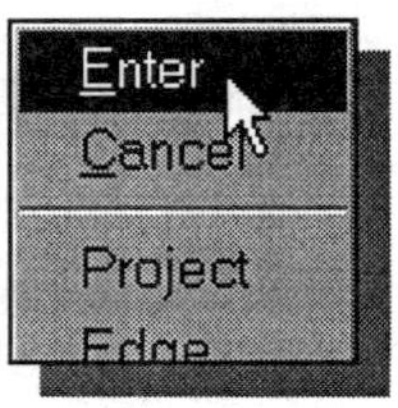

17. Inside the graphics window, right-mouse-click once to display the option menu and select **Enter** to end the *EXTEND* command.

Using the *Tabulated Surface* option

- In AutoCAD, the *TABSURF* command allows us to construct a polygon mesh representing a general tabulated surface defined by a path curve and a direction vector.

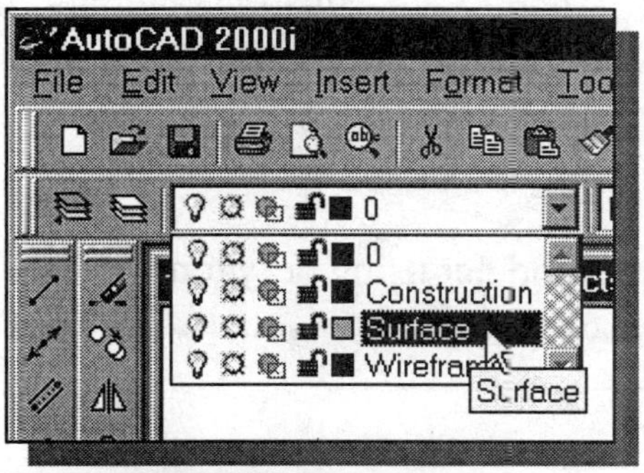

1. Set the ***Surface*** layer as the *Current layer* by choosing the layer name in the *Layer Control* box as shown.

- We will place the surface model on a different layer than the wireframe model.

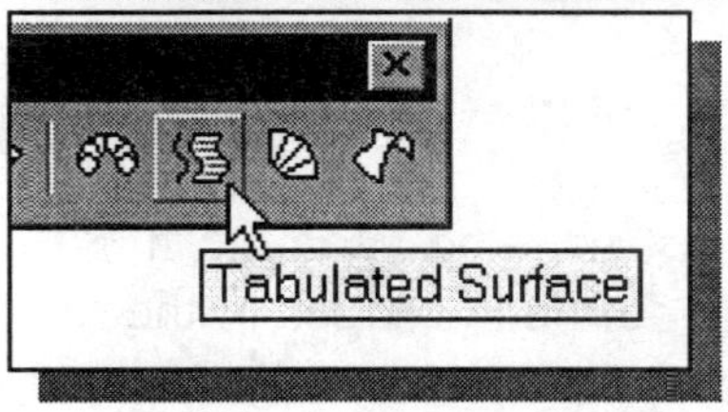

2. Pick ***Tabulated Surface*** in the *Surfaces* toolbar as shown.

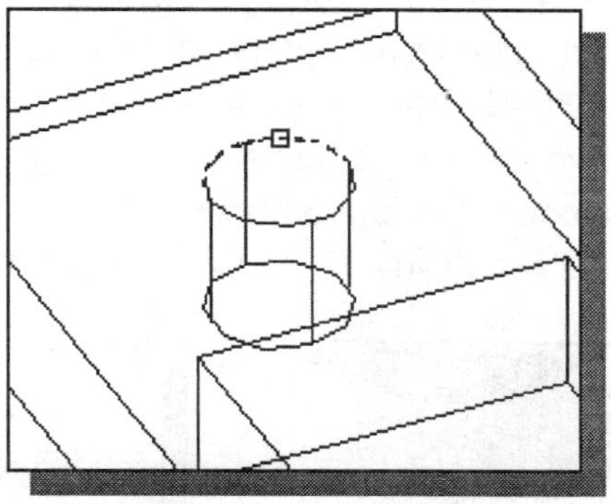

3. In the command prompt area, the message *"Select object for path curve:"* is displayed. Choose the upper arc as shown.

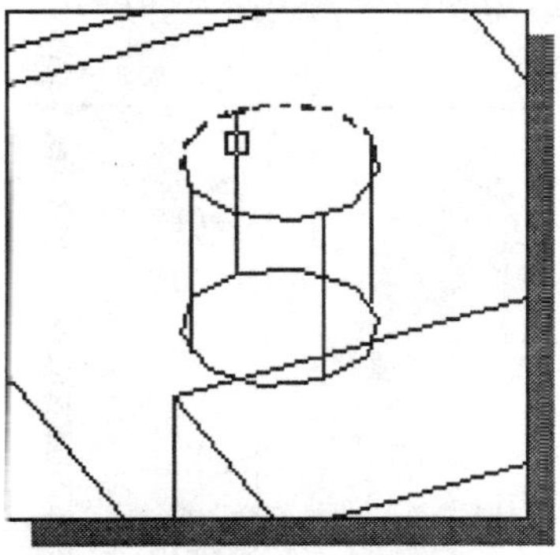

4. In the command prompt area, the message *"Select object for direction vector:"* is displayed. Choose the vertical line near the top endpoint as shown. Note that the endpoint of the line is used as a reference point to determine the direction of the polygon mesh.

5. On your own, use the ***ORBIT*** and ***SHADED*** commands to examine the constructed polygons.

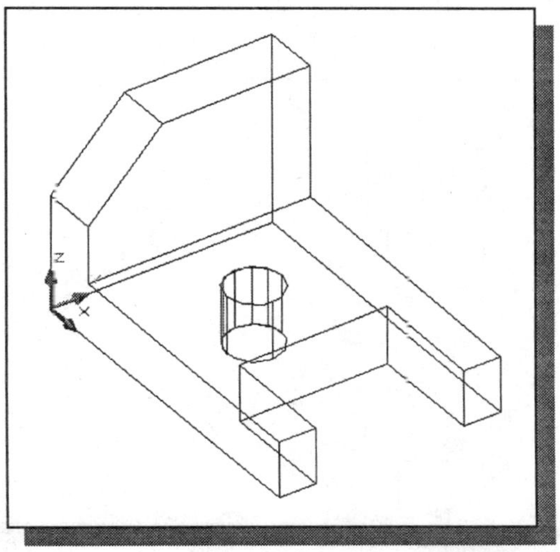

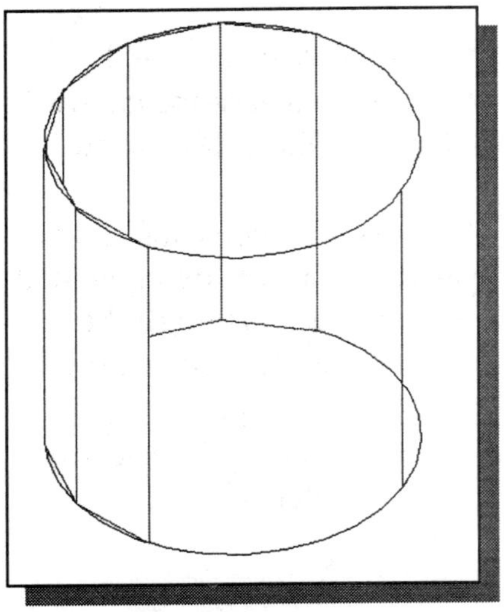

- Exactly six polygons are created and positioned along the selected *path curve*, the upper arc, with the *TABULATED SURFACE* command. This is set by the **SurfTab1** variable. We can adjust number of segments to use by typing the word, **surftab1**, at the command prompt.

❖ Note that a surface modeler using polygons to approximate true curves is called a *faceted surface modeler*.

Using the *Ruled Surface* option

- In AutoCAD, the *RULESURF* command allows us to construct a polygon mesh between two objects. We can use two different objects to define the edges of the ruled surface: lines, points, arcs, circles, ellipses, elliptical arcs, polylines, or splines. The two objects to be used as the *rails* of a ruled surface mesh must both be either open or closed. For open curves, AutoCAD starts construction of the ruled surface based on the locations of the specified points on the curves.

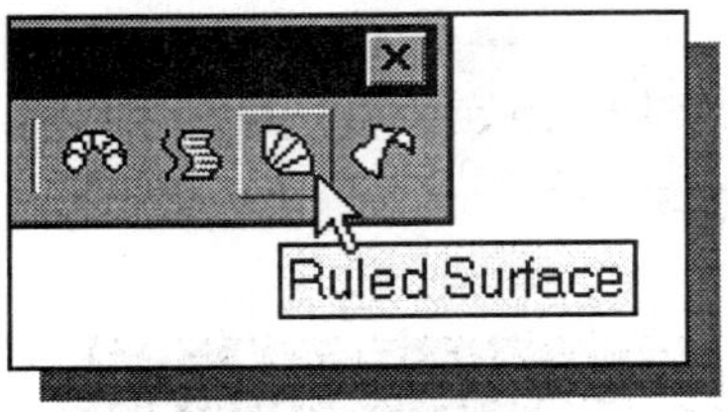

1. Pick ***Ruled Surface*** in the *Surfaces* toolbar as shown.

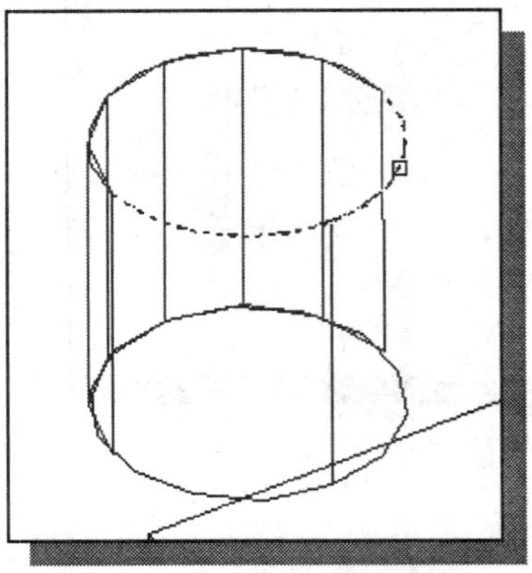

2. In the command prompt area, the message *"Select first defining curve:"* is displayed. Choose the lower arc by clicking on the right side as shown.

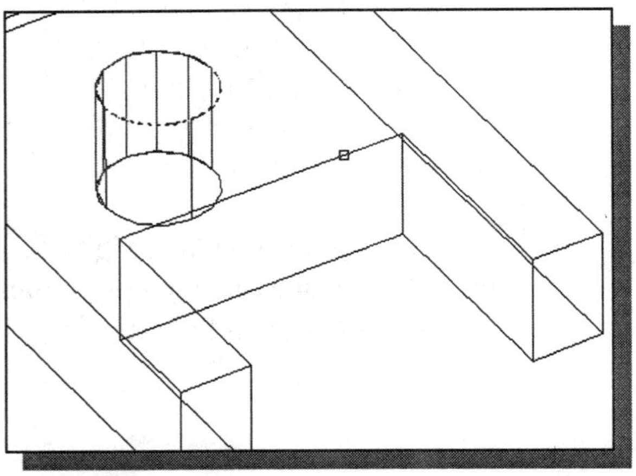

3. In the command prompt area, the message *"Select second defining curve:"* is displayed. Choose the inside straight edge on the right side as shown.

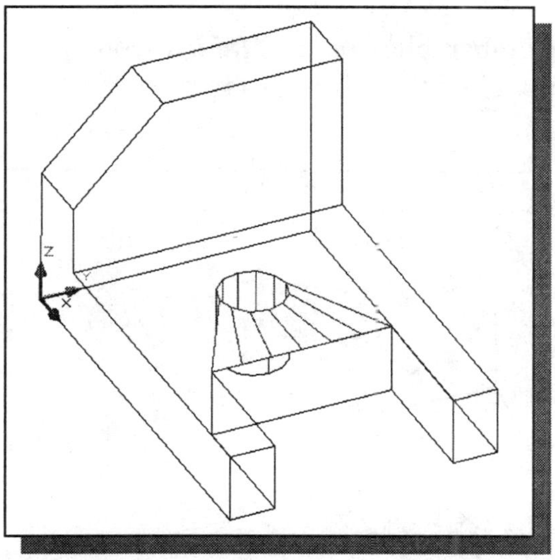

❖ Exactly six polygons are created and positioned along the two *defining curves* with the *RULED SURFACE* command.

- Note that the created polygons are grouped together and all polygons are being treated as one object. To hide the edges of the polygons, it is necessary to separate the polygon into individual entities.

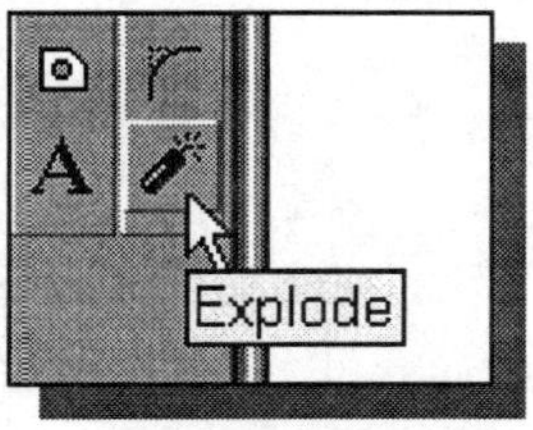

4. Select ***Explode*** in the *Modify* toolbar.

5. In the command prompt area, the message *"Select objects:"* is displayed. Select any edge of the ruled surface and notice that all six polygons are selected.

6. Inside the graphics window, right-mouse-click once to accept the selection and the polygons are separated into individual objects.

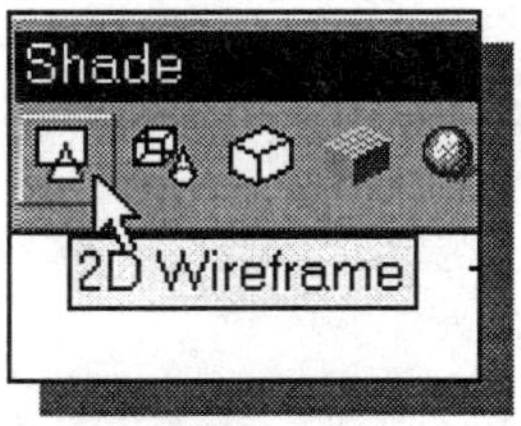

7. Select ***2D wireframe*** in the *Shade* toolbar to display the entities in wireframe mode.

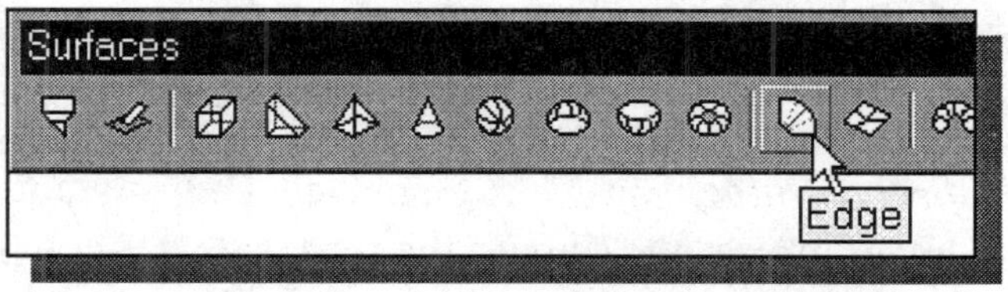

8. Select ***Edge***, with the left-mouse-button, in the *Surfaces* toolbar.

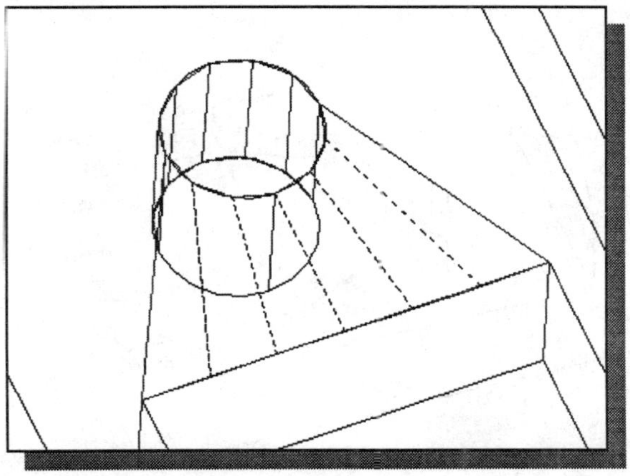

9. In the command prompt area, the message *"Specify edge of 3dface to toggle visibility or [Display]:"* is displayed. Pick the five edges inside the ruled surface as shown.

10. Inside the graphics window, **right-mouse-click** to activate the option menu and select **Enter** to end the *EDGE* command.

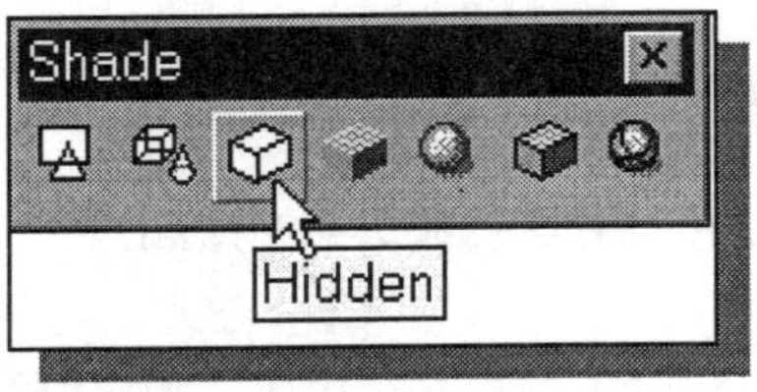

11. In the *Shade* toolbar, click on the ***Hidden*** icon to display the model with hidden lines removed.

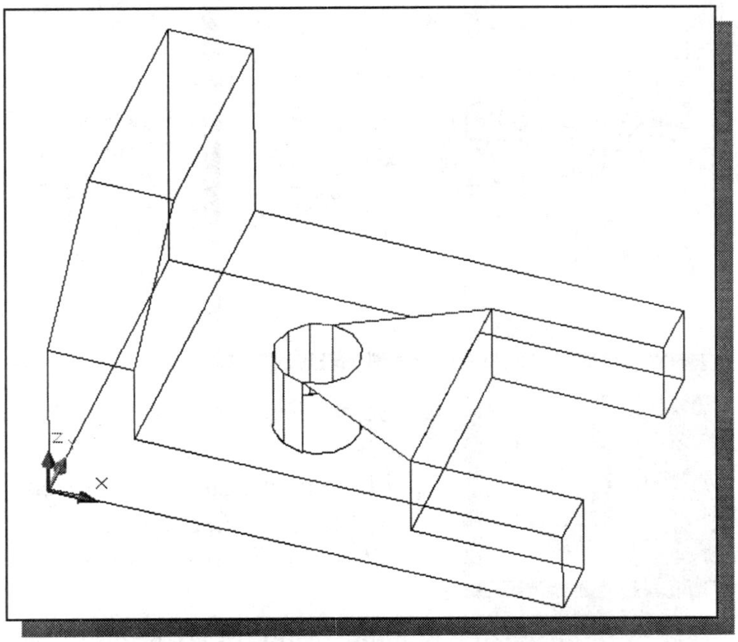

- The selected edges are removed from the display so that the face of the ruled surface appears to be more realistic.

12. On your own, repeat the above steps and create another ruled surface as shown. (Hint: Use the *Realtime Zoom* function to assist the selection of the arc.)

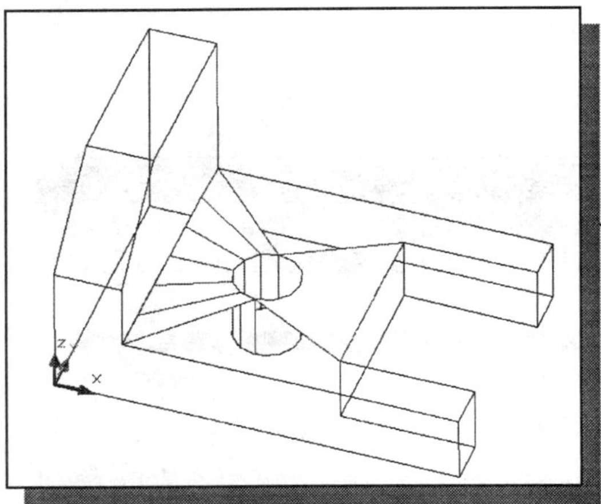

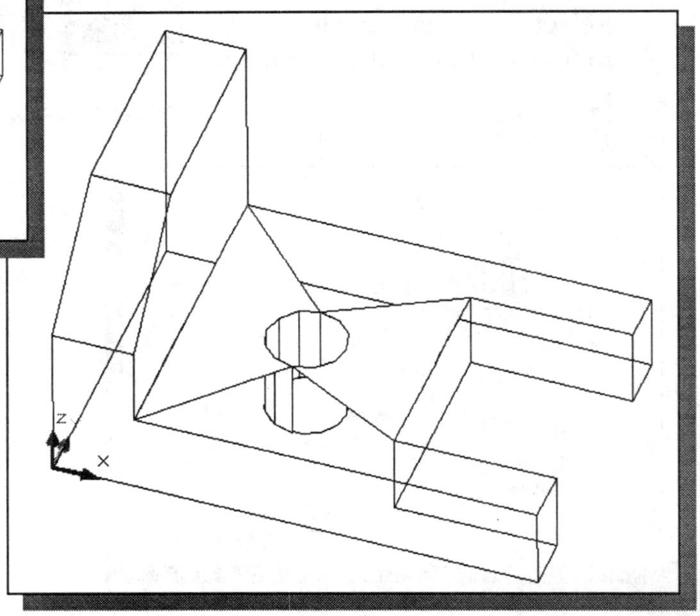

13. On your own, use the *Ruled Surface* option to create a polygon mesh for the other arc on the top surface. What is required to perform such an operation?

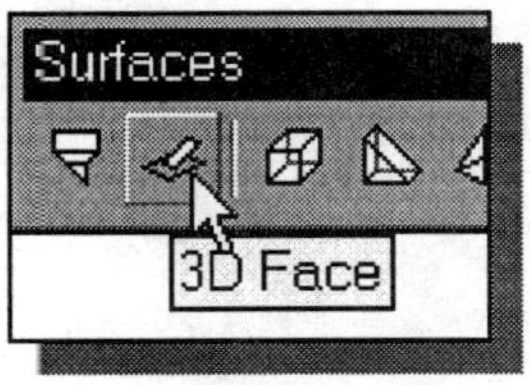

14. Select the ***3D Face*** in the *Surface* toolbar.

- On your own, complete the surface model as shown.

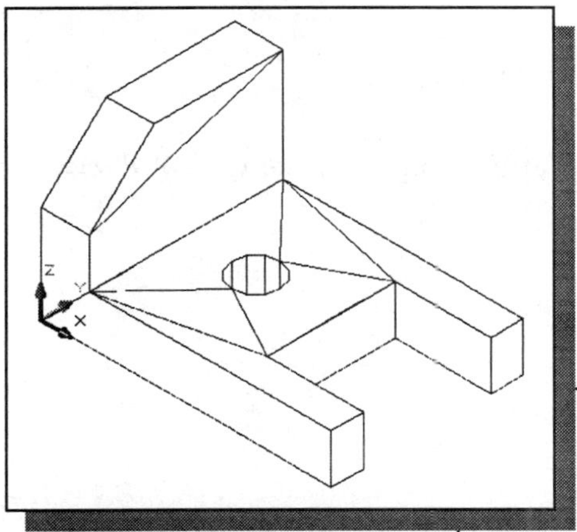

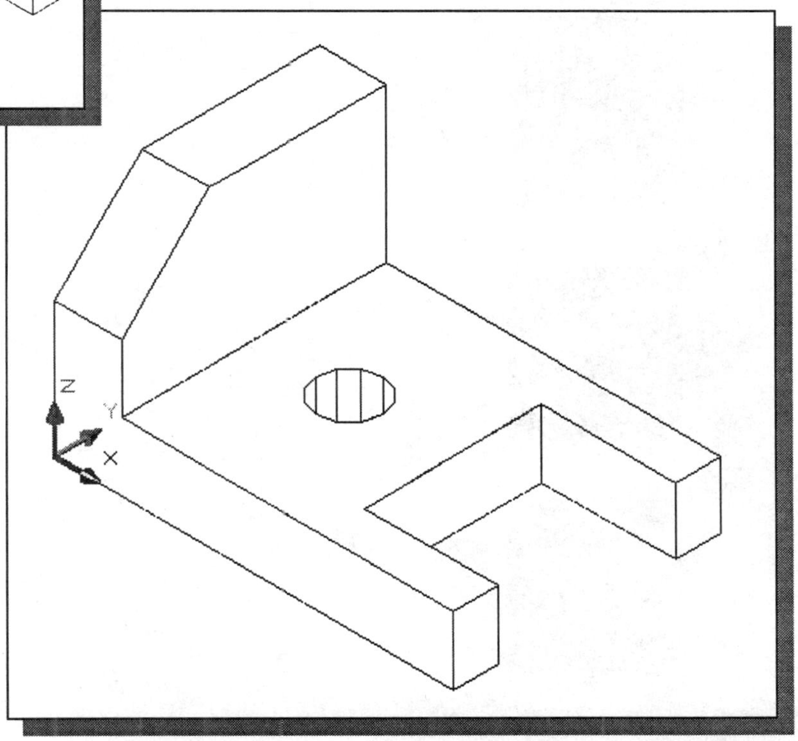

Questions:

1. List and describe three differences between *Wireframe models* and *Surface models*?

2. List and describe the three types of surfaces available in AutoCAD.

3. List and describe two different Shading options in AutoCAD.

4. What is the difference between the *2D solid* and *3D Face commands* in AutoCAD?

5. List and describe two predefined surface models in AutoCAD.

6. What is the difference between *Tabulated Surface* and *Ruled Surface* in AutoCAD?

7. Identify and describe the following commands:

a)

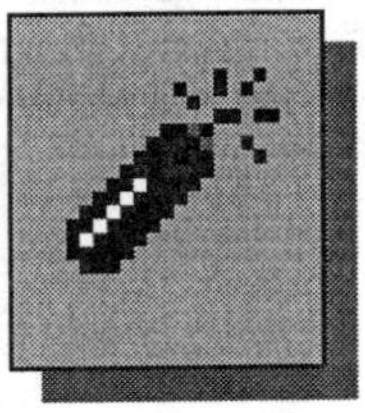

Explode

b)

3D Face

c)

Ruled Surface

d)

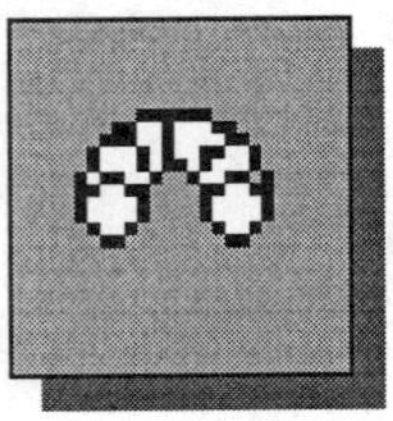

Revolved Surface

Exercises: All dimensions are in inches.

1.

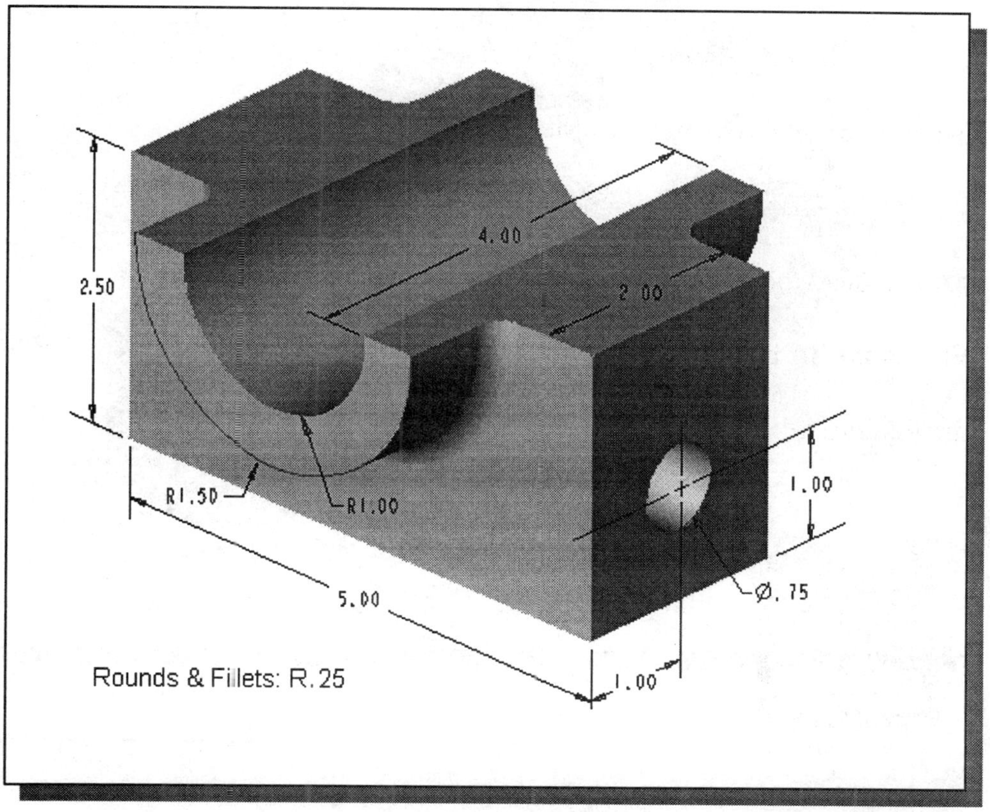

2.

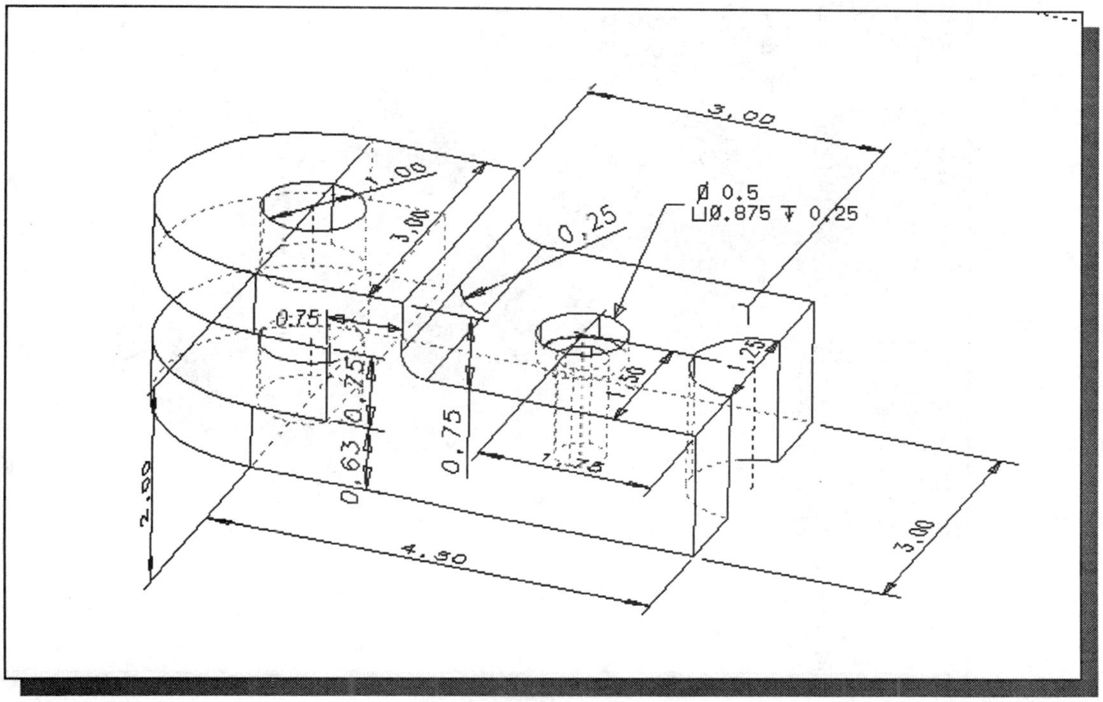

3.

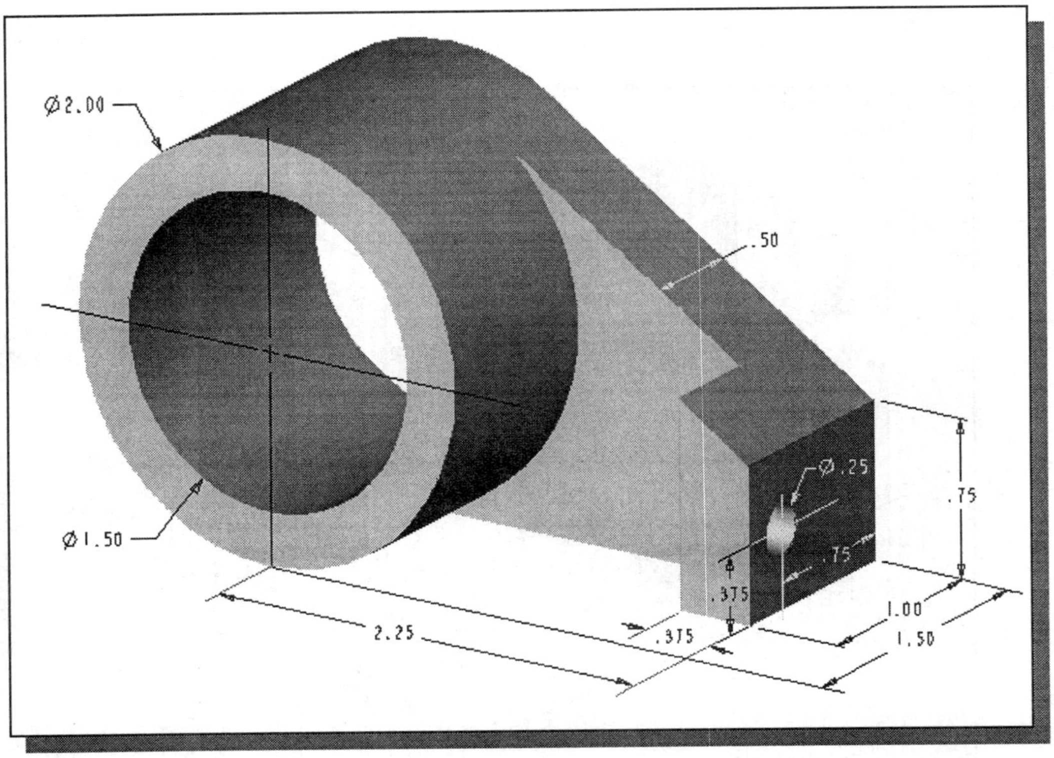
Ø2.00
.50
Ø.25
.75
Ø1.50
.75
.375
1.00
2.25
.375
1.50

4.

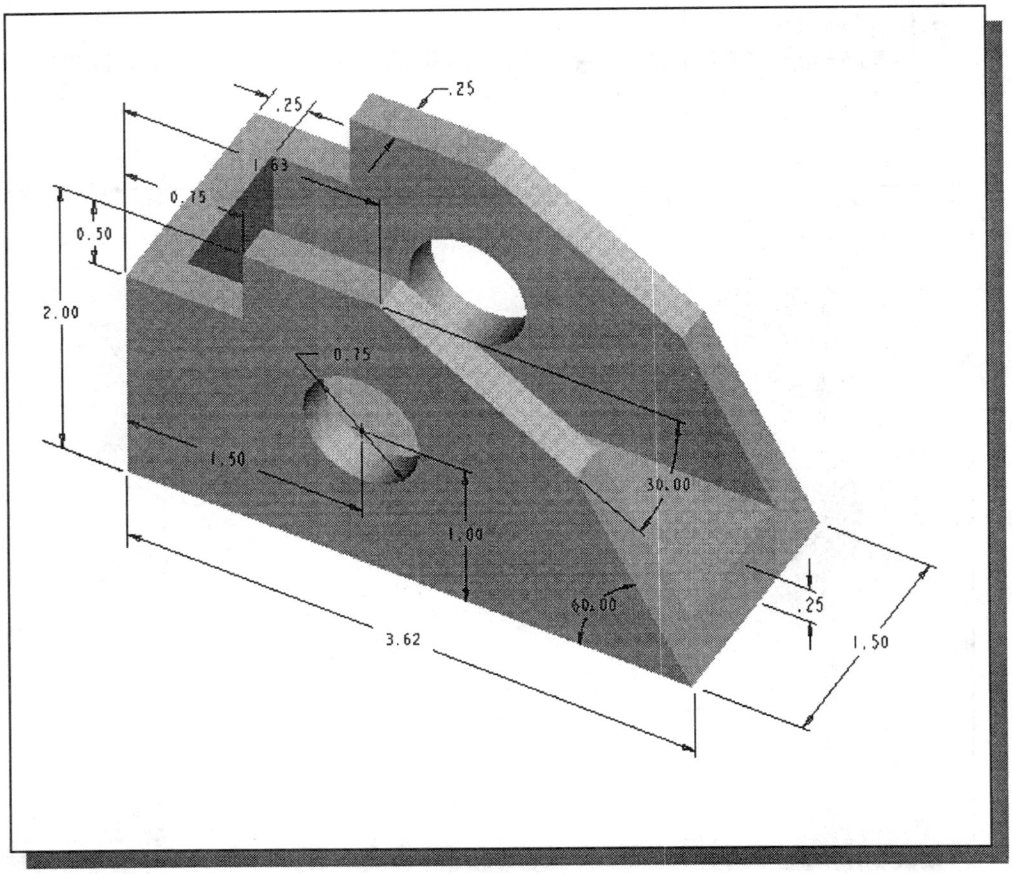
.25
.25
1.63
0.75
0.50
2.00
0.75
1.50
30.00
1.00
.25
60.00
3.62
1.50

Chapter 6
Solid Modeling - Constructive Solid Geometry

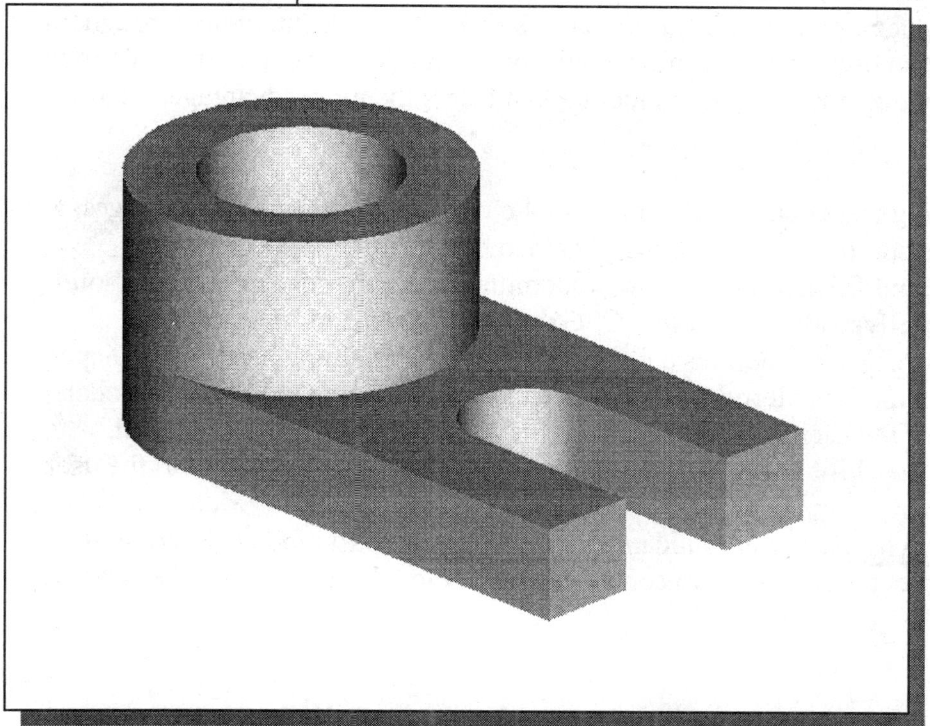

Learning Objectives

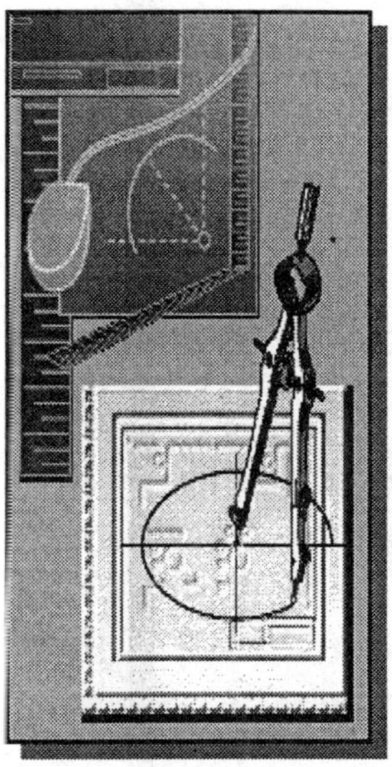

- Understand the Constructive Solid Geometry Concept.
- Create a Binary Tree.
- Understand the basic Boolean Operations.
- Create Solids using AutoCAD Primitive Solids.
- Generate Shaded SOLID images.
- Use the Dynamic Rotation – 3D Orbit command.

Introduction

In the previous chapters, we have looked at wireframe modeling and surface modeling. Wireframe modeling describes only the corners and edges of designs. Surface modeling describes part surfaces but not interiors. Although surface models are fairly good representations of the actual designs. Designers are still required to interactively examine surface models to insure that the various surfaces on a model are contiguous throughout. Many of the concepts used in 3D wireframe and surface modelers are incorporated in the solid modeling scheme, but it is solid modeling that offers the most advantages as a design tool.

In the solid modeling presentation scheme, the solid definitions include nodes, edges, and surfaces, and it is a complete and unambiguous mathematical representation of a precisely enclosed and filled volume. Two predominant methods for representing solid models are **constructive solid geometry** (CSG) representation and **boundary representation** (B-rep). CSG defines a model in terms of combining basic solid shapes and B-rep defines a model in terms of its edges and surfaces. AutoCAD's solid modeler is a hybrid modeler; the user interface and construction techniques are CSG-based, whereas the B-rep capabilities are invoked automatically and are transparent to the user.

In this chapter, we will discuss the fundamental concepts of solid modeling. We will demonstrate the procedure required to construct a solid model using AutoCAD's CSG-based user interface.

The *Guide-Block* Design

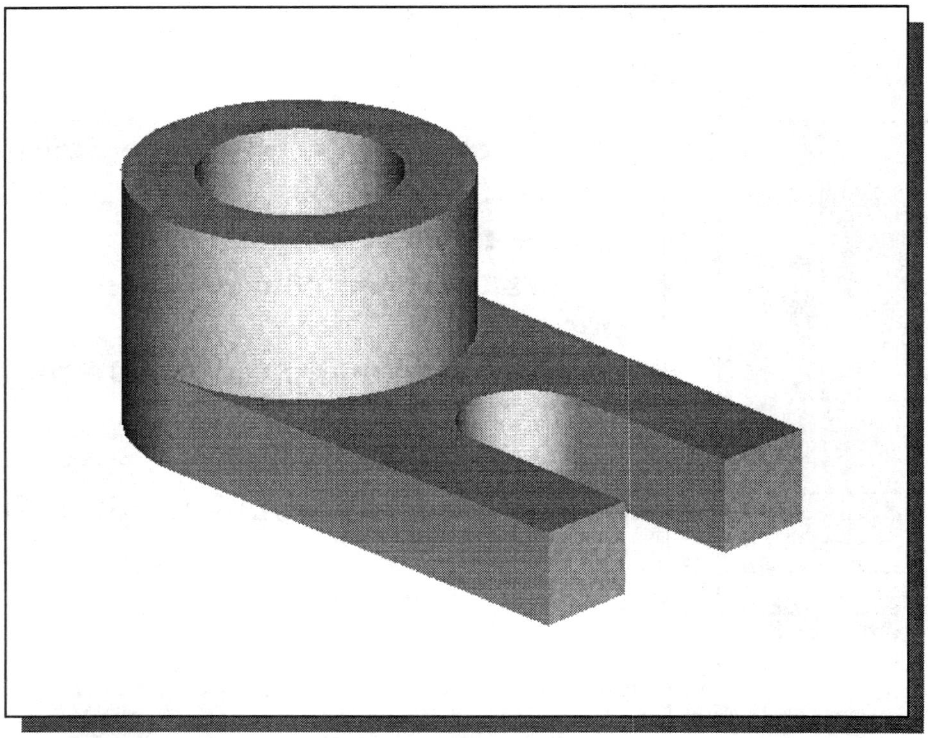

Constructive Solid Geometry concept

In the 1980s, one of the main advancements in **Solid Modeling** was the development of the **Constructive Solid Geometry** (CSG) method. CSG describes the solid model as the combination of basic three-dimensional shapes (**primitive solids**). The basic primitive solid set typically includes: Rectangular-prism (Block), Cylinder, Cone, Sphere, and Torus (Donut). Two solid objects can be combined into one object in various ways, these operations are known as **Boolean operations**. There are three basic Boolean operations: **UNION (Join), SUBTRACT (Cut),** and **INTERSECT**. The UNION operation combines the two volumes included in the different solids into a single solid. The SUBTRACT operation subtracts the volume of one solid object from the other solid object. The INTERSECT operation keeps only the volume common to both solid objects. The CSG method is also known as the **Machinist's Approach**, as the method is parallel to machine shop practices.

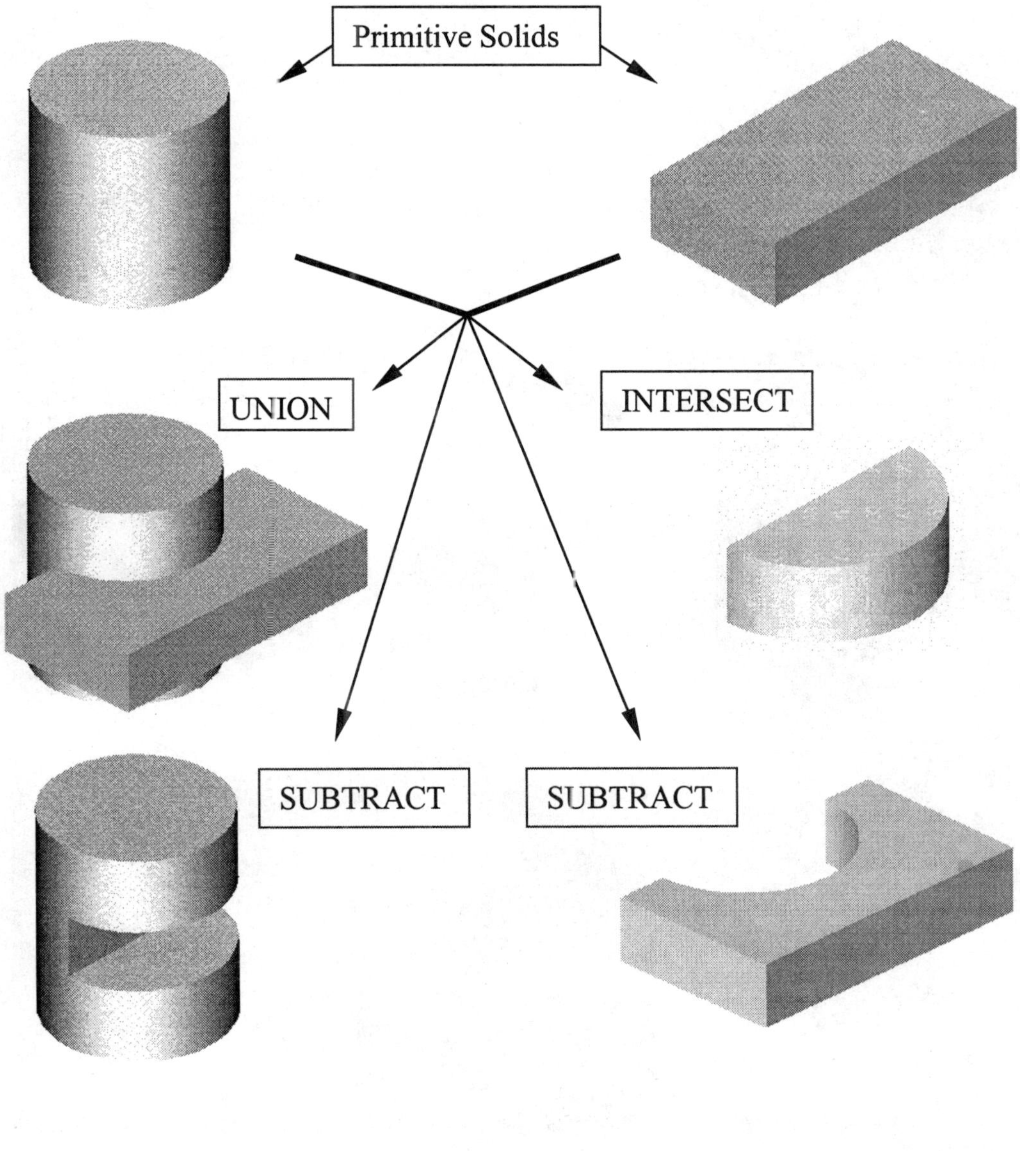

Binary Tree

CSG is also referred to as the method used to store a solid model in the database. The resulting solid can be easily represented by what is called a **binary tree**. In a binary tree, the terminal branches (leaves) are the various primitives that are linked together to make the final solid object (the root). The binary tree is an effective way to represent the steps required to construct the solid model. Complicated solid models can be modeled by considering the different combinations of Boolean operations required in the binary tree. This provides a convenient and intuitive way of modeling that imitates the manufacturing process. A binary tree is an effective way to plan your modeling strategy before you start creating anything.

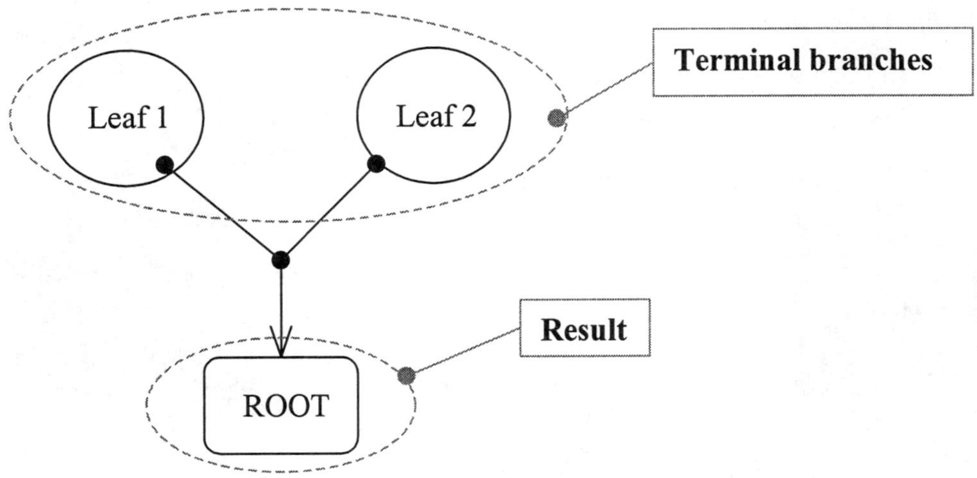

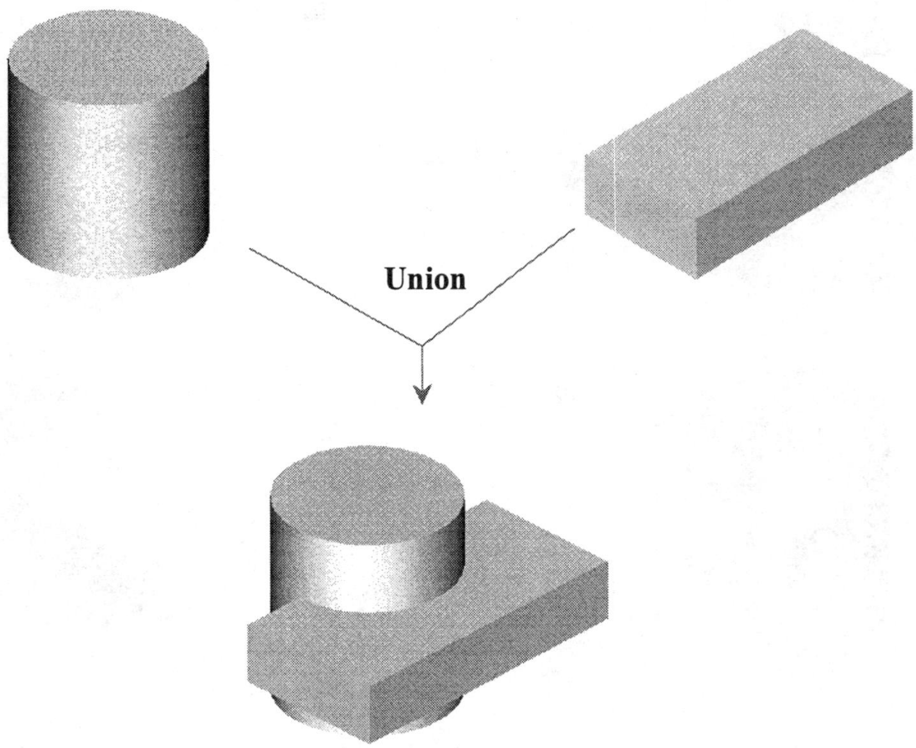

The *Guide-Block* CSG Binary Tree

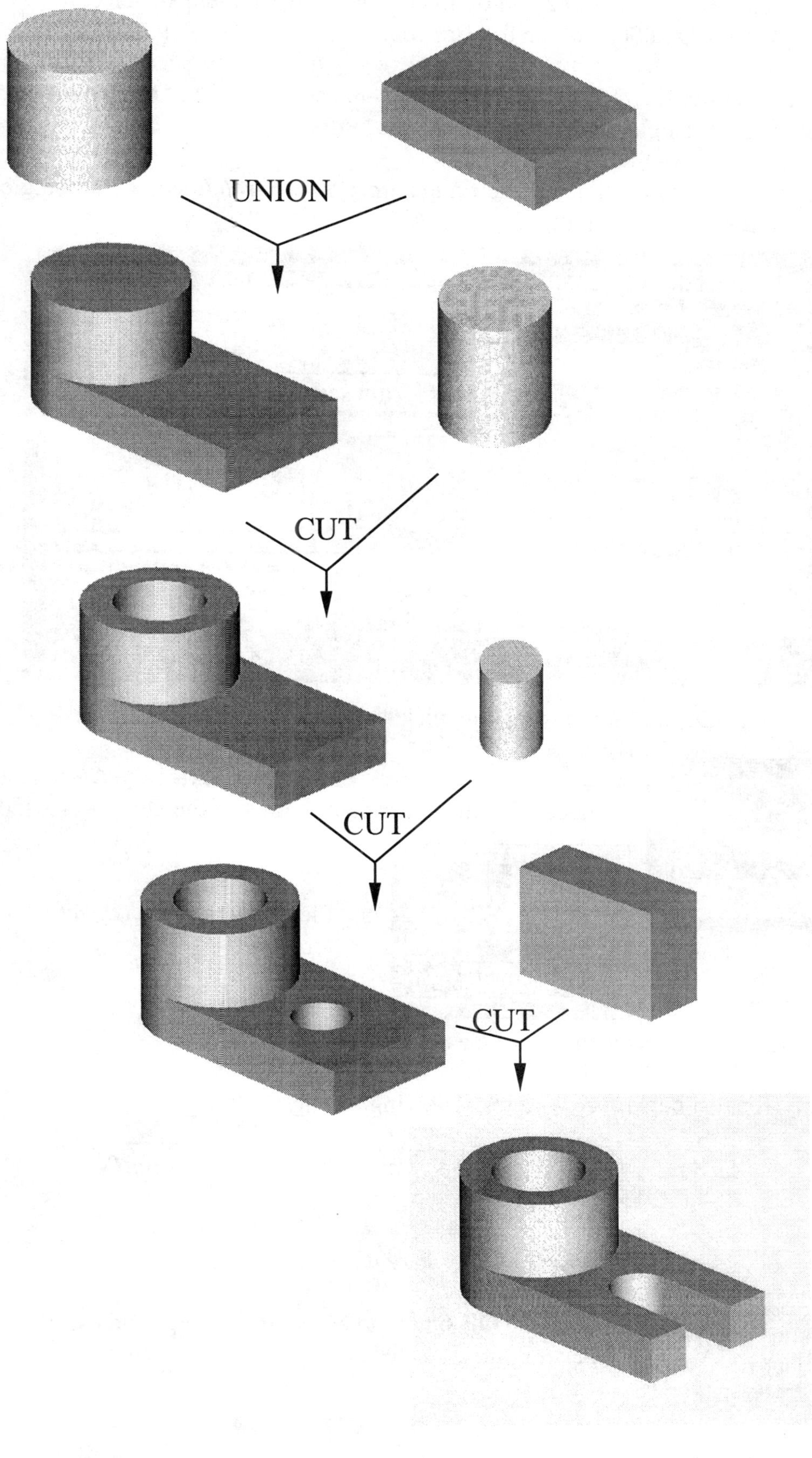

Starting Up AutoCAD 2000i

1. Select the AutoCAD 2000i option on the *Program* menu or select the AutoCAD 2000i icon on the *Desktop*.

2. In the *AutoCAD Today* startup dialog box, select the **Create Drawings** tab with the single click of the left-mouse-button.

3. In the startup dialog box, select the ***Start from Scratch*** icon with a single click of the left-mouse-button.

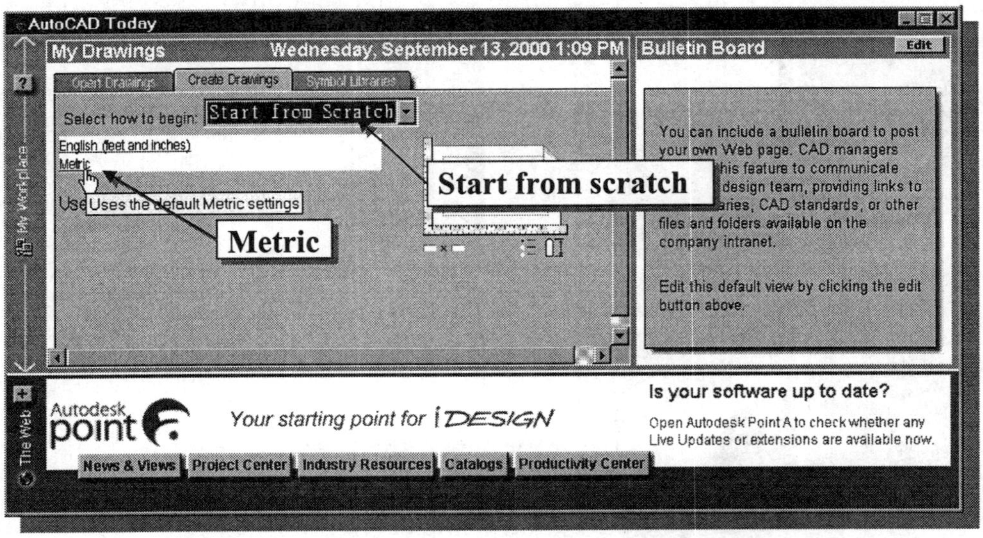

4. In the *Default Settings* section, pick **Metric** as the drawing units.

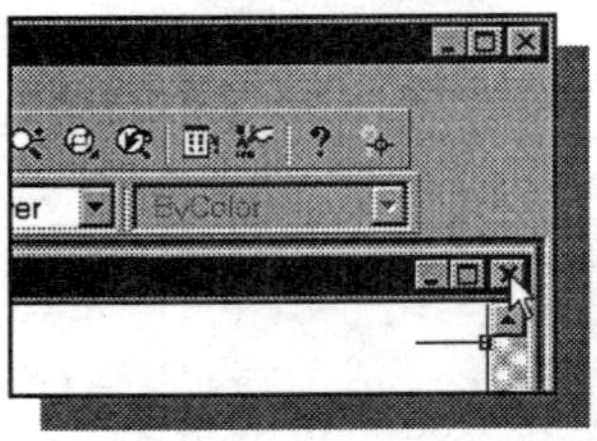

5. Close the *Drawing1* window by clicking the ***Close*** icon located at the upper-right-corner of the *Drawing1* window.

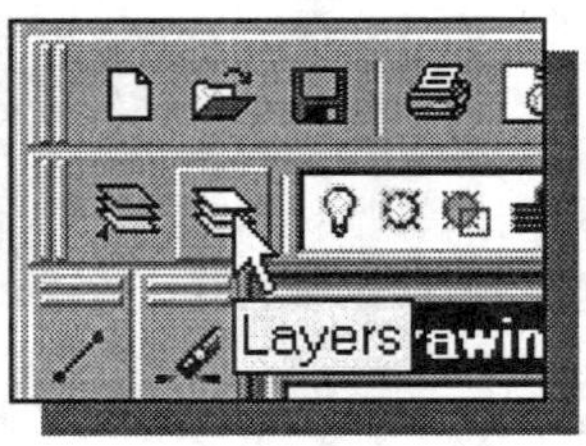

6. Pick ***Layers*** in the *Object Properties* toolbar.

7. Click the ***New*** icon to create a new layer.

8. Create a **new layer** with the following settings:

Layer	***Color***	***LineType***
Solid_Objects	**Cyan**	**Continuous**

9. Set layer ***Solid_Objects*** as the *Current layer*.

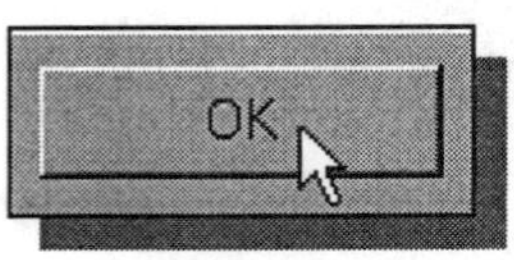

10. Click on the **OK** button to accept the settings and exit the *Layer Properties Manager* dialog box.

Creating the first 3D object

1. In the *Status Bar* area, reset the option buttons so that only *POLAR, OSNAP, OTRACK*, and *MODEL* are switched ***ON***.

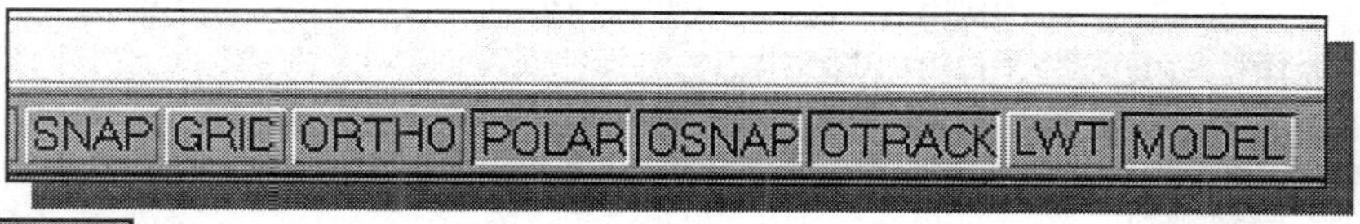

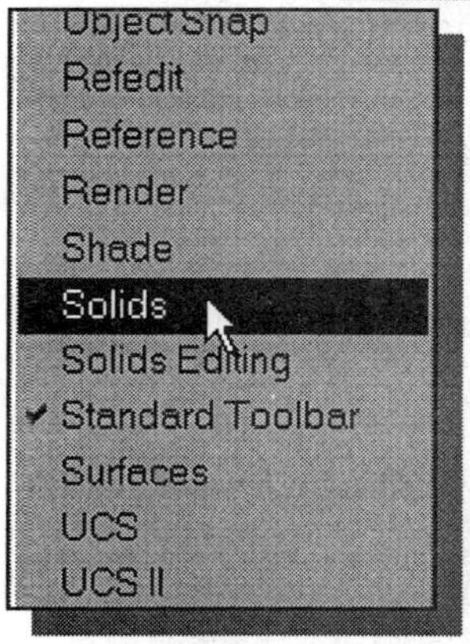

2. Move the cursor to the *Standard* toolbar area and **right-click** on any icon of the *Standard* toolbar to display a list of toolbar menu groups.

3. Select ***Solids***, with the left-mouse-button, to display the *Solids* toolbar on the screen.

➢ The first section of the *Solids* toolbar contains the basic set of solids available in AutoCAD 2000i.

- We will first create a **75 x 50 x 15** rectangular block.

4. In the *Solids* toolbar, click on the ***Box*** icon. In the command prompt area, the message *"Specify corner of box or [Ccenter] <0,0,0>:"* is displayed.

5. Pick a location that is near the lower-left corner of the graphics window.

6. In the command prompt area, the message *"Specify corner or [Cube/Length]:"* is displayed. Enter: **@75,50 [ENTER]**.

7. In the command prompt area, the message *"Specify Height:"* is displayed. Enter: **15 [ENTER]**.

Viewing the 3D block

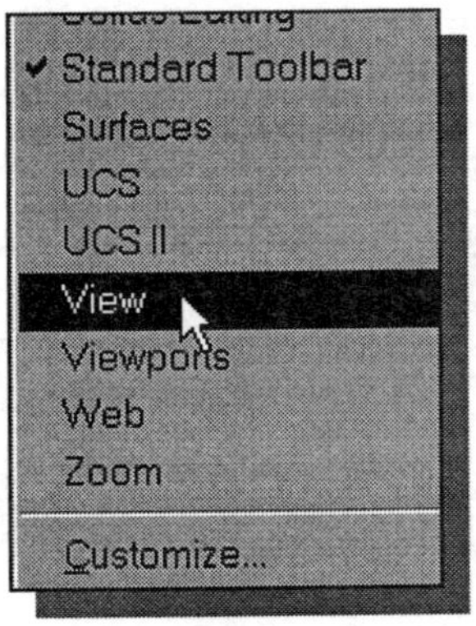

1. Move the cursor to the *Standard* toolbar area and **right-click** on any icon of the *Standard* toolbar to display a list of toolbar menu groups.

2. Select ***View***, with the left-mouse-button, to display the *View* toolbar on the screen.

➢ The *View* toolbar contains two sections of icons that allow us to quickly switch to standard 2D and 3D views.

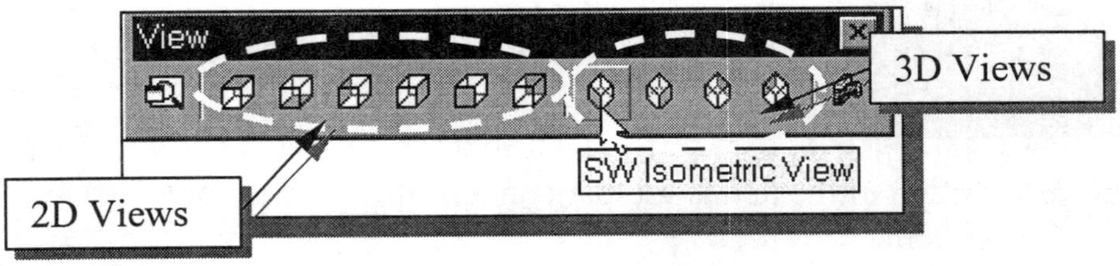

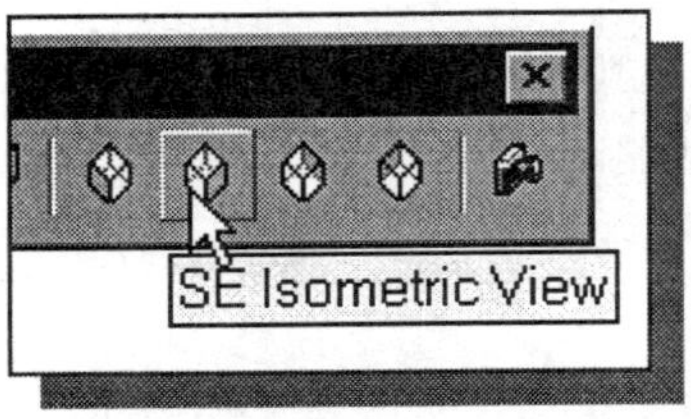

3. In the *View* toolbar, click on the ***SE Isometric View*** icon.

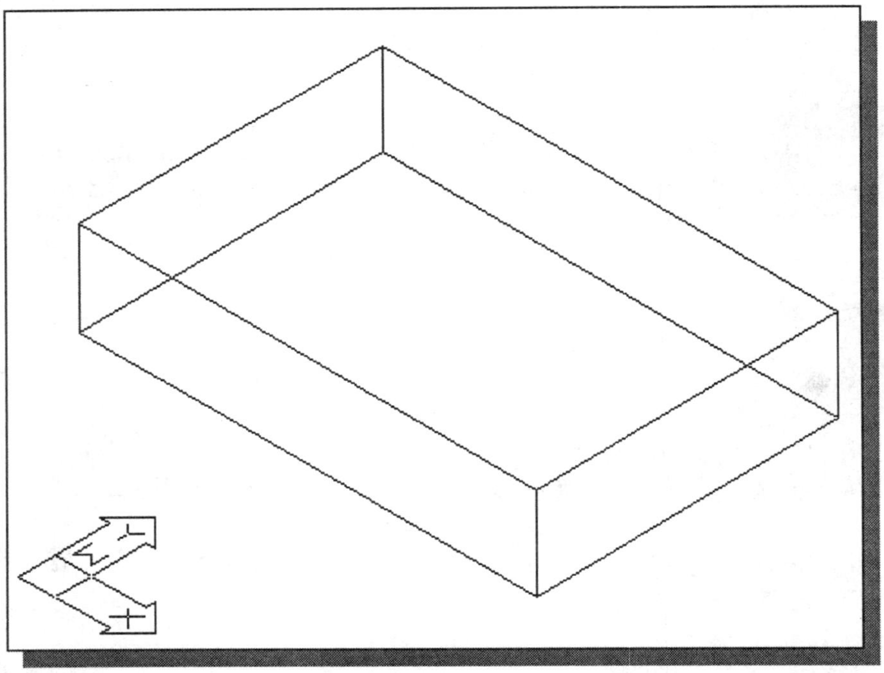

Creating the second solid feature

- We will next create a cylinder block as the second solid feature.

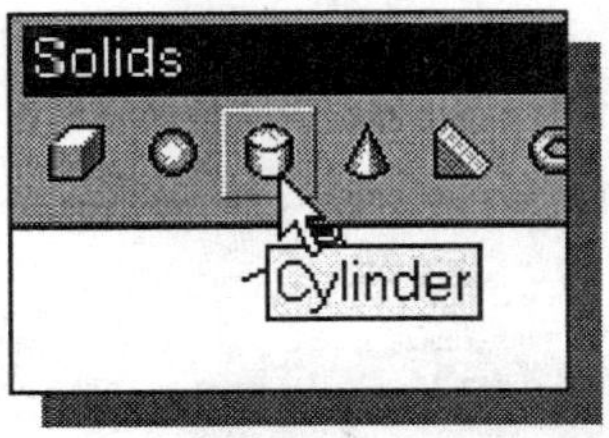

1. In the *Solids* toolbar, click on the ***Cylinder*** icon. In the command prompt area, the message *"Specify center point for base cylinder or [Elliptical] <0,0,0>:"* is displayed.

2. Inside the graphics window, press down the **[SHIFT]** key and **right-mouse-click** once to bring up the *Object Snap* shortcut menu.

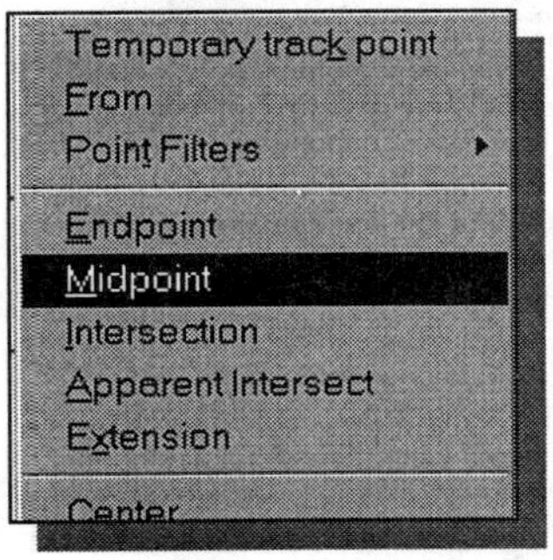

3. Select the **Midpoint** option in the shortcut menu. Snap to and select the midpoint of the left-bottom edge of the rectangular block as shown.

4. In the command prompt area, the message *"Specify radius for base of cylinder or [Diameter]:"* is displayed. Snap to and select one of the endpoints of the bottom edge of the rectangular block.

5. In the command prompt area, the message *"Specify height of cylinder or [Center of other end]:"* is displayed. Enter: **40 [ENTER]**.

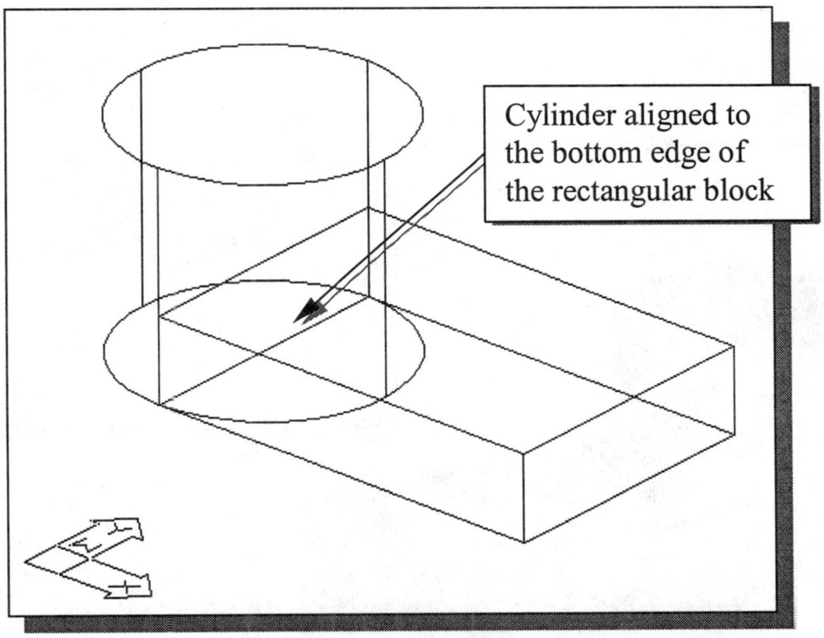

- Two solid objects, one rectangular box and one cylinder, are displayed on the screen.

Boolean operation - *UNION*

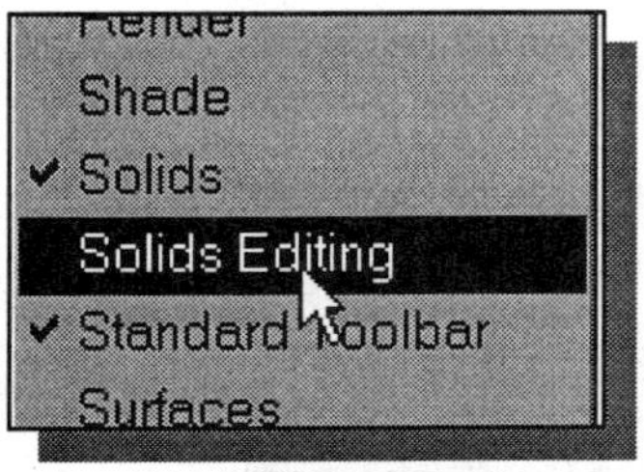

1. Move the cursor to the *Standard* toolbar area and **right-click** on any icon of the *Standard* toolbar to display a list of toolbar menu groups.

2. Select ***Solids Editing***, with the left-mouse-button, to display the *Solids Editing* toolbar on the screen.

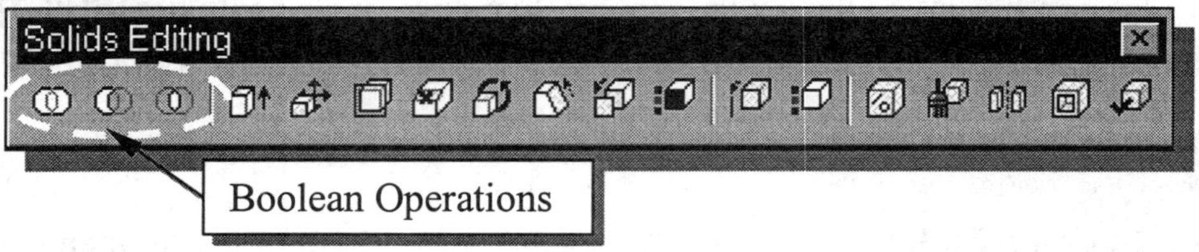

➢ The first section of the *Solids Editing* toolbar contains the basic set of Boolean operation icons.

3. In the *Solids Editing* toolbar, click on the ***Union*** icon. In the command prompt area, the message *"Select Objects:"* is displayed.

4. Pick both solids by clicking on their edges.

5. Inside the graphics window, **right-mouse-click** to accept the selection and proceed with the *UNION* command.

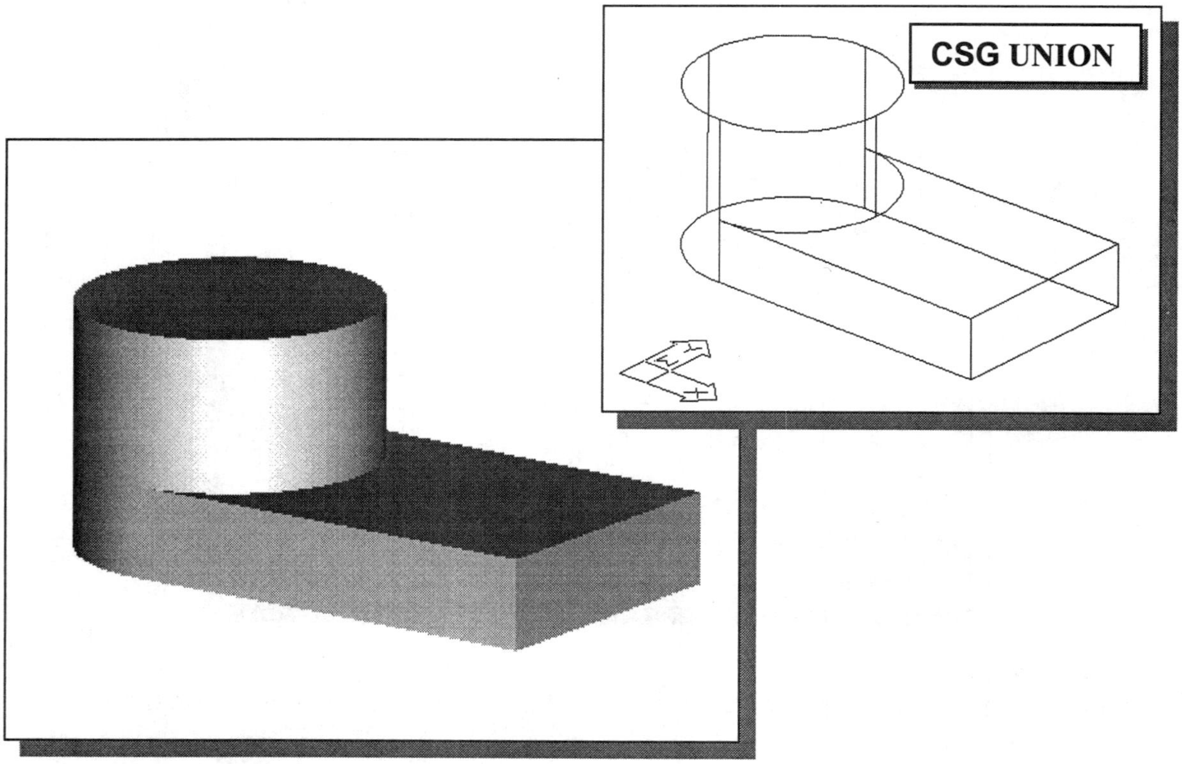

Creating the second cylinder feature

- We will create another cylinder as the next solid feature.

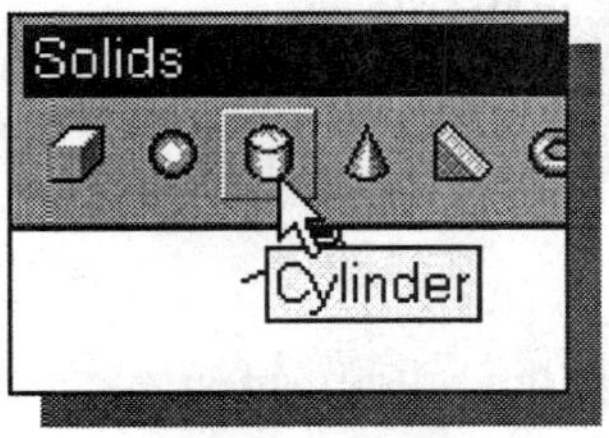

1. In the *Solids* toolbar, click on the ***Cylinder*** icon. In the command prompt area, the message *"Specify center point for base cylinder or [Elliptical] <0,0,0>:"* is displayed.

2. Inside the graphics window, press down the **[SHIFT]** key and **right-mouse-click** once to bring up the *Object Snap* shortcut menu.

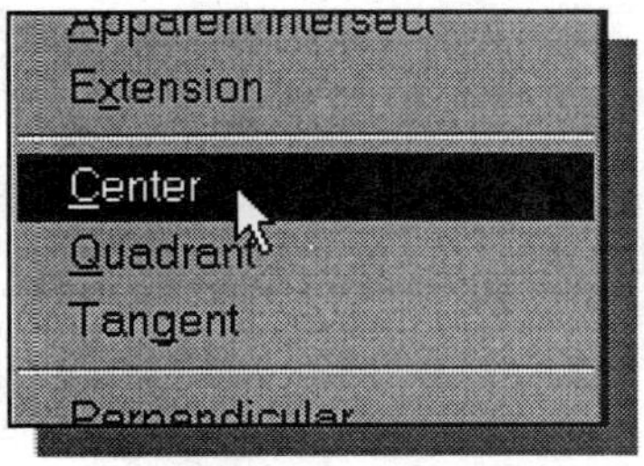

3. Select the **Center** option in the shortcut menu.

4. Snap to and select the **center of the circle** that is at the top of the solid block.

5. In the command prompt area, the message *"Specify radius for base of cylinder or [Diameter]:"* is displayed. Enter: **15 [ENTER]**.

6. In the command prompt area, the message *"Specify height of cylinder or [Center of other end]:"* is displayed. Enter: **-50 [ENTER]**.

(The negative value will extrude the cylinder downward, in the negative Z direction.)

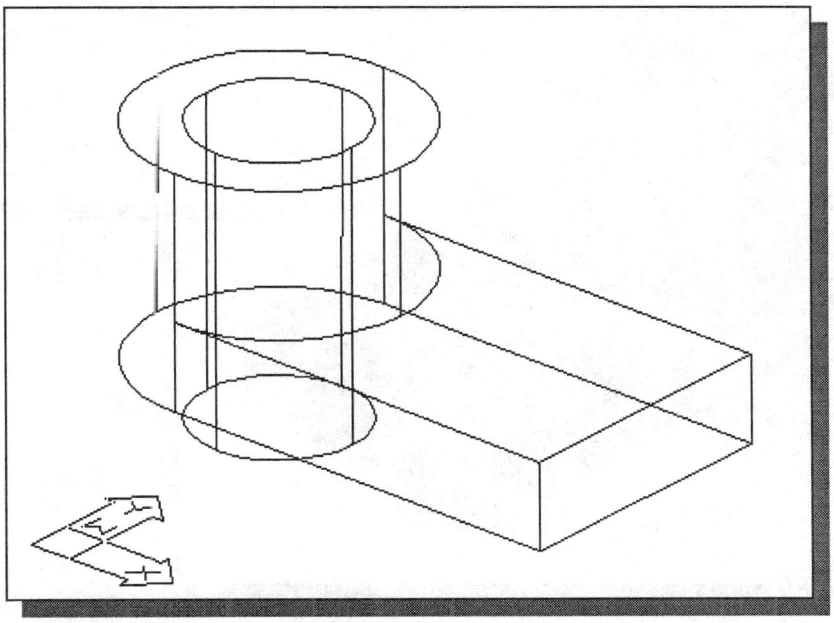

- Two solid objects, the base block and a cylinder, are displayed on the screen. On your own, use the *FRONT VIEW* and *TOP VIEW* options to confirm the top of the two solids are aligned. (Before continuing, restore the view as shown; including the *Coordinate* icon.)

Boolean operation - *SUBTRACT*

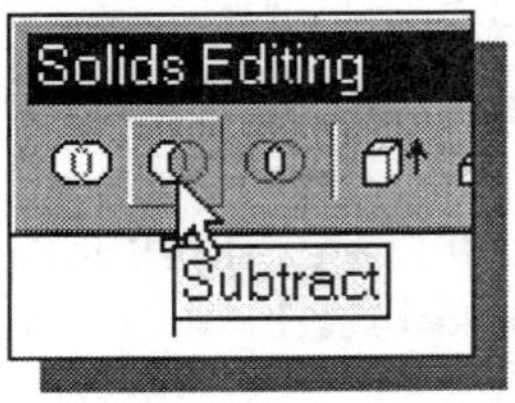

1. In the *Solids Editing* toolbar, click on the ***Subtract*** icon. In the command prompt area, the message *"_subtract Select solids and regions to subtract from .. Select Objects:"* is displayed.

2. Pick the base block solid by clicking on one of the straight edges.

3. Inside the graphics window, **right-mouse-click** to accept the selection and proceed with the *SUBTRACT* command.

4. In the command prompt area, the message *" Select solids and regions to subtract .. Select Objects:"* is displayed.

5. Pick the cylinder block by clicking on one of the circular edges.

6. Inside the graphics window, **right-mouse-click** to accept the selection and proceed with the *SUBTRACT* command.

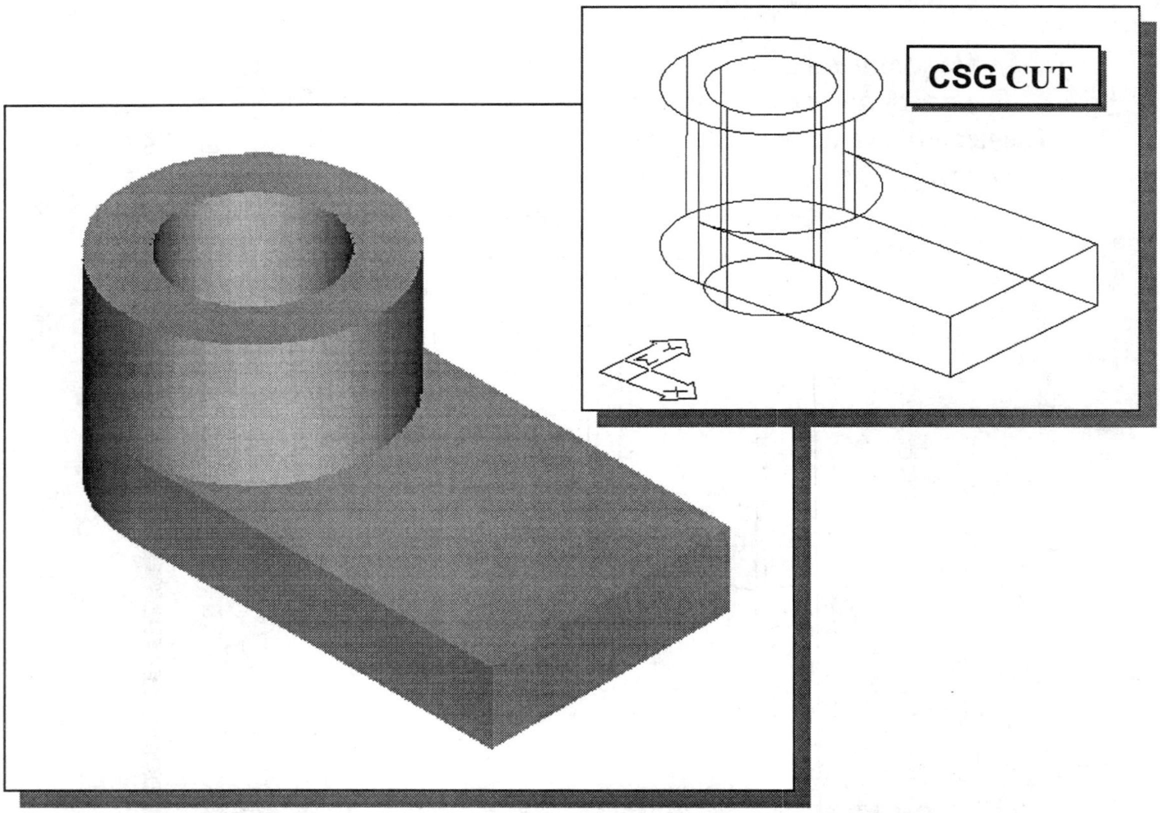

Creating another solid feature

- As can be seen, the CSG construction approach is quite straightforward. The main task is in positioning and aligning the solid blocks prior to applying a Boolean operation.

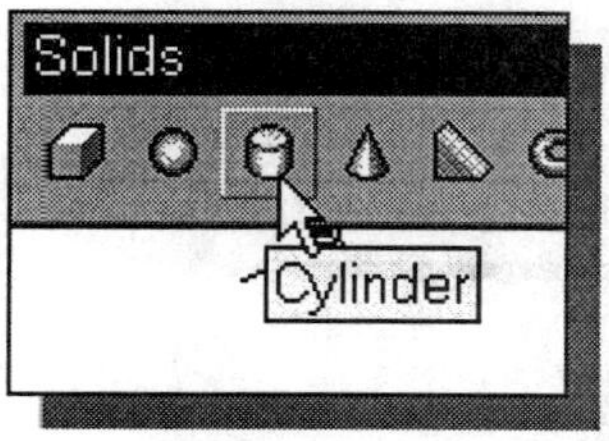

1. In the *Solids* toolbar, click on the ***Cylinder*** icon. In the command prompt area, the message *"Specify center point for base cylinder or [Elliptical] <0,0,0>:"* is displayed.

2. Inside the graphics window, press down the **[SHIFT]** key and **right-mouse-click** once to bring up the *Object Snap* shortcut menu.

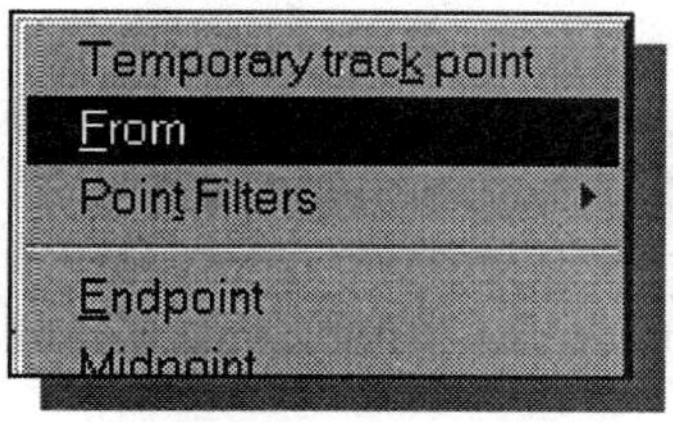

3. Select the **From** option in the shortcut menu.

4. Snap to the top-front corner of the base block and enter: **@-30,25 [ENTER]**.

5. In the command prompt area, the message *"Specify radius for base of cylinder or [Diameter]:"* is displayed. Enter: **10 [ENTER]**.

6. In the command prompt area, the message *"Specify height of cylinder or [Center of other end]:"* is displayed. Enter: **-30 [ENTER]**.

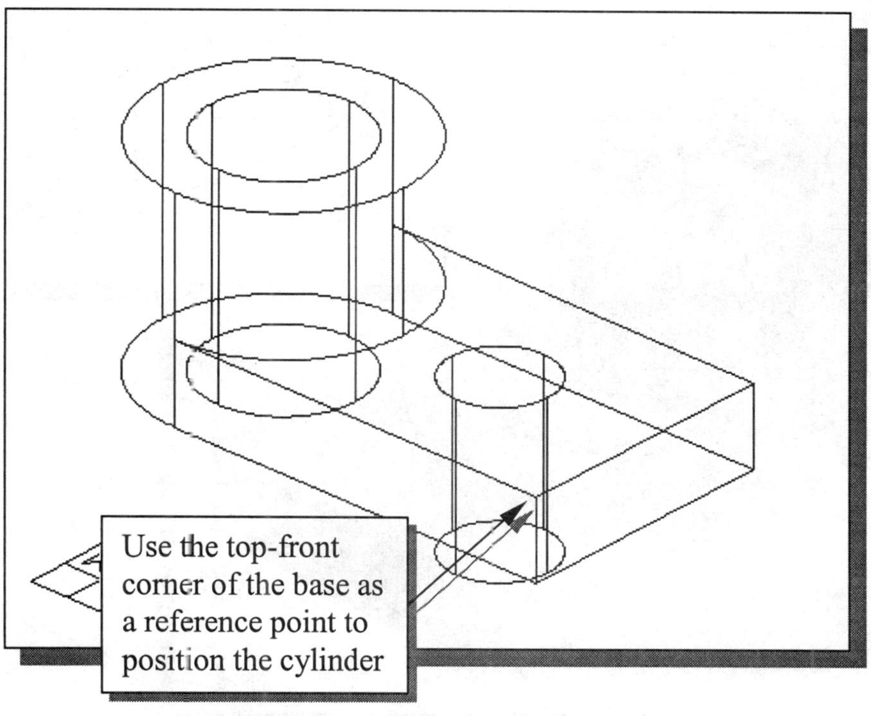

7. On your own, perform the Boolean ***SUBTRACT*** operation.

Shaded SOLID

1. Move the cursor to the *Standard* toolbar area and **right-click** on any icon of the *Standard* toolbar to display a list of toolbar menu groups.

2. Select ***Shade***, with the left-mouse-button, to display the *Shade* toolbar on the screen.

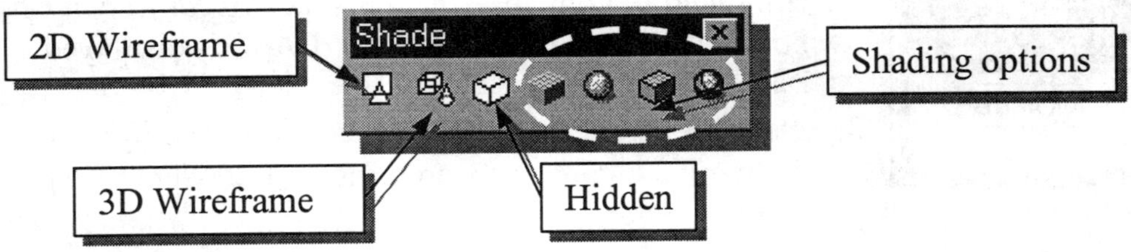

3. In the *Shade* toolbar, click on the ***Gouraud Shaded*** icon. This method produces a relatively smooth shaded solid.

➢ On your own, examine the effects of the other *Shading* options.

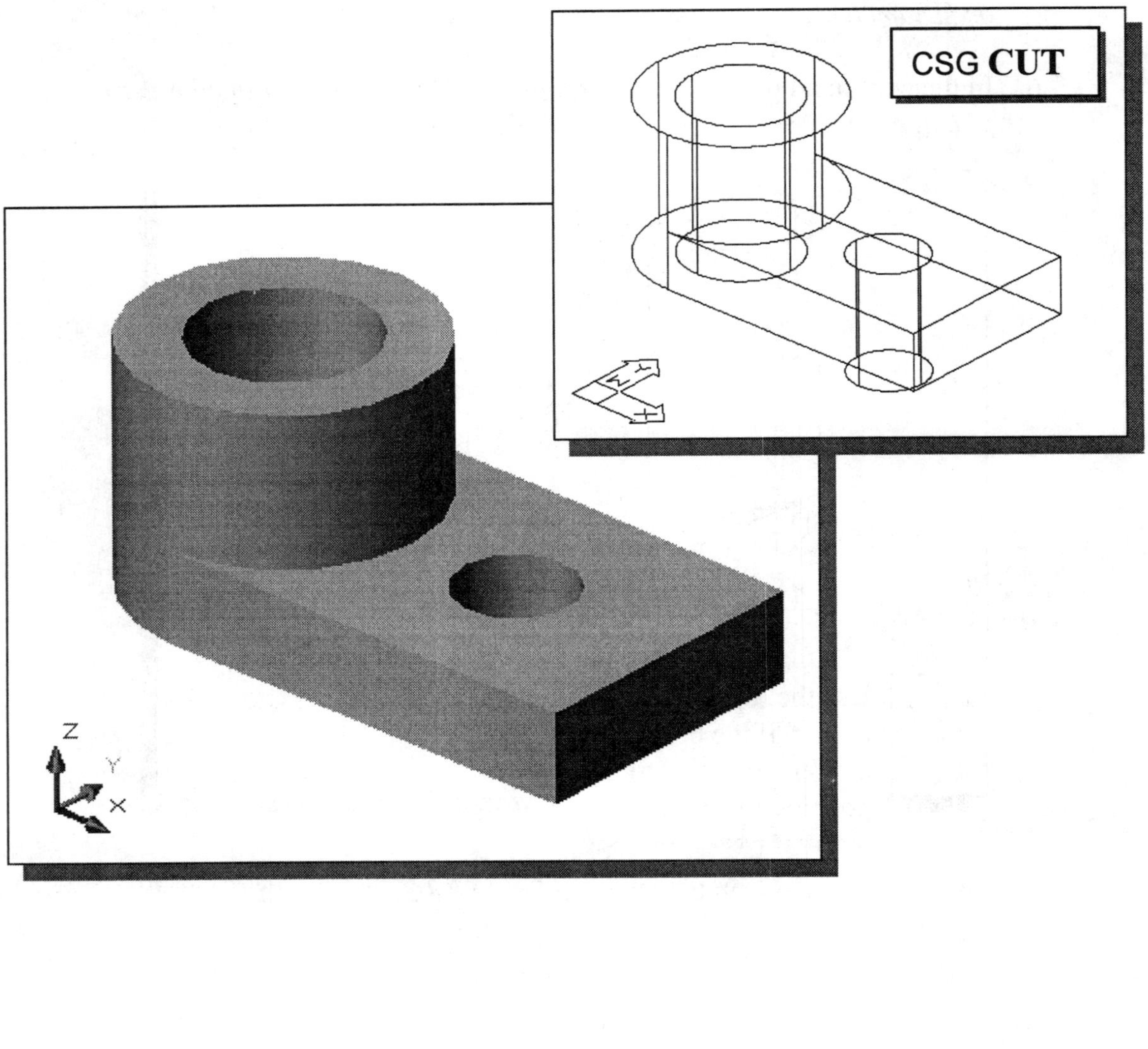

Creating the final feature

- We will create a rectangular cut as the final solid feature of the part. In the previous sections, with some careful planning, we positioned the solid blocks at the correct space locations while we were creating the solids. It is also possible to take a more general approach to orient and position solid blocks in space coordinates.

1. In the *Solids* toolbar, click on the ***Box*** icon. In the command prompt area, the message *"Specify corner of box or [Ccenter] <0,0,0>:"* is displayed.

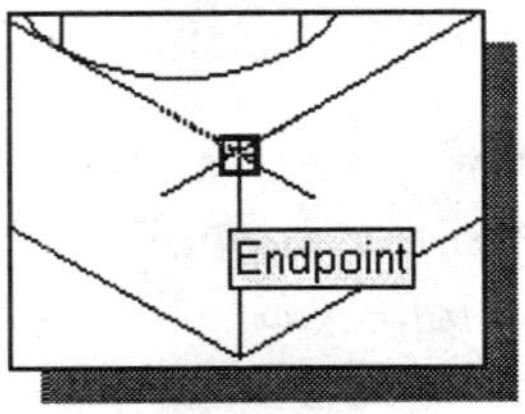

2. Snap to and select the **top-front corner** of the base block.

3. In the command prompt area, the message *"Specify corner or [Cube/Length]:"* is displayed. Enter: **@-30,30 [ENTER]**.

4. In the command prompt area, the message *"Specify Height:"* is displayed. Enter: **-20 [ENTER]**.

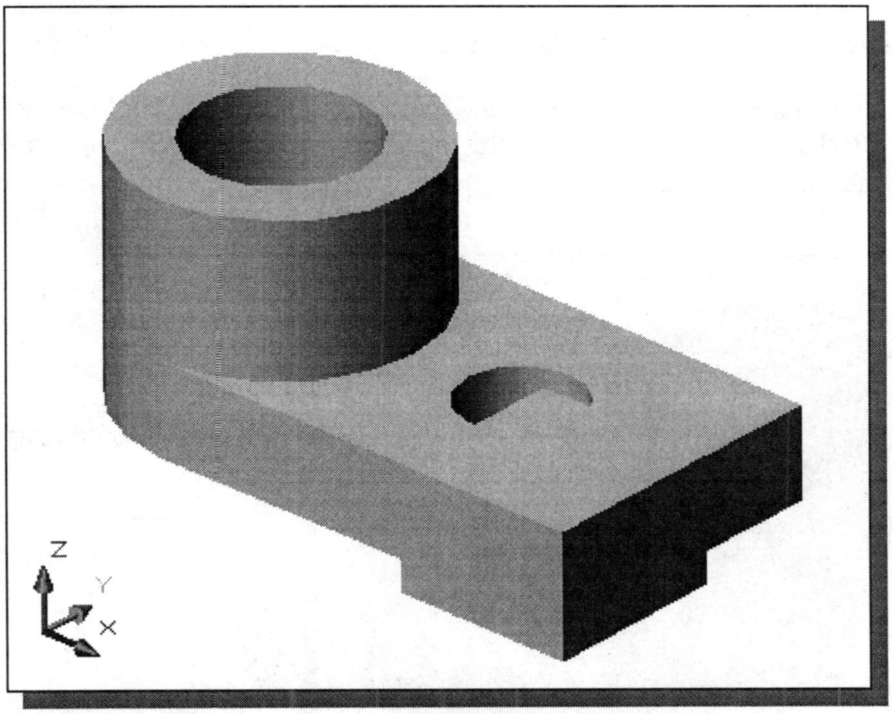

➢ Two overlapping solids appear on the screen. We will use the *editing tools* to orient the cutter, the rectangular block, to its correct location.

Rotating the rectangular block

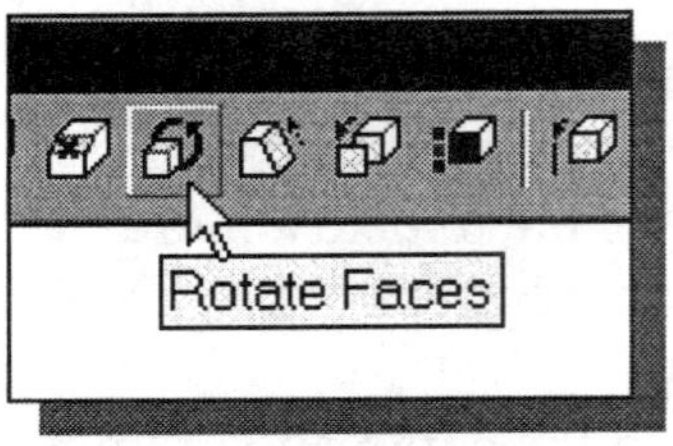

1. In the *Solids Editing* toolbar, click on the ***Rotate Faces*** icon. In the command prompt area, the message *"Select Faces or [Undo/Remove/All]:"* is displayed.

2. Select the edges of the rectangular block until **all edges are highlighted** as shown.

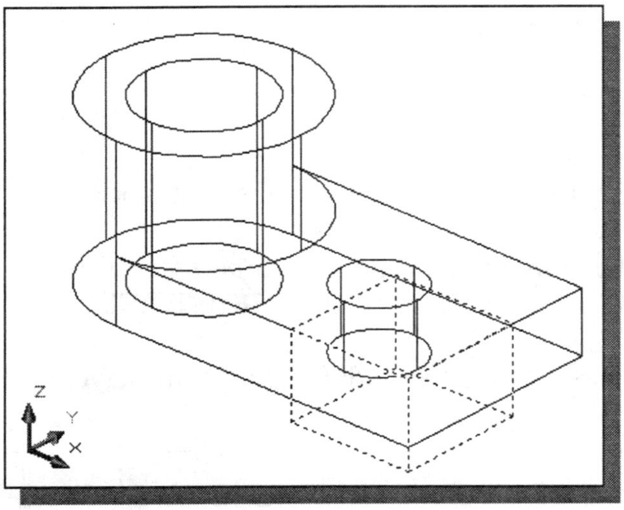

3. Inside the graphics window, **right-mouse-click** and select **Enter** in the popup option menu to proceed with the *ROTATE* command.

4. In the command prompt area, the message *"Specify an axis point or [Axis by object /View /Xaxis /Yaxis /Zaxis]<2 points>:"* is displayed. Inside the graphics window, **right-mouse-click** and select **Xaxis** in the popup option menu to proceed with the *ROTATE* command.

5. In the command prompt area, the message *"Specify the origin of the rotation <0,0,0>:"* is displayed. Pick the top-front corner of the rectangular block as the rotation origin.

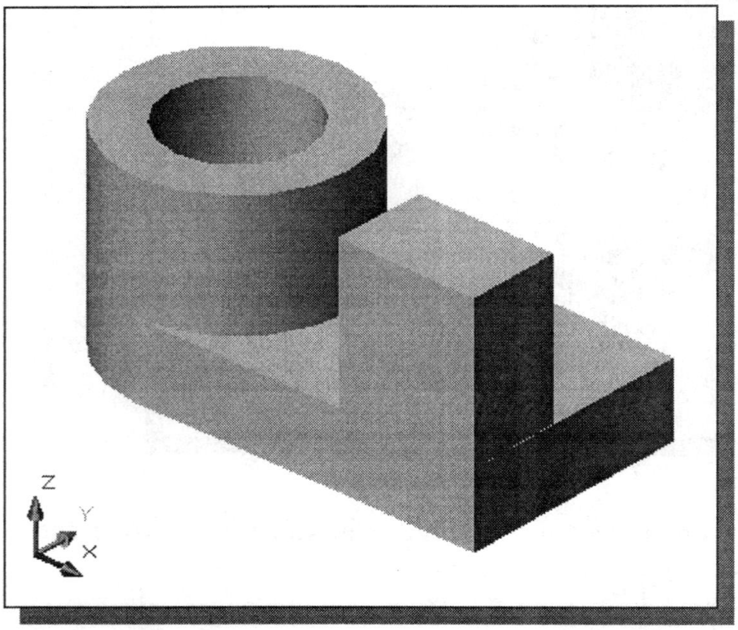

6. In the command prompt area, the message *"Specify a rotation angle or [Reference]:"* is displayed. Enter: **90 [ENTER]**.

7. Inside the graphics window, **right-mouse-click** and select **Exit** in the popup menu.

8. **Right-mouse-click** inside the graphics window and select **Exit** to exit the *ROTATE* command.

Moving the Rectangular Block

1. **Pre-select** the rectangular block by left-clicking on any edge of the block.

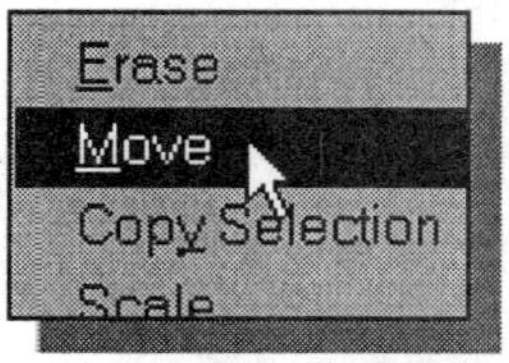

2. Inside the graphics window, **right-mouse-click** and select **Move** in the popup menu. In the command prompt area, the message *"Specify base point or displacement:"* is displayed.

3. Snap to and select the **top-front corner** of the rectangular block as the reference point.

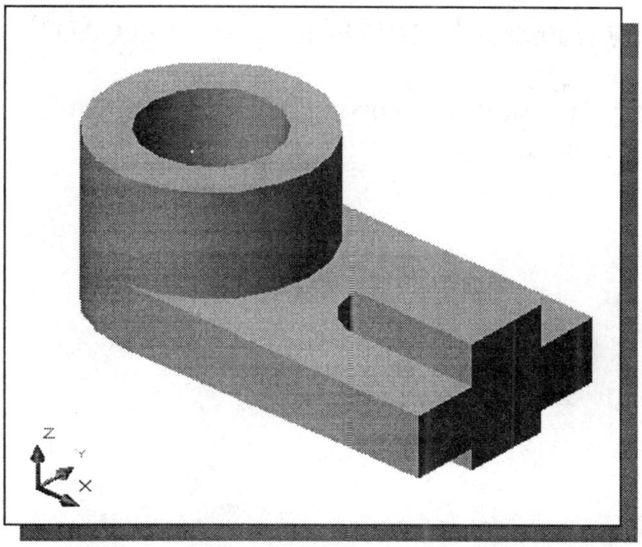

4. In the command prompt area, the message *"Specify second point of displacement or <use first point as displacement>:"* is displayed. Enter: **@0,15,-20 [ENTER]**.

5. On your own, use the ***3D ORBIT*** command to examine the model.

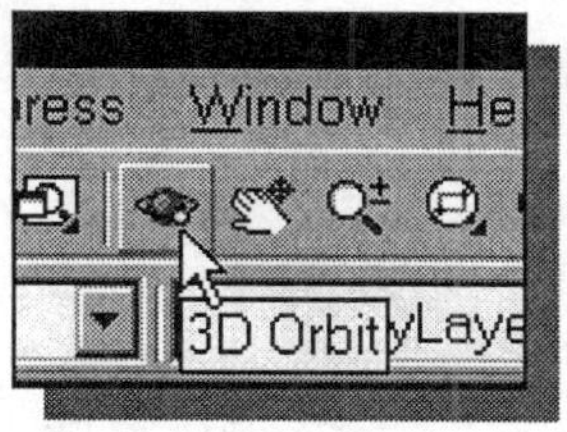

6. On your own, perform the *SUBTRACT BOOLEAN* operation and complete the model.

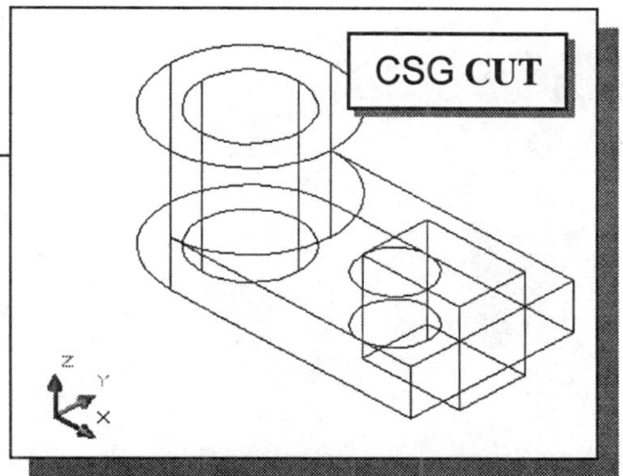

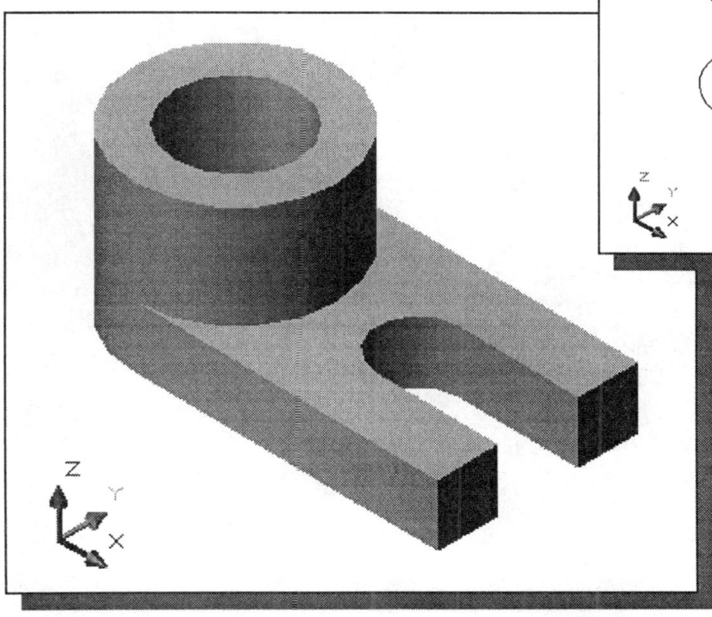

Questions:

1. What are the three basic Boolean operations commonly used in computer geometric modeling software?

2. What is a *primitive solid*?

3. What does *CSG* stand for?

4. Which Boolean operation keeps only the volume common to the two solid objects?

5. What is the difference between a *CUT* feature and a *UNION* feature in AutoCAD?

6. Using the CSG concept, create Binary Tree sketches showing the steps you plan to use to create the two models shown on the next page:

Ex.1)

Ex.2)

Exercises: All dimensions are in inches

1.

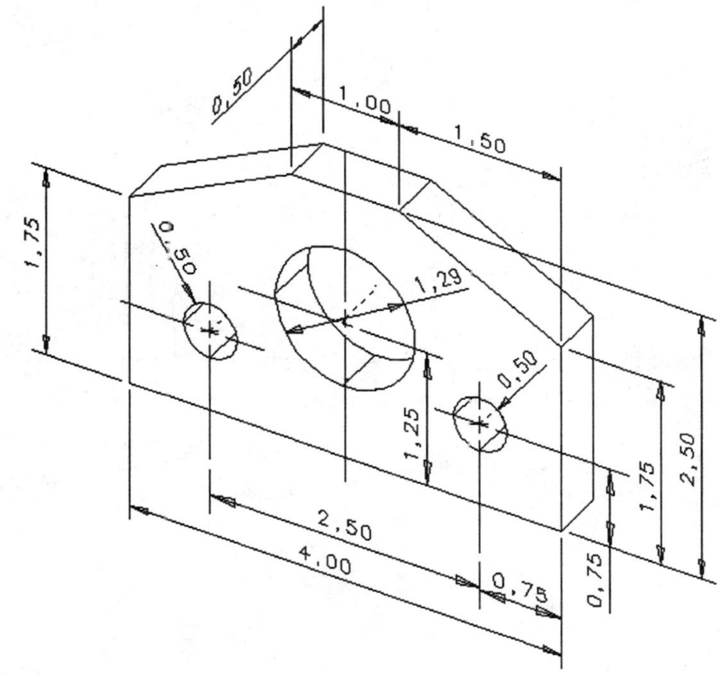

2.

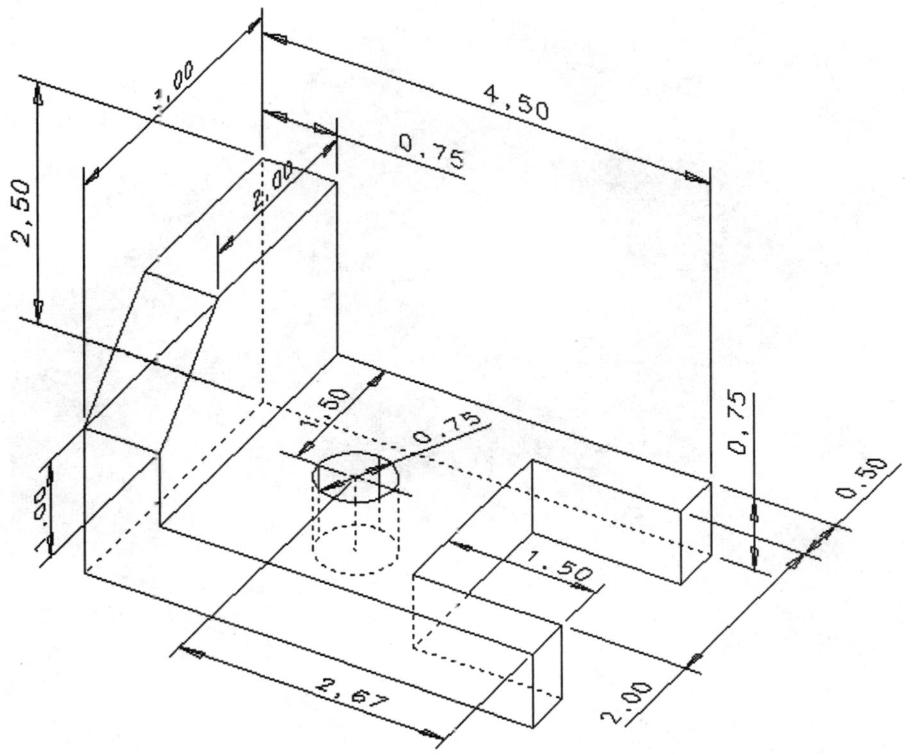

3.

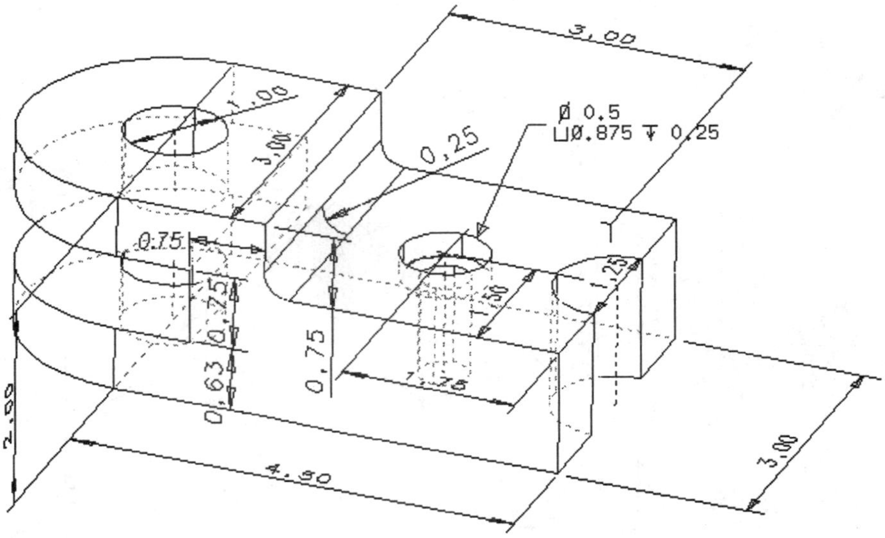
3.00
1.00
3.00
0.25
Ø 0.5
⌴Ø.875 ↧ 0.25
0.75
0.75
0.63
0.75
1.50
1.25
1.75
2.00
4.50
3.00

4.

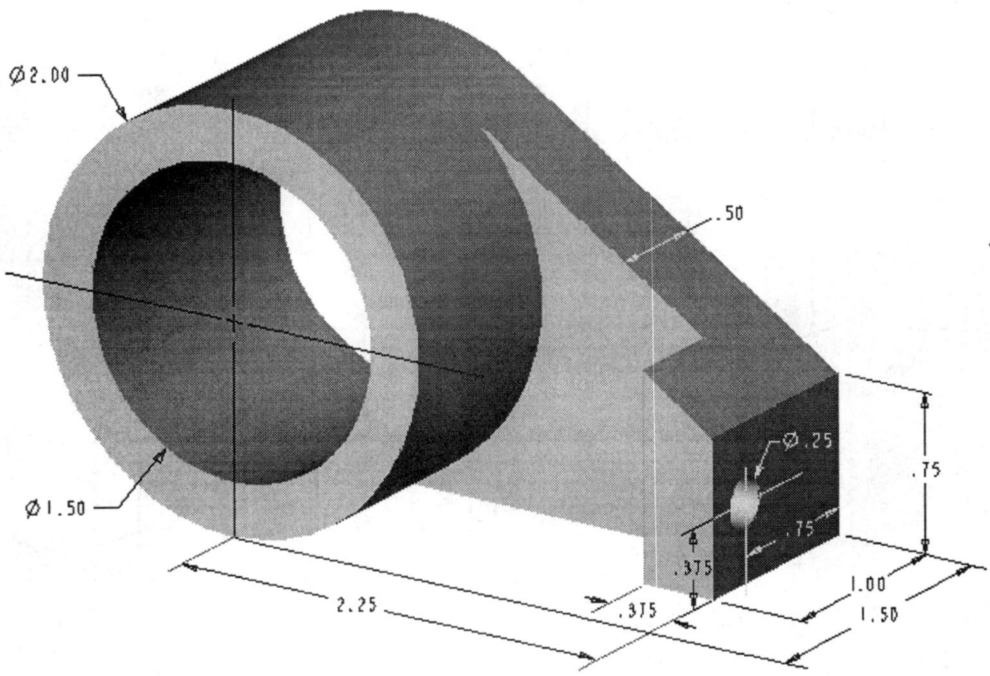
Ø2.00
.50
Ø.25
.75
.75
Ø1.50
.375
.375
2.25
1.00
1.50

Chapter 7
Regions, Extrude and Solid Modeling

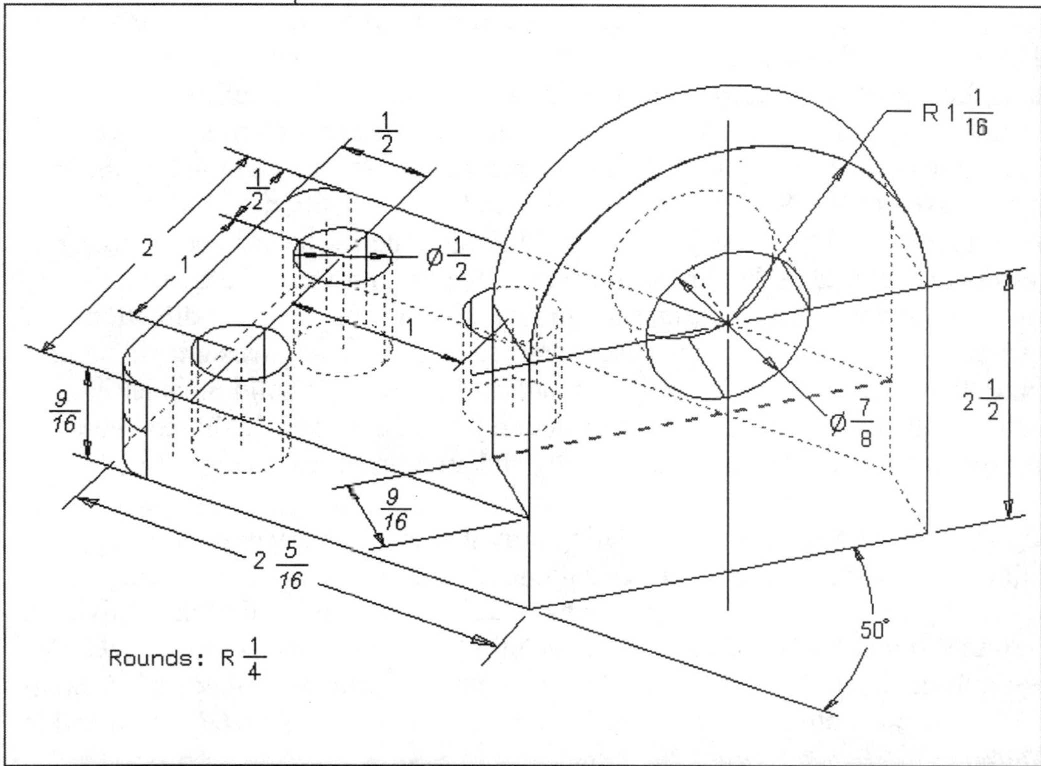

Learning Objectives

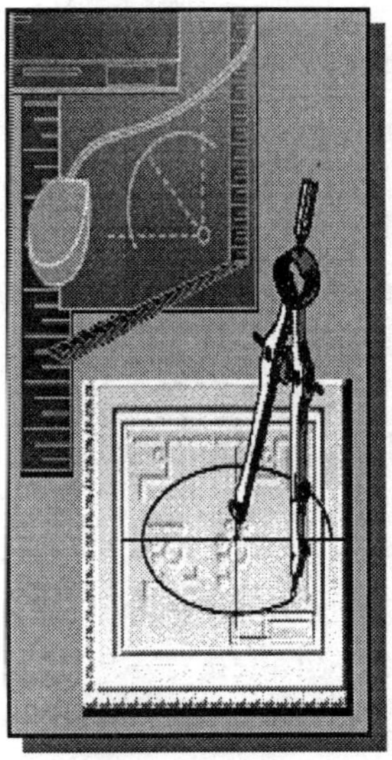

- Use 2D Extrusion method to create Solid Models.
- Understand and Create Regions.
- Use the basic GRIPS Editing commands.
- Edit 3D geometry with the Rotate and Move commands.
- Examine the Mass Properties of Solids.
- Understand the concept of Boundary-Representation modeling approach.

Introduction

AutoCAD provides many powerful modeling and design-tools, and there are many different approaches to accomplish solid modeling tasks. The CSG approach, as illustrated in the previous chapter, allows designers to create solid models by using a set of predefined shapes to simulate the manufacturing process. Using only a limited set of predefined solids becomes less efficient as more complex geometric definitions are involved. Another solid modeling method, parallel to the development of the CSG approach, is the **Boundary Representation (B-rep)** approach. CSG defines a model in terms of combining basic solid shapes and B-rep defines a model in terms of its edges and surfaces. Two of the most important solid construction operations based on the B-rep approach are **Extrude** and **Revolve**. The *Extrude* and *Revolve* options can be used to convert two-dimensional filled polygons into 3D solid models. This concept of using two-dimensional sketches of the three-dimensional features proves to be an effective way to construct solid models. Many designs are in fact the same shape in one direction. Computer input and output devices we use today are largely two-dimensional in nature, which makes this modeling technique quite practical. AutoCAD's solid modeler is a hybrid modeler; the user interface and construction techniques are CSG-based, whereas the B-rep capabilities are invoked automatically and are transparent to the user.

It is important to point out that solid modeling provides us with very powerful design tools. With the abundant tools available in solid modeling software, the modeling techniques are limited only to the imaginations of the designer. Instead of the individual 2D views, one should concentrate on the 3D features of designs. In this chapter, *the V-Block* design from chapter four is revisited to introduce the solid modeling tools available in *A*utoCAD. The procedure to creating solid models using the ***EXTRUDE*** command is demonstrated.

The *V-Block* Design

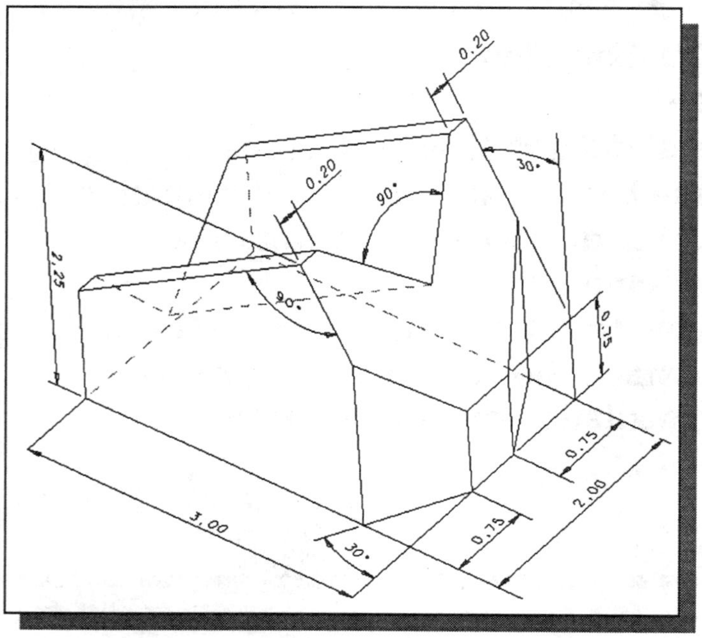

➢ Make a rough sketch of a CSG binary tree showing the steps that can be used to construct the design. What are the advantages and limitations of using the CSG approach in creating the design? What other tools could be helpful to the modeling task at hand? Take a few minutes to consider these questions and you are encouraged to construct the design on your own prior to going through the tutorial.

Starting Up AutoCAD® 2000i

1. Select the AutoCAD® 2000i option on the *Program* menu or select the AutoCAD® 2000i icon on the *Desktop*. Once the program is loaded into the memory, the AutoCAD® 2000i drawing screen and the *AutoCAD Today* startup dialog box will appear on the screen.

2. In the *AutoCAD Today* startup dialog box, select the **Create Drawings** tab with a single click of the left-mouse-button.

3. Confirm the startup option is set to ***Start from Scratch***, as shown in the figure below.

4. In the *Default Settings* section, pick **English (feet and Inches)** as the drawing units.

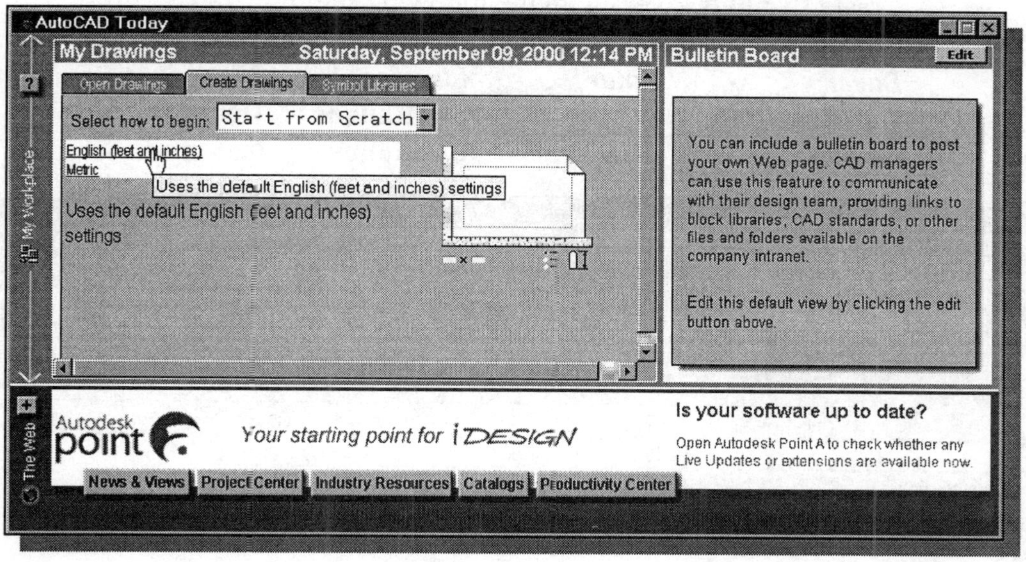

❖ Note that two graphics window are available. The *Drawing1.dwg* uses the default units set during the installation of AutoCAD 2000i. The units used in the second graphics window, the *Drawing2.dwg* window, are set to the English units, inches and feet.

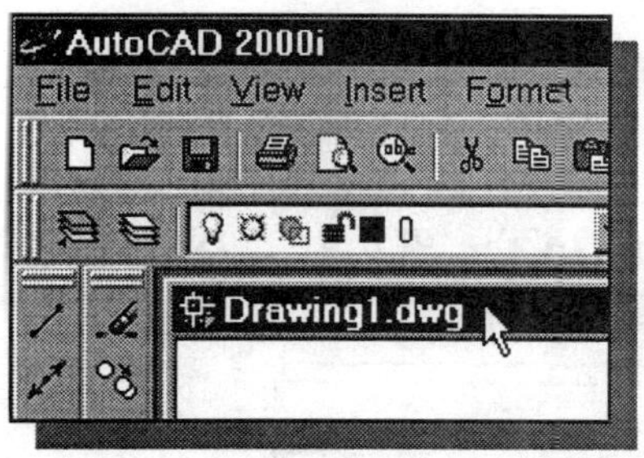

5. Switch to the *Drawing1* window by left-clicking once in the title area of the window.

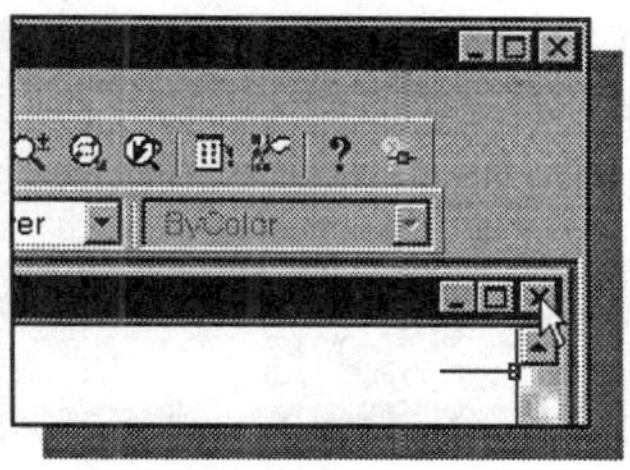

6. Close the window by clicking the ***Close*** icon located at the upper-right-corner of the *Drawing1* window.

Layers setup

1. Pick ***Layers*** in the *Object Properties* toolbar.

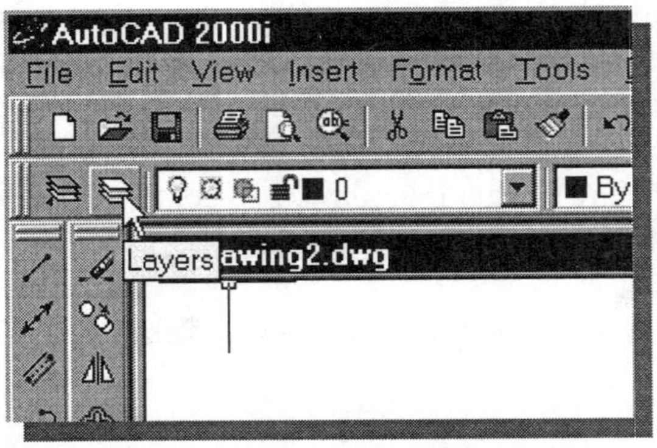

2. Click on the ***New*** icon to create new layers.

3. Create **two new layers** with the following settings:

Layer	***Color***	***LineType***	***LineWeight***
Construction	**White**	**Continuous**	**Default**
Object	**Cyan**	**Continuous**	**0.30mm**

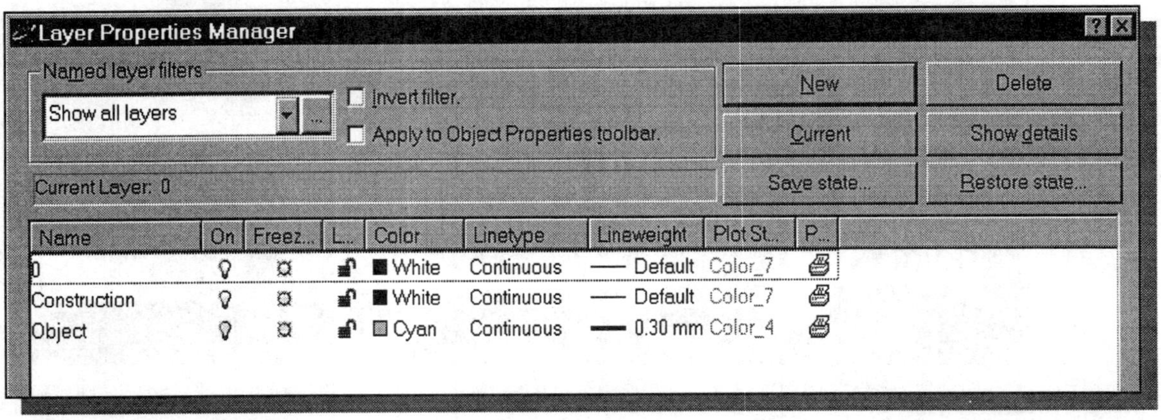

4. Highlight the layer ***Construction*** in the list of layers.

5. Click on the ***Current*** icon to set layer ***Construction*** as the *Current layer*.

6. Click on the **OK** button to accept the settings and exit the *Layer Properties Manager* dialog box.

7. In the *Status Bar* area, reset the options and turn ***ON*** the *POLAR, OSNAP, OTRACK, LWT* and *MODEL* options.

Setting up a 2D sketch

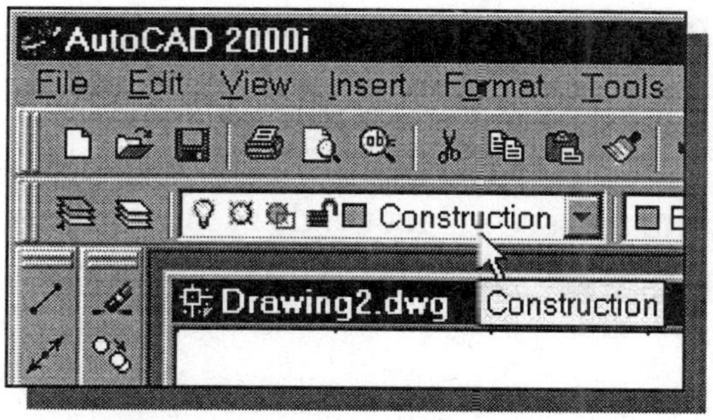

1. In the *Layer Control* box, confirm layer *Construction* is set as the *Current layer.*

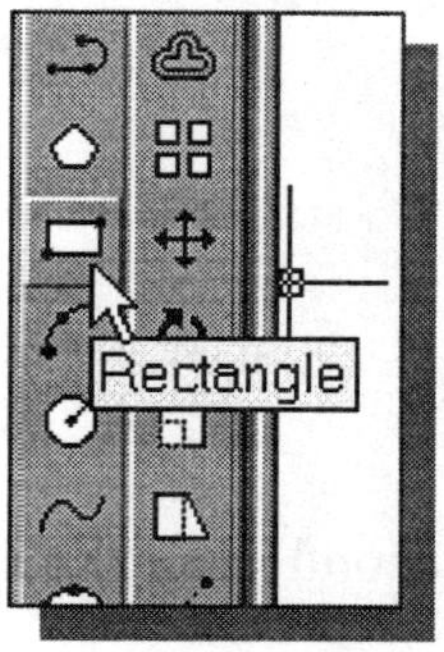

2. Select the ***Rectangle*** icon in the *Draw* toolbar. In the command prompt area, the message *"Specify first corner point or [Chamfer/Elevation/Fillet/Thickness/Width]:"* is displayed.

3. Place the first corner-point of the rectangle near the lower left corner of the screen. Do not be overly concerned about the actual coordinates of the selected location; the CAD drawing space is as big as you can imagine.

4. We will create a 3" x 2.25" rectangle. Enter **@3,2.25 [ENTER]**.

❖ The *RECTANGLE* command creates rectangles as *polyline* features, which means all segments of a rectangle are created as a single object.

5. We will next make a copy of the rectangle. Pick ***Copy Object*** in the *Modify* toolbar.

6. Pick any edge of the rectangle we just created.

7. Inside the graphics window, **right-mouse-click** to accept the selection.

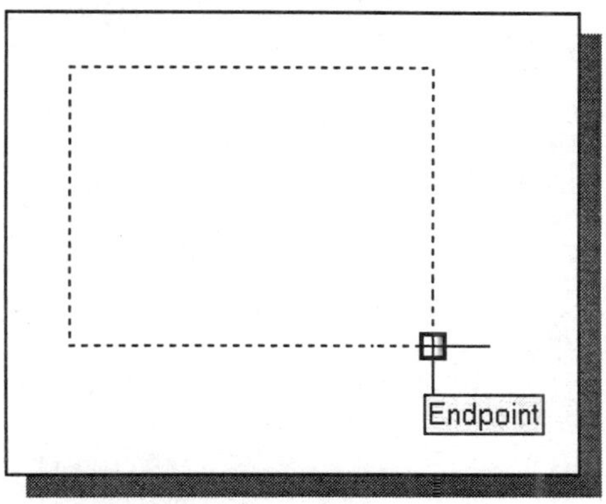

8. In the command prompt area, the message "*Specify base point or displacement, or [Multiple]:*" is displayed. Pick the lower right corner of the rectangle as the base point. A copy of the rectangle is attached to the cursor at the selected base point.

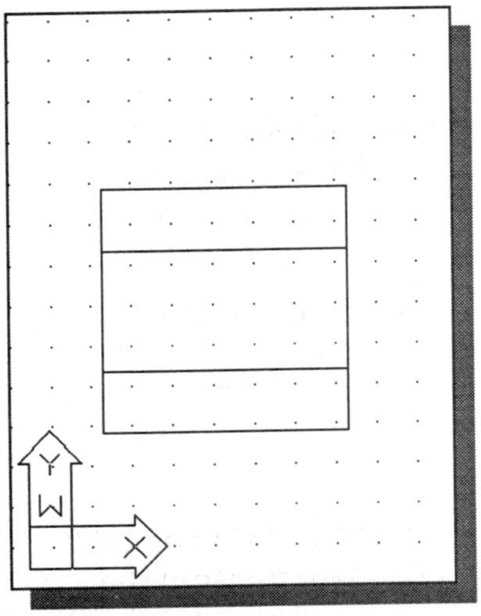

9. In the command prompt area, the message *"Specify second point of displacement, or <use first point as displacement>:"* is displayed. Enter: **@0,0.75 [ENTER]**.

❖ This will position the second rectangle at the location for the 30-degree angle that is needed in the design.

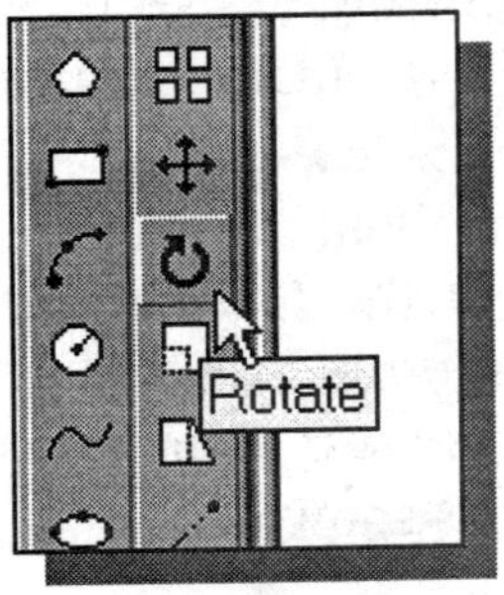

10. Pick ***Rotate*** in the *Modify* toolbar as shown.

11. Pick the top horizontal line on the screen. The second rectangle, the copy we just created, is selected.

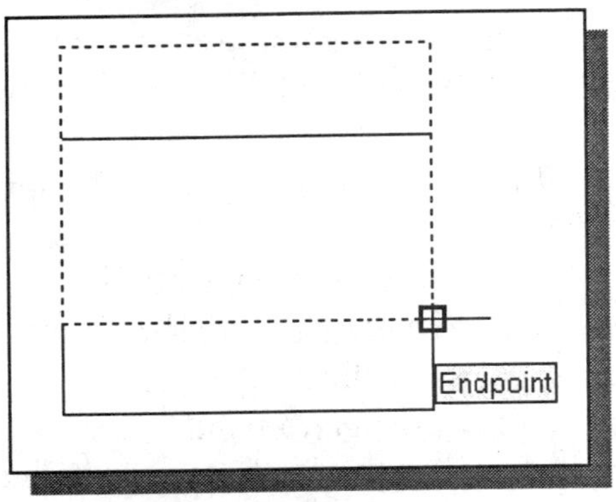

12. Inside the graphics window, **right-mouse-click** to accept the selection.

13. In the command prompt area, the message *"Specify base point:"* is displayed. Pick the lower right corner of the selected rectangle as the base point.

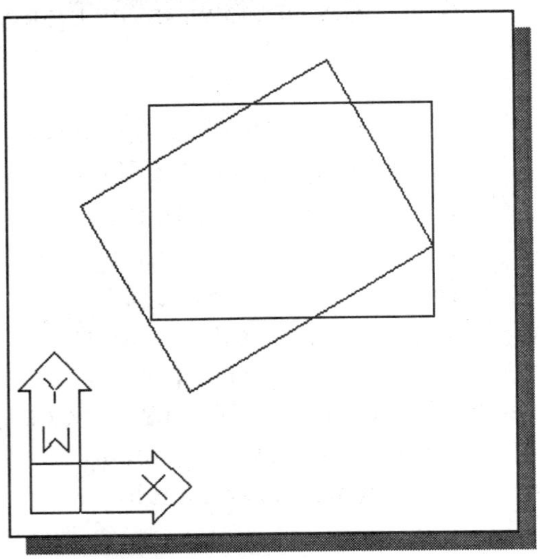

14. In the command prompt area, the message *"Specify the rotation angle or [Reference]:"* is displayed. Enter: **30 [ENTER]**.

Defining the Front edges of the design

1. In the *Status Bar* area, right-mouse-click on any of the *POLAR* options to bring up the option menu.

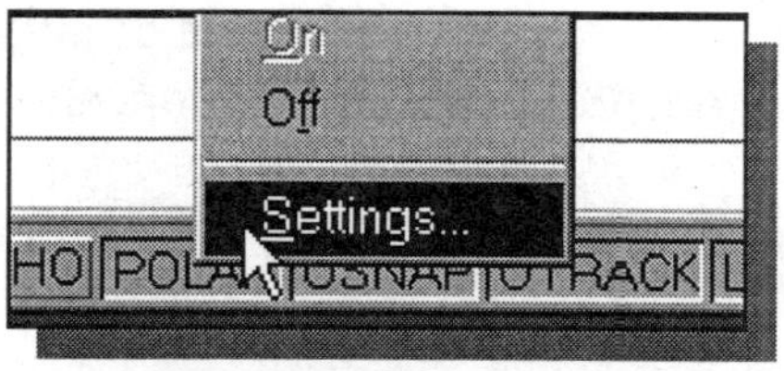

2. Select **Settings** in the option menu as shown.

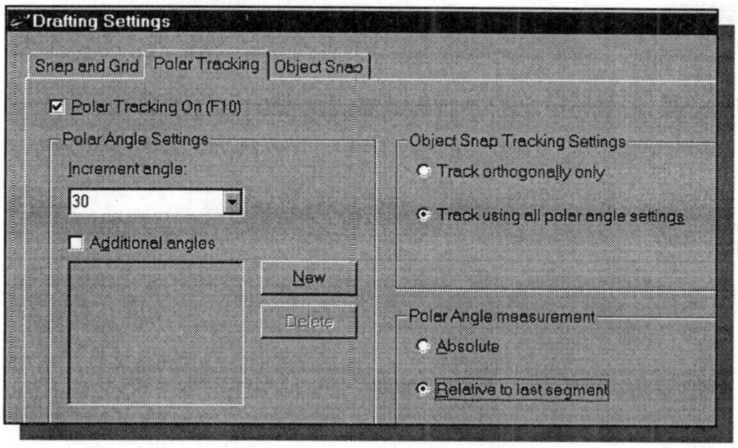

3. In the *Drafting Settings* window, confirm the Increment angle is set to **30** in the *Polar Angle Settings* area.

4. Switch on the ***Track using all polar angle settings*** and ***Relative to last segment*** options as shown.

5. In the *Drafting Settings* window, click on the **Object Snap** tab to display and set the *Object Snap* options.

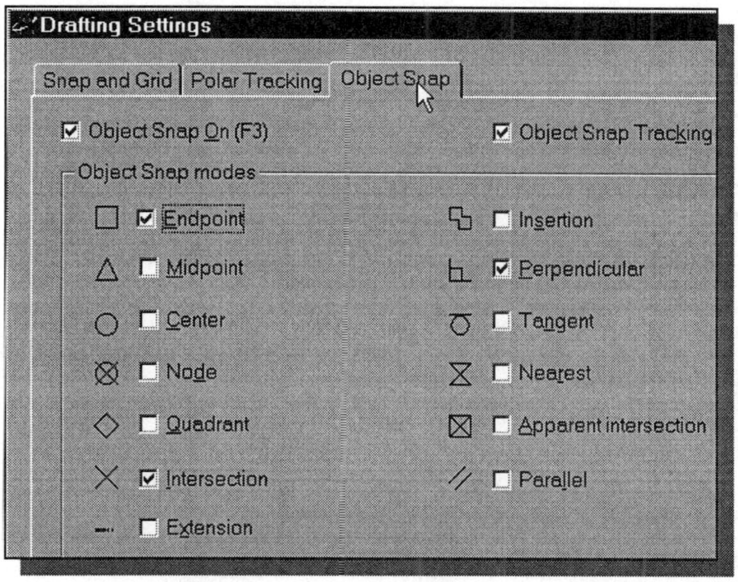

6. On your own, reset the *Object Snap modes* so that only the *Endpoint*, *Intersection* and *Perpendicular* are switched ***ON*** as shown in the figure.

7. In the *Drafting Settings* window, click **OK** to accept the settings.

- The AuotCAD *AutoTrack*™ feature includes two tracking options: *POLAR* tracking and *OBJECT SNAP* tracking. When the *POLAR* option is turned on, alignment markers are displayed to help us create objects at precise positions and angles.

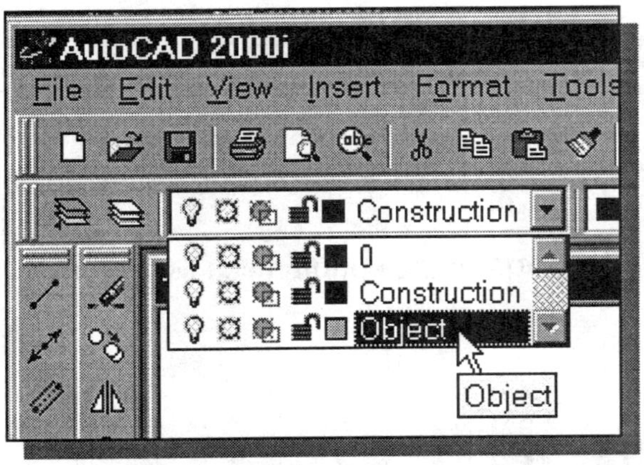

8. On the *Object Properties* toolbar, choose the *Layer Control* box with the left-mouse-button.

9. Move the cursor over the name of layer *Object*; the tool tip *"Object"* appears.

10. **Left-mouse-click once** and layer *Object* is set as the *Current layer*.

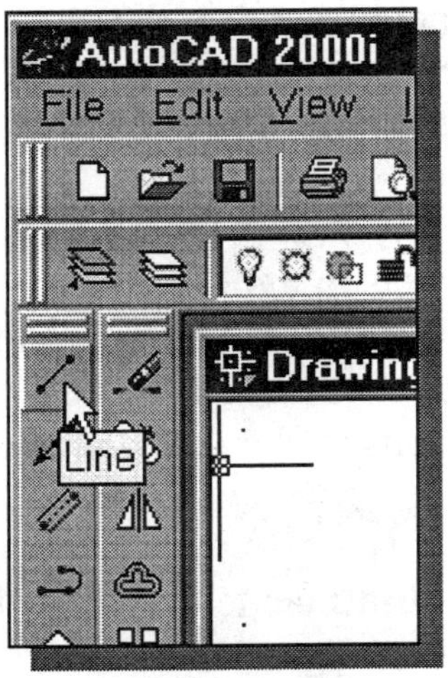

11. Select the ***Line*** command icon in the *Draw* toolbar.

12. In the command prompt area, the message *"_line Specify first point:"* is displayed. Pick the **lower-left corner** of the bottom horizontal line in the front-view as the starting point of the line segments.

13. Pick the **lower-right corner** of the bottom horizontal line in the front-view as the second point.

14. Select the **third** and **fourth** points as shown in the below figure.

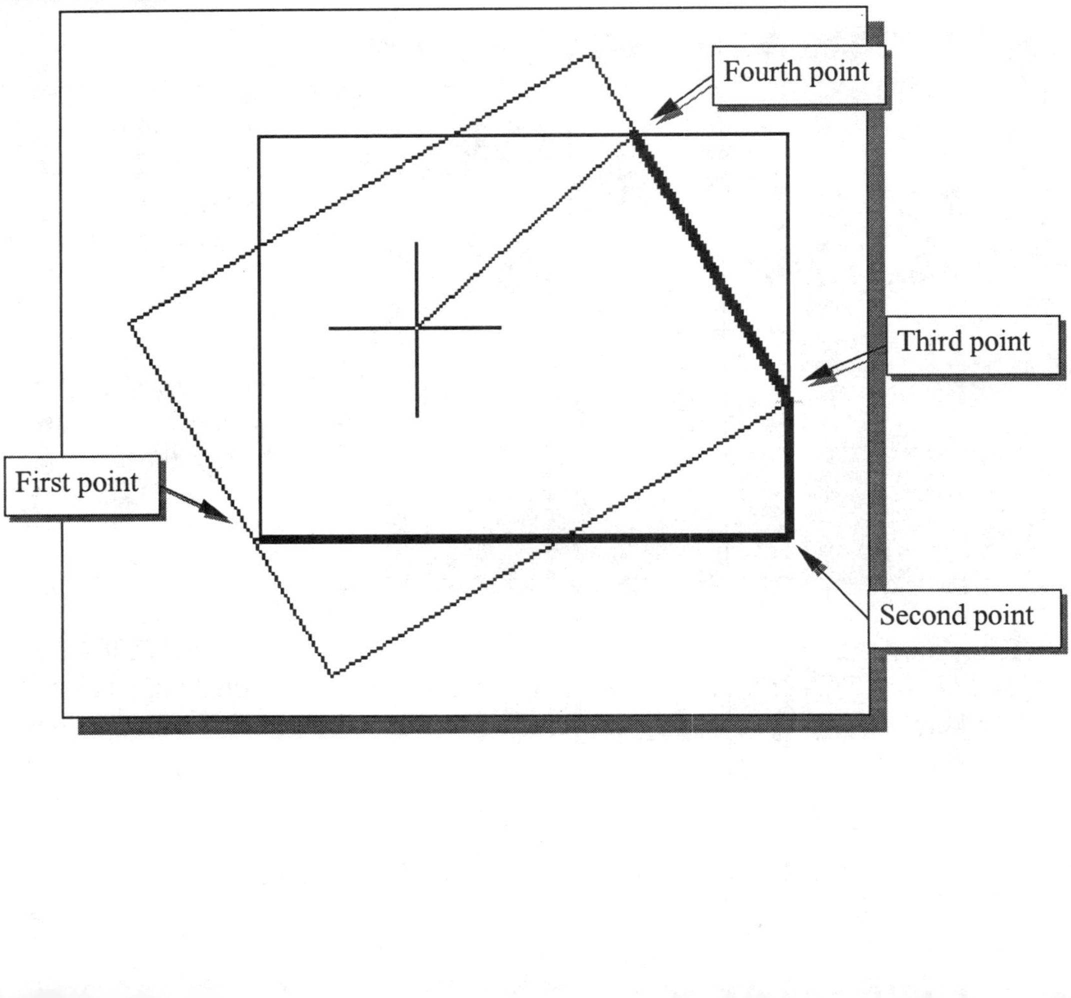

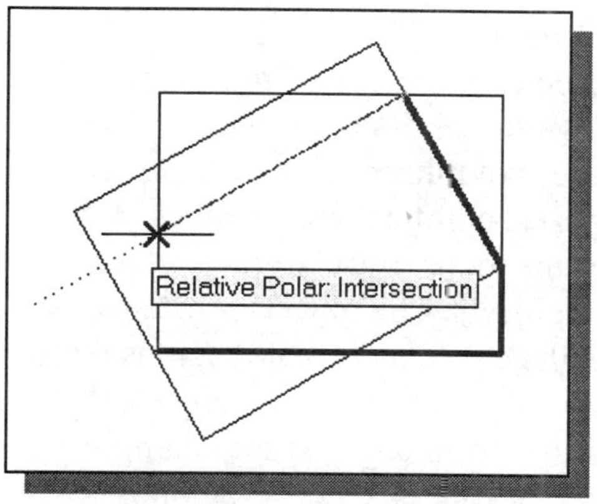

15. Move the cursor near the left vertical line and notice the *AutoTrack* feature automatically snaps the cursor to the intersection point.

16. Left-click at the intersection point as shown.

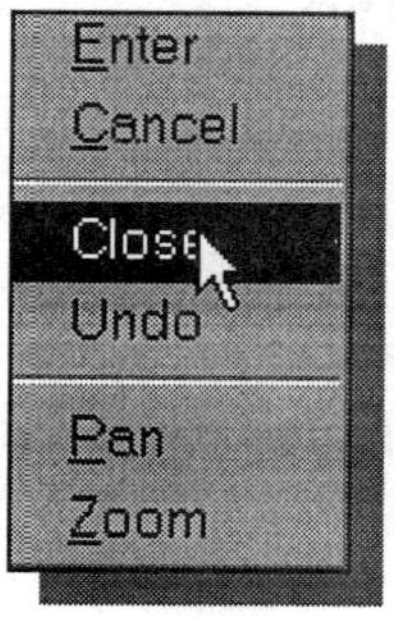

17. Inside the graphics window, **right-mouse-click** once to bring up the popup menu.

18. Pick **Close** in the popup menu. The *Close* option will create a line segment connecting the last point to the first point of the line sequence.

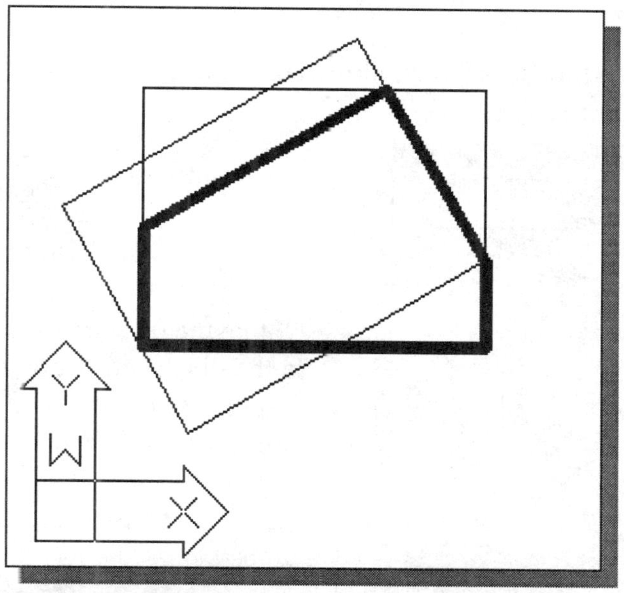

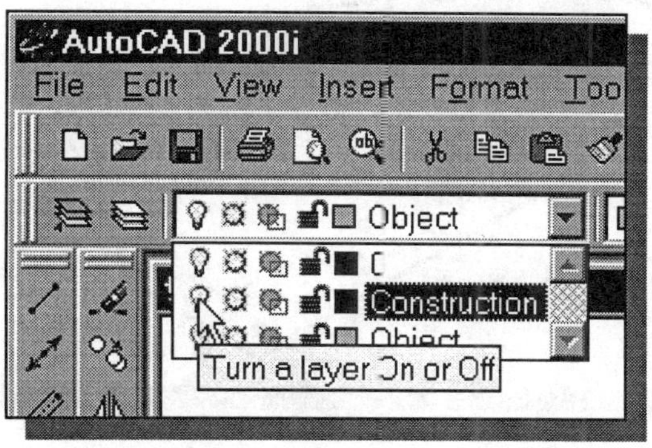

19. On your own, turn ***OFF*** the display of the *Construction Layer* by using the left-mouse-button.

20. Move the cursor into the graphics window and **left-mouse-click once** to accept the layer control settings.

Creating a Region

- In AutoCAD, **Regions** are 2D enclosed areas, which can be created from one or more closed shapes called **loops**. A *loop* is a curve or a sequence of connected curves that defines an area on a plane with a boundary that does not intersect itself. *Loops* can be combinations of lines, polylines, circles, arcs, ellipses, elliptical arcs, splines, 3D faces, traces, and solids. The objects that make up the loops must either be closed or form closed areas by sharing endpoints with other objects. The objects must also be coplanar, which means they must be on the same plane. We can create regions out of multiple loops and out of open curves whose endpoints are connected. Objects that intersect with themselves or with other objects cannot form regions; for example, intersecting lines, intersecting arcs or self-intersecting curves. Once a region is created, we can analyze properties such as its area and moments of inertia.

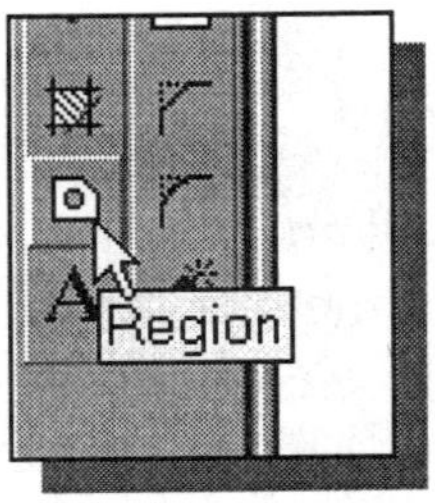

1. Select the ***Region*** command icon in the *Draw* toolbar.

2. In the command prompt area, the message *"Select objects:"* is displayed. Select displayed entities by creating a selection window enclosing all objects.

3. Inside the graphics window, **right-mouse-click** to accept the selection and create a region.

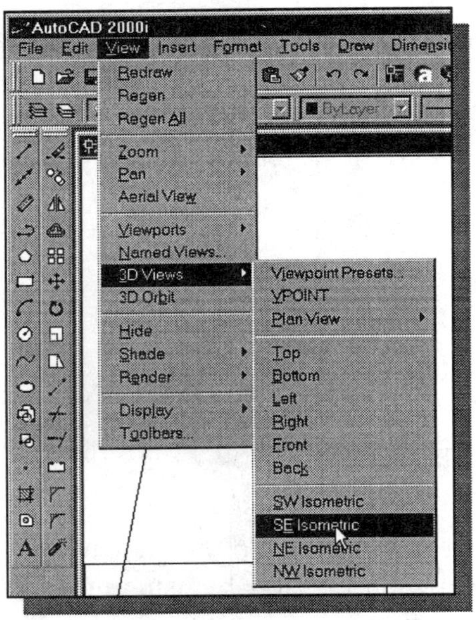

4. In the pull-down menus, select:

   [View] => [3D Views] => [SE Isometric]

- Notice the orientation of the 2D region in relation to the displayed AutoCAD user coordinate system. By default, the 2D sketch-plane is aligned to the XY plane of the world coordinate system.

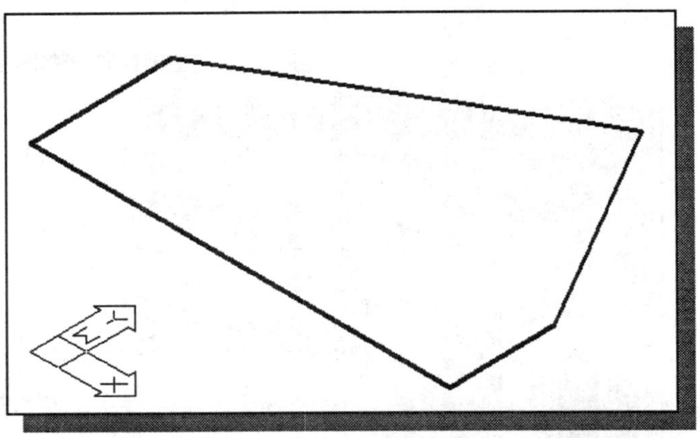

Solids Toolbar

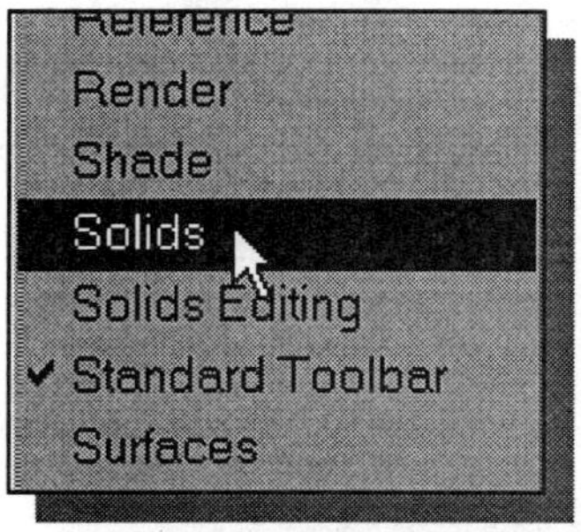

1. Move the cursor to the *Standard* toolbar area and **right-mouse-click** once on any icon in the toolbar area to display a list of toolbar menu groups.

2. Select **Solids**, with the left-mouse-button, to display the *Solids* toolbar on the screen.

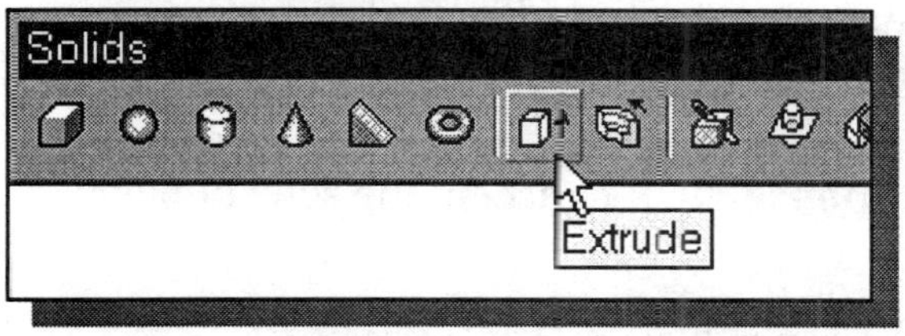

3. Select ***Extrude*** in the *Solids* toolbar as shown.

4. In the command prompt area, the message *"Select objects:"* is displayed. Select the region by clicking on any of the displayed segments.

5. Inside the graphics window, **right-mouse-click** to accept the selection and proceed with the extrude command.

6. In the command prompt area, the message *"Specify height of extrusion or [path]:"* is displayed. Enter: **2.0** [**ENTER**].

7. In the command prompt area, the message *"Specify angle of taper for extrusion <0>:"* is displayed. Enter: **0.0** [**ENTER**].

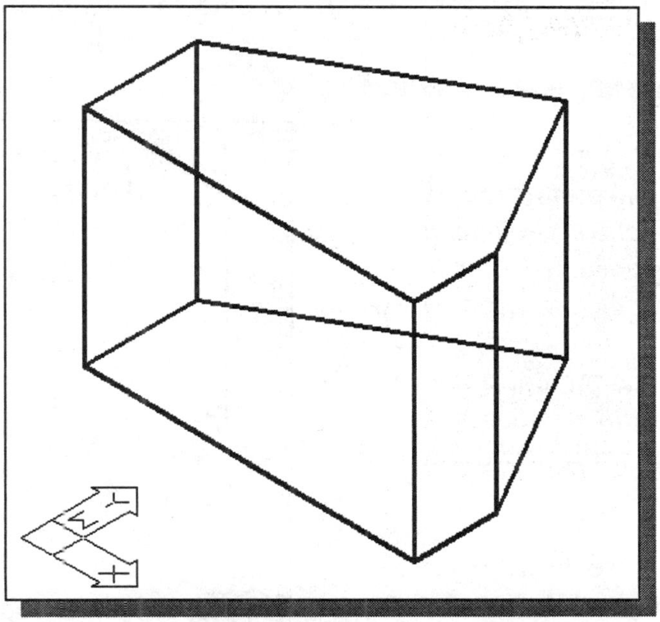

- Note that the orientation and position of solid models, in relations to the world coordinate system, can be adjusted using the *MOVE* and *ROTATE 3D* commands.

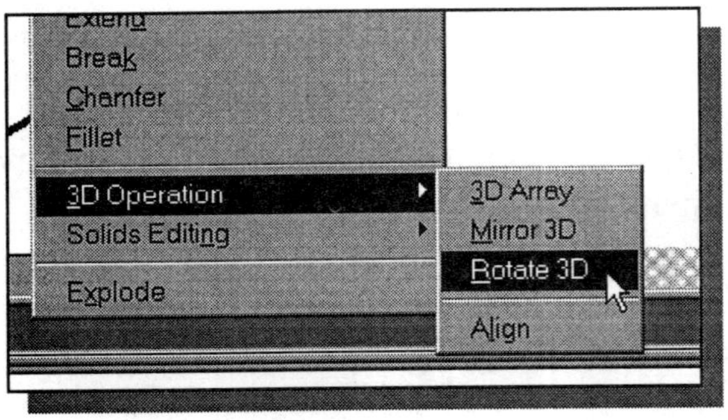

8. In the pull-down menus, select:

   [Modify] => [3D Operation] => [Rotate 3D]

9. In the command prompt area, the message *"Select objects:"* is displayed. Select the solid model by clicking on any of the displayed edges of the model.

10. Inside the graphics window, **right-mouse-click** to accept the selection and proceed with the extrude command.

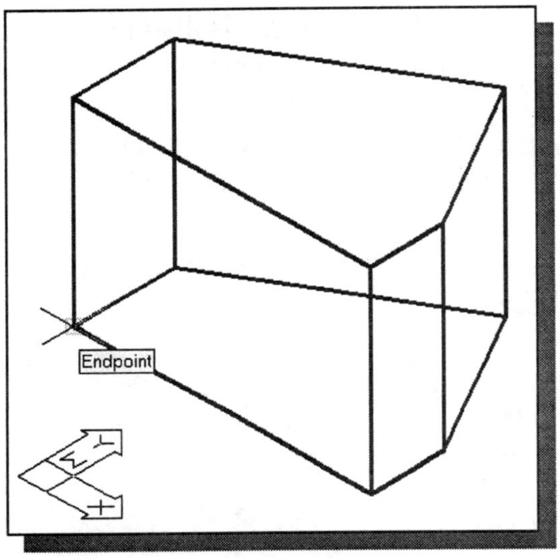

11. In the command prompt area, the message *"Specify first point on axis or define axis by [Object/Last/View/Xaxis/Yaxis/Zaxis/2point s]:"* is displayed. Select the lower-left corner of the model as shown

- Note that the ***ROTATE 3D*** command requires the definition of a *direction vector*, which is used as the axis of rotation. The rotation follows the conventional engineering *right-hand rule*. The first point defines the base of the direction vector.

12. In the command prompt area, the message *"Specify second point on axis:"* is displayed. Select the lower-right corner of the model as shown

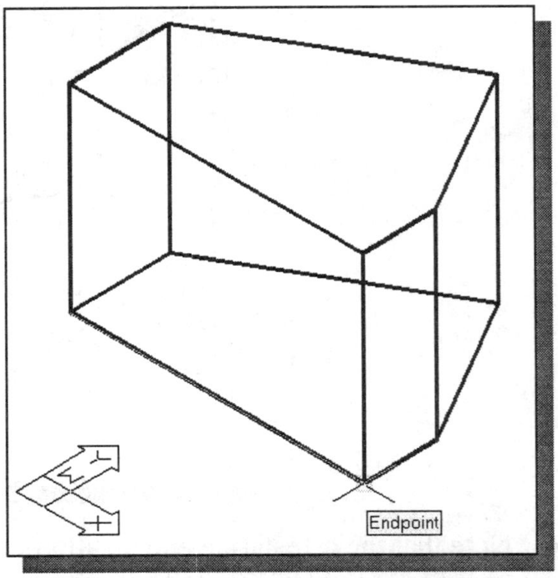

13. In the command prompt area, the message *"Specify rotation angle or [Reference]:"* is displayed. Enter: **90 [ENTER]**

14. On your own, use the available ***SHADE*** commands to examine the created solid object.

Creating a 2D sketch at the Base of the Model

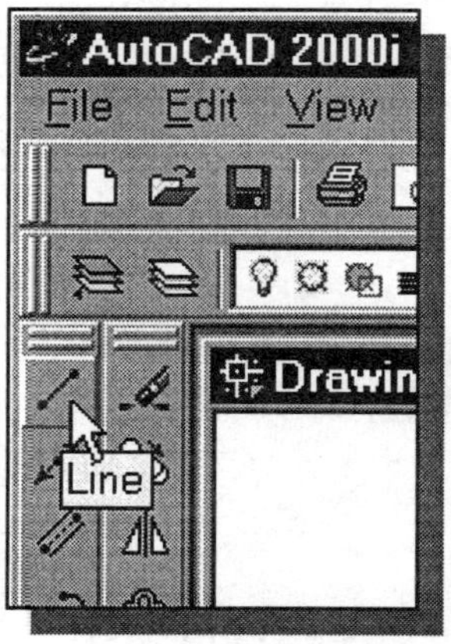

1. Select the ***Line*** command icon in the *Draw* toolbar. In the command prompt area, the message *"_line Specify first point:"* is displayed.

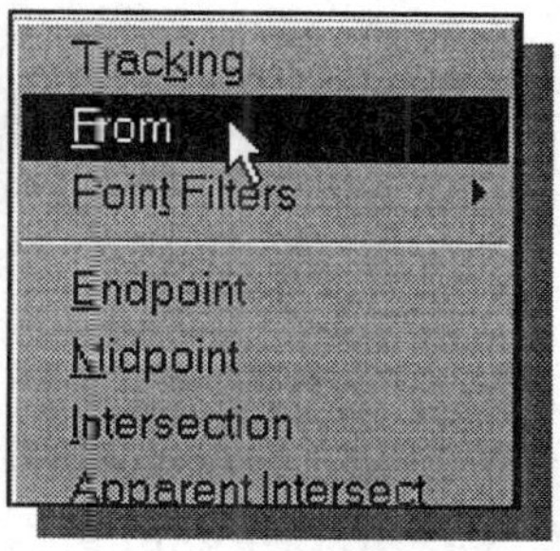

2. Inside the graphics window, hold down the **[SHIFT]** key and **right-mouse-click** once to bring up the *Object Snap* shortcut menu.

3. Select the **From** option in popup window.

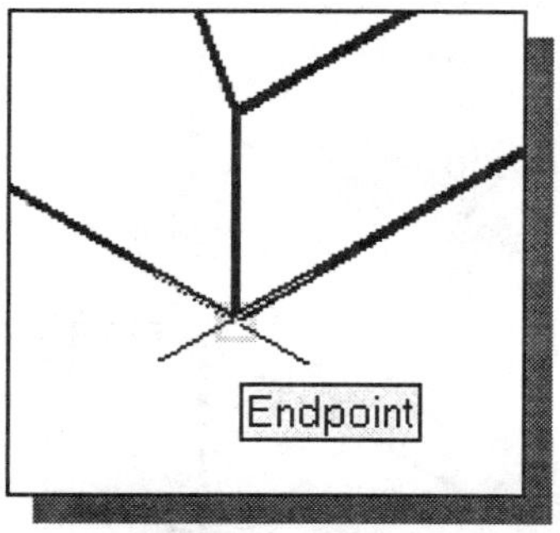

4. Pick the lower-right corner of the solid model as the base point as shown in the figure.

5. We will place the first point above the selected corner. Enter: **@0,0.75 [ENTER]**

- Note the orientation of the world XY-plane.

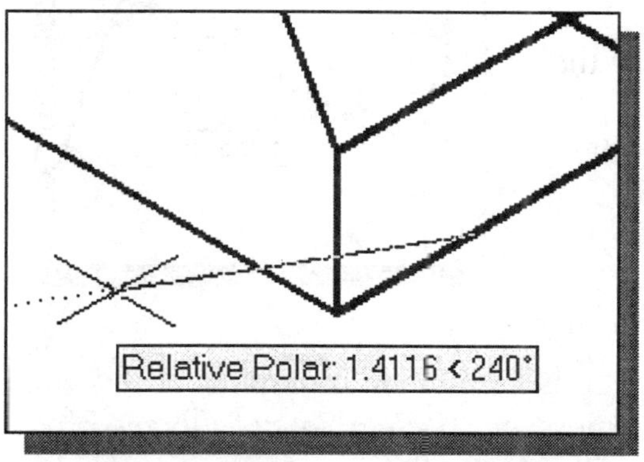

6. In the command prompt area, the message *"Specify next point or [Undo]:"* is displayed. Using the *Polar Tracking* option (30 degrees increment), create a line that is about 1.4 inches long as shown in the figure.

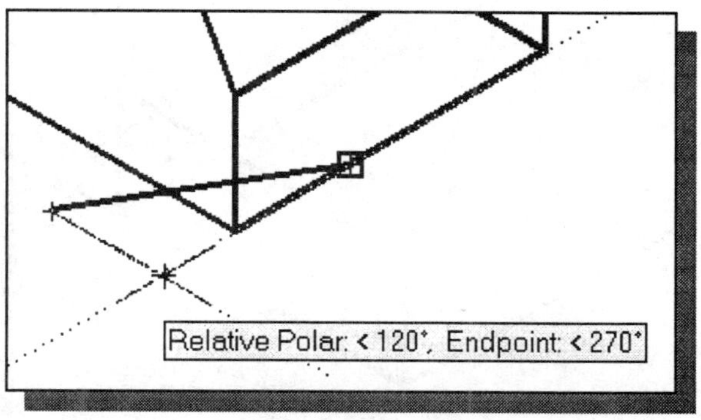

7. Move the cursor on top of the starting point of the last line to activate the *OTRACK* option and select the location that forms a 90-degrees angle as shown.

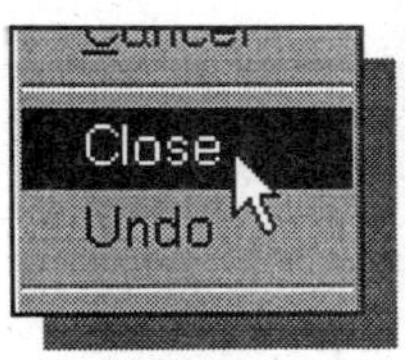

8. Inside the graphics window, **right-mouse-click** to activate the option menu and select **Close** with the left-mouse-button to create a line connecting to the starting point of the line-segments and end the *LINE* command.

Creating a copy of the 2D sketch

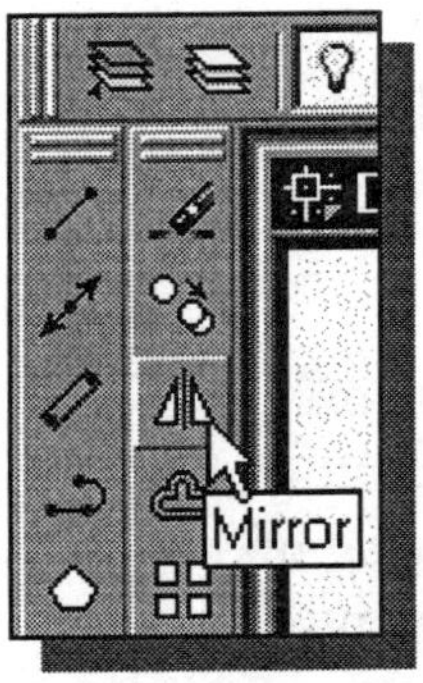

1. Click on the ***Mirror*** icon in the *Modify* toolbar.
2. In the command prompt area, the message *"Select objects:"* is displayed. Select the three line-segments we just created.
3. Inside the graphics window, **right-mouse-click** to accept the selection and proceed with the *EXTRUDE* command.

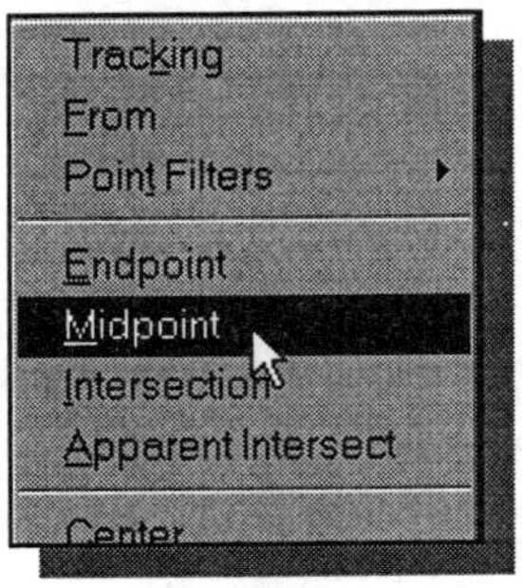

4. Inside the graphics window, hold down the **[SHIFT]** key and **right-mouse-click** once to bring up the *Object Snap* shortcut menu.
5. Select the **Midpoint** option in popup window.

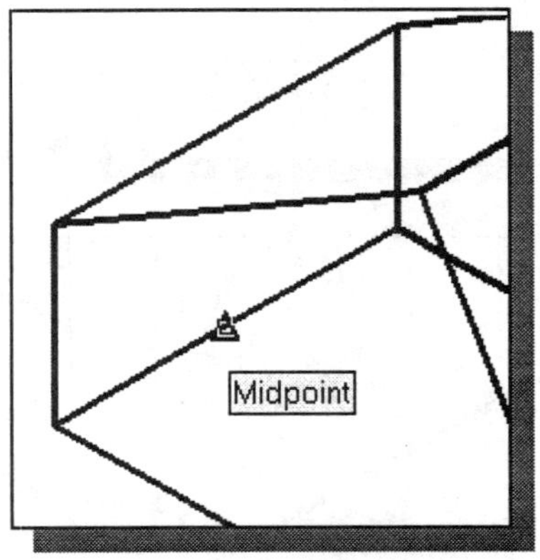

6. Click on the bottom-left edge of the model. With the *Midpoint snap* option, the midpoint of the edge is selected.
7. Move the cursor toward the right-vertical line in the active viewport, left-click once when the ***Perpendicular*** tooltip is displayed as shown in the below figure.

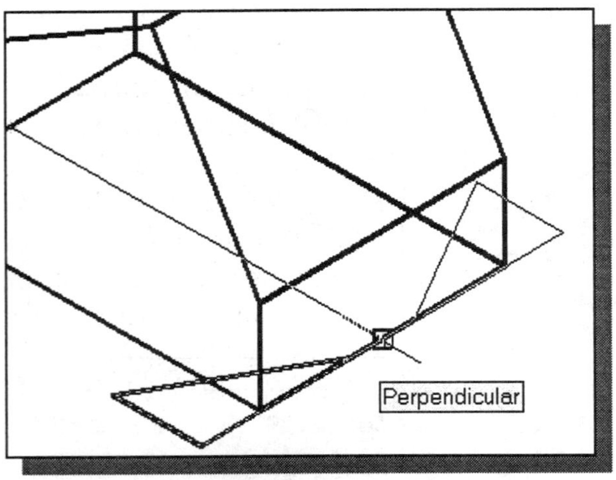

8. In the command prompt area, the message *"Delete Source Objects? [Yes/No] <N>:"* is displayed. Inside the graphics window, **right-mouse-click** once to bring up the option menu and select **No** to keep both sets of objects.

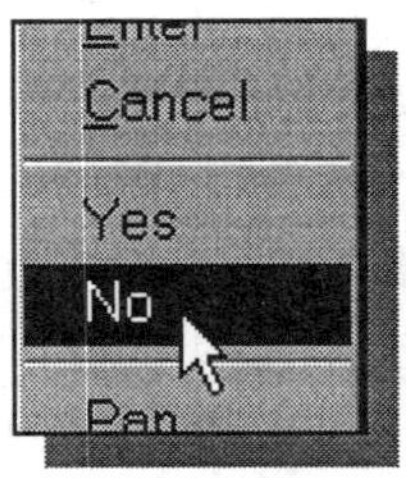

Creating the cutter solids

- The two triangular shapes will be the extruded in the Z-direction to form two solids that can be used to create the two vertical cuts.

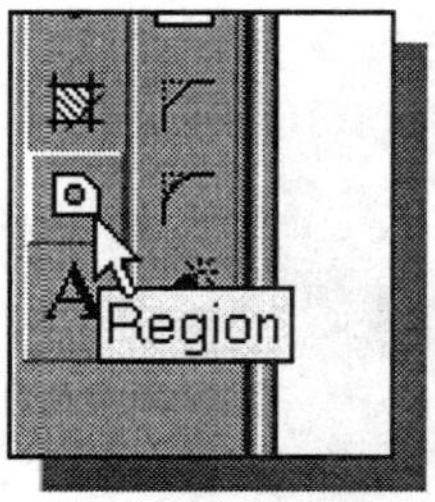

1. Select the ***Region*** command icon in the *Draw* toolbar.
2. In the command prompt area, the message *"Select objects:"* is displayed. Select the six line segments we just created.
3. Inside the graphics window, **right-mouse-click** to accept the selection and create two regions.

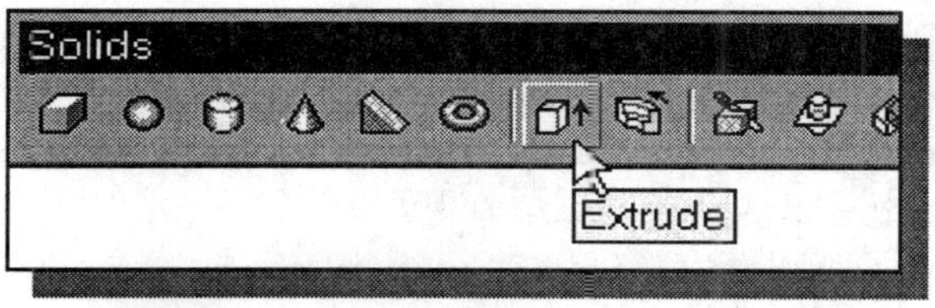

4. Select ***Extrude*** in the *Solids* toolbar as shown.
5. In the command prompt area, the message *"Select objects:"* is displayed. Select the two regions by clicking on the two triangular regions.
6. Inside the graphics window, **right-mouse-click** to accept the selection and proceed with the *EXTRUDE* command.
7. In the command prompt area, the message *"Specify height of extrusion or [path]:"* is displayed. Enter: **2.5 [ENTER]**.
8. In the command prompt area, the message *"Specify angle of taper for extrusion <0>:"* is displayed. Enter: **0.0 [ENTER]**.

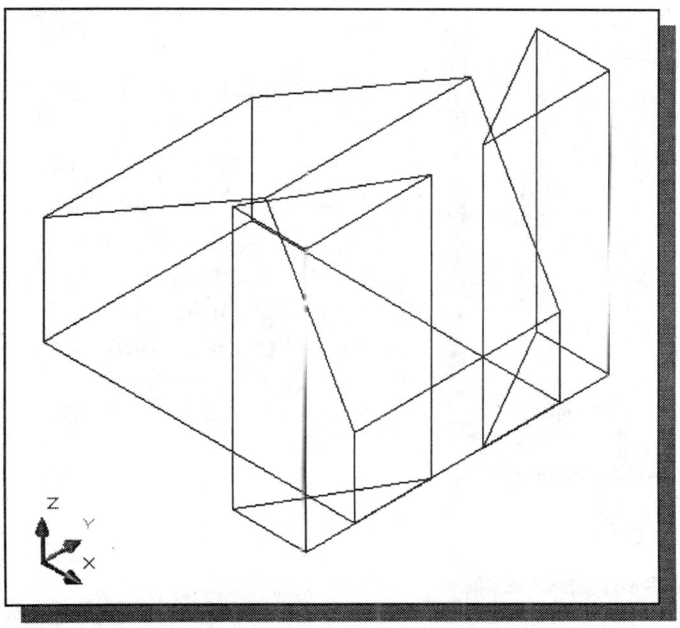

- Note that the two cutters were intentionally made larger than the dimensions shown on the design. In fact, we could create a single cutter, instead of the two we have created, provided the two triangular shapes are included and positioned at the proper locations.

Boolean operation - *Subtract*

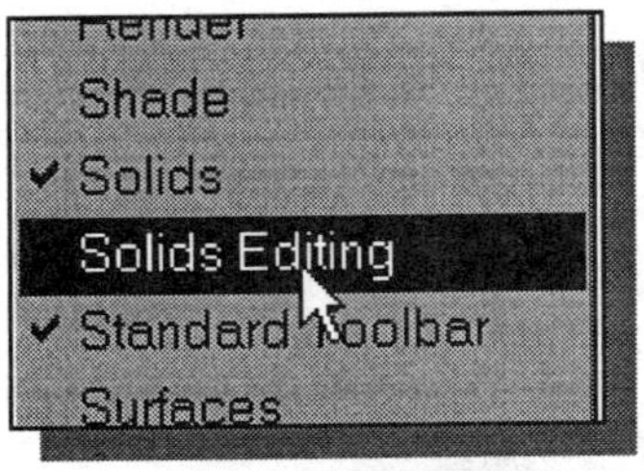

1. Move the cursor to the *Standard* toolbar area and **right-click** on any icon of the *Standard* toolbar to display a list of toolbar menu groups.

2. Select ***Solids Editing***, with the left-mouse-button, to display the *Solids Editing* toolbar on the screen.

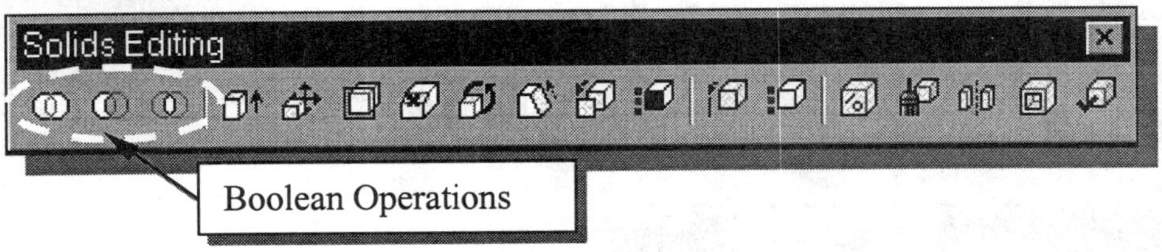

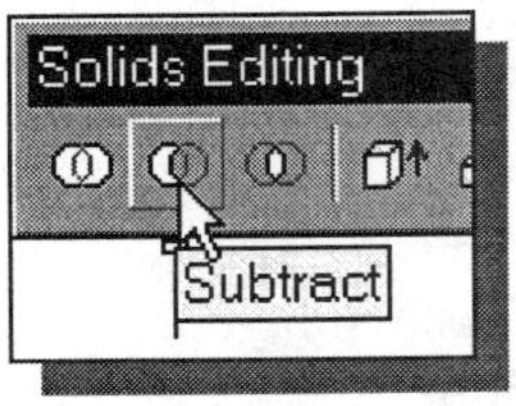

3. In the *Solids Editing* toolbar, click on the ***Subtract*** icon. In the command prompt area, the message *"_subtract Select solids and regions to subtract from .. Select Objects:"* is displayed.

4. Pick the base block solid by clicking on one of the edges.

5. Inside the graphics window, **right-mouse-click** to accept the selection and proceed with the *SUBTRACT* command.

6. In the command prompt area, the message *" Select solids and regions to subtract .. Select Objects:"* is displayed. Pick the two triangular blocks by clicking on the edges of the two cutters.

7. Inside the graphics window, **right-mouse-click** to accept the selection and proceed with the *SUBTRACT* command.

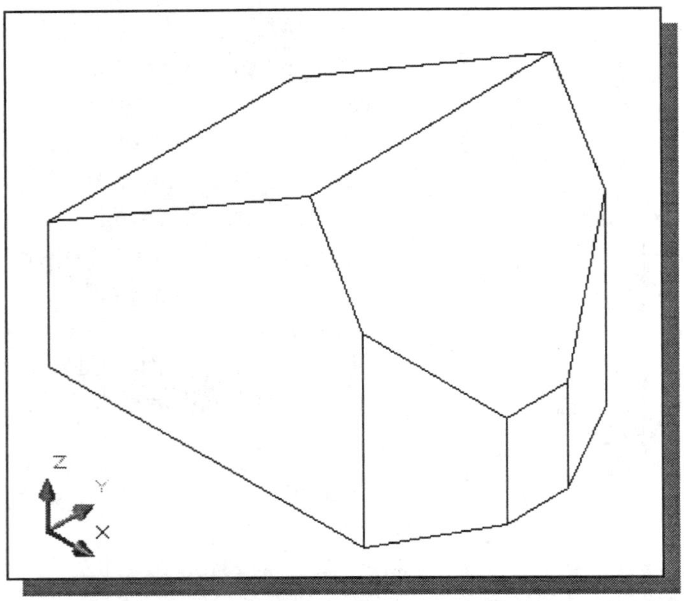

- Note that the two cut features are created fairly quickly. In comparison to the wireframe or surface models created in the previous chapters, the solid modeling approach is much more straight forward and parallel to the manufacturing processes.

Mass properties of the solid model

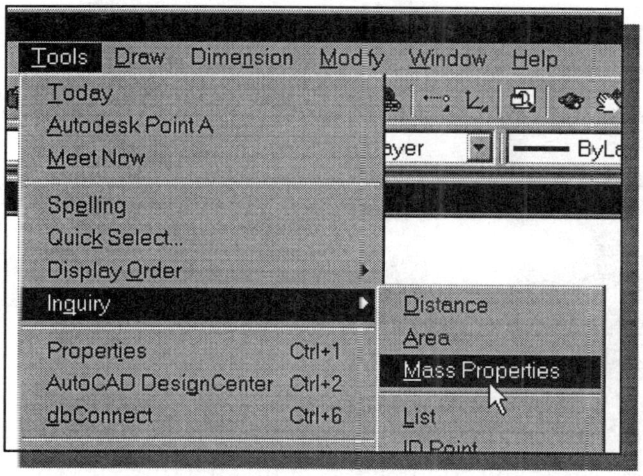

1. In the pull-down menus, select:

   [Tools] => [Inquiry] => [Mass Properties]

2. In the command prompt area, the message *"Select objects:"* is displayed. Select the solid model by clicking on any of the displayed edges of the model.

3. Inside the graphics window, **right-mouse-click** to accept the selection and proceed with the extrude command.

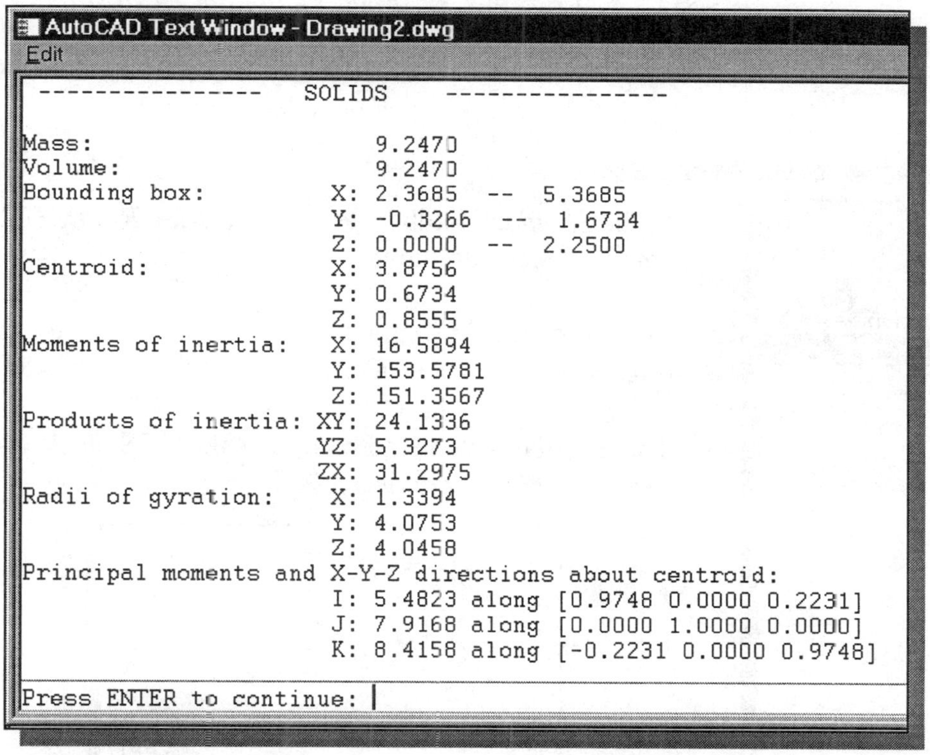

- In the *AutoCAD Text Window*, a list of properties related to the created solid model is displayed. The *Mass* and *Volume* properties are listed as the same since a mass density of one is used for the calculation.

4. Press the **ENTER** key twice to close the *AutoCAD Text Window*.

Align the UCS to the inclined face

➢ We will create an UCS plane aligning to the inclined face of the design.

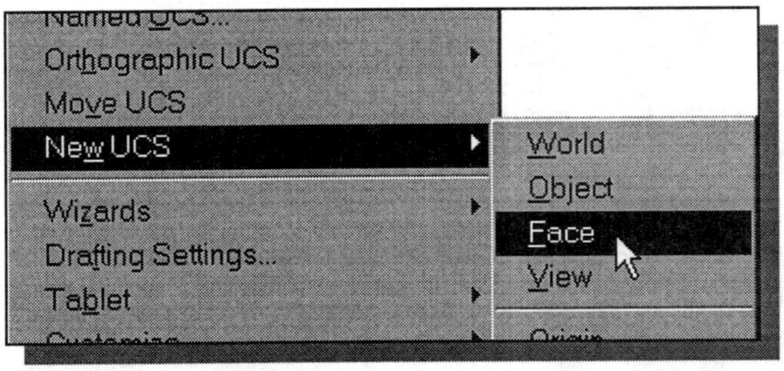

1. In the pull-down menus, select:

   [Tools] => [New UCS] => [Face]

- Note that other options are also available to aid the orientation of new UCS planes.

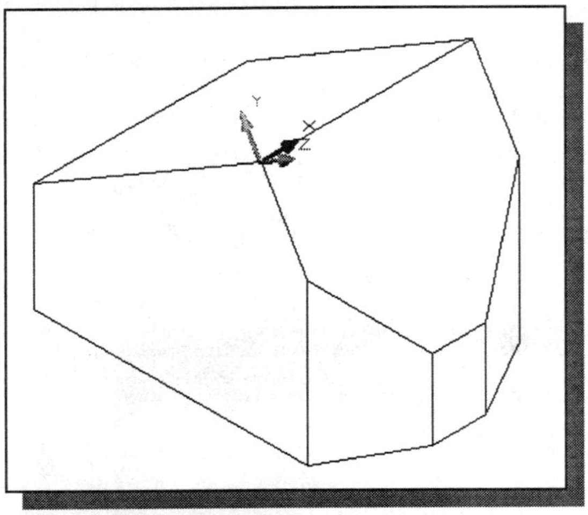

2. In the command prompt area, the message *"Select face of solid object:"* is displayed. Pick the inclined face by clicking on the surface near the upper-left corner.

3. In the command prompt area, the message *"Enter an option [Next/Xflip/Yflip] <accept>:"* is displayed. Press the **ENTER** key to accept the new UCS positioned as shown.

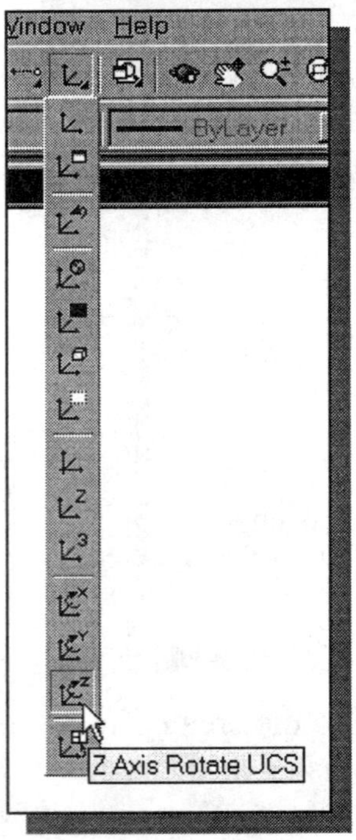

4. In the *Standard* toolbar, select the ***Z Axis Rotate UCS*** command icon as shown.

5. In the command prompt area, the message *"Specify rotation angle about Z-axis <90>:"* is displayed. Enter: **-45** [**ENTER**].

- The negative value entered rotates the UCS clockwise about the current UCS Z-axis.

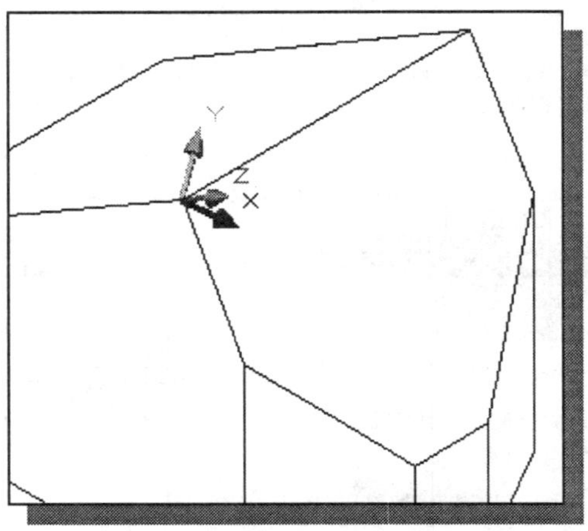

Creating the V-cut

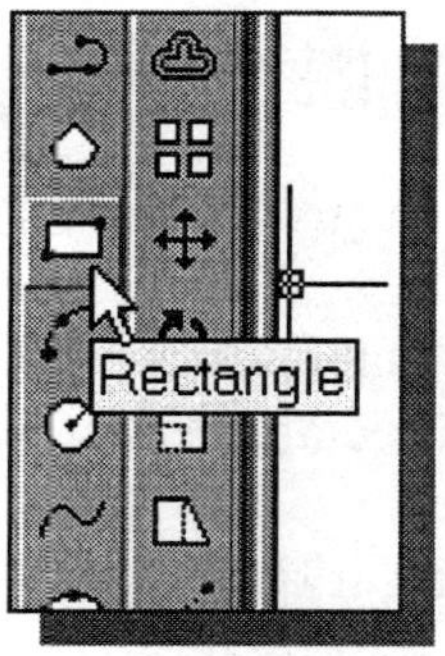

1. Select the ***Rectangle*** icon in the *Draw* toolbar. In the command prompt area, the message *"Specify first corner point or [Chamfer/Elevation/Fillet/Thickness/Width]:"* is displayed.

2. Inside the graphics window, hold down the **[SHIFT]** key and **right-mouse-click** once to bring up the *Object Snap* shortcut menu.

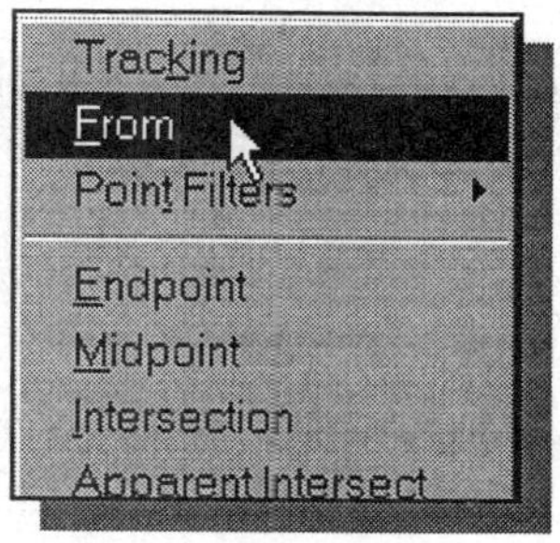

3. Select the **From** option in popup window.

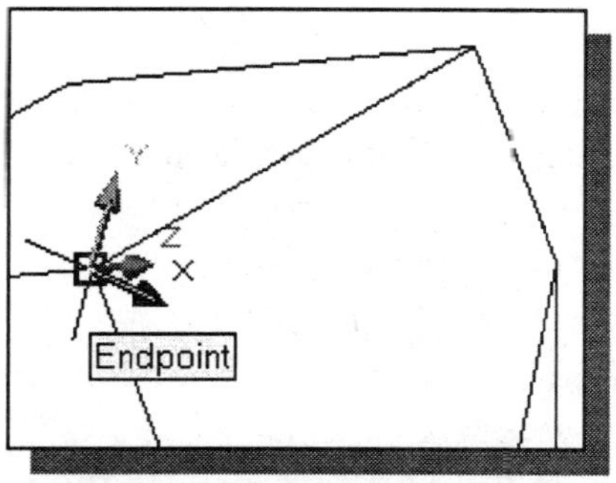

4. Pick the upper-left corner of the inclined surface as the base point as shown in the figure.

5. We will place the first point above the selected corner. Enter: **@0.2<45 [ENTER]**

6. Inside the graphics window, hold down the **[SHIFT]** key and **right-mouse-click** once to bring up the *Object Snap* shortcut menu.

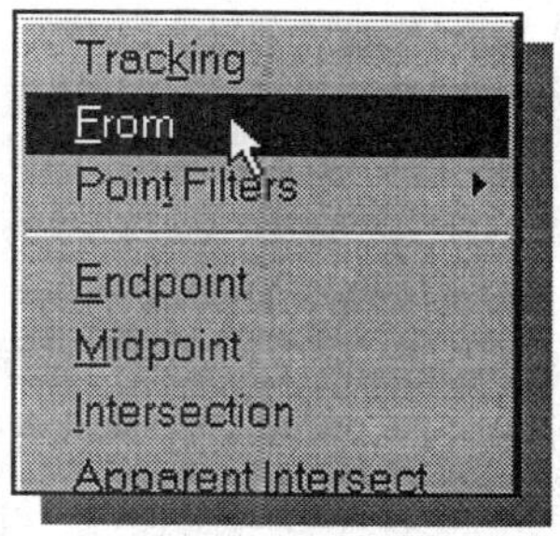

7. Select the **From** option in popup window.

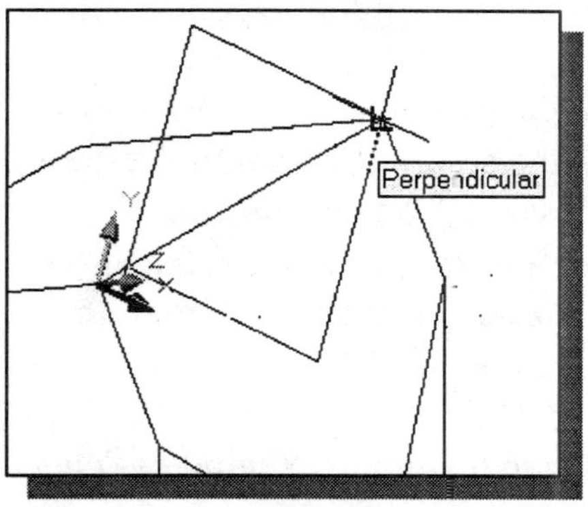

8. Pick the upper-right corner of the inclined surface as the base point as shown in the figure.

9. We will place the first point above the selected corner. Enter: **@0.2<-135 [ENTER]**

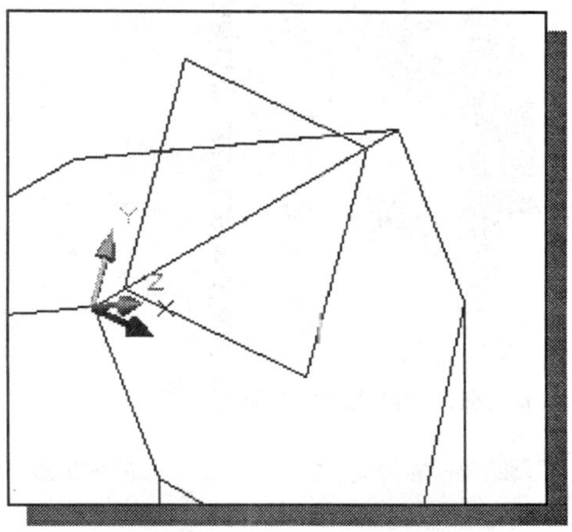

- The above procedure of creating the rectangle at the proper location is simplified by first orienting the UCS.

❖ Note that a rectangle is a valid filled polygon and therefore can be extruded into a solid object.

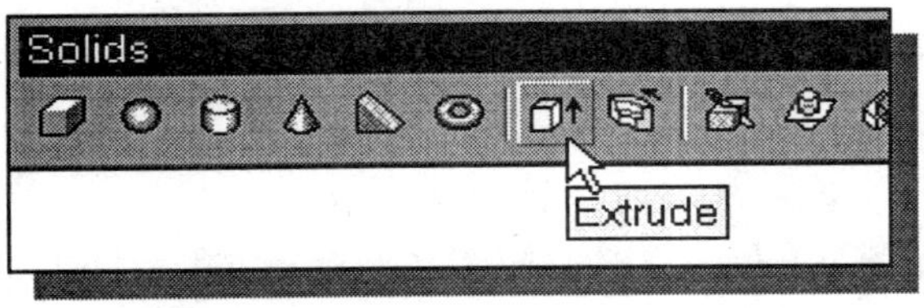

10. Select ***Extrude*** in the *Solids* toolbar as shown.

11. In the command prompt area, the message *"Select objects:"* is displayed. Select the rectangle by clicking on the any edges of the created rectangle.

12. Inside the graphics window, **right-mouse-click** to accept the selection and proceed with the extrude command.

13. In the command prompt area, the message *"Specify height of extrusion or [path]:"* is displayed. Enter: **-4.5 [ENTER]**.

- The negative number indicates the extrusion direction, which needs to be in the negative Z-direction of the current UCS.

14. In the command prompt area, the message *"Specify angle of taper for extrusion <0>:"* is displayed. Enter: **0.0 [ENTER]**.

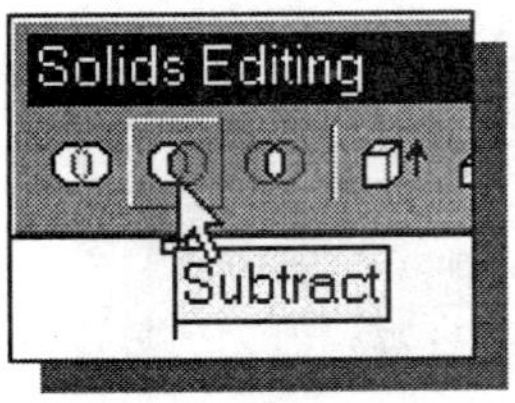

15. In the *Solids Editing* toolbar, click on the ***Subtract*** icon. In the command prompt area, the message *"_subtract Select solids and regions to subtract from .. Select Objects:"* is displayed.

16. Pick the base solid block by clicking on one of the edges.

17. Inside the graphics window, **right-mouse-click** to accept the selection and proceed with the *SUBTRACT* command.

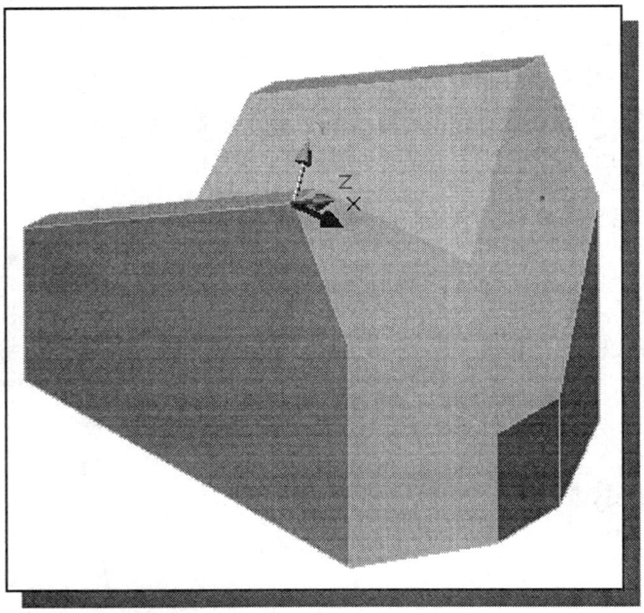

18. In the command prompt area, the message *" Select solids and regions to subtract .. Select Objects:"* is displayed. Pick the rectangular block.

19. Inside the graphics window, **right-mouse-click** to accept the selection and proceed with the *SUBTRACT* command.

- On your own, use the dynamic viewing commands to examine the completed solid model.

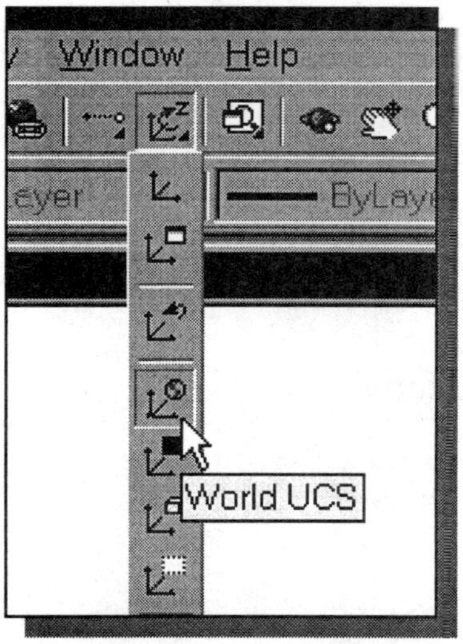

20. In the *Standard* toolbar, select the ***World UCS*** command icon as shown.

- The *WORLD UCS* command aligns the UCS to the world coordinate system.

21. On your own, reset the display to 2D wireframe.

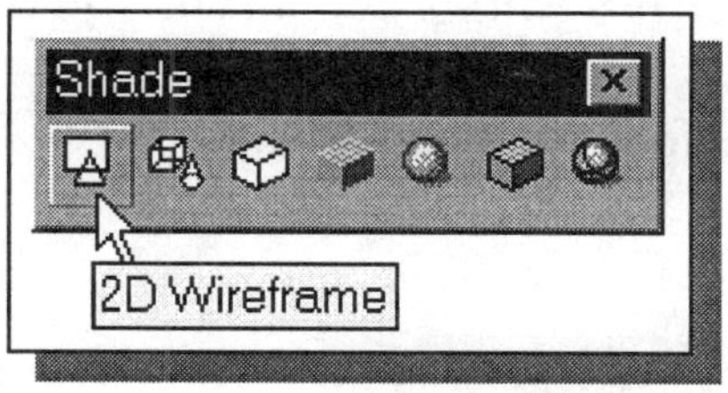

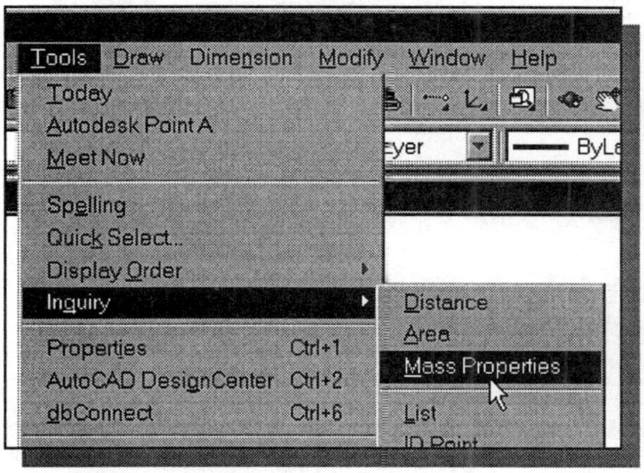

22. In the pull-down menus, select:

    [Tools] => [Inquiry] => [Mass Properties]

23. In the command prompt area, the message *"Select objects:"* is displayed. Select the solid model by clicking on any of the displayed edges of the model.

24. Inside the graphics window, **right-mouse-click** to accept the selection.

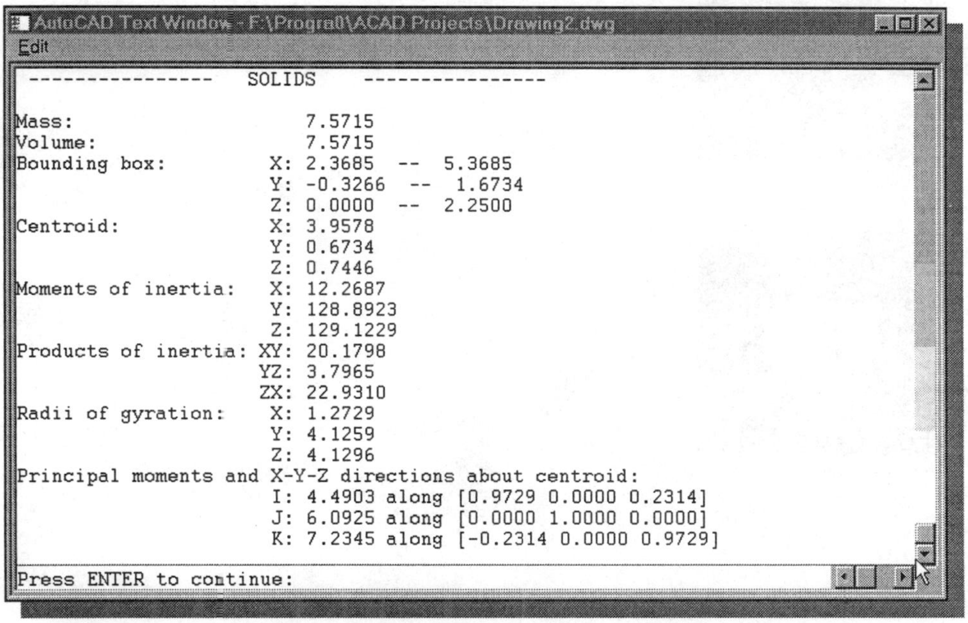

- On your own, compare the displayed values to those shown on page 7-18.

Questions:

1. What is an auxiliary view and why would it be important?

2. When is a line viewed as a point? How can a line be shown in true length?

3. What is a GRIP? What are the advantages of using the GRIPS?

4. List three GRIPS editing commands you have used in the tutorial.

5. Identify the following commands:

(a)

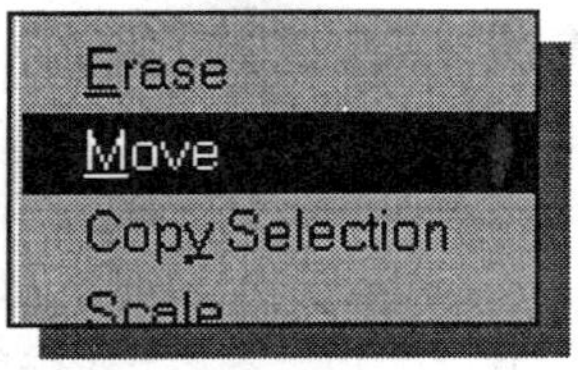

(b)

(c)

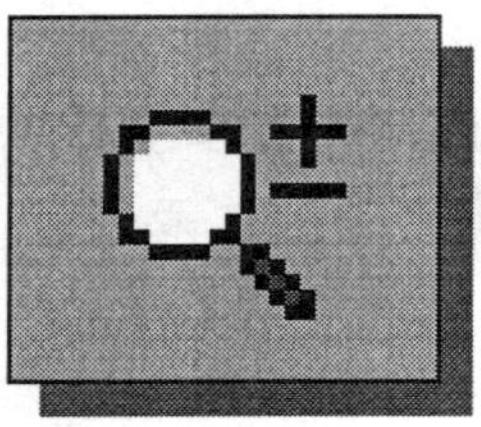

(d)

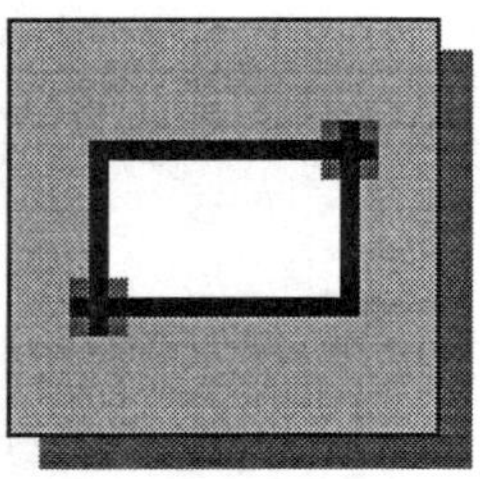

Exercises:

1.

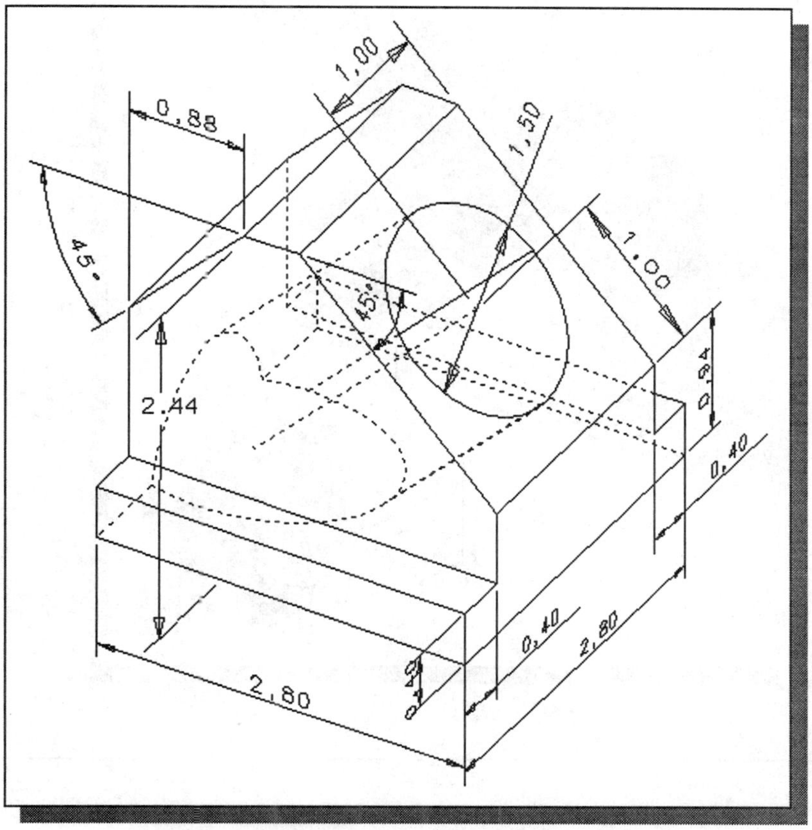

2.

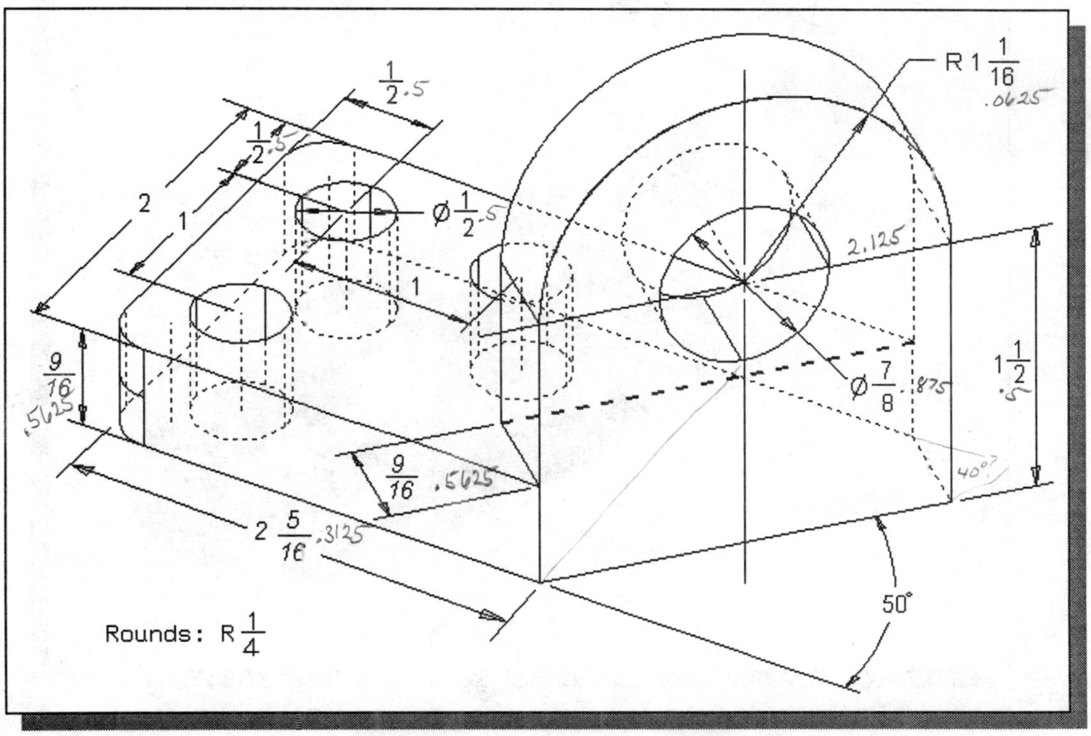

3.

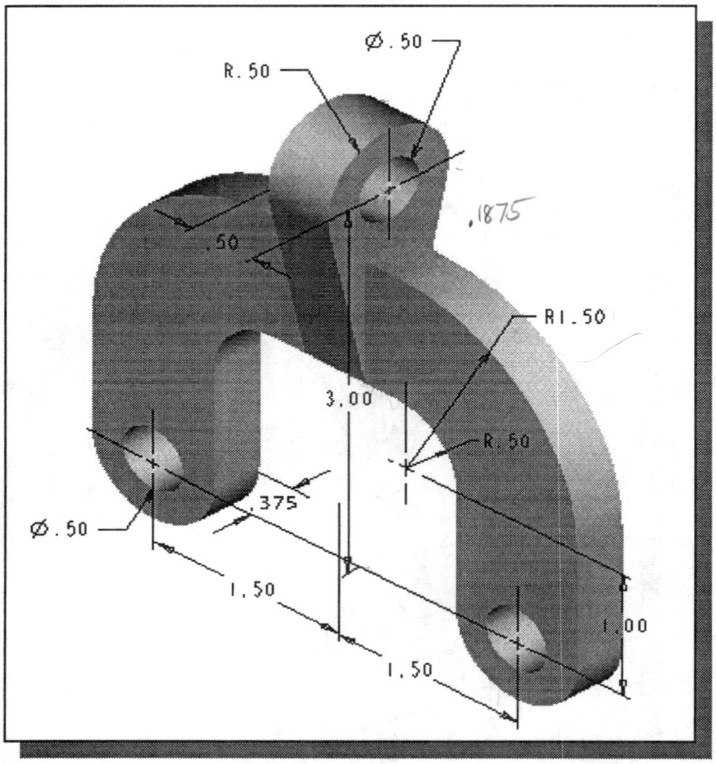

Ø.50
R.50
.50
R1.50
3.00
R.50
.375
Ø.50
1.50
1.00
1.50

4.

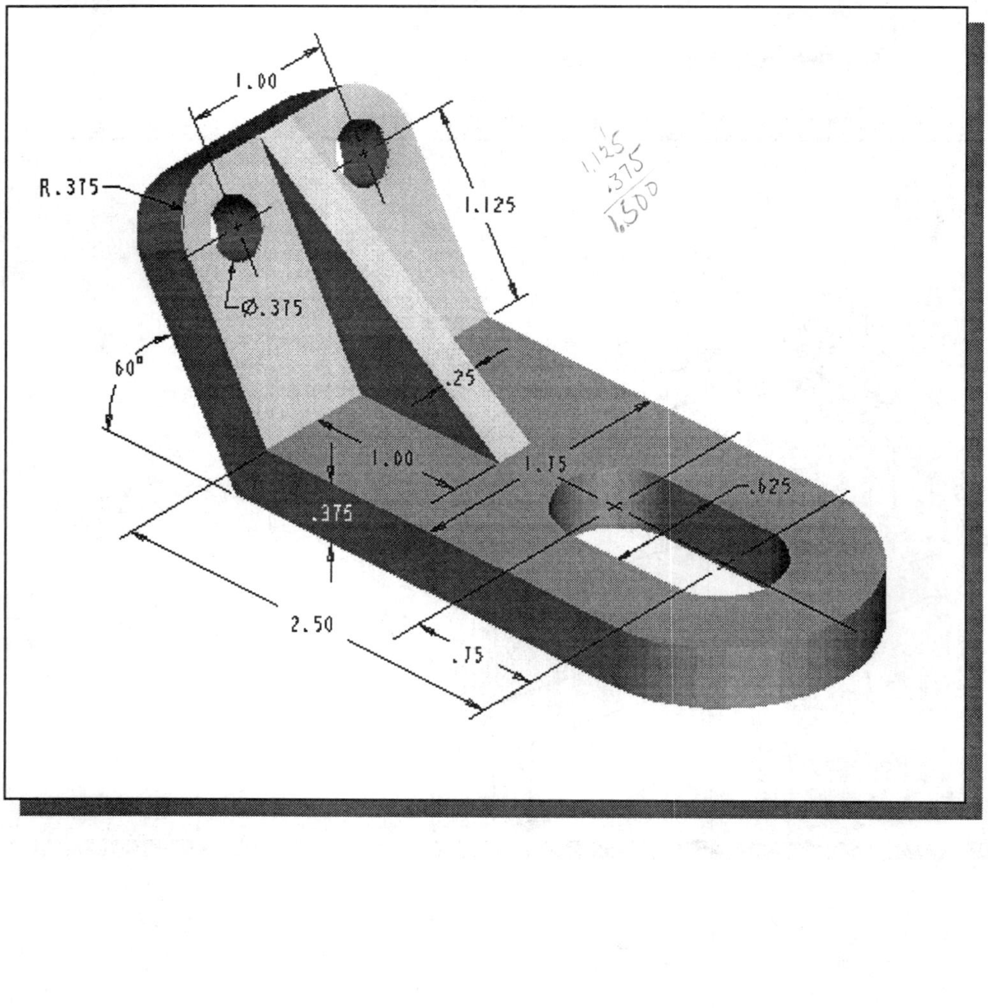

1.00
R.375
1.125
Ø.375
60°
.25
1.00
1.75
.625
.375
2.50
.75

Chapter 8
Multiview Drawings From 3D Models

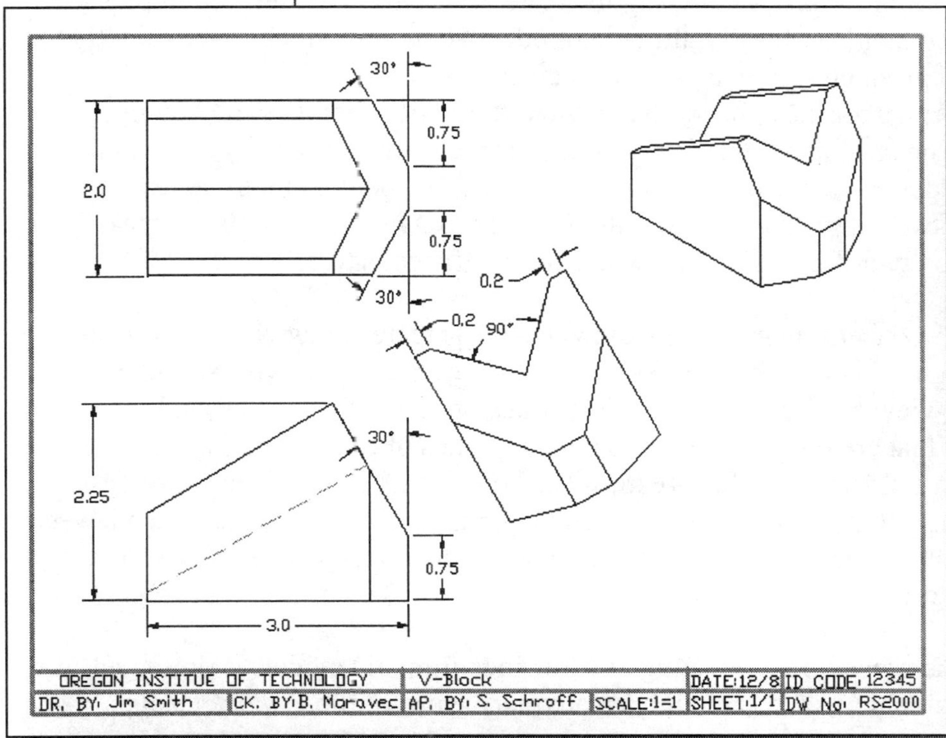

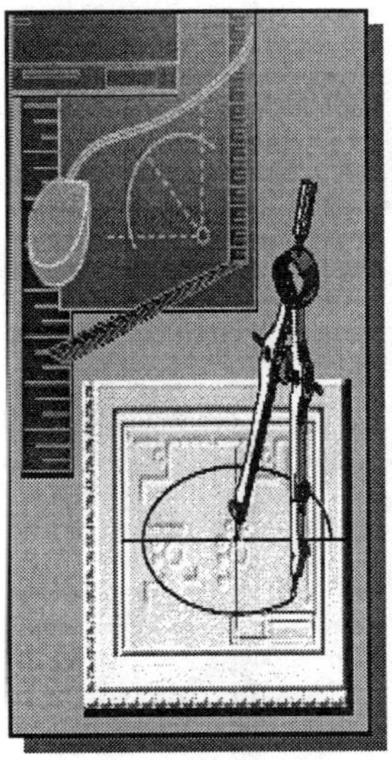

Learning Objectives

- Create Multiview drawings from 3D models.
- Create Borders and Title Block in the Layout mode.
- Create 2D projections from 3D models.
- Create multiple Viewports in Paper Space.
- Align and position 2D projected views in Layout mode.

Introduction

With the capabilities of solid modeling software, the importance of two-dimensional drafting is decreasing. Drafting is now considered as one of the downstream applications of using solid modeling. In many production facilities, solid models are being used to generate machine tool paths for *computer numerical control* (CNC) machine tools. Solid models can also used in *rapid prototyping* to create 3D physical models out of plastic resins, powdered metal, etc. Ideally, the solid model database should be used directly to generate the final product. However, many organizations still require the use of two-dimensional drawings for the applications in their production facilities. In AutoCAD, model views can be used to automatically create 2D views in AutoCAD *paper space*. Using the 3D model as the starting point for a design, 3D modeling tools can easily create all the necessary two-dimensional views. In this sense, 3D modeling tools are making the process of creating two-dimensional drawings more efficient and effective.

An important rule concerning multiview drawings is to create enough views to accurately describe the design. This usually requires two or three of the regular views, such as a front-view, a top-view and/or a side-view. Many designs have features located on inclined surfaces that are not parallel to the regular planes of projection. To truly describe the feature, the true shape of the feature must be shown using an **auxiliary view**. An *auxiliary view* has a line of sight that is perpendicular to the inclined surface, as viewed looking directly at the inclined surface. An *auxiliary view* is a supplementary view that can be constructed from any of the regular views.

In this chapter, the procedure of creating 2D drawings from 3D models is presented. We will create orthographic views, including an auxiliary view, of the *V-block* design.

The *V-Block* Design

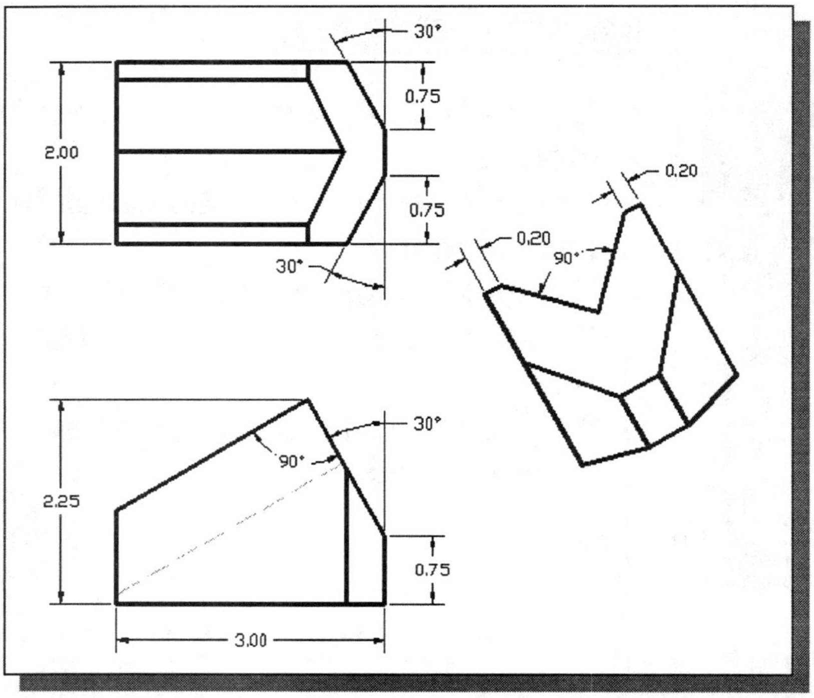

Starting Up AutoCAD® 2000i

1. Select the AutoCAD® 2000i option on the *Program* menu or select the AutoCAD® 2000i icon on the *Desktop*. Once the program is loaded into the memory, the AutoCAD® 2000i drawing screen and the *AutoCAD Today* startup dialog box will appear on the screen.

2. In the *AutoCAD Today* startup dialog box, select the **Open Drawings** tab with a single click of the left-mouse-button.

3. Open the *V-block* solid model created in the previous chapter by clicking on the corresponding filename. (Use the *Browse* option to locate the solid model file if it is not displayed.)

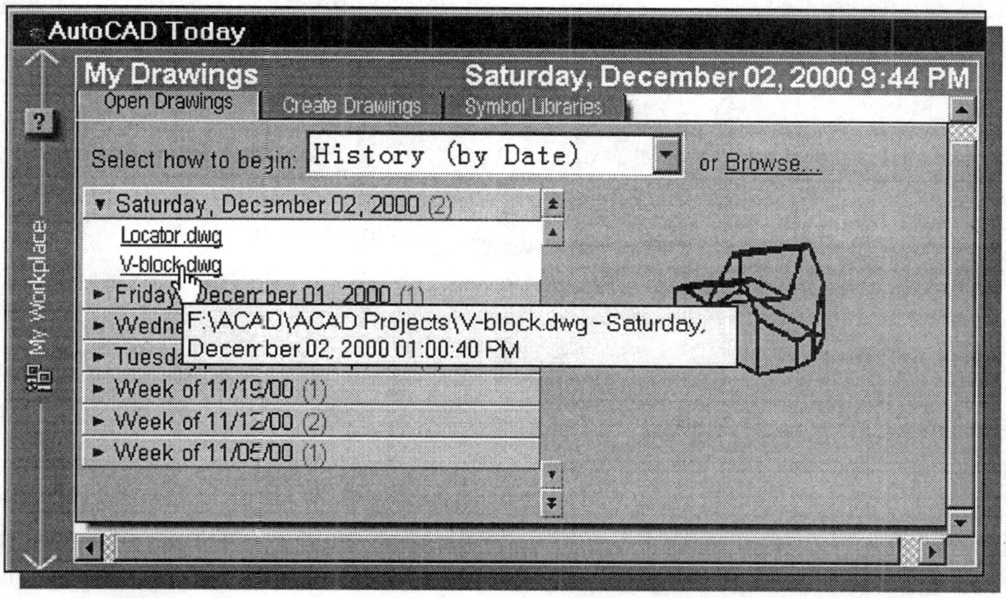

- The *V-block* solid model is retrieved and displayed in the graphics window.

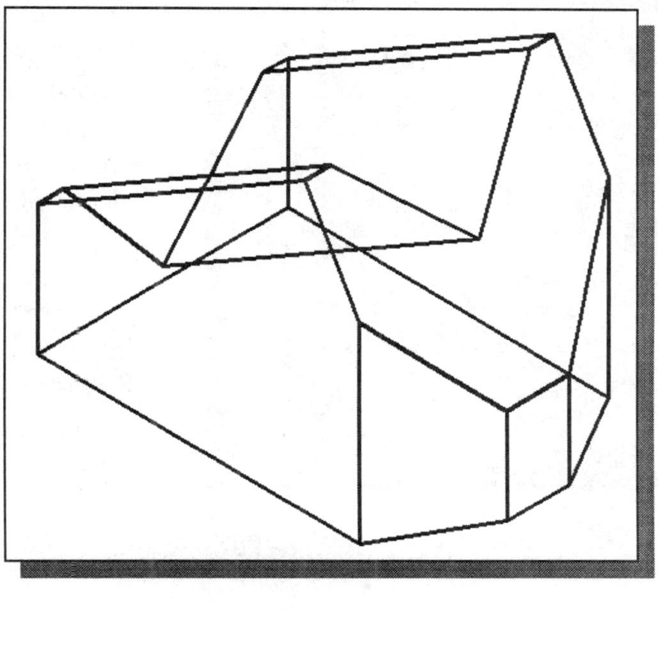

AutoCAD Paper Space

- Until now, we have been working in ***model space*** to create our design in **full size**. Once the 3D model is constructed, we can arrange our design on a two-dimensional sheet of paper so that the plotted hardcopy is exactly what we want. This two-dimensional sheet of paper is known as ***paper space*** in AutoCAD. We can place borders and title blocks on *paper space*, the objects that are less critical to our design.

1. In the *Standard* toolbar, select the ***World UCS*** command icon as shown.

- The default 2D views generated in *paper space* are oriented based on the *World Coordinate System*. It is always a good idea to align the UCS to the WCS prior to entering the AutoCAD paper space.

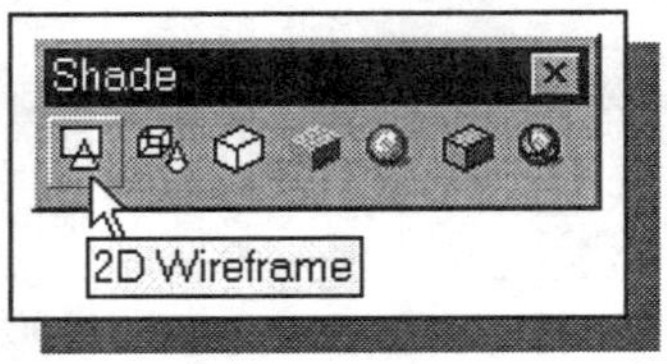

2. On your own, reset the display to *2D Wireframe*.

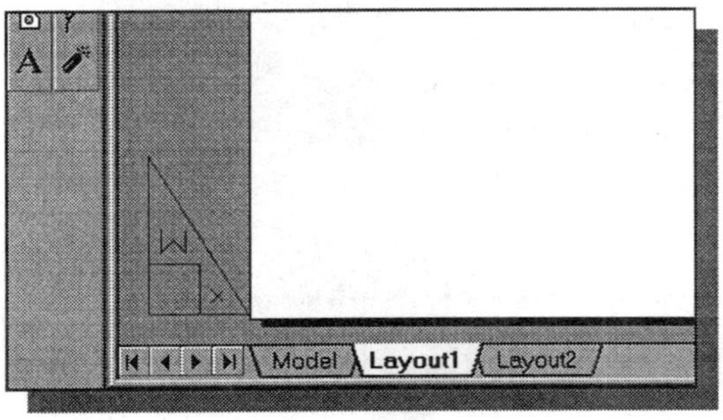

3. Pick the **Layout1** tab to switch to the two-dimensional paper space. The *Page Setup* dialog box appears.

4. In the *Page Setup* dialog box, select a plotter/printer that is available to your system. Consult with your instructor or technical support personnel if you have difficulty identifying the hardware.

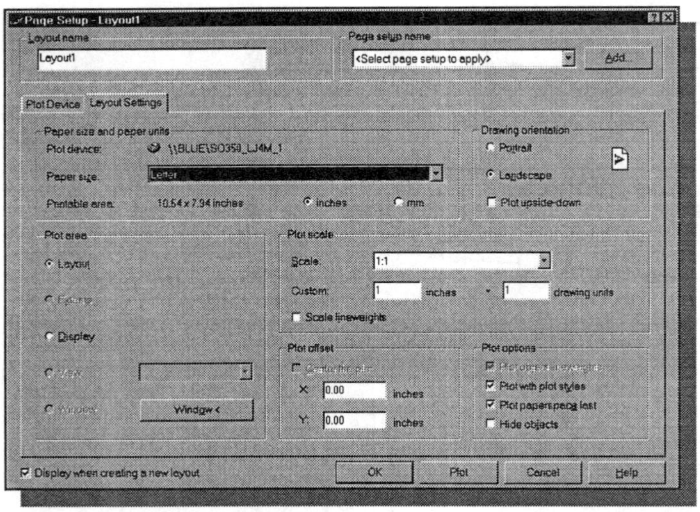

❖ In this chapter, we will demonstrate the plotting procedure for an A-size plot on a LaserJet printer. The procedure described here is also applicable to other types of printers and plotters.

5. Confirm the *Paper size* is set to *Letter* or equivalent (8.5" by 11") and the *Drawing orientation* is set to *Landscape*.

6. Click on the **OK** button to accept the settings and exit the *Page Setup* dialog box.

❖ In the graphics window, a rectangular outline on a gray background indicates the paper size. The dashed lines displayed within the paper indicate the *printable area*. The 3D model appears inside a solid rectangle, which is known as a **viewport**. Note that the orientation of the model is identical to that of the model space.

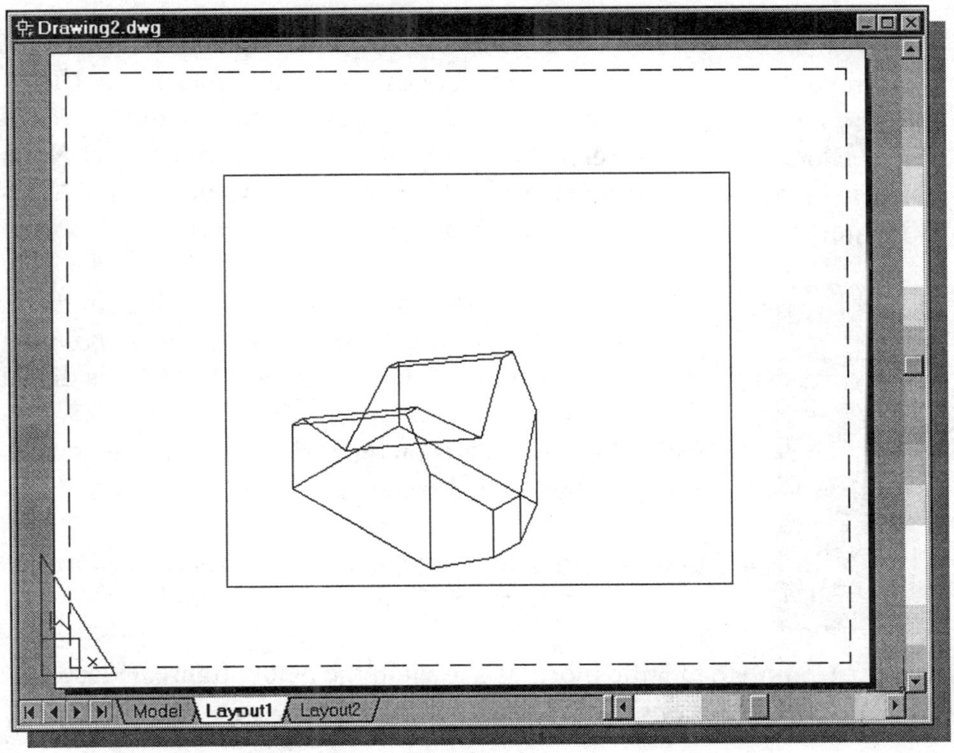

Deleting the displayed viewport

- Viewports can be considered as objects with a view into model space that we can move and resize. Floating viewports can be overlapping or separated from one another. We can also create new viewports, as well as deleting them.

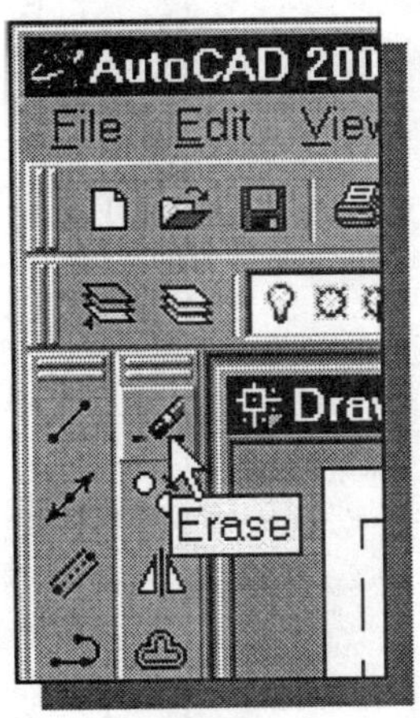

1. Pick ***Erase*** in the *Modify* toolbar.

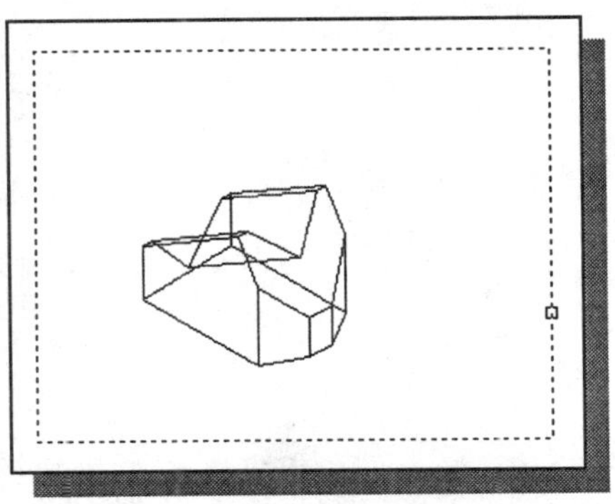

2. The message *"Select objects"* is displayed in the command prompt area and AutoCAD awaits us to select the objects to erase. Pick the viewport by clicking on one of the edges of the viewport border.

3. Inside the graphics window, **right-mouse-click** to accept the selection and delete the viewport.

Adding borders and title block in the layout

➢ AutoCAD 2000i allows us to create plots/prints to any exact scale on the paper. We can place borders and title blocks on *paper space*, the objects that are less critical to our design.

1. On your own, create two new layers and set *Title_Block* as the *Current layer*.

Layer	*Color*	*LineType*	*Lineweight*	*PlotStyle*
Title_Block	**Green**	**Continuous**	**1.2mm**	**Normal**
Dimensions	**Magenta**	**Continuous**	**Default**	**Normal**
Viewport	**White/Black**	**Continuous**	**Default**	**Normal**

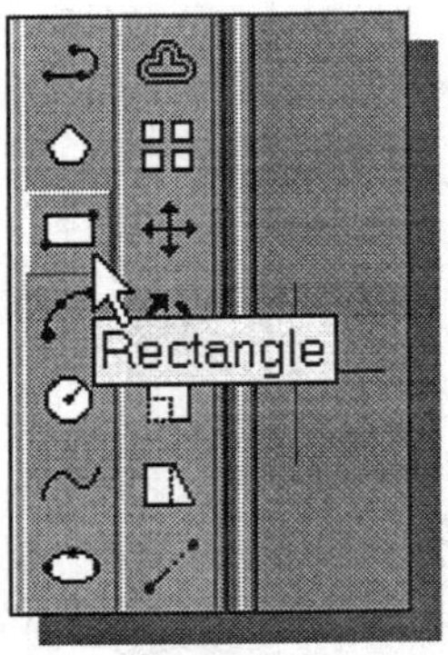

2. Select the ***Rectangle*** icon in the *Draw* toolbar. In the command prompt area, the message *"Specify first corner point or [Chamfer/Elevation/Fillet/Thickness/Width]:"* is displayed.

3. Pick a location that is on the inside and near the lower left corner of the dashed rectangle.

4. In the command prompt area, use the *relative coordinate entry method* and create a 10.25"X7.75" rectangle.

5. Complete the title block as shown in the below figure. (Place the *TEXT* in the *Dimensions* layer.)

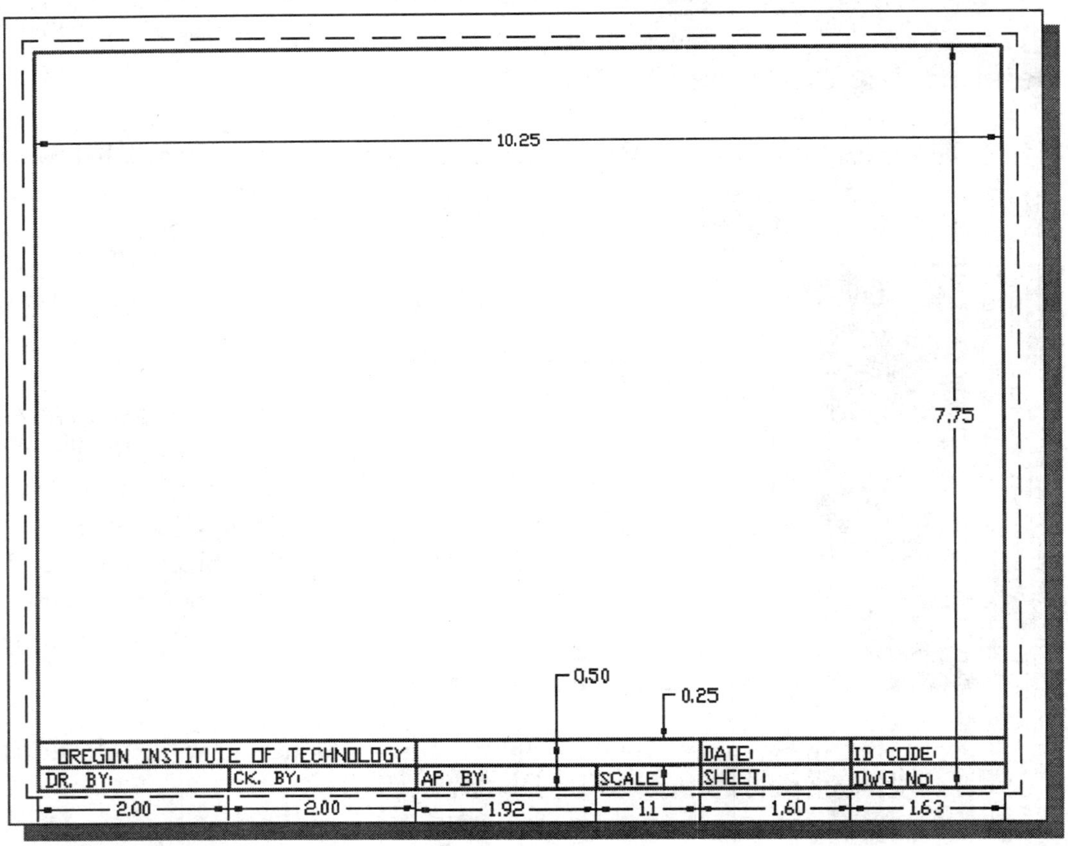

Setting up Viewports inside the Titleblock

- Viewports can be used in both model mode and in layout mode. In *model mode*, only *tiled viewports* (viewports cannot overlap each other) can be created. In *layout mode, floating viewports* (viewports can overlap each other) can be created to set up standard 2D views from 3D models.

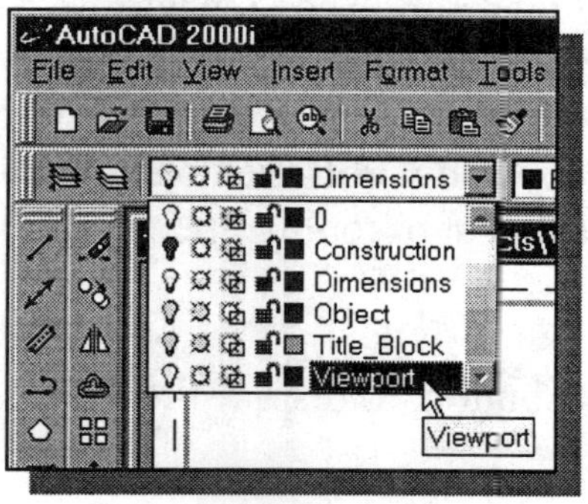

1. In the *Object Properties* toolbar area, select the ***Layer Control*** box and set layer *Viewport* layer as the *Current layer*.

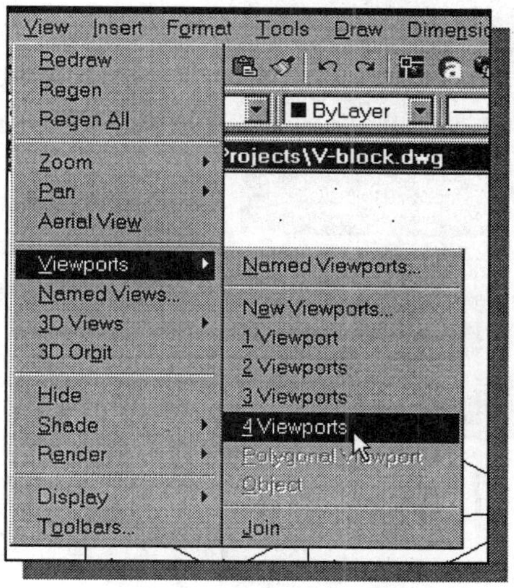

2. In the pull-down menus, select:

[View] => [Viewports] => [4 viewports]

3. In the command prompt area, the message *"Specify first corner of viewport or [Fit] <Fit>:"* is displayed. Pick a corner near the lower-left corner of the created border as shown in the below figure.

4. In the command prompt area, the message *"Specify opposite corner:"* is displayed. Pick a corner near the upper-right corner of the border as shown.

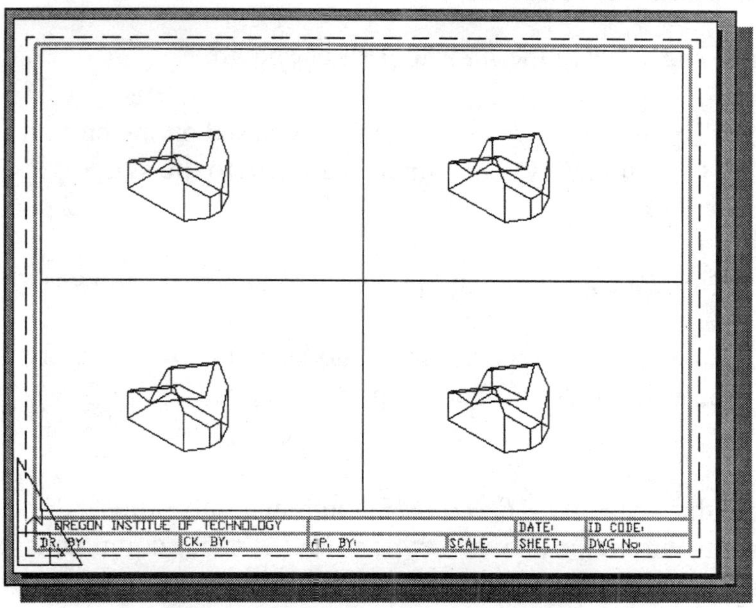

- Four viewports, with rectangular viewport borders, displaying the same isometric view are created.

Setting up the standard views

➢ AutoCAD allows us to control the display of the model inside the created viewports. This is accomplished by switching to *model mode* within each viewport. In *layout mode*, either the *paper space* is activated or one of the created viewport is activated at one time. When a viewport is activated, the model space of the viewport is opened, the model mode commands become available with the viewport. The viewport with the darker border is the active viewport.

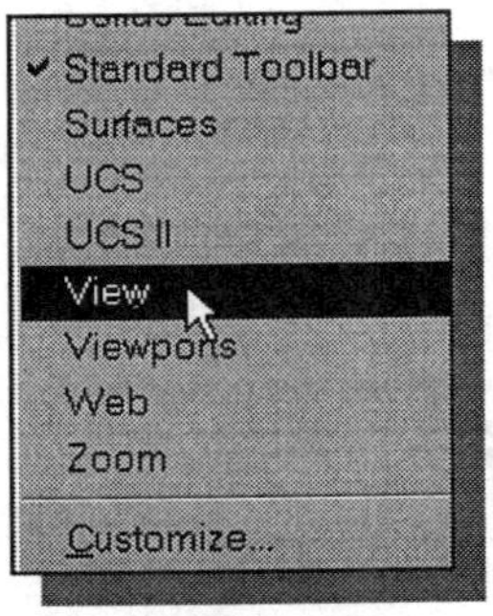

1. Move the cursor on top of any icon and **right-click** on any icon of the *Standard* toolbar to display a list of toolbar menu groups.

2. Select **View**, with the left-mouse-button, to display the *View* toolbar on the screen.

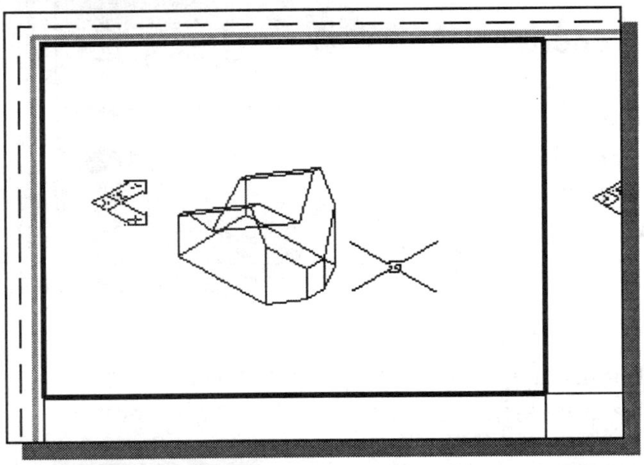

3. Move the cursor inside the upper-left viewport.

4. Double-click with the left-mouse-button to activate the viewport.

- Note the darker border and the cursor-display of the active viewport.

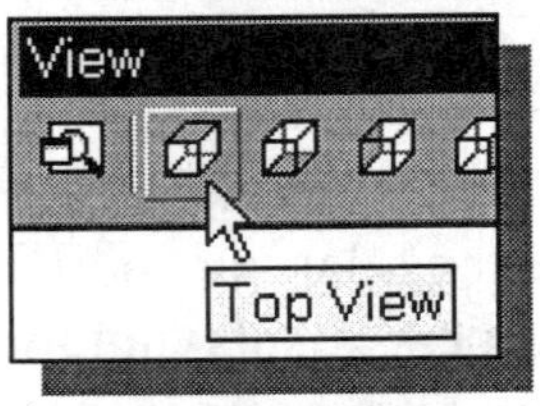

5. Pick ***Top View*** in the *View* toolbar as shown.

- The display is changed to the top view based on the current User Coordinate System, which is aligned to the WCS.

6. Pick ***Pan Realtime*** in the *Standard* toolbar as shown.

7. On your own, reposition the model so that it is roughly near the center of the viewport.

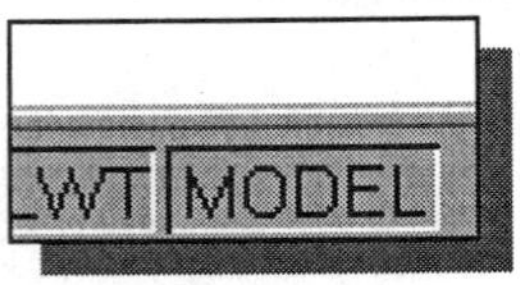

- Note that the ***PAN REALTIME*** command only adjusts the display within the active viewport. Model space commands are only available in the active viewport.

- On your own, experiment with other display related commands, such as *3D ORBIT* and *ZOOM*.

8. Move the cursor inside the lower-right viewport. Left-clicking once inside the viewport to activate the viewport.

9. On your own, repeat the above steps and set the four viewports to display the standard four engineering views, as shown in the below figure. (The standard four engineering views are: **Top**, **Front**, **Right**, and **Isometric**)

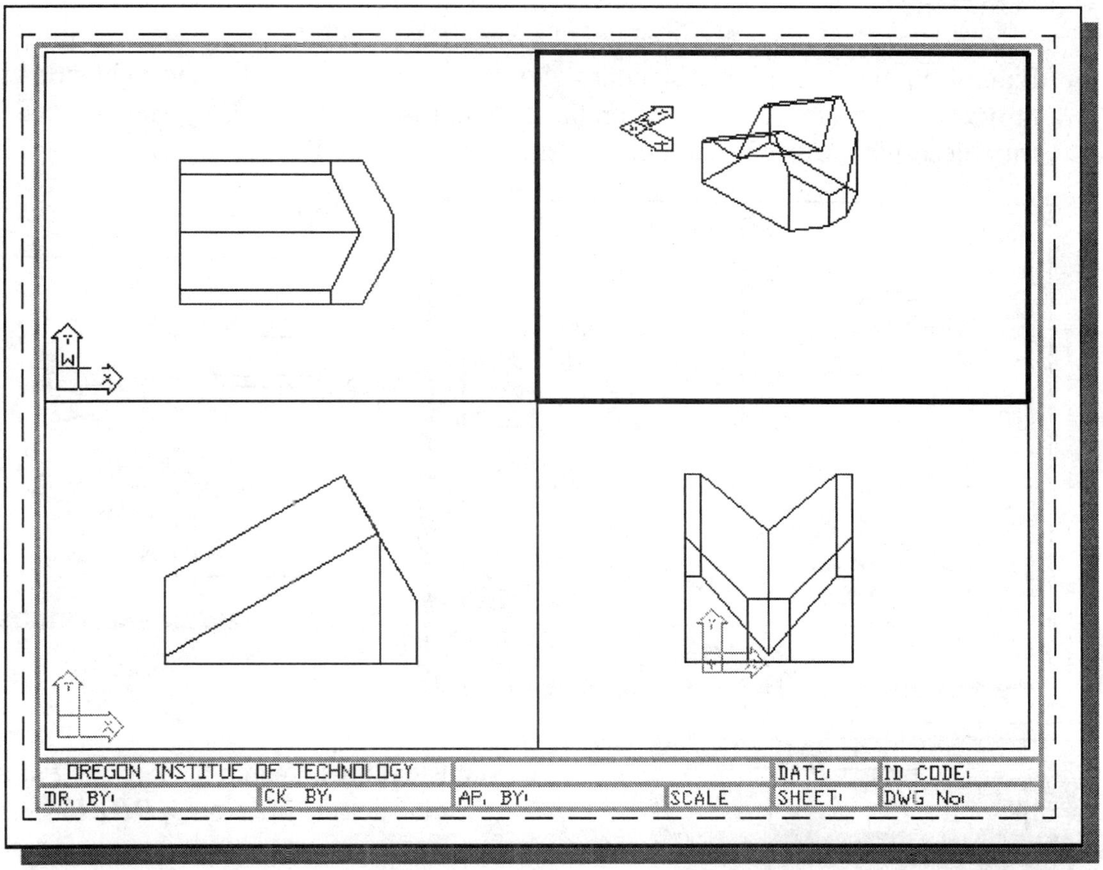

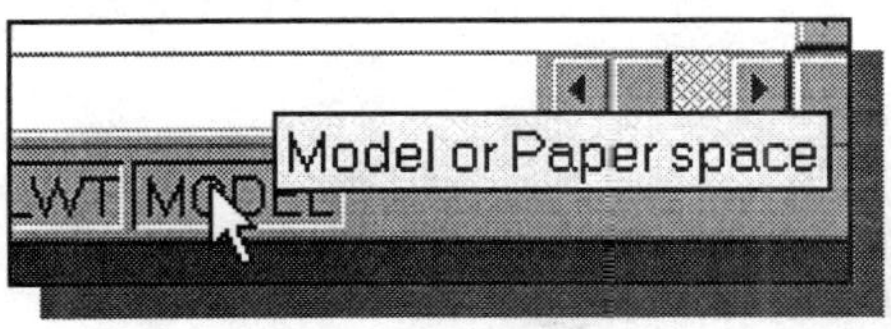

10. In the status bar area, switch back to the ***Paper Space*** by left-clicking once on ***MODEL***.

11. Click on ***PAPER*** to switch back to *MODEL* space and note the last active viewport is activated again.

- The 3D model is displayed in all viewports; note that there is <u>only one 3D model</u>. The multiple viewports simply allow us to view the same model from different angles simultaneously. This approach assures the correctness and accuracy of the 2D views of the model since the views are generated from the database of the same 3D model.

Determining the necessary 2D views

- Multiview drawings usually require two or three of the regular views, such as a front-view, a top-view and/or a side-view. Many designs have features located on inclined surfaces that are not parallel to the regular planes of projection. For the *V-block* design, to truly describe the V-cut feature, the true shape of the feature must be shown using an **auxiliary view**. An *auxiliary view* has a line of sight that is perpendicular to the inclined surface, as viewed looking directly at the inclined surface. An *auxiliary view* is a supplementary view that can be constructed from any of the regular views.

➢ Examining the current four standard views, we can conclude that the right side view provides no crucial information on the design. Instead, an *auxiliary view* is needed to truly describe the V-cut feature.

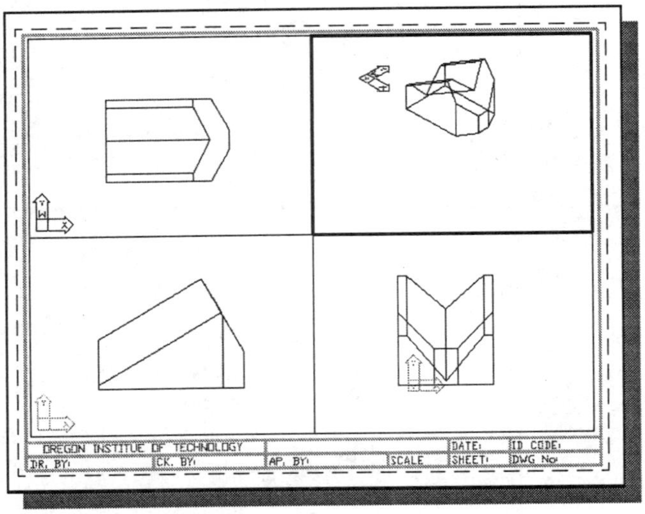

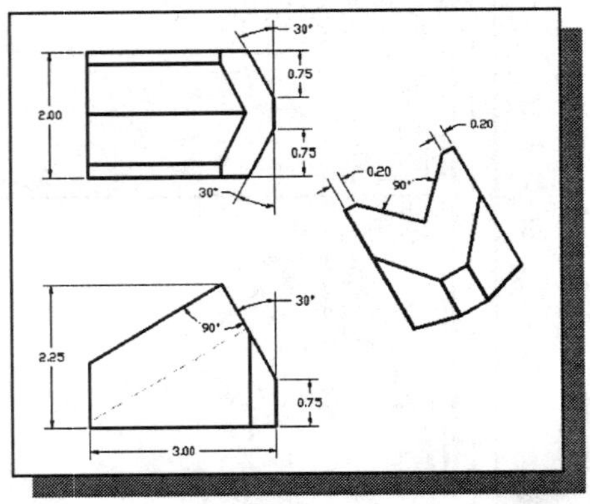

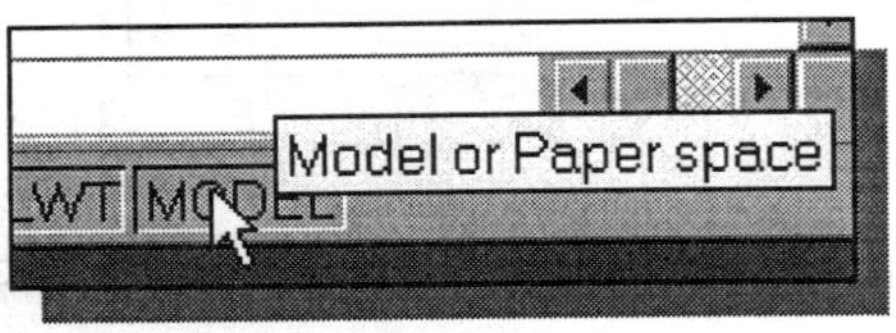

1. In the status bar area, switch back to the ***Paper Space*** by left-clicking once on ***MODEL***.

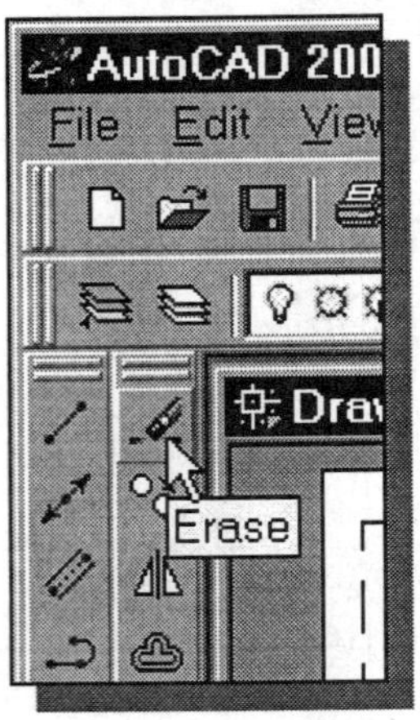

2. Pick ***Erase*** in the *Modify* toolbar.

3. The message *"Select objects"* is displayed in the command prompt area and AutoCAD awaits us to select the objects to erase. Pick the lower-right viewport by clicking on one of the edges of the viewport border.

4. Inside the graphics window, **right-mouse-click** to accept the selection and delete the viewport.

Establishing an auxiliary view in Model Mode

- AutoCAD provides us with many options to establish new viewpoints. The easiest approach is to create a new UCS aligned to the inclined plane of the design and then adjust the display view to the UCS.

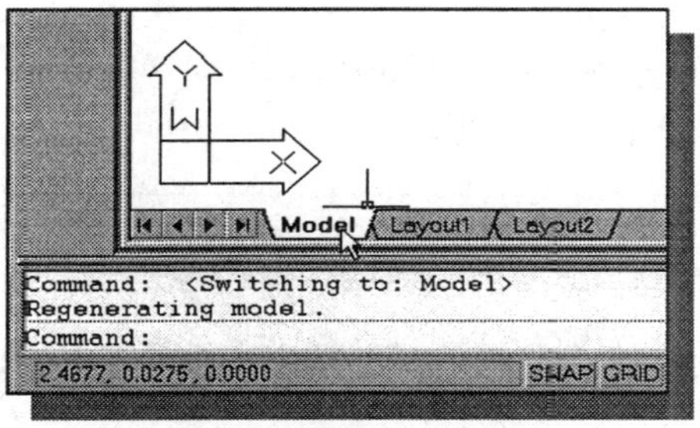

1. Pick the **Model** tab to switch back to model space.

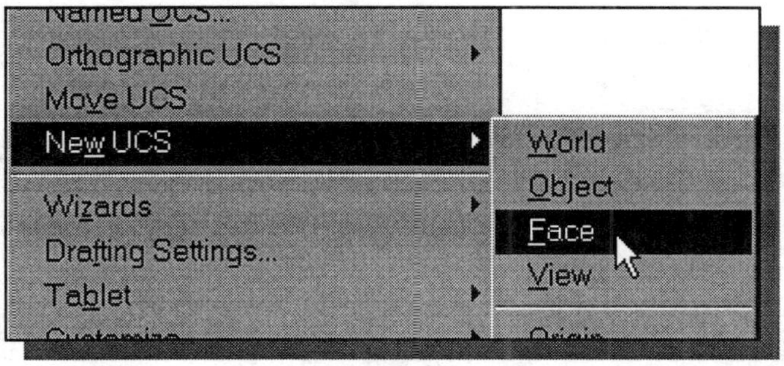

2. In the pull-down menus, select:

   [Tools] => [New UCS] => [Face]

3. In the command prompt area, the message *"Select face of solid object:"* is displayed. Pick the inclined face by clicking on the surface near the bottom edge of the surface.

4. In the command prompt area, the message *"Enter an option [Next/Xflip/Yflip] <accept>:"* is displayed. Press the **ENTER** key once to accept the new UCS positioned as shown.

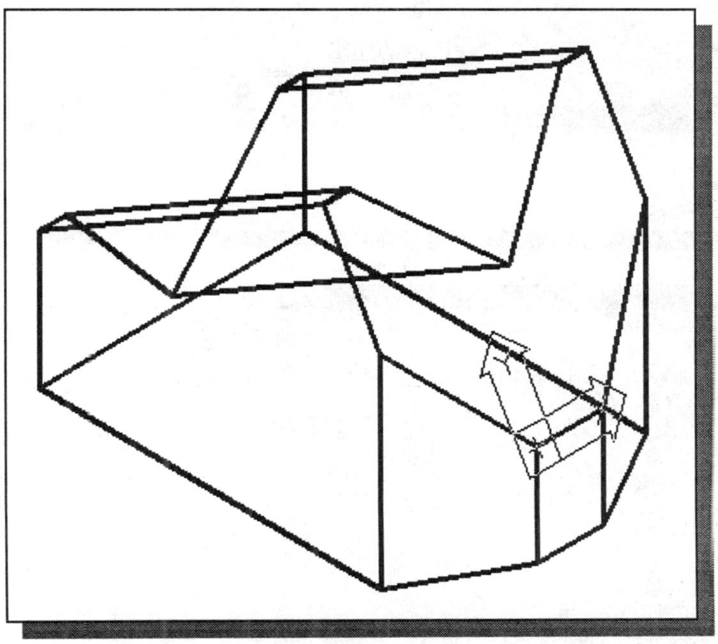

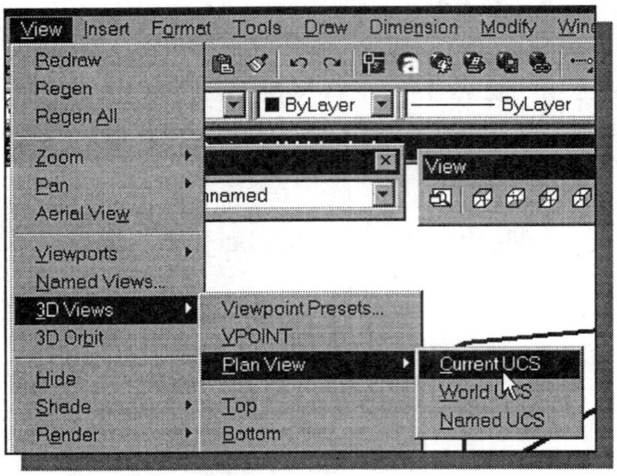

5. In the pull-down menus, select

[View] => [3-D Views] => [Plan View] => [Current UCS]

- The graphics window is now adjusted to display the current UCS plane.

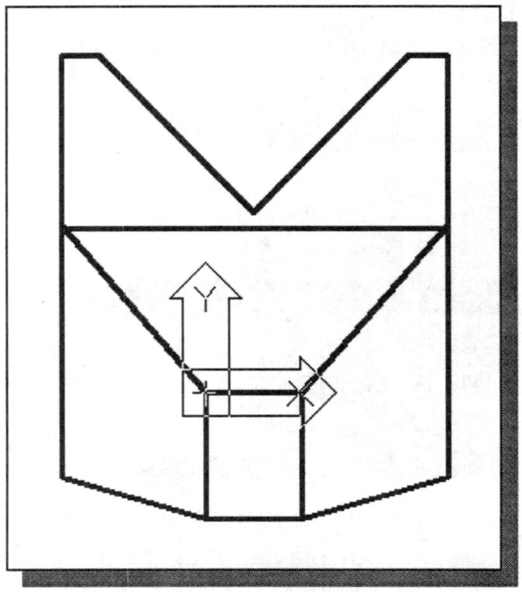

- Note the orientation of the UCS in the display view. This is the auxiliary view that is needed in the multview drawing.

6. Click on the ***Named Views*** icon in the *View* toolbar.

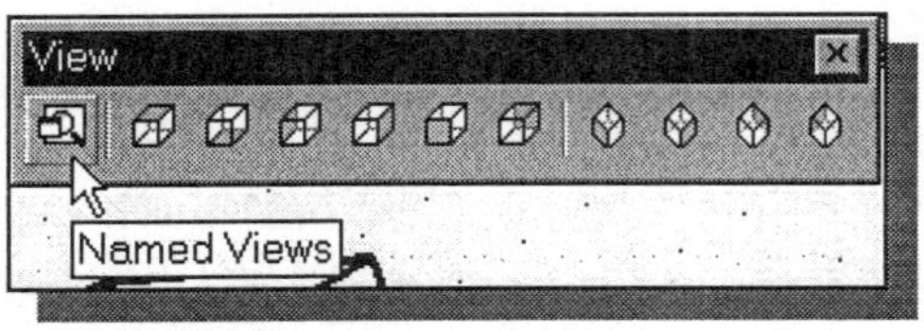

7. In the *View* dialog box, click on the **NEW** button to create a new named view.

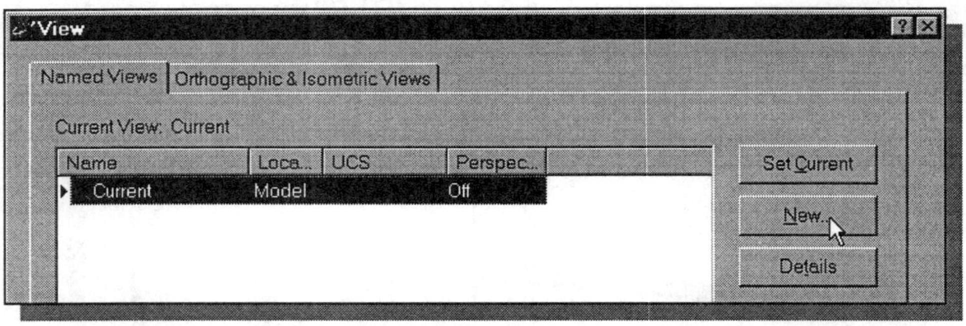

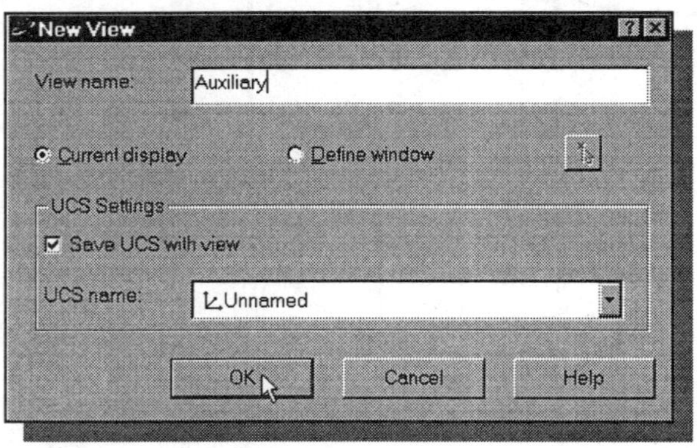

8. In the *New View* dialog box, enter ***Auxiliary*** as the new *View name* and confirm the ***Current display*** option and the ***Save UCS with view*** option are switched ***ON*** as shown.

9. Click on the **OK** button to accept the settings and create the named view.

10. In the *View* dialog box, the new named view (*Auxiliary*) is added to the *Named Views* list. We can also switch to this view by using the **Set Current** option.

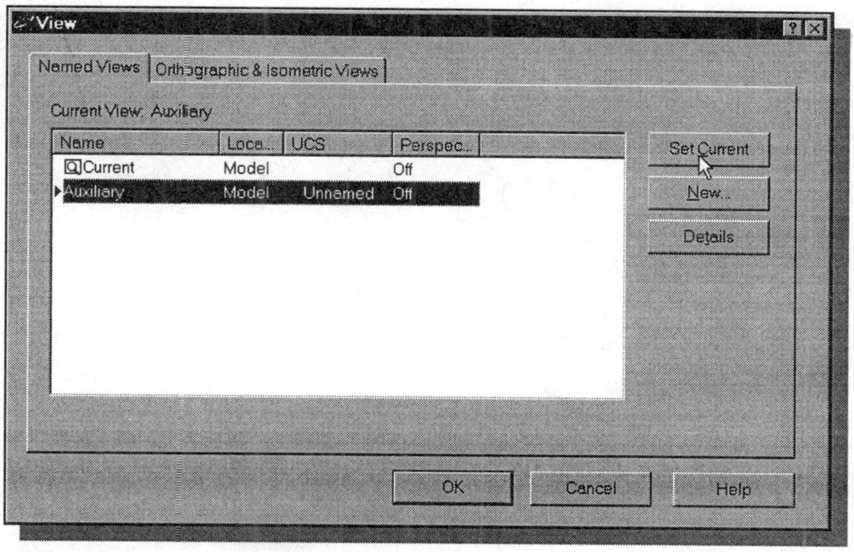

11. Click on the **OK** button to accept the settings.

Adding a viewport for an Auxiliary view

1. Pick the **Layout1** tab to switch back to the two-dimensional paper space.

2. In the status bar area, reset the option buttons so that only *LWT* and *PAPER* are switched ***ON***.

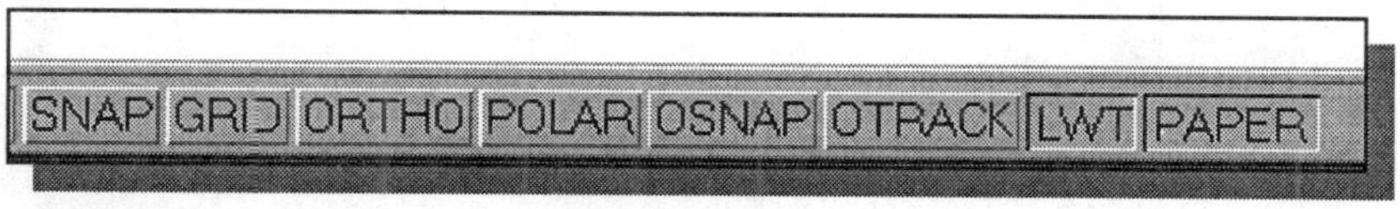

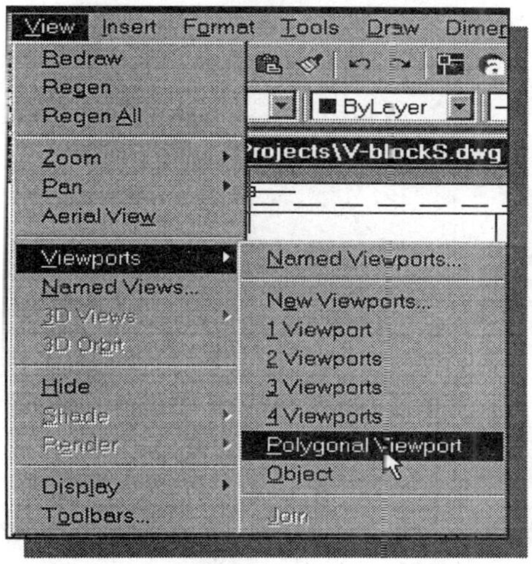

3. In the pull-down menus, select

[View] => [Viewports] => [Polygonal Viewport]

- In AutoCAD 2000i, viewports can be of arbitrary polygonal shapes. In the layout mode, the viewports can also overlap each other. We will create a four-sided viewport overlapping the other viewports.

4. In the command prompt area, the message *"Specify start point:"* is displayed. Create a four-sided shape as shown. (Hint: use the ***Close*** option to assure the last segment is connected to the start point.)

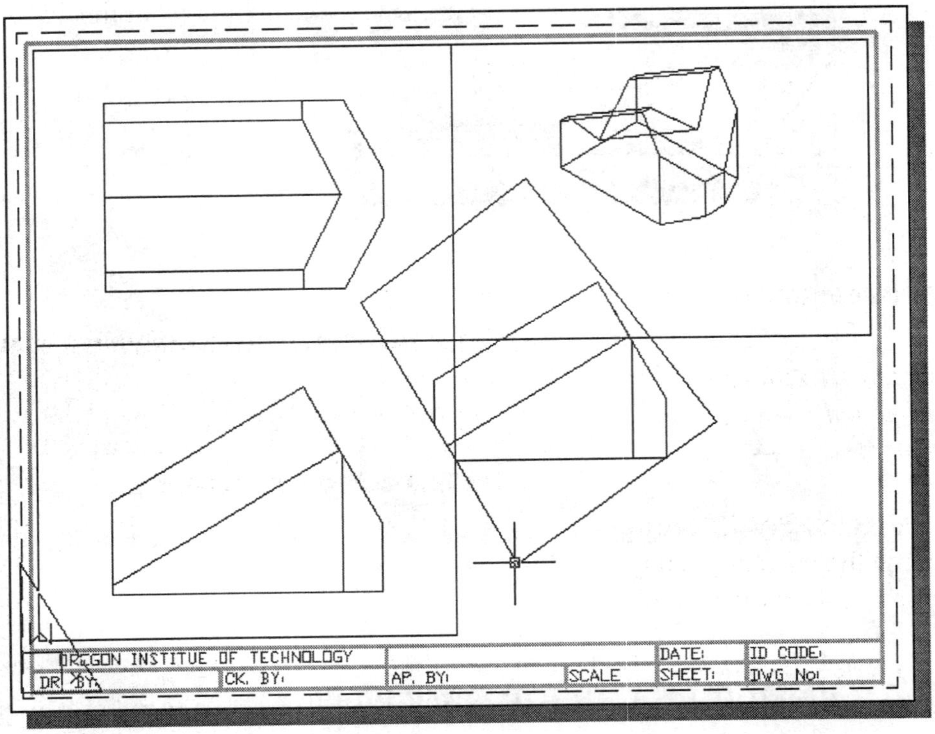

5. Pick one of the edges of the viewport border and notice the four grip-points are displayed.

6. Adjust the size and shape of the viewport by dragging the grip-points.

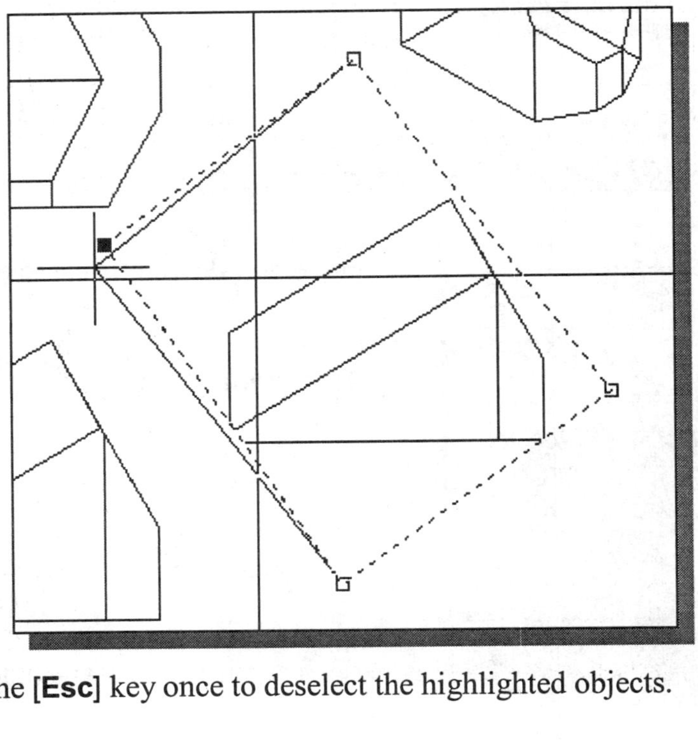

7. Press the **[Esc]** key once to deselect the highlighted objects.

8. Double-click inside the viewport we just created to activate the viewport.

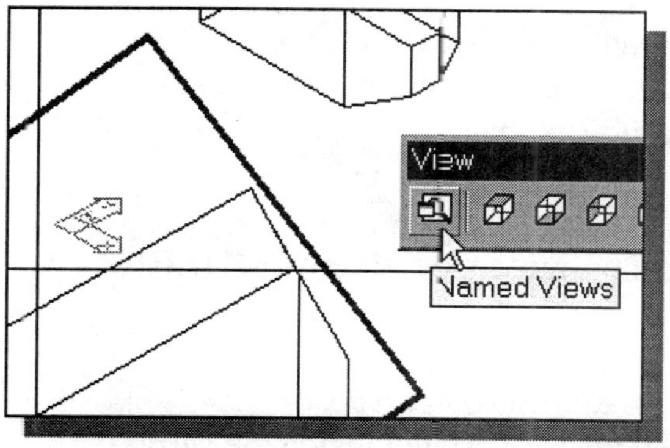

9. Pick ***Named Views*** in the *View* toolbar.

10. Pick the ***Auxiliary*** view in the *Named Views* list as shown.

11. Click on the **Set Current** to change the current display to the saved *Auxiliary* view.

12. Click **OK** to accept the settings.

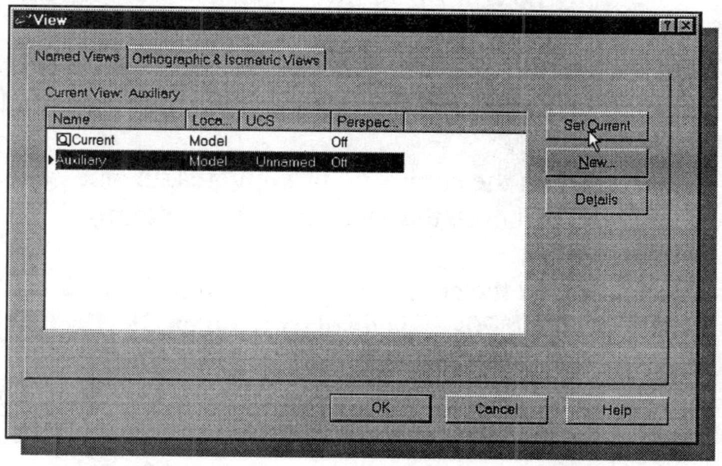

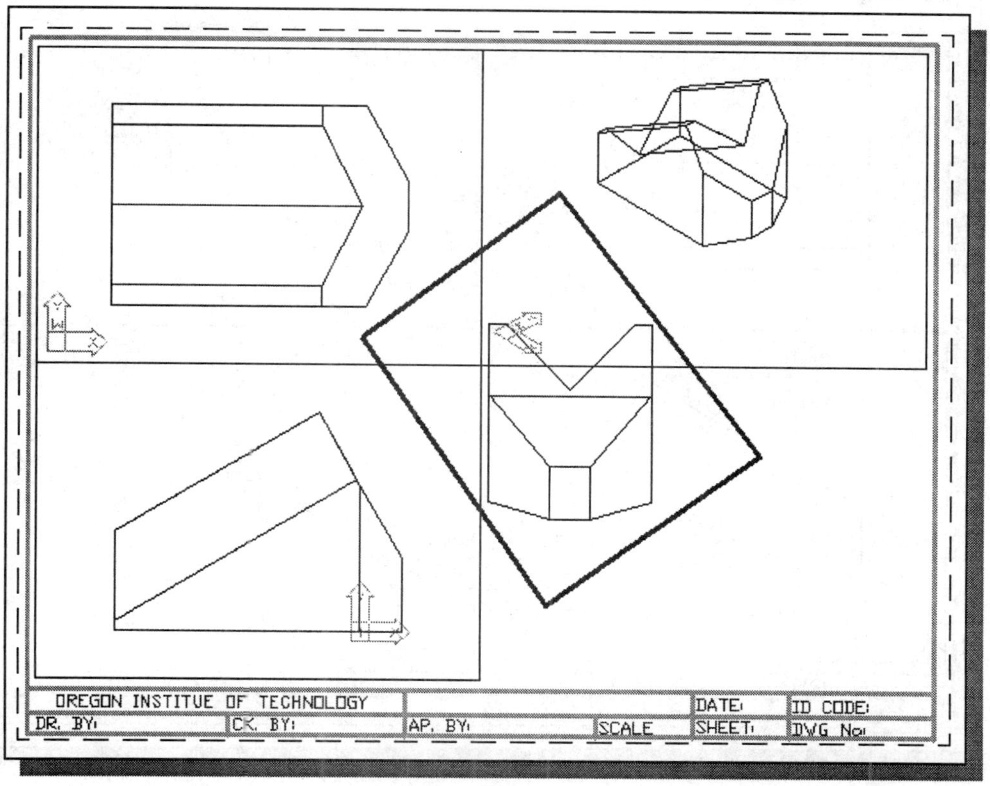

Using the *DVIEW* command

- We can use the *DVIEW* command to zoom, pan, and twist views. We can also use *DVIEW* to remove objects from in front of and behind a clipping plane and to remove hidden lines during a dynamic viewing operation.

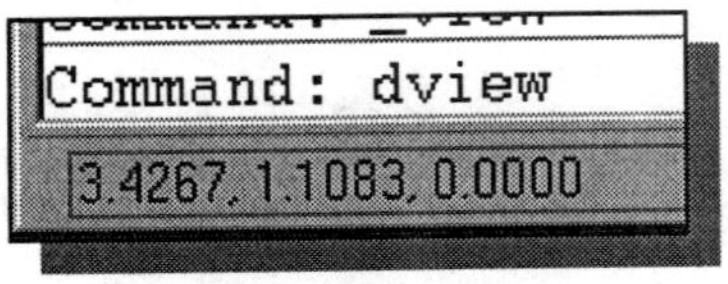

1. At the command prompt, enter: **dview [ENTER]**

2. In the command prompt area, the message *"Select objects or <use DVIEWBLOCK>:"* is displayed. Pick the solid model inside the active viewport.

3. Inside the active viewport, **right-mouse-click** once to accept the selection.

4. In the command prompt area, the message *"Enter option:"* is displayed. Choose the *Twist* option by entering: **TW [ENTER]**

5. In the command prompt area, the message *"Specify the view twist angle <0.00>:"* is displayed. Enter: **30 [ENTER]**

6. Press the **ENTER** key once to end the *DVIEW* command.

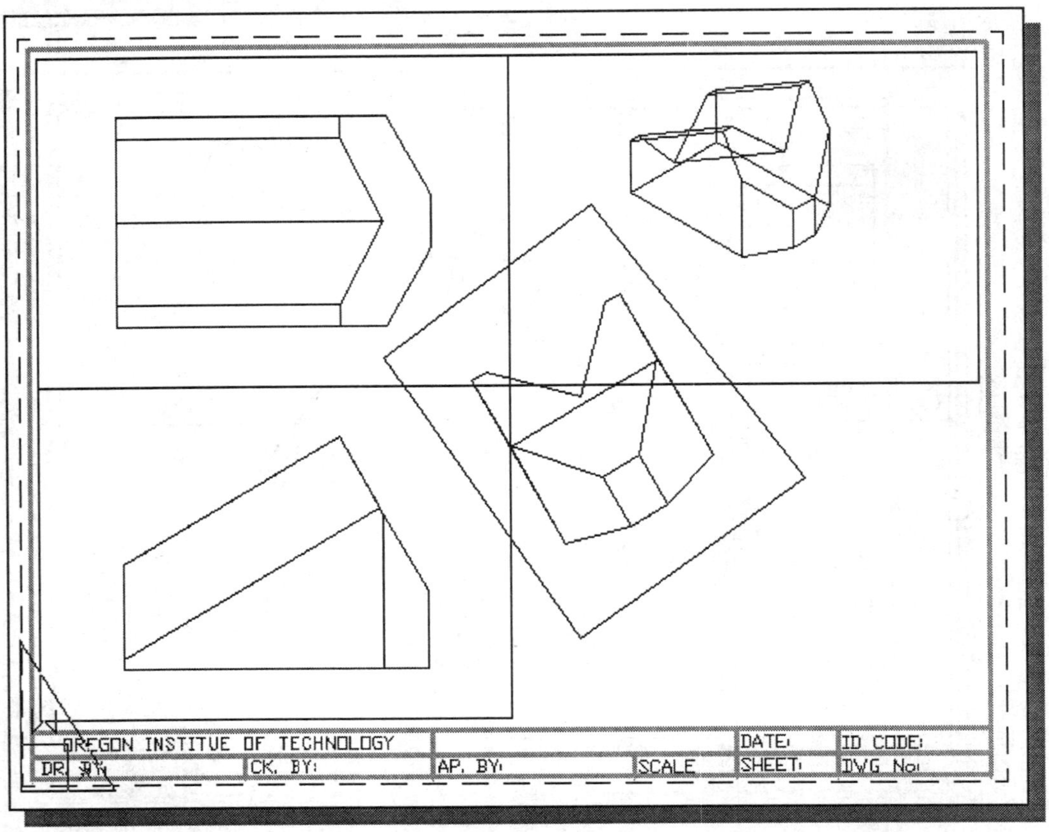

Adjusting the Viewport Scale

- A uniform scale for the 2D views is necessary for view alignments and dimensioning the features.

1. Pick ***Properties*** in the *Standard* toolbar as shown.

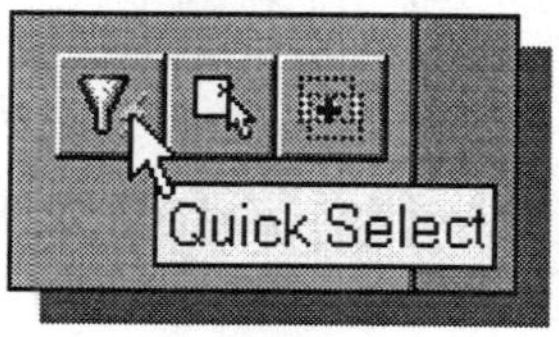

2. In the *Properties* window, click on the ***Quick Select*** button.

- The *Quick Select* option allows us to select items based on the object properties.

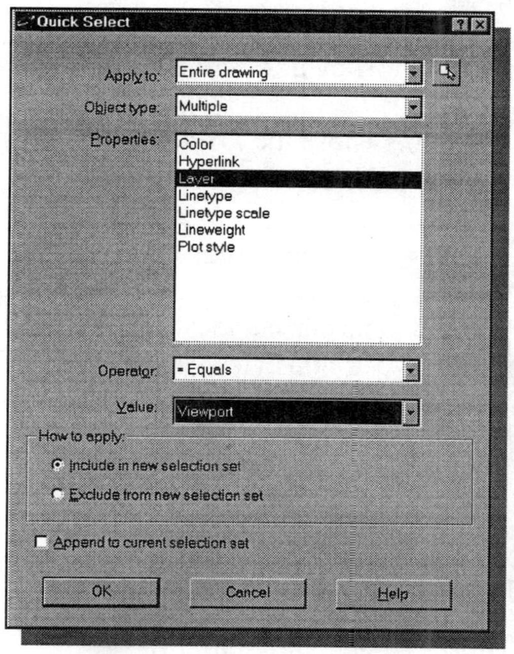

3. In the *Quick Select* window, choose ***Layer*** in the *Properties* list and set the selection operation to ***Equal Viewport*** as shown in the figure.

4. Click **OK** to accept the setting and proceed to select objects matching the quick select settings.

- Note the four viewports are selected.

5. Click on the **Alphabetic** tab to list properties in alphabetical orders.

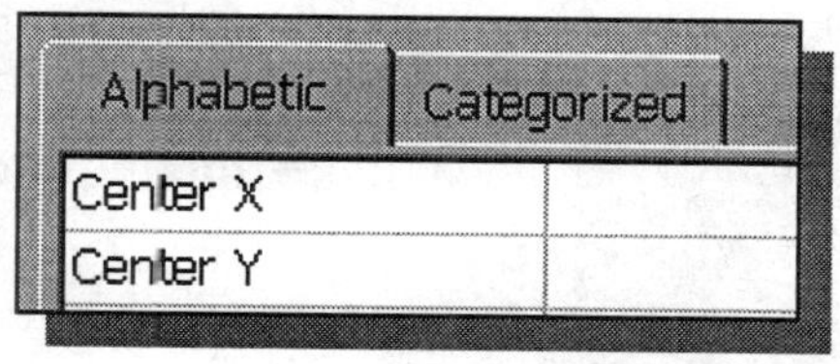

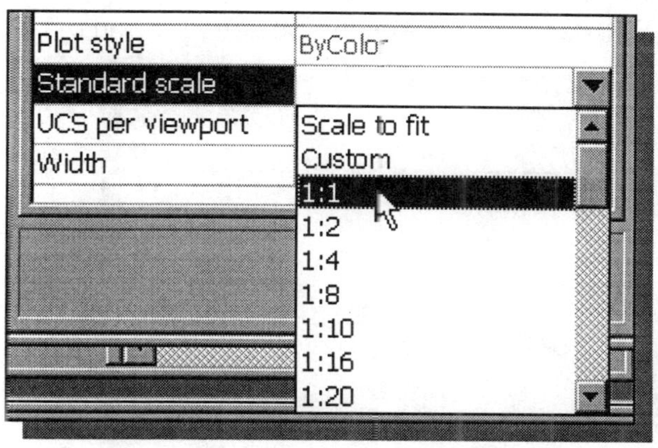

6. Pick the ***Standard scale*** property as shown.

7. Select **1:1** to set the scale to one to one. This will set all displayed views to *Full* scale.

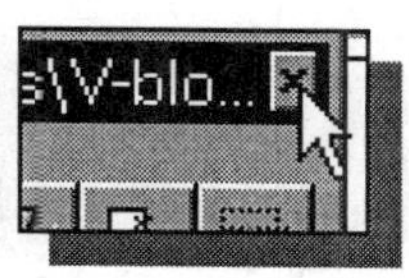

8. Click on the [**X**] button to close the dialogue box.

Locking the Base view

1. Pre-select the lower-left viewport by clicking on one of the viewport borders.

2. Pick ***Properties*** in the *Standard* toolbar as shown.

3. Click on the **Categorized** tab to list properties in categorized order.

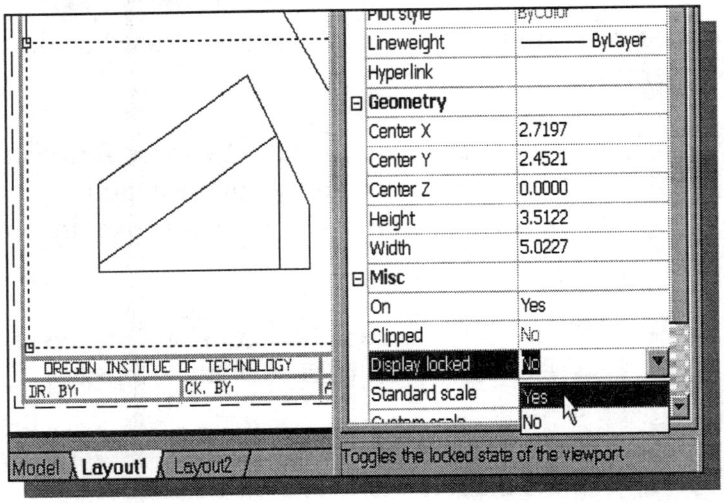

4. Pick ***Display Locked*** option in the *Property* lists.

5. Set the option to ***Yes*** as shown.

6. Close the *Properties* window by clicking on the [**X**].

- By setting this option, the displayed view is locked at its current location. We will use this view as the base

Aligning the 2D views

- We will create two construction lines to assist the alignments of the 2D views.

1. Click **Construction Line** in the *Draw* toolbar as shown.

2. On your own, create two construction lines aligned to the upper-left corner of the *Front* view as shown. (Hint: turn ***ON*** the *SNAP* and *OTRACK* options to help the constructions.)

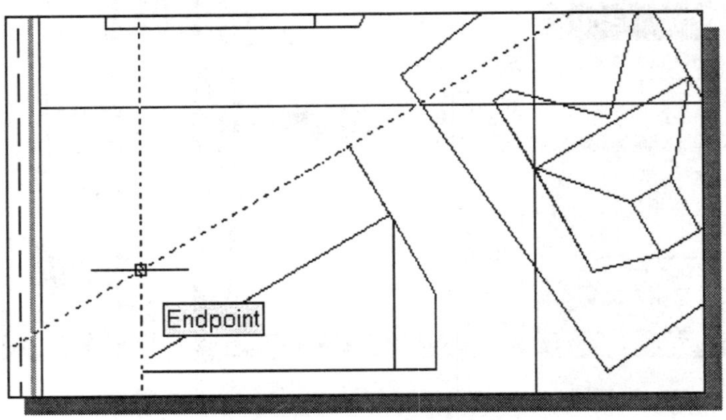

3. Double-click inside the upper-left viewport to activate the viewport.

4. Pick ***Pan Realtime*** in the *Standard* toolbar as shown.

5. On your own, reposition the displayed *Top* view so that it is aligned vertically to the *Front* view. Use the vertical construction line to assist the alignment.

6. Repeat the above steps and reposition the *Auxiliary* view so that it is aligned to the *Front* view as shown in the below figure.

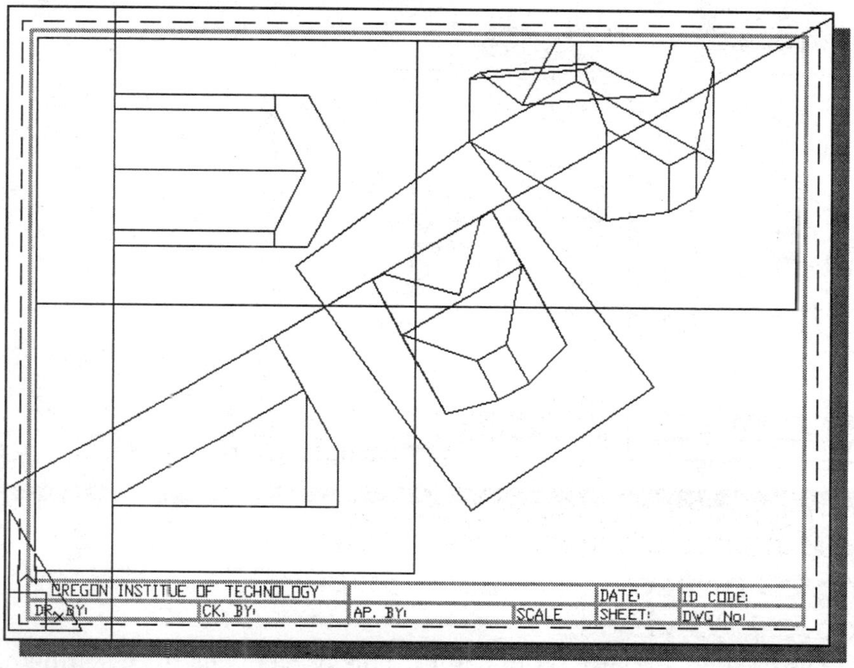

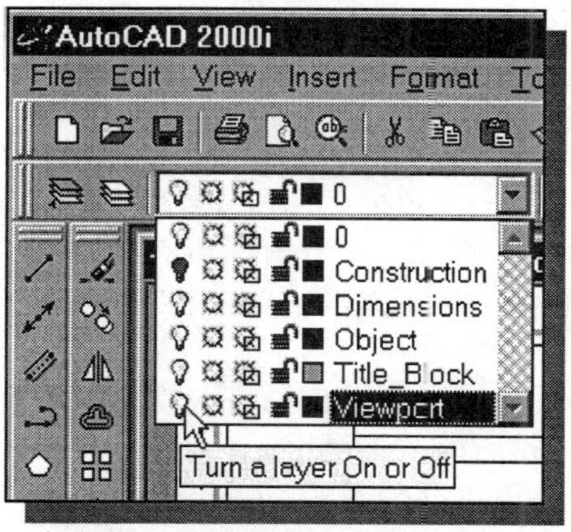

7. Turn ***OFF*** layer *Viewport* in the *Layer Control* box as shown.

- Note that the viewport borders and the two construction lines are switched off since they are placed in the layer *Viewport.*

8. Double-click on the *Isometric* view and note the upper-right viewport is activated.

9. Click ***Zoom Realtime*** in the *Standard* toolbar as shown.

10. On your own, resize and reposition the *Isometric* view so that it does not overlap with the *Auxiliary* view.

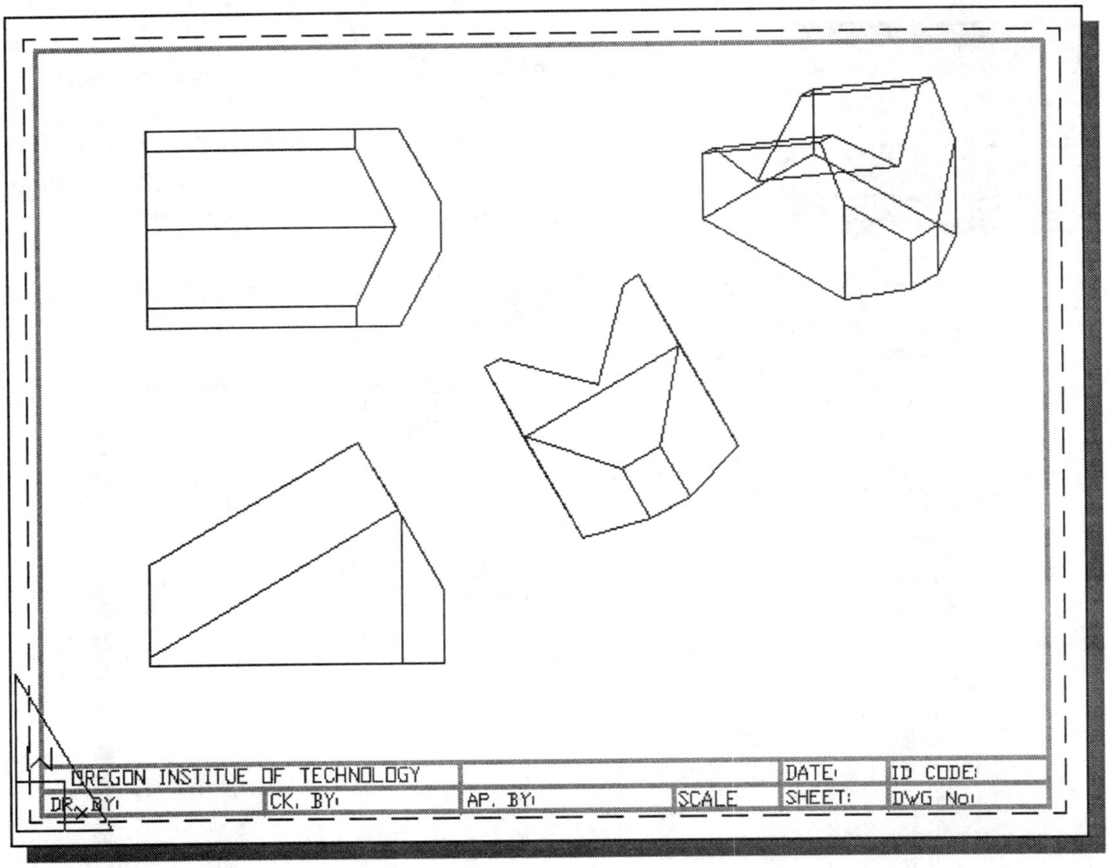

Creating 2D projected entities - SOLPROF

- The views created are still 3D in nature. This prevents us from setting color or linetype for individual edges, so that hidden features can be described correctly based on engineering drafting standards. To overcome that problem, we will generate 2D entities from the established viewports. We can then use layer controls to set color and linetype options, which allows us to distinguish visible and hidden objects in individual views.

1. Double-click inside the upper-left viewport to activate the viewport.

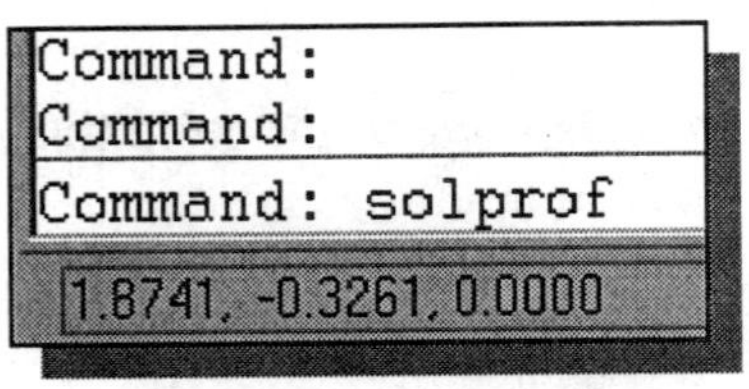

2. At the command prompt, enter: **solprof** [**ENTER**]
3. In the command prompt area, the message *"Select objects:"* is displayed. Pick the solid model inside the active viewport.
4. Inside the active viewport, **right-mouse-click** once to accept the selection.
5. In the command prompt area, the message *"Display hidden profile lines on separate layer? [Yes/No] <Y>:"* is displayed. Enter: **Y** [**ENTER**]

6. In the command prompt area, the message *"Project profile lines onto a plane? [Yes/No] <Y>:"* is displayed. Enter: **Y** **[ENTER]**

7. In the command prompt area, the message *"Delete tangential edges? [Yes/No] <Y>:'* is displayed. Enter: **Y** **[ENTER]**

- The display in the layout appears to be the same before the *SOLPROF* command was executed. Projected 2D entities (profile lines) are created in the view direction of the viewport.

8. Pick the **Model** tab to switch back to the 3D model space.

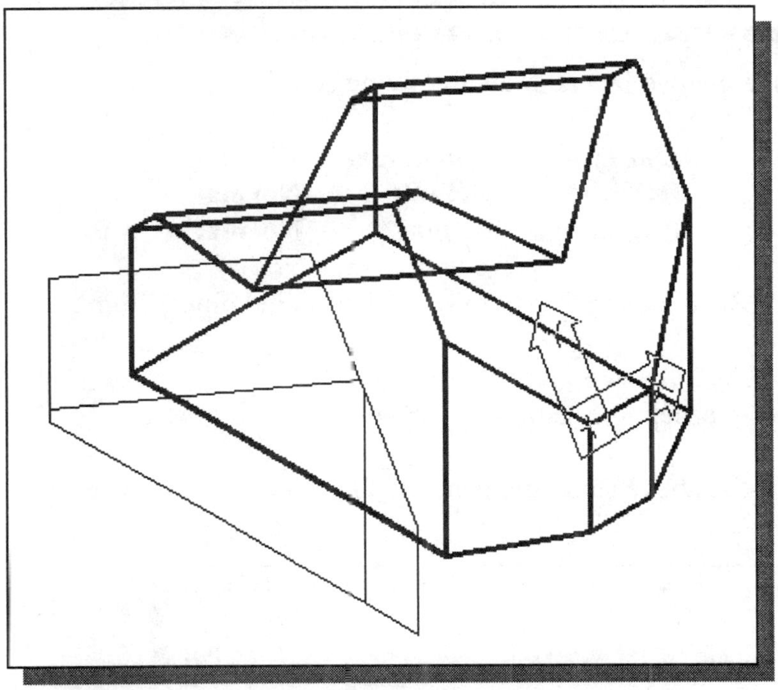

- The projected 2D entities appear in model space. Note that the locations of the projected entities might be at a different location on your screen than is displayed in the figure.

9. Pick the **Layout1** tab to switch back to the two-dimensional paper space.

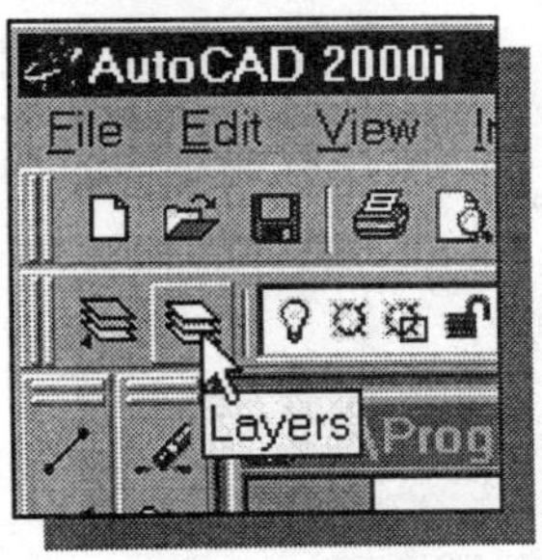

10. Click on the ***Layers*** icon in the *Object Properties* toolbar.

- Note that two additional layers are created by the *SOLPROF* command. The *PV-xx* layer is for the projected visible lines and *PH-xx* layer is for the projected hidden lines.

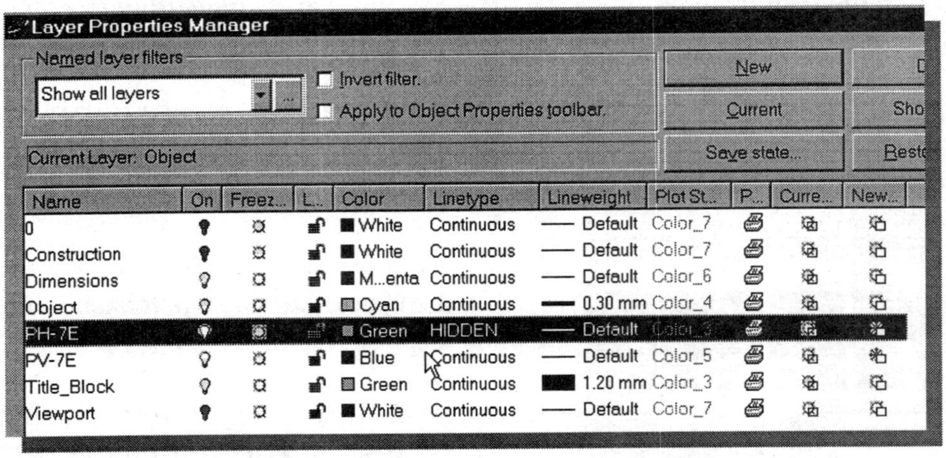

11. On your own, change the two layers to the following settings:

Layer	***Color***	***LineType***	***Lineweight***	***PlotStyle***
PH-xx	**Green**	**HIDDEN**	**Default**	**Normal**
PV-xx	**Blue**	**Continuous**	**0.3mm**	**Normal**

12. On your own, ***FREEZE*** the layer *Object* to remove the solid object from the display.

13. Click the **OK** button to accept the settings.

14. On your own, repeat the above steps and generate 2D projected entities for the other three views.

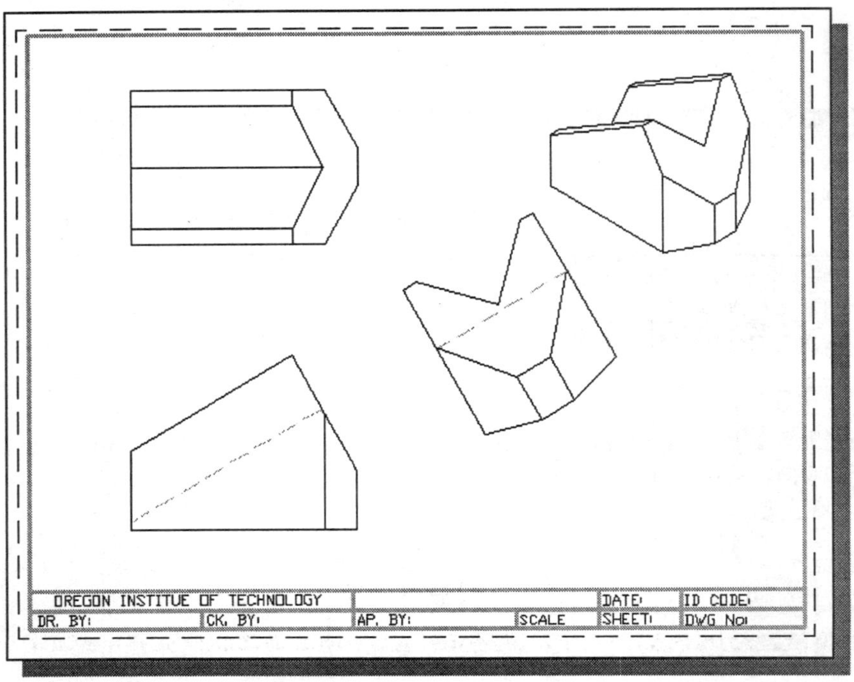

Completing the 2D drawing

- Dimensions and notes can be placed in the model space or the paper space. From a design/modeling perspective, it is generally agreed that the dimensions should be placed in the 2D paper space.

1. Confirm the active mode is set to **paper space** as shown in the status bar area.

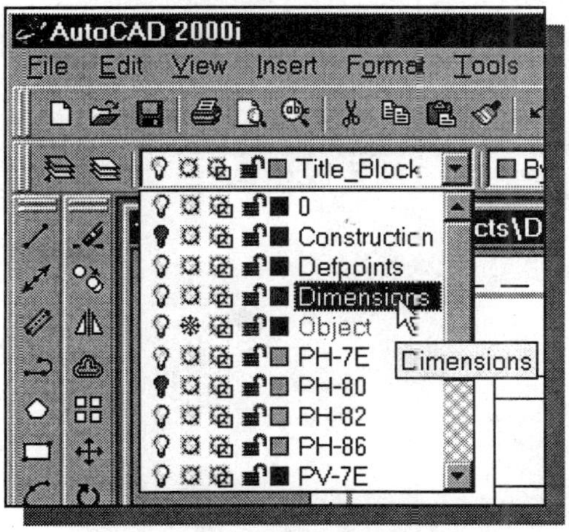

2. On your own, set layer ***Dimensions*** as the *Current layer* in the *Layer Properties box* as shown.

3. Move the cursor to the *Standard* toolbar area and **right-mouse-click** on any icon in the *Standard* toolbar to display a list of toolbar menu groups.

4. Select ***Dimension***, with the left-mouse-button, to display the *Dimension* toolbar on the screen.

5. On your own, create the necessary dimensions and complete the 2D drawing as shown.

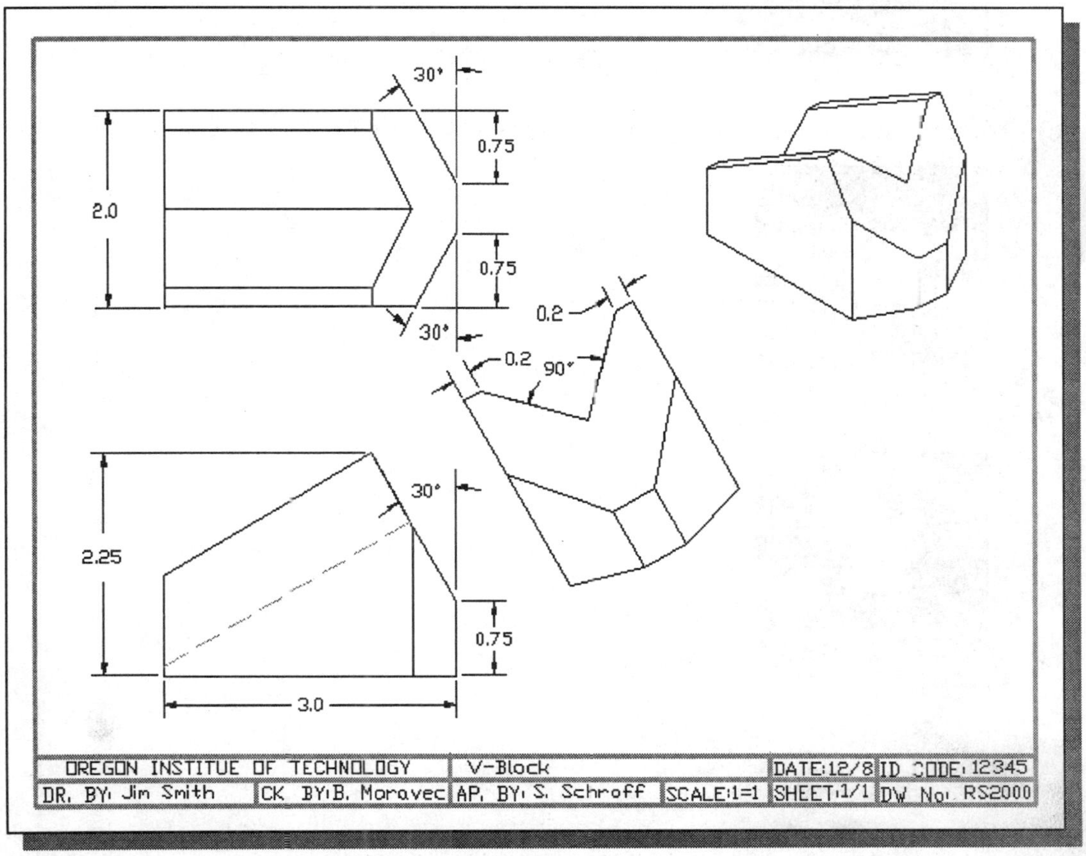

Questions:

1. What is an auxiliary view and why would it be important?

2. When is a line viewed as a point? How can a line be shown in true length?

3. Why and when should you use the *SOLPROF* command?

4. List and describe the differences between *Model Space* and *Paper Space* in AutoCAD?

5. Why and when should you use the DVIEW command?

6. Identify the following commands:

(a)

(b)

(c)

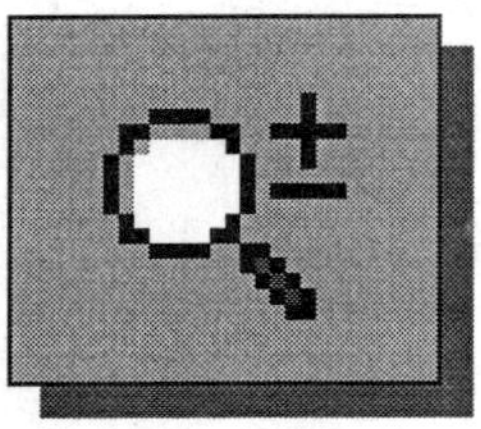

(d)

Exercises: Create Multiview drawings for the following designs.
(All dimensions are in inches.)

1.

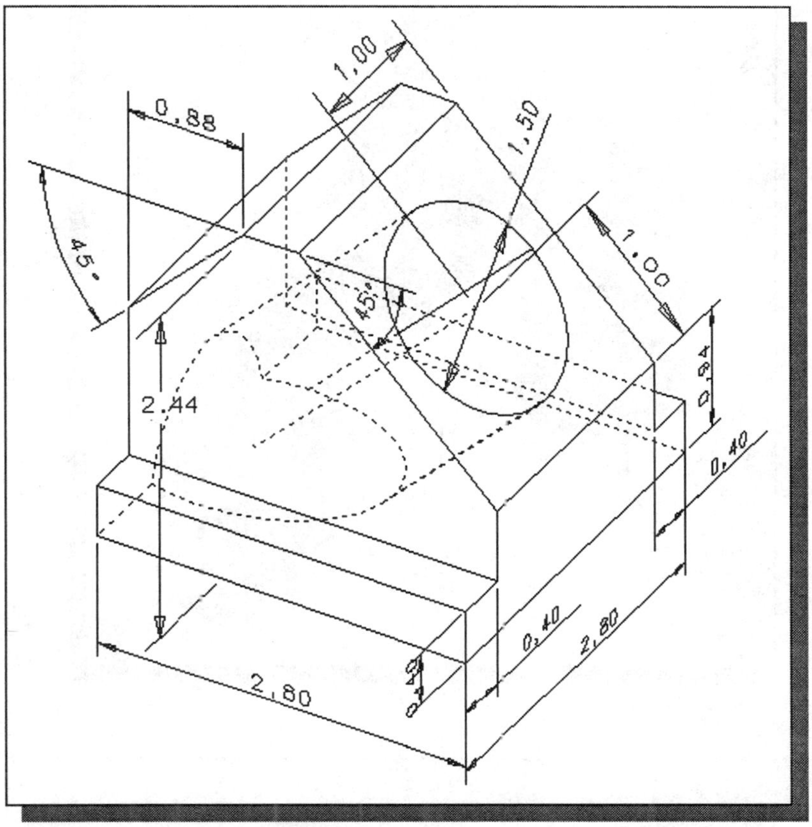

2.

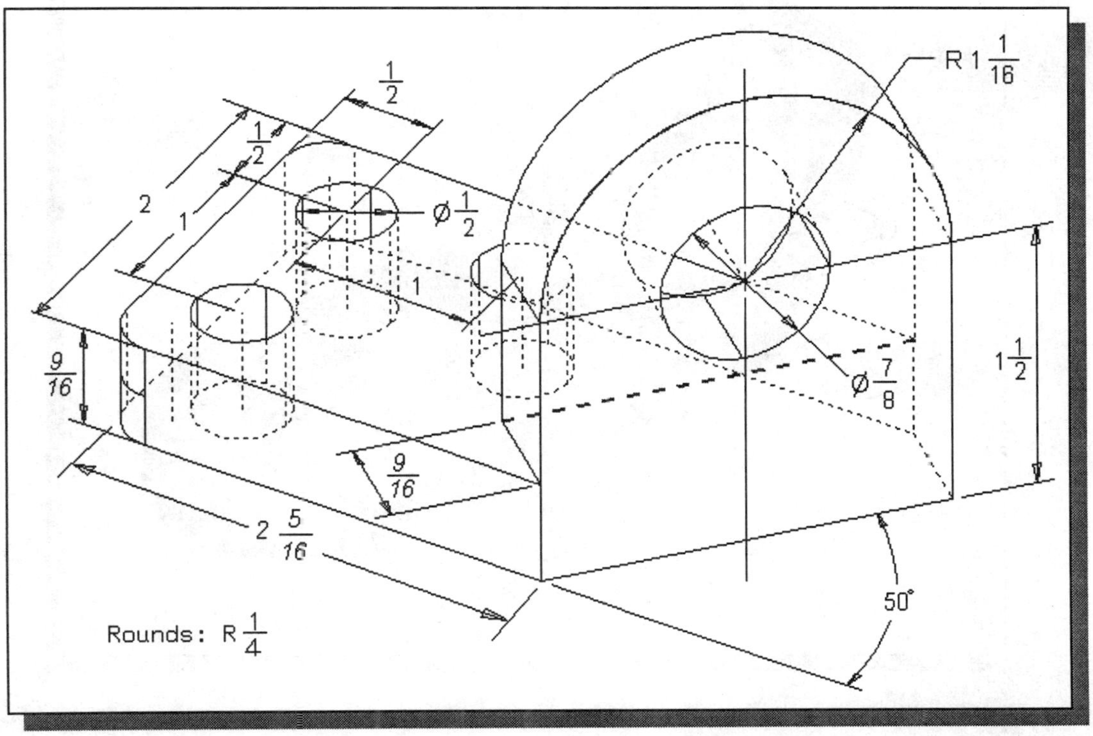

3.

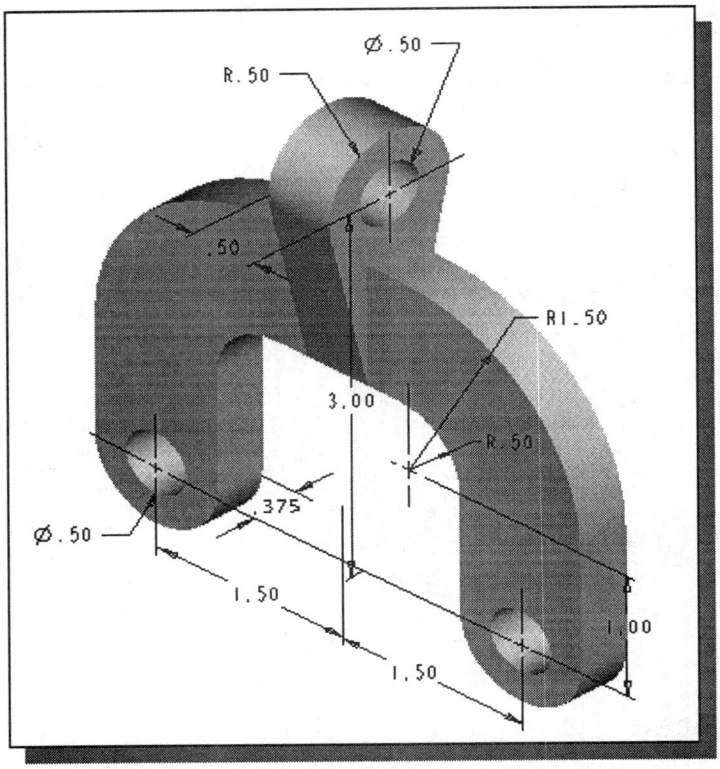

Ø.50
R.50
.50
R1.50
3.00
R.50
.375
Ø.50
1.50
1.00
1.50

4.

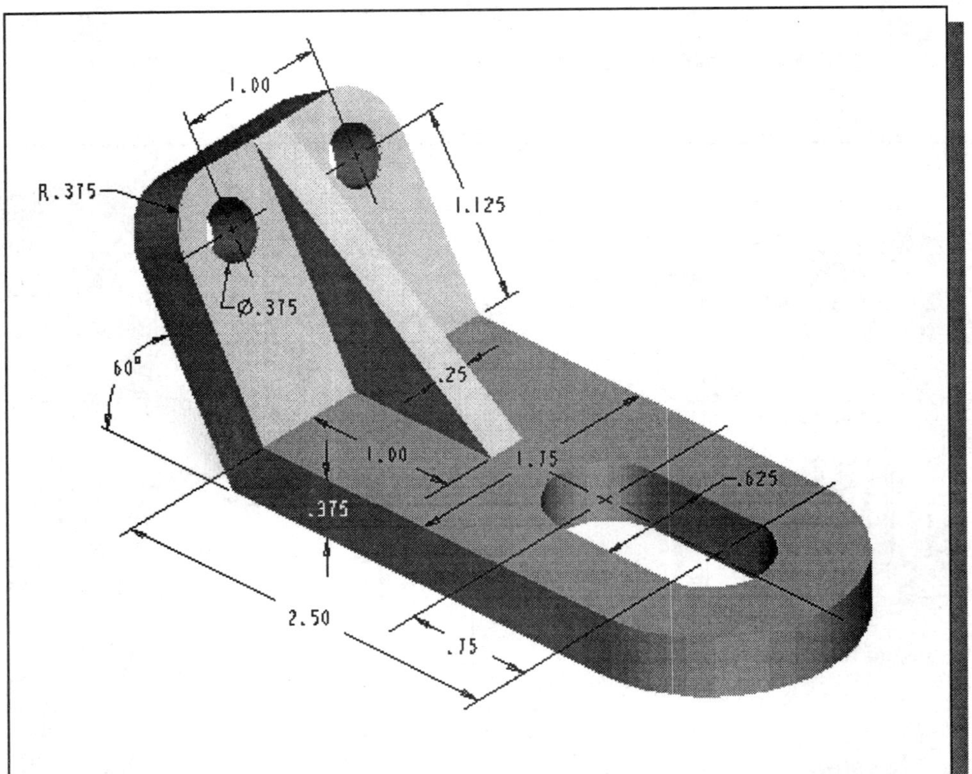

1.00
R.375
1.125
Ø.375
60°
.25
1.00
1.75
.625
.375
2.50
.75

Chapter 9
Symmetrical Features in Designs

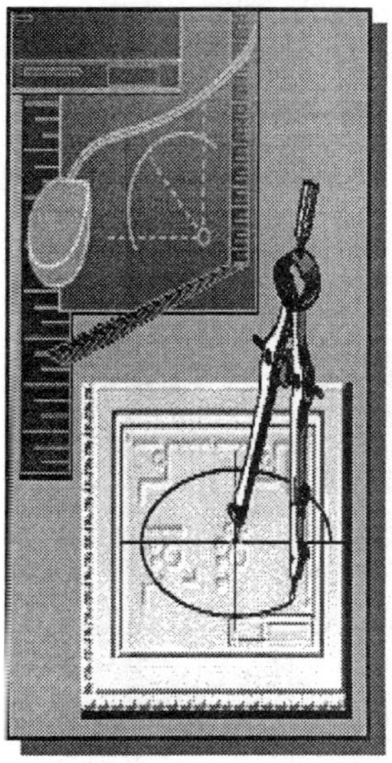

Learning Objectives

- Create Revolved Features.
- Use the Mirror Part Command.
- Understand and Create Construction Geometry.
- Create Combined Parts.
- Create and Modify Feature Arrays.
- Apply Constraints to Construction Geometry.
- Create Symmetrical Features in Designs.

Introduction

In solid modeling, it is important to identify and determine the features that exist in the design. *Modern solid modeling systems* enable us to build complex designs by working on smaller and simpler units. This approach simplifies the modeling process and allows us to concentrate on the characteristics of the design. Symmetry is an important characteristic that is often seen in designs. Symmetrical features can be easily accomplished by the assortments of tools that are available in feature-based modeling systems, such as AutoCAD.

The modeling technique of extruding two-dimensional sketches along a straight line to form three-dimensional features, as illustrated in the previous chapters, is an effective way to construct solid models. For designs that involve cylindrical shapes, shapes that are symmetrical about an axis, revolving two-dimensional sketches about an axis can form the needed three-dimensional features. In solid modeling, this type of feature is called a **Revolved Feature**.

In AutoCAD, besides using the *REVOLVE* command to create revolved features, several options are also available to handle symmetrical features. For example, we can create multiple identical copies of symmetrical features with the ***ARRAY*** command, or create mirror images of models using the ***MIRROR*** command. In this chapter, the construction and modeling techniques of these more advanced features are illustrated.

A Revolved Design: *PULLEY*

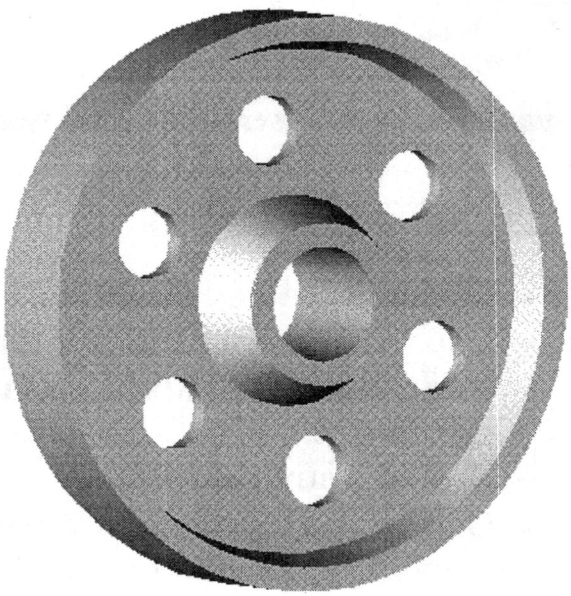

- ❖ Based on your knowledge of AutoCAD, how many features would you use to create the design? Which feature would you choose as the starting point for creating the model? Identify the symmetrical features in the design and consider other possibilities in creating the design. You are encouraged to create the model on your own prior to following through the tutorial.

Modeling Strategy - A Revolved Design

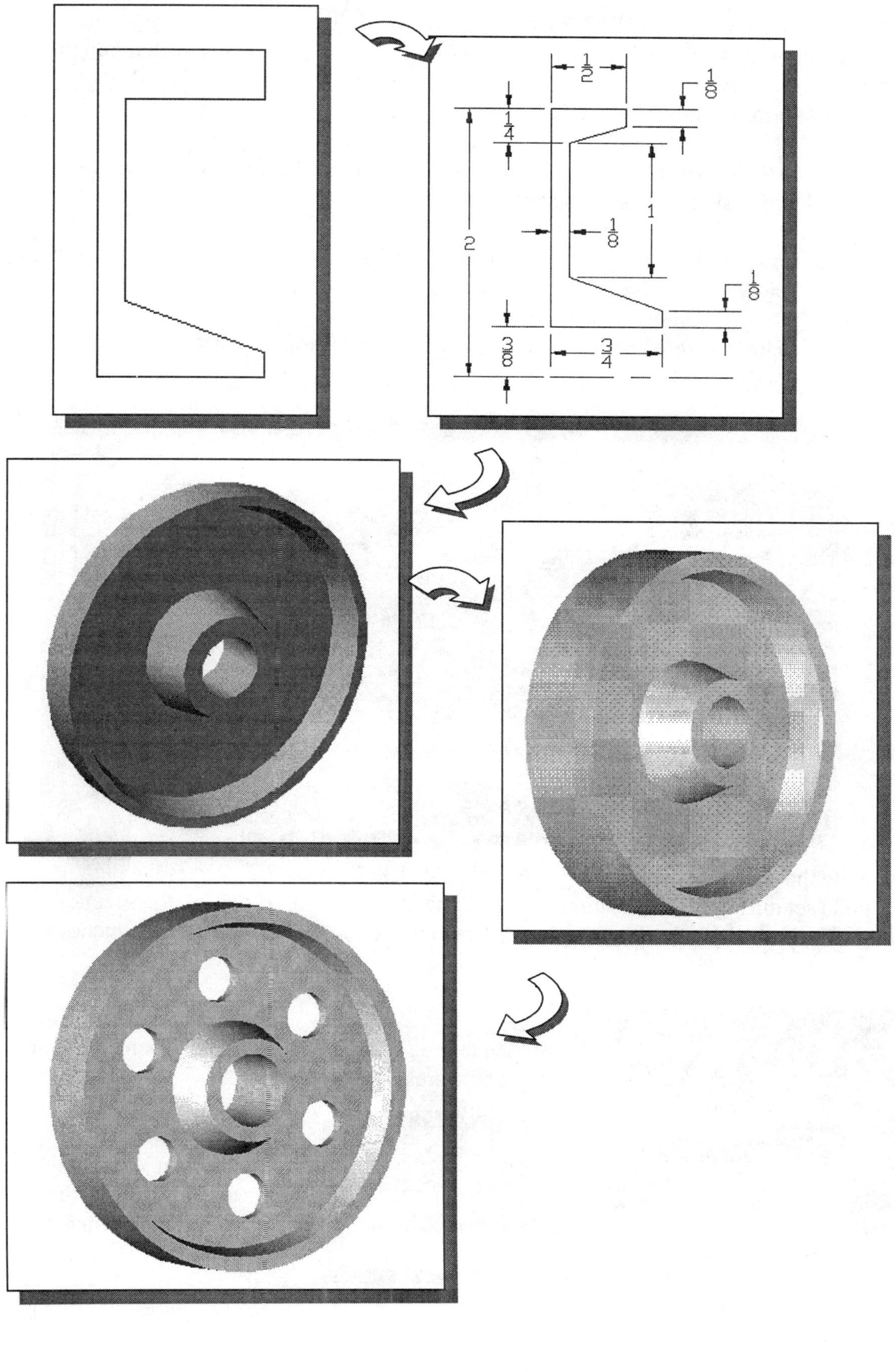

Starting Up AutoCAD® 2000i

1. Select the AutoCAD® 2000i option on the *Program* menu or select the AutoCAD® 2000i icon on the *Desktop*. Once the program is loaded into the memory, the AutoCAD® 2000i drawing screen and the *AutoCAD Today* startup dialog box will appear on the screen.

2. In the *AutoCAD Today* startup dialog box, select the **Create Drawings** tab with a single click of the left-mouse-button.

3. Confirm the startup option is set to ***Start from Scratch***, as shown in the figure below.

4. In the *Default Settings* section, pick **English (feet and Inches)** as the drawing units.

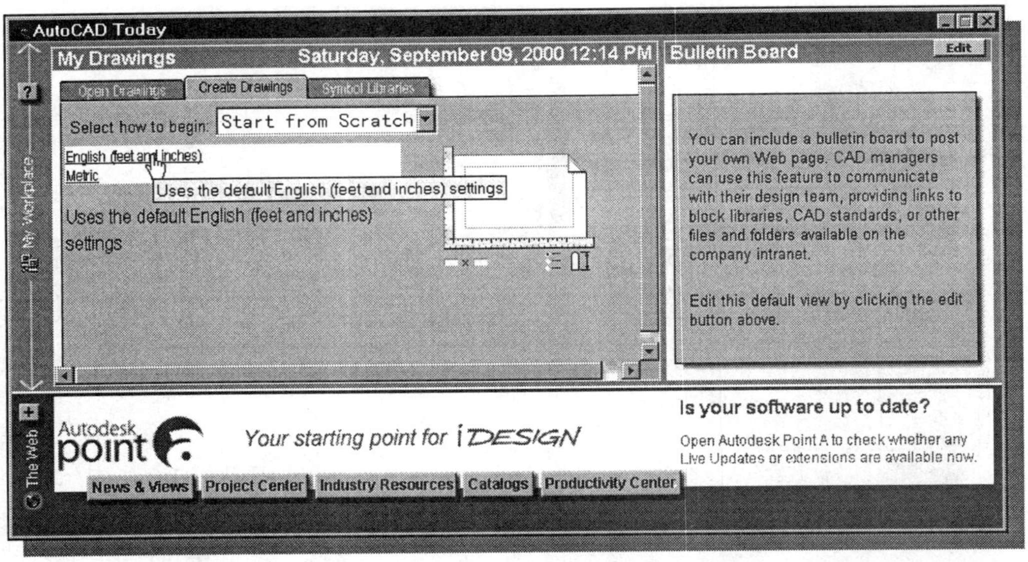

❖ Note that two graphics window are available. The *Drawing1.dwg* uses the default units set during the installation of AutoCAD 2000i. The units used in the second graphics window, the *Drawing2.dwg* window, are set to the English units, inches and feet.

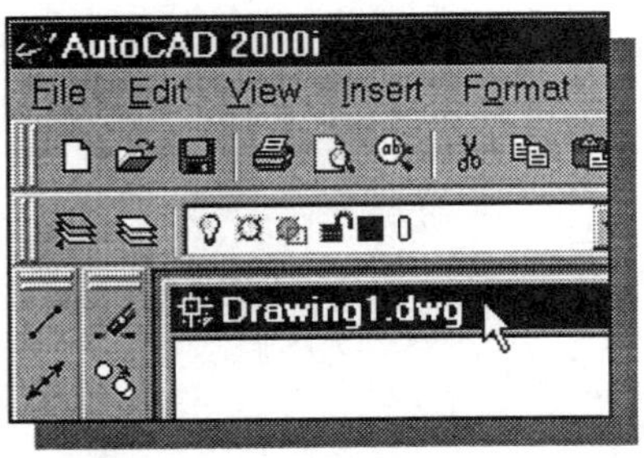

5. Switch to the *Drawing1* window by left-clicking once in the title area of the window.

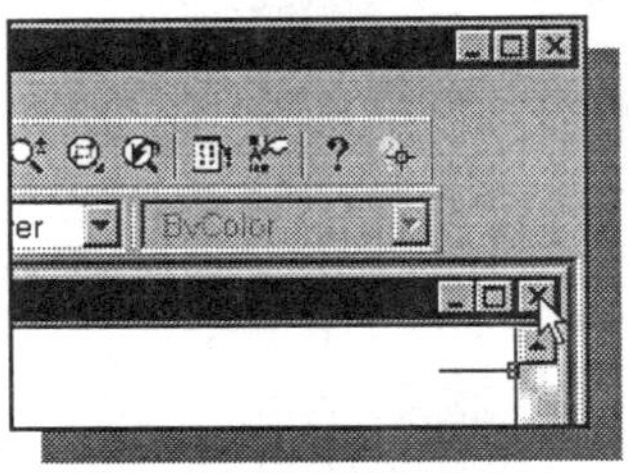

6. Close the window by clicking the ***Close*** icon located at the upper-right-corner of the *Drawing1* window.

Layers setup

1. Pick ***Layers*** in the *Object Properties* toolbar.

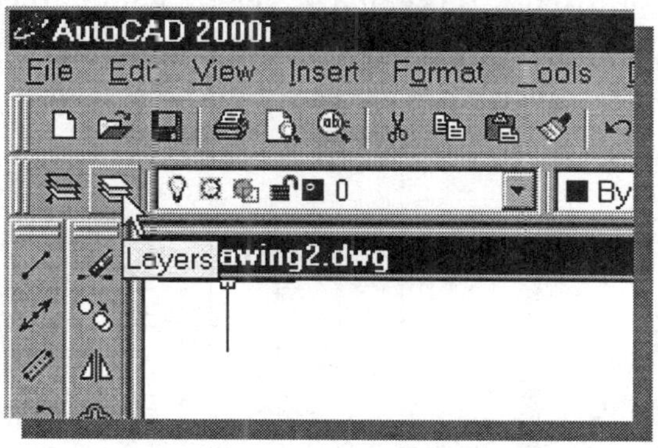

2. Click on the ***New*** icon to create new layers.

3. Create **two new layers** with the following settings:

Layer	***Color***	***LineType***	***LineWeight***
Center_lines	**Red**	**Continuous**	**Default**
Dimensions	**Megenta**	**Continuous**	**Default**
Object_lines	**Cyan**	**Continuous**	**0.30mm**

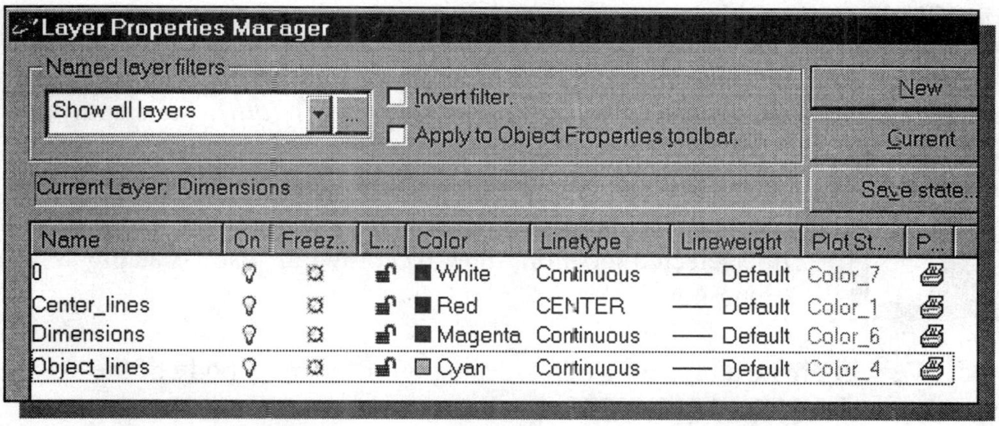

4. Highlight the layer ***Object_lines*** in the list of layers.

5. Click on the ***Current*** icon to set layer ***Object_lines*** as the *Current layer*.

6. Click on the **OK** button to accept the settings and exit the *Layer Properties Manager* dialog box.

7. In the status bar area, reset the options and turn ***ON*** the *POLAR, OSNAP, OTRACK, LWT* and *MODEL* options.

Setting up a 2D sketch for the Revolved feature

- Note that the pulley design is symmetrical about a horizontal axis as well as a vertical axis, which allows us to simplify the 2D sketch as shown below. Instead of creating the 2D sketch by the *LINE* command, we will use some of the more advanced editing options available with the *REGION* command.

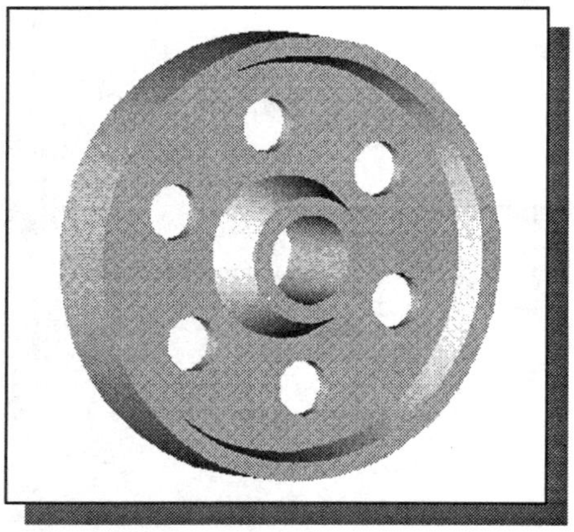

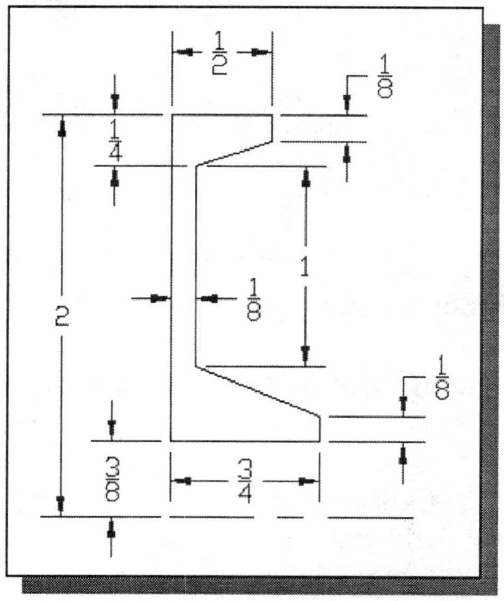

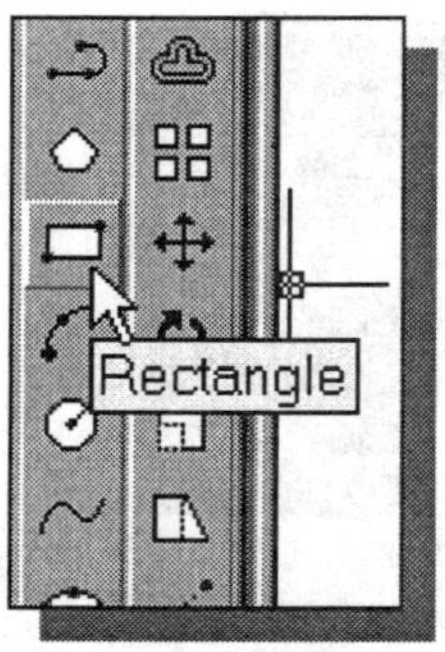

1. Select the ***Rectangle*** icon in the *Draw* toolbar. In the command prompt area, the message *"Specify first corner point or [Chamfer/Elevation/Fillet/Thickness/Width]:"* is displayed.

2. Place the first corner-point of the rectangle near the center of the screen. Do not be overly concerned about the actual coordinates of the selected location; the CAD drawing space is as big as you can imagine.

3. We will create a 0.75" x 1.625" rectangle for the main body of the sketch. Enter **@0.75,1.625 [ENTER]**.

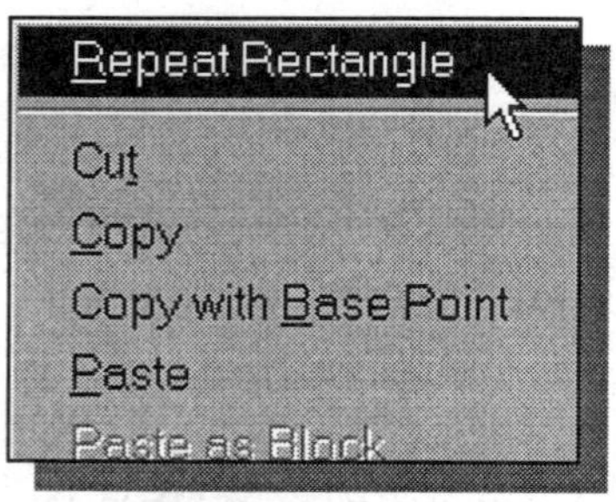

4. Inside the graphics window, click once with the **right-mouse-button** to bring up the popup option menu.

5. Pick **Repeat Rectangle**, with the left-mouse-button, in the popup menu to repeat the last command.

6. Place the first corner-point of the rectangle toward the right side of the previous rectangle.

7. We will create a 0.625" x 1.0" rectangle as a cutter sketch. Enter **@0.625,1.0 [ENTER]**.

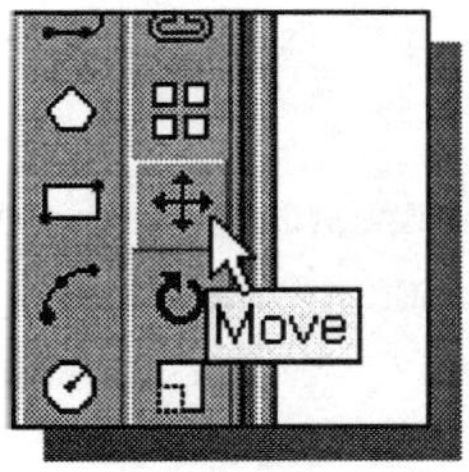

8. Select the ***Move*** icon in the *Draw* toolbar.

9. In the command prompt area, the message *"Select Objects:"* is displayed. Pick the cutter rectangle, the smaller rectangle, to move.

10. Inside the graphics window, **right-mouse-click** to accept the selection.

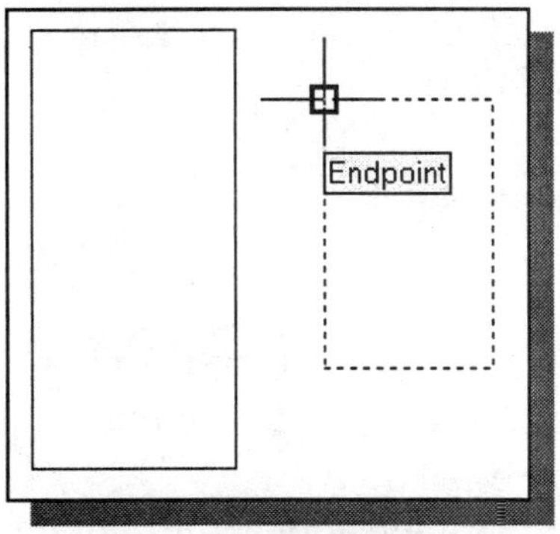

11. In the command prompt area, the message *"Specify base point or displacement:"* is displayed. Pick the upper-left corner of the smaller rectangle as shown.

12. Inside the graphics window, hold down the **[SHIFT]** key and **right-mouse-click** once to bring up the *Object Snap* shortcut menu.

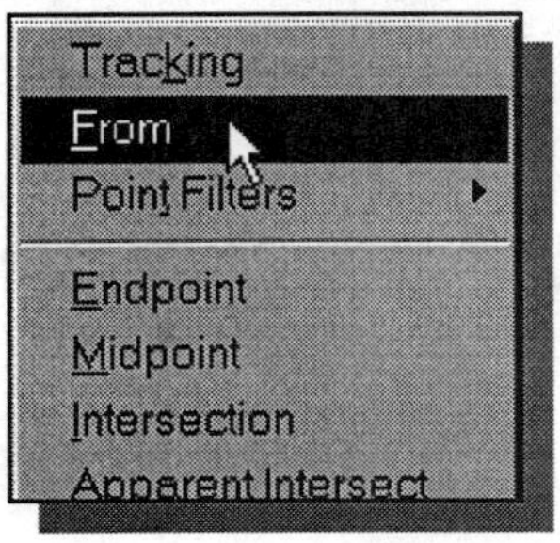

13. Select the **From** option in popup window.

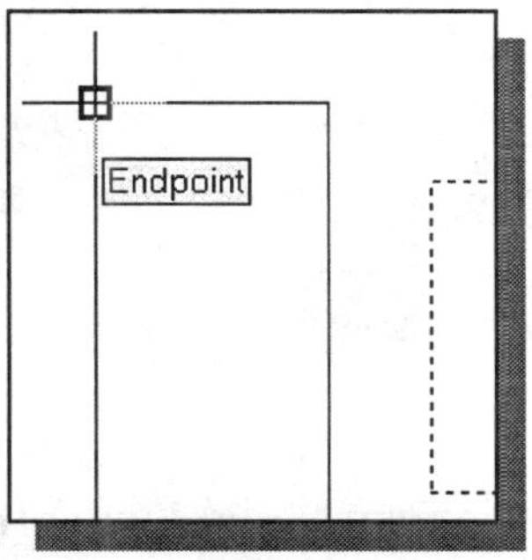

14. Pick the upper-left corner of the larger rectangle as shown.

15. In the command prompt area, the message *"Specify base point or displacement: _from Base point: <Offset>:"* is displayed. Enter: **@0.125,-0.25 [ENTER]**

16. Pre-select the smaller rectangle to activate the grip-editing function.

17. Pick the lower-right grip point displayed along the right vertical edge.

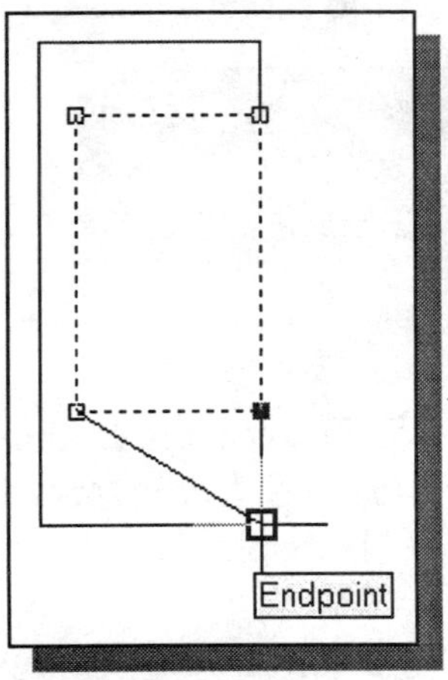

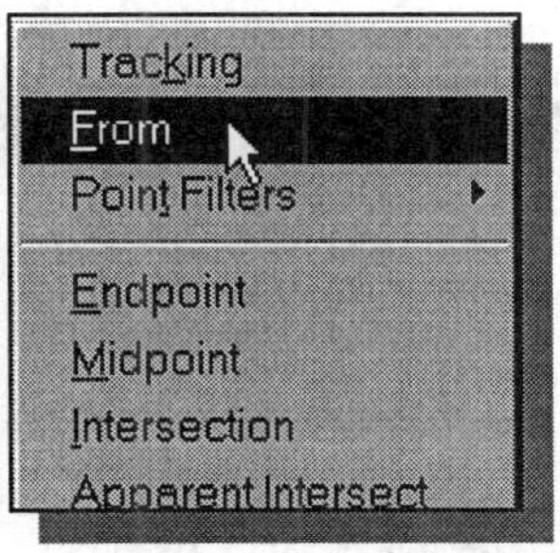

18. Inside the graphics window, hold down the **[SHIFT]** key and **right-mouse-click** once to bring up the *Object Snap* shortcut menu.

19. Select the **From** option in popup window.

20. Pick the lower-right corner of the larger rectangle.

21. At the command prompt: **@0,0.125 [ENTER]**

22. Press the **[Esc]** key twice to deselect the highlighted entities.

Perform 2D Boolean Operations

- AutoCAD's 2D regions are special types of filled polygons. We can create composite 2D regions by applying *Boolean operations* to subtract, find the intersection, or combine two or more regions.

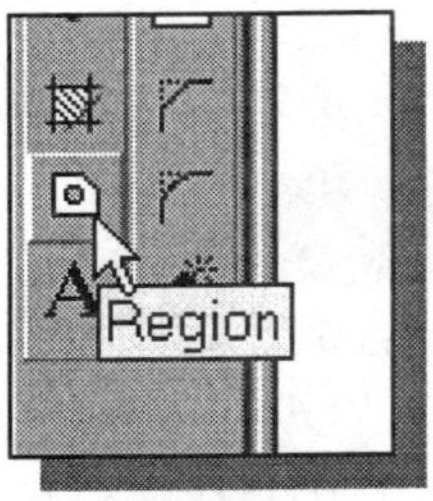

1. Select the ***Region*** command icon in the *Draw* toolbar.
2. In the command prompt area, the message *"Select objects:"* is displayed. Select the polygon we just edited.
3. Inside the graphics window, **right-mouse-click** to accept the selection and create a region.

4. Inside the graphics window, click once with the **right-mouse-button** to bring up the popup option menu.
5. Pick **Repeat Region**, with the left-mouse-button, in the popup menu to repeat the last command.
6. In the command prompt area, the message *"Select objects:"* is displayed. Select the rectangle by clicking on one of the edges.
7. Inside the graphics window, **right-mouse-click** to accept the selection and create a region.

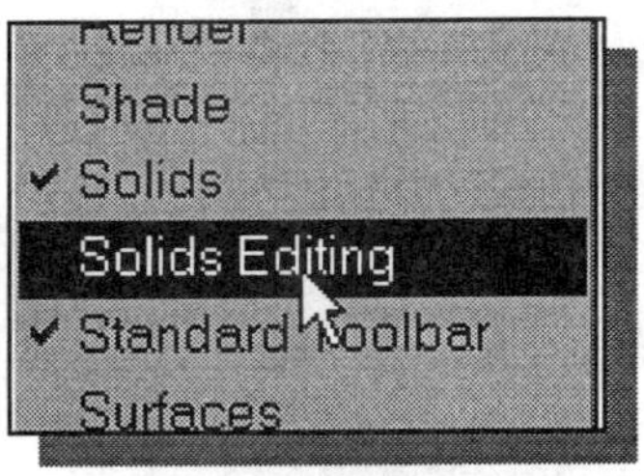

8. Move the cursor to the *Standard* toolbar area and **right-click** on any icon of the *Standard* toolbar to display a list of toolbar menu groups.
9. Select ***Solids Editing***, with the left-mouse-button, to display the *Solids Editing* toolbar on the screen.

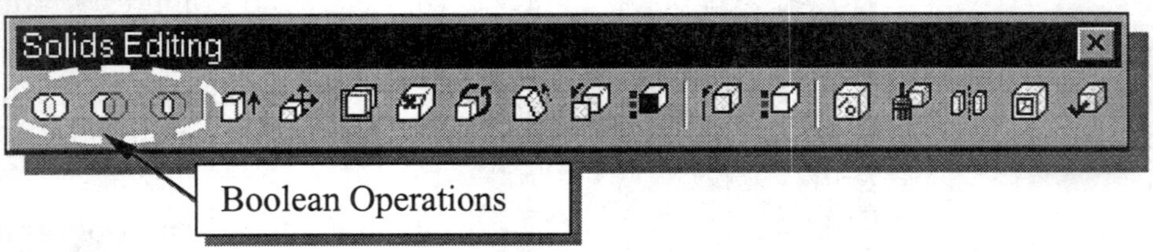

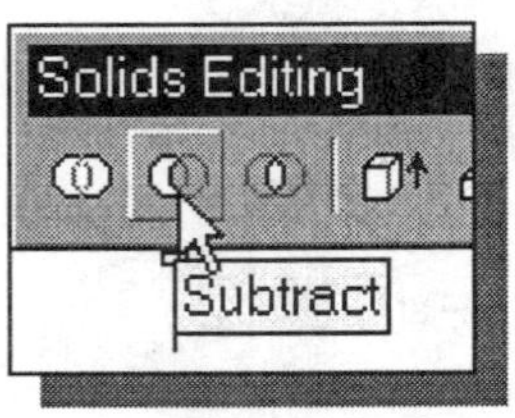

10. In the *Solids Editing* toolbar, click on the ***Subtract*** icon. In the command prompt area, the message *"_subtract Select solids and regions to subtract from .. Select Objects:"* is displayed.
11. Pick the **rectangle** by clicking on one of the edges.

12. Inside the graphics window, **right-mouse-click** to accept the selection and proceed with the *SUBTRACT* command.

13. In the command prompt area, the message *" Select solids and regions to subtract .. Select Objects:"* is displayed. Pick the four-sided **polygon** by clicking on one of the edges.

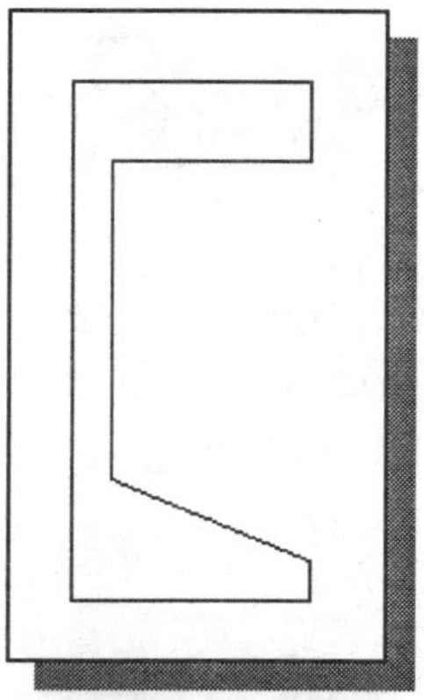

14. Inside the graphics window, **right-mouse-click** to accept the selection and proceed with the *SUBTRACT* command. The completed 2D sketch is as shown.

- AutoCAD's region is a special type of geometric entity. It was developed based on the CSG solid modeling approach and is valuable in the sense that it provides a different method to construct complex geometric shapes. In many cases, the Boolean operations are more efficient than creating geometry by entering point-to-point coordinates.

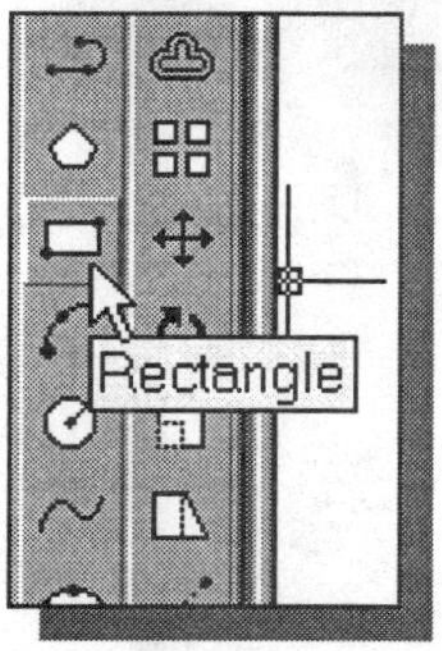

15. Select the ***Rectangle*** icon in the *Draw* toolbar.

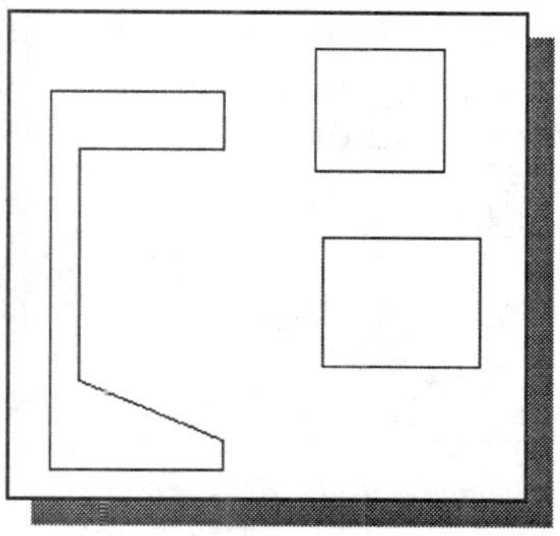

16. On your own, create two rectangles of arbitrary sizes as shown. We will use these two rectangles to shape the upper regions of the design.

17. On your own, convert the two rectangles into two **regions**.

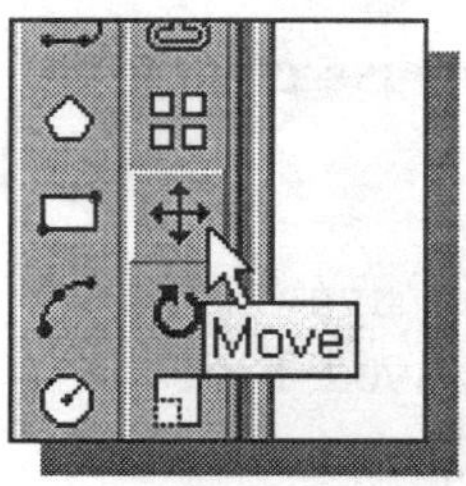

18. Select the ***Move*** icon in the *Draw* toolbar.

19. In the command prompt area, the message *"Select Objects:"* is displayed. Pick one of the rectangles to move.

20. Inside the graphics window, **right-mouse-click** to accept the selection.

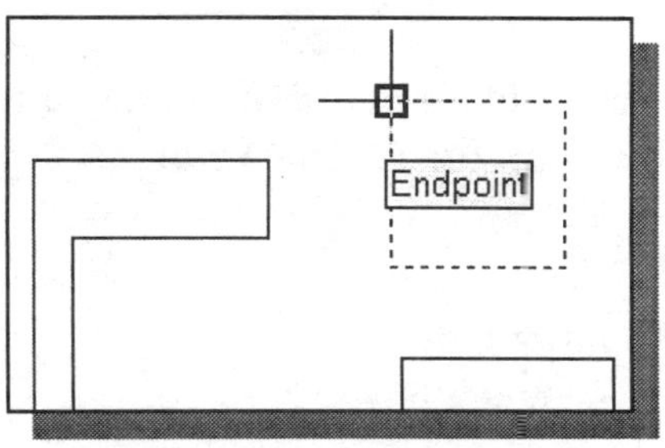

21. In the command prompt area, the message *"Specify base point or displacement:"* is displayed. Pick the upper-left corner of the selected rectangle as shown.

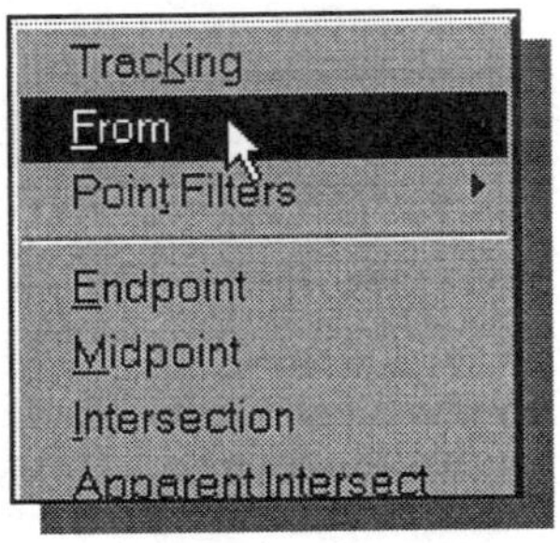

22. Inside the graphics window, hold down the **[SHIFT]** key and **right-mouse-click** once to bring up the *Object Snap* shortcut menu.

23. Select the **From** option in popup window.

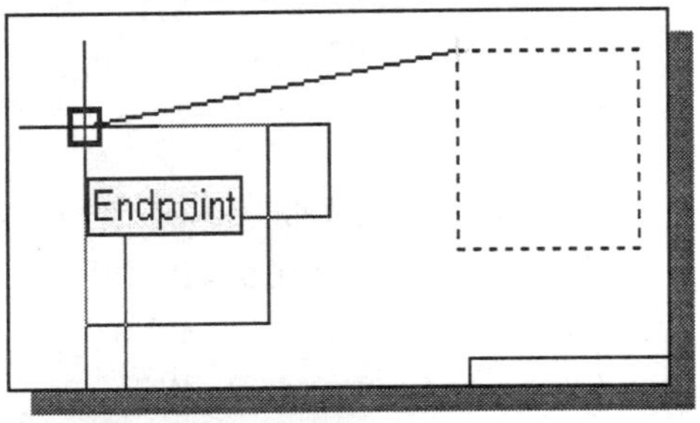

24. Pick the upper-left corner of the larger rectangle as shown.

25. In the command prompt area, the message *"Specify base point or displacement: _from Base point: <Offset>:"* is displayed.
    Enter: **@0.5,0.0 [ENTER]**

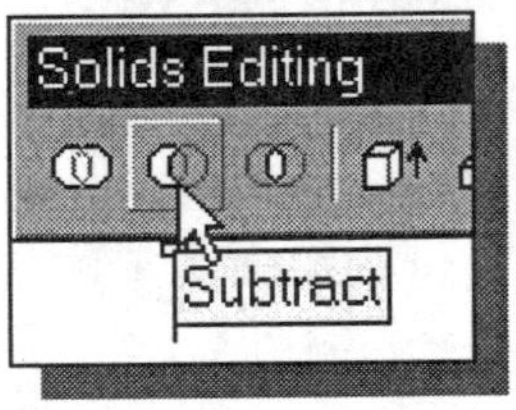

26. On your own, perform the **Boolean *SUBTRACT*** operation and create the 2D sketch as shown.

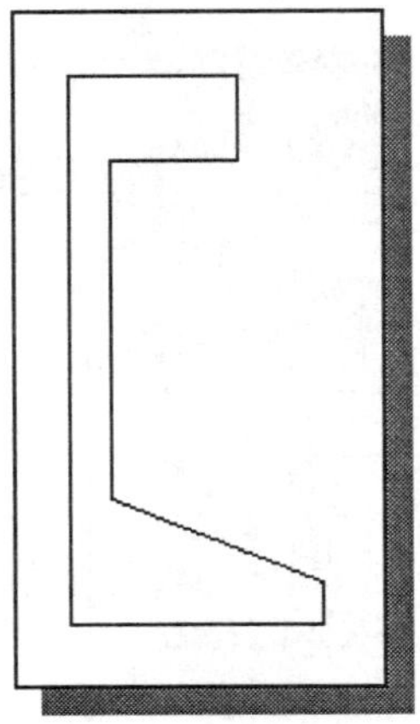

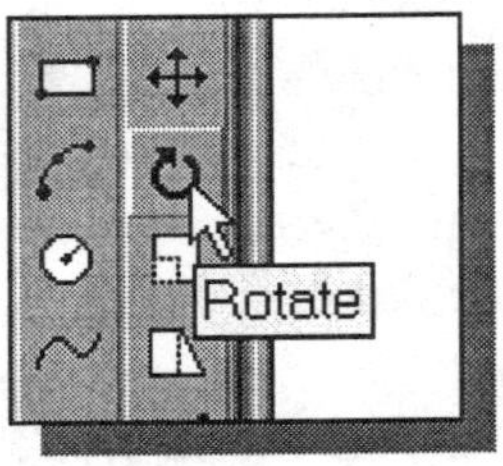

27. Select the ***Rotate*** icon in the *Modify* toolbar.

28. In the command prompt area, the message *"Select Objects:"* is displayed. Pick the rectangle to rotate.

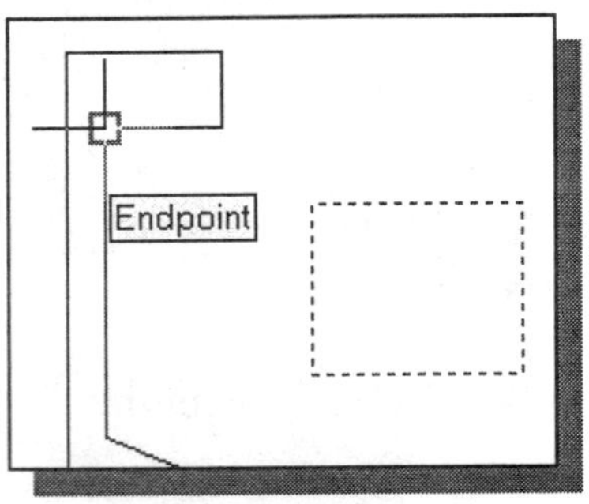

29. Inside the graphics window, **right-mouse-click** to accept the selection.

30. In the command prompt area, the message *"Specify base point or displacement:"* is displayed. Pick the inside corner of the 2D sketch as shown.

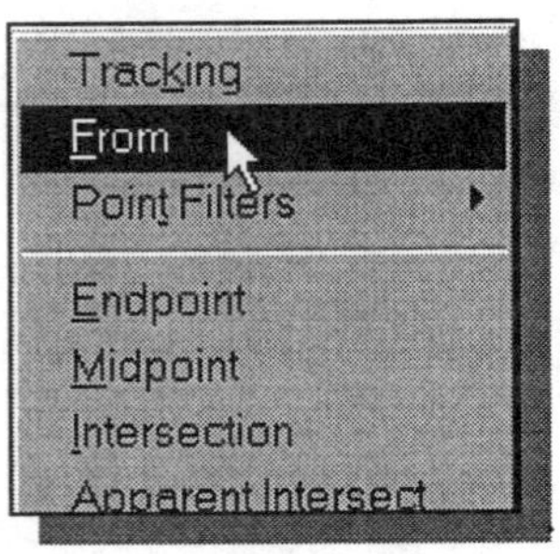

31. Inside the graphics window, hold down the **[SHIFT]** key and **right-mouse-click** once to bring up the *Object Snap* shortcut menu.

32. Select the **From** option in popup window.

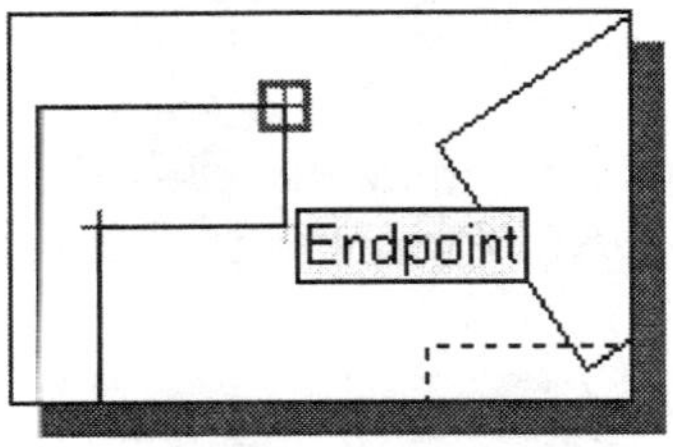

33. Pick the upper-left corner of the 2D sketch as shown.

34. At the command prompt: **@0,-0.125 [ENTER]**

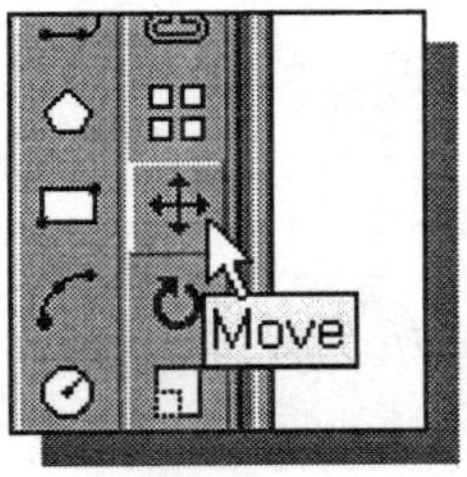

35. Select the ***Move*** icon in the *Draw* toolbar.

36. In the command prompt area, the message *"Select Objects:"* is displayed. Pick the rotated rectangles to move.

37. Inside the graphics window, **right-mouse-click** to accept the selection.

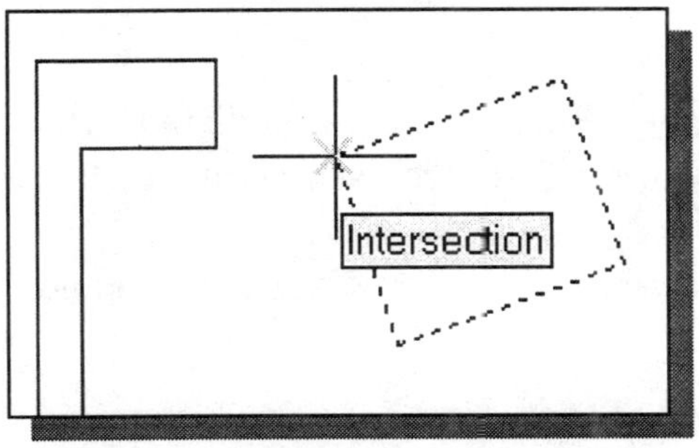

38. In the command prompt area, the message *"Specify base point or displacement:"* is displayed. Pick the upper-left corner of the selected rectangle as shown.

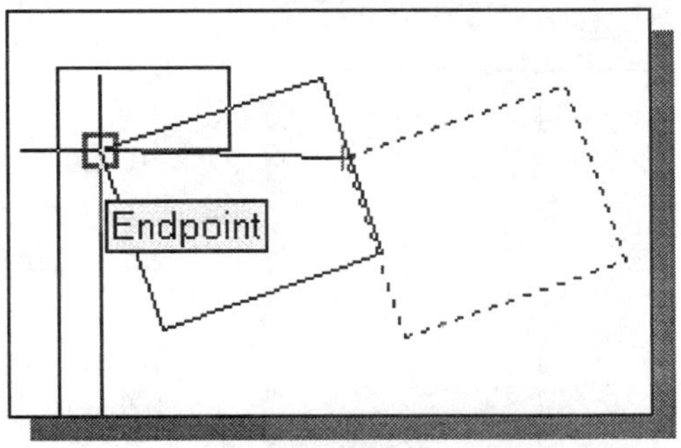

39. In the command prompt area, the message *"Specify base point or displacement:"* is displayed. Pick the inside corner of the 2D sketch as shown.

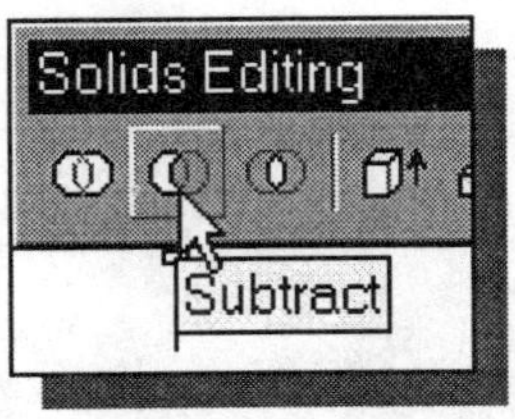

40. On your own, perform the **Boolean *SUBTRACT*** operation and complete the 2D sketch as shown.

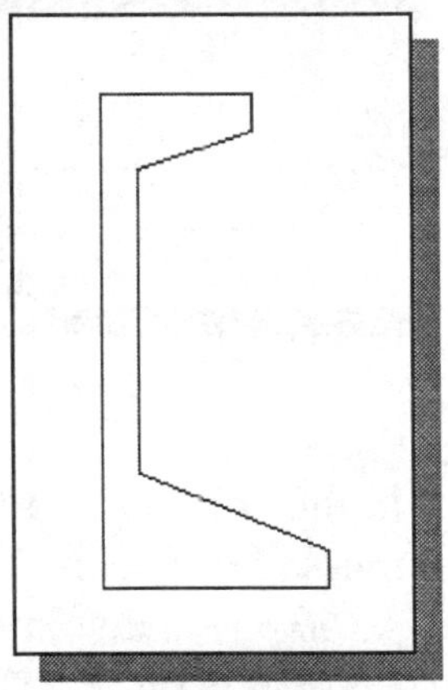

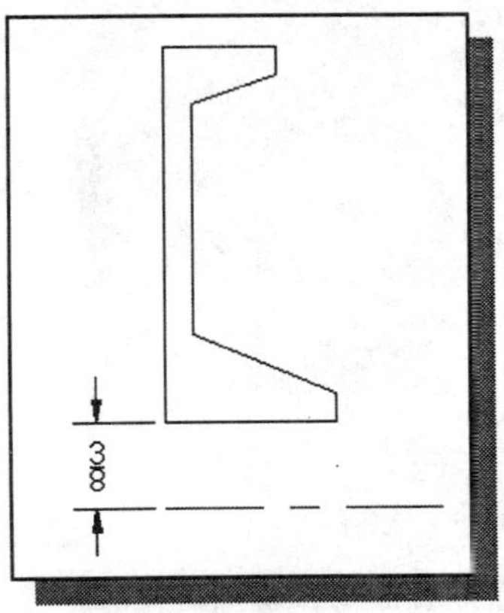

41. On your own, create a centerline that is 3/8 below the 2D sketch as shown. This line will be used as the axis of rotation for the revolved feature. (Trim the line so that the left endpoint is aligned to the left edge of the 2D sketch.)

Creating the Revolved Feature

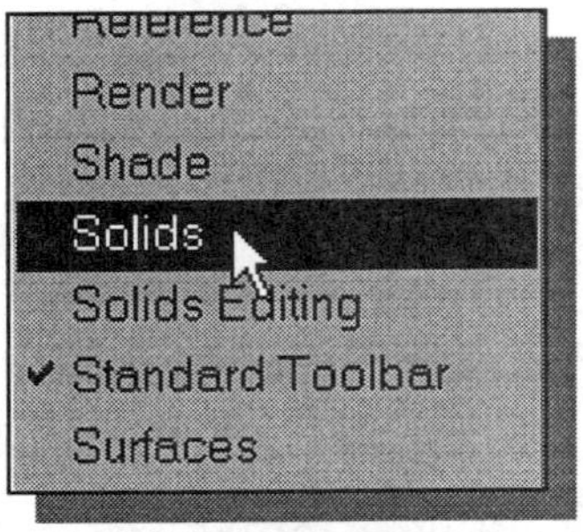

1. Move the cursor to the *Standard* toolbar area and **right-mouse-click** once on any icon in the toolbar area to display a list of toolbar menu groups.

2. Select ***Solids***, with the left-mouse-button, to display the *Solids* toolbar on the screen.

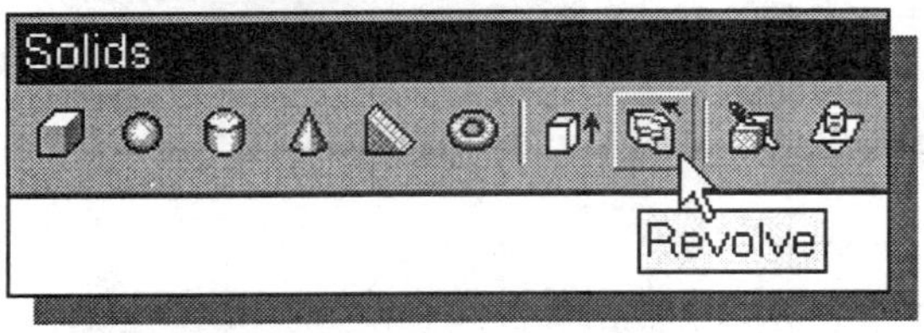

3. Select ***Revolve*** in the *Solids* toolbar as shown.

4. In the command prompt area, the message *"Select objects:"* is displayed. Select the 2D region by clicking on any of the displayed segments.

5. Inside the graphics window, **right-mouse-click** to accept the selection and proceed with the *REVOLVE* command.

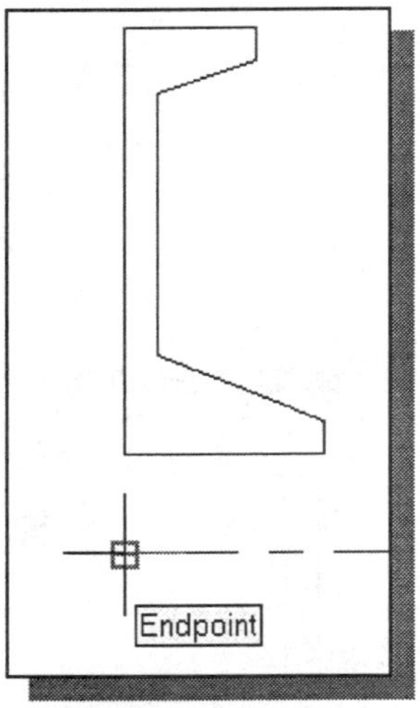

6. In the command prompt area, the message *"Define axis by [Object/X (axis)/Y (axis)}]:"* is displayed. Pick the **left endpoint of the centerline** as shown.

7. In the command prompt area, the message *"Specify endpoint of axis:"* is displayed. Pick the **right endpoint of the centerline**.

8. In the command prompt area, the message *"Specify angle of revolution <360>:"* is displayed.
   Enter: **360.0 [ENTER]**

- The revolved feature is created as shown.

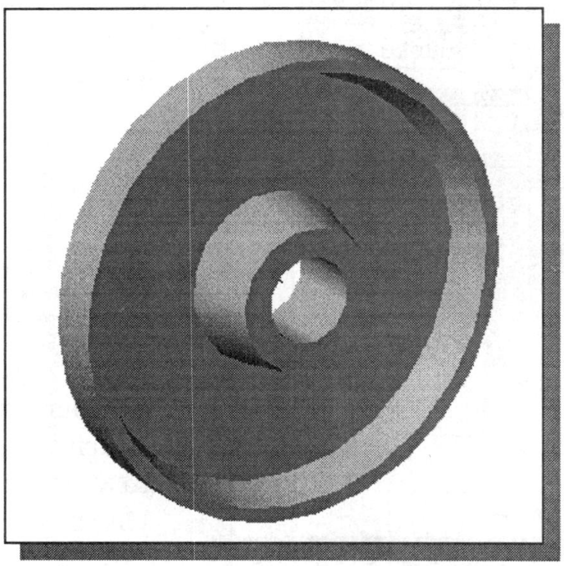

Mirroring Part

- In AutoCAD, we can mirror a 2D sketch or a 3D part about a line or a specified surface. We can define the line by selecting existing points or by picking locations on the screen. We can physically flip the part about a reference plane or create a new mirrored part.

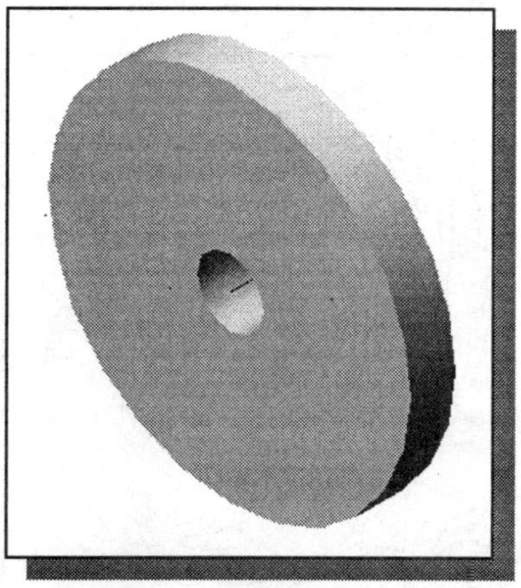

1. On your own, change the display to ***SW Isometric*** view or use the ***3D ORBIT*** command to display the flat face of the solid model.

2. In the pull down menus, select
   [Modify] => [3D Operation] => [Mirror 3D]

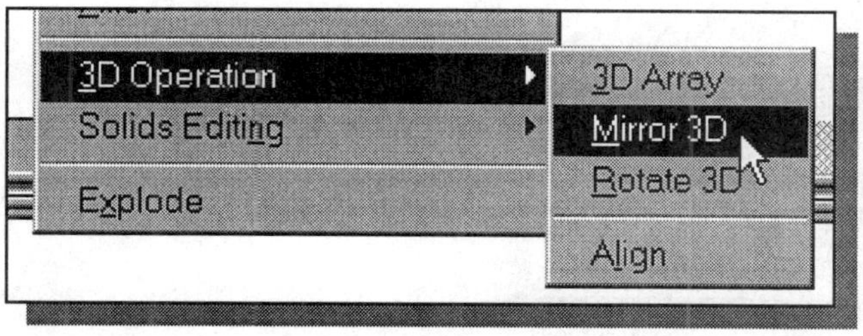

3. In the command prompt area, the message "*Select objects:*" is displayed. Select any edge of the 3D model.

4. Inside the graphics window, **right-mouse-click** to accept the selection.

5. In the command prompt area, the message "*Specify first point of mirror plane (3 points) or [Object/Last/Zaxis/View/XY/YZ/ZX/3points] <3points>:*" is displayed. Choose the YZ plane by entering: **YZ [ENTER]**

6. In the command prompt area, the message "*Select point on YZ plane <0,0,0>:*" is displayed. Pick the **left endpoint of the centerline**.

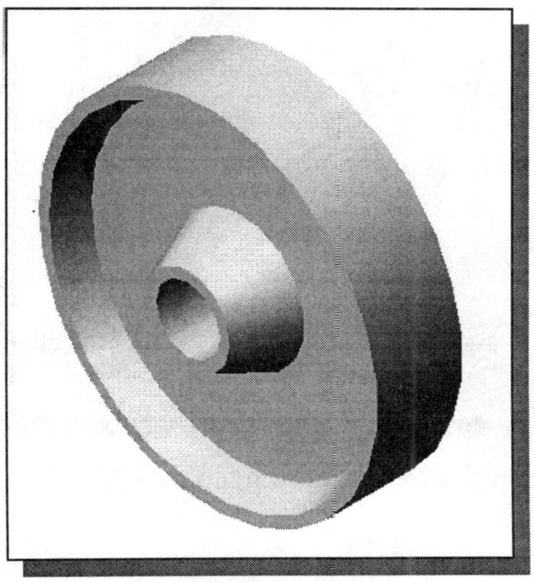

7. In the command prompt area, the message "*Delete source objects? [Yes/No] <N>:*" is displayed. Inside the graphics window, **right-mouse-click** to bring up the option menu and select **No** to create a new part.

Combining Parts

- We have created two separate parts with the *MIRROR 3D* command. We will combine the two parts into a single part using the CSG *Boolean operations*.

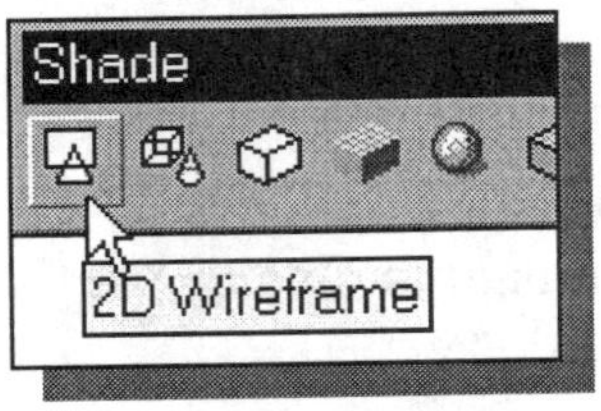

1. Select ***2D Wireframe*** by left-clicking once on the icon in the *Shade* toolbar.

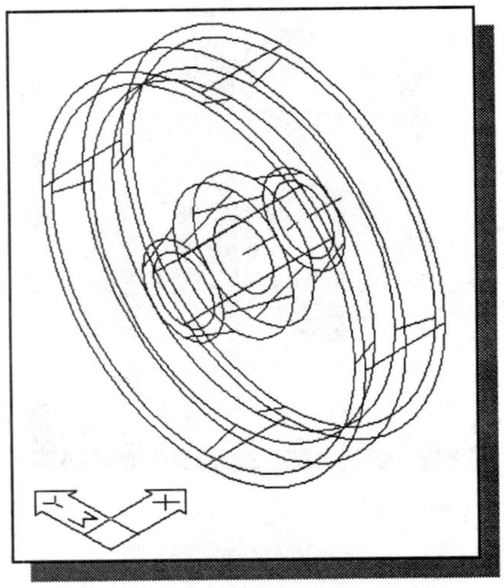

- Note the edges separating the two parts displayed on the screen.

2. Pick ***Union*** in the *Solids Editing* toolbar as shown.

3. In the command prompt area, the message "*Select Objects:*" is displayed. Pick the two parts.

4. Inside the graphics window, **right-mouse-click** to accept the selection and proceed with the *UNION* command to combine the two parts into a single part.

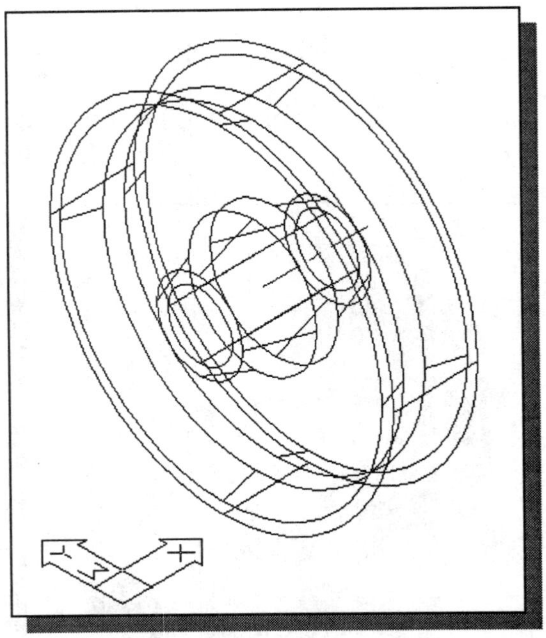

- Reset the display to ***2D Wireframe*** mode before proceeding to the next section.

3D ARRAY

- In AutoCAD, existing 2D and/or 3D features can be easily duplicated. The ***ARRAY*** command allows us to create both rectangular and polar arrays of features.

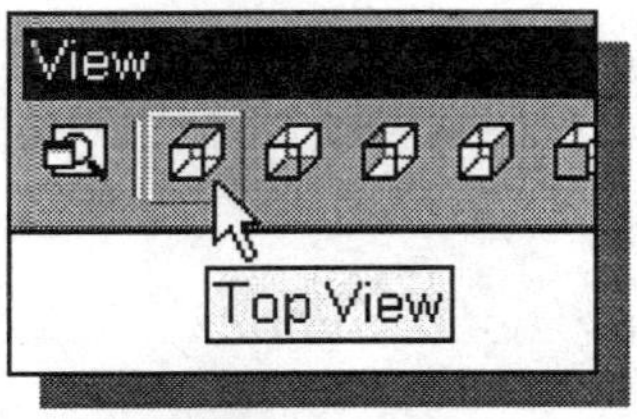

1. In the *View* toolbar, select the ***Top View*** option to reset the display.

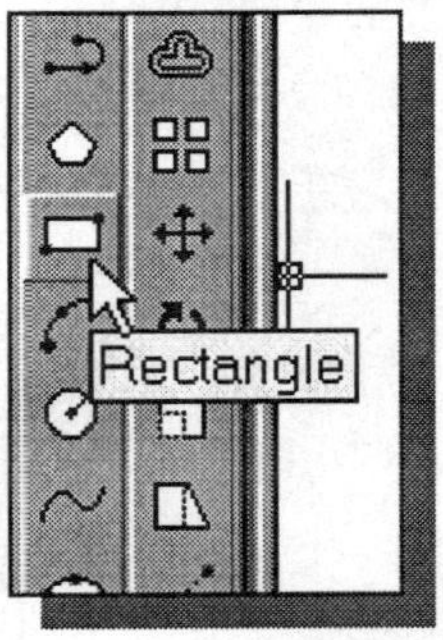

2. Select the ***Rectangle*** icon in the *Draw* toolbar.
3. On your own, create a rectangle that is **1.0" x .25"** toward the right side of the solid model.
4. On your own, convert the rectangle into a *Region.*

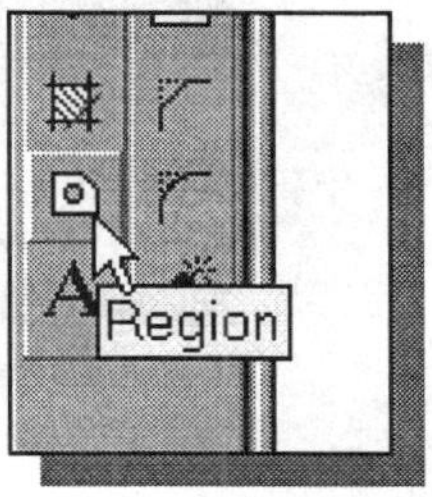

- The rectangle will be used to create a cylindrical solid model. The cylinder will be used to generate a polar array using the *Array* command.

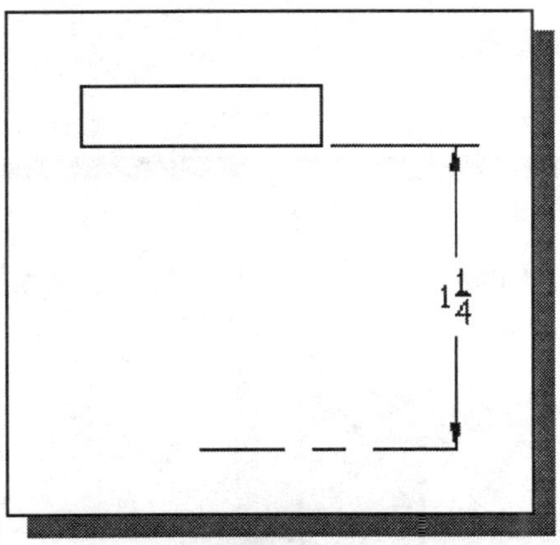

5. On your own, create a centerline that is **1¼"** below the rectangle with the left endpoint aligned to the center of the rectangle as shown.

- The centerline will be used as the axis of rotation to create the *polar array.*

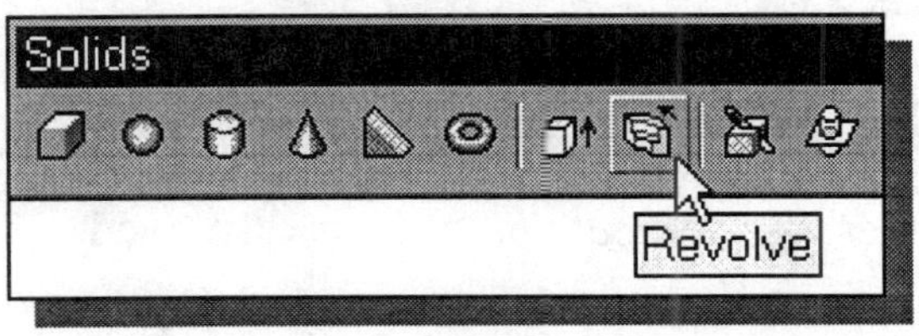

6. Select ***Revolve*** in the *Solids* toolbar as shown.
7. In the command prompt area, the message *"Select objects:"* is displayed. Select the rectangular region by clicking on any of the displayed segments.
8. Inside the graphics window, **right-mouse-click** to accept the selection and proceed with the *REVOLVE* command.

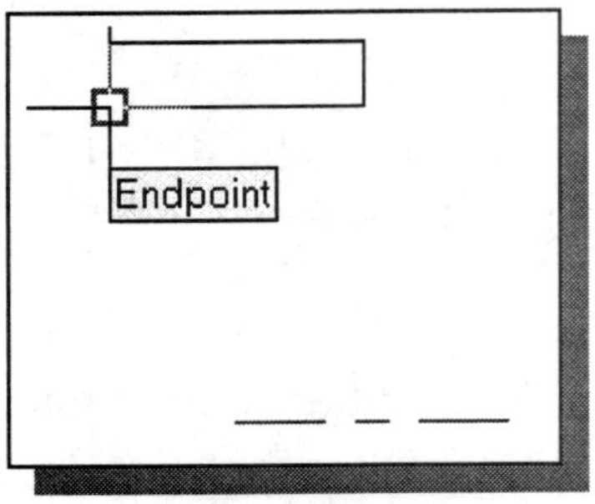

9. In the command prompt area, the message *"Define axis by [Object/X (axis)/Y (axis)}]:"* is displayed. Pick the **lower-left corner** of the region as shown.

10. In the command prompt area, the message *"Specify endpoint of axis:"* is displayed. Pick the **lower-right corner** of the region.

11. In the command prompt area, the message *"Specify angle of revolution <360>:"* is displayed.
    Enter: **360.0** **[ENTER]**

12. In the *View* toolbar, click on the ***SE Isometric View*** icon.

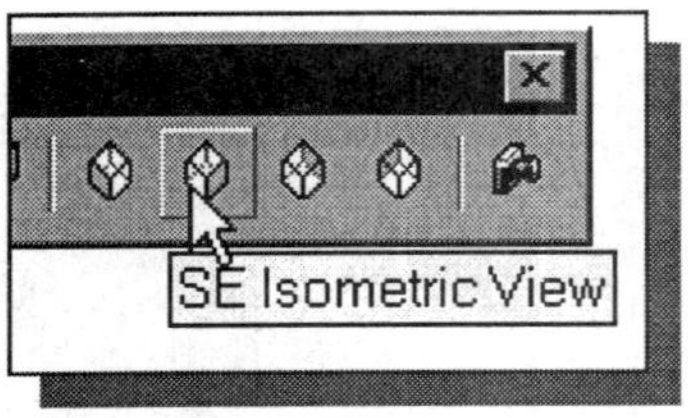

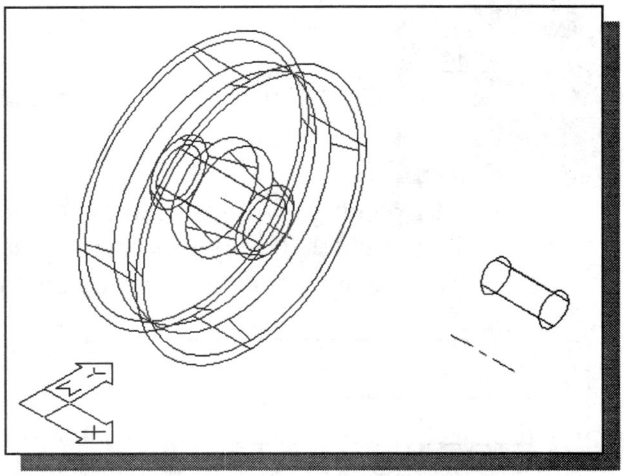

13. In the pull down menus, select
    [Modify] => [3D Operation] => [3D Array]

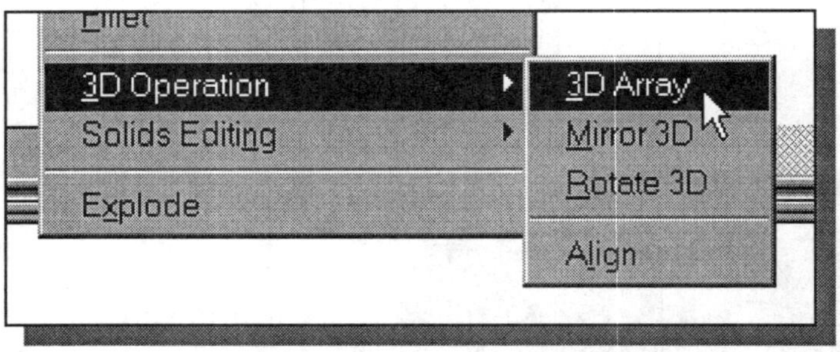

14. In the command prompt area, the message *"Select objects:"* is displayed. Select any edge of the cylinder.

15. Inside the graphics window, **right-mouse-click** to accept the selection.

16. In the command prompt area, the message *"Enter the type of array [Rectangular/Polar] <R>:"* is displayed. Choose the *Polar* option by entering: **P** **[ENTER]**

17. In the command prompt area, the message "*Enter the number of items in the array:*" is displayed. We will create 6 items by entering: **6 [ENTER]**

18. In the command prompt area, the message "*Specify the angle to fill (+=ccw, -=cw) <360>:*" is displayed. Enter: **360 [ENTER]**

19. In the command prompt area, the message "*Rotate arrayed objects?[Yes/No] <Y>:*" is displayed. Enter: **N [ENTER]**

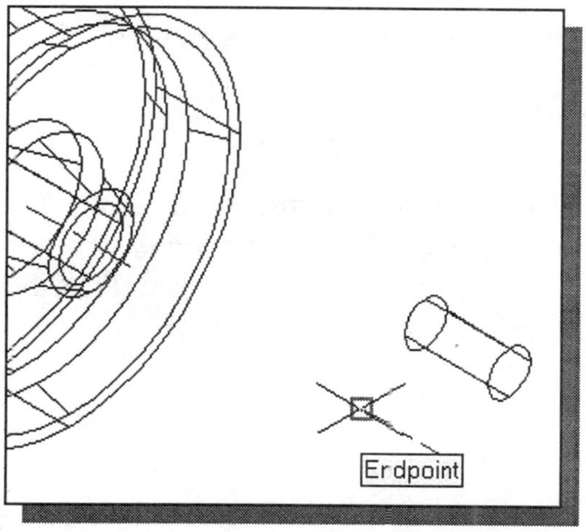

20. In the command prompt area, the message "*Specify center point of array:*" is displayed. Pick the left endpoint of the centerline as shown.

21. In the command prompt area, the message "*Specify second point on axis of rotation:*" is displayed. Pick the right endpoint of the centerline as shown.

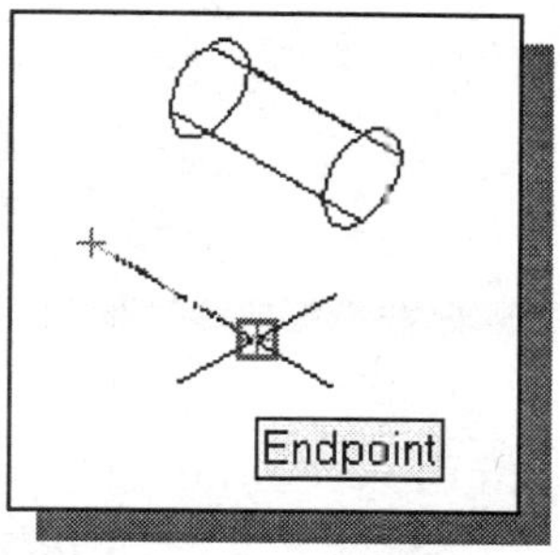

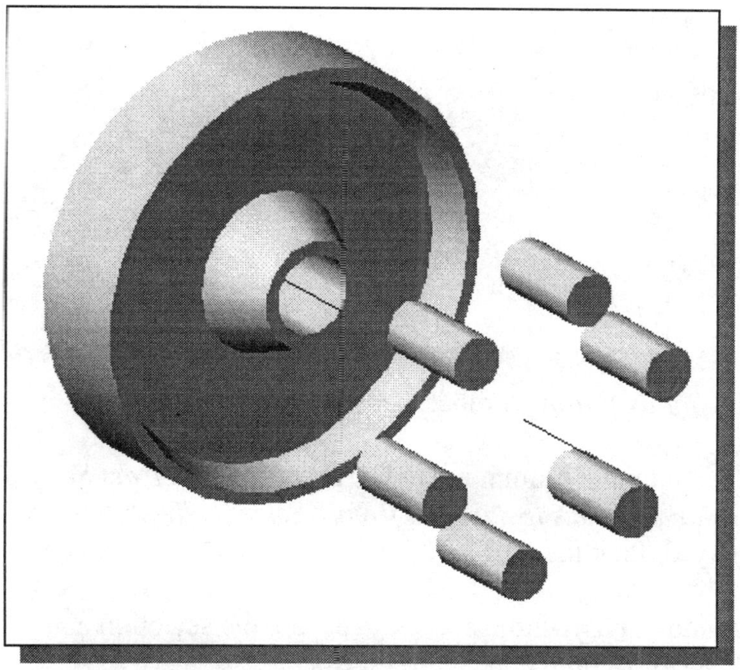

Position and perform the Cut

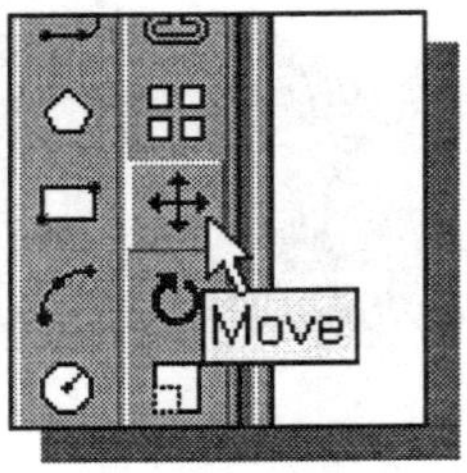

1. Select the ***Move*** icon in the *Draw* toolbar.

2. In the command prompt area, the message *"Select Objects:"* is displayed. Pick the six cylinders we just created.

3. Inside the graphics window, **right-mouse-click** to accept the selection.

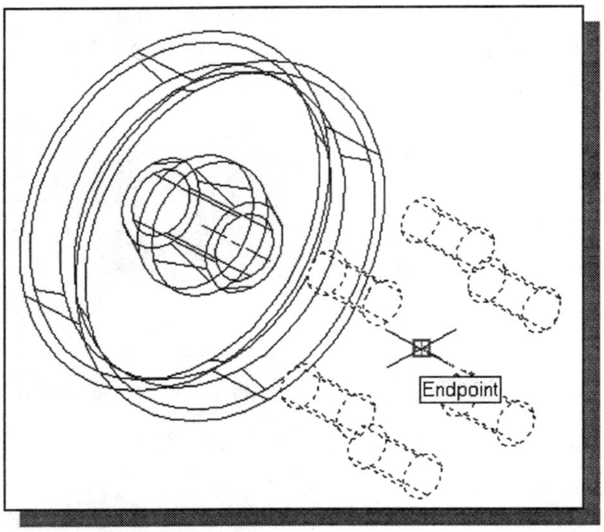

4. In the command prompt area, the message *"Specify base point or displacement:"* is displayed. Pick the left endpoint the polar array centerline as shown.

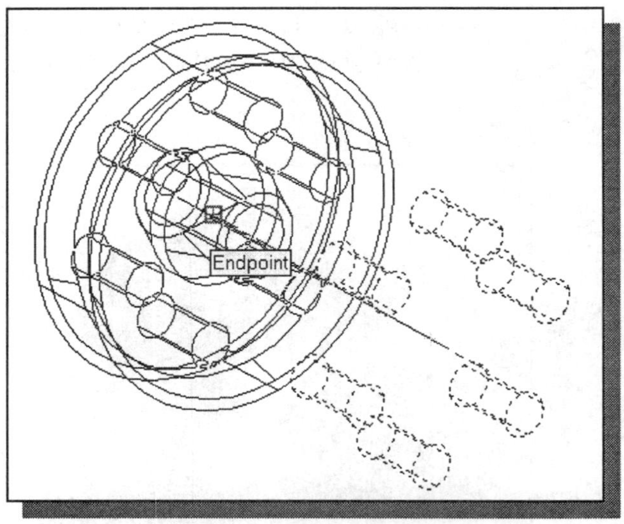

5. In the command prompt area, the message *"Specify base point or displacement:"* is displayed. Pick the left endpoint of the centerline of the *PULLEY* as shown.

6. In the *Solids Editing* toolbar, click on the ***Subtract*** icon.

7. In the command prompt area, the message *"_subtract Select solids and regions to subtract from .. Select Objects:"* is displayed. Pick the *PULLEY* by clicking on one of the edges.

8. Inside the graphics window, **right-mouse-click** to accept the selection and proceed with the *SUBTRACT* command.

9. In the command prompt area, the message *" Select solids and regions to subtract .. Select Objects: "* is displayed.

10. Pick the six cylinder blocks by clicking on the circular edges.

11. Inside the graphics window, **right-mouse-click** to accept the selection and proceed with the *SUBTRACT* command.

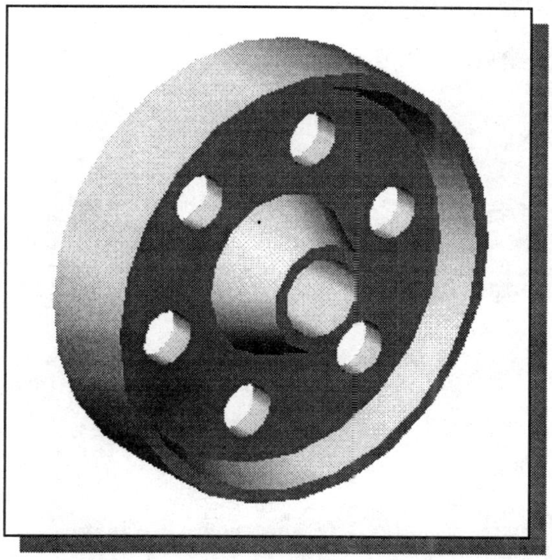

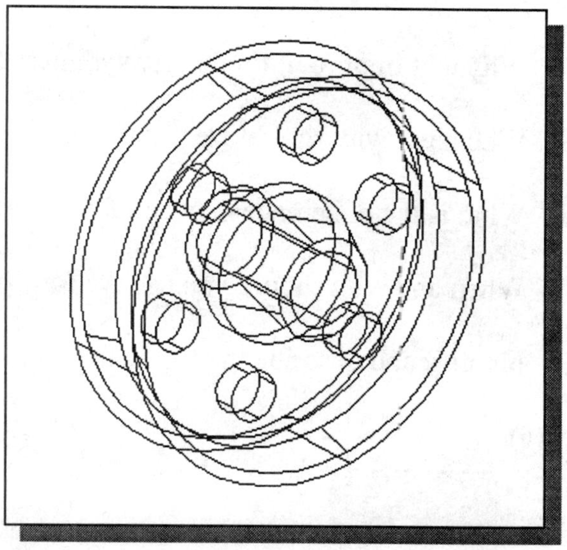

- On your own, create the 2D drawing from the 3D model as shown.

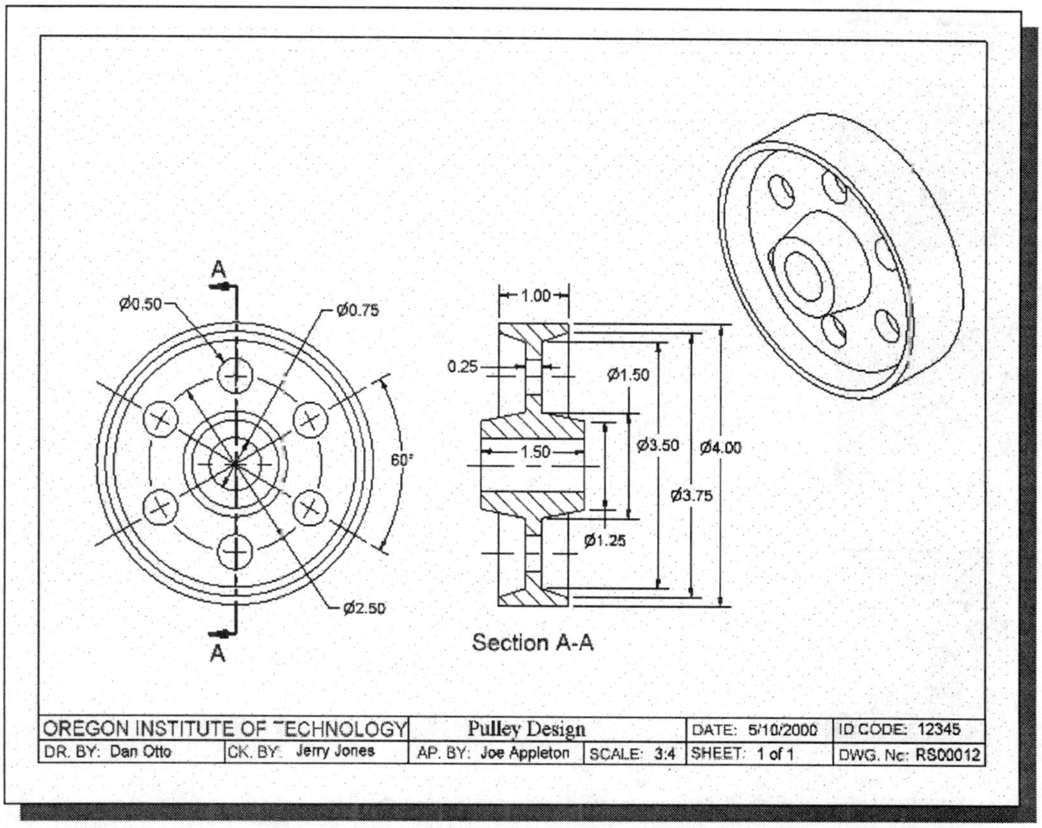

Questions:

1. List the different symmetrical features created in the *PULLEY* design.
2. What are the advantages of using *Regions*?
3. Describe the steps required in using the *Mirror Part* command.
4. Why is it important to identify symmetrical features in designs?
5. When and why should we use the *Array* option?
6. What is the difference between *Rectangular Array* and *Polar Array*?
7. When and why should you use the *Revolve* command in AutoCAD?
8. Identify and describe the following commands:

(a)

(b)

(c)

(d)

Exercises:

1.

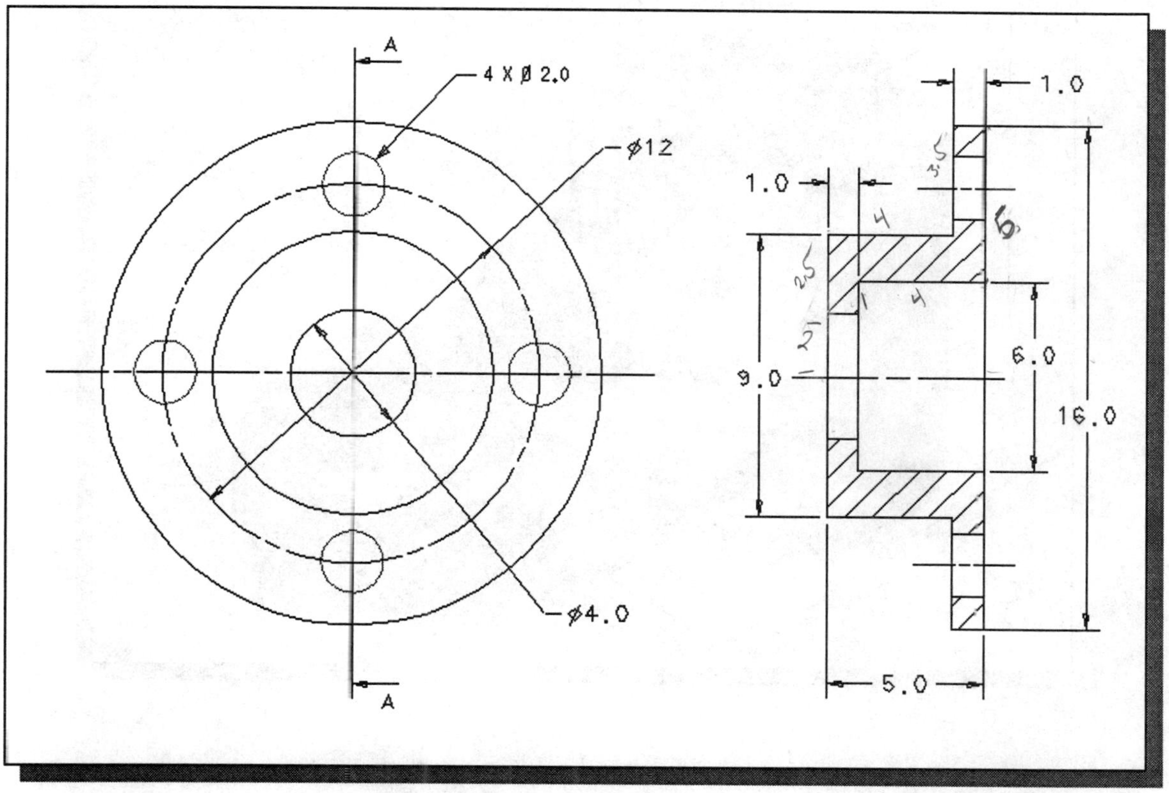

2. Plate thickness : 0.125 inch

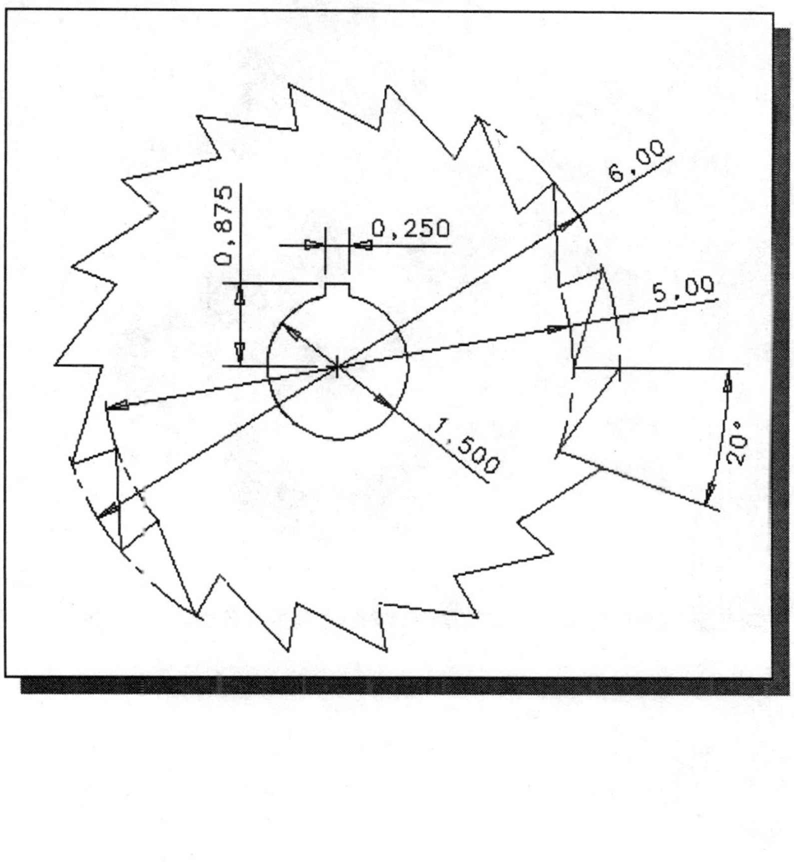

3.

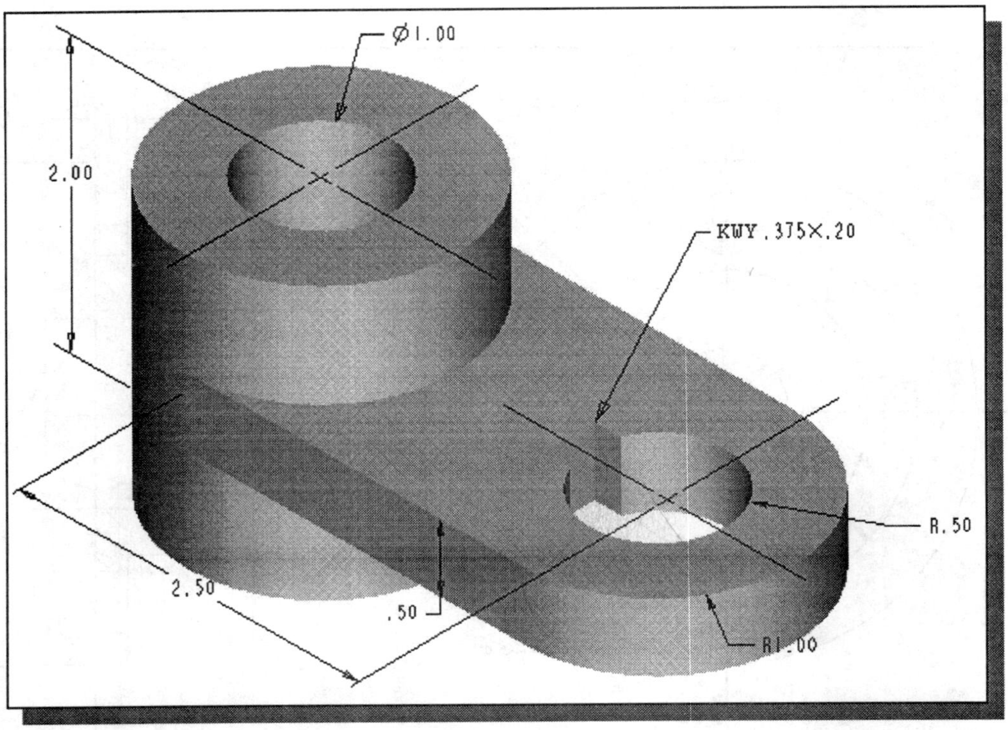
Ø1.00
2.00
KWY.375×.20
R.50
2.50
.50
R1.00

4.

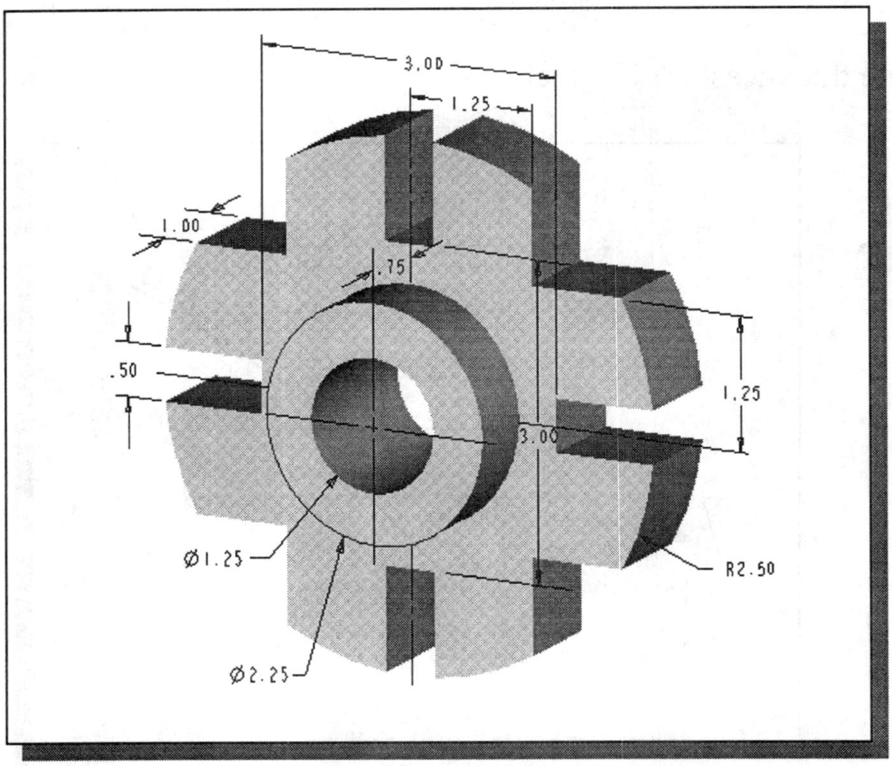
3.00
1.25
1.00
.75
.50
1.25
3.00
Ø1.25
R2.50
Ø2.25

5.

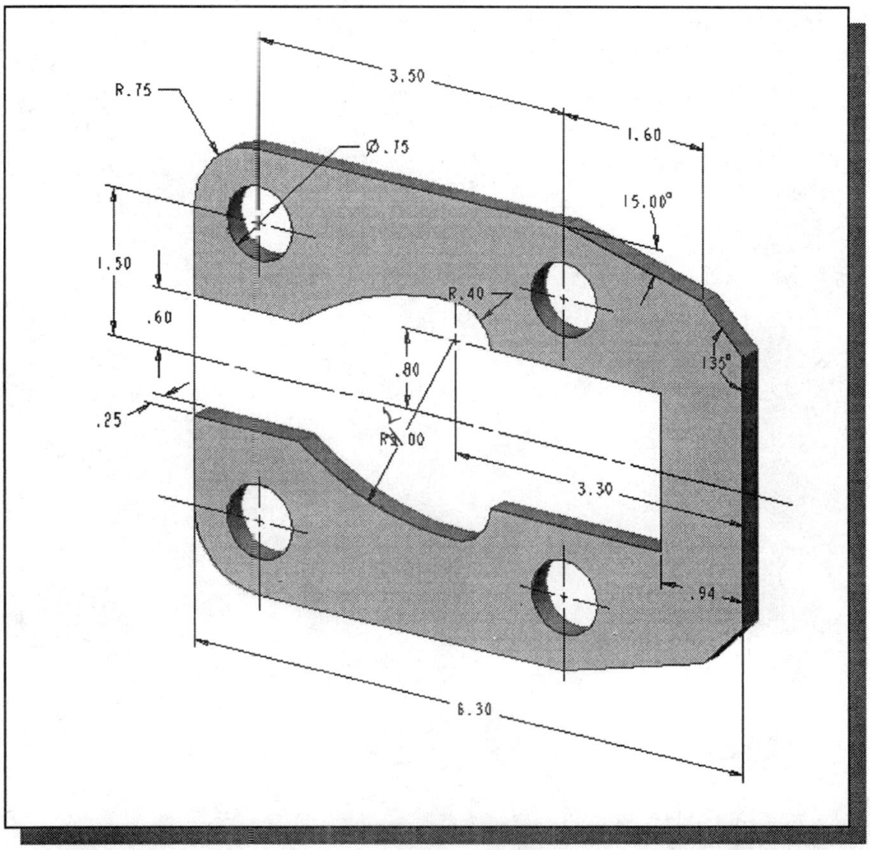

6. Plate thickness: 0.25

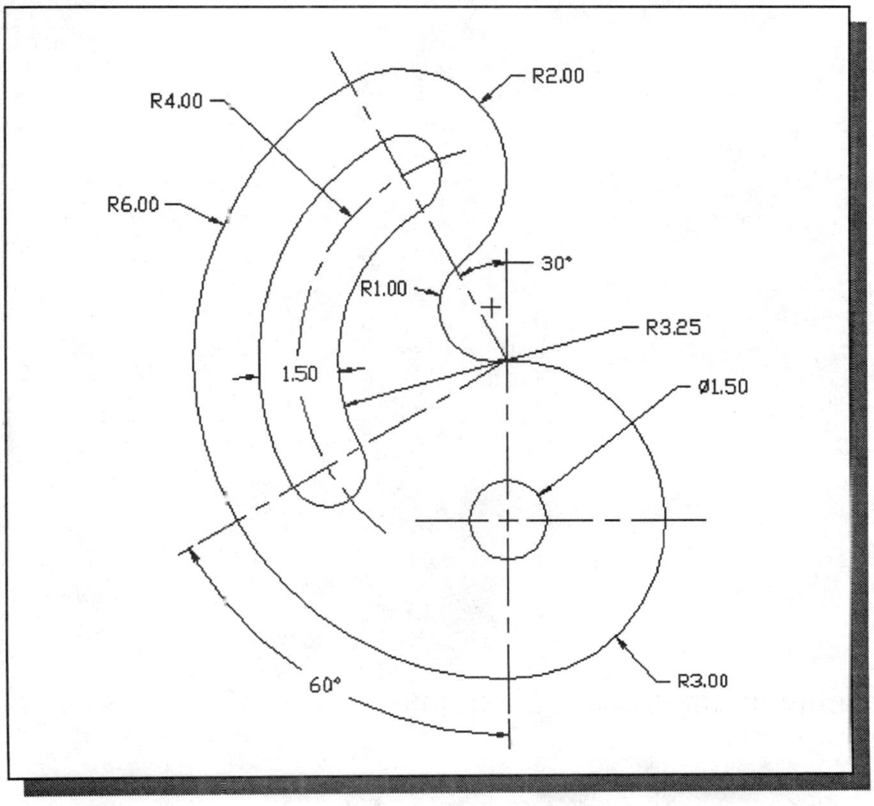

Notes:

Chapter 10

Advanced Modeling Tools & Techniques

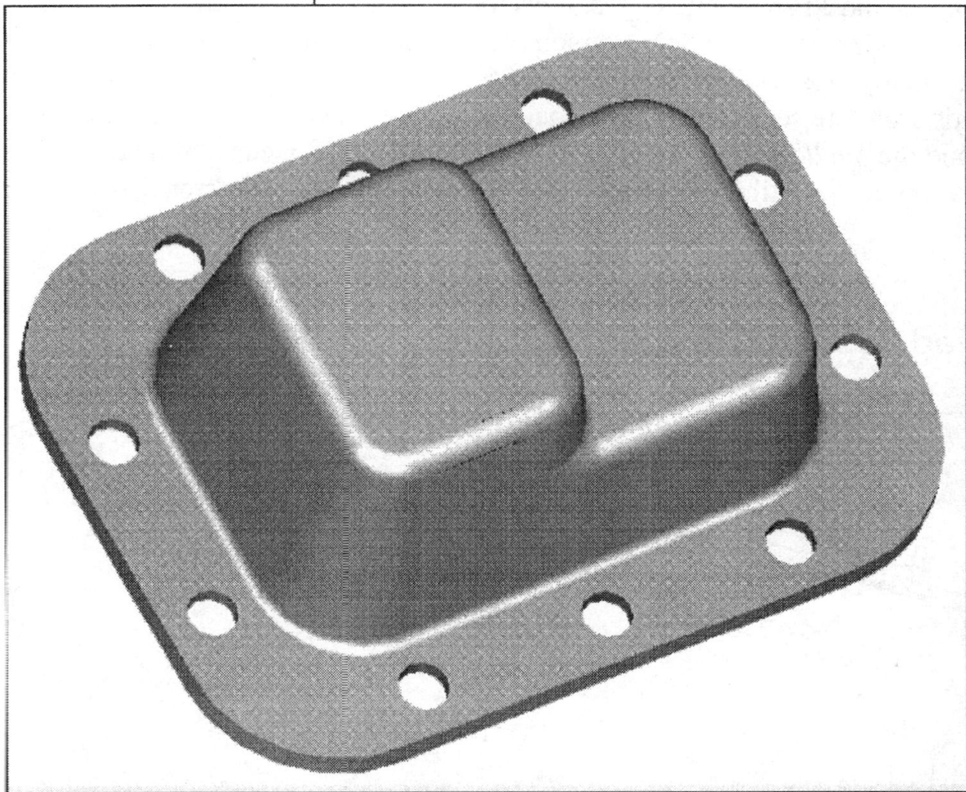

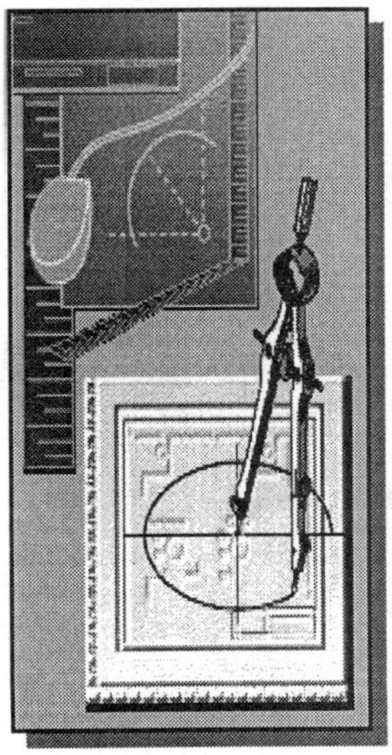

Learning Objectives

- Create Draft Angle Features.
- Use the 3D Rounds & Fillets command.
- Create Rectangular Patterns.
- Use the Shell command.
- Use the Copy Faces command.

Introduction

AutoCAD provides an assortment of three-dimensional construction tools to make the creation of solid models easier and more efficient. In this chapter, we will examine the procedures to create the *Draft Angle* feature, the *Shell* feature and also for creating three-dimensional *Rounds* and *Fillets* along edges of a solid model. These features are common characteristics of molded parts. The three-dimensional *FILLETS* and the *SHELL* commands will usually create complex three-dimensional spatial curves and surfaces. These commands are more sensitive to the associated geometric entities. For this reason, the *3D Fillets* and the *Shell* features are created last, after all associated solid features are created. In this chapter, we will also examine the different methods of referencing to existing surfaces.

A Thin-walled Design: *OIL SINK*

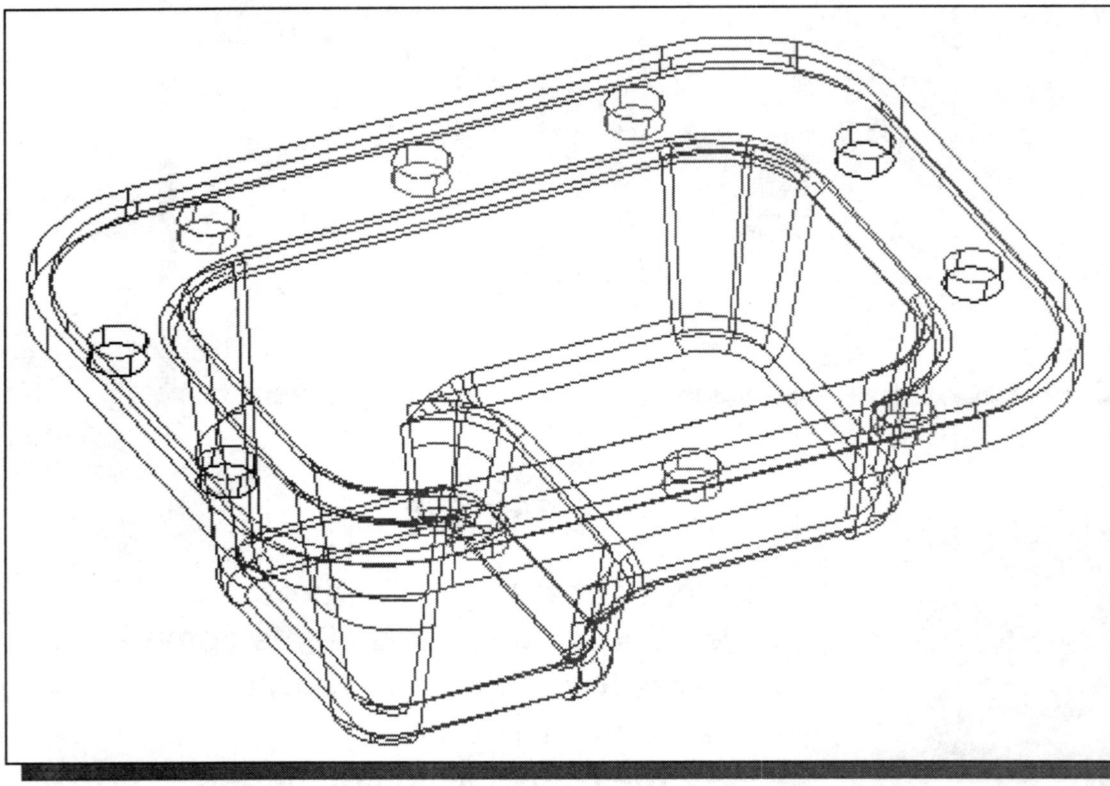

❖ Based on your knowledge of AutoCAD so far, how many features would you use to create the design? Which feature would you choose as the starting point in creating the model? What are the more difficult features involved in the design? What is your choice in arranging the order of the features? Take a few minutes to consider these questions and do preliminary planning by sketching on a piece of paper. You are also encouraged to create the design on your own prior to following through the tutorial.

Modeling Strategy

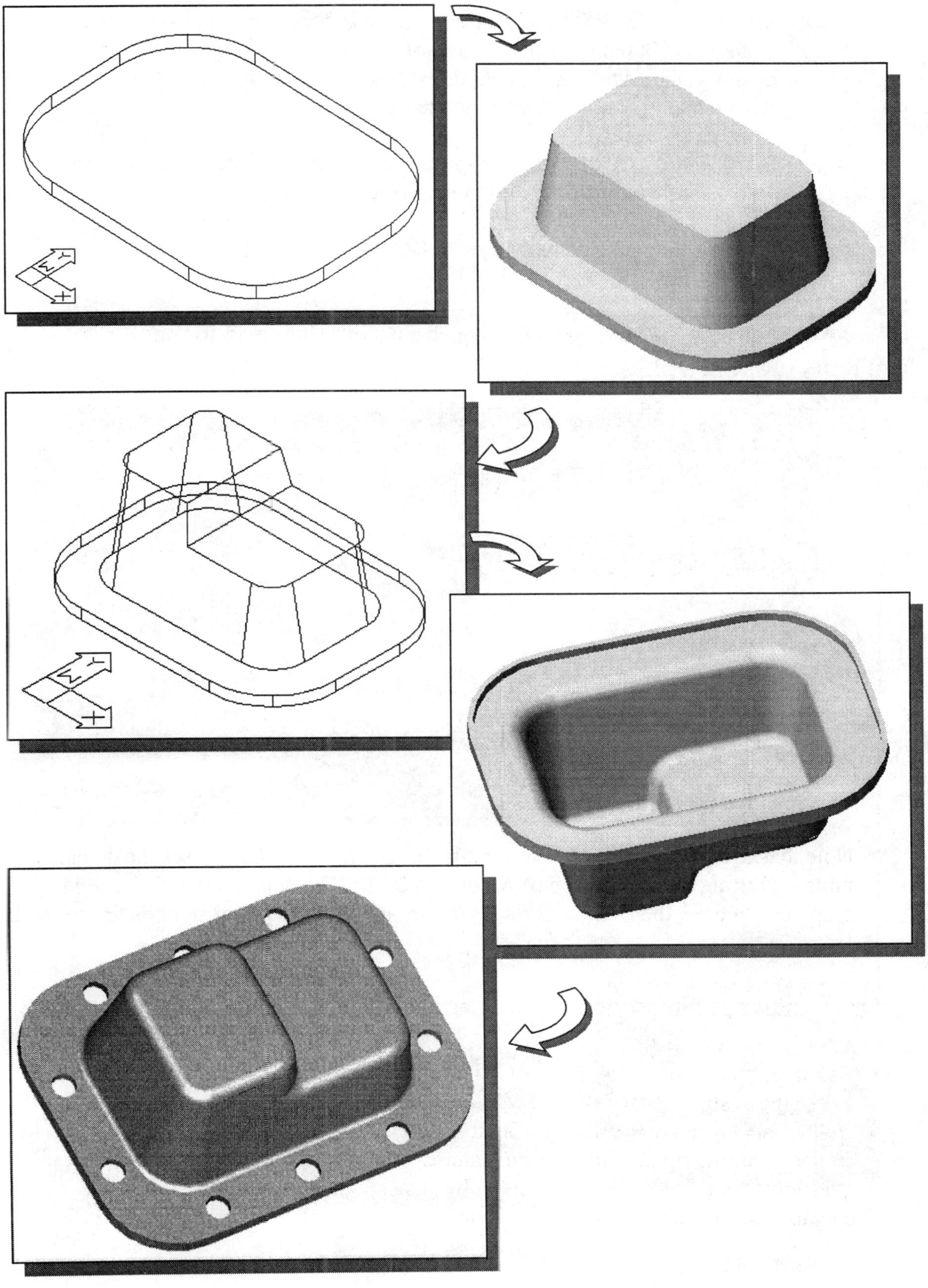

Starting Up AutoCAD® 2000i

1. Select the AutoCAD® 2000i option on the *Program* menu or select the AutoCAD® 2000i icon on the *Desktop*. Once the program is loaded into the memory, the AutoCAD® 2000i drawing screen and the *AutoCAD Today* startup dialog box will appear on the screen.

2. In the *AutoCAD Today* startup dialog box, select the **Create Drawings** tab with a single click of the left-mouse-button.

3. Confirm the startup option is set to **Start from Scratch**, as shown in the figure below.

4. In the *Default Settings* section, pick **English (feet and Inches)** as the drawing units.

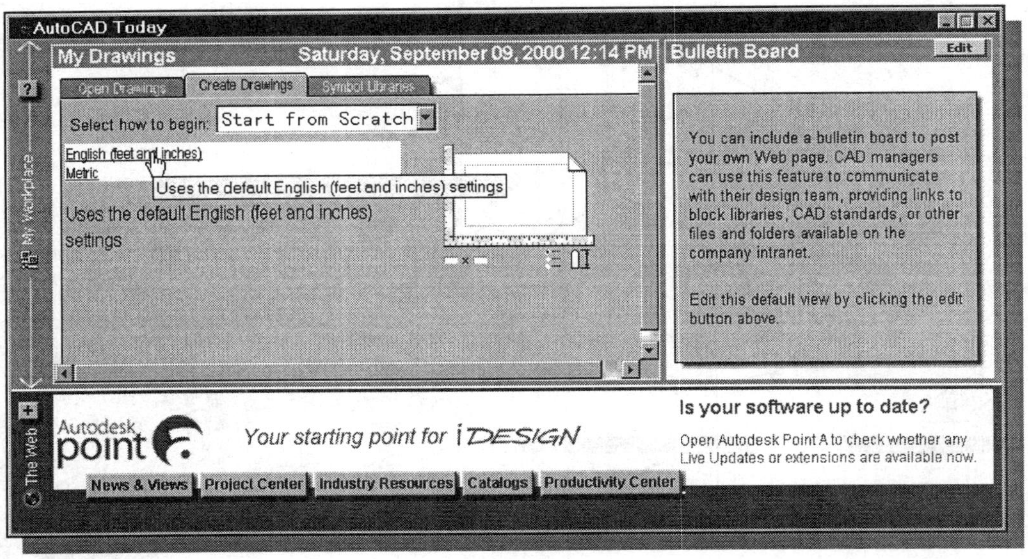

❖ Note that two graphics window are available. The *Drawing1.dwg* uses the default units set during the installation of AutoCAD 2000i. The units used in the second graphics window, the *Drawing2.dwg* window, are set to the English units, inches and feet.

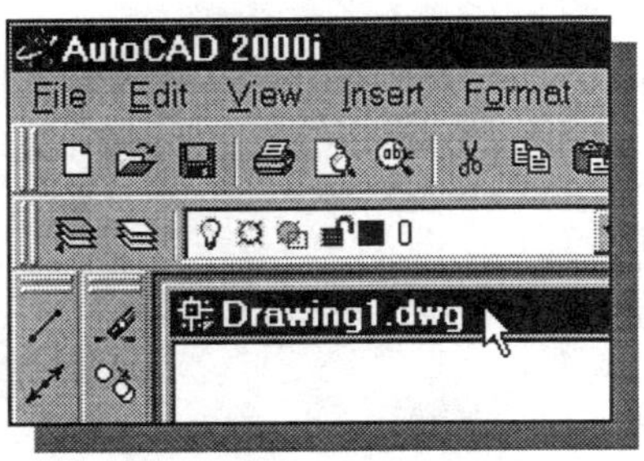

5. Switch to the *Drawing1* window by left-clicking once in the title area of the window.

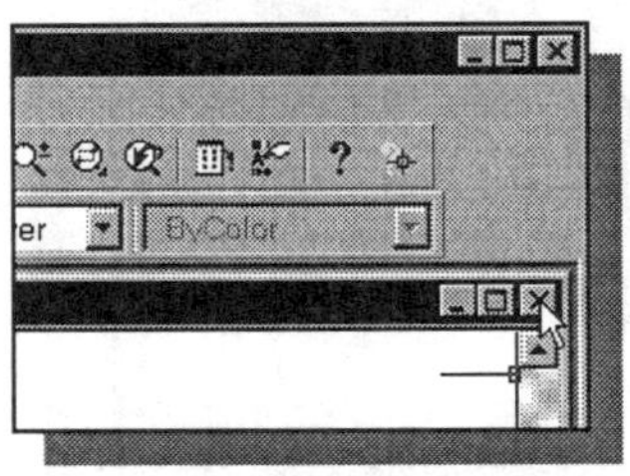

6. Close the window by clicking the ***Close*** icon located at the upper-right-corner of the *Drawing1* window.

Layers setup

1. Pick ***Layers*** in the *Object Properties* toolbar.

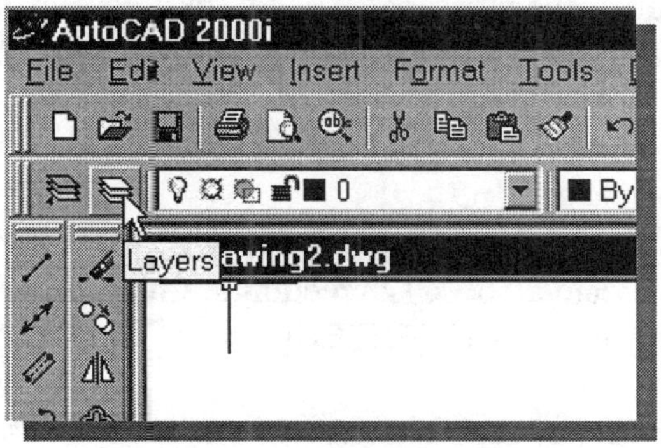

2. Click on the ***New*** icon to create new layers.

3. Create **two new layers** with the following settings:

Layer	***Color***	***LineType***	***LineWeight***
Center_lines	**Red**	**Continuous**	**Default**
Dimensions	**Megenta**	**Continuous**	**Default**
Object_lines	**Cyan**	**Continuous**	**0.30mm**

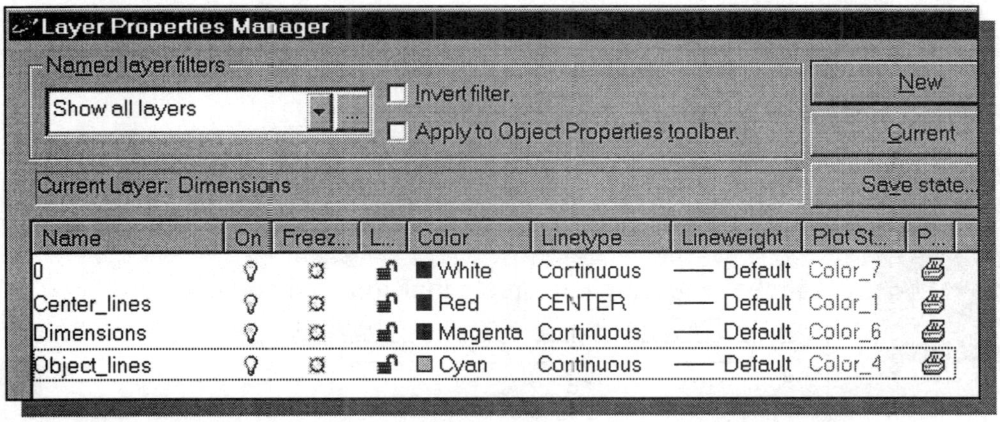

4. Highlight the layer ***Object_lines*** in the list of layers.

5. Click on the ***Current*** icon to set layer ***Object_lines*** as the *Current layer*.

6. Click on the **OK** button to accept the settings and exit the *Layer Properties Manager* dialog box.

7. In the status bar area, reset the options and turn ***ON*** the *POLAR, OSNAP, OTRACK, LWT* and *MODEL* options.

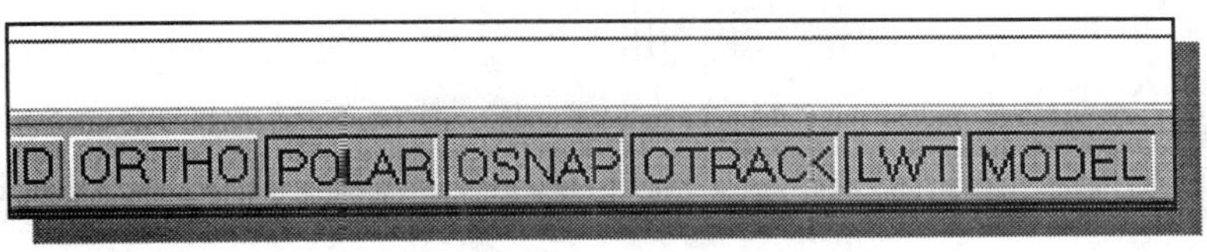

The First Extruded Feature

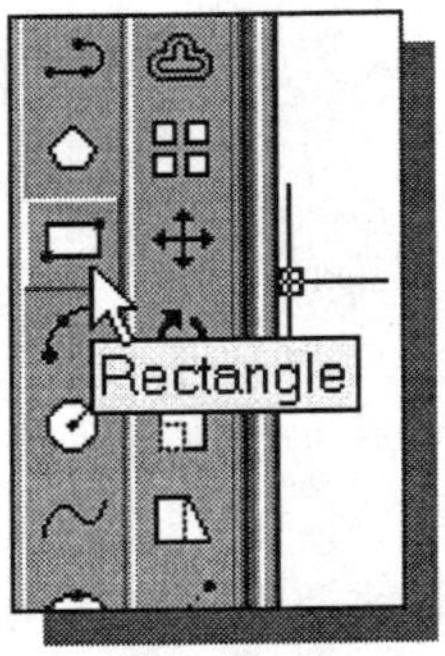

1. Select the ***Rectangle*** icon in the *Draw* toolbar. In the command prompt area, the message *"Specify first corner point or [Chamfer/Elevation/Fillet/Thickness/Width]:"* is displayed.

2. Place the first corner-point of the rectangle near the lower-left corner of the screen.

3. We will create a 16" x 12" rectangle for the main body of the sketch. Enter **@16,12 [ENTER]**.

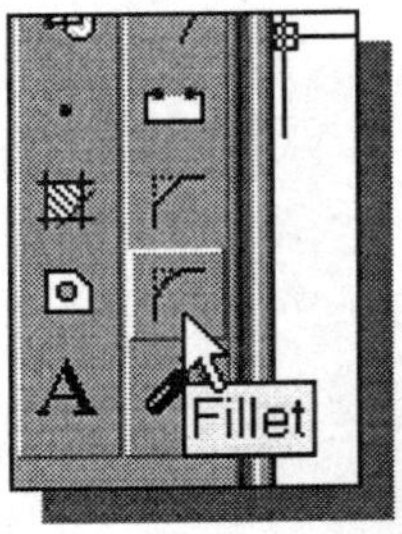

4. Select the ***Fillet*** command icon in the *Modify* toolbar. In the command prompt area, the message *"Select first object or [Polyline/Radius/Trim]:"* is displayed.

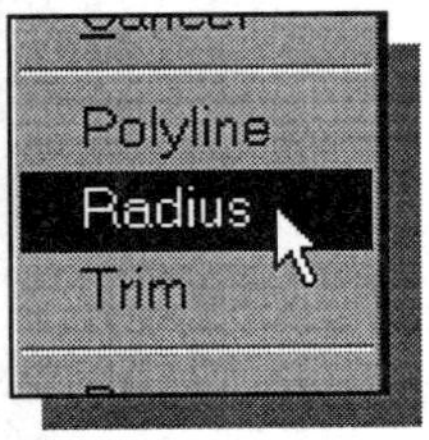

5. Inside the graphics window, **right-mouse-click** to activate the option menu and select the **Radius** option with the left-mouse-button to specify the radius of the fillet.

6. In the command prompt area, the message *"Specify fillet radius:"* is displayed.
   Specify fillet radius: **4.0 [ENTER]**

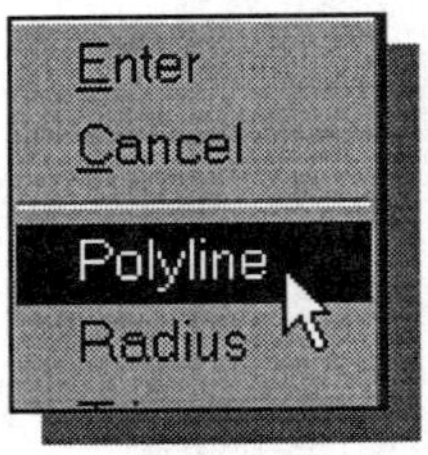

7. Inside the graphics window, **right-mouse-click** to activate the option menu and select the **Polyline** option.

8. Pick the rectangle to create four rounded corners.

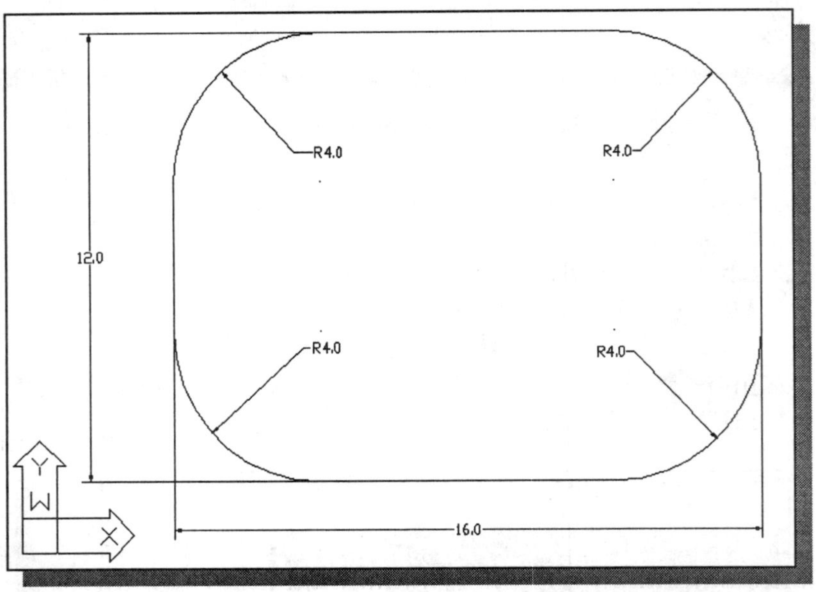

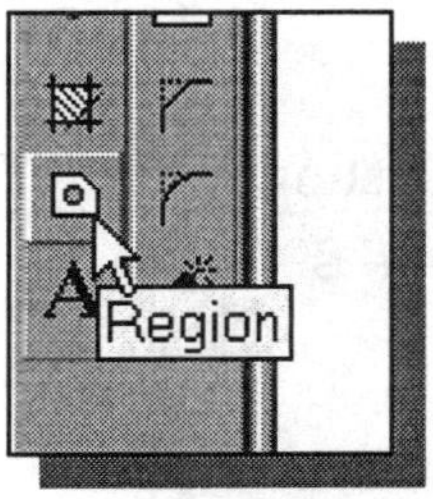

9. Select the ***Region*** command icon in the *Draw* toolbar.

10. In the command prompt area, the message *"Select objects:"* is displayed. Select the polyline by clicking on any segments of the 2D sketch.

11. Inside the graphics window, **right-mouse-click** to accept the selection and create a region.

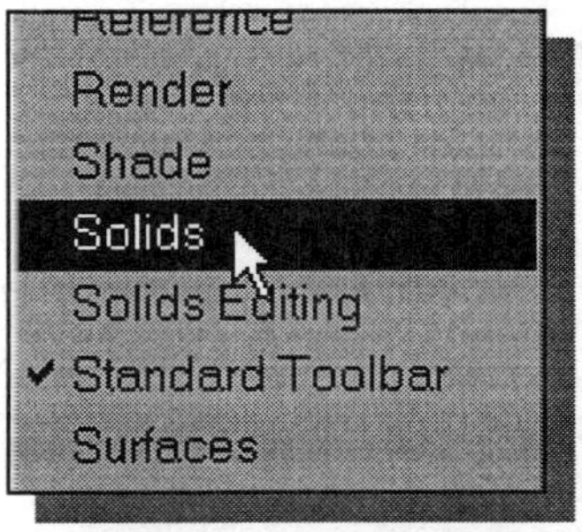

12. Move the cursor to the *Standard* toolbar area and **right-mouse-click** once on any icon in the toolbar area to display a list of toolbar menu groups.

13. Select **Solids**, with the left-mouse-button, to display the *Solids* toolbar on the screen.

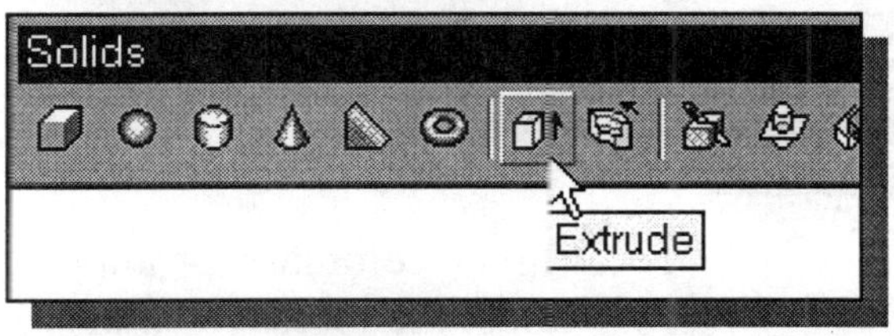

14. Select ***Extrude*** in the *Solids* toolbar as shown.

15. In the command prompt area, the message *"Select objects:"* is displayed. Select the region by clicking on any of the displayed segments.

16. Inside the graphics window, **right-mouse-click** to accept the selection and proceed with the extrude command.

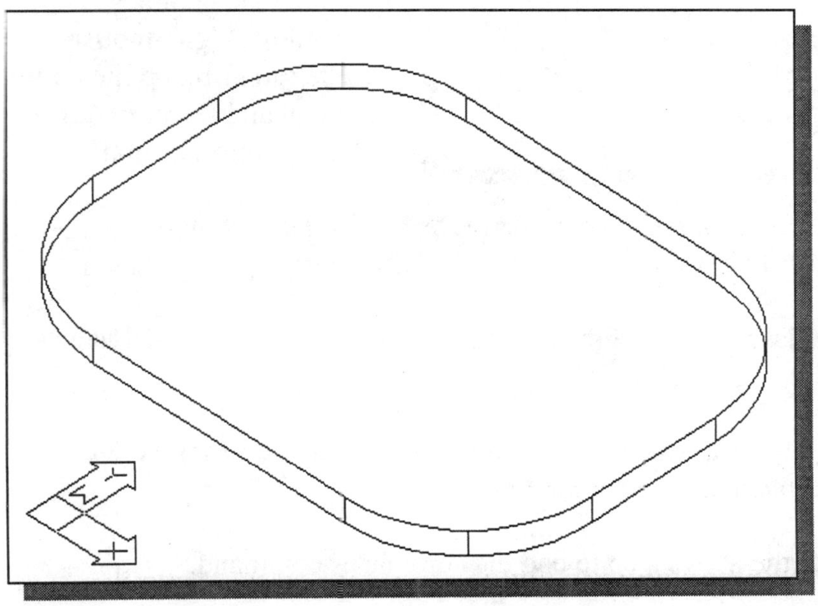

17. In the command prompt area, the message *"Specify height of extrusion or [path]:"* is displayed. Enter: **0.625 [ENTER]**

18. In the command prompt area, the message *"Specify angle of taper for extrusion <0>:"* is displayed. Enter: **0.0 [[ENTER]**

Create an Offset geometry from an Extracted surface

- In AutoCAD, several options are available to create geometry from existing solid features. We will use the *COPY FACES* command to assist constructing geometry from the existing surfaces.

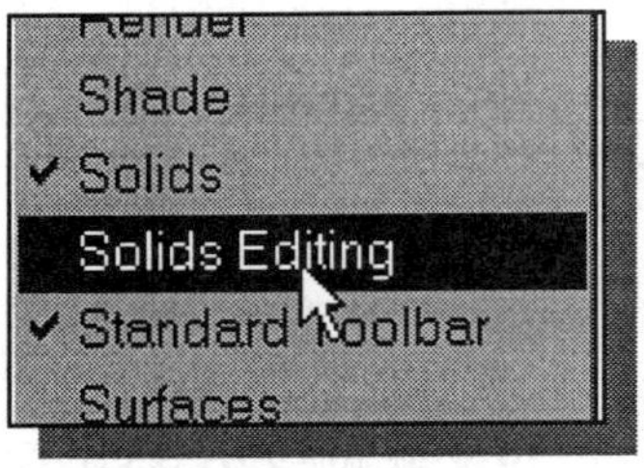

1. Move the cursor to the *Standard* toolbar area and **right-click** on any icon of the *Standard* toolbar to display a list of toolbar menu groups.

2. Select ***Solids Editing***, with the left-mouse-button, to display the *Solids Editing* toolbar on the screen.

3. Click on the ***Copy Faces*** icon to activate the command.

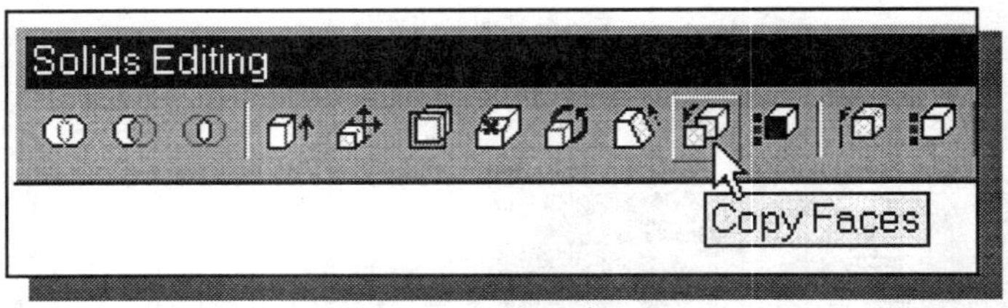

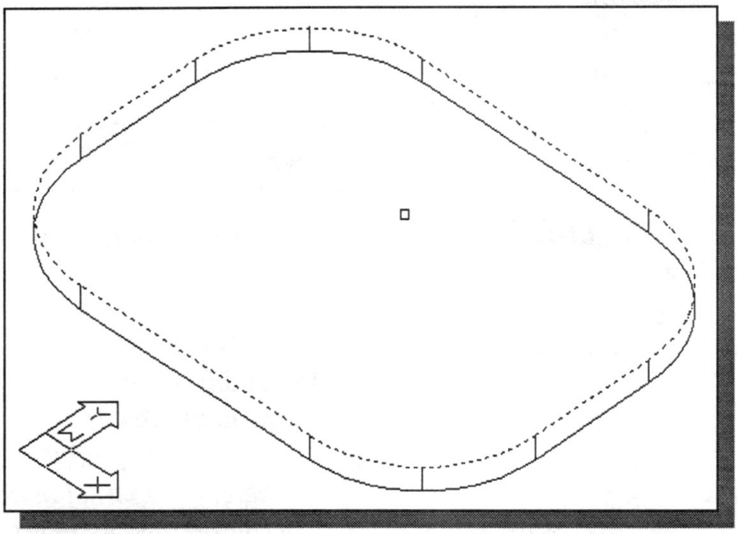

4. In the command prompt area, the message *"Select faces or [Undo/ Remove/ All]:"* is displayed. Pick the upper surface by clicking on the inside of the surface as shown.

5. Inside the graphics window, **right-mouse-click** to bring up the option menu and select **Enter** to accept the selection.

6. In the command prompt area, the message *"Specify a base point or displacement:"* is displayed. Enter: **20,0 [ENTER]**

7. Inside the graphics window, **right-mouse-click** to accept the entered values.

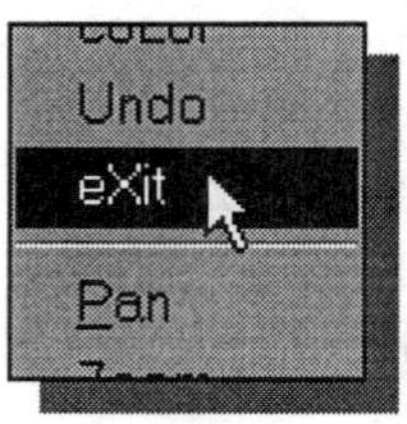

8. Inside the graphics window, **right-mouse-click** to bring up the option menu and select **Exit.**

9. Repeat the above step to end the copy faces command.

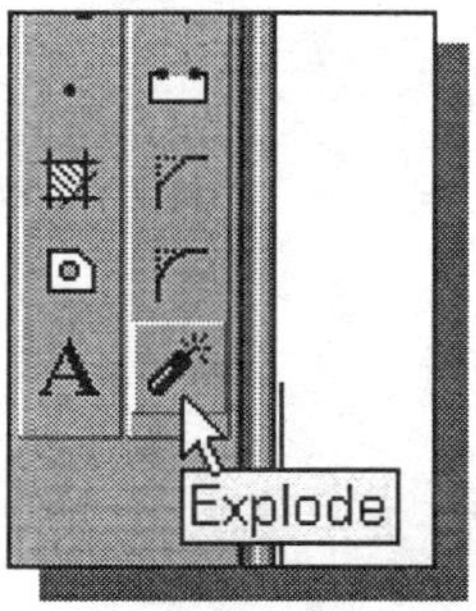

10. Select the ***Explode*** command icon in the *Modify* toolbar. In the command prompt area, the message *"Select objects:"* is displayed.

11. Pick the *surface* we just created.

12. Inside the graphics window, **right-mouse-click** to end the *EXPLODE* command.

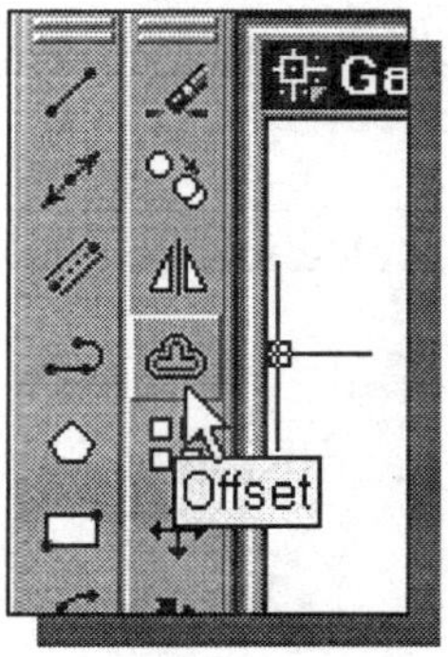

13. Select the ***Offset*** command icon in the *Modify* toolbar. In the command prompt area, the message *"Specify offset distance or [Through]:"* is displayed.
Specify offset distance or [Through]: **2.0 [ENTER]**

14. On your own, create a set of entities on the inside of the exploded surface as shown.

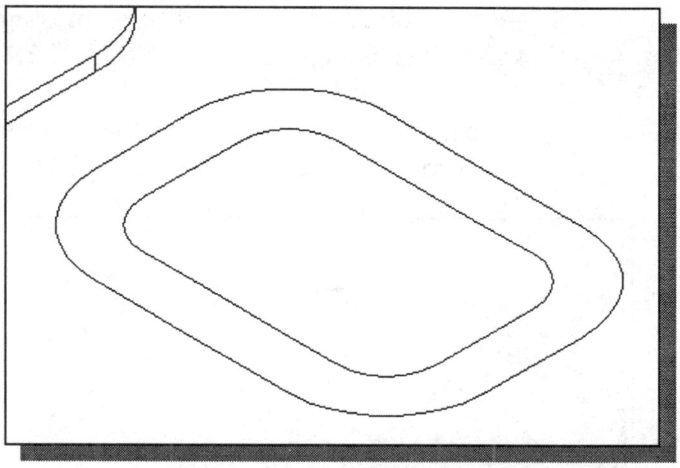

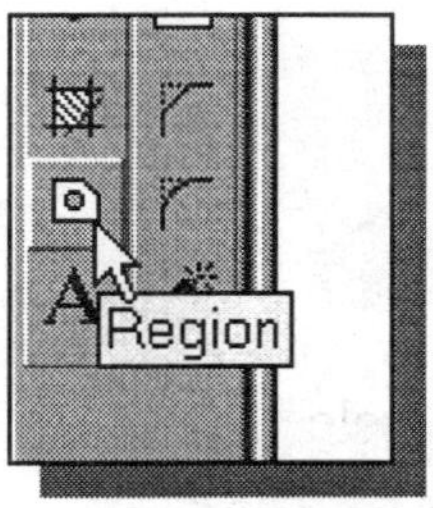

15. Select the ***Region*** command icon in the *Draw* toolbar.

16. In the command prompt area, the message *"Select objects:"* is displayed. Select the entities we just created with the *OFFSET* command.

17. Inside the graphics window, **right-mouse-click** to accept the selection and create a region.

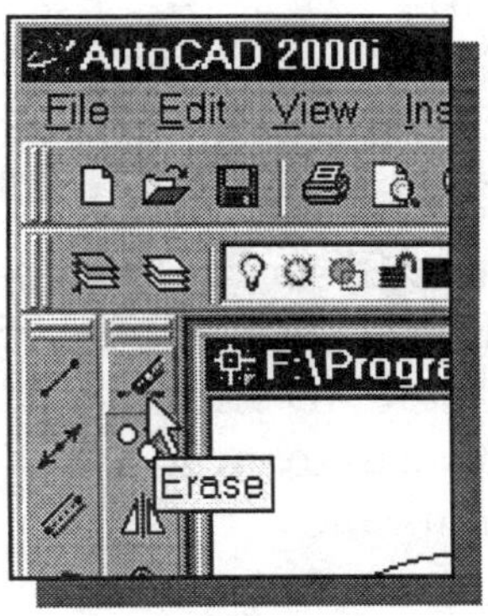

18. Select the ***Erase*** command icon in the *Modify* toolbar.

19. In the command prompt area, the message *"Select objects:"* is displayed. Select the entities that were created with the *COPY FACES* command.

20. Inside the graphics window, **right-mouse-click** to accept the selection and end the *ERASE* command.

Extrude with Draft Angle

1. Select ***Extrude*** in the *Solids* toolbar as shown.

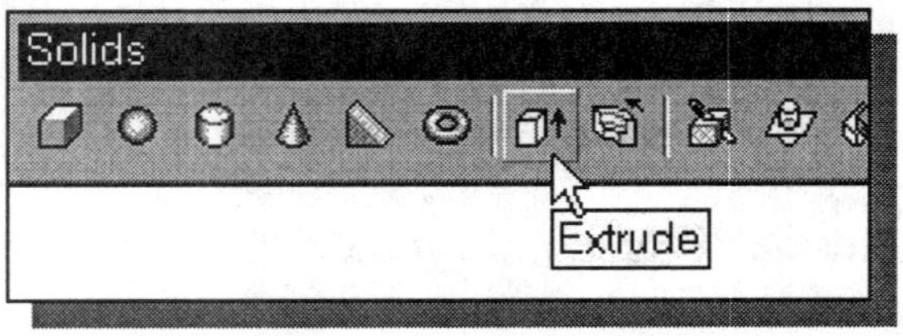

2. In the command prompt area, the message *"Select objects:"* is displayed. Select the 2D region by clicking on any of the displayed segments.

3. Inside the graphics window, **right-mouse-click** to accept the selection and proceed with the *EXTRUDE* command.

4. In the command prompt area, the message "Specify height of extrusion or [path]:" is displayed. Enter: **4.0 [ENTER]**

5. In the command prompt area, the message "Specify angle of taper for extrusion <0>:" is displayed. Enter: **10.0 [ENTER]**

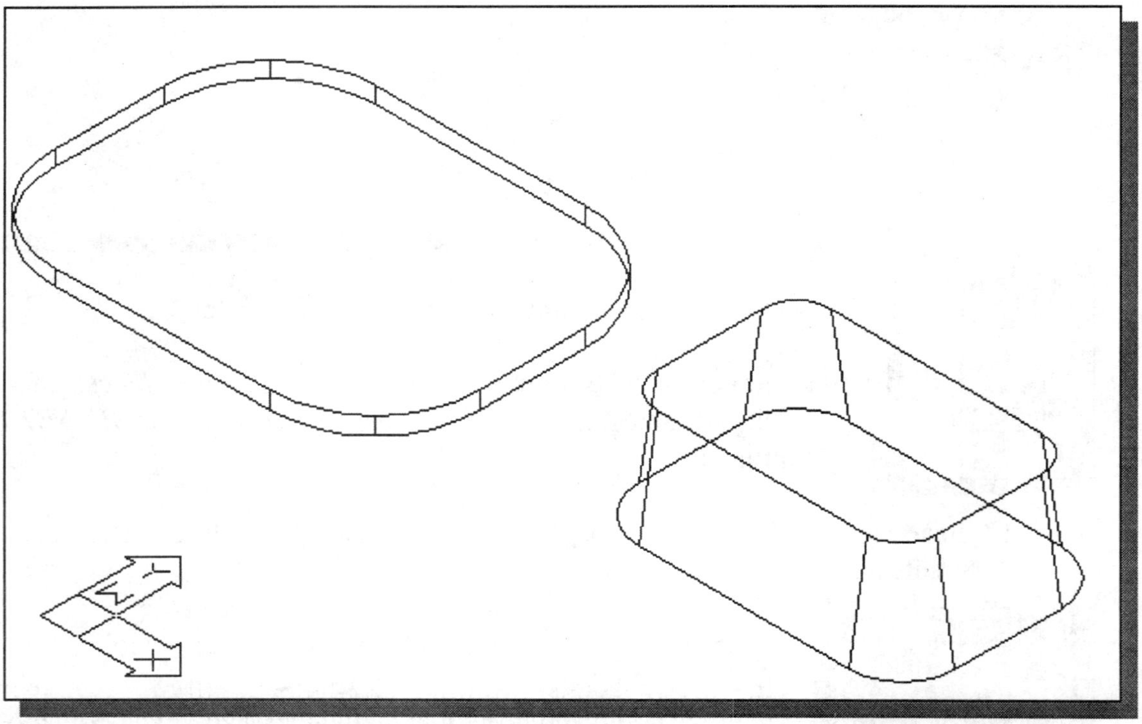

- Note that the second part is created by extruding an extracted surface from the first solid model. The ability to extract and re-use existing surface-geometry is an important aspect of solid modeling. Also note that AutoCAD allows us to create multiple parts in a single drawing file, which allows us to create assembly models under the same deign environment.

Aligning the parts

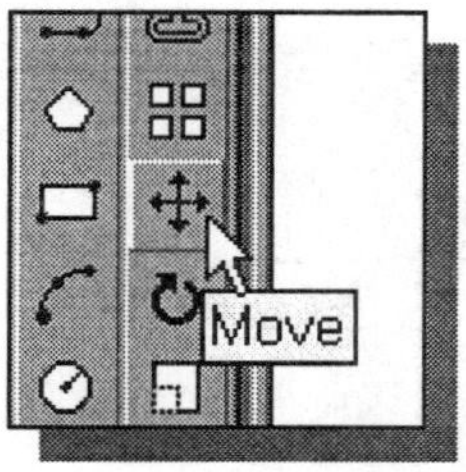

1. Select the ***Move*** icon in the *Draw* toolbar.

2. In the command prompt area, the message *"Select Objects:"* is displayed. Pick the *second part* we just created.

3. Inside the graphics window, **right-mouse-click** to accept the selection.

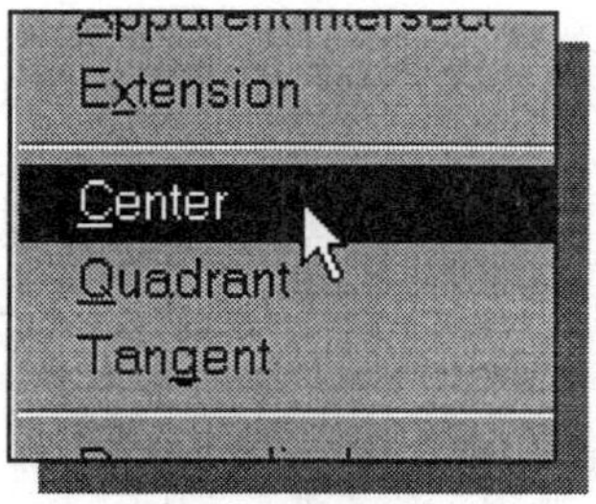

4. Inside the graphics window, hold down the **[SHIFT]** key and **right-mouse-click** once to bring up the *Object Snap* shortcut menu.

5. Select the **Center** option in popup window.

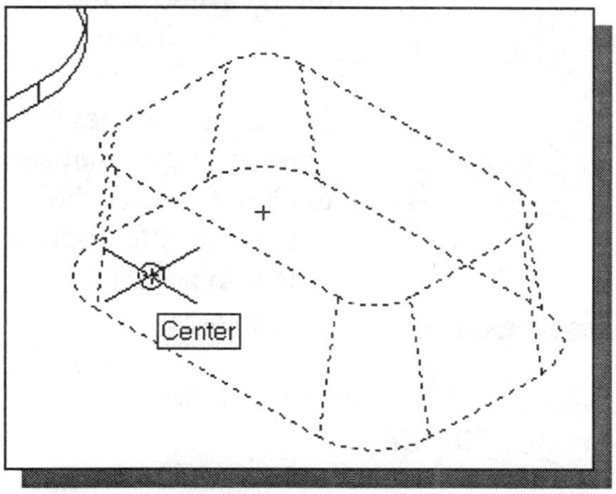

6. Pick the center of the bottom-left arc as shown in the figure.

7. In the command prompt area, the message *"Specify second point of displacement:"* is displayed. Pick the corresponding center point on the top surface of the solid model as shown.

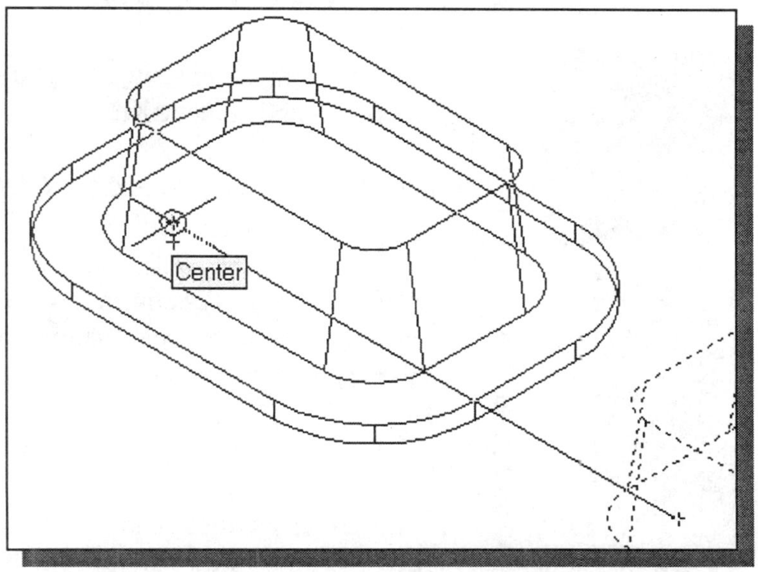

Create another Extracted Surface

1. Click on the ***Copy Faces*** icon to activate the command.

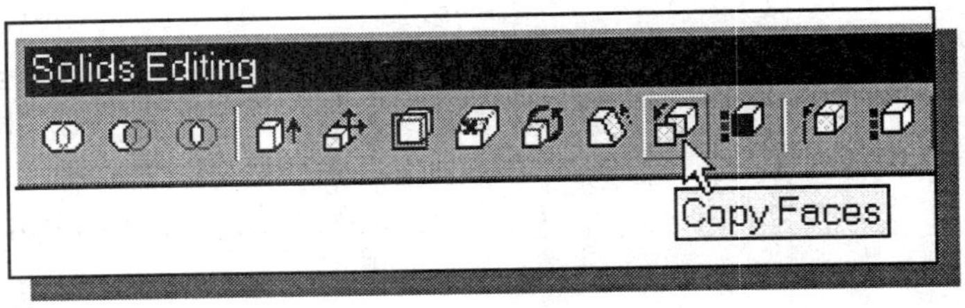

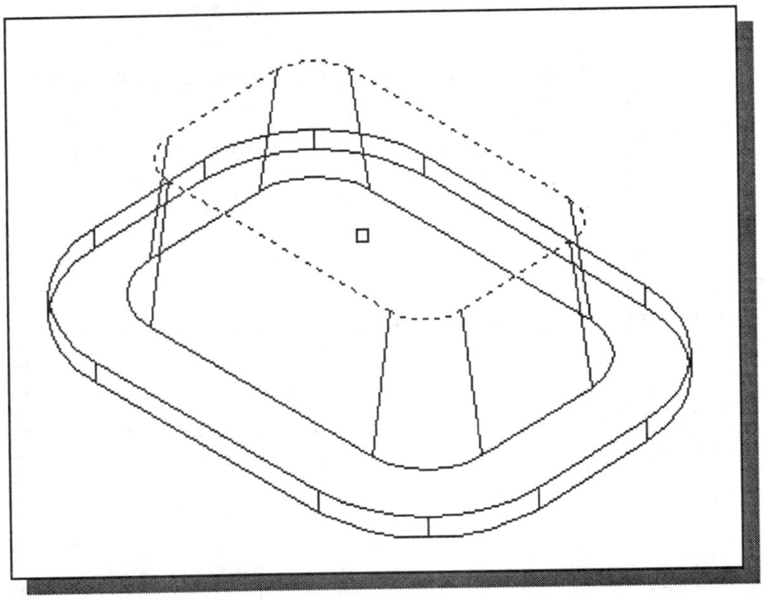

2. In the command prompt area, the message *"Select faces or [Undo/ Remove/ All]:"* is displayed. Pick the top surface of the tapered part by clicking on the inside of the surface as shown.

3. Inside the graphics window, **right-mouse-click** to bring up the option menu and select **Enter** to accept the selection.

4. In the command prompt area, the message *"Specify a base point or displacement:"* is displayed. Enter: **20,0 [ENTER]**

5. Inside the graphics window, **right-mouse-click** to accept the entered values.

6. Inside the graphics window, **right-mouse-click** to bring up the option menu and select **eXit.**

7. Repeat the above step to end the *COPY FACES* command.

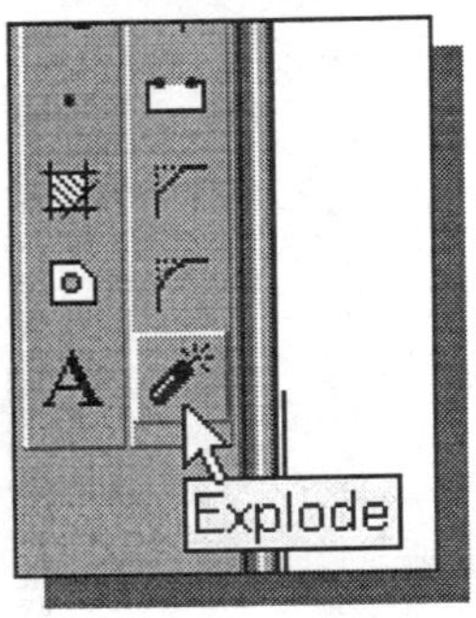

8. Select the ***Explode*** command icon in the *Modify* toolbar. In the command prompt area, the message *"Select objects:"* is displayed.

9. Pick the *surface* we just created.

10. Inside the graphics window, **right-mouse-click** to end the *EXPLODE* command.

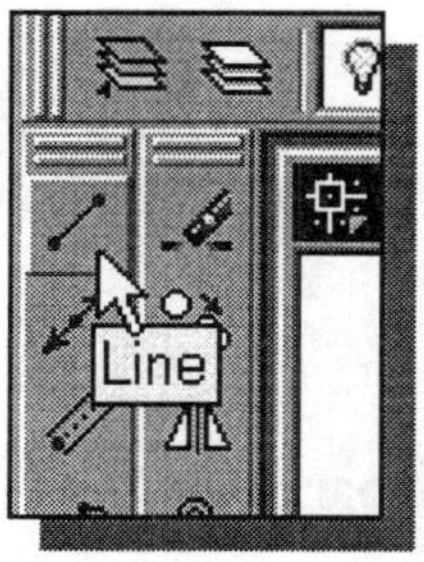

11. Select the ***Line*** command icon in the *Draw* toolbar.

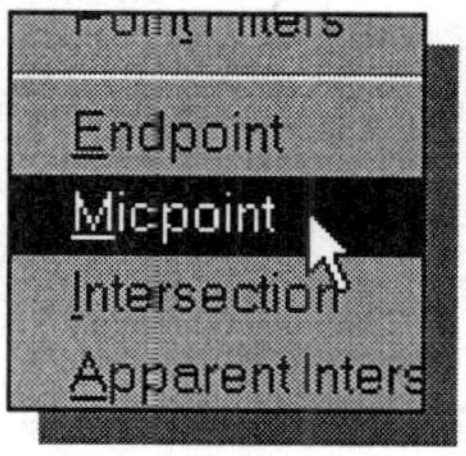

12. Inside the graphics window, hold down the **[SHIFT]** key and **right-mouse-click** once to bring up the *Object Snap* shortcut menu.

13. Select the **Midpoint** option in popup window.

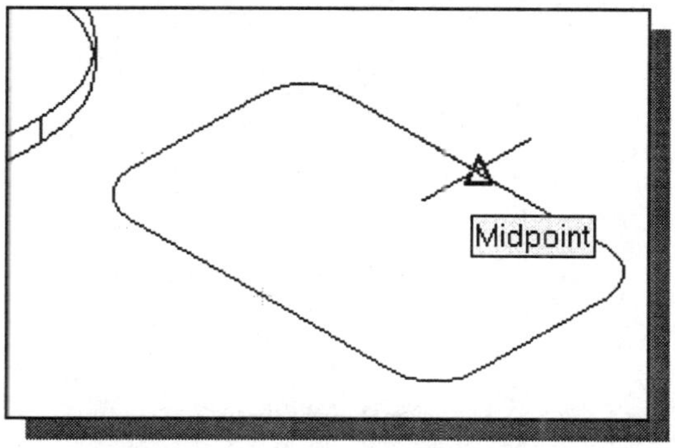

14. In the command prompt area, the message *"_line Specify first point:"* is displayed. Pick the line segment on the extracted surface as shown.

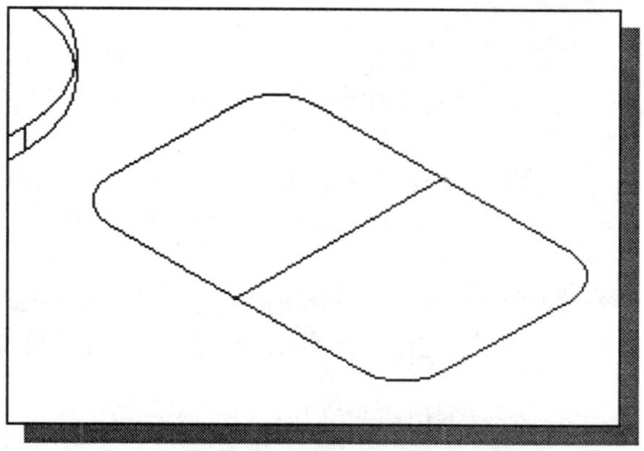

15. On your own, repeat the ***midpoint snap*** option and create a line as shown.

16. Inside the graphics window, **right-mouse-click** once and select **Enter** to end the *LINE* command.

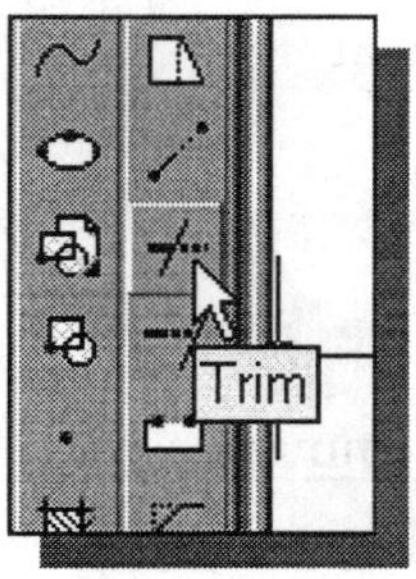

17. Select the ***Trim*** command icon in the *Modify* toolbar.

18. In the command prompt area, the message *"Select boundary edges... Select objects:"* is displayed. Pick the line across the center of the 2D sketch.

19. Inside the graphics window, **right-mouse-click** to proceed with the *TRIM* command.

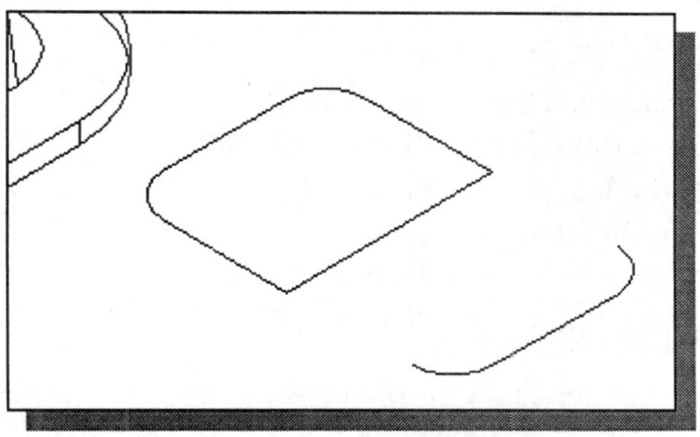

20. The message *"Select object to trim or shift-select object to extend or [Project/ Edge/ Undo]:"* is displayed in the command prompt area. Trim the two lines of the exploded geometry as shown.

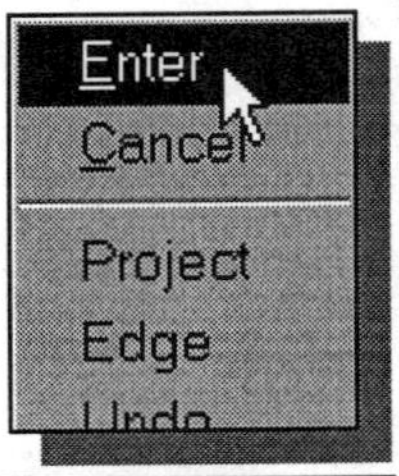

21. Inside the graphics window, **right-mouse-click** to activate the option menu and select **Enter** with the left-mouse-button to end the *TRIM* command.

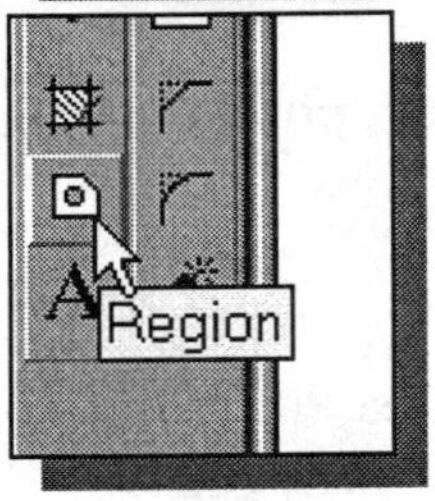

22. Select the ***Region*** command icon in the *Draw* toolbar.

23. In the command prompt area, the message *"Select objects:"* is displayed. Select the entities we just modified.

24. Inside the graphics window, **right-mouse-click** to accept the selection and create a region.

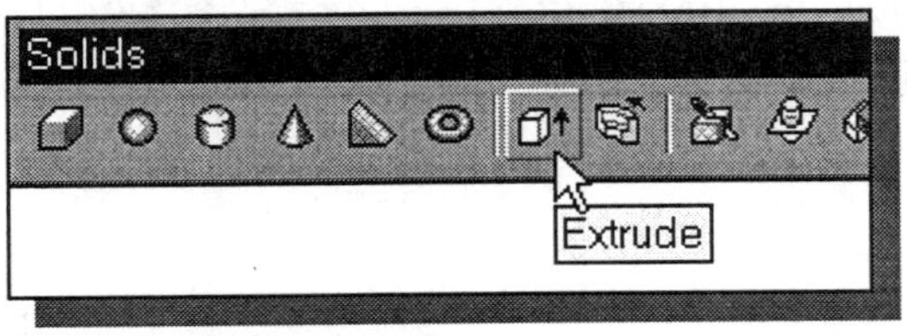

25. Select ***Extrude*** in the *Solids* toolbar as shown.

26. In the command prompt area, the message *"Select objects:"* is displayed. Select the 2D region by clicking on any of the displayed segments.

27. Inside the graphics window, **right-mouse-click** to accept the selection and proceed with the extrude command.

28. In the command prompt area, the message "Specify height of extrusion or [path]:" is displayed. Enter: **2.0 [ENTER]**

29. In the command prompt area, the message "Specify angle of taper for extrusion <0>:" is displayed. Enter: **10.0 [ENTER]**

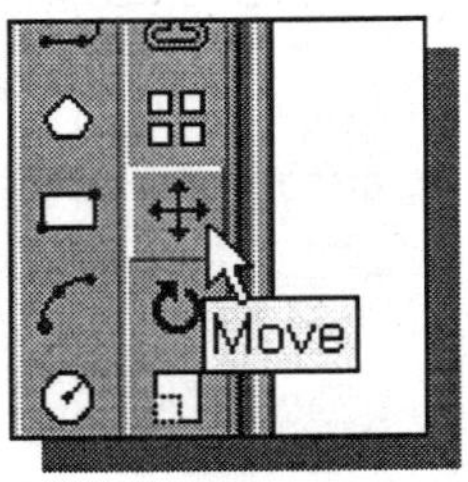

30. Select the ***Move*** icon in the *Draw* toolbar.

31. On your own, reposition the part on top of the other parts as shown.

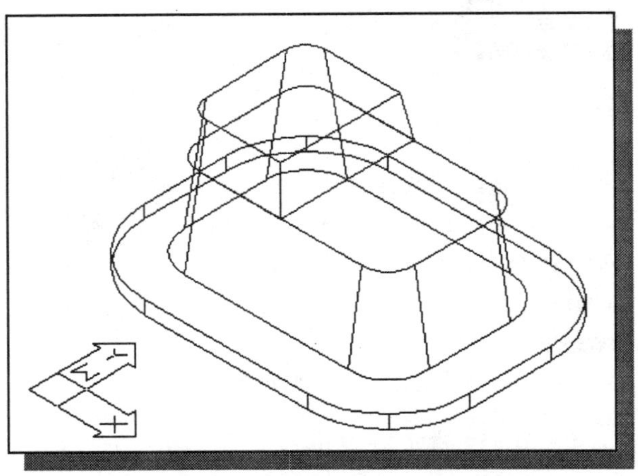

❖ At this point, the <u>three</u> separate parts are positioned and aligned on top of each others. Note that the last part was created without applying or knowing the exact diemensions of the extracted geometry.

Combining parts – Boolean UNION

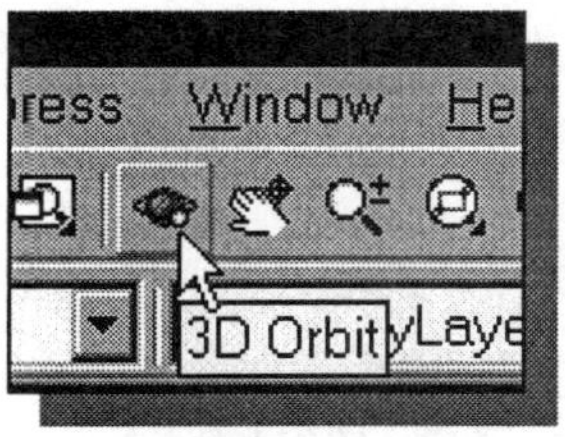

1. Click on the ***3D Orbit*** icon in the *Standard* toolbar.

2. On your own, rotate the created models in 3D space and confirm the three parts are positioned correctly.

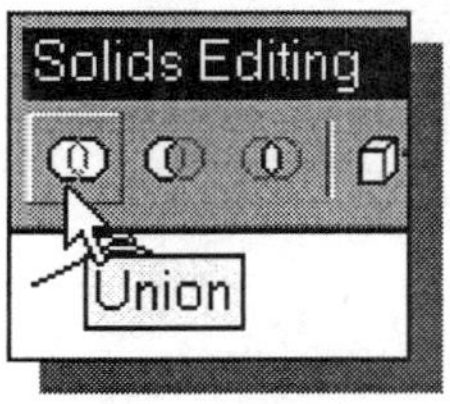

3. In the *Solids Editing* toolbar, click on the ***Union*** icon. In the command prompt area, the message *"Select Objects:"* is displayed.

4. Pick all the solid models by clicking on their edges as shown.

5. Inside the graphics window, **right-mouse-click** to accept the selection and proceed with the *UNION* command.

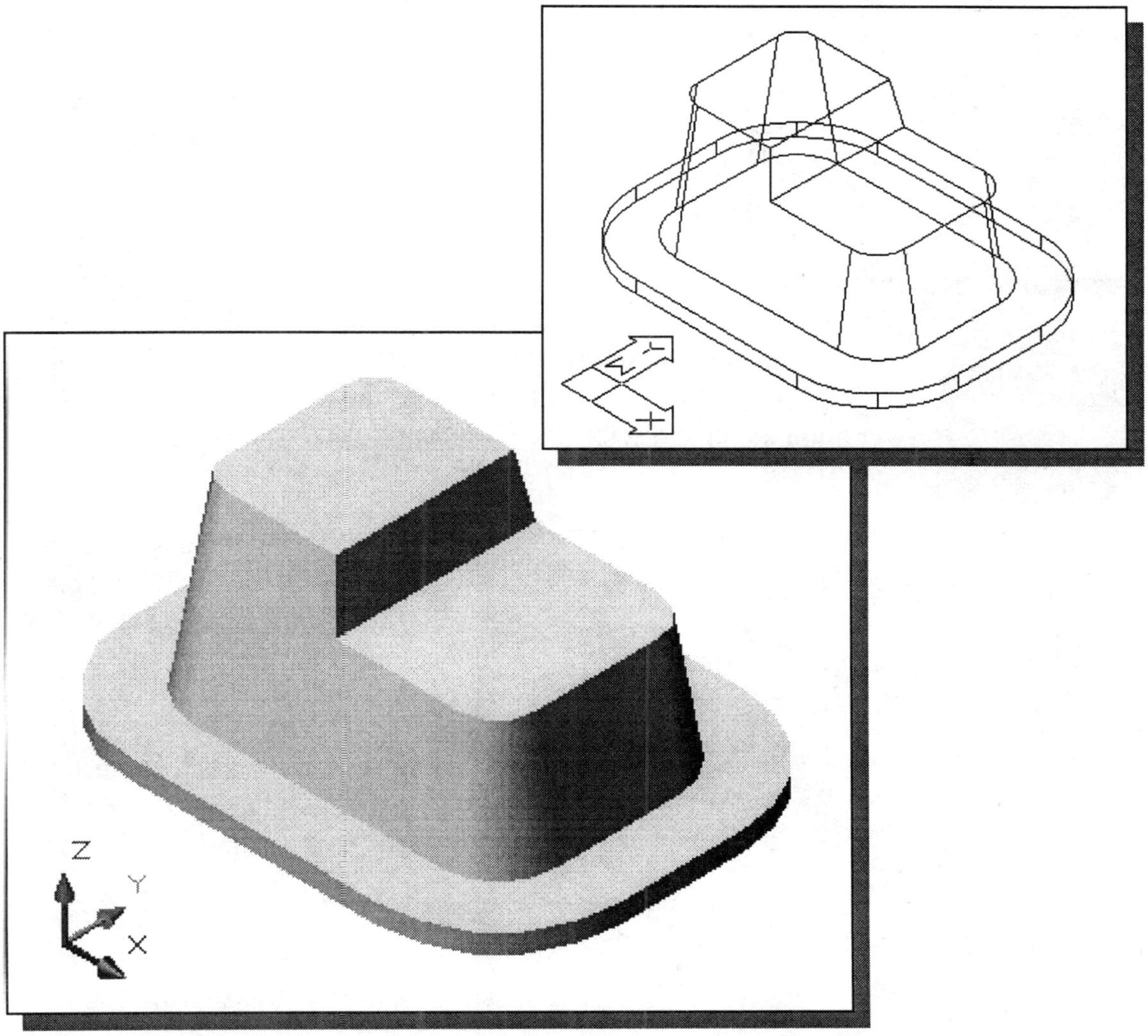

Creating 3D Rounds and Fillets

- In AutoCAD 2000i, the same ***FILLET*** command can be applied to both 2D and 3D designs.

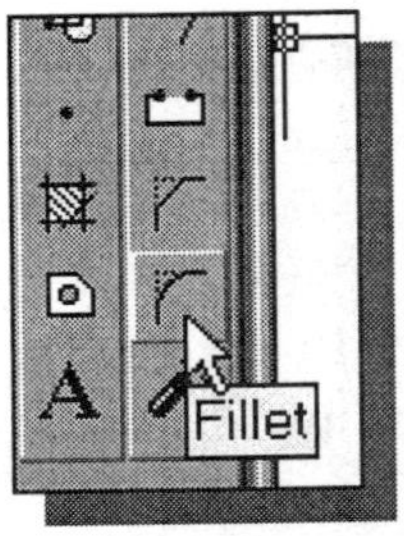

1. Select the ***Fillet*** command icon in the *Modify* toolbar.
2. In the command prompt area, the message *"Select first object or [Polyline/Radius/Trim]:"* is displayed. Inside the graphics window, **right-mouse-click** to activate the option menu and select the **Radius** option with the left-mouse-button to specify the radius of the fillet.
3. In the command prompt area, the message *"Specify fillet radius:"* is displayed.
   Specify fillet radius: **0.75** **[ENTER]**

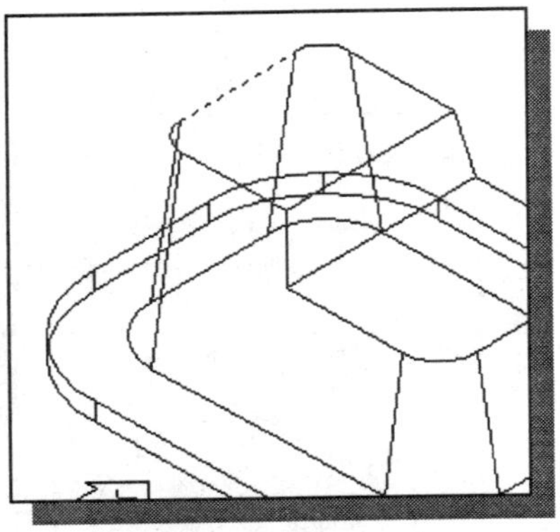

4. Pick the **top back edge** as shown.
5. In the command prompt area, the message *"Enter fillet radius <0.75>:"* is displayed. Right-mouse-click to accept the displayed value.

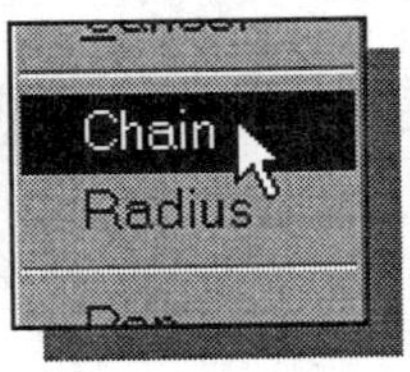

6. In the command prompt area, the message *"Select an edge or [Chain/Radius]:"* is displayed. Right-mouse-click to activate the option menu and select the **Chain** option.

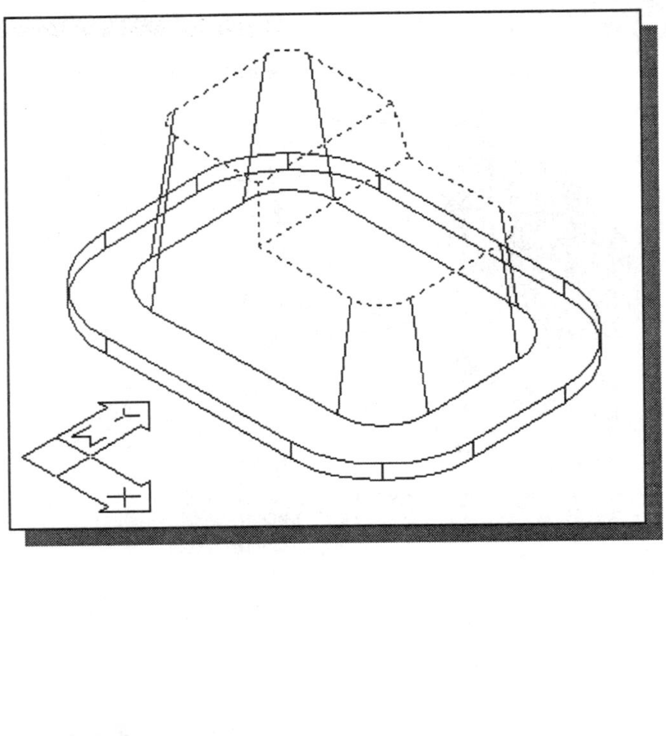

7. In the command prompt area, the message *"Select an edge or [Chain/Radius]:"* is displayed. Select the adjacent curve on the top surface.
8. On your own, select the adjacent edges on the top surfaces as shown in the figure.
9. Press the **ENTER** key or the *right-mouse-button* and select **Enter** to accept the selection.

- The *FILLET* command can be used to create complex 3D curves and surfaces as shown in this example.

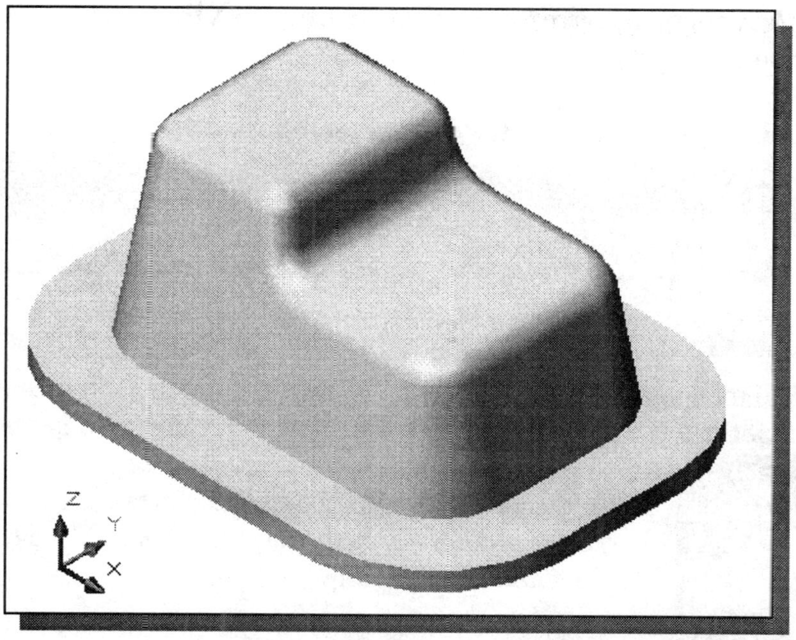

- On your own, create a *chained fillet* of **0.5 radius** at the inside edges as shown.

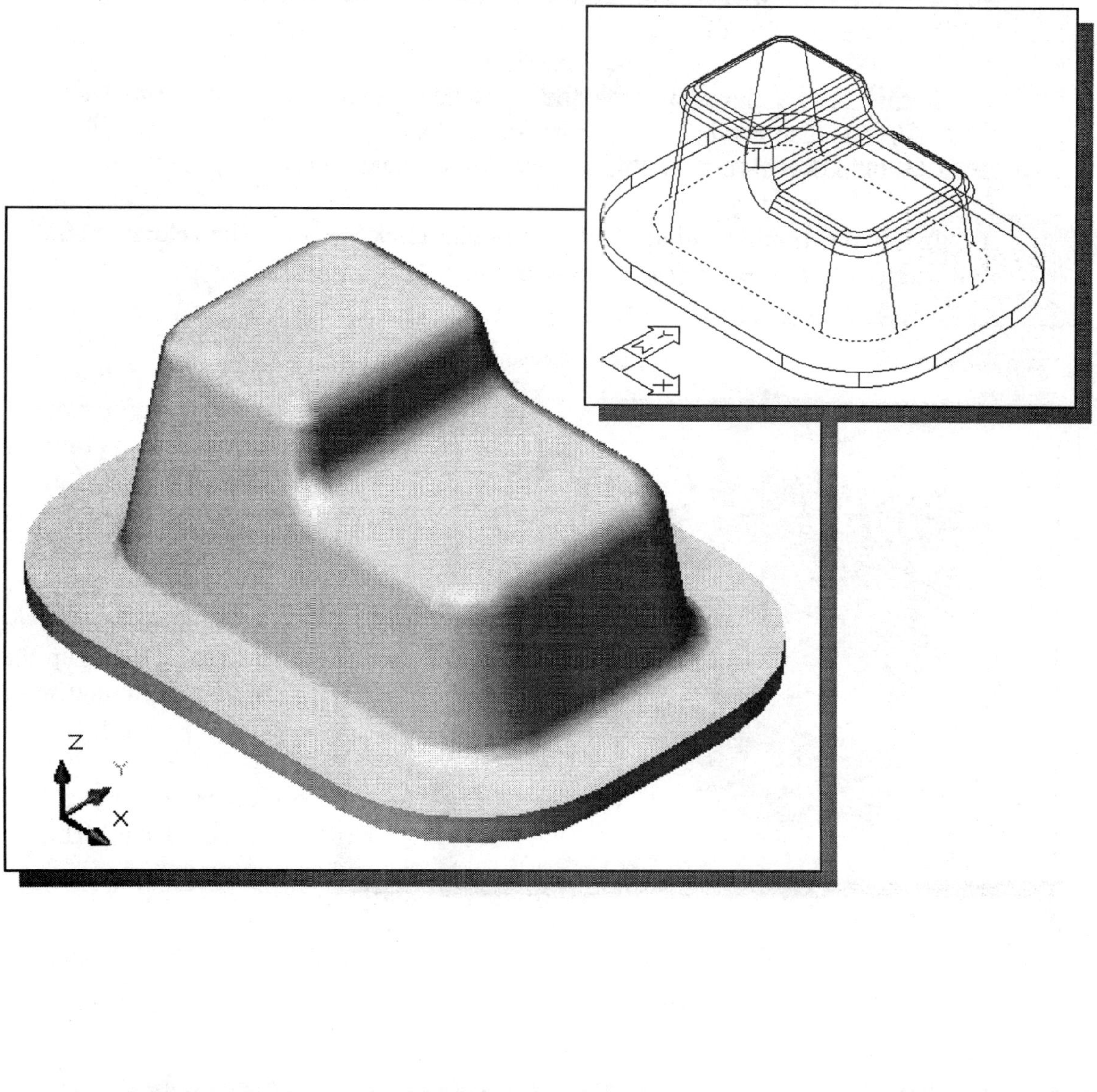

Creating a Shell Feature

- The *SHELL* command can be used to create new faces by offsetting existing ones inside or outside of their original positions.

1. Choose ***Shell*** in the *Solids Editing* toolbar.

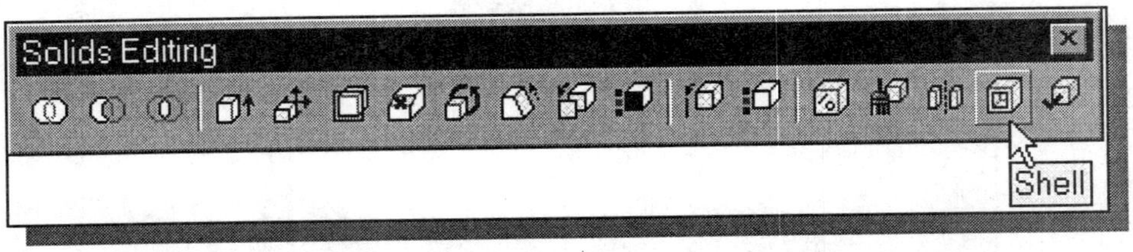

2. The message "*Select a 3D solid:*" is displayed in the command prompt area. Pick the top surface of the 3D solid. Note the entire solid is selected.

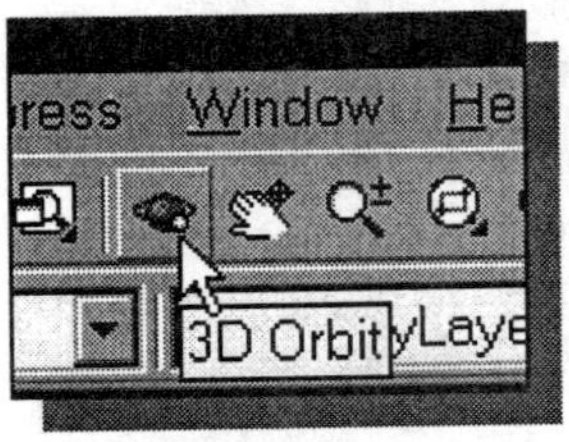

3. In the command prompt area, the message *"Remove faces or [Unco/Add/All]:"* is displayed. Click on the ***3D Orbit*** icon in the *Standard* toolbar.

4. On your own, dynamically rotate the 3D model so that we are viewing the bottom flat side of the *OIL SINK* model.

5. In the command prompt area, the message *"Remove faces or [Undo /Add /All]:"* is displayed. Select the bottom flat side of the *OIL SINK* model. (AutoCAD will remove this surface before creating the shell feature.)

6. Inside the graphics window, **right-mouse-click** to accept the selection and proceed with the *SHELL* command.

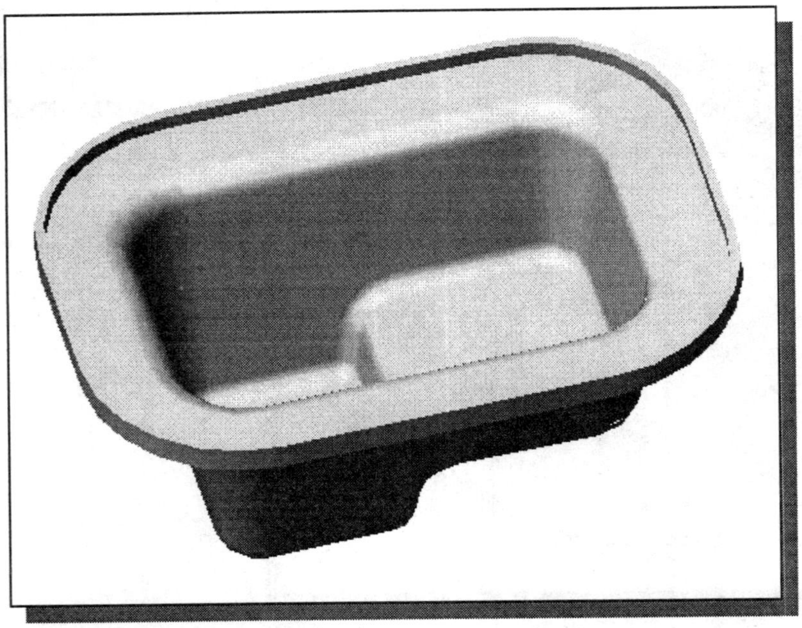

7. In the command prompt area, the message *"Enter the shell offset distance:"* is displayed. Set the thickness to **0.25.**

8. Press the **ENTER** key or the **middle-mouse-button** to bring up the option menu and select **Exit** to continue.

9. Repeat the above step and **Exit** the *SHELL* command.

Creating a Rectangular Array Cut feature

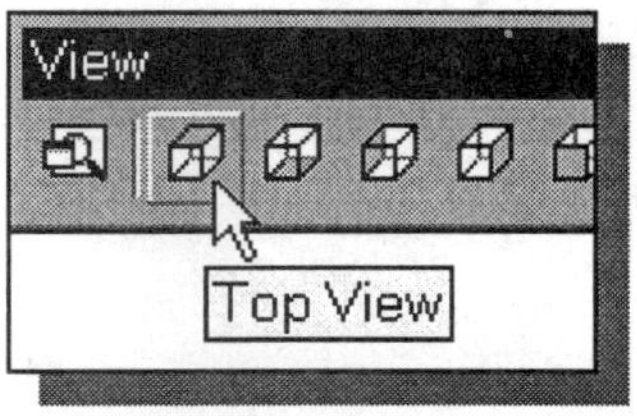

1. In the *View* toolbar, select the ***Top View*** option to reset the display to the XY plane of the coordinate system.

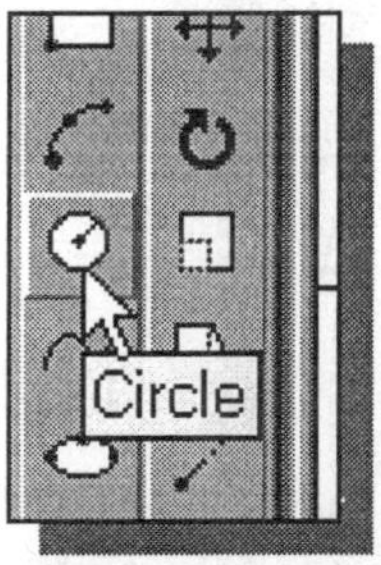

2. Select the ***Circle*** icon in the *Draw* toolbar.

3. On your own, create a circle (diameter 0.75) that is toward the right side of the solid model. Note that **circles** are valid *regions*.

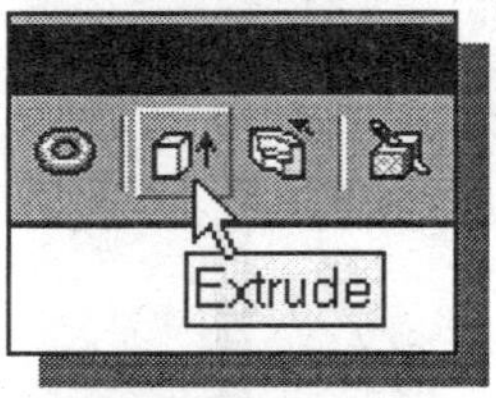

4. On your own, extrude the region into a **1**" high cylinder.

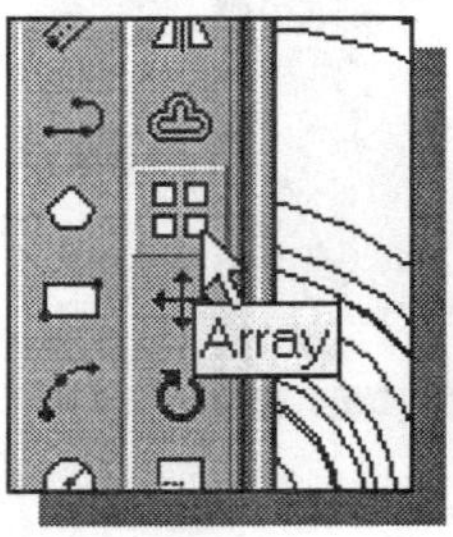

5. Select ***Array*** in the *Modify* toolbar as shown.

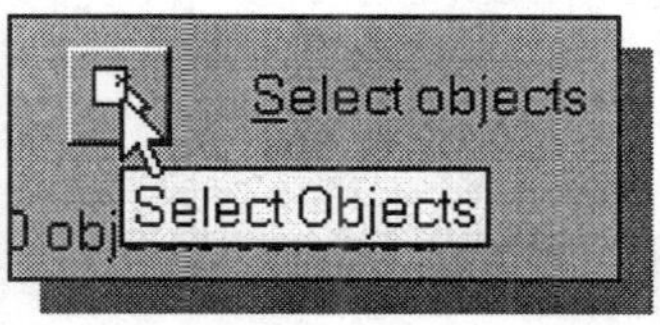

6. Click on the **Select Objects** button.

7. Select the cylinder.

8. Inside the graphics window, **right-mouse-click** to accept the selection and return to the *ARRAY* command.

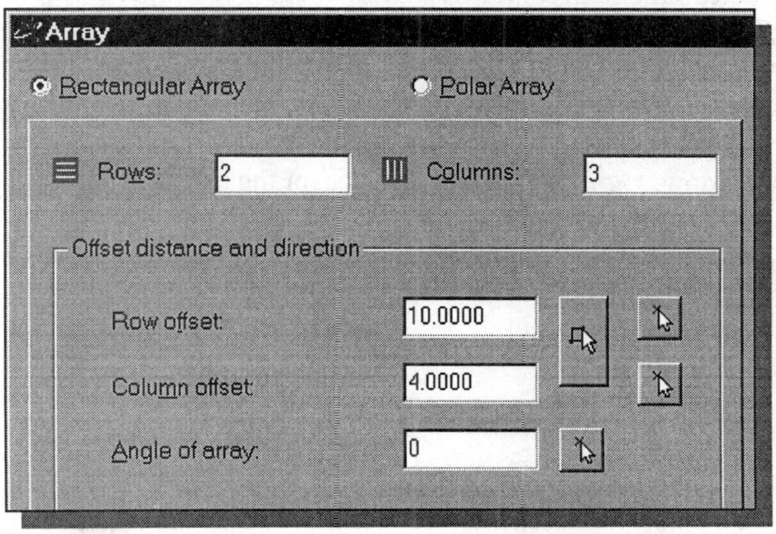

9. In the array window, fill in the items as shown: **Rectangular array, 2 rows** with **10" offset** and **3 columns** with **4" offset**.

10. Click on the **OK** button to accept the settings.

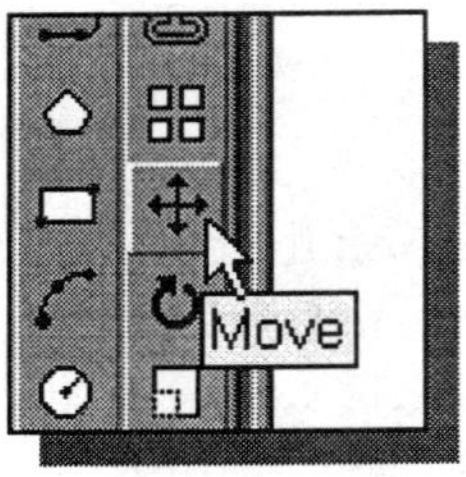

11. Select the ***Move*** icon in the *Draw* toolbar.

12. On your own, reposition the six cylinders as shown in the figure below. Make sure the cylinders pass through the *OIL PAN* model before proceeding to the next step.

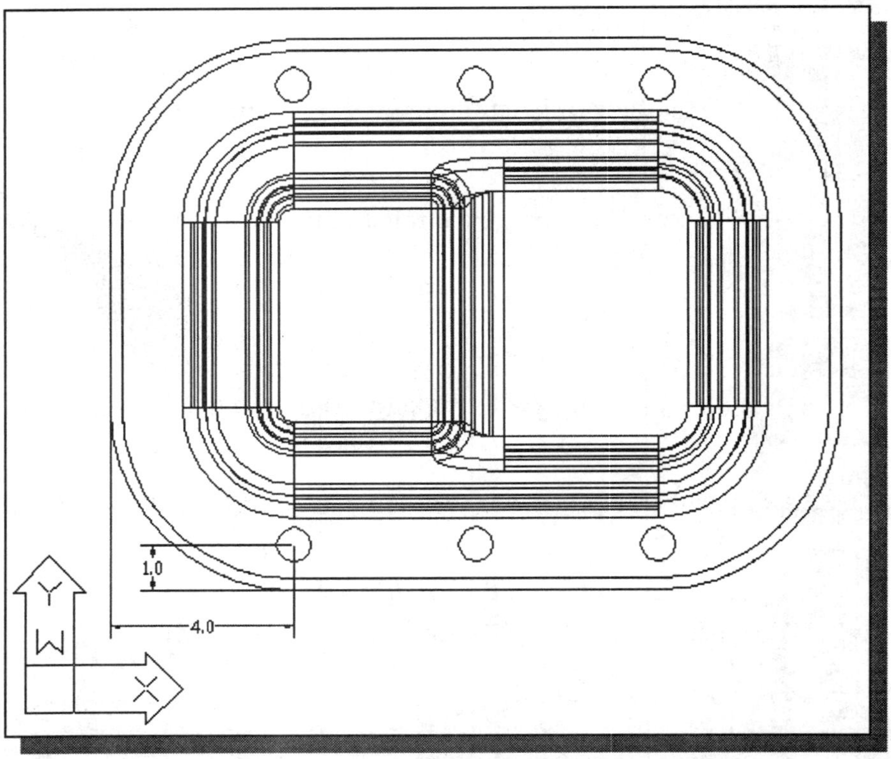

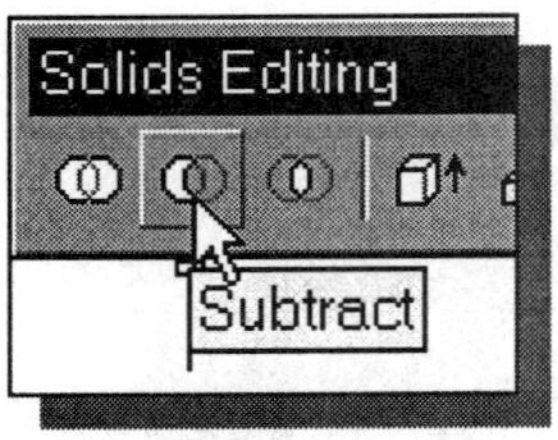

13. In the *Solids Editing* toolbar, click on the ***Subtract*** icon.

14. In the command prompt area, the message *"_subtract Select solids and regions to subtract from .. Select Objects:"* is displayed. Pick the *OIL PAN* model by clicking on one of the edges.

15. Inside the graphics window, **right-mouse-click** to accept the selection and proceed with the *SUBTRACT* command.

16. In the command prompt area, the message *" Select solids and regions to subtract .. Select Objects:"* is displayed.

17. Pick the six cylinder blocks by clicking on the circular edges.

18. Inside the graphics window, **right-mouse-click** to accept the selection and proceed with the *SUBTRACT* command.

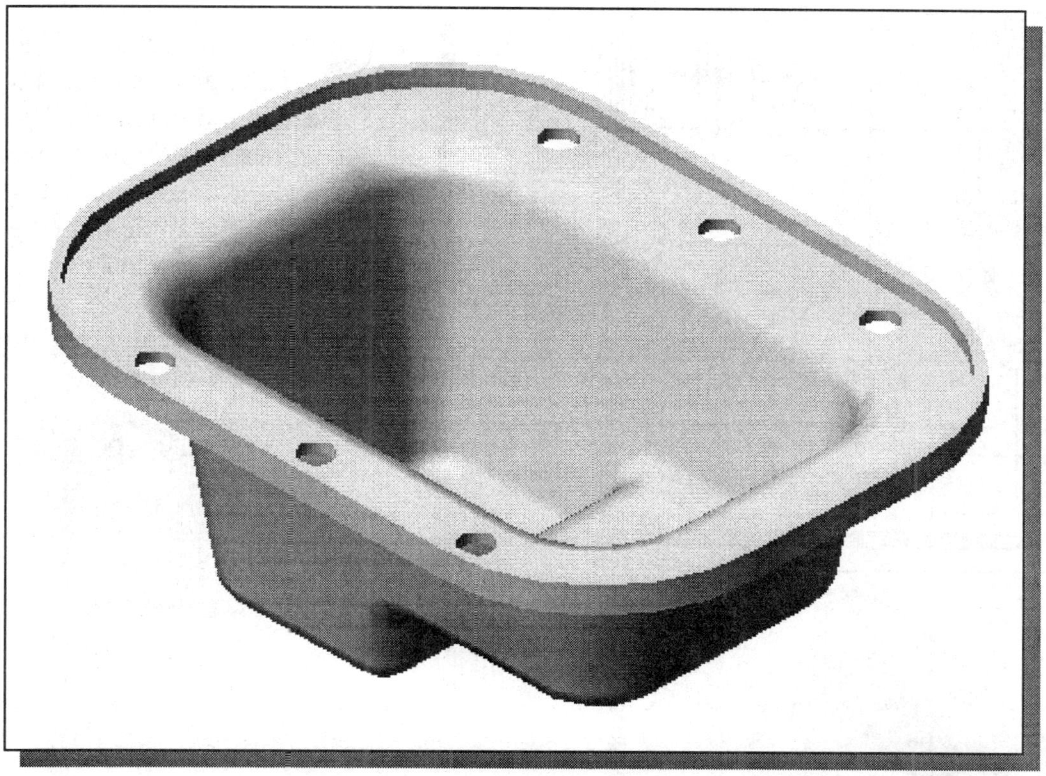

Creating Another Rectangular Array cut feature

1. On your own, repeat the above steps and create another rectangular array as shown (circular hole: diameter 0.75, ***Rectangular array***, ***2 rows*** with ***4" offset*** and ***2 columns*** with ***14" offset***.)

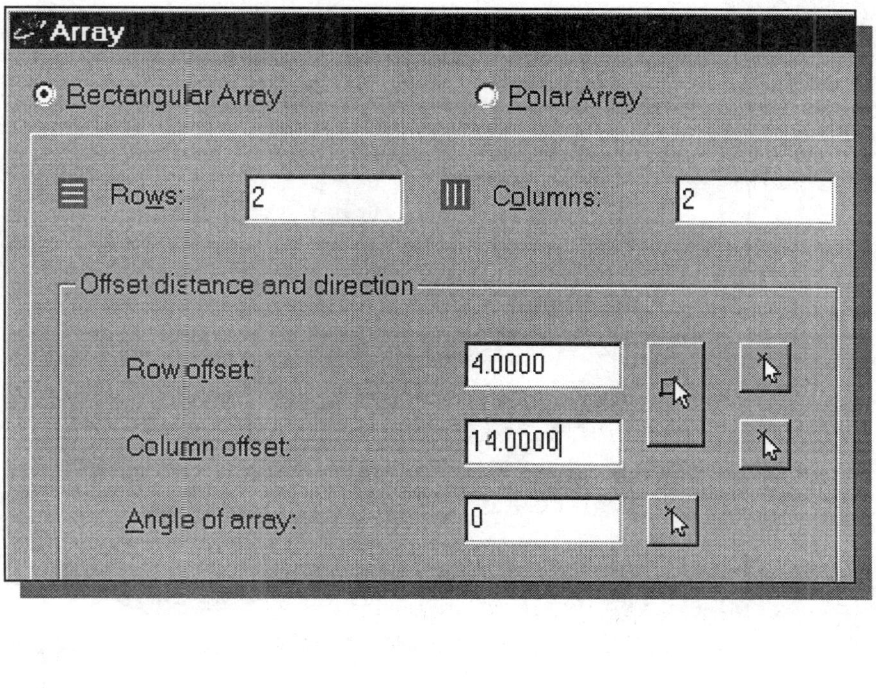

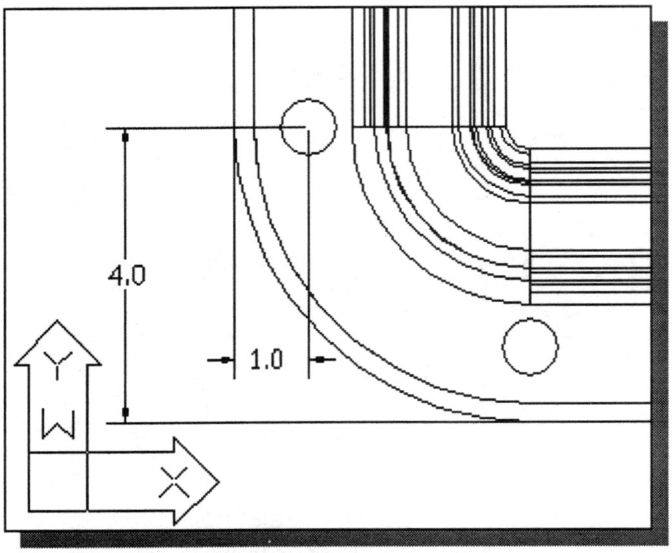

2. On your own, reposition the rectangular array so that the lower-left cylinder is located at 4.0 inches away from the bottom edge of the base feature and 1.0 inch away from the left edge of the *OIL PAN* model.

3. Complete the model with the ***SUBTRACT*** command.

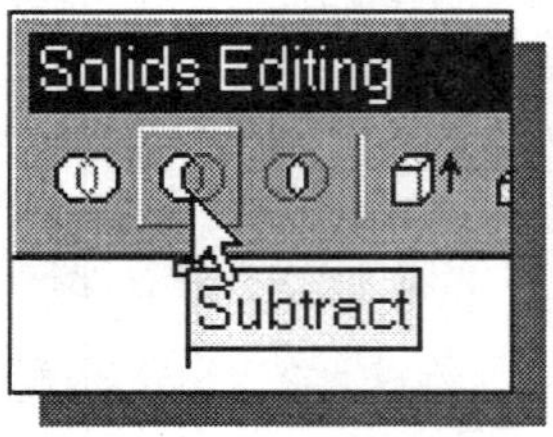

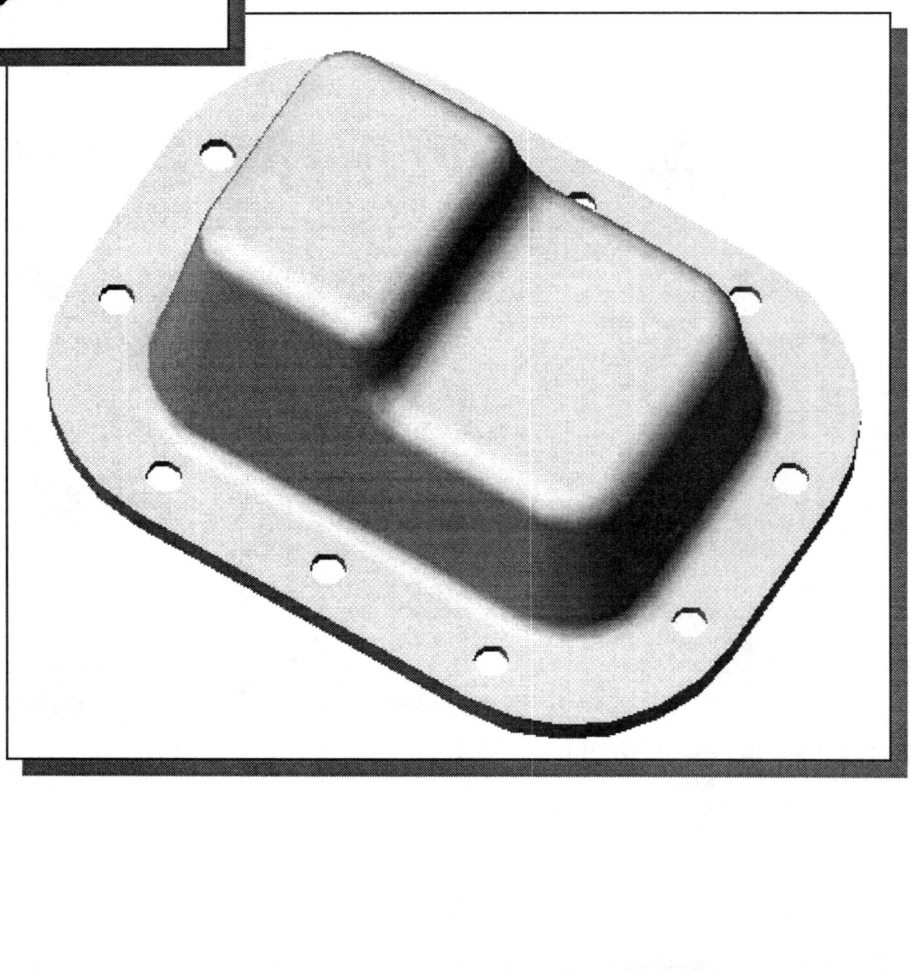

Conclusion

Design includes all activities involved from the original concept to the finished product. Design is the process by which products are created and modified. For many years designers sought ways to describe and analyze three-dimensional designs without building physical models. With the advancements in computer technology, the creation of computer solid models on computers offers a wide range of benefits. Solid models are easier to interpret and can be easily altered. Solid models can also be analyzed using finite element analysis software, and simulation of real-life loads can be applied to the models and the results graphically displayed.

Throughout this text, various modeling techniques have been presented. Mastering these techniques will enable you to create intelligent and flexible solid models. The goal is to make use of the tools provided by AutoCAD and to successfully perform solid models of the product. In many instances, only a single approach to the modeling tasks was presented; you are encouraged to repeat all of the chapters and develop different ways of thinking in accomplishing the same tasks. We have only scratched the surface of AutoCAD's functionality. The more time you spend using the system, the easier it will be to perform solid modeling with AutoCAD.

Questions:

1. Describe the method to create *Draft Angle* features in AutoCAD.

2. List and describe the differences between *Cut with a Pattern* and *Cut Each One Individually*?

3. Which command is used to create *3D rounded corners* in AutoCAD?

4. What elements are required to define a *Rectangular Array* in AutoCAD?

5. How do we create a thin-walled part in AutoCAD? What elements are required to perform the operation?

6. Identify the following commands:

(a)

Extrude

(b)

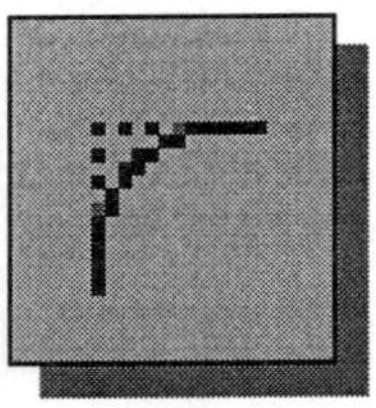

Fillet

(c)

copy faces

(d)

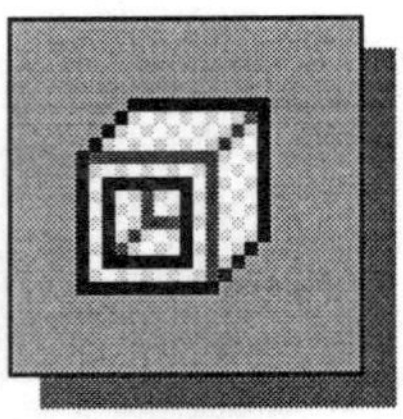

shell

Exercise:

1. Dimensions are in inches

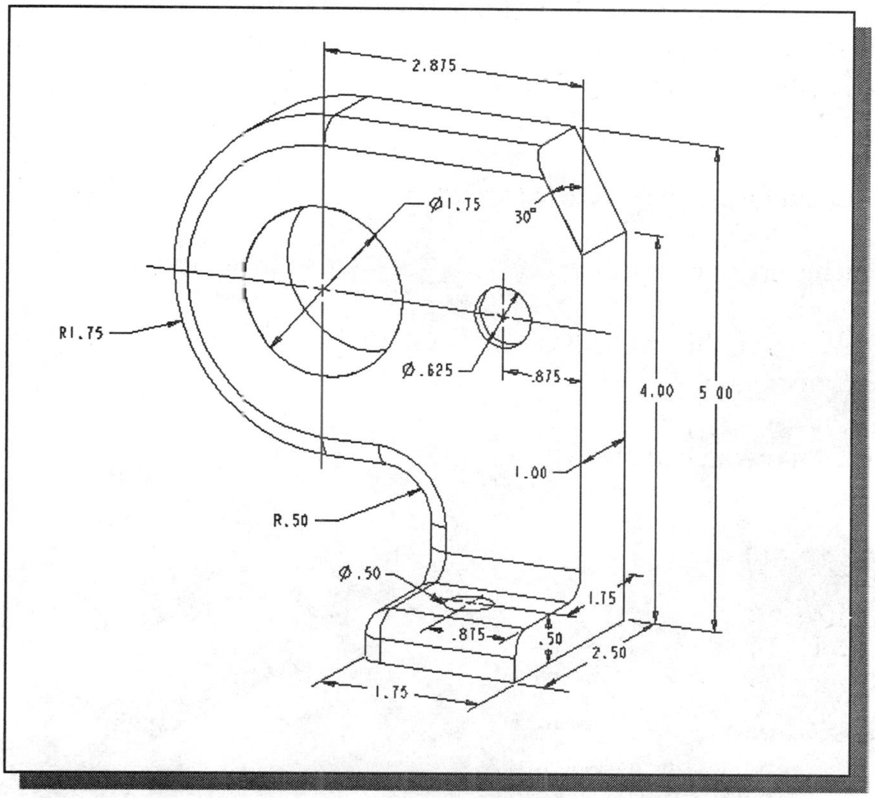

2. Dimensions are in millimeters

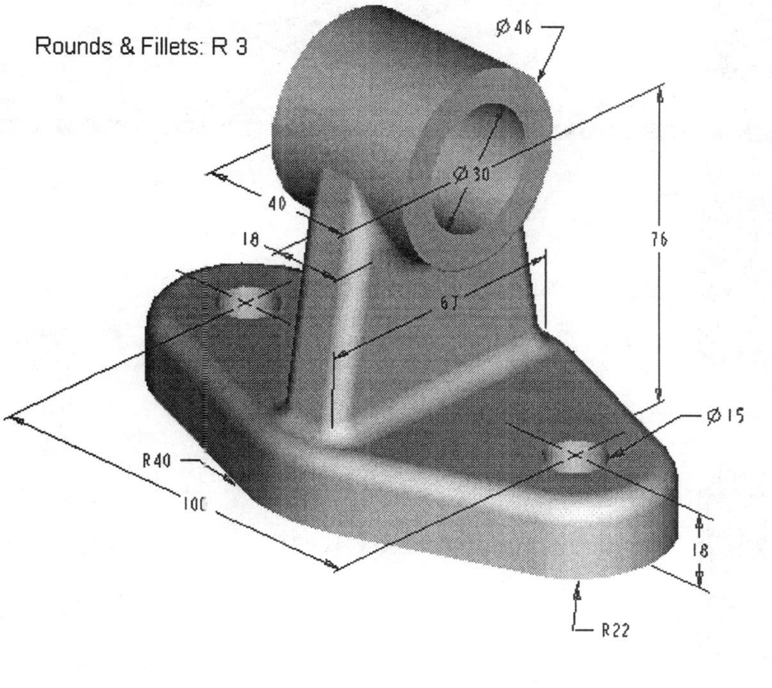

3. Leveling Device: All dimensions are in millimeters

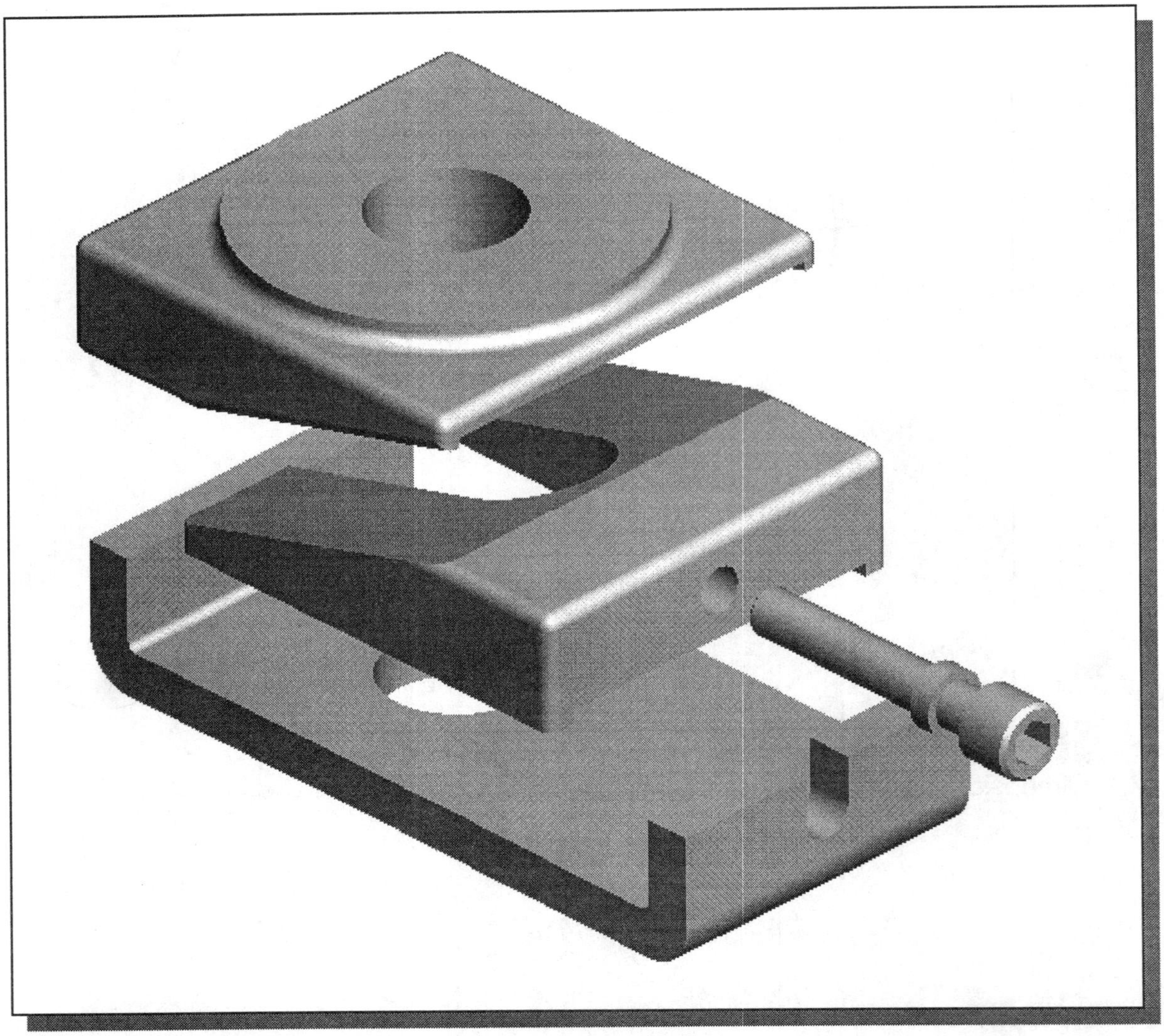

1. *Base Plate*

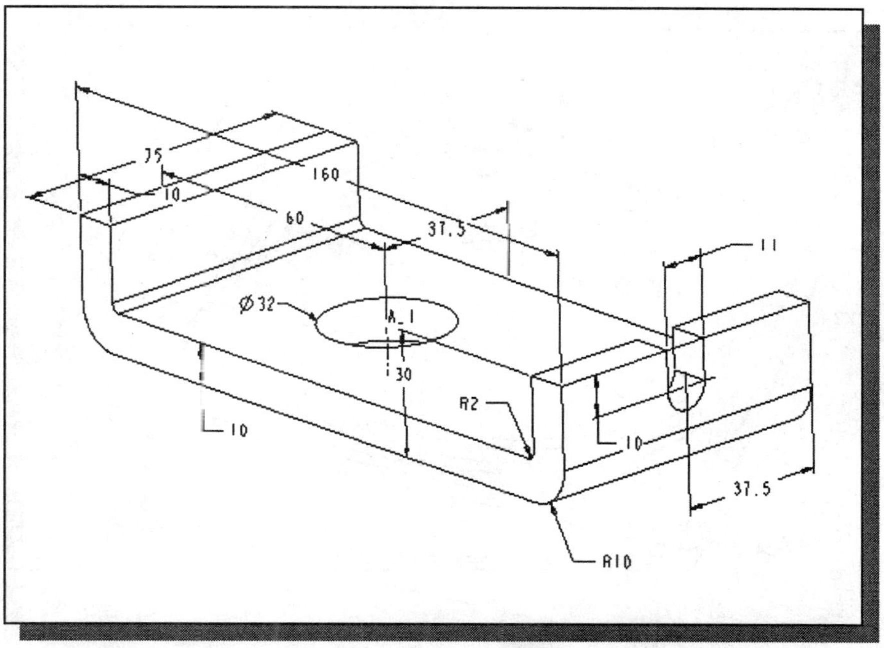

2. *Sliding Block*

(Rounds & Fillets: R3)

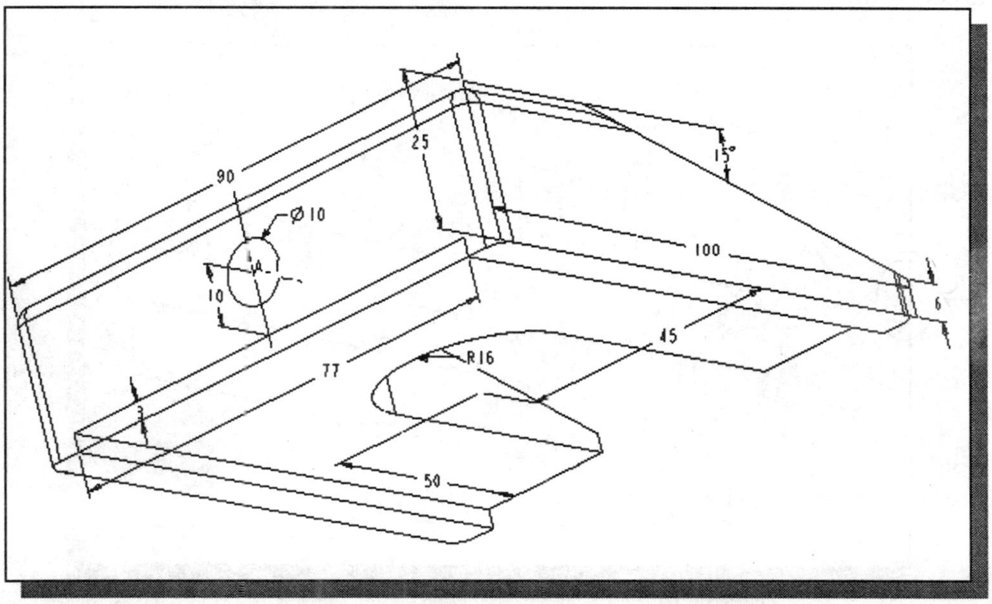

3. Lifting Block

(Rounds & Fillets: R3)

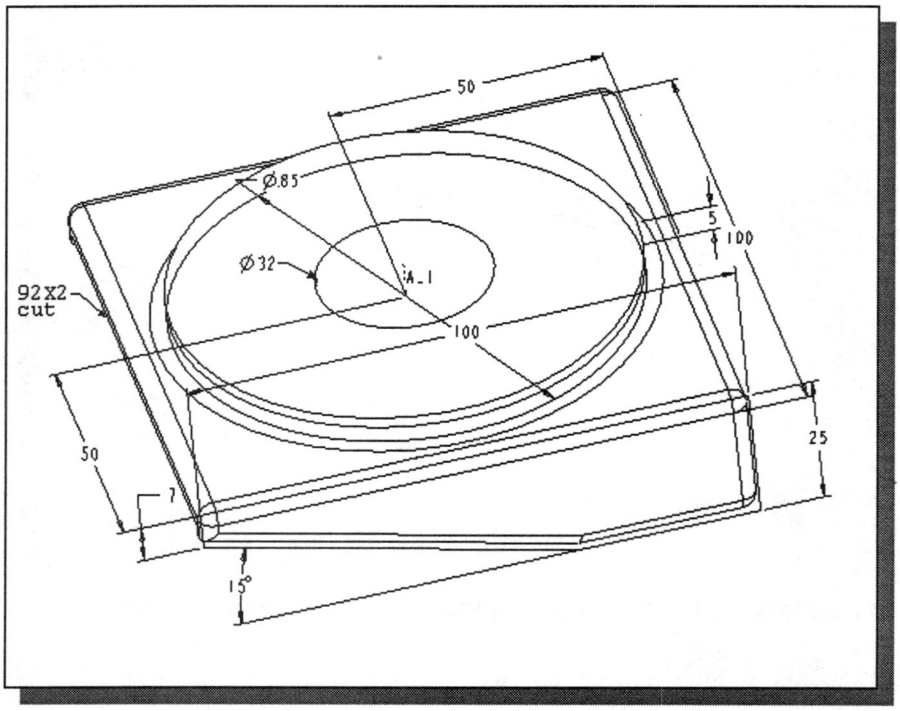

4. Adjusting Screw

(Threads Omitted)

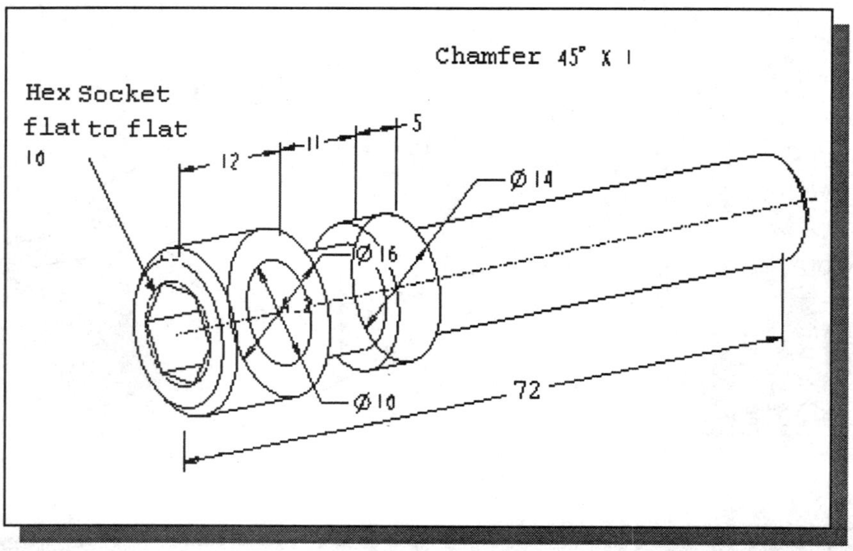

INDEX

A

B

C

D

E

F

G

H

T

U

V

W

X

Y

Z

Notes

Notes

Notes

Notes

Notes

Notes

Notes

Notes

Notes

Notes

Notes